Lecture Notes in Artificial Intellige

Subseries of Lecture Notes in Computer Science
Edited by J. G. Carbonell and J. Siekmann

Lecture Notes in Computer Science

Edited by G. Goos, J. Hartmanis, and J. van Leeuwen

Springer
Berlin
Heidelberg
New York
Barcelona
Hong Kong
London
Milan
Paris
Tokyo

Floriana Esposito (Ed.)

AI*IA 2001:
Advances in
Artificial Intelligence

7th Congress of the Italian Association for Artificial Intelligence
Bari, Italy, September 25-28, 2001
Proceedings

 Springer

Series Editors

Jaime G. Carbonell, Carnegie Mellon University, Pittsburgh, PA, USA
Jörg Siekmann, University of Saarland, Saabrücken, Germany

Volume Editor

Floriana Esposito
University of Bari, Computer Science Department
via Orabona 4, 70125 Bari, Italy
E-mail: esposito@di.uniba.it

Cataloging-in-Publication Data applied for

Die Deutsche Bibliothek - CIP-Einheitsaufnahme

Advances in artificial intelligence : Bari, Italy, September 25 - 28, 2001 ;
proceedings / Floriana Esposito (ed.). - Berlin ; Heidelberg ; New York ;
Barcelona ; Hong Kong ; London ; Milan ; Paris ; Tokyo : Springer, 2001
     (... congress of the Italian Association for Artificial Intelligence, AIIA ... ; 7)
     (Lecture notes in computer science ; 2175 : Lecture notes in artificial
     intelligence)
     ISBN 3-540-42601-9

CR Subject Classification (1998): I.2

ISBN 3-540-42601-9 Springer-Verlag Berlin Heidelberg New York

Springer-Verlag Berlin Heidelberg New York
a member of BertelsmannSpringer Science+Business Media GmbH

http://www.springer.de

© Springer-Verlag Berlin Heidelberg 2001
Printed in Germany

Typesetting: Camera-ready by author, data conversion by Boller Mediendesign
Printed on acid-free paper   SPIN: 10840444   06/3142   5 4 3 2 1 0

Preface

This book contains 41 papers (25 long and 16 short ones) accepted and presented during the scientific track of the seventh Conference of the Italian Association for Artificial Intelligence (AI*IA). The conference, held in Bari this year, follows those previously organized in Trento ('89), Palermo ('91), Turin ('93), Florence ('95), Rome ('97), and Bologna ('99). It is the traditional biennial appointment of Italian academic and industrial researchers working in the field of artificial intelligence and is based on talks given by international experts, presentations of scientific works, system and prototype demonstrations, tutorials, round-table discussions, and workshops on topics of interest from both a methodological and a technological point of view.

In the selection of the papers for the scientific track, the Program Committee has chosen long papers from those contributions that presented a complete work and short papers from those reporting ongoing research. The committee has enforced the rule that only original and unpublished work could be considered for inclusion in these proceedings. The papers, distributed among seven specific topics, report significant research at an international level, in various areas of Artificial Intelligence ranging from Machine Learning to Planning and Control, from Automatic Reasoning to Knowledge Representation, from Robotics to Intelligent Multiagent Systems and Natural Language Processing. The quality of the papers and the hard work of the researchers are witness to a massive research activity mainly devoted to the theoretical aspects of AI, but clearly aimed at consolidating the results that have already been achieved.

Many people contributed in different ways to the success of the conference and to this volume. First of all, the authors who continue to show their enthusiastic interest in AI research and the members of the Program Committee who efficiently handle the reviewing of the consistently high number of submitted papers. They provided three reviews for each manuscript, by relying on the support of valuable additional reviewers. The members of the organizing committee, Fiorella de Rosis, Donato Malerba, Sebastiano Pizzutilo, Giovanni Semeraro deserve my gratitude. A special thank to Berardina De Carolis, Nicola Fanizzi, and Stefano Ferilli who worked hard at solving supporting problems before and during the conference. I wish to thank the Dipartimento di Informatica of the University of Bari and the Director Carlo dell'Aquila for encouraging and sustaining us in the organization of the event. The financial support of the University of Bari, Italy, for partially covering the publication costs of this book is also gratefully acknowledged.

July 2001   Floriana Esposito

Organizing Committee

Berardina DE CAROLIS (Univ. Bari)
Fiorella DE ROSIS (Univ. Bari)
Donato MALERBA (Univ. Bari)
Giovanni SEMERARO (Univ. Bari)

Tutorials: Maria Teresa PAZIENZA
(Univ. Roma Tor Vergata)

Demonstrations: Sebastiano PIZZUTILO (Univ. Bari)

Program Committee

Program Chair: Floriana ESPOSITO (Univ. Bari)

Program Committee: Giovanni ADORNI (Univ. Parma)
Luigia AIELLO CARLUCCI (Univ. Roma
La Sapienza)
Massimo ANDRETTA (Montecatini, Ravenna)
Andrea BONARINI (Politecnico Milano)
Amedeo CAPPELLI (CNR Pisa)
Cristiano CASTELFRANCHI (CNR Roma)
Salvatore GAGLIO (Univ. Palermo)
Attilio GIORDANA (Univ. Piemonte Orientale)
Enrico GIUNCHIGLIA (Univ. Genova)
Nicola GUARINO (CNR Padova)
Leonardo LESMO (Univ. Torino)
Paola MELLO (Univ. Bologna)
Alfredo MILANI (Univ. Perugia)
Eliana MINICOZZI (Univ. Napoli)
Luisa SANSEVERINO (Centro Ricerche FIAT)
M. Teresa PAZIENZA (Univ. Roma Tor Vergata)
Giovanni SODA (Univ. Firenze)
Oliviero STOCK (IRST, Trento)
Furio SUGGI LIVERANI (Illy, Trieste)
Piero TORASSO (Univ. Torino)
Franco TURINI (Univ. Pisa)

Referees

Fabio ABBATTISTA
Liliana ARDISSONO
Edoardo ARDIZZONE
Marco BAIOLETTI
Federico BERGENTI
Monica BIANCHINI
Guido BOELLA
Marco BOTTA
Andrea BRACCIALI
Antonio BROGI
Stefano CAGNONI
Giovanna CASTELLANO
Claudio CASTELLINI
Antonio CHELLA
Massimo COPPOLA
Rita CUCCHIARA
Berardina DE CAROLIS
Giuseppe DE GIACOMO

Fiorella DE ROSIS
Francesco M. DONINI
Rino FALCONE
Nicola FANIZZI
Stefano FERILLI
Paolo FRASCONI
Cesare FURLANELLO
Aldo GANGEMI
Laura GIORDANO
Evelina LAMMA
Alberto LAVELLI
Alessandro LENCI
Paolo LIBERATORE
Vincenzo LOMBARDO
Donato MALERBA
Stefano MARCUGINI
Simone MARINAI
Fabio MASSACCI

Michela MILANO
Daniele NARDI
Fabio PATERNÒ
Roberto PEDONE
Maurizio PIAGGIO
Giovanni PILATO
Vito PIRRELLI
Alessandra RAFFAETÀ
Francesco RICCI
Fabrizio RIGUZZI
Andrea ROLI
Maria SIMI
D. THESEIDER DUPRÉ
Paolo TORRONI
Achille VARZI
Gianni VERCELLI

Table of Contents

Knowledge Representation

Multi-agent Systems

Natural Language Processing

Perception, Vision, and Robotics

Planning and Scheduling

A Monte Carlo Approach to Hard Relational Learning Problems

A. Serra and A. Giordana

Dipartimento di Scienze e Tecnologie Avanzate, Universita del Piemonte Orientale,
C.Borsalino 54, 15100 Alessandria, Italy

Abstract. A previous research has shown that most learning strategies fail to learn relational concepts when descriptions involving more than three variables are required. The reason resides in the emergence of a phase transition in the *covering test*. After an in depth analysis of this aspect, this paper proposes an alternative learning strategy, combining a Monte Carlo stochastic search with local deterministic search. This approach offers two main benefits: on the one hand, substantial advantages over more traditional search algorithms, in terms of increased learning ability, and, on the other, the possibility of an a- priori estimation of the cost for solving a learning problem, under specific assumptions about the target concept.

1 Introduction

In a recent paper Giordana et al. [4] have shown that relational learning becomes very hard when the target concept requires descriptions involving more than three variables. The reason is related to the presence of a phase transition in the covering test [9, 3], i.e., an abrupt change in the probability that an inductive hypothesis covers a given example, when the hypothesis and the example sizes reach some critical values. Moreover, any top-down learner will search for discriminant hypotheses in the phase transition region [4, 3], and, finally, heuristics commonly used to guide top-down relational learning [10, 1] become useful only in the same region. The consequence is that the top-down induction process is blind in its first steps, so that the path to the correct concept definition is very easily lost.

This paper offers two major contributions. First, an estimate of the "difficulty" of a learning problem is proposed, in terms of the density of sub-formulas of the target concept in the hypothesis space. Moreover, an estimate of the probability of detecting one of these is also given, as a function of the target concept location with respect to the phase transition.

Second, an induction algorithm, combining a Monte Carlo stochastic search [2] with local deterministic search, is proposed to (partially) avoid the pitfall that causes top-down search to fail. The new algorithm directly jumps into a region of the hypothesis space where the information gain heuristics has good chance of being successful, continuing its search exploiting a classical hill climbing strategy. The complexity of this algorithm is analyzed in a probabilistic framework,

F. Esposito (Ed.): AI*IA 2001, LNAI 2175, pp. 1–10, 2001.

and it is proposed as a measure of the difficulty of the induction task. Finally, the algorithm has been experimentally evaluated on the set of hard induction problems provided by [4], and it shows a good agreement with the theoretical estimates.

2   Hard Relational Problems

Relational languages [7] are appealing for describing highly structured data. However, complex relational features may be hard to discover during the very learning process; in fact, finding substructures can be considered a learning problem of its own [5]. For the sake of exemplification, let us consider the data set in Figure 1. The cue discriminating structures (b) and (c) from structures (a) and (d) is the presence of at least one pentagonal ring. Such a cue can be simply described by the logical formula

bound-to(x,y), bound-to(y,z), bound-to(z,w), bound-to(w,v), bound-to(v,x),

where variables x, y, z, w and v are instantiated to vertices, and the predicates bound-to(.,.) denote edges of the graphs. Capturing this cue in a propositional language requires that one already knows what he/she is searching for.

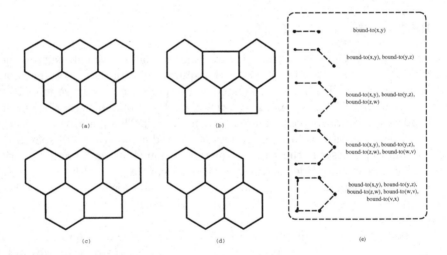

Fig. 1. Example of data requiring relational features to be discovered. Examples (a) and (d) cannot be distinguished from (b) and (c) until a ring of at least five edges is constructed. (e) Sequence of hypotheses that a general-to-specific strategy should generate in order to learn a five edge ring description in predicated logic.

On the other hand, the same cue is difficult to learn also for relational/ILP learners [6, 10, 1, 7, 8]. In fact, a FOIL-like general-to-specific learning strat-

egy requires the construction of the sequence of hypotheses: "bound-to(x,y)",
"bound-to(x,y) ∧ bound-to(y,z)", and so on, corresponding to growing portions
of the ring (see Figure 1-(e)). As all elements in the sequence have a rather large
number of models both in the positive and in the negative examples, heuristics
such as *information gain* [10] or *MDL* [11] do not assign any special relevance
to them until the last element is generated, and the number of models drops to
zero on the negative examples. Then, a general-to-specific strategy is likely to
be misled by the presence of other constructs, which may have a slightly higher
information gain.

This problem has been detected both in real and artificial learning problems
[3], and has been investigated in [4], where the results summarized in the following have been obtained. Let L be the complexity of a structured example e,
measured by the number of atomic components, and let m be the number of literals in a conjunctive formula φ, in a first order logic language. Representing the
pair (e, φ) as a point (m_φ, L_e) in the plane (m, L), three regions have been found
(see Figure 2(a)): the YES-region, the *mushy*-region, and the NO-region. In a
point (m, L) located in the YES-region, it is highly probable that any formula
φ with m literals has many different models on a randomly selected example
e. Instead, in the mushy region (or phase transition region) a formula has, in
average, 0.5 probability of having a model on e, whereas this probability is close
to 0 in the NO-region. Let us now consider an inductive hypothesis φ and a
set of learning examples $\mathcal{E}_L$. When the points defined by pairing every example
$e \in \mathcal{E}_L$ to φ fall in the YES-region, there is no chance of deciding if it is a good
or a bad hypothesis, because in both cases it will have a comparable number of
models on the positives and negative examples in $\mathcal{E}_L$. Then, a learner following
a general-to-specific strategy is blind until the hypotheses are complex enough
to reach the border of the mushy region.

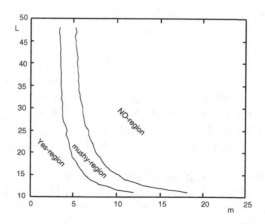

Fig. 2. Regions characterizing the (m, L)-plane.

3   A Stochastic Approach

In absence of admissible heuristics, stochastic search may be a valid alternative. Moreover, stochastic search may be successfully combined with deterministic search when the search space is structured into regions such that, after entering in a given region R, there exists admissible heuristics able to guide the search toward the locally best solution existing in R. Examples of how Monte Carlo search can be combined with deterministic search in classical search problems, such as the k-queens, can be found in [2].

Let P_G be the probability that φ is subformula of ω, the number τ of trials required to find at least one generalization of ω with confidence confidence $1 - \epsilon$, is

$$1 - \epsilon = 1 - (1 - P_G)^\tau. \tag{1}$$

Solving (1) with respect to τ we obtain

$$\tau = \frac{\log \epsilon}{\log (1 - P_G)} \tag{2}$$

An analytical method for estimating P_G will be supplied in the next section.

The algorithm we propose is based on a two step strategy. The first step creates a hypothesis φ_μ with a complexity m_μ sufficiently close to the border between the YES-region and the mushy region, by randomly sampling the hypothesis space. The second step performs a general-to-specific search starting from φ_μ according to a hill-climbing strategy guided by the information gain heuristics.

Algorithm T^4
let $m_\mu = \mu_0$ and let $\hat{\omega} = \emptyset$
while the learning set $\mathcal{E}_L$ is not fully covered do:
1. Generate a set Φ of τ hypotheses of complexity m_μ, randomly selected.
2. Rank hypotheses in Φ according to their information gain with respect to the formula $True$ that covers all examples, by definition.
3. Starting from the top ranked hypothesis, apply the hill-climbing specialization step to the K best ranked hypotheses.
4. Add to $\hat{\omega}$ the best hypothesis produced in the previous step.
5. Declare *covered* all the examples verified by some element in $\hat{\omega}$

It is immediate to verify that, if the target concept has a conjunctive description ω in the hypothesis space H, and τ is large enough, algorithm T^4 will find ω or at least a generalization $\hat{\omega}$ of it, correct on the learning set $\mathcal{E}_L$. Otherwise, it will produce a disjunctive description.

However, the question we want to answer is: assuming to know the complexity m_ω and the number of variables n_ω in ω what is the complexity τ we should allocate to Algorithm T^4.

4   Evaluation the Hypothesis Space Size

In the following we will provide methods for computing or estimating the size of the hypothesis space in dependence of the complexity of the concept description language. Moreover, we will provide an estimate of the probability of finding a generalization of the target concept by randomly sampling the hypothesis space.

4.1   Estimating the Hypothesis Space Size for a Function Free Language

Let $\mathbf{P}$ be the union of a set $\mathbf{B}$ of binary predicates and a set $\mathbf{U} = \{\beta_j(\mathbf{x}) | 0 \leq j \leq m_U\}$ of unary predicates.

We will first estimate the number of possible hypotheses consisting of t_B binary literals built on r variables. Let m_B be the cardinality of $\mathbf{B}$ and let m_U be the cardinality of $\mathbf{U}$. Let moreover $\mathbf{L}_{B,r}$ be the set of literals built on $\mathbf{B}$ and r variables. The cardinality of set $\mathbf{L}_{B,r}$ is $r \cdot r \cdot m_B$

Then the number of syntactically different formulas containing t_B binary literals and up to r different variables is $\binom{r \cdot r \cdot m_B}{t_B}$. By subtracting, from this quantity, the number of formulas having less than r variables, the number of syntactically different formulas containing exactly r variables

$$M_s(m_B, t_B, r) = \binom{r \cdot r \cdot m_B}{t_B} - \sum_{i=1}^{r-1} \binom{r}{r-i} M_s(m_B, t_B, r-i) \qquad (3)$$

is obtained.

Notice that syntactically different formulas can be semantically equivalent, being unifiable by properly renaming the variables. For instance, formula $\alpha_1(x_1, x_2) \wedge \alpha_2(x_2, x_3)$ is unifiable with $\alpha_1(x_2, x_3) \wedge \alpha_2(x_3, x_1)$ and hence they cover the same models in any learning instance. Actually, the complexity of a learning task depends upon the number of semantically different hypotheses.

In order to estimate the number $M(m_B, t_B, r)$ of semantically different hypotheses with r variables, we observe that the maximum number of syntactic variants a formula may have is $r!$. Then, the following relation holds:

$$M_s(m_B, t_B, r) \geq M(m_B, t_B, r) \geq \frac{M_s(m_B, t_B, r)}{r!} \qquad (4)$$

We will choose the central value $\hat{M}(m_B, t_B, r) = \frac{M_s(m_B, t_B, r)}{2}\left(1 + \frac{1}{r!}\right)$ of the interval $[M_s(m_B, t_B, r), \frac{M_s(m_B, t_B, r)}{r!}]$ as an approximation of $M(m_B, t_B, r)$.

Let $\varphi_B(x_1, x_2, \dots, x_r)$ a syntactic instance of a hypothesis containing only binary predicates. Let moreover β a unary literal built on one of the variables $x_1, \dots, x_r$. It is immediate to verify that the formula $\varphi_B(x_1, x_2, \dots, x_r) \wedge \beta$, for any β, is a syntactic instance of semantically different hypothesis. More in general, let $\varphi(x_1, x_2, \dots, x_r)$ a formula containing both binary and unary predicates, any formula $\psi(x_1, x_2, \dots, x_r) = \varphi(x_1, x_2, \dots, x_r) \wedge \beta$, being $\beta \notin \varphi(x_1, x_2, \dots, x_r)$, is semantically different from any other conjunction $\varphi(x_1, x_2, \ldots, x_r) \wedge \beta'$ if $\beta' \neq \beta$. On the basis of this observation, we conclude that the complexity of the hypothesis space for hypotheses $\varphi = \varphi_B \wedge \varphi_U$, being φ_U a formula of only unary literals, lies in the interval:

$$M_s(m_B, t_B, r) \cdot M_s(m_U, t_U, r) \geq M(m, t, r) \geq \frac{M_s(m_B, t_B, r) \cdot M_s(m_U, t_U, r)}{r!} \tag{5}$$

where $t = t_B + t_U$, $m = m_B + m_U$, and

$$M_s(m_U, t_U, r) = \sum_{i=1}^{m_U} \binom{m_U}{i} M_s(m_U, t_U - i, r - 1)$$

is the number of formulas having up to r variable made of unary literals selected from set $\mathbf{U}$. We will approximate $M(m, t, r)$ with the value

$$\hat{M}(m, t, r) = M_s(m_B, t_B, r) \cdot M_s(m_B, t_U, r) \left(1 + \frac{1}{r!}\right) \tag{6}$$

4.2   Estimating the Frequency of Concept Generalizations

The last problem we will face is that of estimating the frequency of generalizations ψ_ω, of a concept ω, existing in a space of semantically different hypotheses. In other words, this is equivalent to estimate the probability $P(\psi_\omega | \omega)$ assuming that ω exists. Let $M_G(\omega, t, r)$ be the number of semantically different generalizations of t literals and r variables we may expect for a concept ω of t_ω literals, and r_ω variables $(r_\omega \geq r)$. The number of existing generalizations of t literals having number $\hat{M}_G(\omega, t)$ of variables between 1 and r_ω is precisely evaluated by the expression

$$\hat{M}_G(\omega, t) = \binom{t_\omega}{t}. \tag{7}$$

Evaluating the generalizations of exactly r variables, is impossible if ω is not known. As, for values of t, t_ω close to the mushy region, it has been found that $\hat{M}_G(\omega, t)$ is quite close to $M_G(\omega, t, r)$, we will use $\hat{M}_G(\omega, t)$ as an estimate of $M_G(\omega, t, r)$.

Then an approximation of $\hat{P}_G(\omega, m, t, r)$ can be obtained as the ratio

$$\hat{P}_G(\omega, m, t, r) = \frac{\hat{M}_G(\omega, t)}{\hat{M}(m, t, r)}. \tag{8}$$

5   An Experimental Evaluation

Algorithm T^4 has been tested on the set of 451 artificial learning problems described in [4].

The artificial learning problem set has been generated by imposing that all target concept be describable using only binary predicates and exactly four variables ($n = 4$). Moreover, it has been required that all binary predicates have an extension of $N = 100$ tuples on any learning example. Given n and N, let (m, L) be a point in the plane (m, L). A set of 451 points has been sampled in the plane (m, L). Then, for each point, a learning problem $\Pi_{m,L}$ has been built up from the 4-tuple $(n = 4, N = 100, m, L)$. A target concept ω with m literals and n variables has been built up, and then a training set $\mathcal{E}_L$ and a test set $\mathcal{E}_T$ have been generated. Let Λ be a set of L constants; every example is a collection of m relational tables of size N obtained by sampling the binary table $\Lambda \times \Lambda$. In order to generate balanced training and test sets in each point of the (m, L) plane, the random generation of the examples has been modified in order to obtain examples with models also in the NO-region, and examples without models also in the YES-region (see [4] for more details). The result has been the generation of training and test sets, $\mathcal{E}_L$ and $\mathcal{E}_T$, each one with 100 positive and 100 negative examples in each (m, L) point.

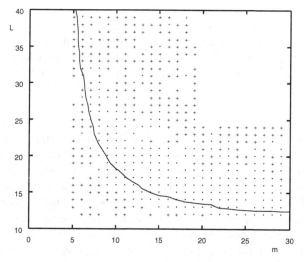

Fig. 3. Results obtained with FOIL: *Failure region* (legend ".") and *success region* (legend "+"), for $n = 4$ and $N = 100$. The contour plot corresponds to the value $P_{sol} = 0.5$ of the probability that randomly generated covering test is positive.

Some details about the problems lying in the mushy region are reported in Table 1. The first five columns report the number m of predicates in the concept description language, the number L of components in every single learning instance, the critical value m_c of the center of the mushy region, and the value for t_μ and r, chosen for every single run. The eleventh column reports the error rate on $\mathcal{E}_T$ for the solution selected by the algorithm. Columns from 6 to 10 report

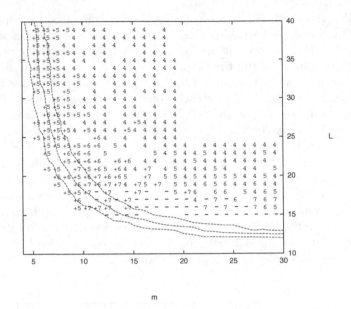

Fig. 4. Results obtained by Algorithm T^4. The numbers denote the minimum value that was necessary to assume for m_μ in order to solve the learning problem. When the number is prefixed by "+", it means that $n = 4$ has been assumed, otherwise $n = 3$. Symbol "-" means that the problem has not been solved.

the values of $M(m, t_\mu, r)$ (computed by expression (6)), the real value of M_G, the estimated value $\hat{M}_G$ (assuming a concept of 4 variables lying close to the phase transition), the size $M_S(m, t_\mu, r)$ of the syntactic hypothesis space, the probability P_G computed from the values in column 6 and 7, and the number of trials τ. The results obtained by FOIL on this set of problems is summarized in Figure 3. It appears that most problems beyond FOILS's capability have been solved. Anyhow, for low L some problems have been found beyond the complexity affordable with the available computational resources. A problem was considered solved when the error rate on the test set of the learned concept definition was smaller than 20%. Figure 3 shows a large area, across the mushy region, where FOIL systematically fails.

Algorithm T^4 has been run on the problems lying in the mushy region and in the NO-region obtaining the results described in Figure 4. In all experiments, we started with minimal assumptions about the difficulty of the problems, scaling up until the problem T^4 was not able to find a good solution or the predicted complexity was not affordable. More specifically, in the area where the problems are easy to solve, we started with $r = 3$ and $m_\mu = 4$, and usually T^4 found the solution at the first attempt. In the more difficult region (the blind spot), we started with $r = 4$ and $m_\mu = m_c - 6$ increasing m_μ up to reach $m_c - 1$, when necessary. Parameter τ was determined using (6), by requiring confidence $1 - \epsilon = 0.999$. The number K of hypotheses refined at each run was chosen $K =$

Table 1. Results obtained by adding a stochastic search step to the basic hill climbing strategy. Horizontal lines separate the results reported for different problems. Rows between two horizontal lines refer to a same problem.

m	L	m_c	t_μ	r	M [10^3]	M_G [10^3]	$\tilde{M}_G$ [10^3]	M_S [10^3]	P_G	$\tau_{0.999}$	Err %
7	36	6	4	4	22.82	0.03	0.035	40.320	0.0011947	5778	100%
7	35	6	4	4	22.82	0.03	0.035	40.320	0.0011947	5778	100%
7	34	6	4	4	22.82	0.03	0.035	40.320	0.0011947	5778	100%
7	33	6	4	4	22.82	0.03	0.035	40.320	0.0011947	5778	100%
7	32	6	4	4	22.82	0.03	0.035	40.320	0.0011947	5778	47%
			5	4	190.68	0.02	0.021	725.760	0.0000996	69379	100%
8	31	6	4	4	45.64	0.05	0.07	80.640	0.0011758	5871	53%
			5	4	508.48	0.05	0.056	1935.360	0.0000980	70497	100%
8	30	7	4	4	45.64	0.05	0.07	80.640	0.0011758	5871	49%
			5	4	508.48	0.05	0.056	1935.360	0.0000980	70497	100%
8	29	7	4	4	45.64	0.05	0.07	80.640	0.0011758	5871	51%
			5	4	508.48	0.05	0.056	1935.360	0.0000980	70497	100%
8	28	7	4	4	45.64	0.05	0.07	80.640	0.0011758	5871	50%
			5	4	508.48	0.05	0.056	1935.360	0.0000980	70497	100%
8	27	7	4	4	45.64	0.05	0.07	80.640	0.0011758	5871	48%
			5	4	508.48	0.05	0.056	1935.360	0.0000980	70497	100%
9	26	7	4	4	82.15	0.10	0.126	145.152	0.0011665	5918	49%
			5	4	1144.08	0.11	0126	4354.560	0.0000972	71056	100%
9	24	8	4	4	82.15	0.10	0.126	145.152	0.0011665	5918	50%
			5	4	1144.08	0.11	0.126	4354.560	0.0000972	71056	100%
10	23	8	4	4	136.92	0.16	0.21	241.920	0.0011619	5941	51%
			5	4	2288.16	0.22	0.252	8709.120	0.0000968	71336	48%
			6	4	24497.76	0.20	0.21	174182.400	0.0000081	856074	100%
10	22	8	4	4	136.92	0.16	0.21	241.920	0.0011619	5941	49%
			5	4	2288.16	0.252	0.22	8709.120	0.0000968	71336	52%
			6	4	24497.76	0.20	0.210	174182.400	0.0000081	856074	100%
11	21	9	4	4	215.16	0.25	0.33	380.160	0.0011597	5953	48%
			5	4	4194.96	0.41	0.462	15966.720	0.0000966	71476	50%
			6	4	53895.07	0.43	0.462	383201.280	0.0000081	857753	100%
12	20	9	4	4	322.74	0.37	0.495	570.240	0.0011585	5959	51%
			5	4	7191.36	0.69	0.792	27371.520	0.0000965	71581	50%
			6	4	107790.14	0.87	0.924	766402.560	0.0000080	858592	100%
13	19	10	4	4	466.18	0.54	0.715	823.680	0.0011580	5961	50%
			5	4	11685.96	1.13	01.287	44478.720	0.0000965	71581	49%
			6	4	200181.70	1.61	1.716	1423319.040	0.0000080	859012	49%
			7	4	2481967.49	1.66	1.716	29889699.840	0.0000007	10308184	100%

$\tau/100$. Given the high confidence required, the stochastic step always succeeded in finding at least one generalization of the target concept. Nevertheless, the hill climbing step did not succeed to find a correct generalization until t_μ was not close enough to the mushy region. Even if the t_μ and r was known in advantage, for the most complex problems, several trials have been done with smaller r and m_μ. It appears that a good generalization has been obtained always and only when the values t_μ, τ, predicted by the theory have been used.

All runs have been done using a cluster of 20 Pentium III, 800Mz.

6   Discussion

We have shown that combining stochastic search with local deterministic search it is possible to learn approximated concept descriptions where no known classical algorithm was successful. Even if the algorithm is used under the stringent assumption that a conjunctive concept description exists, it is not difficult to extend it in order to cope with more general concept descriptions. For instance, disjunctive descriptions can be learned by integrating T^4 with a set covering algorithm as it is made in most relational learner [10, 1].

However, this is not the fundamental result that emerges from the framework we propose. In our opinion, the most important outcome is the method for estimating the complexity of a learning problem: given a specific hypothesis about the structure of the concept, we have a method for predicting the expected cost for testing the hypothesis. Moreover, a criterion for deciding on-line when stop testing the hypothesis is provided.

A second important result is a negative one, and concerns the possibility of learning descriptions with many variables. Even considering quite simple concept description languages, the task looks hard for many concepts requiring at least 4 variables. Increasing the number of variables, the complexity rises up exponentially. Considering the presence of irrelevant predicates, the analysis we performed still holds, but the the density of sub-formulas of the target concept close to the phase transition becomes even more tiny, and so the difficulty will increase further.

References

[1] M. Botta and A. Giordana. SMART+: A multi-strategy learning tool. In *IJCAI-93, Proceedings of the Thirteenth International Joint Conference on Artificial Intelligence*, pages 937–943, Chambéry, France, 1993.

[2] G. Brassard and P. Bratley. *Algorithmics: Theory and Practice*. Prentice Hall, Englewood Cliffs, NJ, 1988.

[3] A. Giordana and L. Saitta. Phase transitions in relational learning. *Machine Learning*, 41:217–251, 2000.

[4] A. Giordana, L. Saitta, and M. Sebag amd M. Botta. An experimental study of phase transitions in matching. In *Proceedings of th 17th International Conference on Machine Learning*, pages 311,318, Stanford, CA, 2000.

[5] Dehaspe L., Toivonen H., and King R.D. Finding frequent substructures in chemical compounds. In *Int Conf. on Knowledge Discovery and Data Mining*, pages 30–36, New York, NY, 1998.

[6] R. Michalski. A theory and methodology of inductive learning. In R. Michalski, J. Carbonell, and T. Mitchell, editors, *Machine Learning: An Artificial Intelligence Approach*, pages 83–134, Los Altos, CA, 1983. Morgan Kaufmann.

[7] S. Muggleton, editor. *Inductive Logic Programming*. Academic Press, London, UK, 1992.

[8] S. Muggleton. Inverse entailment and PROGOL. *New Gen. Comput.*, 13:245–286, 1995.

[9] P. Prosser. An empirical study of phase transitions in binary constraint satisfaction problems. *Artificial Intelligence*, 81:81–110, 1996.

[10] R. Quinlan. Learning logical definitions from relations. *Machine Learning*, 5:239–266, 1990.

[11] J. Rissanen. Modeling by shortest data description. *Automatica*, 14:465–471, 1978.

Boosting as a Monte Carlo Algorithm

Roberto Esposito, Lorenza Saitta

Dipartimento di Informatica, Università di Torino
Corso Svizzera 185, Torino, Italy
esposito@di.unito.it
DISTA, Università del Piemonte Orientale "Amedeo Avogadro",
Corso Borsalino 54, Alessandria, Italy
saitta@mfn.unipmn.it

Abstract. A new view of majority voting as a Monte Carlo stochastic algorithm is presented in this paper. The relation between the two approches allows Adaboost's example weighting strategy to be compared with the greedy covering strategy used for a long time in Machine Learning. Even though one may expect that the greedy strategy is very much prone to overfitting, extensive experimental results do not support this guess. The greedy strategy does not clearly show overfitting, it runs in at least one order of magnitude less time, it reaches zero error on the training set in few trials, and the error on the test set is most of the time comparable, if not lower, than that exhibited by Adaboost.

1 Introduction

Majority voting classification algorithms, such as boosting [Schapire, 1990] or bagging [Breiman, 1996] are very popular nowdays because of the superior performances shown experimentally on a number of data sets (see, for example, [Bauer & Kohavi, 1999; Quinlan, 1996]). Majority voting methods increase the accuracy of classifiers acquired by *weak learners* combining their predictions.

An intriguing property of these algorithms is their robustness with respect to overfitting. In fact, their generalization error does not appear, usually, to increase, even when the number of voting classifiers ranges in the thousands. A rather convincing argument to explain this behaviour is that boosting increases the number of learning examples with a large classification *margin* [Schapire et al., 1998].

Given a class of hypotheses, and the empirical classification errors on a set of examples of the single classifiers belonging to the class, it is possible to upper bound the training error of the composite classification rule in terms of them, and to upper bound, in probability, the generalization error, as well. However, these last bounds are too loose to be useful in practice, even though they are consistent with the qualitative behaviour of the classification error observed experimentally. Moreover, it is possible to estimate the minimum number of iterations necessary to achieve a desired error on the learning set, with high probability. In this paper we concentrate, for the sake of simplicity, on the case of binary classification.

F. Esposito (Ed.): AI*IA 2001, LNAI 2175, pp. 11-19, 2001.

In the effort to understand why and when boosting works, links with other approaches, such as logistic regression and game theory [Freund & Schapire, 1996b], have been established,. In this paper we offer a new perspective, relating majority voting with Monte Carlo stochastic algorithms [Brassard & Bratley, 1988]. In fact, the Monte Carlo approach offers a technique to increase the performance of a simple algorithm by repeatedly running it on the same problem instance. Monte Carlo algorithms have been studied for a long time and they offer several results that can possibly be transferred to the majority voting framework. For instance, realistic bounds on the number of iterations necessary to reach a given level of performances were already available [Brassard & Bratley, 1988, p. 265].

In addition, a subclass of Monte Carlo algorithms shows particularly interesting properties with respect to the link between performance increase and number of iterations. Then, a natural question is whether they correspond to some class of machine learning algorithms, which these properties could be transferred to. As it turns out, the answer is yes, and these special Monte Carlo algorithms correspond to the well known *greedy covering* strategy, where covered examples are removed at each run and majority voting becomes an "at least one" combination rule. Then, while Monte Carlo theory suggests that these algorithms are particularly good, machine learning experience tells us that they are not. Understanding where the relationship breaks down may help in deepening our knowledge of both majority voting and greedy covering. In order to clarify the above issue, we have taken an experimental approach, using several artificially generated learning problems and also some "natural" ones.

2 Monte Carlo Algorithms

Given a class Π of problems, a Monte Carlo algorithm is a stochastic algorithm that, applied to any instance $x \in \Pi$, always outputs an answer, but, occasionally, this answer is incorrect [Brassard & Bratley, 1988]. In order for an algorithm to be Monte Carlo, any problem instance must have the same probability of being incorrect [1]. More precisely, let p be a real number such that $1/2 < p < 1$. A Monte Carlo algorithm is *p-correct* if the probability that it returns a correct answer is at least p on any problem instance. The difference $(p - 1/2)$ is the *advantage* of the algorithm. Moreover, a Monte Carlo algorithm is said to be *consistent* if it never outputs two different correct solutions to the same instance.

The probability of success of a consistent Monte Carlo algorithm can be increased by running the algorithm several time on the same instance, and choosing the most frequent answer [2]. More precisely, let ε and η be two positive real numbers, such that ε

---

[1] This statement is different from saying that the algorithm is correct on most problem instances, being only incorrect on a small subset of them.

[2] The consistency of the algorithm is fundamental for the amplification. For instance, running three times a consistent 0.75-correct Monte Carlo algorithm MC and taking the most frequent answer leads to a 0.84-correct algorithm, whereas the resulting algorithm is only 0.71-correct, should MC be not consistent.

$+ \eta < 1/2$. Let MC(x) be a consistent and $(1/2 + \varepsilon)$-correct Monte Carlo algorithm. If we define

$$n(\varepsilon) = -\frac{2}{\lg_2(1 - 4\varepsilon^2)} \tag{1}$$

it is sufficient to call MC at least

$$T = \lceil n(\varepsilon) \lg_2(1/\eta) \rceil \tag{2}$$

times on x, and to returns the most frequent answer[3], to obtain an algorithm that is still consistent and also $(1-\eta)$-correct. We have *amplified* the advantage of MC(x). A more accurate bound than (2) can be obtained by running a consistent and $(1/2 + \varepsilon)$-correct algorithm a number $T = (2m - 1)$ of times; the resulting algorithm is $(1 - \eta)$-correct, where:

$$\eta = 1/2 - \varepsilon \sum_{i=0}^{m-1} \text{Bin}(2i, i)\left(\frac{1}{4} - \varepsilon^2\right)^i \cdot \frac{(1 - 4\varepsilon^2)^m}{4\varepsilon\sqrt{\pi m}} \tag{3}$$

2.1 Biased Monte Carlo Algorithms

Let us consider now a Monte Carlo algorithm solving a decision problem, with only two answers: *true* and *false*. Suppose moreover that the algorithm is always correct when it outputs *true*, errors being only possible on the answer *false*. Such an algorithm is said to be a *true-biased* Monte Carlo. With a true-biased Monte Carlo algorithm, majority voting on a sequence of runs is superfluous, because it is sufficient that the answer *true* be output a single time. More importantly, amplification occurs also for biased p-correct algorithms with $p \leq 1/2$, provided that p > 0. More formally:

Definition 1 – Let Π be a class of problem and let s_0 be a possible output of a Monte Carlo algorithm MC(x). MC(x) is s_0-*biased* if there exists a subset X of Π such that:
a. MC(x) is always correct on instance x whenever $x \notin X$,
b. The correct solution to any $x \in X$ is s_0, but MC(x) may not always return the correct answer on these instances.

It is easy to prove [Brassard & Bratley, 1988, p. 266] the following:

Theorem 1 (*Brassard & Bratley*) – Running k times a consistent, s_0-biased, p-correct Monte Carlo algorithm (with $0<p<1$) yields a consistent, s_0-biased, $[1 - (1- p)^k]$-correct algorithm.

---

[3] Taking the most frequent answer corresponds to an unweighted majority voting. It is possible to modify the decision procedure so that weighted voting results. However, this issue is not central to the paper, and will not be considered further.

Then, in order to achieve a correctness level of (1- η), it is sufficient to run the algorithm at least a number of times:

$$T - \frac{\lg_2 \eta}{\lg_2(1-p)} \qquad (4)$$

Table 1 reports a comparison among the numbers of repetitions for unbiased and biased algorithms, according to (2), (3) and (4).

Table 1. Comparison among numbers of repetitions.

$1-\varepsilon$	$1-\eta$	T Bound (2)	T Bound (3)	T Bound (4)
0.55	0.95	596	269	4
0.55	0.99	918	367	6
0.10	0.99	—	—	11

From Table 1 biased algorithms appear to be much more effective and highly desirable.

3 Relations between Majority Voting and Monte Carlo Algorithms

Let us consider now a learning context in which a weak learner A acquires decision rules $h(x) : X \rightarrow Y$, belonging to a set H. X is a set of instances and $Y = \{+1, -1\}$ is a binary set of classes. Let us call *positive* the instances labelled $+1$. Let $\mathcal{E}_t$ be a subset of X, such that $|\mathcal{E}_t| = N$, and $\mathcal{E}_t = \mathcal{POS} \cup \mathcal{NEG}$. Let MC(x) be a Monte Carlo algorithm that takes as input a random instance x and outputs a class label $h_t(x) \in Y$. The instance belongs to $\mathcal{E}_t$ but MC(x) does not know. MC(x) can be defined as in Figure 1.

MC(x) is a Monte Carlo algorithm, because the probability ε_t of misclassifying x (i.e., the generalization error of $h_t(x)$) is uniform over all instances x. Moreover, MC is consistent, because the correct answer (class label) is unique.

If we run MC(x) T times on instance x and take as answer the most frequent one, it is immediate to see that MC(x) corresponds to a majority voting classification algorithm. Different combination schemes, such as boosting or bagging, correspond to different ways of choosing the set at each run. Then, for the error ε of the combined decision, formulas (2) and (3) hold. As we may notice, formula (2) is the same as the one derived by Shapire [1990], whereas formula (3) is an improvement thereupon, which is more close to experimental results [Quinlan, 1996; Bauer & Kohavi, 1999].

If we now consider biased Monte Carlo algorithms, we may wonder to what kind of combined classifiers they might correspond to. If a correspondence can be established, it would be reasonable to expect that the learning counterpart shows at least two advantages over more generic boosting methods: first of all, comparable error rates with a much smaller numbers of individual classifiers, and, second, the possibility of using very rough weak learners, because their error rate only needs to be greater than zero. Actually, it turns out that the learning counterpart of a consistent, true-biased and p-correct Monte Carlo algorithm is a greedy covering algorithm of the AQ-type, with the set of positive examples as the S set in Definition 1. In fact, let us consider as weak learner A an algorithm that covers some positive examples and no negative ones. Then, at each repetition of MC(x), we eliminate the already covered positive examples. At the end, when no positive example is left, the majority voting rule becomes an "at least one" rule.

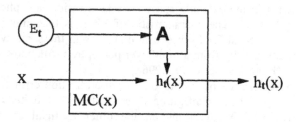

Fig. 1. Monte Carlo algorithm MC(x) classifies instance x into a binary set of classes Y. MC(x) exploits a subset $\mathcal{E}_t$ of training examples from X, applies A to $\mathcal{E}_t$ and outputs $h_t(x)$, which is used to classify x. MC(x) does not know that x belongs to the learning set $\mathcal{E}_t$.

In fact, it is sufficient that one among the $h_t(x)$'s says +1 to classify the example as positive, due to the bias. If we look at Adaboost, this algorithm partially satisfies the biasedness requirement. In fact, even though successive runs are not independent, the weighting process simulates the elimination of already classified examples: actually, correctly classified examples are not really eliminated, but only considered less important than not yet correctly classified ones. The process of deleting covered examples is a limiting process of this weighting procedure.

The idea of obtaining much smaller classifiers is appealing, as one of the drawback of boosting is the generation of incomprehensible classification rules. However, the machine learning field has dealt a long time with greedy covering algorithms, which did not prove to be very robust with respect to generalization error. Then, a pertinent question would be: why? The previous observation suggested us to test the following hypotheses:

1. A GCA allows very simple learners to be boosted in few runs, without bothering about their recognition rate (provided that it is greater than zero).
2. GCA's should be prone to overfitting, whereas (most of the times) Adaboost is not. Then, increasing the number of basic classifiers should let the test error of a GCA increase, contrarily to what happens to Adaboost.
3. The different behaviour of Adaboost and GCA with respect to generalization is reflected in the evolution of margin distributions, if it is true that large margins are the reason underlying Adaboost's robustness.

In order to test the previous hypotheses, we performed experiments on a set of artificial datasets, reported in the following section.

4 Experimental Setting

We now describe the experimental setting used to test Adaboost and GCA algorithms. The following three subsections will describe the learning task, the two tested algorithms and the datasets used for experiments.

4.1 Weak Learner

Both Adaboost and the GCA use a very simple weak learner, called MCK, that was designed on purpose. This learner induces *spherical stumps*, i.e. the basic classifiers $h_t(x)$ are spheres in the example space: if x falls inside the sphere, then $h_t(x) = 1$, otherwise $h_t(x) = -1$. The characteristic of MCK is that individual classifiers are local, and hence they differ from decision stumps in the same way as Radial Basis Function neural net differ from a multilayer perceptron. Adaboost's implementation is the same as in [Freund & Schapire, 1996a].

In order to explore the behaviour of the generalization error for high redundancy level, Adaboost has been configured to stop after 20.000 iterations on "difficult" datasets, after "10.000" iterations on the other artificial ones, and after 6.000 iterations on the "Splice Junction" dataset. For MCK, we have used two strategies: first, the iteration of MCK stops when a zero error is reached, which happens when no positive example is left uncovered. But we have also continued to add classifiers, as in Adaboost, in the hope to show that this added redundancy would let the test error increase. Then, in this case, the GCA has been iterated for up to 1,000 runs.

4.2 Datasets

We created nine artificial datasets. Eight of them contain examples of concepts that ly in a two-dimensional Euclidean space. Figure 2 shows these concepts. In addition, a 5-dimensional, sphere-like concept (D8.Hyperspheres, N = 5000), and the "Splice Junction" dataset (D9.Splice, N = 3190) from Irvine repository have been considered. N is the total number of examples in the dataset.

4.3 Experimental Results

Even though the same analysis has been performed on all the datasets, detailed results are described only for D4.Asia, because they all showed similar patterns of bahviour. In particular, the results have been summarized into Figure 3.

The graphs reported in Figure 3 are typical of the two dimensional cases. An interesting feature of these graphs is the fact that even though Adaboost may be better in the long run, for small number of trials the simpler GCA strategy is often better with respect to not only the training error (which reaches zero in few runs), but also with respect on the test set.

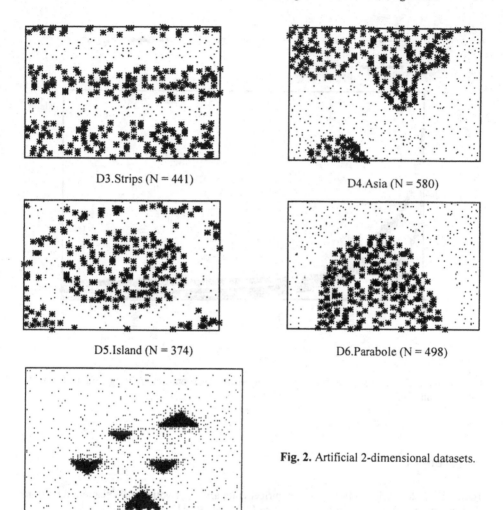

D3.Strips (N = 441)

D4.Asia (N = 580)

D5.Island (N = 374)

D6.Parabole (N = 498)

Fig. 2. Artificial 2-dimensional datasets.

D7.Triangles (N = 1135)

5 Conclusions

Relating majority voting procedures with similar approaches can shed light on the reasons and conditions under which it may work. According to the experimentation provided, there is still a need for investigation on at least two issues: the influence of the very methods of combination, and the type of example distribution modification (reweighting). However, further experiments are necessary to draw more precise conclusions.

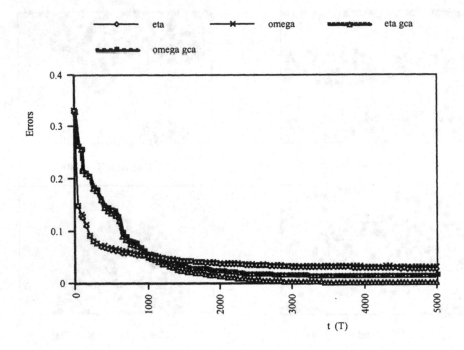

Fig. 3. Results for the dataset D4.Asia. Empirical error on the training and test sets for Adaboost and GCA.

References

Bauer, E., & Kohavi, R. (1999). "An empirical comparison of voting classifcation algorithms: Bagging, boosting, and variants". *Machine Learning, 30,* 113-142.

Brassard G., and Bratley P. (1988). *Algorithmics: Theory and Practice.* Prentice Hall, Englewood Cliffs, NJ.

Breiman, L. (1996). Bagging predictors. *Machine Learning, 24,* 123-140.

Freund, Y. & Schapire, R. E. (1996a). Experiments with a new boosting algorithm. Machine Learning: Proceedings of the Thirteen International Conference (pp. 148-156).

Freund, Y. & Schapire, R. E. (1996b). Game theory, on-line prediction and boosting. In Proceedings of the Ninth Annual Conference on Computational Learning Theory, (pp. 325-332).

Freund, Y. & Schapire, R. E. (1997). A decision-theoretic generalization of on-line learning and an application to boosting. *Journal of Computer and System Sciences, 55,* 119-139.

Kong, E. B., & Dietterich, T. G. (1995). "Error-correcting output coding corrects bias and variance". In *Proceedings of the Twelfth International Conference on Machine Learning* (Lake Tahoe, CA), pp. 313-321.

Quinlan, J. R. (1996). Bagging, boosting, and C4.5. Proceedings of the Thirteenth National Conference on Artificial Intelligence, (pp. 725-730).

Schapire, R. E., Freund, Y., Bartlett, P. & Lee, W. S. (1998). "Boosting the margin: A new explanation for the effectiveness of voting methods". *The Annals of Statistics, 26*, 1651-1686.

Schapire, R. E. (1990). The strength of weak learnability. Machine Learning, 5(2), 197-227.

Shawe-Taylor, J., Bartlett, P. L., Williamson, R. C., & Anthony, M. (1996). "A framework for structural risk minimisation". In Proceedings of the Ninth Annual Conference on Computational Learning Theory, (pp. 68-76)

Stepwise Induction of Model Trees

Donato Malerba   Annalisa Appice   Antonia Bellino
Michelangelo Ceci   Domenico Pallotta

Dipartimento di Informatica, Università degli Studi di Bari
via Orabona 4, 70125 Bari, Italy
{malerba, appice, bellino, ceci, pallotta}@di.uniba.it

Abstract. Regression trees are tree-based models used to solve those prediction problems in which the response variable is numeric. They differ from the better-known classification or decision trees only in that they have a numeric value rather than a class label associated with the leaves. Model trees are an extension of regression trees in the sense that they associate leaves with multivariate linear models. In this paper a method for the data-driven construction of model trees is presented, namely the Stepwise Model Tree Induction (SMOTI) method. Its main characteristic is the induction of trees with two types of nodes: regression nodes, which perform only straight-line regression, and splitting nodes, which partition the sample space. In this way, the multivariate linear model associated to each leaf is efficiently built stepwise. SMOTI has been evaluated in an empirical study and compared to other model tree induction systems.

1 Introduction

Many problems encountered in practice involve the prediction of a continuous numeric attribute associated with a case. More formally, given a set of observed data $(\mathbf{x}, y) \in \mathcal{X} \times \mathcal{Y}$, where $\mathcal{X}$ denotes the feature space spanned by m independent (or predictor) variables x_i (both numerical and categorical), the goal is to predict the dependent (or response) variable Y which is continuous. This problem has been approached in many ways, such as standard regression, neural nets, and regression trees [1]. A *regression tree* approximates a function $y=g(\mathbf{x})$ by means of a piecewise *constant* one. *Model trees* generalize the concept of regression trees in the sense that they approximate the function above by a piecewise *linear* function, that is they associate leaves with multivariate linear models. The problem of inducing model trees from a training set has received attention both in statistics [2,9] and in machine learning. Some of the model tree induction systems developed are: M5 [8], RETIS [4], M5' [12], RegTree [5], and HTL [10,11]. All these systems perform a *top-down* induction of models trees (TDIMT) by building the tree structure through recursive partitioning of the training set and by associating leaves with models. During the construction of the tree there are three main problems to be solved: Choosing the best partition of a region of the feature space, determining the leaves of the tree and choosing a model for each leaf. Since an exhaustive exploration of all possible

F. Esposito (Ed.): AI*IA 2001, LNAI 2175, pp. 20-32, 2001.

solutions is not possible in practice, several heuristics have been proposed to solve such problems.

In this paper we present the current state of the art of research on TDIMT and, starting from the strengths and weaknesses of some approaches, we propose a new method, named Stepwise Model Tree Induction (SMOTI), which tries to match the coherence of the heuristic evaluation function, used to choose the best partition, with the type of model associated to the leaves. SMOTI constructs model trees stepwise, by adding, at each step, either a regression node or a splitting node. Regression nodes perform straight-line regression, while splitting nodes partition the sample space. The multivariate linear model associated to each leaf is obtained by composing the effect of regression nodes along the path from the root to the leaf.

The background and motivation of this work is described in the next section, while in Section 3 the method SMOTI is introduced, and its computational complexity is analyzed. Finally, in Section 4 some experimental results on eight different data sets are reported and commented on.

2. Background and Motivation

In tree-structured regression models the partitioning process is guided by a heuristic *evaluation function* that chooses the best split of observations into subgroups. In CART (Classification And Regression Trees), a well-known system for the induction of regression trees [1], the quality of the constructed tree T is measured by the mean square error $R^*(T)$: The lower the $R^*(T)$ the better. A sample estimate of the *mean square error* is:

$$R(T) = \frac{1}{N} \sum_{t \in \tilde{T}} \sum_{x_i \in t} (y_i - \bar{y}(t))^2$$

where N is the number of training examples (x_i, y_i), $\tilde{T}$ is the set of leaves of the tree, and $\bar{y}(t)$ is the sample mean of the response variable, computed on the observations in the node t. In other words, $R(T)$ is the sum of the resubstitution estimates of risk $R(t)$ at the leaves of the tree. By denoting with $s^2(t)$ the sample variance of the response variable at a node t, $R(T)$ can be rewritten as:

$$R(T) = \sum_{t \in \tilde{T}} R(t) = \sum_{t \in \tilde{T}} \frac{N(t)}{N} s^2(t) = \sum_{t \in \tilde{T}} p(t) s^2(t)$$

where $N(t)$ is the number of observations in the node t and $p(t)$ is the probability that a training case reaches the leaf t. When the observations in a leaf t are sub-divided into two groups, we obtain a new tree T', where t is an internal node with two children, say, t_L and t_R. Different splits generate distinct trees T', and the choice of the best split is made on the grounds of the corresponding $R(T')$. More precisely, the minimization of $R(T')$ is equivalent to minimizing $p(t_L)s^2(t_L) + p(t_R)s^2(t_R)$, the contribution to $R(T')$ given by the split.

This heuristic criterion conceived for a regression tree learning problem has also been used in some TDIMT systems, such as HTL. In his system M5, Quinlan adopts a similar criterion, using the sample standard deviation $s(t)$ instead of the sample variance $s^2(t)$. The evaluation function used by AID [6] is *Fisher's correlation coefficient*, η^2:

$$\eta^2 = \frac{N(t_L)(\bar{y}(t_L)-\bar{y}(t))^2 + N(t_R)(\bar{y}(t_R)-\bar{y}(t))^2}{\sum\limits_{j=1}^{N}(y_j-\bar{y}(t))^2}$$

where $\bar{y}(t_L)$ ($\bar{y}(t_R)$) is the sample mean of the dependent variable computed on the set of the $N(t_L)$ ($N(t_R)$) cases falling in the left (right) child node. Briefly, the numerator is the deviance between two groups (left and right), while the denominator is the total deviance. This coefficient ranges between 0 and 1; when η^2 is close to 1, there is no variance *within* the groups. AID chooses the partition that maximizes η^2. Actually, the maximization of the deviance between two groups and the minimization of $p(t_L)s^2(t_L)+p(t_R)s^2(t_R)$ lead to the same partitioning.

The problem with these evaluation functions is that they do not take into account the models associated with the leaves of the tree. In principle, the optimal split should be chosen on the basis of the fit of each *model* to the data. In practice, many TDIMT systems choose the optimal split on the basis of the spread of observations with respect to the *sample mean*. However, a model associated to a leaf is generally more sophisticated than the sample mean. Therefore, *the evaluation function is incoherent with respect to the model tree being built.*

To illustrate the problem, let us consider the following dataset with twenty cases and only one independent variable:

| x | -1.0 | -0.8 | -0.7 | -0.5 | -0.3 | -0.1 | 0.0 | 0.2 | 0.3 | 0.4 | 0.5 | 0.6 | 0.7 | 1.0 | 1.1 | 1.2 | 1.5 | 1.7 | 1.9 | 2.0 |
| y | 0.3 | 0.1 | 0.2 | 0.7 | 0.8 | 0.5 | 1.1 | 1.5 | 1.1 | 1.2 | 1.6 | 1.2 | 1.5 | 0.8 | 1.1 | 0.7 | 0.9 | 0.1 | 0.4 | 0.2 |

The scatter plot of the data set is given in Figure 1a; the values of the independent variable range between -1.0 and 2.0. The best model tree is reported in Figure 1b. It is obtained by partitioning the training observations into two subgroups: $X \leq 0.4$ and $X > 0.4$. It shows the flexibility and the power of model trees, since a simple linear regression on the whole data set would give the dashed line in Figure 1a.

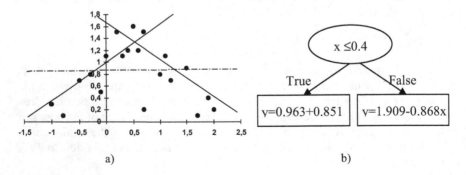

a)   b)

Fig. 1. A split node t with two straight-line regression models in the leaves.

Nevertheless, neither M5 nor HTL are able to find this model tree. The system Cubist (http://www.rulequest.com), a commercial version of M5, splits the data at x = -0.1 and builds the following models:

$X \le -0.1$: $Y = 0.78 + 0.175*X$
$X > -0.1$: $Y = 1.143 - 0.281*X$

The problem illustrated above is caused by the net separation of the *splitting* stage from the *predictive* one. This separation seems to be inherited by regression tree learners, such as AID and CART, but a careful study of the heuristic criteria used in these systems shows that the evaluation functions do take into account the models built in the leaves. Indeed, the models are the sample means which play a role in the computation of $R(T)$ and η^2. However, when we try to use the same heuristic criteria for model tree induction we are rating the effectiveness of a partition with respect to different models from the ones chosen in the subsequent predictive stage.

This problem cannot potentially occur in RETIS, whose heuristic criterion is to minimize $p(t_L)s^2(t_L) + p(t_R)s^2(t_R)$, where $s^2(t_L)$ $(s^2(t_R))$ is now computed as the mean square error with respect to the regression plane g_L (g_R) found for the left (right) child:

$$s^2(t_L) = \frac{1}{N(t_L)} \sum_{x_i \in t_L} (y_i - g_L(x_i))^2 \qquad \left(s^2(t_R) = \frac{1}{N(t_R)} \sum_{x_i \in t_R} (y_i - g_R(x_i))^2 \right)$$

In practice, for each possible partitioning the best regression planes at leaves are chosen, so that the selection of the optimal partitioning can be based on the result of the prediction stage. This corresponds to a look-ahead strategy with depth one, as in traditional top-down induction of decision/regression trees.

The weakness of the RETIS heuristic evaluation function is its high computational complexity, especially when all independent variables are continuous. For instance, in the case of N training observations, described by m independent continuous variables, the selection of the first split takes time $O(mNlogN)$ to sort all values of the m variables, plus time required to test $(N-1)m$ distinct cut points, at worst. Each test, in turn, requires the computation of two regression planes on the m independent variables. The coefficients of each linear regression function are computed according to the formula $(\mathbf{X'X})^{-1}\mathbf{X'y}$, where $\mathbf{y}$ is the $N(t)$-dimensional vector of values taken by the response variable in node t, while $\mathbf{X}$ is an $N(t)(m+1)$ matrix of observations, plus a column with only 1s [3]. The complexity of the computation of $\mathbf{X'X}$ is $N(t)(m+1)^2$, the complexity of the inversion of an $(m+1)(m+1)$ matrix is $O((m+1)^3)$, and the complexity of the computation of the product of an $(m+1)(m+1)$ matrix with an $N(t)$-dimensional vector is $N(t)(m+1)$. In general, $N(t) > m$, thus the computation of the regression function takes time $O(N(t)(m+1)^2)$. When $N(t_L)$ is small, $N(t_R)$ is almost equal to N. Thus, for at least one of the children $N(t)$ is proportional to N. To sum up, the choice of the first split takes time $O(N(N-1)m(m+1)^2)$, which is cubic in m and square in N.

In order to reduce the computational time, we could adopt a forward stepwise strategy, according to which a multiple linear regression model is built step-by-step. The proposed method is illustrated in the next section.

3. Stepwise Construction of Model Trees

To reduce the computational time a multiple linear regression model is built stepwise, according to a new forward strategy, named SMOTI, which considers *regression steps* and *splitting tests* at the same level. In this way, the development of a tree structure is not only determined by a recursive partitioning procedure, but also by some intermediate prediction functions. This means that that there are two types of nodes in the tree: regression nodes and splitting nodes. Regression nodes perform only straight-line regressions, since a multivariate linear regression model can be built stepwise by regressing Y on one single variable at a time. Regression and splitting nodes pass down observations to their children in two different ways. For a splitting node t, only a subgroup of the $N(t)$ observations in t is passed to each child, and no change is made on the variables. For a regression node t, all the observations are passed down to its only child, but the values of the independent variables not included in the model are transformed, to remove the linear effect of those variables already included. Thus, descendants of a regression node will operate on a modified training set. Indeed, according to the statistical theory of linear regression, the incremental construction of a multiple linear regression model is made by removing the linear effect of introduced variables each time a new independent variable is added to the model [3]. For instance, let us consider the problem of building a multiple regression model with two independent variables through a sequence of straight-line regressions:

$$Y = a + bX_1 + cX_2$$

We start regressing Y on X_1, so that the model:

$$Y = a_1 + b_1 X_1.$$

is built. This fitted equation does not predict Y exactly. By adding the new variable X_2, the prediction might improve. Instead of starting from scratch and building a model with both X_1 and X_2, we can build a linear model for X_2 given X_1:

$$X_2 = a_2 + b_2 X_1$$

then compute the residuals on X_2:

$$X'_2 = X_2 - (a_2 + b_2 X_1)$$

and finally regress Y on X'_2 alone:

$$Y = a_3 + b_3 X'_2.$$

By substituting the equation of X'_2 in the last equation we have:

$$Y = a_3 + b_3 X_2 - a_2 b_3 - b_2 b_3 X_1.$$

It can be proven that this last model coincides with the first model built, that is $a = a_3 - a_2 b_3$, $b = -b_2 b_3$ and $c = b_3$. This explains why SMOTI removes the linear effect of variables already included in the model (X_1) from variables to be selected for the next regression step (X_2).

In SMOTI the validity of either a regression step on a variable X_i or a splitting test on the same variable is based on two distinct evaluation measures, $\pi(X_i, Y)$ and $\sigma(X_i, Y)$ respectively. The variable X_i is of a continuous type in the former case, and of any

type in the latter case. Both $\pi(X_i,Y)$ and $\sigma(X_i,Y)$ are mean square errors, therefore they can be actually compared to choose between three different possibilities:
1. growing the model tree by adding a regression node t;
2. growing the model tree by adding a splitting node t;
3. stop growing the tree at node t.

As pointed out in Section 2, the evaluation measure $\sigma(X_i,Y)$ should be coherently defined on the basis of the multivariate linear model to be associated with each leaf. In the case of SMOTI it is sufficient to consider a straight-line regression associated to each leaf t_R (t_L), since regression nodes along the path from the root to t_R (t_L) already partially define a multivariate regression model (see Figure 2).

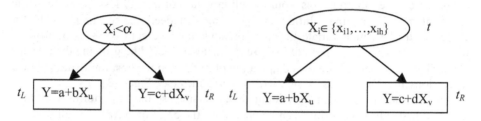

Fig. 2. A split node t with two straight-line regression models in the leaves. The variable is continuous in the left tree and discrete in the right tree.

If X_i is continuous and α is a threshold value for X_i then $\sigma(X_i,Y)$ is defined as:

$$\sigma(X_i,Y) = \frac{N(t_L)}{N(t)} R(t_L) + \frac{N(t_R)}{N(t)} R(t_R)$$

where $N(t)$ is the number of cases reaching t, $N(t_L)$ $(N(t_R))$ is the number of cases passed down to the left (right) child, and $R(t_L)$ $(R(t_R))$ is the resubstitution error of the left (right) child, computed as follows:

$$R(t_L) = \sqrt{\frac{1}{N(t_L)} \sum_{j=1}^{N(t_L)} (y_j - \hat{y}_j)^2} \qquad \left(R(t_R) = \sqrt{\frac{1}{N(t_R)} \sum_{j=1}^{N(t_R)} (y_j - \hat{y}_j)^2} \right).$$

The estimate:

$$\hat{y}_j = a_0 + \sum_{s=1}^{m} a_s x_s$$

is computed by combining the straight-line regression associated to the leaf t_L (t_R) with all univariate regression lines associated to regression nodes along the path from the root to t_L (t_R).

If X_i is discrete, SMOTI partitions attribute values into two sets, so that binary trees are always built. Partitioning is based on the same criterion applied in CART [1, pp. 247], which reduces the search for the best subset of categories from 2^{k-1} to $k-1$, where k is the number of distinct values for X_i. More precisely, if $S_{X_i} = \{x_{i_1}, x_{i_2}, ..., x_{i_k}\}$ is the set of distinct values of X_i, S_{X_i} is sorted according to the average over all y_i in t. The best split is in the form: $X_i \in \{x_{i_1}, ..., x_{i_h}\}$, $h= 1, ..., k-1$. For all $k-1$ possible splits, the evaluation measure $\sigma(X_i, Y)$ is computed as in the case of continuous variables.

The evaluation of the effectiveness of a regression step $Y=a+bX_i$ at node t cannot be naïvely based on the resubstitution error $R(t)$:

$$R(t) = \sqrt{\frac{1}{N(t)} \sum_{j=1}^{N(t)} (y_j - \hat{y}_j)^2}$$

where the estimator $\hat{y}_i$ is computed by combining the straight-line regression associated to t with all univariate regression lines associated to regression nodes along the path from the root to t. This would result in values of $\pi(X_i, Y)$ less than or equal to values of $\sigma(X_i, Y)$ for some splitting test involving X_i. Indeed, the splitting test "looks-ahead" to the best multivariate linear regressions after the split on X_i is performed, while the regression step does not. A fairer comparison would be growing the tree at a further level in order to base the computation of $\pi(X_i, Y)$ on the best multivariate linear regressions after the regression step on X_i is performed (see Figure 3).

Let t' be the child of the regression node t, and suppose that it performs a splitting test. The best splitting test in t' can be chosen on the basis of $\sigma(X_j, Y)$ for all possible variables X_j, as indicated above. Then $\pi(X_i, Y)$ can be defined as follows:

$\pi(X_i, Y) = min \{ R(t), \sigma(X_j, Y) \text{ for all possible variables } X_j \}$.

Having defined both $\pi(X_i, Y)$ and $\sigma(X_i, Y)$, the criterion for selecting the best node is fully characterized as well. A weight w $(1-w)$ is associated to splitting (regression) nodes, so as to express the user preference for model trees with splitting tests (regression steps). Therefore, SMOTI actually compares the weighted values $w\sigma(X_i, Y)$ and $(1-w)\pi(X_i, Y)$ while selecting a node. At each step of the model tree induction process, SMOTI chooses the apparently most promising node according to a greedy strategy. A continuous variable selected for a regression step is eliminated from further consideration, so that it can appear only once in a regression node along a path from the root to a leaf.

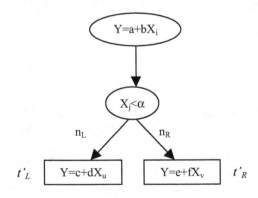

Fig. 3. Evaluation of a regression step at node t, based on the best splitting test below.

In SMOTI three different stopping criteria are implemented. The first one uses the partial F-test to evaluate the contribution of a new independent variable to the model [3]. The second stopping criterion adopted by SMOTI requires the number of cases in each node to be greater than a minimum value. The third criterion stops the induction process when all continuous variables along the path from the root to the current node are used in regression steps and there are no discrete variables in the training set.

The computational complexity of the model tree induction algorithm is highly dependent on the choice of the best splitting test or regression step for a given node. For regression steps, the worst case complexity is $O(NmlogN)$, where N is the number of examples in the training set and m is the number of independent variables. For splitting tests, the worst case complexity is $O(N+NlogN)$, where the component $NlogN$ is due to the quicksort algorithm. Therefore, the worst case complexity for the selection of any node is $O(Nm^2 logN)$, since there are m independent variables.

It is noteworthy that SMOTI is more efficient than RETIS at building model trees and defines the best partitioning of the feature space coherently with respect to the model tree being built.

4. Observations on Experimental Results

SMOTI has been implemented as a module of a knowledge discovery system and has been empirically evaluated on six datasets are taken from either the UCI Machine Learning Repository (URL: http://www.ics.uci.edu/~mlearn/MLRepository.html) or the site of the system HTL (URL: http://www.ncc.up.pt/~ltorgo/Regression/DataSets.html). They are listed in Table 1 and they all have a continuous variable to be predicted.

Table 1. Datasets used in the empirical evaluation of SMOTI.

Dataset	No. cases	No. attributes	Continuous	Discrete
Abalone	2889	8	7	1
Auto	398	8	5	3
Housing	506	14	14	0
Machine CPU	209	6	0	6
Pyrimidines	74	27	27	0
Price	159	16	15	1

Each dataset is analyzed by means of a 10-fold cross-validation, that is, the dataset is firstly divided into ten blocks of near-equal size and distribution of class values, and then, for every block, SMOTI is trained on the remaining blocks and tested on the hold-out block.

The system performance is evaluated on the basis of both the average resubstitution error and the average number of leaves. For pairwise comparison of methods, the non-parametric Wilcoxon signed rank test is used [7], since the number of folds (or "independent" trials) is relatively low and does not justify the application of parametric tests, such as the t-test. In the Wilcoxon signed rank test, the summations on both positive and negative ranks, namely W+ and W-, are used to determine the winner. In all experiments reported in this empirical study, the significance level α is set to 0.05.

4.1 Effect of Node Weighting

The first experiment aims at investigating the effect of node weighting on the predictive accuracy and complexity of the tree. A weight greater than 0.5 gives preferentiality to splitting tests, while a weight lower than 0.5 favors the selection of regression nodes. In terms of complexity of model trees, this means that the number of leaves in the tree-structure is generally higher when the weight is greater than 0.5. This intuition has been confirmed by experimental results, as can be seen in Figure 4.

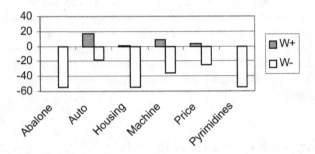

Fig. 4. Summations of positive and negative signed ranks used to compare the number of leaves in model trees built with $w=0.5$ and $w=0.6$. Differences are statistically significant for the databases Abalone, Housing, and Pyrimidine, meaning that in these cases the size of the model trees built with $w=0.5$ is significantly lower than the size of the model trees built with $w=0.6$.

It is noteworthy that, for higher values of the weight, regression nodes are often selected near the leaves of the tree, so that they can give only a local contribution to the approximation of the underlying function with a model tree. On the contrary, for lower values of the weight regression node they tend to be selected at the root, so that they give a global contribution to the approximation of the underlying function. In other words, the weight represents the trade-off between global regression models that span the whole feature space and are built using all training cases and local regression models, which fit fewer data falling in smaller portions of the feature space.

The weighting factor also affects the predictive accuracy of the induced model, as reported in Table 2. In each of the ten trials per dataset, predictive accuracy is estimated by the mean square error, computed on the corresponding validation set. Experimental results show that by increasing the weight, that is favoring the selection of splitting nodes, it is possible to obtain more accurate model trees. Moreover, we also observed that for weight values higher than 0.6 the situation does not change with respect to the case $w=0.6$, while for weight values lower than 0.5 the accuracy is lower than that observed with $w=0.5$. The conclusion is that, in almost all data sets considered, local regression steps are preferred.

Table 2. Results of the Wilcoxon signed rank test on the accuracy of the induced model. The best value is in boldface, while the statistically significant values (p≤α/2) are in italics.

Data set	00.5 vs 0.52			0.5 vs 0.56			0.5 vs 0.6		
	p	W+	W-	p	W+	W-	p	W+	W-
Abalone	0.083	45	**10**	*0.004*	54	*1*	*0.004*	54	*1*
Auto	0.556	34	**21**	0.492	35	**20**	1.000	28	**27**
Housing	0.492	**20**	35	0.275	39	**16**	0.432	36	**19**
Machine	0.064	46	**9**	0.064	46	**9**	0.064	46	**9**
Price	0.083	45	**10**	0.232	**40**	15	0.432	36	**19**
Pyrimidines	*0.002*	55	*0*	0.106	11	**44**	0.064	46	**9**

4.2 Comparison with Other Systems

SMOTI has also been compared to two other TDMTI systems, namely a trial version of Cubist and M5'. Since the trial version of Cubist worked only for data sets of at most 200 cases and 50 attributes, the comparison with Quinlan's system was possible only for four databases, namely Machine CPU, Price, and Pyrimidines. On the contrary, the comparison with M5' was performed on all collected data sets.

When possible, two statistics were collected for comparison purposes: the average number of leaves and the average MSE of the trees. Actually, Cubist did not report the average MSE, but it was derived from other statistics printed in the report file. On the contrary, it was impossible to derive the average number of leaves from statistics made available to the user. Experimental results are shown in Table 3.

Table 3. Tree size and predictive accuracy for three different systems: SMOTI, M5' and Cubist.

Data Sets	SMOTI 0.5		SMOTI 0.6		M5'		Cubist	
	Av. No. Leaves	Av. MSE	Av. No. Leaves	Av. MSE	Av. No. Leaves	Av. MSE	Av. No. Leaves	Av. MSE
Abalone	320,2	6,15	373,5	3,44	304,1	*2,62*		
Auto	31,7	7,87	31,9	7,92	24,6	*3,19*		
Housing	28,1	12,1	44,1	8,3	48,4	*3,89*		
Machine	15,6	296,05	17,1	70,11	15,2	59,69		50,07
Price	11,1	3220,51	13,6	2646,17	16,9	2150,74		2512,37
Pyrimidines	1	0,12	6,1	0,08	3,4	0,09		0,09

As pointed out before, SMOTI generates more accurate model trees when splitting tests are favored by setting the weight to 0.6. However, even in the best case, SMOTI does not perform as well as M5' and Cubist with almost all data sets. Some differences between SMOTI 0.6 and M5' are statistically significant and are reported in italics. These results, which are unfavorable to SMOTI, seem to confirm the presence of a common factor to many of the data sets used in the experiments on regression and model trees: no general behavior was noted for the underlying function to be approximated, and it can be better represented as a composition of many definite local behaviors.

4.3 Experiments on Laboratory-Sized Data Sets

In order to better understand the behavior of SMOTI, the system has been tested on laboratory-sized data sets randomly generated for seven different model trees. These model trees were automatically built for learning problems with nine independent variables (five continuous and four discrete), where continuous variables take values in the unit interval [0,1], while discrete variables take values in the set {A,B,C,D,E,F,G}. The model tree building procedure is recursively defined on the maximum depth of the tree to be generated. The choice of adding a regression or a splitting node is random and depends on a parameter $\theta \in [0,100]$: the probability of selecting a splitting node is θ%; conversely, the probability of selecting a regression node is $(100-\theta)$%. Therefore, the returned model trees have a variable number of regression/splitting nodes and leaves, while the depth of the tree is kept under control. In the experiments reported in this paper θ is fixed to 0.5 while the depth is set to 5.

Ten data points were randomly generated for each leaf, so that the size of the data set associated to a model tree depends on the number of leaves in the tree itself. Data points are generated according to the different multivariate linear models associated to the leaves. The error added to each model is distributed normally, with zero mean and variance σ^2, which is kept constant for all leaves. The value of σ^2 set for the experimentation is 0.001, which means that for almost 90% of generated data points the effect of the error is ±0.095, according to Chebyshev's inequality. The effect of the error is not marginal, given that both independent variables and their coefficients range in the unit interval.

Table 4. Results for the model tree built with parameters θ=0.5, depth=5, and σ^2=0.001.

w	T. depth	I. depth	T. # regr. nodes	I. #regr. nodes	T. # split. nodes	I. # split. nodes	T. # leaves	I. # leaves	Av. MSE SMOTI	Av. MSE. M5'
0.5	5	9	4	5	4	6	5	7	0.24	0.35
0.55		7		1		8		9	0.61	
0.5	5	5	4	2	6	9	7	10	0.2	0.36
0.55		5		1		9		10	0.15	
0.5	5	8	3	3	7	10	8	11	0.19	0.3
0.55		8		1		11		12	0.17	
0.5	5	10	2	5	5	9	6	10	0.53	0.27
0.55		6		1		9		10	0.32	
0.5	5	9	4	6	7	11	8	12	0.56	0.24
0.55		5		1		9		10	0.68	
0.5	5	0	4	0	0	0	1	1	0.16	0.29
0.55		0		0		0		1	0.16	
0.5	5	12	3	5	5	16	6	17	0.15	0.25
0.55		8		2		17		18	0.16	

Each dataset was analyzed by means of a 10-fold cross-validation. In order to study the effect of the weight, two different values were considered: w=0.5 and w=0.55. Experimental results are reported in Table 4. The properties of the original model trees (T. depth, T. number of regression nodes, T. number of splitting nodes, T. number of leaves) are compared to the corresponding properties of the induced tree (denoted by the initial I). The last two columns list the average mean square error reported by SMOTI and M5′. Results show that SMOTI over-partition the feature space, since the number of splitting nodes in the induced trees is always greater than the number of splitting nodes in the theoretical model tree. This is true even in the case of w=0.5. No similar regularity can be detected for regression nodes. Interestingly, in many cases SMOTI performs better than M5′ with respect to average MSE, even for the standard parameter setting like w=0.5. These results reverse negative results obtained with UCI data sets and confirm that SMOTI works quite well when both global and local behaviors are mixed up in the underlying models.

5. Conclusions

In the paper, a novel method, called stepwise model tree induction (SMOTI), has been presented. The main advantage of SMOTI is that it efficiently generates model trees with multiple regression models in the leaves. Model trees generated by SMOTI include two types of nodes: regression nodes and splitting nodes. A weight associated to the type of node allows the user to express a preference for either local regression or global regression.

Experimental results proved empirically the effect of the weight. A comparison with two other TDMTI systems has been reported for six datasets typically used to test regression tree induction algorithms. A justification of the unfavorable results for SMOTI may be the absence of a global behavior in the underlying model. An empirical comparison with M5′ on laboratory-sized data sets proved that SMOTI can induce more accurate model trees when both global and local behaviors are mixed up in the underlying model. In the future, we plan to investigate the effect of pruning model trees. To date, no study on the simplification techniques for model trees has been presented in the literature. There are several possible approaches, some based on the direct control of tree size, and others based on the extension of the set of tests considered. Both a theoretical and an empirical evaluation of these approaches in terms of accuracy and interpretability would be helpful in practical applications.

Acknowledgments

This work is part of the MURST COFIN-1999 project on "Statistical Models for Classification and Segmentation of Complex Data Structures: Methodologies, Software and Applications." The authors thank Lynn Rudd for her help in reading the paper and Marcello Lucente for his collaboration in conducting the experiments.

References

1. Breiman L., Friedman J., Olshen R., & Stone J.: *Classification and regression tree*, Wadsworth & Brooks, 1984.
2. Ciampi A.: Generalized regression trees, *Computational Statistics and Data Analysis*, 12, pp. 57-78, 1991.
3. Draper N.R., & Smith H.: *Applied regression analysis*, John Wiley & Sons, 1982.
4. Karalic A.: Linear regression in regression tree leaves, in *Proceedings of ISSEK '92 (International School for Synthesis of Expert Knowledge)*, Bled, Slovenia, 1992.
5. Lanubile A., & Malerba D.: Induction of regression trees with RegTree, in *Book of Short Papers on Classification and Data Analysis*, Pescara, Italy, pp. 253-260, 1997.
6. Morgan J.N., & Sonquist J.A.: Problems in the analysis of survey data, and a proposal, in *American Statistical Association Journal*, pp. 415-434, 1963.
7. Orkin, M., Drogin, R.: *Vital Statistics*, McGraw Hill, New York (1990).
8. Quinlan J. R.: Learning with continuous classes, in Proceedings AI'92, Adams & Sterling (Eds.), World Scientific, pp. 343-348, 1992.
9. Siciliano R., & Mola F.: Modelling for recursive partitioning in variable selection, in *COMPSTAT '94*, Dutter R., & Grossman W. (Eds.), Physica-Verlag, pp. 172-177, 1994.
10. Torgo L.: Kernel Regression Trees, in *Poster Papers of the 9th European Conference on Machine Learning (ECML 97)*, M. van Someren, & G. Widmer (Eds.), Prague, Czech Republic, pp. 118-127, 1997.
11. Torgo L.: Functional Models for Regression Tree Leaves, in *Proceedings of the Fourteenth International Conference (ICML '97)*, D. Fisher (Ed.), Nashville, Tennessee, pp. 385-393, 1997.
12. Wang Y., & Witten I.H.: Inducing Model Trees for Continuous Classes, in *Poster Papers of the 9th European Conference on Machine Learning (ECML 97)*, M. van Someren, & G. Widmer (Eds.), Prague, Czech Republic, pp. 128-137, 1997.

Evaluation Methods for Focused Crawling

Andrea Passerini, Paolo Frasconi, and Giovanni Soda

DSI, University of Florence, ITALY
{passerini,paolo,giovanni}@dsi.ing.unifi.it

Abstract. The exponential growth of documents available in the World Wide Web makes it increasingly difficult to discover relevant information on a specific topic. In this context, growing interest is emerging in *focused crawling*, a technique that dynamically browses the Internet by choosing directions that maximize the probability of discovering relevant pages, given a specific topic. Predicting the relevance of a document before seeing its contents (i.e., relying on the parent pages only) is one of the central problem in focused crawling because it can save significant bandwidth resources. In this paper, we study three different evaluation functions for predicting the relevance of a hyperlink with respect to the target topic. We show that classification based on the anchor text is more accurate than classification based on the whole page. Moreover, we introduce a method that combines both the anchor and the whole parent document, using a Bayesian representation of the Web graph structure. The latter method obtains further accuracy improvements.

1   Introduction

The World Wide Web is experiencing an exponential growth, both in size and number of users. The quantity and variety of documentation available poses the problem of discovering information relevant to a specific topic of interest. The instruments developed to easen information recovering in the Internet suffer from various limitations. *Web directories* cannot realize exhaustive taxonomies and have a high mantainance cost due to the need for human classification of new documents. *Search engines* allow only searches by keywords, and cannot compete with dynamysm of the Internet in terms of coverage, novelty, and consistence of information [6]. These limitations suggest to experience different solutions, trying to provide focused, consistent and possibly new information related to a specific topic of interest. *Focused crawling* is a techinque that dynamically browses the Web looking for documents relevant to a certain topic. It employs an evaluation method to choose the best hyperlink to follow at a given time in order to maximize the probability of discovering relevant information, given a topic of interest. This allows to fully exploit limited bandwidth resources. The evaluation methods deal with the problem of predicting relevance of a document without seeing its content, while knowing the contents of a page pointing to the document to be evaluated. A common way to implement this evaluation function is that of training a classifier to predict the relevance of a document to a specific

F. Esposito (Ed.): AI*IA 2001, LNAI 2175, pp. 33–39, 2001.

topic, and using such a relevance, calculated for the visited page, as a score for all the hyperlinks contained in the page [2, 3]. This method, which we shall call *neighbourhood* score, relies on the idea that pages treating a specific topic will point to other pages relevant to that topic. More complex evaluation functions assign each link a different score that depends on the information contained in the context surrounding the hyperlink inside the page [5, 7].

Focused crawling is a rather young technique, and almost no comparisons are available for the different evaluation methods employed. In this paper, we propose a method to compare predicting capabilities of different evaluation functions. We use such a method to compare the neighobourhood score with an evaluation function which assigns each link a different score that depends on their anchor text. The *anchor* score greatly outperforms the neighbourhood score in every experiment performed. We also introduce a method that combines the other two ones, exploiting a Bayesian representation of hypertext connections between documents. Such a method yields further improvements in terms of predicting capability.

2   The Probabilistic Model for Hypertexts

A typical representation of textual documents in information retrieval is the so called *bag of words*. A document is represented as in a vector space whose dimension is the vocabulary size. Vector components are proportional to word frequencies in the document being represented. We restrict to alphabetical words and remove stopwords. Stemming and feature selection did not prove to be effective in this task. Hypertext documents have a structured nature given by HTML tags. We try to mantain part of this structure by using an extension of the bag of words representation. We split the document in three areas associated with HTML tags: 1) META, 2) TITLE and H1, 3) all the remaining tags. A different vocabulary was used for each area.

Naive Bayes is a well known approach to text categorization. The basic underlying assumption is that words in the document are conditionally independent given the class. The associated Bayesian network is shown in Figure 1a, where X_i is the i-th word in the document, and C is the document class. Maximum a posteriori predictions are obtained as

$$c^* = \arg\max_{c_i \in \mathcal{C}} P(c_i) \prod_{j=0}^{|d|} P(w_j|c_i) \tag{1}$$

where $\mathcal{C}$ is the set of candidate classes, w_j are the words in document d ,and $|d|$ is the document length. Given a set of training examples for each class, the a priori class probabilities $P(c_i)$ are obtained as the number of training documents belonging to each class divided by the total number of training documents, while the probabilities associated to words are given by:

$$P(w_j|c_i) = \frac{n_{ji} + 1}{n_i + |V|} \tag{2}$$

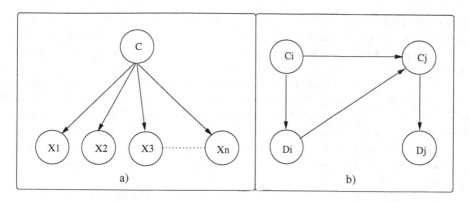

Fig. 1. a) Structure of a Naive Bayes classifier. b) Bayesian model for two linked documents.

where n_{ji} is the number of times word w_j occurs in documents of class c_i, n_i is the total number of words occurrences in documents of class c_i, and $|V|$ is the size of the vocabulary.

We suggest an extension of the Naive Bayes classifier in order to exploit the structured representation given by HTML tags. We associate multiple random variables with a word, depending on the tag context (TC) in which it can be found inside a document, and use a different vocabulary for each tag context. The class probability is calculated as:

$$c^* = \arg\max_{c_i \in C} P(c_i) \prod_{k=1}^{m} \left(\prod_{j=0}^{|d_{V_k}|} P(w_{d_{V_k}j}|c_i) \right) \qquad (3)$$

where m is the number of TC being considered, d_{V_k} the fraction of words in d belonging to TC V_k, and $w_{d_{V_k}j}$ the jth of these words. Probabilities associated with words are given by:

$$P(w_{kj}|c_i) = \frac{n_{kji} + 1}{n_{ki} + |V_k|} \qquad (4)$$

where n_{kji} is the number of occurrences of word w_j in the kth TC of documents of class c_i, n_{ki} is the total number of words occurrences in the kth TC of documents of class c_i, and $|V_k|$ is the size of the kth vocabulary.

This classifier proved to perform better than regular Naive Bayes in classifying HTML documents, and we shall employ it in developing the evaluation functions for hyperlinks.

3   Evaluation Methods for Hyperlinks

In order to assign a relevance score to hyperlinks inside a document, we must implement an evaluation function that predicts the probability that the document pointed by an hyperlink belongs to the class of interest. While different evaluation functions have been proposed, no significant comparison experiments are available in the literature. In this paper, we compare three different evaluation fuctions, that we named: *Neighbourhood* score, *Anchor* score, *Transition* score.

The first method we implement is the simplest and commonest one. It assigns to all hyperlinks inside a document the same relevance, given by the class a posteriori probability of the document containing them. We call this method *neighbourhood* score, because it is based on the assumption that relevant pages for a given class will point to other relevant pages for the same class. We calculate such a probability by the extended Naive Bayes classifier described in previous section.

The second method, called *anchor* score, assigns each hyperlink a different score depending on the text of its anchor, that is the text that can be clicked when viewing the document with a browser, or the text contained in the ALT tag in case of a clickable image. We employ a Naive Bayes classifier trained on the anchor text of hyperlinks whose pointed page class was known. This method is opposite to the neighbourhood one because it doesn't take in account neither the remaining text of the document containing the hyperlink to classify nor its class.

The third method, called *transition* score, aims to merge the two contributions of neighbourhood and anchor score into a single evaluation function. In this case, we use a Bayesian network model for the relationship between two documents connected by a hyperlink. The model is shown in Figure 1b, where D_i is a document, with associated class C_i, which contains a hyperlink pointing to a document D_j with associated class C_j. We are interested in estimating information related to edge $D_i \rightarrow C_j$, that is probability that a hyperlink in D_i points to a document of class C_j, when C_j is the class of interest. Named D_{ij} a hyperlink inside D_i, we can represent the probability that the class of the document pointed by that link is C_j as:

$$P(C_j|D_{i,j}) = \sum_{C_k \in C} \left(\frac{P(D_{i,j}|C_j, C_k)P(C_j|C_k)P(C_k|D_{i,j})}{P(D_{i,j}|C_k)} \right) \qquad (5)$$

where probability is summed over all the possible classes $C_k \in C$ of D_i, and we applied product rule and then Bayes theorem to the first term of the product. Unfortunately equation 5 has too many parameters to be estimated, and some simplifying assumption is necessary. We use the assumption that the link is independent of the class of the document containing it, that is $D_{i,j} \perp C_k$. With such an assumption the equation becomes:

$$P(C_j|D_{i,j}) = \frac{P(D_{i,j}|C_j)\sum_{C_k \in C} P(C_j|C_k)P(C_k|D_{i,j})}{P(D_{i,j})} \qquad (6)$$

In the above equation, $P(C_k|D_{i,j})$ is the probability of class C_k given link $D_{i,j}$. This is the neighbourhood score contribution, i.e. the a posteriori probability of the class given the document in which the link is contained. $P(C_j|C_k)$ represents the *transition* probability, that is the probability that a generic document of class C_k has a link pointing to a document of class C_j. Finally, $P(D_{i,j}|C_k)$ is the probability that a link $D_{i,j}$ is contained in a document of class C_k. $P(D_{i,j})$ is the a priori probability of a link $D_{i,j}$.

4   Experimental Results

In order to compare performances of the proposed evaluation methods, we developed a dataset of documents containing labeled hyperlinks, i.e. hyperlinks pointing to pages whose class was known. To generate such a set, we started from a dataset provided by the *World Wide Web Knowledge Base*[1] project, consisting of pages from computer science departments of United States Universities. We merged together the classes referring to personal homepages (faculty members, staff and students) obtaining five classes: *Course* for university courses, *Department* for department homepages, *Homepage* for personal homepages, *Project* for research projects and *Other* for pages not belonging to any of the other classes. We then collected all the *backlinks* of these pages, that is documents containing links pointing to one of such pages. In order to have more than one labeled hyperlink per document, we also collected part of the other links contained inside backlink documents, and manually classified the corresponding pages. In this way, each example consists of a labeled hyperlink and the document containing the link itself.

We divided the examples in a training set of 35,606 examples and a test set of 10,829 examples. For each evaluation method proposed, we trained the corresponding classifier on the training set and verified its performances on the test set. The following tables show the results in accuracy and recall, together with the confusion matrices, for the three methods proposed (table 1). Anchor score outperforms neighbourhood score of 39.69%, meaning that, when present, anchor text alone gives much better information about the page pointed by the link than the document cointaining the link itself.

Adding transition probabilities yields a 10% prediction error reduction. Modeling the probability of transition between classes, weighted by the a posteriori probability of the class of the starting document, helps to disambiguate in the case of rare hyperlinks, like for example a department homepage directly pointing to a specific course homepage.

5   Conclusions

In this paper, we showed that an evaluation function based on anchor text can greatly outperform the common approach of assigning the same score to all links contained in a given page.

---

[1] the dataset is available on-line at:
  http://www.cs.cmu.edu/afs/cs.cmu.edu/project/theo-20/www/data

Class	0	1	2	3	4	Class Total	Recall (%)
0 course	217	.	851	208	4	1280	16.95
1 dept.	56	2	1233	197	54	1542	0.13
2 home	102	1	1818	754	748	3423	53.11
3 other	96	3	2542	1039	52	3732	27.84
4 project	8	.	508	281	55	852	6.46

Neighbourhood score (**28.91%** accuracy)

Class	0	1	2	3	4	Class Total	Recall (%)
0 course	882	101	37	78	182	1280	68.91
1 dept.	117	1303	32	26	64	1542	84.50
2 home	261	161	2560	334	107	3423	74.79
3 other	476	266	139	2040	811	3732	54.66
4 project	63	42	17	86	644	852	75.59

Anchor score (**68.60%** accuracy)

Class	0	1	2	3	4	Class Total	Recall (%)
0 course	673	92	73	255	187	1280	52.58
1 dept.	39	1302	55	99	47	1542	84.44
2 home	43	114	2779	368	119	3423	81.19
3 other	165	283	180	2402	702	3732	64.36
4 project	17	33	32	161	609	852	71.48

Transition score (**71.71%** accuracy)

Table 1. Total Accuracies and Confusion matrices (row is actual, column is predicted).

We furthermore proposed an evaluation function exploiting a Bayesian representation of connection between documents, showing that it further increases predicting accuracy. The problem of this approach is that anchor score does not contribute to the evaluation when the anchor text is empty. A further development is to extend the text used for anchor score to some context of the hyperlink itself. Using context for hyperlink score has been proposed by previous works [7], but there is no evidence of its benefit, especially for the difficulty to define and extract a consistent context without introducing greater noise. We are trying to apply the idea of using a link context path [1] to extract such a context. Regarding focused crawling, we are studying techniques to choose directions to follow when no relevant documents are available in the fringe of search, and longer distance predictions must be made [4, 7].

References

[1] G. Attardi, S. Di Marco, and D. Salvi. Categorization by context. *Journal of Universal Computer Science*, 4(9):719–736, 1998.
[2] P. De Bra, G.-J. Houben, Y. Kornatzky, and R. Post. Information retrieval in distributed hypertexts. In *Proceedings of RIAO'94, Intelligent Multimedia, Information Retrieval Systems and Management*, New York, NY, 1994.

[3] S. Chakrabarti, M. van der Berg, and B. Dom. Focused crawling: a new approach to topic-specific web resource discovery. In *Proceedings of the 8th International World Wide Web Conference*, Toronto, Canada, 1999.

[4] M. Diligenti, F.M. Coetzee, S. Lawrence, C.L. Giles, and M. Gori. Focused crawling using context graphs. In *Proceedings of the 6th International Conference on Very Large Databases, VLDB 2000*, Cairo, Egypt, 2000.

[5] M. Hersovici, M. Jacovi, Y.S. Maarek, D. Pelleg, M. Shtalheim, and S. Ur. The shark-search algorithm — an application: tailored web site mapping. In *Proceedings of the 7th International World Wide Web Conference (WWW7)*, Brisbane, Australia, 1998.

[6] S. Lawrence and C.L. Giles. Accessibility of information on the web. *Nature*, 400:107–109, July 1999.

[7] J. Rennie and A. McCallum. Using reinforcement learning to spider the web efficiently. In *Proceedings of the 16th International Conference on Machine Learning (ICML'99)*, 1999.

A Knowledge-Based Neurocomputing Approach to Extract Refined Linguistic Rules from Data

Giovanna Castellano and Anna Maria Fanelli

Università degli Studi di Bari, Dipartimento di Informatica
Via E. Orabona, 4 - 70126 Bari - ITALY
{castellano,fanelli}@di.uniba.it

Abstract. This paper proposes a knowledge-based neurocomputing approach to extract and refine a set of linguistic rules from data. A neural network is designed along with its learning algorithm that allows simultaneous definition of the structure and the parameters of the rule base. The network can be regarded both as an adaptive rule-based system with the capability of learning fuzzy rules from data, and as a connectionist architecture provided with linguistic meaning. Experimental results on two well-known classification problems illustrate the effectiveness of the proposed approach.

1 Introduction

Even if neural networks can model complex systems with a high degree of accuracy, they are usually difficult to interpret. This can constitute a severe limitation in applications where reliability and comprehensibility of the model may be of critical importance. In order to overcome this limitation, various attempts have been made to provide neural network models with explanatory facilities, leading to the so-called *knowledge-based neurocomputing* (KBN), an area which concerns the use and representation of explicit knowledge within the neurocomputing paradigm [1], [2], [3]. The key assumption of KBN is that knowledge is obtainable from, or can be represented by a neurocomputing system, in a comprehensible form, i.e. in a symbolic or well-structured form, such as Boolean functions, automata, rules, or similar ways.

A form of explicit knowledge representation and processing is provided by fuzzy inference methods that are based on reasoning-oriented mechanisms and allow knowledge representation in the form of intuitive linguistic rules. In this context, fuzzy rule extraction becomes the most important issue within the KBN approach. The rules determine a reasoning algorithm for a fuzzy system approximating the network function and the network learning provides knowledge created automatically [4], [5], [6].

In this paper, we propose a KBN approach to extract and refine a set of linguistic rules from data within the framework of fuzzy reasoning systems. A neural network architecture is designed whose topology maps the adopted knowledge representation in the form of fuzzy rules. Along with this architecture, a ANN

F. Esposito (Ed.): AI*IA 2001, LNAI 2175, pp. 40–50, 2001.

Fuzzy Rule (ANN-FR) learning algorithm is defined which allow the network to self-organize its structure and parameters so as to generate a set of fuzzy rules that adequately represent a given data set. The algorithm involves two phases: a rule extraction phase via unsupervised learning and a rule refinement phase via supervised learning, with an effort to enhance the extracted fuzzy rules in terms of accurate approximation of the mapping underlying the relations among data. Once the learning is completed, the network architecture encodes the knowledge learned in the form of fuzzy rules and processes data following fuzzy reasoning principles. Simulations on two classification problems confirm the effectiveness of the proposed KBN approach.

2 The ANN Architecture

Within a KBN approach, the knowledge representation adopted influences the architecture of the neurocomputing system, which must be constrained to allow correspondence with such knowledge representation. In our case, we represent knowledge in the form of fuzzy rules:

$$R_k : \text{IF } (x_1 \text{ is } A_1^k) \text{ AND } \cdots (x_n \text{ is } A_n^k) \text{ THEN } (y_1 \text{ is } v_{k1}) \text{ AND } \cdots (y_m \text{ is } v_{km})$$

where R_k is the kth rule $(1 \leq k \leq K)$, $\{x_i\}_{i=1...n}$ are the input variables, $\{y_j\}_{j=1...m}$ are the output variables, A_i^k are fuzzy sets defined on the input variables, and v_{kj} are fuzzy singletons defined on the output variables. Fuzzy sets A_i^k are defined by Gaussian membership functions

$$\mu_{ik}(x_i) = \exp\left(- \frac{(x_i - c_{ik})^2}{\sigma_{ik}^2} \right)$$

where c_{ik} and σ_{ik} are the center and the width of the Gaussian function, respectively. The inferred crisp output value for any input $\overline{x}^0 = (x_1^0, x_2^0, \ldots, x_n^0)$ is calculated as:

$$y_j(0) = \frac{\sum_{k=1}^{K} \mu_k(\overline{x}^0) v_{kj}}{\sum_{k=1}^{K} \mu_k(\overline{x}^0)} \tag{1}$$

where $\mu_k(\overline{x}^0) = \prod_{i=1}^{n} \mu_{ik}(x_i^0)$.

A neural network architecture is designed so that it maps to the described knowledge representation and processing, i.e. it encodes a set of fuzzy rules in its topology, and processes information in a way that matches the fuzzy reasoning scheme adopted. The network topology is comprised of three layers with the following meaning:

1. The first layer calculates the membership values $\mu_{ik}(x_i)$. Each node of this layer has 2 free parameters (center and width of Gaussian function).
2. The second layer computes the activation strength of each rule, by multiplying the corresponding input membership values. Nodes of this layer have no free parameters.

3. The third layer determines the output values $y_j, j = 1 \ldots m$, according to (1). Connections between the second and the third layer are weighted by the free parameters v_{kj}.

The architecture of this neural network is depicted in Fig.1, where nodes representing the premise part of a fuzzy rule are enclosed in a gray circle, representing a *meta-node* of the network. The weights of the network correspond to the Gaussian membership functions parameters $\{c_{ik}\}$, $\{\sigma_{ik}\}$ and to the consequent singletons $\{v_{kj}\}$. In other words, each meta-node k is associated with two premise weight vectors $\bar{c}_k = (c_{1k}, \ldots, c_{nk})$, $\bar{\sigma}_k = (\sigma_{1k}, \ldots, \sigma_{nk})$ and one consequent weight vector $\bar{v}_k = (v_{k1}, \ldots, v_{km})$.

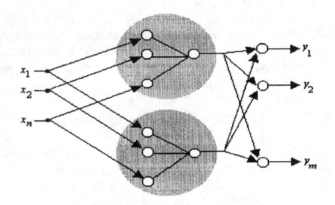

Fig. 1. The neural network.

3 The ANN-FR Learning Algorithm

To allow the proposed network to discover fuzzy rules from a set of input-output data $D_N = \{(\bar{x}(t), \bar{y}(t))\}_{t=1}^{N}$ describing an input-output mapping, we have defined a ANN-FR learning algorithm, that comprises an unsupervised learning phase for rule extraction and a supervised learning phase for rule refinement.

For sake of rule creation, a competitive learning scheme is defined that is able to find the number of rules through identification of the network structure. The algorithm involves only the meta-nodes of the network. When a n-dimensional vector $\bar{x}$ is presented, such nodes compete and the node whose weight vector $\bar{c}$ is closest to the vector $\bar{x}$ is chosen as winner, while the second winner is marked as the *rival*. Then, the weight vector of the winner is rewarded, i.e. updated so as to become closer to the current input vector $\bar{x}$, while the weight vector of the rival is punished, i.e. updated so as to move it away from $\bar{x}$. This mechanism tries to push the weight vector of the rival node far away from the cluster towards which the weight vector of the winner is moving, thus implicitly making sure that each cluster is represented by only one weight vector. The use of this reward/punishment mechanism, that gradually drives the weight vectors of extra nodes far away from the distribution of the data, allows the appropriate number of meta-nodes, and hence the number of rules, to be automatically selected.

To perform this kind of competition, the closeness between an input vector and a weight vector can be measured by any distance measure. In [7], [8], [9], the authors have used the standard Euclidean distance, yielding learning algorithms suitable for detecting prototypes of hyper-spherical shaped clusters. However, clustering with Euclidean distance has the undesirable property of splitting large as well as elongated clusters under some circumstances. Indeed, it has been noted that most clusters in real data sets are neither well-isolated nor have the spherical shape. Other distance measures, such as the Mahalanobis distance, can be used to find hyper-ellipsoidal shaped clusters [10], [11].

Based on these ideas, we have developed an adaptive competitive learning based on the above described reward-punishment mechanism for elliptical clustering. This is accomplished by using the Mahalanobis distance in place of the Euclidean distance to evaluate the closeness between a pattern and a cluster center. The squared Mahalanobis distance between a pattern vector $\overline{x}$ and a center vector $\overline{c}_k$ is defined as follows:

$$d_M(\overline{x}, \overline{c}_k) = (\overline{x} - \overline{c}_k)^T \Sigma_k^{-1} (\overline{x} - \overline{c}_k) \tag{2}$$

where Σ_k^{-1} is the inverse of the $[n \times n]$ covariance matrix of the kth cluster, defined as:

$$\Sigma_k = \frac{1}{N_k} \sum_{t=1}^{N_k} I_k(\overline{x}(t)) \left(\overline{x}(t) - \overline{c}_k\right) \left(\overline{x}(t) - \overline{c}_k\right)^T \tag{3}$$

where N_k is the total number of data points that belong to the kth cluster and $I_k(\cdot)$ is defined as follows:

$$I_k(\overline{x}) = \begin{cases} 1 & \text{if } \overline{x} \text{ belongs to cluster } k \\ 0 & \text{otherwise} \end{cases}$$

There are, however, a number of difficulties associated with incorporating the Mahalanobis distance in the competitive learning:

- the computation of (2) requires the computation of the inverse of the sample covariance matrix every time a pattern changes its cluster category, which obviously requires a high computational cost.
- if the number of patterns belonging to a cluster is small with respect to the input dimensionality n, then the $[n \times n]$ sample covariance matrix may be singular, leading to numerical problems in the computation of its inverse.

To overcome the problems tied to the computation of inverse of covariance matrices, we have derived a direct update for such matrices. In the same way the weight vector of the winner (resp. rival) "moves" towards (resp. away) the input vector presented, the covariance matrix moves towards (resp. away) the covariance matrix represented by that input vector. Therefore, when an input vector $\bar{x}$ is presented, the covariance matrix of the winner must be updated as follows:

$$\Sigma_w = \Sigma_w + \alpha_w \left((\bar{x} - \bar{c}_w)(\bar{x} - \bar{c}_w)^T - \Sigma_w \right)$$
$$= (1 - \alpha_w)\Sigma_w + \alpha_w \left((\bar{x} - \bar{c}_w)(\bar{x} - \bar{c}_w)^T \right) \tag{4}$$

while for the rival we have:

$$\Sigma_r = \Sigma_r - \alpha_r \left((\bar{x} - \bar{c}_r)(\bar{x} - \bar{c}_r)^T - \Sigma_r \right)$$
$$= (1 + \alpha_r)\Sigma_r - \alpha_r \left((\bar{x} - \bar{c}_r)(\bar{x} - \bar{c}_r)^T \right) \tag{5}$$

where α_w and α_r are the learning rate for the winner and the rival, respectively.

These rules, however, are impractical since to perform the competition, that is to find the winner and the rival nodes, the computation of the inverse Σ_k^{-1} is needed after each presentation of an input vector. To avoid such a computation, we propose a rule to update the inverse Σ_k^{-1} directly. To do so, we make for convenience the following positions:

$$\overline{m}_k = (\bar{x} - \bar{c}_k)$$

$$\lambda_k = \overline{m}_k^T \Sigma_k^{-1} \overline{m}_k$$

First, we derive the update formulas for the winner. The derivation is based on the following well-known result:

$$\sum_{n=0}^{\infty} (-\beta x)^{-1} \approx (1 + \beta x)^{-1}$$

Using the update formula for the covariance matrix (4), we can write:

$$\Sigma_w^{-1} = \left((1 - \alpha_w)\Sigma_w + \alpha_w(\overline{m}_w \cdot \overline{m}_w^T) \right)^{-1}$$

$$= \frac{\Sigma_w^{-1}}{1 - \alpha_w} \left(I + \frac{\alpha_w}{1 - \alpha_w} \Sigma_w^{-1}(\overline{m}_w \cdot \overline{m}_w^T) \right)^{-1} \qquad \text{put} \quad \beta_w = \frac{\alpha_w}{1 - \alpha_w}$$

$$= \frac{\Sigma_w^{-1}}{1 - \alpha_w} \left(I + \beta_w \Sigma_w^{-1}(\overline{m}_w \cdot \overline{m}_w^T) \right)^{-1}$$

$$= \frac{\Sigma_w^{-1}}{1 - \alpha_w} \left(I - \beta_w \Sigma_w^{-1}(\overline{m}_w \cdot \overline{m}_w^T) + \beta_w^2 \Sigma_w^{-1}(\overline{m}_w \cdot \lambda_w \cdot \overline{m}_w^T) - \beta_w^3 ... \right)$$

$$= \frac{\Sigma_w^{-1}}{1 - \alpha_w} \left(I - \beta_w \Sigma_w^{-1} (\overline{m}_w \cdot \overline{m}_w^T)(1 - \beta_w \lambda_w + \beta_w^2 \lambda_w^2 - ...) \right)$$

$$= \frac{\Sigma_w^{-1}}{1 - \alpha_w} \left(I - \beta_w \Sigma_w^{-1} (\overline{m}_w \cdot \overline{m}_w^T) \left(\frac{1}{1 + \beta_w \lambda_w} \right) \right)$$

$$= \frac{\Sigma_w^{-1}}{1 - \alpha_w} - \frac{\beta_w}{1 - \alpha_w} \frac{(\Sigma_w^{-1} \overline{m}_w)^T \cdot (\Sigma_w^{-1} \overline{m}_w)}{1 + \beta_w \lambda_w} \tag{6}$$

The corresponding update formula for the rival is derived analogously:

$$\Sigma_r^{-1} = \frac{\Sigma_r^{-1}}{1 + \alpha_r} - \frac{\beta_r}{1 + \alpha_r} \frac{(\Sigma_r^{-1} \overline{m}_r)^T \cdot (\Sigma_r^{-1} \overline{m}_r)}{1 + \beta_r \lambda_r} \tag{7}$$

Using (6) and (7), the inverse of the covariance matrix can be updated directly for the winner and the rival unit, respectively.

Summarizing, starting with H meta-nodes (rules), the proposed competitive learning dynamically finds a set of K nodes ($K \leq H$) whose weight vectors $\overline{c}_k, k = 1, \ldots, K$, represent the centers of ellipsoidal clusters in the input space. The components of each weight vector $\overline{c}_k$ represent the initial center values of the Gaussian membership functions in the premise part of the kth rule. To complete the definition of premise parameters of fuzzy rules, the weights $\{\sigma_{ik}\}$ representing the widths of the membership functions are derived using the following heuristic:

$$\sigma_{ik} = \max_{t=1...N_k} |x_i(t) - c_{ik}|, \qquad \text{for } i = 1, \ldots, n$$

where N_k is the number of input vectors belonging to the kth cluster. Finally, initial values of weights $\{v_{kj}\}$ representing rule consequent parameters are obtained using the cluster membership values $\mu_k(\overline{x}(t))$ and the target vectors $\overline{y}(t) = (y_1(t), \ldots, y_m(t))$, for all training patterns $t = 1, \ldots, N$ as follows:

$$v_{kj} = \frac{\sum_{t=1}^N \mu_k(\overline{x}(t)) y_j(t)}{\sum_{t=1}^N \mu_k(\overline{x}(t))}$$

The resulting unsupervised phase of the ANN-FR algorithm based on the adaptive competitive learning above described is given below:

Unsupervised phase of ANN-FR Algorithm

BEGIN

1. $\tau = 0$;   /* epoch number */
2. Initialize randomly the center vectors $\overline{c}_k, k = 1, \ldots, H$.
3. Initialize the learning rates α_w and α_r for the winner and the rival, respectively, so that $0 \leq \alpha_r \leq \alpha_w \leq 1$.

4. **Repeat**
   (a) $\tau = \tau + 1$;
   (b) For each training input vector $\overline{x}(t), t = 1, \ldots, N$:
       i. For $k = 1, \ldots, H$ compute the distances:

$$D(\overline{x}(t), \overline{c}_k) = \frac{n_k}{\sum_{k=1}^{H} n_k} d_M(\overline{x}(t), \overline{c}_k) \qquad (8)$$

where n_k is the cumulative number of the winning occurrences for the meta-node k and $d_M(\cdot, \cdot)$ is the Mahalanobis distance as defined in (2).

   ii. Determine the winning node w and its rival r according to:

$$w = \arg\min_k D(\overline{x}(t), \overline{c}_k) \qquad r = \arg\min_{k \neq w} D(\overline{x}(t), \overline{c}_k) \qquad (9)$$

   iii. $n_w = n_w + 1$
   iv. Update weight vectors of the winning and the rival nodes:

$$\overline{c}_w = \overline{c}_w + \alpha_w(\overline{x}(t) - \overline{c}_w) \qquad \overline{c}_r = \overline{c}_r - \alpha_r(\overline{x}(t) - \overline{c}_r)$$

   v. Update the inverse of covariance matrix of the winning and the rival, according to (6) and (7), respectively.
   (c) Modify the learning rates α_w and α_r according to a linear decay;
5. **UNTIL** $\frac{1}{H} \sum_{k=1}^{H} \|\overline{c}_k^{(\tau+1)} - \overline{c}_k^{(\tau)}\| \leq \varepsilon$
6. Remove all meta-nodes whose weight vectors $\overline{c}_k$ fall outside the input range.

END

To enhance the extracted fuzzy rules in terms of accurate approximation of the mapping underlying the relations among data, the network enters in the supervised learning phase. This second phase of the ANN-FR algorithm, based on the well-known gradient-descent technique, is aimed to optimally adjusts premise parameters $\{c_{ik}\}$, $\{a_{ik}\}$ and consequent parameters $\{v_{kj}\}$.

4   Application Examples

To show the applicability of the proposed KBN approach to fuzzy rule extraction, we have considered two well-known classification datasets taken from the UCI Repository of Machine Learning databases: the Iris dataset and the Heart Disease dataset. The classification tasks are distinguished for their complexity: the former is quite simple, the latter involves a classification task in a multi-dimensional feature space.

To estimate the performance of the proposed ANN-FR learning algorithm, we carried out a 10-fold cross-validation since both the considered data sets contained few exemplars so that we considered them too small for applying the holdout method, but large enough to use cross validation.

To illustrate the effectiveness of our approach, we have implemented another version of the ANN-FR algorithm that performs spherical clustering by using the Euclidean distance during the competition of the meta-nodes. In the following we denote by ANN-FR(e) and ANN-FR(s) the variants of the algorithm for ellipsoidal and spherical clustering, respectively.

4.1   Iris Dataset

The first benchmark concerns classification of flowers [12]. Three species of Iris flowers (setosa, versicolor and virginica) are known. There are 150 samples for this problem, 50 of each class. A sample is a four-dimensional pattern vector representing four attributes of the Iris flower (sepal length, sepal width, petal length, and petal width).

To perform cross-validation, the whole data set was divided into 10 equally sized parts (15 samples uniformly drawn from the three classes). Each part was used as a test set for the network trained with the remaining 135 data. In each run, the learning was initiated with a guessed structure of the neural network based on a number of 10 rules (meta-nodes) given as a form of a-priori knowledge. Hence, the starting network had 4 inputs, 3 outputs (corresponding to the 3 classes) and 10 meta-nodes. In both variants, the same learning rates $\alpha_w = 0.05$, $\alpha_r = 0.04$ and stopping threshold $\epsilon = 0.0001$ have been used in the unsupervised phase, and the same stopping condition for the supervised learning phase (i.e. 100% classification rate achieved on training set or maximum number of 50 epochs).

Table 1 summarizes the average results obtained by the two algorithms ANN-FR(e) and ANN-FR(s) in terms of number of generated rules and classification rate on training and test set. It can be seen that the two algorithms lead to very similar results in terms of number of generated rules, but they differ in accuracy as the rules produced by ANN-FR(e) yield a better generalization ability than ANN-FR(s). Indeed, the Iris data is a typical example where the data do not have a spherically shaped clusters, but they form elongated ellipsoidal regions. As a consequence, the ANN-FR(e) better captures the structure of data, providing rules that can better generalize.

	Average number of rules	Unsupervised phase		Supervised phase	
		Training set	Test set	Training set	Test set
ANN-FR(s)	3.6	90.15	88.66	94.66	94.66
ANN-FR(e)	3.5	93.33	93.33	96.66	96.00

Table 1. Comparison between the two variants of ANN-FR algorithm on the Iris dataset.

4.2   Heart Disease Dataset

To evaluate the behavior of the proposed approach in the case of multidimensional classification problems with many continuous attributes, we have considered the Heart Disease dataset. This dataset comes from the Cleveland Clinic Foundation and was supplied by Robert Detrano, M.D., Ph.D., of the V.A. Medical Center, Long Beach, CA. The purpose of the dataset is to predict the presence or absence of heart disease given the results of various medical tests carried out on a patient. This database contains 270 examples with 13 attributes. There are two classes: presence or absence of heart disease. There are no missing values. To perform cross validation, the data set was divided into 10 subsets, each with 27 instances, resulting in 10 training sets of 243 samples and as many corresponding test sets of 27 samples.

The unsupervised learning phase of ANN-FR algorithm was initiated with a guessed structure of the neural network based on 20 rules. Hence, the starting network had a structure made of 13 inputs, 2 outputs and 20 meta-nodes. The competitive learning algorithm was run with $\alpha_w = 0.06$, $\alpha_r = 0.02$ and $\epsilon = 0.0001$ and required on the average 21 steps to converge, i.e. to establish the structure and the parameters of the network, providing an initial fuzzy rule base. In the ten trials, a number of clusters between 12-15 were produced by ANN-FR(e) while a number of rules between 10-16 were produced by ANN-FR(s).

Then the supervised learning phase was applied for 100 epochs. The classification results obtained in the ten trials are summarized in Table 2 together with the average number of rules. As before, we remark a different behavior in terms of accuracy between fuzzy rule bases developed by ANN-FR(e) and ANN-FR(s), which confirms the superiority of ANN-FR(e). Conversely, as far as the quality in terms of structure simplicity is concerned, the two versions of the ANN-FR algorithm seem to produce very similar results.

To evaluate the effectiveness of such results, they were compared with those obtained through a 10-fold cross validation (as in our case) by some state-of-art approaches. Table 3 summarizes the comparative results in terms of generalization ability. It can be seen that our approach compares favorably with all these approaches, providing in most cases a higher accuracy.

	Average number of rules	Unsupervised phase		Supervised phase	
		Training set	Test set	Training set	Test set
ANN-FR(s)	12.3	63.95	62.96	70.96	68.15
ANN-FR(e)	13.4	70.41	71.82	87.53	81.11

Table 2. Comparison between the two variants of ANN-FR algorithm on the Heart Disease dataset.

classifier	class. rate
NN-DT [13]	82.8
C4.5 [13]	72.0
CART [13]	77.8
OC1 [13]	73.7
Augmented Bayes network [14]	78.7
Naive Bayes [14]	72.5
TAN network [14]	73.5
C4.5-AP [15]	82.2
C4.5 [15]	80.0
ANN-FR(e)	81.1

Table 3. Comparison among different classification approaches on the Heart Disease dataset.

5   Conclusions

In this paper, a KBN approach has been proposed to extract and refine linguistic rules from data. The rules, in the form of those used in fuzzy reasoning mechanism, are obtained through learning of a neural network whose topology allows representation of knowledge in the form of fuzzy rules. The only a-priori information needed for the rule extraction process is an initial guessed number of rules represented as meta-nodes in the network. According to the KBN paradigm, our approach can be considered as a way to characterize the behavior of a neural network by means of a set of fuzzy rules that can be easily understood.

The validity of the proposed KBN approach has been illustrated on two well-known classification benchmarks, with the aim to extract useful knowledge about a classification task, rather than to build a neural model with optimal classification ability. The promising results obtained on the two benchmarks encourage the application of our methodology in respect to a wider range of real-world problems. These applications are the subject of our on-going research projects.

References

1. Cloete, I., Zurada, J.M., eds., Knowledge-based neurocomputing, The MIT Press, Cambridge, Massachussets, (2000).
2. Shavlik, J.W., Combining symbolic and neural learning, Machine Learning, 14:321-331, (1994).
3. Setiono, R., Liu, H., Symbolic representation of neural networks, IEEE Computer, 29(3):71-77, (1996).
4. Wang, L.X., Mendel, J., Generating fuzzy rules by learning from examples, IEEE Trans. Syst., Man, and Cyb., 22: 1414-1427, (1992).
5. Sun, C.T., Rule-base structure identification in an adaptive-network-based fuzzy inference system, IEEE Trans. on Fuzzy Systems, 2(1):64-73, (1994).

6. Lozowski, A., Zurada, J.M., Extraction of linguistic rules from data via neural networks and fuzzy approximation, in I. Cloete and J.M. Zurada, eds., Knowledge-based neurocomputing, The MIT Press, Cambridge, Massachussets, pp. 403-417, (2000).

7. Xu, L., Krzyzak, A., Oja, E., Rival Penalized Competitive Learning for clustering analysis, RBF net, and curve detection, IEEE Trans. on Neural Networks, 4(4):636-649, (1993).

8. Castellano, G., Fanelli, A.M., Fuzzy inference and rule extraction using a neural network, Neural Network World Journal , 3:361-371, (2000).

9. Luk, A., Lien, S., Rival rewarded & randomly rewarded rival competitive learning, in Proc. of IEEE Int. Joint Conference on Neural Networks, Washington, USA, (1999).

10. Mao, J., Jain, A.K., A self-organizing network for hyperellipsoidal clustering (HEC), IEEE Trans. on Neural Networks, 7(1):16-19, (1996).

11. De Backer, S., Scheunders, P., A competitive elliptical clustering algorithm, Pattern Recognition Letters, 20(11-13):1141-1147, (1999).

12. Fisher, R.A., The use of multiple measurements in taxonomic problems, Ann. Eugen., 7:179-188, (1936).

13. Setiono, R., Liu, H., A connectionist approach to generating oblique decision trees, IEEE Trans. on Systems, Man and Cybernetics- Part B: Cybernetics, 29(3):440-443, (1999).

14. Keogh, E.J., Pazzani, M.J, Learning Augmented Bayesian Classifiers: a Comparison of Distribution-based and Classification-based Approaches, Proc. of 7th International Workshop on AI and Statistics, Fort Lauderdale, Florida, pp.225-230, (1999).

15. Kohavi, R., John, G.H., Automatic Parameter Selection by Minimizing Estimated Error, Proc. of the 12th International Conference on Machine Learning, San Francisco, CA, (1995).

RBF Networks Exploiting Supervised Data in the Adaptation of Hidden Neuron Parameters

Palma Blonda[1], Andrea Baraldi[2], Annarita D'Addabbo[1], Cristina Tarantino[1], and Roberto De Blasi[3]

[1] IESI-CNR, via G.Amendola 166/5, 70126 Bari, Italy
{blonda, daddabbo, cristina}@iesi.ba.cnr.it
http://www.iesi.ba.cnr.it
[2] ISAO-CNR, via Gobetti 101, 40129 Bologna, Italy
{a.baraldi}@isao.bo.cnr.it
[3] Cattedra e Servizio di Neuroradiologia, University of Bari, P.za G. Cesare, 11, 70126 Bari, Italy

Abstract. Radial Basis Function (RBF) classifiers, which consist of an hidden and an output layer, are traditionally trained with a two-stage hybrid learning approach. This approach combines an unsupervised (data-driven) first stage to adapt RBF hidden layer parameters with a supervised (error-driven) second stage to learn RBF output weights. Several simple strategies that exploit labeled data in the adaptation of centers and spread parameters of RBF hidden units may be pursued. Some of these strategies have been shown to reduce traditional weaknesses of RBF classificaton, while typical advantages are maintained, e.g., fast training, easy implementation, low responses to outliers. In this work, we compare a traditional RBF two-stage hybrid learning procedure with an RBF two-stage learning technique exploiting labeled data to adapt hidden unit parameters. Two data sets were analized: the first consisted of multitemporal remote sensed data; the second consisted of Magnetic Resonance images ...

1 Introduction

The Radial Basis Function (RBF) neural network model overcomes some of the problems related to the computational cost of the Multilayer Perceptron (MLP) learning phase [1] in the classification of large data sets. With respect to MLP, RBF [1]: i) employs simpler architectures to perform complex mappings, ii) is faster to train, iii) provides low output responses to inputs that fall into regions of the data space where there are no training samples, iv) may exploit localized basis functions such that learning of each input sample affects a specialized subset of the network parameters, v) allows a closed form linear optimization of the output weights when a two-stage learning strategy is employed, and vi) is easily interpretable if RBFs are well localized (e.g., a Gaussian RBF is well localized when its adjustable parameter σ does not tend to either zero or infinity). The disadvantage of RBF networks is that the classification error strongly

F. Esposito (Ed.): AI*IA 2001, LNAI 2175, pp. 51–56, 2001.

depends on the selection of the number, centers and widths of basis functions. A two-stage hybrid learning framework is traditionally employed to train RBF networks. It combines a first stage unsupervised learning (data-driven) strategy for the RBF hidden layer with a supervised learning (error-driven) mechanism for the RBF output layer. In this learning framework, if the number of RBFs increases, then there is no guarantee of improving the system's performance on a set of unobserved labeled data samples. This stems from the fact that the unsupervised learning (clustering) algorithm may locate the additional RBFs in regions of the input space where they are either useless or harmful in implementing the desired (input, output) mapping [2], i.e., the distribution of RBFs in the input space as computed by the unsupervised learning technique does not reflect the local complexity of the classification or regression problem at hand. For example, unsupervised methods may form *mixed* clusters of input vectors that are closely spaced in the input space but belong to different classes [2]. To avoid this problem, the density of RBFs must be made independent of input vector density, but dependent on the complexity of the desired (input, output) mapping, i.e., density of RBFs must be computed on the basis of the supervised training set. Thus, several error-driven (supervised) learning algorithms, either one- or two-stage, have been proposed for RBF networks in recent years. Unlike MLP, it has been proved that when a one-stage gradient descent of a sum-of-squares error learning technique is applied, for example, to a Gaussian RBF (GRBF) network, it is unsuccessful because [3]: i) it does not ensure that GRBFs will remain localized, i.e., spread parameters may become very large and GRBF responses may become very broad; and ii) it has practically no effect on the positions (centers) of GRBFs. To overcome these limitations a simple strategy has been adopted, recently, [4] to exploit labeled data in the adaptation of parameters in the RBF hidden layer. RBF centers are determined by running a clustering algorithm separately on different training sets, where each training set is associated with a different output class, according to the scheme in Figure 1. Each colour in the figure identifies a clustering module trained with only the input data associated to a specific output class.

It has been proved that this simple strategy reduces instability of the classification error as a function of the number of basis functions, while typical advantages of RBF networks are maintained (e.g., fast training, easy implementation, low responses to outliers) [4].

In the framework of an RBF two-stage training approach, different clustering techniques can be employed to detect RBF centers in the hidden layer. Among others, interesting clustering approaches recently published in the literature are:

• The Fully self-Organizing Adaptive Resonance Theory (FOSART) algorithm, which is a constructive (growing), on-line learning, topology-preserving, soft-to-hard competitive, minimum-distance-to-means clustering network. Proposed as a new synthesis between properties of Fuzzy-ART and other successful clustering algorithms such as the Self-Organizing Map and Neural Gas to extend the capabilities of these separate approaches, FOSART is capable of: i) generating processing units and lateral connections on an example-driven basis, and ii) removing processing units and lateral connections on a mini-batch basis. To run, FOSART requires the user to define a normal adimensional threshold $\rho \in (0, 1]$ such that coarser grouping of input patterns is obtained when the vigilance parameter is lowered [5], [6].

• The Enhanced Linde-Buzo-Gray (ELBG) algorithm, which is a batch learning, non-constructive clustering system whose distorsion error is reduced by applying a standard LBG optimization criteria locally, and where codewords are allowed to move through non-contiguous Voronoi regions [7], [8]. To the best of our knowledge, this latter feature characterizes ELBG, along with the LBG-Utility algorithm proposed in [9], among all clustering algorithms proposed in the literature.

Our goal is to apply the RBF two-stage training approach developed in [4], where labeled data is employed in the adaptation of centers and widths of the RBF hidden layer, to data classification. This RBF learning approach is compared with a traditional RBF two-stage hybrid learning procedure in the classification of two different data sets.

2 Experimental Data Sets

2.1 MR Images

The dataset consisted of images PD, T2 weighted Spin Echo (SE) and the T1 Magnetization-prepared rapid gradient echo (MP-RAGE) sequence of a patient with multiple sclerosis lesions. The MP-RAGE slices of the whole head were acquired at 4 mm of thickness by a Siemens Impact 1.0 Tesla to be analyzed with the corresponding SE s. The image size is 256 by 256 pixels. Areas of interest interactively selected, in the raw images, by an expert neuroradiologist belong to classes: white matter, gray matter, CSF, pathologic lesions, background, other. A portion of the labelled were employed for training the classifier, the remaining pixels for test.

2.2 Remote Sensed Data

The input data set consisted of three SAR ERS1/ERS2 tandem pair images depicting an area featuring slope instability phenomena in the Campanian Apennines of Southern Italy. From each tandem pair, four features were extracted per pixel: the backscattering mean intensity, the interferometric coherence, the backscattering intensity texture and the backscattering intensity change. In the study area, 40×40 Km wide, seven classes were considered: I) layover; II) rocks; III) farmland; IV) water; V) erosion; VI) woods; and VII) urban areas. Class erosion identifies areas affected by and/or susceptible to mass movement-related processes. The supervised data set consisting of 27,948 pixels was extracted through *in situ* inspections and interpretation of aerial photographs. For each class, half of the supervised samples were randomly selected for training while the rest was used for testing.

3   On the Selection of Basis Function Parameters

In [4], to take into account the class-membership of training samples in the adptation of RBF centers and widths, Bruzzone adopts two simple strategies. To avoid the creation of *mixed* clusters, RBF centers are detected by running a clustering algorithm separately on training samples which have been grouped based on their output label. To compute RBF widths, the following criterion is employed. Given basis function BF_q^i, whose center is μ_q^i, $q = 1, ..., C$, $i \in \{1, ...L\}$, where C is the number of hidden units and L is the number of output labels, if M (e.g., $M = 3$) cluster centers closest to μ_q^i are associated to the i-th class, then the q-th basis function is not considered located on any decision boundary between classes and its width is computed with the p-nearest neighbor (p-nn) technique, where $M \geq p$ (e.g., if $M = 3$ and $p = 2$, then the width of the q-th basis function is equal to the average distance between μ_q^i and its two nearest cluster centers). Otherwise, the choice of the width of the q-th basis function is more conservative to avoid large overlapping between neighboring basis functions: in particular, this width is set equal to the standard deviation computed over all training samples belonging to basis function BF_q^i.

4   Clustering Strategy

In RBF first stage learning, FOSART was employed to initialize ELBG. This network combination is interesting owing to the complementary functional features of the two separate algorithms. On the one hand, FOSART is on-line learning, constructive and cannot shift codewords through non-contiguous Voronoi regions. On the other hand, ELBG is non-constructive, batch learning and capable of moving codewords through contiguous as well as non-contiguous Voronoi regions to reduce the distorsion error.

5   Experiments

RBF-1 and RBF-2 represents the two RBF networks trained with the Bruzzone and the traditional two-stage hybrid learning algorithm respectively. For each data set, two classification experiments were carried out.

Experiment 1: RBF-1 training and test
• RBF center initialization: employing the same vigilance threshold ρ, FOSART was run separately on each training set associated with a different output class (such that the number of detected clusters per class increases with the complexity of the class distribution).
• RBF center detection: ELBG was run separately on each training set.

Experiment 2: RBF-2 training and test
• RBF center initialization: FOSART was run once on the whole training set. Parameter ρ was adjusted until FOSART detected a number of clusters (approximately) equal to the overall number of clusters detected in Experiment 1.
• RBF center detection: ELBG was run once on the whole training set.

6   Results

The results obtained with RBF-1 scheme were compared with those obtained by RBF-2. Both RBF-1 and RBF-2 used a gradient descent technique in the supervised phase. In addition, these results were compared with those of a two-stage learning system consisting of a ELBG clustering algorithm combined with a second stage Majority Vote (MV) mechanism.

For the remote sensed data set, Table 1 reports the number of detected clusters per class obtained in RBF-1 scheme for different ρ values. and the percentage of the overall testing accuracy obtained with RBF-1, RBF-2 and the Majority Vote. Figure 1 shows the classification purity (%) for each class as a function of hidden layer nodes obtained with RBF1 and RBF2.

Table 1. RBF-1 classification of Remote Sensed Data

	ELBG								RBF1	RBF2	MV
ρ	Output nodes per class							TOT	OA%	OA%	OA%
	I	II	III	IV	V	VI	VII				
0.6	6	3	3	4	4	3	9	32	77.7	71.3	66.9
0.7	17	6	12	8	12	7	27	89	80.1	78.4	73.2
0.75	28	13	21	14	21	11	47	155	81.0	79.9	74.4
0.8	69	19	37	23	38	18	100	304	82.2	81.6	78.1

For the MR images, the results show the same trend as in the previous case. Infact, in the case of a total number of 224 nodes in the hidden layer, the percentage of the Overall Accuracy (OA) with RBF1 was equal to 87.3% in training and to 85.9% in test, whereas the OA obtained with RBF2 was equal to 84.1% in training and 81.2% in test respectively.

7   Conclusions

In line with theoretical expectations, our experiments show that: 1) when the number of processing unit in the hidden layer is the same, RBF-1 and RBF-2 perform better than a two-stage learning system consisting of a first stage ELBG clustering algorithm combined with a second stage mayority vote mechanism; 2) RBF-2 requires more hidden units than RBF-1 to reach the same classification error; and 3) the RBF-1 classification error is more stable than the classification error of RBF-2 with respect to changes in the number of hidden units.

8   Acknowledgments

This work was supported by the Italian Space Agency (ASI), contract ROPR 100296. The remote sensed images were provided by the ESA AO3-320 project.

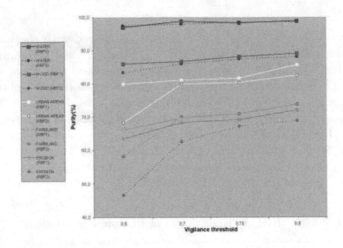

Fig. 1. Percentage of purity for each class in RBF-1 and RBF-2

The MR images were provided by Cattedra e Servizio di Neuroradiologia, University of Bari.

References

1. C. M. Bishop, *Neural Networks for Pattern Recognition*, Clarendon Press: Oxford (UK), 1995.
2. N. Karayiannis, "Growing radial basis neural networks: Merging supervised and unsupervised learning with network growth techniques," *IEEE Trans. on Neural Neworks*, vol. 8, no. 6, pp. 1492-1506, 1997.
3. N. Karayiannis, "Reformulated radial basis neural networks trained by gradient descent," *IEEE Trans. on Neural Networks*, under review, 1998.
4. L. Bruzzone and D. F. Prieto, "A technique for the selection of kernel-function parameters in RBF neural networks for classification of remote-sensing images," *IEEE Trans. Geosci. and Remote Sensing*, vol. 37, no.2, pp. 1179-1184, 1999.
5. A. Baraldi and P. Blonda, "A survey of fuzzy neural networks for pattern recognition: Part II," *IEEE Trans. Systems, Man and Cybernetics - Part B: Cybernetics*, vol. 29, no. 6, pp. 786-801, Dec. 1999.
6. A. Baraldi, P. Blonda, F. Parmiggiani, and G. Satalino, "Contextual clustering for image segmentation," *Optical Engineering*, vol. 39, no. 4, pp. 1-17, April 2000.
7. M. Russo and G. Patanè, "The Enhanced-LBG algorithm," *IEEE Trans. Knowledge and Data Engineering*, subm. 2000.
8. G. Patanè and M. Russo, "ELBG implementation," *IEEE Trans. Knowledge and Data Engineering* , subm. 2000.
9. B. Fritzke, "The LBG-U method for vector quantization - An improvement over LBG inspired from neural networks," *Neural Processing Letters*, vol. 5, no. 1, 1997.

A New Machine Learning Approach to Fingerprint Classification

Yuan Yao[1], Gian Luca Marcialis[2], Massimiliano Pontil[1,3], Paolo Frasconi[4], and
Fabio Roli[2]

[1] Dept. of Mathematics, City University of Hong Kong
mayyao@cityu.edu.hk
[2] DIEE University of Cagliari, Italy
{marcialis,roli}@diee.unica.it
[3] DII, University of Siena, Italy
mapontil@cityu.edu.hk
[4] DSI, University of Florence, Italy
paolo@dsi.unifi.it

Abstract. We present new fingerprint classification algorithms based
on two machine learning approaches: support vector machines (SVMs),
and recursive neural networks (RNNs). RNNs are trained on a structured
representation of the fingerprint image. They are also used to extract a
set of distributed features which can be integrated in the SVMs. SVMs
are combined with a new error correcting code scheme which, unlike
previous systems, can also exploit information contained in ambiguous
fingerprint images. Experimental results indicate the benefit of integrating global and structured representations and suggest that SVMs are a
promising approach for fingerprint classification.

1 Introduction

The pattern recognition problem studied in this paper consists of classifying fingerprint images into one out of five categories: whorl (W), right loop (R), left
loop (L), arch (A), and tented arch (T). These categories were defined during
early investigations about fingerprint structure [4] and have been used extensively since then. The task is important because classification can be employed
as a preliminary step for reducing complexity of database search in the problem
of automatic fingerprint matching [5]: If a query image can be classified with
high accuracy, the subsequent matching algorithm only needs to compare stored
images belonging to the same class.

In this paper, we propose new fingerprint classification algorithms based on
two machine learning approaches: support vector machines (SVMs), and recursive neural networks (RNNs). SVMs are a relatively new technique for pattern
classification and regression that is well-founded in statistical learning theory [8].
One of the main attractions of using SVMs is that they are capable of learning
in *sparse, high-dimensional spaces* with very few training examples. RNNs are
connectionist architectures designed for solving the supervised learning problem

F. Esposito (Ed.): AI*IA 2001, LNAI 2175, pp. 57–63, 2001.

when the instance space is comprised of labeled graphs [2]. This architecture can exploit structural information in the data, which improves the discrimination of certain pairs of classes. RNNs are also used to extract a distributed vectorial representation of the relational graph associated with a fingerprint. This vector is regarded as an additional set of features subsequently used as inputs for the SVM classifier. An important issue in fingerprint classification is the problem of ambiguous examples: some fingerprints are assigned to two classes simultaneously, i.e. they have double labels. In order to address this issue, we designed an error correcting code [1] scheme of SVM classifiers based on a new type of decoding distance. This approach has two main advantages: (a) It can tolerate the presence of ambiguous fingerprint images in the training set, and (b) It can effectively identify the most difficult fingerprint images in the test set. By rejecting these images the accuracy of the system improves significantly.

The paper is organized as follows: In Section 2 we briefly describe SVM's theory and discuss how to combine SVM classifiers for multi-class classification tasks. Section 3 briefly presents RNNs. In Section 4 we report the experimental results. Section 5 concludes the paper.

2   Support Vector Machines

SVMs [8] perform pattern recognition for two-class problems by determining the separating hyperplane with maximum distance or *margin* to the closest points of the training set. These points are called *support vectors*. If the data is not linearly separable in the input space, a non-linear transformation $\Phi(\cdot)$ can be applied which maps the data points $\mathbf{x} \in \mathbb{R}^n$ into a Hilbert space $\mathcal{H}$. The mapping $\Phi(\cdot)$ is represented by a kernel function $K(\cdot, \cdot)$ which defines an inner product in $\mathcal{H}$, i.e. $K(\mathbf{x}, \mathbf{t}) = \Phi(\mathbf{x}) \cdot \Phi(\mathbf{t})$. The decision function of the SVM has the form: $f(\mathbf{x}) = \sum_{i=1}^{\ell} \alpha_i c_i K(\mathbf{x}_i, \mathbf{x})$, where ℓ is the number of data points, and $c_i \in \{-1, 1\}$ is the class label of training point $\mathbf{x}_i$. Coefficients α_i can be found by solving a quadratic programming problem with linear constraints. An important kernel function is the Gaussian kernel: $K(\mathbf{x}, \mathbf{y}) = \exp(-\|\mathbf{x} - \mathbf{y}\|/2\sigma^2)$, with σ the variance of the gaussian. See [8] for more information on SVMs.

2.1   Multi-class Classification with Error Correcting Codes

Standard approaches to solve q-class problems with SVMs are: (a) One-vs-all: We train q SVMs, each of which separates a single class from all remaining classes [8]; (b) Pairwise: We train $\frac{q(q-1)}{2}$ machines, each of which separates a pair of classes. These two classification schemes are two extreme approaches: the first uses all the data, the second the smallest portion of the data. In practice, it can be more effective to use intermediate classification strategies in the style of error-correcting codes (ECCs) [1]. In this case, each classifier is trained to separate a subset of classes from another disjoint subset of classes (the union of these two subsets does not need to cover all the classes). For example the first set could consist of classes A and T and the second of classes R,L and W. By doing so, we associate each class with a row of the "coding matrix" $M \in \{-1, 0, 1\}^{q \times s}$, where s denotes the number of classifiers. $M_{ij} = -1$ or 1 means that points in class i are regarded as negative or positive examples for training the classifier j. $M_{ij} = 0$ says that points in class i are not used for training the j-th classifier. ECCs allows a more accurate use of ambiguous examples, since each SVM is in charge of generating one codebit only, whose value discriminates between two disjoint sets of classes. If a fingerprint has labels all belonging to the same set for a particular codebit, then clearly we can keep this example in the training set without introducing any labeling noise. As an example consider fingerprints with double labels A and T. These examples are discarded by the one-vs-all classifiers of class A and T, and the pairwise classifier A-vs-T. However they are used to train the classifier AT-vs-RLW. A test point is classified in the class whose row in the coding matrix has minimum distance to the output raw of the classifiers. Let $\mathbf{m}$ be a row of the coding matrix, $\mathbf{f}$ the real output vector of the classifiers, and γ_i the margin of the i-th classifier. The simplest and most commonly used distance is the Hamming distance $d(\mathbf{f}, \mathbf{m}) = \sum_{i=1}^{s} 1 - \mathrm{sign}(f_i m_i)$. We will also use two other distance measures which take in account the margin of the classifiers: The margin weighted Euclidean distance, $d(\mathbf{m}, \mathbf{f}) = \sum_{i=1}^{s} \gamma_i (1 - f_i m_i)$, and the soft margin distance $d(\mathbf{f}, \mathbf{m}) = \sum_{j=1}^{s} |1 - f_i m_i|_+$. In the later expression, the function $|x|_+$ is equal to x, when $x > 0$, and zero otherwise.

3   Recursive Neural Networks

A RNN [2] is a connectionist model designed to solve supervised learning problems such as classification or regression when the output prediction is conditioned on a hierarchical data structure, like the structural representation of fingerprints of [6]. The input to the network is a labeled direct positional acyclic graph (DPAG) U (see [2] for a definition), where the label $U(v)$ at each vertex v is a real-value feature vector associated with a fingerprint region, as described above. A hidden state vector $X(v) \in R^n$ is associated with each node v. This vector contains a distributed representation of the subgraph dominated by v (i.e. all the vertices that can be reached starting a directed path from v). The state vector is computed by a state transition function which combines the state vectors of v's children with a vector encoding of the label of v:

$$X(v) = f(X(w_1), \cdots, X(w_k), U(v)),$$

where $\{w_1, \cdots, w_k\}$ is the ordered set of v's children. Computation proceeds recursively from the frontier to the supersource (the vertex dominating all other vertices). Transition function f is computed by a multilayer perceptron, which is replicated at each node in the DPAG, sharing weights among replicas. Classification with RNNs is performed by adding an output function g that maps the hidden state vector $X(s)$ associated with the supersource to the class label. The state vector $X(s)$ is a distributed representation of the entire input DPAG and encodes features of the input DPAG deemed to be relevant for discrimination amongst classes. In the subsequent experiments, the components of the state vector at the supersource are thus used as an additional set of features.

4   Experimental Results

Our system was validated the NIST Database 4 [9]. This Database consists of 4000 images analyzed by a human expert and labeled with one *or more* of the five structural classes W, R, L, A, and T (more than one class is assigned in cases where ambiguity could not be resolved by the human expert). Previous works on the same dataset either rejected ambiguous examples in the training set (loosing in this way part of the training data), or used the first label as a target (potentially introducing output noise). Fingerprints were represented with the structured representation of [6] (22 real value features) as well as with FingerCode features [5] (192 real features).

4.1   Stacked Integration of Flat and Structural Classifiers

In a first set of experiments we investigated the potentialities of the combination of flat and structural methods. We coupled our structural approach with the flat neural network proposed in [5]. In these experiments, we used a "stacked" approach for combining classifiers, with a k-nearest neighbor as the additional classifier for combination [3].

Comparison between Vector-Based and Structural Classification. We have trained a multi-layer perceptron (MLP) using the FingerCode feature vector as input. The best test set performance was obtained with 28 hidden units. The overall accuracy is 86% at 1.8% rejection rate. For comparison, the structural approach described in [6] achieves the performance of 71.5% only. This low accuracy is mainly due to the large degree of confusion among L, R and T, while A and W are well discriminated. Afterwards, we analyzed the degree of complementarity between the two above classifiers. To this end, we assessed the performance of an ideal "oracle" that, for each input fingerprint, always selects the best of the two classifiers. Such an oracle provides an overall accuracy of 92.5% at 1.8% rejection rate. This value obviously represents a very tight upper bound for any combination method applied to the two classifiers. However, it points out the potential benefit of combining the flat and structural classifiers.

Combined Flat and Structural Classification. A k-nearest neighbor classifier (with a value of $k = 113$) was used for combining the flat and structural classifiers. Such metaclassifier takes the outputs of the two above classifiers as inputs and provides the final fingerprint classification as output. Such combination attains 87.9% accuracy at 1.8% rejection rate, outperforming the MLP classifier discussed above. This result indicates that accuracy can be improved by exploiting structural information. In particular, we observed that such combination improves the performances related to A and W classes.

4.2   Results with SVMs

We compared the three types of multi-class classification schemes discussed in section 2.1. SVMs were trained using the SVMFu code (`http://five-percent-`

`nation.mit.edu/SvmFu`) on a 550MHz Pentium-II PC. Training on 2000 examples takes about 10s for pairwise classifiers and about 20s for one-vs-all classifiers.

One-vs-All SVMs. We trained five one-vs-all SVM classifiers using both gaussian kernels and polynomials of degree between 2 and 6. The best result was obtained with the gaussian kernel with $\sigma = 1$: 88.0% at 1.8% rejection rate. The best polynomial SVM was of degree 3 and achieved a performance of 84.5% only. Then, in the remaining experiments we used only the Gaussian kernel.

Pairwise SVMs. We trained the ten pairwise SVMs. The test set accuracy increases to 88.4%, improving of 2.4% the MLP accuracy reported above.

Error-Correction SVM Scheme. Three sets of SVM classifiers were used to construct the coding matrix: 5 one-vs-al classifiers, 10 two-vs-three classifiers and 10 pairwise classifiers. The three kinds of decoding distances discussed in Section 2.1 were compared: (i) Hamming distance: 88.0%, (ii) Margin weighted Euclidean distance: 89.1%, (iii) Soft margin distance: 88.8% (all results are at 1.8% rejection rate). This results confirm the advantage of incorporating the margin of the classifiers inside the decoding distance. We have also trained the ECC of SVMs for the four classes task (classes A and T merged together) using the margin weighted Euclidean distance. The obtained accuracy is of 93.7% at 1.8% rejection rate. For comparison, the accuracy reported in [5] for the sole MPL's is 92.1%, while the cascade of $k-$NN and MLP yields 94.8%. This series of experiments indicate the advantage of the ECC scheme over the first two to the better exploiting information contained in multiple labeled examples.

Analysis of the Margin. We measured the margin and the number of support vectors of each SVM classifier used in our experiments (the training error of each individual classifier was always equal to zero). The number of support vectors ranges between $1/5$ and $1/2$ of the number of training points. As expected the margin decreases for those classifiers which involve difficult pairs of classes. Among the pairwise classifiers, the A-T classifier has the smallest margin. The margin of the T-vs-all and A-vs-all is also small. However the margin of the AT-vs-RLW classifier increases, which might explain why our error correcting strategy works well.

Rejection versus Accuracy. Let d_1 be the minimum distance of the output vector of the classifiers from the coding row, and d_2 the second minimum distance. Rejection can be decided by looking at the difference $\Delta = d_2 - d_1$. A large value of Δ indicates high confidence in classification; when Δ is smaller than a given threshold we reject the data. The rejection rate is controlled by this threshold. Table 1 shows the accuracy-rejection tradeoff obtained in our experiments. Notice that the accuracy of the system increases sharply with the rejection rate. At 20% and 32.5% rejection, the system shows a moderate improvement over the best results in [5].

Table 1. Accuracy vs. rejection rate for the ECC scheme of SVMs (Margin weighted Euclidean decoding) trained on FingerCode features.

Rejection Rate:	1.8%	8.5%	20%	32.5%
5 Classes:	89.1%	90.6%	93.9%	96.2%
4 Classes:	93.7%	95.4%	97.1%	98.4%

4.3 Combining Flat and Structural Features with SVM and ECC

We have trained SVMs on both FingerCode and RNN-extracted features and used the ECC scheme with margin weighted Euclidean decoding. The confusion matrix is summarized in Table 2a. The performance improves to 90.0% at 1.8% rejection rate. If we compare this performance to the performance obtained with FingerCode features only (89.1%), we observe the benefit of integrating global and structural representations. This effect is especially clear in the accuracy

Table 2. (a): Confusion matrix for the ECC of SVMs (Margin weighted Euclidean decoding) trained on both FingerCode and RNN-extracted features. (b): Accuracy vs. rejection rate for the ECC of SVM classifiers trained on the union of FingerCode and RNN- extracted features.

	W	R	L	A	T
W	366	18	8	2	0
R	5	354	0	7	29
L	6	1	357	2	13
A	0	2	2	396	33
T	1	8	12	48	294

(a)

Rejection Rate:	1.8%	8.5%	20.0%	32.5%
5 Classes:	90.0%	92.2%	95.6%	97.6%
4 Classes:	94.7%	96.6%	98.4%	99.2%

(b)

vs. rejection rate results. As shown in Table 2b, the accuracy sharply increases with the rejection rate, improving significantly over the results obtained with FingerCode features only (see Table 1).

5 Conclusions

In this paper have studied the combination of flat and structured representations for fingerprint classification. RNNs were used for process this structural representation and to extract a distributed vectorial representation of the fingerprint. This vectorial representation was integrated with other global representations, showing significant improvement over global features only. Experiment were performed on the NIST Database 4. The best performance was obtained with an error correcting code of SVMs. This method can tolerate the presence of ambiguous examples in the training set and shown to be precise to identify difficult test images, then sharply improving the accuracy of the system at a higher rejection rate.

Acknowledgments: We wish to thank R. Cappelli and D. Maltoni for useful discussions and A. Jain for providing us the dataset of preprocessed NIST-4 fingerprints. This work was partially supported by CERG grant No. 9040457.

References

1. T. G. Dietterich and G. Bakiri. Solving multiclass learning problems via error-correcting output codes. *Journal of Artificial Intelligence Research*, 1995.
2. P.Frasconi, M.Gori, and A.Sperduti. A general framework for adaptive processing of data structures. IEEE Trans on Neural Networks, 9(5), pp 768-786, 1998.
3. G.Giacinto, F.Roli, L.Bruzzone. Combination of Neural and Statistical Algorithms for Supervised Classification of Remote-Sensing Images. Pattern Recognition Letters, May 2000, 21 (5) pp. 385-397.
4. E.R. Henry. *Classification and Uses of Finger Prints*. Routledge, London, 1900.
5. A.K. Jain, S. Prabhakar, and L. Hong. A multichannel approach to fingerprint classification. *PAMI*, 21 (4):348–359, 1999.
6. G. Marcialis, F Roli, and P. Frasconi. Fingerprint classification by combination of flat and structural approaches. Proc. of AVBPA 2001, June 2001, pp. 241- 246.
7. M. Pontil and A. Verri. Support vector machines for 3-d object recognition. *IEEE Trans. PAMI*, pages 637–646, 1998.
8. V. N. Vapnik. *Statistical Learning Theory*. Wiley, New York, 1998.
9. C.I. Watson and C.L. Wilson. National Inst. of Standards and Technology, 1992.

An Automatic Accompanist Based on
Hidden Markov Models

Nicola Orio

Ircam – 1, pl. Igor Stravinsky, 75004 Paris, France
Nicola.Orio@ircam.fr

Abstract. The behavior of a human accompanist is simulated using a hidden Markov model. The model is divided in two levels. The lower level models directly the incoming signal, without requiring analysis techniques that are prone to errors; the higher level models the performance, taking into account all the possible errors made by the musician. Alignment is performed through a decoding technique alternative to classic Viterbi decoding. A novel technique for the training is also proposed. After the performance has been aligned with the score, the information is used to compute local tempo and drive the automatic accomaniment.

1   Introduction

This paper presents a possible solution to the problem of automatic real-time synchronization between musicians and computers, which is normally addressed in the literature as *intelligent automatic accompaniment* or *score following*. There are some applications for an automatic accompanist. For example, music students need to rehearse pieces where an accompaniment is required, but they may not easily find experienced accompanists to play with. The use of a prerecorded accompaniment is totally inadequate when expressive parameters are to be changed. Moreover, a student is likely to perform a number of mistakes when practicing, thus demanding for an intelligent system able to continuously resynchronize itself with the human player. Another application is for contemporary concerts that require synchronization between musicians and electronics. Forcing the musicians to follow the synthetic part means to reduce their expressiveness. A solution can be given by a computer system that listens to the musicians and drives the synthesis in response.

From these two examples, it can be seen that human-computer interaction has to be achieved through the audio channel. In fact, not only is audio the natural medium for the communication, but it eliminates the need for musicians to interact with other devices when playing. The automatic accompanist is then required to recognize users' intentions by listening only to their music performance. Furthermore, the system should react in real-time. Being time one of the main features of music, the delay introduced by the computation should not exceed the human perceptual thresholds in time discrimination of events.

An approach is proposed for the automatic recognition of sound events based on the modeling of sound features through a hidden Markov model (HMM). The

F. Esposito (Ed.): AI*IA 2001, LNAI 2175, pp. 64–69, 2001.

computation of the player position on the score is performed through decoding. A novel approach for the training of the HMM is proposed in order to optimize the probability of a correct decoding.

1.1 Background

The first task for an automatic accompanist is to match soloist performance with a score. This is a special case of sequence alignment, which has been extensively addressed in different areas. Even if music can be seen both as a sequence of symbols, as in molecular genetics, and as a sequence of acoustic parameters, as in speech recognition, score-performance matching has some peculiarities. Real-time constraints demand techniques that are robust even when only partial information is available. They are required techniques particularly suitable for local alignment and dealing with two sources of mismatch: analysis and performer errors. While analysis errors have been well explored there is no extensive study on the latter.

It seems promising to apply the techniques used in other research areas to score following. HMMs have become extremely popular in speech recognition, because of their outstanding results in comparison with approximate string matching and dynamic time warping. HMMs are probabilistic finite-state automata. At each transition, which is ruled by a probability function, the new state emits a symbol with a given probability. Finding the optimal sequence of states corresponding to a sequence of observations is called *decoding*. A complete discussion on theory and applications of HMMs can be found in [3] and in [5].

1.2 Previous Works on Automatic Intelligent Accompanist

The first approaches to score following were based on MIDI (Musical Instruments Digital Interface) instruments. Dannenberg proposed a technique based on classical approximate string matching, with some heuristics added to improve the performances [2]. Vercoe proposed a similar technique, where also timing was considered and a method for training the system after rehearsals was presented [8]. A simpler approach, due to Puckette [4], compares each incoming event with the list of expected events and the first exact match is chosen. Raphael [6] was the first who developed a system based on HMMs. States emit the expected sound features. Each note in the score is modeled by a sequence of states, depending on its length. A similar approach has been proposed by Cano and coworkers [1], where states of the HMM are specialized to emit respectively the attack, the sustain, and the decay of the notes but time features are not used. In both cases, Viterbi decoding is used to compute the alignment and the HMMs are strictly left-to-right, thus not dealing explicitly with performer's errors.

It can be noted that the proposed techniques can be divided in *note* and *signal* approaches. The former considers only musician's errors as a cause of mismatch, while the latter trusts the musician and focuses on errors due to incorrect sound features extraction.

2   The Intelligent Accompanist

The methodology presented in this paper joins the signal and the note approaches, through the use of a statistical model based on a two-level HMM. Alternative training and decoding techniques, more suitable for score following than classical approaches, are proposed.

2.1   Modeling the Signal

The *lower level* models the incoming audio signal and its states emit the expected features of the signal directly. This approach overcomes the problems of errors introduced by typical analysis techniques: Instead of analyzing the signal, a comparison of its features is performed with the expected ones. The only processing required is a fast Fourier transform, which gives a frequency representation of the signal. Currently, Fourier analysis is performed on a window of 1024 points with an hop-size of 512 points that, for a sampling rate of 44.1 kHz, introduces about 10 ms of delay. States emit a given pattern in the spectrum, with some simplifications. Instead of emitting a given spectrum, which may vary dramatically, a more general feature is emitted. This is the ratio of the energy carried by the first harmonics to the overall signal energy. The computation of partials energy can be carried out by taking the energy output by a bank of bandpass filters, each filter centered at one of the harmonics of the expected note. Good results have been obtained by using eight bandpass filters, with a band of a semitone.

Each note of the score is modeled using three classes of states: the first emits the note onset; the second emits the steady part of the signal (duration is modeled using a chain of states); the third emits a possible silence after the note. The network for a single note is reported in Figure 1. The emissions of the three classes of states are given by continuous probability density functions (pdf). Extensive test highlighted that the exponential pdf is the most suitable. The approach allows synchronization of polyphonic signals and trills, by changing the filterbank according to the superposition of the different expected events.

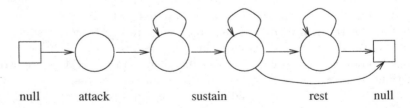

null   attack   sustain   rest   null

Fig. 1. Graphical representation of the lower level (two null states are added).

2.2   Modeling the Performance

The *higher level* models the performance and its states represent the events in the score. They are constituted by a HMM of the lower level. Notes in the score will be referred to as *note states* (n-states). Other events (e.g., rests, noise, trills) are treated in the same way. A simple chain of n-states, as in [6] and [1], proved to be effective only when few errors were present in the performance.

To deal with errors, a second category of states has been introduced. They will be referred to as *ghost states* (g-states). Each g-state represents the situation of a local mismatch. There is a parallel g-state for each n-state, dealing with three kinds of errors: wrong, extra, and skip notes. A n-state is connected to the following n-state and g-state. When there is no error, the most probable path will be going through n-states, while in case of errors, alternative paths through g-states become more probable. Emission probabilities of g-states are computed to minimize the probability of emitting the correct note. They can be computed using the same features extracted at the lower level. In Figure 2 it is depicted the same segment of the higher level, different paths are shown depending on performance correctness.

2.3   Training the HMM

There are some difficulties in training the HMM, because of the lack of a database of performances with errors. In the present work, emission probabilities of the lower level are trained from sound examples, taken from the database Studio On Line [7]. The parameters μ of each exponential pdf have been calculated through the analysis of all the samples in the database. Transition probabilities of the higher level are trained from examples of performances, which are automatically generated considering all the possible errors affecting from one to four notes. Normally, training of HMM is performed using Baum-Welch method.

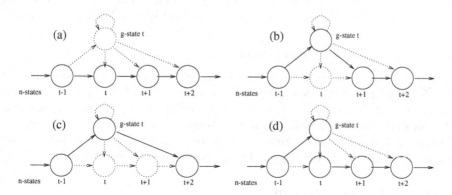

Fig. 2. Graphical representation of states at the higher level at time t. Different paths are related to: correct (a), wrong (b), skip(c), and extra (d) notes.

Experiments showed that this procedure is not suitable, because the meaning of the states (n-states vs. g-states) is lost. A novel technique for the training of HMMs is proposed, which maximizes the probability of being in the correct last state when a sequence of observations is given. Hence, instead of maximizing $P(o_1, \ldots, o_t \mid \lambda)$ it maximizes $P(q_t = v_t, o_1, \ldots, o_t \mid \lambda)$ where v_t is the correct last state, $o_1, \ldots, o_t$ are the observation until time t, and λ represents the model. The maximization is extended to all the possible performances, which are correct performances as well as the ones with errors, considering all their possible lengths from two notes to the complete performance. The training is then carried out by automatically computing both the sequences of observations and the sequences of correct positions in the HMM network. A technique has been developed, using Lagrange multipliers for the maximization and a dynamic programming approach for the computation of the probabilities.

2.4 Synchronization

Real-time alignment can be carried out through decoding. The Viterbi algorithm is the most popular technique for finding the optimal path along an HMM. Viterbi decoding is of global optimality, because it maximizes the probability of the whole state sequences given the observations. Global optimality may not be the best choice. In fact, for real-time alignment the main goal is to find the state locally corresponding to the actual note. This is a particular case of another optimality criterion, already introduced in the literature [3], where the probability of local alignments of each individual state is maximized.

This criterion may be applied by considering the optimal alignment of only the last state, that is the one corresponding to the current position in the score. The decoding of the last state is performed through the following maximization:

$$q_t = \arg\max P(q_t = v_t, o_1, \ldots, o_t \mid \lambda) \qquad (1)$$

which can be efficiently computed. This approach is coherent with the training procedure that has been previously introduced. The comparison with Viterbi showed lower delay in detecting note changes and higher robustness to errors.

2.5 Playing the Accompaniment

After the alignment is performed, the information on local time can be computed. This is used to drive the automatic accompaniment. Only correct matches are used to update the internal representation of local time. The human accompanist, who does not play mechanically at a fixed tempo, is simulated by simply adding a given randomness to onset time of the notes. The system can be set to react to particular events, which trigger the accompaniment when the tempo is free.

3 Experimental Results

Tests have been developed on a number of performances of classical and contemporary music, taken from recordings. Unfortunately, at least for our study, only few errors were present in these recordings. Different monophonic and polyphonic instruments and the voice have been used. In all the tests the alignment was successfully achieved.

Robustness to errors has been tested by using the same performance and altering the score. This allowed to extensively test the methodology, even if a database of real performances (with real errors) will be more appropriate. A correct alignment was always achieved, but these encouraging results have yet to be tested in real environments.

4   Conclusions and Future Work

A methodology aimed at an intelligent automatic accompanist has been developed. It is based on the modeling of the listening behavior of a human accompanist through a two-level HMM. A novel approach for the identification of relevant sound features has been developed, as well as a new technique for the training of HMMs. Results, even if not completely tested, are satisfactory particularly for scores that other systems are still not able to follow, such as polyphonic music.

Future steps on the research will regard the use of time information as a supplementary feature for the alignment. The use of local time will be explored as a way to choose between alternatives when a mismatch occurs. Pitch information is not sufficient to determine, for instance, if a mismatch is due to wrong or extra notes, and requires additional information on the performance. The use of time will help to make the correct choice before having to collect new information. Extensive tests with music students and professional musicians will be carried out for a complete evaluation of the methodology.

References

1. Cano, P., Loscos, A., Bonada, J.: Score-Performance Matching using HMMs. In Proc. of the ICMC, San Francisco (1999) 441–444
2. Dannenberg, R.B.: Recent Work In Real-Time Music Understanding By Computer. In Sundberg, Nord, and Carlson (Eds.), *Music, Language, Speech, and Brain*, Macmillan Publishers, London, UK (1991) 194–202
3. Durbin, R., Eddy, S., Krogh, A., Mitchison, G.: *Biological sequence analysis*. Cambridge University Press, Cambridge, UK (2000) 46–133
4. Puckette, M.S.: EXPLODE: A User Interface for Sequencing and Score Following. In Proc. of the ICMC, San Francisco (1990) 259–261
5. Rabiner, L. and Juang, B.H.: *Fundamentals of speech recognition* Prentice Hall, Englewood Cliffs, NJ (1993) 321–389
6. Raphael, C.: Automatic Segmentation of Acoustic Musical Signals Using Hidden Markov Models. IEEE Transactions on Pattern Analysis and Machine Intelligence, **21**(4) (1999) 360–370
7. Studio On Line, http://sol.ircam.fr, visited on 27 June 2001
8. Vercoe, B. and Puckette, M.S.: Synthetic Rehearsal: Training the Synthetic Performer. In Proc. of the ICMC, San Francisco, CA (1985) 275–278

Resampling vs Reweighting in Boosting a Relational Weak Learner

Marco Botta

Dipartimento di Informatica, Università di Torino, Corso Svizzera 185 – 10149 Torino – Italy
botta@di.unito.it

Abstract. Boosting is a powerful and thoroughly investigated learning technique that improves the accuracy of any given learning algorithm by weighting training examples and hypotheses. Several authors contributed to the general boosting learning framework with theoretical and experimental results, mainly in the propositional learning framework. In a previous paper, we investigated the applicability of Freund and Schapire's AdaBoost.M1 algorithm to a first order logic weak learner. In this paper, we extend the weak learner in order to directly deal with weighted instances and compare two ways to apply boosting to such a weak learner: resampling instances at each round and using weighted instances.

1 Introduction

This paper focuses on supervised learning from examples in first order logic languages [22,4], also called *relational learning* [25], which has been extensively studied from a theoretical and experimental point of view in Inductive Logic Programming (ILP) [23]. In particular, we are interested in the classification task of structured instances, i.e. the recognition of an object or event as an instance of a given class. Medical and fault diagnosis, prognosis, image recognition, text categorization, adaptive user profiling, can be seen as specific instances of such a classification task.

A wide spectrum of learning algorithms, based on different approaches ranging from logic induction [24,25,5] to Artificial Neural Networks [6] and Genetic Algorithms [2,18], are now available for acquiring first order theories.

All these approaches favor readability and interpretability of the learned classification theories. However, it often happens that the learned knowledge is not as meaningful and understandable as expected by a human expert. Moreover, when error rates are high, it is questionable whether what has been learned should be considered "knowledge", thus how relevant is to obtain readable theories in these cases.

In the propositional framework, several recent approaches, such as boosting [17], bagging [9] and arching [10], favor, instead, classification accuracy by repeatedly learn theories calling a so called *weak learner* and somehow combining the acquired theories. These methods generally improved performances with respect to sophisticated learners [16], despite the readability of the learned classification theory.

In this paper, we investigate the effectiveness of one of the above-mentioned methods, namely boosting, in a first order logic setting and compare two ways to implement it. Boosting uses all instances at each repetition, and maintains a *weight* for

F. Esposito (Ed.): AI*IA 2001, LNAI 2175, pp. 70–80, 2001.

each instance in the training set that reflects its importance; adjusting the weights causes the learner to focus on different instances and so leads to different classifiers. The multiple classifiers are assigned different voting strengths on the basis of their accuracy and combined by voting to form a composite classifier.

Even though almost all existing FOL learning systems can be used as weak learners, they are not usually able to directly take into account weighted instances. In order to boost these systems, a subset of the training instances is sampled according to the weights associated to the instances, and these (unweighted) resampled examples can be used to train the weak learner. We refer to this method as boosting by *resampling*, as opposed to boosting by *reweighting*, as done in [16], when the weak learner is able to use weighted instances.

Quinlan [27] performed a similar study by boosting FFOIL, an adaptation of FOIL [25] for functional relations, but he only used boosting by resampling, as FFOIL is not able to weigh instances. He found that boosting improves performances of first order learners, as well, but we reached a somewhat different conclusion by comparing the obtained results to the best published ones.

The paper is organized as follows: Section 2 introduces the weak learner WWIL, an extension of WIL [7] that directly manages weighted instances; Section 3 briefly overviews the AdaBoost.M1 algorithm, Section 4 describes the experimental setting and results obtained, and Section 5 presents some discussion and concludes the paper.

2   The Weighted Weak Learner

In order for the boosting methodology to be affordable and convenient, the weak learning algorithm should be fast. In the propositional framework, there are a quite large number of learning algorithms (see, for instance, [8,26]) that meet this constraint. In first order logic, learning algorithms tend to be quite slow, due to the complexity of the search space they have to explore. We devised an extremely straightforward learning algorithm, called WIL (Weak Inductive Learner) [7], that builds a set of decision rules, resembling the way FOIL [25] works, and further extended in WWIL (Weighted Weak Inductive Learner) to directly manage weighted instances. First, let us briefly introduce the learning framework.

We assume the reader is familiar with standard logic programming terminology and only recall here a few notions. Examples processed by WWIL are represented by specifying their elementary components, called *objects*, plus a set of their *properties* such as "color" or "length", and *relationships*, such as "relative position". This representation is close to the one adopted in object oriented databases (see [19] for a more detailed description), and naturally regresses to attribute-value representation when instances are composed by a single object. Theories consists of sets of clauses with the following format:

$$Head \leftarrow L_1 \wedge ... \wedge L_n$$

where *Head* is a positive literal (a concept to learn) and each L_i is a positive or negated literal. Recursive clauses, i.e. clauses with the same literal both in the head and in the body, are not allowed. Moreover, clauses are *range-restricted*, i.e., variables in the head of a clause must also appear in its body.

A sketch of the algorithm is reported in Fig. 1.

Algorithm WWIL
Input: set of N examples $<(Ex_1,y_1),...,(Ex_N,y_N)>$ with labels $y_i \in Y = \{1,...,k\}$. Note
      that examples may be structured.
  vector **w** specifying instance weights
  float γ specifying percentage of positive instances to cover
  a set Λ of literals
  integer μ specifying number of allowed literals in a clause (default ∞)
Set *Theory* = $\varnothing$
Do for $j = 1, 2, ..., k$
    Set *PosInstances* = $\{(Ex_i,y_i) \mid y_i = y_j \}$, *ToCover* = $|PosInstances|*\gamma$
    While $|PosInstances|$ > *ToCover*
        Set *body* = *true*
        Set *clause* = $y_j \leftarrow body$
        While *clause* covers some negative example $\wedge |body|$ < μ
            find the literal *L* to add to the right-hand side of *clause* that maximizes
            an Information Gain IG_w measure. All variabilizations of each
            literal in Λ consistent with *body* are considered and scored in this
            step.
            update *body* = *body* $\wedge L$
      End
      Remove from *PosInstances* examples covered by *clause*
      Add clause to Theory: *Theory* = *Theory* $\cup$ {*clause*}
    End
Endfor

Fig. 1. The first-order weak learning algorithm WWIL with weights.

The inner loop of WWIL is responsible to find a clause as consistent and complete as possible. Once such a clause is found, it is added to the theory, the PosInstances set is updated by removing the covered instances, and these steps repeated until enough positive instances are covered. This process is performed for each concept to learn, so WWIL solves *k* binary problems (one-vs-all approach [1]) and simply combines their outputs according to the following scheme: a score, that measures how good a clause is, is associated to every clause; then, the label(s) predicted by clause(s) with the highest score is(are) associated to the instance. Notice that, in this way, multiple labels can be assigned to an instance and no tie breaking is used (classification is ambiguous and considered an error in AdaBoost). Moreover, it should be pointed out that by setting $\gamma = \dfrac{1}{|PosIntances|}$ only one clause is built in the inner loop, and by further setting μ to 1, clauses will have only one literal, thus mimicking the *FindDecRule* and *FindAttrTest* algorithms [16], respectively, designed for the propositional framework.

The only difference with respect to its predecessor WIL [7], is the way the Information Gain measure IG_w that guides the selection of the best literal to add to a clause, is computed. IG_w is a generalization of the classical Information Gain measure used in FOIL [25] that accounts for weighted instances. Given a clause φ and a literal L, let $\psi = \varphi \wedge L$. The IG_w measure is computed as follows:

$$IG_w(\varphi,\psi,\overline{w}) = pos(\psi,\overline{w})\left(\log_2 \frac{pos*(\psi,\overline{w})}{pos*(\psi,\overline{w}) + neg*(\psi,\overline{w})} - \log_2 \frac{pos*(\varphi,\overline{w})}{pos*(\varphi,\overline{w}) + neg*(\varphi,\overline{w})} \right)$$

where $pos(\varphi,\overline{w}) = \displaystyle\sum_{Ex_i \in PosInstances} w_i$ is the number of positive instances covered by φ,

$pos*(\varphi,\overline{w}) = \displaystyle\sum_{Ex_i \in PosInstances} w_i * t_i$ is the number of substitutions for variables of φ in

positive instances covered by φ, and $neg*(\varphi,\overline{w}) = \displaystyle\sum_{Ex_i \notin PosInstances} w_i * t_i$ is the number

of substitutions for variables of φ in negative instances covered by φ (t_i is the number of substitutions of variables of φ in instance Ex_i). When all values w_i are set to 1, this equation is similar to the Information Gain measure and is exactly the one used in WIL.

3 Boosting

The version of boosting used in this paper is AdaBoost.M1 [17]. It maintains a weight for each instance – the higher the weight, the more the instance influences the learned theory. At each round, the vector of weights is adjusted to reflect the performance of the corresponding theory, with the result that the weight of misclassified instances is increased. The final classification theory aggregates the learned theories by voting, where each theory's vote is a function of its accuracy.

The AdaBoost.M1 algorithm is sketched in Fig. 2.

Algorithm AdaBoost.M1
Input: set of N examples $<(Ex_1,y_1),\ldots,(Ex_N,y_N)>$ with labels $y_i \in Y = \{1,\ldots,k\}$
distribution D over the N examples
weak learner algorithm **WWIL**
integer T specifying number of iterations
Initialize the weight vector $w_i^1 = D_i$ for $i = 1,\ldots,N$.
Do for $t = 1, 2, \ldots, T$

1. Set $D^t = \dfrac{\mathbf{w}^t}{\sum_{i=1}^{N} w_i^t}$

2. Call **WWIL** providing it with distribution D^t as weight vector; get back a hypothesis $h_t : X \to Y$

3. Calculate the error of

$$h_t : \varepsilon_t = \sum_{i=1}^{N} D_i^t \|h_t(Ex_i) \neq y_i\|.$$

If $\varepsilon_t > \frac{1}{2}$ or $\varepsilon_t = 0$, then set $T = t\text{-}1$ and abort the loop.

4. Set $\beta_t = \varepsilon_t /(1\text{-}\varepsilon_t)$.

5. Set the new weights vector to be

$$w_i^{t+1} = w_i^t \beta_t^{1-\|h_t(Ex_i) \neq y_i\|}$$

Output the hypothesis

$$h_f(Ex) = \arg\max_{y \in Y} \sum_{t=1}^{T} \left(\log \frac{1}{\beta_t} \right) \|h_t(Ex) = y\|$$

Fig. 2. Simple multi-class version of AdaBoost. For any predicate π, $\|\pi\|$ is 1 if π holds, and 0 otherwise.

The algorithm takes as input a training set (Ex_1, y_1), ..., (Ex_N, y_N) where each Ex_i belongs to an instance space X, and each label y_i is in some label set Y. A weak learning algorithm is called at every round to find a weak hypothesis $h_t : X \rightarrow Y$ appropriate for distribution D^t. The goodness of a weak hypothesis is measured by its error:

$$\varepsilon_t = \Pr_{i \sim D^t} [h_t(Ex_i) \neq y_i] = \sum_{i:h_t(Ex_i) \neq y_i} D_i^t .$$

The error is measured with respect to the distribution D^t on which the weak learner was trained. Once the weak hypothesis h_t has been received, AdaBoost.M1 chooses a parameter β_t measuring the importance of that hypothesis. The final hypothesis h_f for a given instance Ex outputs the label that maximizes the sum of the weights of the weak hypotheses predicting that label.

In the experiments reported in the next section, we compare boosting by resampling, in which at every round t, exactly N instances are randomly sampled with replacement according to distribution D^t, to boosting by reweighting, in which distribution D^t is directly passed to WWIL.

4   Experimental Setting

We conducted a number of experiments on a collection of 7 first-order learning problems that show different properties and seemed to be a good test bench for the presented algorithm. Moreover, we experimentally checked the correctness of the implementation by running the algorithm on a propositional learning problem. A brief description of the selected learning problems follows.

Splice-junctions. The first problem we considered, the *Splice Junctions* dataset, comes from molecular biology and has been provided by Jude Shavlik [30]. The problem is that of identifying boundaries between coding (exons) and non-coding (introns) regions of genes occurring in eukaryote DNA. The dataset consists of 3190 DNA sequences, collected from the GeneBank. Each sequence is represented as a string of length 60 from the alphabet {a,t,c,g}. The sequences are labeled according to three classes. Sequences containing a donor site belong to the E/I class (25% of the dataset); the ones containing an acceptor site to the class I/E (25% of the dataset);

finally, sequences that do not contain any site belong to the N (Neither) class (50% of the dataset).

Mutagenesis. The first FOL problem we considered is represented by the *Mutagenesis* dataset, a challenging problem widely used in the ILP community for testing induction algorithms in FOL [21]. More recently, the problem has been proposed as a *real* Data Mining application [11]. The problem consists in learning rules for discriminating substances (aromatic and etheroaromatic nitro compounds occurring in car emissions) having carcinogenic properties on the basis of their chemical structure. The dataset contains 188 aromatic compounds (each example describes a single compound), of which 118 present positive levels of mutagenicity and therefore are labeled as positive examples, and the remaining 60 form the negative ones. The difficulty mainly lies in the complexity of matching formulas in FOL, which strongly limits the exploration capabilities of any induction system.

Train-check-out. This is an artificial dataset built to test the generalization ability of FONN [6], a learning algorithm that refines numerical constants in first order classification rules. The problem consists in deciding whether a train must not be allowed to transit on a given line (check-out procedure followed by a railway inspector), depending on the characteristics of the line. Two instances of the problem, *Trains2* and *Trains3* [6], of different complexity, have been considered in the experiments.

SpeechRecognition. The fourth learning problem concerns the recognition of the ten digits spoken in Italian [3] as isolated words, starting from the time evolution of two rough features, i.e., the zero-crossing and the total energy of the signal. The features are extracted from the signal using classical signal processing algorithms and are then described using a set of primitives, as proposed by DeMori et al. [12]. The learning set consists of 219 instances, while 100 instances are used for testing.

OfficeDocuments. This learning problem is a natural dataset derived from a real-world application of digitized office document classification [14]. The task is that of classifying single page documents by using only information about the page layout structure. A page layout is produced by segmenting the document and by grouping together some segments (or blocks) that satisfy predetermined requirements such as closeness, same type, and so on. Blocks and segments are described by categorical attributes, such as the frame type (text, line, graphics, and so on), by numerical attributes, such as width, length and positions of blocks, and relational properties, such as alignment of blocks (two blocks are aligned at left or right, bottom or top, etc.). Instances are classified into 8 classes, four corresponding to printed letters from the same company, three to magazine indexes, and the last one to a reject class representing ``the rest of the world''.

DocumentUnderstanding. In this learning problem, tha task is that of identifying the purpose served by components of single-page letters (see [15] for a complete description of the application). There are five concepts to be learned, namely *sender* of the letter, *receiver, logotype, reference number* and *date,* in terms of operational predicates such as *height, width, position, type, relative position* and *relative alignment* of objects in a document. The dataset consists of 30 documents composed of 364 objects, 35 of which are instances of concept *sender,* 39 are instances of *receiver,* 30 of *logotype,* 45 of *reference number* and 37 of *date.* The remainder objects are just blocks of text or lines.

ArtificialCharacters. The last learning problem concerns an artificial dataset that bears many resemblances to a real-world one: ten capital letters of the English alphabet have been chosen and described in terms of segments, as though acquired from a tablet. Each segment is described by the initial and final coordinates (x,y) in a Cartesian plane. From these basic features, other features can be extracted, such as the length of a segment, its orientation, its preceding and following segments, and so on. Some of these features are numerical by nature, whereas others are categorical. Here, we took the original dataset of 6000 instances[1] and split it into 6 folds of 1000 instances each (100 instances per class), that are used for learning, while an independent test set of 10000 instances (1000 per class), is used for testing.

5   Experimental Results

Table 1 reports the results obtained on the 8 problems by running AdaBoost.M1 for 50 rounds, evaluating performances at the first ((W)WIL no boosting) and last round ((W)WIL + boosting by resampling and reweighting). Results using no boosting or boosting by resampling are the same for both WIL and WWIL. WWIL is called with γ = 0.7 (so that it must cover at least 70% of positive instances). For *Trains2*, *Trains3* (5 folds) and *ArtificialCharacters* (6 folds), AdaBoost.M1 has been run on each learning set, the learned theory tested on the testset and results are averaged. For *Splice-junctions*, *Speech* and *OfficeDocuments* we performed 10 runs of AdaBoost.M1 (when using resampling) and averaged the results (only 1 run was possible when using reweighting). For *Mutagenesis* we performed 10-fold cross-validation. Finally, for *DocumentUnderstanding*, we performed a 30-fold cross-validation, by omiting all information about components of a letter at each fold, learning a theory, and testing on the omitted letter.

Table 1. Results obtained on the test benches by WWIL. ± indicates standard deviation. Arrows state whether error is decreasing, increasing or stable in the last 10 rounds. In the last column, numbers in square bracket are references to papers publishing the best performances.

LEARNING PROBLEM	(W)WIL (NO BOOSTING)	(W)WIL + BOOSTING BY RESAMPLING	WWIL + BOOSTING BY REWEIGHTING	BEST PUBLISHED RESULT (ERROR RATE %)
SPLICE-JUNCTIONS	24.1	4.2±0.27 ↓	6.8 ≈	4.0 [16]
TRAINS2	19.92±1.38	11.6±0.80 ≈	8.58±1.72 ↓	19.97±1.9 [6]
TRAINS3	18.17±4.14	24.59±0.65 ↑	7.58±0.96 ↓	12.76±5.4 [6]
MUTAGENESIS	27.22±10.37	7.7±6.6 ↓	16.11±5.79 ≈	6.4 [29]
SPEECH	36.7±3.35	16±2.19 ↓	20 ≈	18.0 [6]
DOCUMENT UNDERSTANDING	15.49±14.82	5.67±7.84 ≈	4.89±7.77 ↓	3.0 [27]
OFFICE DOCUMENTS	8.30±1.87	2.32±0.91 ≈	4.43 ≈	1.82 [6]
ARTIFICIAL CHARACTERS	30.74±1.29	5.65±0.78 ↓	8.76±0.78 ↑	1.08±1.25 [6]

---

[1] Available in the ML repository at UCI.

By comparing the results reported in column two to those reported in columns three and four of Table 1, it is clear that boosting greatly improves performances of the weak learner WWIL when using both resampling and reweighting. In particular, boosting by resampling improves in 7 out of 8 problems (error is reduced by about 322% on average) and boosting by reweighting improves in all problems (error is reduced by 231% on average). This confirms Quinlan's statement that 'boosting is advantageous for first-order learning in general' [27]. However, this is not the only conclusion one can draw from these experiments.

First of all, by comparing the results reported in columns three and four to those in column five of Table 1, only in two cases (*Trains2* and *Trains3*) out of 8, boosting WWIL outperformed a fully featured (i.e., explicitly configured to solve the problem) first-order learning system. In one case (*Trains3*), boosting by resampling degrades performances: this is a somewhat unexpected result given the kind of learning problem. Also Quinlan [27] noted that boosting sometimes degrades performances; in this case, it might be due to small learning sets, since when boosting by reweighting is used (thus considering all instances) better performances are obtained.

A second observation concerns the two boosting strategies we tried. A somewhat surprising result is that boosting by resampling is better than boosting by reweighting in 5 out of 8 cases, whereas in the propositional framework the opposite is generally true [16,28]. We thought that, since reweighting always provides all instances to the weak learner (even if they might have small weights), WWIL tends to overfit the data, as it looks for consistent hypotheses. To test this conjecture, we modified WWIL inner loop termination condition (*clause* covers some negative example $\land |body| < \mu$), allowing for the generation of slightly inconsistent hypotheses (*clause* covers less than $\tau\%$ negative examples $\land |body| < \mu$), set $\tau - 5$ and 10 and repeated some of the experiments. We found that in 5 out of 8 cases performances are further improved by reducing the error rate of about 10% on average. For instance, on the *splice-junctions* dataset, we obtained 3.7% error rate, that is also the best result we are aware of.

It should be pointed out that the best result for the *Mutagenesis* dataset has been obtained by STILL as its best hit with very careful setting of the parameters, while average error rates are around 11%, as also obtained by other systems (see [29] for further details). Also the results on the *ArtificialCharacters* dataset need a further comment. The best results have been obtained by running a powerful learning system such as Smart+ [5] provided with qualitative background knowledge and a more expressive representation language, and refining the learned knowledge with NTR [6] for a total running time of several hours on a Pentium II 400 Mhz processor. Each round of WWIL took about 50 seconds. This means that there should be room for improvements by performing a larger number of rounds.

For what concerns the running times, WWIL is as fast as expected. For instance, on the *mutagenesis* dataset it took 10.5 CPU seconds per round, on average; on the *Trains2* dataset it took 4 CPU seconds per round, whereas on the *Speech* dataset it took 6.3 CPU seconds per round (all timings have been measured on a Pentium III 600 Mhz processor with 196 Mbytes RAM, running Linux Slackware 7.1).

6   Discussion and Conclusions

From the reported results, boosting seems effective also in solving problems represented in first order logic languages, at the cost of interpretability of the acquired knowledge. The weak learner WWIL, being really weak, is greatly improved by boosting, but as Quinlan's results show [27] it is not clear how much boosting a more sophisticated learner can increase performances. A more thorough analysis is required, because it seems that the better the weak learner, the less improvement boosting provides. Furthermore, as pointed out above, performances after 50 rounds are still worse than the best published ones in most cases. As reported in Table 1, on four cases performances constantly decrease in the last 10 rounds, so there is hope to get close to the best results with more rounds. Moreover, it seems that boosting by reweighting can indeed improve performances over resampling, provided that a slight inconsistency of the acquired theory is allowed (anyhow, this point needs further investigation).

Another issue concerns multi-class learning problems, such as the *Speech* and *ArtificialCharacters* datasets. The classification strategy adopted by WWIL is quite simple; by using more sophisticated combination strategies, such as those suggested by Dietterich & Bakiri [13] and Allwein et al. [1] that are orthogonal to the application of boosting, performances might further be improved.

Future work will be devoted to study the convergence property of the algorithm on long runs (1000 rounds). Moreover, one interesting aspect of AdaBoost is that it calls the weak learner several times on different sampling of the learning instances, focusing the search on the most difficult ones. An investigation of the effects of this strategy on really hard relational problems may reveal a way to overcome the limitations of greedy search heuristics [20].

Acknowledgements

The author is grateful to Attilio Giordana and Roberto Esposito for their helpful comments and discussions during the development and writing process.

References

1.   E. L. Allwein, R. E. Schapire and Y. Singer (2000). Reducing multiclass to binary: A unifying approach for margin classifiers. *Journal of Machine Learning Research, 1*, 113-141.

2.   C. Anglano, A. Giordana, G. Lo Bello and L. Saitta (1998). An Experimental Evaluation of Coevolutive Concept Learning. *Proc. 15th Int. Conf. on Machine Learning* (Madison, WI, 1998), pp. 19-27.

3.   F. Bergadano, A. Giordana and L. Saitta (1988). Learning Concepts in Noisy Environment. *IEEE Transaction on Pattern Analysis and Machine Intelligence, PAMI-10*, 555-578.

4.   F. Bergadano, A. Giordana and L. Saitta (1991). *Machine Learning: An Integrated Framework and its Applications*. Hellis Horwood, Chichester, UK.

5. M. Botta and A. Giordana (1993). Smart+: A MultiStrategy Learning Tool. *Proc. of the 13th Int. Joint Conf. on Artificial Intelligence,* (Chambery, France, 1993), pp. 937-943.
6. M. Botta and R. Piola (2000). Refining Numerical Constants in Structured First Order Logic Theories. *Machine Learning Journal, 38,* 109-131.
7. M. Botta (2001). WIL: a First Order Logic Weak Learner for Boosting. *Technical Report RT 60/01,* Dipartimento di Informatica, Università di Torino, http://www.di.unito.it/~botta/rt60-01.pdf.
8. L. Breiman, J. H. Friedman, R. A. Olshen and C. J. Stone (1984). *Classification and Regression Trees.* Wadsworth & Brooks.
9. L. Breiman (1996). Bagging Predictors. *Machine Learning, 24,* 123-140.
10. L. Breiman (1998). Arcing Classifiers. *The Annals of Statistics, 26,* 801-849.
11. L. Dehaspe, H. Toivonen and R. King (1998). Finding frequent substructures in chemical compounds. *Proc. of the 4th Int. Conf. On Knowledge Disciovery and Data Mining* (New York, NY, 1998), pp. 30-66.
12. R. DeMori, A. Giordana, P. Laface and L. Saitta (1984). An Expert System for Mapping Acoustic Cues into Phoenetic Features. *Information Sciences, 33,* 115-155.
13. T. G. Dietterich and G Bakiri (1995). Solving Multiclass Learning Problems via Error-Correcting Output Codes. *Journal of AI Research, 2,* 263-286.
14. F. Esposito, D. Malerba and G. Semeraro (1992). Classification in noisy environments using a distance measure between structural symbolic descriptions. *IEEE Transactions on Pattern Analisys and Machine Intelligence, PAMI-14(3),* 390-402.
15. F. Esposito, D. Malerba, G. Semeraro, and M. Pazzani (1993). A Machine Learning Approach to Document Understanding. *Proc. of the 2nd International Workshop on Multistrategy Learning,* (Harpers Ferry, WV, 1993), pp. 276-292.
16. Y. Freund and R. E. Schapire (1996). Experiments with a New Boosting Algorithm. *Proc. of the 13th Int. Conf. on Machine Learning,* (Bari, Italy, 1996), pp. 148-156.
17. Y. Freund and R. E. Schapire (1997). A decision-theoretic generalization of on-line learning and an application to boosting. *Journal of Computer and System Sciences, 55,* 119-139.
18. A. Giordana and F. Neri (1996). Search-intensive Concept Induction. *Evolutionary Computation, 3,* 375-416.
19. A. Giordana, F. Neri, L. Saitta and M. Botta (1997). Integrating Multiple Learning Strategies in First Order Logics. *Machine Learning, 27,* 209-240.
20. A. Giordana, L. Saitta and M. Botta (1999). An Experimental Study of Phase Transitions in Matching. *Proc. 16th Int. Joint Conf. on Artificial Intelligence,* (Stockholm, Sweden, 1999), pp. 1198-1203.
21. R. King, A. Srinivasan and M. Stenberg (1995). Relating chemical activity to structure: an examination of ILP successes. *New Generation Computing, 13.*
22. R. S. Michalski (1983). A Theory and Methodology of Inductive Learning. *Artificial Intelligence, 20,* 111-161.
23. S. Muggleton (Ed.). (1992). *Inductive Logic Programming.* Academic Press, London. UK.
24. S. Muggleton (1995). Inverse Entailment and Progol. *New Generation Computing, 13,* 245-286.
25. J. R. Quinlan (1990). Learning Logical Definitions from Relations. *Machine Learning, 5,* 239-266.
26. J. R. Quinlan (1993). *C4.5: Programs for Machine Learning.* Morgan Kaufmann.
27. J. R. Quinlan (1996). Boosting First-Order Learning. *LNAI, 1160,* 143-155.
28. J. R. Quinlan (1996). Bagging, Boosting, and C4.5. *Proc. of the 14th AAAI,* (Portland, OR, 1996), pp. 725-730.

29. M. Sebag and C. Rouveirol (1997). Tractable Induction and Classification in First Order Logic via Stochastic Matching. *Proc. of the 15th Int. Joint Conf. On Artificial Intelligence*, (Nagoya, Japan, 1997), pp. 888-893.
30. G. Towell and J. Shavlik (1994). Knowledge Based Artificial Neural Networks. *Artificial Intelligence, 70*, 119-166.

Learning Logic Models
for Automated Text Categorization

Stefano Ferilli, Nicola Fanizzi, and Giovanni Semeraro

Dipartimento di Informatica
Università di Bari
via E. Orabona, 4 - 70125 Bari - Italia
{ferilli, fanizzi, semeraro}@di.uniba.it

Abstract. This work addresses a logical approach to text categorization inside a framework aimed at full automatic paper document processing. The logic representation of sentences required by the adopted learning algorithm is obtained by detecting structure in raw text trough a parser. A preliminary experimentation proved that the logic approach is able to capture the semantics underlying some kind of sentences, even if the assessment of the efficiency of such a method, as well as a comparison with other related approaches, has still to be carried out.

1 Introduction

Statistical approaches have been so far extensively used for learning tasks related to Natural Language Processing [SN97], despite of their limitations in flexibility and expressivity [Cus99]. Conversely, logical approaches may have a relevant impact at the level of semantic interpretation [Moo99]. Attempts to exploit first-order logic have already been made; however, they just define simple properties about textual sources, regarded, for instance, as bags of words [JSR99] or as semi-structured texts [Fre00]. Such properties are often loosely related with the grammar of the underlying language [Coh96]. We aim at exploiting a logic representation to take advantage of the grammatical structure of the texts, according to the assumption that a more knowledge intensive technique is likely to perform better when applied on the tasks of Text Categorization/Information Extraction.

When no background knowledge about the language structure is available, one of the fundamental problems with the adoption of logic learning techniques is that a structured representation of sentences is required on which the learning algorithm can be run. Hence, the need for parsers that are able to discover such a structure starting from raw, unstructured text. Such a preprocessing step obviously affects the performance of the whole approach, since noise coming from wrongly parsed sentences could have a negative influence towards the model to be induced. Further problems are due to the intrinsic computational complexity of these methods, as a drawback of the expressive power gained through relations.

After presenting in Section 2 the first-order learning system INTHELEX, Section 3 shows the results of applying it to text categorization for the inference of some simple events related to foreign commerce. Lastly, Section 4 draws some preliminary conclusions on this research and outlines future work issues.

F. Esposito (Ed.): AI*IA 2001, LNAI 2175, pp. 81–86, 2001.
© Springer-Verlag Berlin Heidelberg 2001

2   The Learning System

INTHELEX (INcremental THEory Learner from EXamples) is a learning system for the induction of *hierarchical* logic theories from examples [ESFF00]. It is *fully incremental*, meaning that, in addition to the possibility of refining a previously generated version of the theory, learning can also start from an empty theory and from the first available example. INTHELEX can learn simultaneously *multiple concepts*, possibly related to each other; furthermore, it is a *closed loop* learning system — i.e. a system in which the learned theory is checked for validity on any new example; in case of failure, a revision process is activated in order to restore completeness and consistency. Incremental learning is necessary when either incomplete information is available at the time of initial theory generation, or the nature of the concepts evolves dynamically. In any case, it is useful to consider learning as a closed loop process, where feedback on performance is used to activate the theory revision phase [Bec85].

In particular, INTHELEX learns theories expressed as sets of Datalog^{OI} clauses [SEM$^+$98] from positive and negative examples. It adopts a *full memory storage* strategy [RM85] – i.e., it retains all the available examples, so to guarantee validity of the learned theories on all of them — and it incorporates two refinement operators, one for generalizing hypotheses that reject positive examples, and the other for specializing hypotheses that explain negative examples. Both such operators, when applied, change the *answer set* of the theory, i.e. the set of examples it accounts for. Therefore, it is a system for theory revision rather than for *theory restructuring* [Wro96].

In order to perform its task, INTHELEX exploits a (possibly empty) previous theory, a graph describing the dependence relationships among the concepts to be learned, and a historical memory of all the past examples that led to the current theory. The revision process can be summarized as follows: Whenever a new example is taken into account, it is stored in the base of processed examples and a preliminary saturation phase is performed, that preserves all the specific information contained in the original example while adding higher level concepts. Then, the current theory is checked against it.

If it is positive and not covered, generalization must be performed. The system chooses a clause to be generalized among those that define the example concept. Then, the lgg$_{OI}$ of this clause and the example is computed [SEM$^+$98]. If one of the lgg$_{OI}$'s is consistent with all the past negative examples, then it replaces the chosen clause in the theory, or else a new clause is chosen to compute the lgg$_{OI}$. If no clause can be generalized in a consistent way, the system checks if the example itself, with the constants properly turned into variables, is consistent with the past negative examples. If so, such a clause is added to the theory, or else the example itself is added as an exception.

If the example is negative and covered, specialization is needed. Among the program clauses occurring in the SLD-derivation of the example, INTHELEX tries to specialize one at the lowest possible level in dependency graph by adding to it one (or more) positive literal(s), which characterize all the past positive examples and can discriminate them from the current negative one. In case of failure, it tries to add the negation of a literal, that is able to discriminate the negative example from all the past positive ones, to the clause related to the concept the example is an instance of. If none of the clauses thus obtained makes the theory complete, the negative example is added to the theory as an exception. New incoming observations are always checked against the exceptions before applying the rules that define the concept they refer to.

Another peculiarity in INTHELEX is the integration of multistrategy operators that allow for the solution of the theory revision problem. Namely, abduction and abstraction are exploited to perform a pre-processing of incoming information. The former aims at completing possibly partial information in the examples (adding more details); the latter removes superfluous details from the description of both the examples and the theory. Thus, even if with opposite perspectives, both aim at reducing the computational effort required to learn a correct theory with respect to the incoming examples.

Specifically, an embedded abductive proof procedure helps INTHELEX at managing situations in which not only the set of all observations is partially known, but each observation could be incomplete too [ESFF00]. Abduction can be exploited as a means for identifying learning problems hidden in the new observation given to the system. Thus, in our system, abduction is preliminarily used to generate suitable or relevant background data on which theory induction is based. The exploitation of abstraction concerns the shift from the language in which the theory is described to a higher level one. In INTHELEX, it is assumed that the abstraction theory is already given (i.e. it has not to be learned by the system), and that the system automatically applies it to the learning problem at hand before processing the examples. The abstraction theory contains information for performing the shift specified by the abstraction operators.

3 Handling Text in Document Processing

The increasing interest on digital libraries has generated a strong demand for the digitization of large corpora of paper documents, coming from the most diverse environments. Classification and Interpretation aim at labelling the documents according to one of some predefined classes and then eliciting the function of the various layout components relating it to spatial information coming from layout analysis. They are referred to as *Document image understanding* [Nag00], and can be carried out based only on the layout structure of the document. Then, going into more detail, OCR can be applied only to the textual components recognized as particularly meaningful (e.g., the title and abstract in a scientific paper). Two more phases can be devised, referred to as *Document understanding* [Nag00]: categorization of the subject of the document [Seb99] and consequent extraction of information that is significant for that particular concern. First order logic offers a unique and natural representation framework both for describing the document structure and for detecting its content. Also, a logic representation allows for an easy understanding of the model inferred automatically when the human intervention is required to adjust it.

In order to obtain, from raw text, the structured representations of sentences that can be expressed in the input language required by the symbolic learner, a parser was used as a pre-processor. In particular, we exploited a prototypical parser for the Italian language, designed to manage texts having a simple and standard phrase structure. Such a parser was validated on a set of 72 sentences drawn from a corpus of articles on foreign commerce available on the Internet, and the results obtained showed an average error of about 25% on the whole set of syntactic items to be recognized.

The experiment on Text Categorization concerned Italian texts on foreign commerce downloaded from the Internet. In the formal representation of texts, we used the following descriptors:

- `sent(e1,e2)` e2 is a sentence from e1
- `subj(e1,e2)` e2 is the subject of e1
- `obj(e1,e2)` e2 is the (direct) object of e1
- `indirect_obj(e1,e2)` e2 is an indirect object of e1
- `rel_subj(e1,e2)` e2 is a clause related to the subject of e1
- `rel_obj(e1,e2)` e2 is a clause related to the object of e1
- `verb(e1,e2)` e2 is the verb of e1
- `lemma(e2)` word e2 has lemma *lemma* (in fact, it is a meta-predicate)[1]
- `infinite(e2)` verb e2 is in an infinite mood
- `finite(e2)` verb e2 is in a finite mood
- `affirmative(e2)` verb e2 is in an affirmative mood
- `negative(e2)` verb e2 is in a negative mood
- `np(e1,e2)` e2 is a 2nd level NP of e1
- `pp(e1,e2)` e2 is a PP of e1

An example for INTHELEX, expressed in such a language, is the following:

```
import(example) ← sent(example,e1), subj(example,e2), np(e2,e3),
          impresa(e3), rel_subj(e1,e4), verb(e4,e5), specializzare(e5),
          infinite(e5), affirmative(e5), pp(e4,e6), distribuzione(e6),
          componente(e6), verb(e1,e7), interessare(e7), finite(e7),
          affirmative(e7), indirect_obj(e1,e8), pp(e8,e9),
          importazione(e9), macchina(e9), produzione(e9), ombrello(e9).
```

Note that the logic language exploited by INTHELEX is so close to the human one that it is easy to guess the original sentence underlying this formal description: "Impresa specializzata nella distribuzione di componenti è interessata all'importazione di macchine per la produzione di ombrelli"[2].

The first experiment aimed at learning the concept of "importation". Starting from the empty theory, INTHELEX was fed with a total of 67 examples, 39 positive (not all explicitly using verb 'importare') and 28 negative. The resulting theory was composed by 9 clauses. Some were slightly different, considering that:

---

[1] This way, information about word lemmas can be exploited during theory refinement, and in the recognition of higher level concepts of which *lemma* is an instance.

[2] Given the proper lemmas translation, also the English equivalent can be guessed: "Enterprise specialized in the distribution of components is interested in the importation of machines for the production of umbrellas".

'impresa' (enterprise), 'società' (society), 'ditta' (firm) and 'agenzia' (agency) are all instances of the concept 'persona giuridica'; 'fornitore' (provider) and 'distributore' (distributor) play the same role (let us call it 'providing_role'); 'cercare' (to look for) and 'interessare' (to interest) are almost synonyms (and hence may be grouped in one category, say 'interest_cat'); 'acquistare' (to buy) and 'importare' (to import) bear more or less the same meaning of acquiring something ('acquisire'). Exploiting the above ontological information as an abstraction theory results in a more compact theory, made up of just 3 rules, thus confirming that the availability of an ontology would improve the compactness and readability of the inferred rules:

```
import(A) ← sent(A,B), subj(B,C), np(C,D), persona_giuridica(D),
            verb(B,E), interest_cat(E), finite(E), affirmative(E),
            obj(B,F), np(F,G), providing_role(G).

import(A) ← sent(A,B), subj(B,C), np(C,D), persona_giuridica(D),
            verb(B,E), interest_cat(E), finite(E), affirmative(E),
            indirect_obj(B,F), pp(F,G), importazione(G).

import(A) ← sent(A,B), subj(B,C), np(C,D), persona_giuridica(D),
            verb(B,E), acquisire(E), finite(E), affirmative(E).
```

For instance, the second clause is to be read as: "Text A concerns importation if it contains a sentence with a subject composed by a NP containing a *persona giuridica*, the verb of the main sentence belongs to the interest category and is in finite affirmative mood, and the indirect object is composed by a PP containing the word *importazione* (importation)".

Another experiment aimed at learning the concept of "specialization" (of someone in some field). The system was run on 40 examples, 24 positive and 16 negative. The resulting theory, without exploiting any additional knowledge, was made up by 5 clauses. By exploiting again the above abstraction theory, the theory is reduced to just 2 rules, saying that a text is about specialization if it is of the kind: "persona giuridica is specialized in *something*" or "persona giuridica, that is specialized in *something*, does *something*" (underlined parts stand for more specific terms, and italic ones are placeholders for unknown terms).

```
specialization(A) ← sent(A,B), subj(B,C), np(C,D), persona_giuridica(D),
            verb(B,E), specializzare(E), finite(E), affirmative(E),
            indirect_obj(B,F), pp(F,_).

specialization(A) ← sent(A,B), subj(B,C), np(C,D), persona_giuridica(D),
            rel_subj(B,E), verb(E,F), specializzare(F), affirmative(F),
            pp(E,_), verb(B,_).
```

4   Conclusions & Future Work

The presented approach proves that learning theories for text categorization can take advantage by the semantic interpretation provided by a logic framework.

This has required structured sentences in a logic representation on which to run our learning algorithms, obtained through a parser.

Future work will concern a more extensive experimentation, also on English texts, and an empirical evaluation of our approach. If good results will be obtained, it will be possible to apply these techniques for semantic indexing of the documents stored in digital libraries, such as CDL [EMS+98].

References

[Bec85]   J. M. Becker. Inductive learning of decision rules with exceptions: Methodology and experimentation. B.s. diss., Dept. of Computer Science, University of Illinois at Urbana-Champaign, Urbana, Illinois, USA, 1985. UIUCDCS-F-85-945.

[Coh96]   W. Cohen. Learning to classify english text with ILP methods. In de Raedt [dR96], pages 124–143.

[Cus99]   J. Cussens, editor. *Learning Language in Logic*, 1999. 1st Workshop on Learning Language in Logic, Workshop Notes.

[dR96]   L. de Raedt, editor. *Advances in Inductive Logic Programming*. IOS Press, Amsterdam, NL, 1996.

[EMS+98]   F. Esposito, D. Malerba, G. Semeraro, N. Fanizzi, and S. Ferilli. Adding machine learning and knowledge intensive techniques to a digital library service. *International Journal of Digital Libraries*, 2(1):3–19, 1998.

[ESFF00]   F. Esposito, G. Semeraro, N. Fanizzi, and S. Ferilli. Multistrategy Theory Revision: Induction and abduction in INTHELEX. *Machine Learning Journal*, 38(1/2):133–156, 2000.

[Fre00]   D. Freitag. Machine learning for information extraction in informal domains. *Machine Learning Journal*, 39:169–202, 2000.

[JSR99]   M. Junker, M. Sintek, and M. Rinck. Learning for text categorization and information extraction with ILP. In Cussens [Cus99], pages 84–93.

[Moo99]   R. Mooney. Learning for semantic interpretation: Scaling up without dumbing down. In Cussens [Cus99], pages 7–15.

[Nag00]   G. Nagy. Twenty years of document image analysis in PAMI. *IEEE Transactions on Pattern Analysis and Machine Intelligence*, 22(1):38–62, 2000.

[RM85]   R. E. Reinke and R. S. Michalski. Incremental learning of concept descriptions: A method and experimental results. In D. Michie, editor, *Machine Intelligence*, volume 11. Edinburgh University Press, 1985.

[Seb99]   F. Sebastiani. Machine learning in automated text categorization. Technical Report Technical Report IEI:B4-31-12-99, CNR - IEI, Pisa, Italy, December 1999. Rev. 2001.

[SEM+98]   G. Semeraro, F. Esposito, D. Malerba, N. Fanizzi, and S. Ferilli. A logic framework for the incremental inductive synthesis of Datalog theories. In N.E. Fuchs, editor, *Proceedings of 7th International Workshop on Logic Program Synthesis and Transformation - LOPSTR97*, volume 1463 of *LNCS*, pages 300–321. Springer, 1998.

[SN97]   L. Saitta and F. Neri. Machine learning for information extraction. In M.T. Pazienza, editor, *Information Extraction*, volume 1299 of *Lecture Notes in Artificial Intelligence*, pages 171–191. Springer, 1997.

[Wro96]   Stefan Wrobel. First order theory refinement. In de Raedt [dR96], pages 14–33.

User Profiling in an Application of Electronic Commerce

Fabio Abbattista, Nicola Fanizzi, Stefano Ferilli, Pasquale Lops,
Giovanni Semeraro

Dipartimento di Informatica, Università di Bari
{fabio,fanizzi,ferilli,lops,semeraro}@di.uniba.it

Abstract. The COGITO[1] project aims at improving consumer-supplier relationships in future e-commerce interfaces featuring agents which can converse with users in written natural language (chatterbots) and extending their capabilities. In this paper we present the personalization component, developed in the COGITO system, that allows for the classification of users accessing an e-commerce web site through Machine Learning techniques. In the final implementation, the resulting user profiles will be further analyzed to automatically extract usage patterns from the data given about user communities. This helps content providers to tailor their offers to the customers' needs, and can be used to generate assumptions about new users, when they start to converse with the system.

1. Introduction

BOL Medien, one of the partner of the COGITO consortium, is one of the European subsidiaries of Bertelsmann AG, Europe's largest media enterprise. One of the main weakness of the BOL web site is represented by the user registration procedure to the My-BOL service, a service for the personalization of product presentation. The users have to fill an initial form that asks for personal identification (e-mail address and password) and some specific information (such as product categories of interest among the list of books/CDs categories available in the store). The main problem of this process is its dependency on users willing in updating their preferences. If users do not remember or do not want spend their time to update preferences, the personalization service will rely on unreliable or wrong data.

The goal of the personalization module, in the COGITO system, is to improve the MyBOL service by dynamically discover users preferences, from data collected in the course of past dialogues with the chatterbot developed for the BOL web site. In this scenario, users accessing the MyBOL service do not have to fill a registration form, and they only have to engage in a conversation with the chatterbot which will support them in searching or buying BOL products. The personalization component of the COGITO system, through the exploitation of data collected in the dialogue history, classifies users on the basis of their preferences and dynamically updates the inferred

---

[1]*COGITO is an EU-funded project in the 5th Framework Programme, (IST-1999-13347)*

F. Esposito (Ed.): AI*IA 2001, LNAI 2175, pp. 87-98, 2001.

classifications. Users classification represents one of the main source of data from which the users recommendations module will receive useful inputs. The other source of data is represented by the evaluations given by users to purchased products and it is used by the collaborative filtering system actually in use in the BOL site. The common flaw of collaborative filtering techniques is represented by the strong dependency of recommendation's effectiveness from a sufficient populated repository of correlate users' evaluations. The integration of these two complementary techniques, the rule-based personalization and the collaborative filtering technique, will improve the whole recommendation process of the BOL's site because each recommendation will take into account individual user preferences and interests as well as evaluations coming from users with very similar tastes.

In the next section we briefly explain what we intend with the term user profile. In section 3 an overview of the profile extractor module is presented, while in section 4 we detail its main components. In section 5 results of some experimental results are reported and section 6 concludes the paper.

2.   User Profiling

The more a system knows about users the better it can serve them effectively. But there are different styles, and even philosophies, to teach computer about user habits, interests, patterns and preference. User Modeling simply means ascertaining a few bits of information about each user, processing that information quickly and providing the results to applications, all without intruding upon the user's consciousness. The final result is the construction of a user model or a user profile.

By user profile we mean all the information collected about a user that logs to a Web site, in order to take into account his/her needs, wishes, and interests. Roughly, a user profile is a structured representation of the user's needs by means of which a retrieval system should act upon one or more goals based on that profile in order to autonomously pursue the goals posed by the user. It is quite obvious that a user profile modeling process requires two steps. We have to decide: *what* has to be represented and *how* this information is effectively represented.

Generally the information stored in a user profile can be conceptually categorized in seven classes, according to their source: *Registration Data, Question & Answer, Legacy Data, Past History, 3rd Party, Current Activity, Open Adapter*.

A user profile is given by a list of attribute-value pairs, in which each attribute is given the proper value on the ground of the specific user it refers to. Each attribute-value pair represents a characteristic of that user. The list of attributes must be finite as well as the possible values related to each attribute. Examples of attributes in that list are: LAST NAME, FIRST NAME, AGE, ADDRESS, JOB, ANNUAL INCOME, PREFERENCES, etc. The attribute list is the same for all the users.

These attributes or features can be divided into three categories: *Explicit,* whose values are given by the user herself/himself (*Registration Data* or *Q & A*); *Existing,* that can be drawn by existing applications, such as anagraphic systems (e.g., ADDRESS, JOB); *Implicit,* are elicited from the behavior of the user, through the history of his/her navigation or just from the current navigation.

For our purposes, a *computational* user profile will be useful to describe univocally a user accessing to a Website. Considering the previous kind of features, the most common approach to build a user profile mixes three techniques [1].

In the first one, buyers have to fill an initial form that asks for personal information and some specific information (such as product categories of interest among the list of categories available in the store). Since only a limited amount of information can be acquired in this way (customers might not be able or willing neither to fill large forms nor to provide personal details and preferences), the approach usually followed is to present the customer with a limited number of fields to fill and to let him/her decide which fields (s)he is willing to fill.

The other two techniques can be used if the customer does not provide information about his/her interests. The second one exploits demographic profiles (available on the market) that give detailed information on the different categories of buyers, and can be used to make predictions on consumer preferences and behavior. The third technique dynamically updates the user model by considering data (e.g. purchases made, number of visits, ...) recorded on past visits to the store.

These three techniques complement each other, allowing one to obtain a more complete customer model. The integration of these techniques allows to implement a profiling system less intrusive with respect of users. They will not be requested to explicitly insert information concerning their preferences, tastes, etc. but they will be able to participate in the management and updating of their personal profile. This will result in an increasing of their trust and confidence in a system able to automatically collect data about their preferences, tastes and interests.

The analysis of these requirements, in the first phase of COGITO project, lead us to adopt machine learning techniques for the implementation of a profiling system able to build user profiles through their past interactions with the system.

3. Profile Extractor Module Architecture

This section describes the COGITO architecture identifying the role and the structure of the Profile Extractor module within the system. The general architecture shows that it is mainly based on five macro modules (Figure 1): *BOL Web-Server; eBrain; Profile Extractor; Prompter; XML Content Manager.*

The overall system architecture is centered on an already exiting chatterbot system, *eBrain*, capable of engaging a conversation with users. The eBrain system kernel provides the basic functionality needed to handle parallel user sessions, parse and analyze written natural language input, invoke appropriate rules from a *Chat Rule Base*, which trigger internal processes (such as database access) and generate the system response in written language. This can be accompanied by graphical animation and the presentation of offers.

The connection to back-end systems is realized through the *Connector* that enables the system to access external services and knowledge sources. In addition to providing an interface to application database, the XML-Content Manager provides a suite of tools for supporting the creation, management and distribution of XML documents and specific Document Type Definitions (DTD).

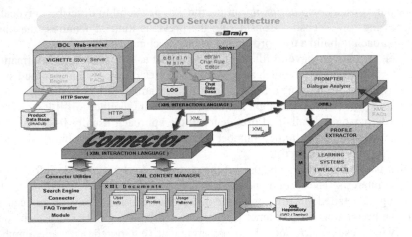

Fig. 1. Cogito Server Architecture.

The Profile Extractor (Figure 2) is the module that allows for the classification of users accessing the COGITO system through Machine Learning techniques, namely the PART algorithm [2].

During a session, user dialogues with the eBrain agent are stored in log files. The Dialog Analyzer receives the log files of past sessions and processes them in order to produce a Structured Dialogue History, representing user interests and preferences.

The goal of the Profile Extractor is to identify, from data stored in the Structured Dialogue History, the main features that are necessary to produce a user profile. The Profile Extractor module is further divided into four sub-modules: the *Learning Problem Manager;* the *Profile Rule Extractor;* the *Classifier* and the *Usage Pattern Extractor* (not yet completely implemented).

The input flow to the Profile Extractor comes from the Dialogue Analyzer module that provides a representation format for dialogue histories. The dialogue analyzer relates the dialogue contributions of an ongoing dialogue between the system and a specific user, thus enabling the identification and extraction of facts about user from the dialogue. These include topics and items (s)he knows/wants/likes/dislikes.

In addition, the user's reaction to the system actions (accept/reject offers, request detailed information etc.) are monitored and a *formal structured dialogue history* is created for every user dialogue.

Dialogue files of user sessions are decomposed to extract facts about information needs, attitudes towards items (e.g. desires), known items, etc. This step produces a *model* of the user representing her/his interests and background in the dialogues.

Supervised machine learning techniques are used for analyzing a number of dialogues of several users, to induce a set of rules, expressed in the same representation language. Such rules can be regarded as the core of an *extractor*, which is able to generate user models from new unclassified incoming structured user logs.

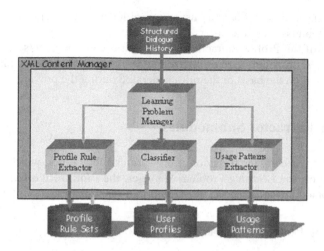

Fig. 2. Profile Extractor Architecture

In the architecture, the Profile Extractor can be seen as an intelligent component capable of automatically assigning a customer to a specific class in order to improve the system usability. This component should help users to accomplish their goals easier (through explanations and suitable interaction modalities performed by the agent). As a consequence, one of the main problems concerns the definition of meaningful classes and the identification of the features that properly describe each of them and characterize the corresponding kind of interaction. In the system, the classes we considered are the book categories.

Thus the main function provided is to automatically assign each buyer to these predefined classes on the ground of information drawn from real sessions (*interaction modeling*). This approach relies on machine learning methods, since interaction modeling can be cast as a supervised learning problem by considering the customer structured dialogue history as a source for training instances for the learning system. By examining the dialogue histories, it is possible to extract some characteristics that are useful for recognizing the buyer. We observed that most of the characteristics that were identified turned out to be application dependent, while only few of them seem to be system dependent.

For instance, relevant characteristics are those concerning the way users exploit the capabilities of the search engine of the BOL Web site. This information constitutes examples exploited to train the learning system in order to induce a set of rules.

After the training phase, the interaction of any user that access to the BOL Website information through a client will generate/update a dialogue history file that will be exploited to provide a new example that the Profile Extractor will classify on the ground of the rules inferred. In this way it is possible to create a personal profile of each customer, which contains information about his/her interests, tastes, preferences. The system is capable of tracking user behavior evolution, so customer profiles may change across multiple interactions. On the ground of the profile, the agent could better support customers during the interaction, providing personal recommendations and purchase incentives and helping users in problematic situations during the search or during the submission of the orders.

The output of the Profile Extractor module is a set of documents in XML format that describe: a set of learning rules inferred by Weka after the training phase and user profiles extracted on the basis of the rules generated during the previous phase.

4.   Profile Extractor Submodules

In this section we specify the behavior of the various submodules, which constitute the Profile Extractor: the Learning Problem Manager, the Profile Rule Extractor and the Classifier submodule, outlining the most important functionalities.

4.1   Learning Problem Manager Submodule

The aim of the Learning Problem Manager (LPM) is to extract from the Structured Dialogue History the most relevant parts of the dialogue and to transform them into a set of examples capable of being processed by the Profile Rule Extractor, the Usage Pattern Extractor and the Classifier modules. The main functions of the LPM are sending training examples to the Profile Rule Extractor module; preparing examples for the testing phase; distributing examples related to the users to be classified.

The information considered for the setting of the examples are the following:

- **User_ID** and **User_name** identifies the user.
- **Personal Data** (Age, Gender, Civil Status, Education, Geographic Area and Job).
- **Access_date** identifies the last access date related to the user.
- **Connections_num** is the total number of connections to the site related to the user.
- **Class_Name** is the class of the BOL category list.
- **Search_num, Search_freq** are number and frequency of searches in the category.
- **Purchase_num, Purchase_freq** are number and frequency of purchases in the category.

From these topics the learning attributes are extracted. The related values are picked up from the structured dialogue history. The results that the LPM submodule supplies are XML documents containing a set of labeled examples with attributes and related values. From these documents it is possible to infer more general information about users in form of abstract rules. By applying these rules, it is possible to extract preferences and tastes (a profile) about users that access the BOL Website. Preferences are a subset of the 10 product categories of the BOL Website: *Belletristik, Computer und Internet, Kinderbucher, Kultur und Geschichte, Nachschlagewerke, Reise, Sachbuch_Und_Ratgeber, Schule und Bildung, Wirtschaft_Und_Soziales, Wissenschaft_Und_Technik,*

4.2   Profile Rule Extractor Submodule

The *Profile Rule Extractor,* has been implemented through one of the WEKA classifiers; WEKA is a machine learning tool freely downloadable on the Web, implemented at the University of Waikato, New Zealand. During a learning session, each example of the dialogue history, representing a single user feature vector, must be pre-classified by a human expert. The WEKA package processes training examples and induces rules for extracting user features from further unclassified examples, to be used by the Classifier module. The main functions of this submodule are summarized as follows:

- Sending the training examples to Weka for extracting the learning rules;
- Sending the rules extracted to the LPM for subsequent storing.

The Profile Rule Extractor input regards XML documents containing training examples to be used for inferring the rules. These examples contain a set of instances each of which is a list of attributes with corresponding values packed by the Learning Problem Manager submodule.

The XML documents prepared by the LPM submodule are sent to the Weka learning system capable of extracting the rules into XML format. An example of learning rules inferred is showed in Figure 3. These rules are referred to a learning session performed on the class *Belletristik*.

4.3 Classifier Submodule

The *Classifier*, performs the profiling task, according to the set of rules induced by the Profile Rule Extractor and the user history. Once a user accesses the system, his history is retrieved in the Structured Dialogue History repository and his characteristic features are singled out, according to the rules that fired. Hence, the rest of the dialogue can benefit from knowing standard information about his interests, his community, etc. The main functions of the Classifier are summarized as follows:

- Performing the test on the basis of some test instances provided by the LPM;
- Classifying new instances according to the rules inferred;
- Extracting the user profiles on the basis of the classification.

The Classifier input regards XML documents containing testing examples to be used for extracting the books categories preferred by the user. These examples contain a set of instances each of which is a list of attributes with corresponding values provided by the Learning Problem Manager submodule.

The XML documents prepared by the LPM sub module are sent to the Weka learning system capable of performing testing and profile extraction.

The results regarding the extraction of user profiles are showed in Figure 4. The general structure of a profile is composed of the set of personal data and a set of

The Rules extracted for class Belletristik are 6:
1. **If** search_freq_Belletristik > 0.3 **Then** Class: yes
2. **ElsIf** age <= 50.0 **And** age > 26.0 **Then** Class: no
3. **ElsIf** search_freq_Belletristik > 0.11 **And** age > 38.0 **Then** Class: yes
4. **ElsIf** search_freq_Nachschlagewerke <= 0.25 **Then** Class: no
5. **ElsIf** search_freq_Belletristik > 0.21 **Then** Class: yes
6. **Otherwise** Class: no

Fig. 3. An example of Learning Rules

preferences and interests of a particular user. In our system, the set of preferences and interests of a particular user consist of the list of the books categories each user likes.

5.   Experimental Results

In this section, we propose two different experiments conducted in order to evaluate the most suitable learning system to embed into the Profile Extractor.

First, a comparison between two different approaches, namely PART [2] and J4.8 [3], regarding the extraction of concepts within Weka has been performed. Then, the most efficient method has been compared with two other learning systems: the tree inducer C4.5 [4] and IBK [3], an implementation of the k-NN classifier employing the Euclidean distance.

J4.8 is an algorithm that implements a later and slightly improved version of C4.5, called C4.5 Revision 8, decision tree learner [4]. The learner treats data in the ARFF format and it can process both training and test data. The output produced can be divided in two parts: the first is a pruned decision tree while the second part gives estimates of its predictive performance, generated by the evaluation module in Weka.

The problem of constructing decision trees can be expressed recursively, using a "Divide and Conquer" approach. First select an attribute to place at the root node and make one branch for each possible value. This splits up the example set into subsets, one for each value of the attribute. This process can be repeated recursively for each branch, using only those instances that actually reach the branch. If at any time all instances at a node have the same classification, the algorithm stops developing that part of the tree.

Nodes in a decision tree involve testing a particular attribute. The only thing left to decide is how to determine which attribute to split on. Since the aim is to find small subtrees, we could choose the attribute that produces the purest daughter nodes. The

Profile for User: 8

AGE	55
GENDER	Male
CIVIL_STATUS	Married
EDUCATION	High_School
GEOGRAPHIC_AREA	Val_Aosta
JOB	Serviceman
CONNECTIONS_NUM	21
SEARCH_NUMBelletristik	1
SEARCH_FREQBelletristik	0.1
PURCHASE_NUMBelletristik	14
PURCHASE_FREQBelletristik	0.14
....	....

The categories preferred by the user are:
Kinderbucher, Kultur_und_Geschichte, Reise

Fig. 4. An example of user profiles

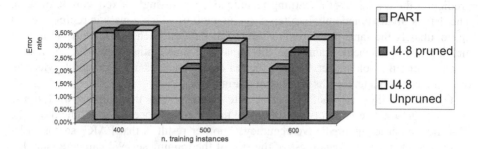

Fig. 5. Error rates related to PART and J4.8

measure of purity used is the Information and is measured in units called *bits*. Associated with a node of the tree, this value represents the expected amount of information that would be needed to specify whether a new instance should be classified in a way or in another one, given that the example reached that node.

Usually the test at a node compares an attribute value with a constant. Leaf nodes give a classification that applies to all instances that reach the leaf or a set of classifications.

5.1   First Experiment

In this experiment we compare performances of PART and J4.8 in order to choose the best decision tree inducer within the Weka suite. Results related to classification errors have been analyzed to determine the most efficient algorithm.

The experimental session is structured as follows. First of all, three sets of respectively 400, 500 and 600 instances have been gathered. These examples simulate information about the interaction with the BOL website. The instances have been sent to PART and J4.8, considering the error rate produced by each learning method.

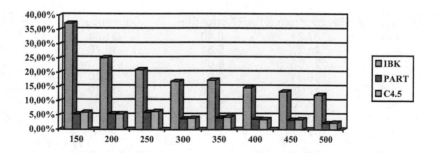

Fig. 6. Error rates related to PART, C4.5 and IBK

Actually, both unpruned and pruned trees have been inferred in order to evaluate the different error percentages. The ten-fold cross validation is the standard way of predicting the error rate of a learning technique given a single, fixed sample of data. The data is divided randomly into ten parts, in each of which a class is represented in approximately the same proportion as in the full dataset. Each part is held out in turn and the learning scheme trained on the remaining nine-tenths; then its error rate is calculated on the holdout set. Finally, the ten error estimates are averaged to yield an overall error estimate. Results are shown in Figure 5.

The results illustrate that the error rate decreases as the number of training instances grows. The reason is that the more the set of instances is large, the more the classifier increases its predictive accuracy. Another result is that PART seems to be more accurate than J4.8 regardless of the size of the training set. We can conclude that the different behaviour of the methods is due to the different approaches they adopt, respectively "Divide and Conquer" for J4.8 and a hybrid method for PART.

5.2   Second Experiment

In this sub section we present experimental results concerning the comparison among PART, C4.5 and IBK using the error rates extracted by the application of the ten-fold cross validation to eight different sets of examples, ranging from 150 to 500 instances. In Figure 6 results are shown. From the results obtained we can observe that the error rate relative to the two rule-based systems is lower than the one by IBK. This conclusion has been confirmed by the application of the Wilcoxon test to the three approaches. This test is a nonparametric test for comparing two treatments. It is defined nonparametric because no assumptions about the distribution of the population data are required. For further details about Wilcoxon test refer to [5].

In this context the test has been performed three times, one for each possible pair of systems. At the end of each experimental session a result table is presented. For each experiment two opposite hypotheses are compared. Finally the test will accept the most probable and reject the other one. Actually, the method first reduces measurement data to ordinal data by replacing the differences between measurements with ranks. The statistic W is obtained by adding together the ranks.

Table 1. Wilcoxon test performed between IBK and PART

Instances #	IBK error rate	PART error rate	Difference	Rank
150	37.24	5.40	-31.84	+8
200	25.27	5.51	-19.76	+7
250	21.06	6.03	-15.03	+6
300	16.91	3.81	-13.10	+4
350	17.35	4.06	-13.29	+5
400	14.70	3.65	-11.05	+3
450	13.29	3.30	-9.99	+2
500	12.17	2.20	-9.97	+1
			W = +36	

Under the null hypothesis that the two populations have the same distribution, we would expect the ranks of the plus and minus differences to be evenly distributed. If H_0 is false, we would expect W to be large (either positively or negatively).

IBK vs. PART In this case, the two hypotheses are:

H_0: the error rates of IBK and PART are not significantly different;

H_a: the error rates of IBK and PART are significantly different;

IBK vs. C4.5 The two hypotheses are:

H_0: the error rates of IBK and C4.5 are not significantly different;

H_a: the error rates of IBK and C4.5 are significantly different;

Table 2. Wilcoxon test performed between IBK and C4.5

Instances #	IBK error rate	C4.5 error rate	Difference	Rank
150	37.24	6.03	-31.21	+8
200	25.27	5.50	-19.77	+7
250	21.06	6.40	-14.66	+6
300	16.91	3.99	-13.25	+5
350	17.35	4.35	-13.00	+4
400	14.70	3.50	-11.20	+3
450	13.29	3.52	-9.77	+1.5
500	12.17	2.40	-9.77	+1.5
			W = +36	

C4.5 vs. PART The two hypotheses are:

H_0: the error rates of C4.5 and PART are not significantly different;

H_a: the error rates of C4.5 and PART are significantly different;

Table 3. Wilcoxon test performed between C4.5 and PART

Instances #	C4.5 error rate	PART error rate	Difference	Rank
150	6.03	5.40	-0.63	+8
200	5.50	5.51	+0.01	-1
250	6.40	6.03	-0.37	+7
300	3.99	3.81	-0.18	+3
350	4.35	4.06	-0.29	+6
400	3.50	3.65	+0.15	-2
450	3.52	3.30	-0.22	+5
500	2.40	2.20	-0.20	+4
			W = +30	

On the basis of the values of the W statistic calculated above, we could deduce the results reported in Table 4. The null hypothesis is accepted or rejected according to the W statistic related to the different levels of significance. The comparison among IBK, PART and C4.5 states that PART and C4.5 are clearly more efficient than IBK, for each significance level considered.

Different results emerged from the comparison between PART and C4.5. In fact, PART seems to be more accurate only at a significance level of 10%. At lower levels, the test does not suggest that the null hypothesis should be rejected and so the two systems behave almost in the same way.

Table 4. Wilcoxon results

	α = 0.1	α = 0.05	α = 0.02	α = 0.01
IBK vs. PART	H_0 rejected	H_0 rejected	H_0 rejected	H_0 rejected
IBK vs. C4.5	H_0 rejected	H_0 rejected	H_0 rejected	H_0 rejected
PART vs. C4.5	H_0 rejected	H_0 accepted	H_0 accepted	H_0 accepted

6. Conclusions

In the previous section we have presented two kinds of experiment. The result emerged from the first experimental session, the comparison between PART and J4.8, is that PART seems to be more accurate than J4.8 regardless of the number of training examples. This is due to the different approaches they adopt, respectively "Divide and Conquer" for J4.8 and a hybrid method for PART.

Regarding the second experimental session, the comparison among IBK, PART and C4.5 states that PART and C4.5 are clearly more efficient than IBK.

Particularly, we can observe that the error rate produced by PART is lower than the one produced by IBK and C4.5. This conclusion has been confirmed by the application of the Wilcoxon test to the three approaches.

Interesting results emerged from the comparison between PART and C4.5. In fact, PART system seems to be more accurate just at a significance level of 10%. At lower levels, the two systems behave almost in the same way. However, by the analysis of all the results gathered, we could state that PART system is certainly the most suitable and efficient for our purposes in the COGITO project, even if the differences in the prediction accuracy with C4.5 system are minimal.

References

[1] Pazzani, M., Billsus D., Learning and Revising User Profiles: The Identification of Interesting Web Sites, Machine Learning, Vol.27, 1997.
[2] Frank E. and Witten I.H., Generating Accurate Rule Sets without Global Optimization, Proceedings of the International Conference on Machine Learning (ICML'98), 1998.
[3] Witten, I.H., Frank, E., Data Mining: Practical Machine Learning Tools and Techniques with Java Implementations. Morgan Kaufmann Publishers, CA. San Francisco, 1999.
[4] Quinlan, J.R., C4.5: Programs for Machine Learning, 1993.
[5] Orkin, M., Drogin, R., Vital Statistic. McGraw-Hill Book Company, 1993.

Computing Spatial Similarity by Games

Marco Aiello

Institute for Logic, Language and Computation, and
Intelligent Sensory and Information Systems
University of Amsterdam
Plantage Muidergracht 24 1018 TV Amsterdam, The Netherlands
aiellom@ieee.org

Abstract. The multi-modal logic $S4_u$, known in the field of qualitative spatial reasoning to be a decidable formalism for expressing topological and mereological properties, can also be exploited to define a distance measure among patterns. Here, we recall the notion of topological distance defined in terms of games over $S4_u$ models, and show how it is effectively computed for a specific class of models: the class of polygons of the real plane, a class of topological models widely used in computer science and AI applications. Finally, we briefly overview an implemented system based on the presented framework. This paper is the practical counterpart of, and continuation to [1].

Keywords: qualitative spatial reasoning, model comparison games, image similarity

1 Introduction

The core of the question we address is *How can I compute how similar two spatial patterns are?* The fundamental issues to solve in order to answer this question involve finding an agreement on spatial representation, finding an agreement on a language to describe spatial patterns, and finding an agreement on a measure of similarity. Our choice here falls onto modal logics, topologically interpreted, and equipped with adequate model comparison games. The language, called $S4_u$, is a multi-modal S4*S5 logic interpreted on topological spaces equipped with valuation functions.

Spatial representation is not only interesting in itself, but also when considering its applications. It is essential in vision, in spatial reasoning for robotics, in geographical information systems, and many more related fields. Of paramount importance in applications is the comparison of spatial patterns, which must be represented in the same way. We consider similarity measures and look at their application to image retrieval. Image retrieval is concerned with the indexing and retrieval of images from a database, according to some desired set of image features. These features can be as diverse as textual annotations, color, texture, object shape, and spatial relationships among objects. The way the features from different images are compared, in order to have a measure of similarity among images, is what really distinguishes an image retrieval architecture from another

F. Esposito (Ed.): AI*IA 2001, LNAI 2175, pp. 99–110, 2001.

one. We refer to [11] for an overview of image retrieval and more specifically to [18] for image similarity measures. Here we concentrate on image retrieval based on spatial relationships at the qualitative level of mereotopology, that is, part-whole relations, topological relations and topological properties of individual regions (see for instance [3, 19, 8]). Other image retrieval systems are based on spatial relationships as the main retrieval feature [20, 15, 9].

The paper is organized as follows. First, we recall the basic facts of the spatial framework and in particular of the similarity measure. The work overviewed in Section 2 is based on [2] and [1], to which we refer the reader for details and examples. In Section 3, we present an algorithm to compute the similarity measure in the case of polygons of the real plane. The techniques described in the paper have been used to implement an image retrieval prototype named IRIS (Image RetrIeval based on Spatial relationships) which is overviewed in Section 4.

2   A General Framework for Mereotopology

The framework we adopt to express spatial properties at the mereotopological level is the multi-modal logic S4*S5, usually referred to as $S4_u$. The language is known in modal logics [13], and has been introduced into spatial reasoning by Bennett [5] to encode decidable fragments of the RCC calculus [17]. For the syntax, axiomatization, truth definition and topological expressive power we refer to [2], while for an analysis of the mereotopological expressive power and a comparison with RCC we refer to [1].

Let us only say that the modal logic is interpreted on topological spaces (à la Tarski [21]) instead of the usual Kripke semantics. Every formula φ of $S4_u$ represents a region. $\Box\varphi$ is interpreted as "interior of the region φ" and $U\varphi$ as "it is the case everywhere that φ."

For $S4_u$ it is possible to define a notion of equivalence resorting to an adequate notion of bisimulation ([6, 14]), after all we are dealing with a modal logic... For a definition and proof of adequacy see [2]. This notion lets us answer questions like *When are two spatial patterns the same?* or *When is a pattern a sub-pattern of another one?* If topological bisimulation is satisfactory from the formal point of view, one needs more to address qualitative spatial reasoning problems and computer vision issues. If two models are not bisimilar, or one does not simulate the other, one must be able to quantify the difference between the two models. Furthermore, this difference should behave in a coherent manner across the class of all models. Informally, one needs to answer questions like: *How different are two spatial patterns?*

To this end, we defined an adequate notion of model comparison game in the Ehrenfeucht-Fraïssé style. The idea is that two players challenge each other on two models. One player (Spoiler) is attempting to prove the difference of the models, while the other one (Duplicator) wants to prove their equivalence. The moves available to the players are those of deciding on which model to play, which type of round to engage, and that of picking points and opens on the two models. A game is played to a fixed number of rounds n. We denote a game by $TG(X, X', n)$, where X and X' are two topological models, i.e., a topological space $\langle X, O \rangle$ equipped with a valuation function ν, and n is the number of rounds. For the precise definition we refer, again, to [2]. The *multi-modal rank* of a $S4_u$ formula is the maximum number of nested modal operators appearing in it (i.e. $\square$, $\diamond$, U and E modalities). The following adequacy of the games with respect to the mereotopological language holds.

Theorem 1 (Adequacy). Duplicator has a winning strategy (w.s.) in n rounds in $TG(X, X', n)$ iff X and X' satisfy the same formulas of multi-modal rank at most n.

Various examples of plays and a discussion of winning strategies can be found in [2]. The interesting result is that of having a game theoretic tool to compare topological models. Given any two models, they can be played upon. If Spoiler has a winning strategy in a certain number of rounds, then the two models are different up to a certain degree. The degree is exactly the minimal number of rounds needed by Spoiler to win. On the other hand, one knows (see [2]) that if Spoiler has no w.s. in any number of rounds, and therefore Duplicator has in all games, including the infinite round game, then the two models are bisimilar.

A way of comparing any two given models is not of great use by itself. It is essential instead to have some kind of measure. It turns out that topo-games can be used to define a distance measure.

Definition 1 (isosceles topo-distance). Consider the space of all topological models T. *Spoiler's shortest possible win* is the function $spw : T \times T \rightarrow I\!N \cup \{\infty\}$, defined as:

$$spw(X_1, X_2) = \begin{cases} n & \text{if Spoiler has a winning strategy in } TG(X_1, X_2, n), \\ & \text{but not in } TG(X_1, X_2, n-1) \\ \infty & \text{if Spoiler does not have a winning strategy in} \\ & TG(X_1, X_2, \infty) \end{cases}$$

The *isosceles topo-model distance (topo-distance, for short)* between X_1 and X_2 is the function $tmd : T \times T \rightarrow [0, 1]$ defined as:

$$tmd(X_1, X_2) = \frac{1}{spw(X_1, X_2)}$$

In [1], it is shown that indeed the above definition is a distance measure on the class of all models for the language:

Theorem 2 (isosceles topo-model distance). tmd is a distance measure on the space of all topological models.

3   Computing Similarities

The fundamental step to move from theory to practice has been taken when shifting from model comparison games to a distance. To complete the journey towards practice one needs to identify ways of effectively computing the distance in cases actually occurring in real life domains. We do not have an answer to the general question of whether the topo-distance is computable for any two topological models or not. Though, by restricting to a specific class of topological models widely used in real life applications, we can show the topo-distance to be computable when one makes an ontological commitment. The commitment consists of considering topological spaces made of polygons. This is common practice in various application domains such as geographical information systems (GIS), in many branches of image retrieval and of computer vision, in robot planning, just to mention the most common.

Consider the real plane $I\!R^2$, any line in $I\!R^2$ cuts it into two open half-planes. We call a half-plane *closed* if it includes the cutting line, *open* otherwise.

Definition 2 (region). A *polygon* is the intersection of finitely many open or closed half-planes. An *atomic region* of $I\!R^2$ is the union of finitely many polygons.

An atomic region is denoted by one propositional letter. More in general, any set of atomic regions, simply called *region*, is denoted by a S4$_u$ formula. The polygons of the plane equipped with a valuation function, denoted by $M_{I\!R^2}$, are in full rights a topological model as defined in Section 2, a basic topological fact. A similar definition of region can be found in [16]. In that article Pratt and Lemon also provide a collection of fundamental results regarding the plane, polygonal ontology just defined (actually one in which the regions are open regular).

From the model theoretic point of view, the advantage of working with $M_{I\!R^2}$ is that we can prove a logical finiteness result and thus give a terminating algorithm to compute the topo-distance. The preliminary step is thus that of proving a finiteness lemma for S4$_u$ over $M_{I\!R^2}$ models.[1]

Lemma 1 (finiteness). There are only finitely many modally definable subsets of a finite set of regions $\{r_i | r_i$ is an atomic region$\}$.

Here is a proof sketch. We work by enumerating cases, i.e., considering boolean combinations of planes, adding to an 'empty' space one half-plane at the time, first to build one region r, and then to build a finite set of regions. The goal is to show that only finitely many possibilities exist. We begin by placing a half plane denoted by r on an empty bidimensional space, Figure 1.a. Let us follow what happens to points in the space from left to right. On the left, points satisfy the formula $E(r \wedge \Box r)$ and its subformulas Er and $E\Box r$. This is true until we reach the frontier point of the half-plane. Either $E(\neg r \wedge \Diamond \Box r)$ or $E(r \wedge \Diamond \Box \neg r)$ are true depending on whether the half-plane is open or closed, respectively. Once the frontier has been passed to the right, the points satisfy $E(\neg r \wedge \Box \neg r)$ and its subformulas $E\neg r$ and $E\Box \neg r$, better seen in Figure 1.¬a. In fact, if we consider negation in the formulas the role of r and $\neg r$ switch. Consider now a second plane in the picture:

---

[1] Of course, in general this is not true. There are infinitely many non equivalent S4$_u$ formulas and one can identify appropriate Kripke models to show this, [7].

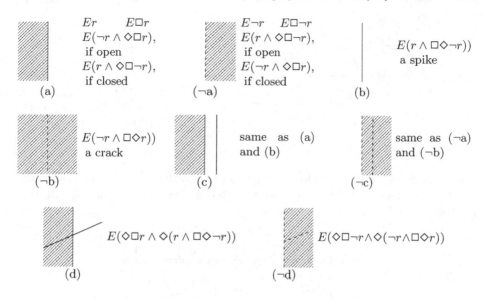

Fig. 1. Basic formulas defined by one region.

- **Intersection:** the intersection may be empty (no new formula), may be a polygon with two sides and vertices (no new formula, the same situation as with one polygon), or it may be a line, the case of two closed polygons that share the side (in this last case depicted in Figure 1.b—*spike*—we have a new formula, namely, $E(r \land \Box \Diamond \neg r)$).
- **Union:** the union may be a polygon with either one or two sides (no new formula), two separated polygons (no new formula), or two open polygons sharing the open side (this last case depicted in Figure 1.¬b—*crack*—is like the spike, one inverts the roles r and $\neg r$ in the formula: $E(\neg r \land \Box \Diamond r)$).

Finally, consider combining cases (a) and (b). By union, we get Figure 1.a, 1.c, 1.d. The only situation bringing new formulas is the latter. In particular, the point where the line intersects the plane satisfies the formula: $E(\Diamond \Box r \land \Diamond(r \land \Box \Diamond \neg r))$. By intersection, we get a segment, or the empty space, thus, no new formula.

The four basic configurations just identified yield no new configuration from the $S4_u$ point of view. To see this, consider the boolean combinations of the above configurations. We begin by negation (complement):

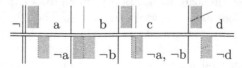

Union straightforwardly follows (where a stands for both a and ¬a, as both configurations always appear together):

∪	a	b	c	d
a	a, ¬b, ¬d	a, c, d	a, ¬b, c, d, ¬d	a, ¬b, d, ¬d
b	a, c, d	b	c, d	d
c	a, ¬b, c, d, ¬d	c, d	a, ¬b, c, d, ¬d	a, ¬b, c, d, ¬d
d	a, ¬b, d, ¬d	d	a, ¬b, c, d, ¬d	a, ¬b, d, ¬d

The table for intersection follows, with the proviso that the combination of the two regions can always be empty (not reported in the table) and again a and ¬a are represented simply by a:

∩	a	b	c	d
a	a, b, c, d	b	a, b, c	a, b, d
b	b	b	b	b
c	a, b, c	b	a, b, c, d	a, b, c, d
d	a, b, d	b	a, b, c, d	a, b, c, d

We call *topo-vector* associated with the region r, notation $\boldsymbol{r}$, an ordered sequence of ten boolean values. The values represent whether the region r satisfies or not the ten formulas $\{Er, E\neg r, E\Box r, E\Box\neg r, E(\neg r \wedge \Diamond\Box r), E(r \wedge \Diamond\Box\neg r), E(r\wedge\Box\Diamond\neg r)), E(\neg r\wedge\Box\Diamond r)), E(\Diamond\Box r\wedge\Diamond(r\wedge\Box\Diamond\neg r)), E(\Diamond\Box\neg r\wedge\Diamond(\neg r\wedge\Box\Diamond r))\}$. The ten formulas are those identified in Figure 1 which we have shown to be the only one definable by boolean combinations of planes denoting the same one region r. For example, the topo-vector associated with a plate—a closed square r in the plane—is {true, true, true, true, false, true, false, false, false, false}.

Adding half-planes with different denotations $r_2, r_3, \ldots$ increases the number of defined formulas. The definition of topo-vector is extended to an entire $M_{\mathbb{R}^2}$ model: $\{ E\bigwedge_i[\neg]r_i,\ E\bigwedge_i\Box[\neg]r_i,\ E(\bigwedge_i[\neg]^+r_i \wedge \bigwedge_i\Diamond\Box[\neg]^*r_i), E(\bigwedge_i[\neg]^+r_i \wedge \bigwedge_i\Box\Diamond[\neg]^*r_i), E(\bigwedge_i\Diamond\Box[\neg]^+r_i\wedge\Diamond(\bigwedge_i[\neg]^+r_i\wedge\bigwedge_i\Box\Diamond[\neg]^*r_i)) \}$, where $[]$ denotes an option and if the option $[]^+$ is used then the option $[]^*$ is not and viceversa. The topo-vector is built such that the modal rank of the formulas is not decreasing going from the positions with lower index to those with higher. The size of such a vector is $5 \cdot 2^i$ where i is the number of denoted regions of the model. The fact that the size of the topo-vector grows exponentially with the number of regions might seem a serious drawback. Though, as we shall show in a moment, the topo-vector stores all the information relevant for $S4_u$ about the model. Furthermore, the size of a topo-vector is most often considerably smaller than that of a topological model. In fact, a topo-vector is of exponential size in the number of regions, while a topological model is of exponetial size in the number of points of the space because of the set of opens. As a final argument, one should add that in practical situations the number of regions is always much smaller than the number of points of the space.

We are now in a position to devise an algorithm to compute the topo-distance between two topological models. The algorithm works by first computing the associated topo-vectors and then comparing them. By the comparison it is possible to establish which formulas differentiate the two models and therefore the distance between the two models. Here is the general algorithm (in pseudo-code) to compute the topo-distance between two topological models M_1 and M_2:

> topo-distance(M_1, M_2)
>> v_1 = topo-vector (M_1)
>> v_2 = topo-vector (M_2)
>> align v_1 and v_2
>> **loop** on v_1 v_2 with index i
>>> **if** $v_1(i) \neq v_2(i)$
>>>> **return** $\frac{1}{\text{modal rank}(v_1(i))}$
>> **return** 0

The idea is of retrieving the topo-vectors associated with the two input models and then looping over their elements. The inequality check can also be thought of as a **xor**, since the elements of the array are booleans. If the condition is never satisfied, the two topo-vectors are identical, the two-models are topo-bisimilar and thus the topo-distance is null. The **align** command makes the topo-vectors of the same length and aligns the formulas of the two, i.e., such that to the same index in the vector corresponds the same formula. If a topo-vector contains a formula that the other one does not, the entry is added to the vector missing it with a false value. To complete the description of the algorithm, we provide the function to compute the topo-vector associated with an $M_{\mathbb{R}^2}$ model:

> topo-vector(M)
>> v = intialized to all false values
>> **loop** on regions r of M with index i
>>> **loop** on atomic regions a of $r(i)$ with index j
>>>> **loop** on vertices v of $a(j)$ with index k
>>>>> update v with the point $v(k)$
>>>>> **if** $v(k)$ is not free
>>>>>> **loop** on intersections x of $a(j)$ with all
>>>>>>> regions of M with index l
>>>>>> update v with the point $x(l)$
>> **return** v

If a point $v(k)$ of an atomic region $a(j)$ is contained in any polygon different from $a(j)$ and it is not contained in any other region, then the condition $v(k)$ is not free is satisfied. Standard computational geometry algorithms exist for this

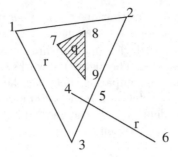

Fig. 2. Computing the topo-vector on a simple model.

task, [10]. When the **update** v **with the point** p function is called, one checks in which case p is (as shown after Lemma 1), then one considers the position of the corresponding topo-vector and puts in a true value. An obvious optimization to the algorithm is to avoid checking points for which all the associated formulas are already true. Consider the simple model of Figure 2 composed of two closed regions r and q. Since there are two regions, the topo-vector will be of size $5 \cdot 2^2 = 20$ elements: $\{E(r \wedge q), E(r \wedge \neg q), \ldots E(\Diamond\Box\neg r \wedge \Diamond\Box\neg p \wedge \Diamond(\neg r \wedge \neg q \wedge \Box\Diamond r \wedge \Box\Diamond q)))\}$. After initialization, the region r is considered and one starts looping on the vertices of its polygons, first the point 1. The point is **free**, it is the vertex of a full polygon (not a segment) and therefore the topo-vector is updated directly in the positions corresponding to $Er \wedge \neg q$, $E\Box r \wedge \Box\neg q$, $Er \wedge \neg q \wedge \Box r \wedge \Box\neg q$, $Er \wedge \neg q \wedge \Diamond\Box r \wedge \Diamond\Box q$. The points 2 and 3 would update the values for the same formula and are not considered. The point 4 falls inside the first polygon of r, the topo-vector does not need update. Intersections are then computed and the point 5 is found. The point needs to update the vector for the formula $E\Diamond\Box r \wedge \Diamond\Box\neg q \wedge \Diamond(r \wedge \neg q \wedge \Box\Diamond\neg r \wedge \Box\Diamond\neg q)$. Finally, the point 6 is considered and the point needs to update the formula $E(r \wedge \neg q \wedge \Diamond\Box\neg r \wedge \Diamond\Box\neg q)$. The algorithm proceeds by considering the second region, q and its vertices 7, 8, and 9. The three vertices all fall inside the region r and provide for the satisfaction of the formulas $Er \wedge q$, $E\Box r \wedge \Box q$, $\ldots$

Lemma 2 (termination). The topo-distance algorithm terminates.

The property is easily shown by noticing that a segment (a side of a polygon) can have at most one intersection with any other segment, that the number of polygons forming a region of $M_{I\!R^2}$ is finite, and that the number of regions of $M_{I\!R^2}$ is finite. Putting this result together with Lemma 1 one gets the hoped decidability result for polygonal topological models.

Theorem 3 (decidability of the topo-distance). In the case of polygonal topological models $M_{I\!R^2}$ over the real plane, the problem of computing the topo-distance among any two models is decidable.

Given the definition of topo-distance, the fact that two models have a null topo-distance implies that in the topo-game Duplicator has a winning strategy in the infinite round game. In the case of $M_{I\!R^2}$, Theorem 3 implies that the two models are topo-bisimilar. Note that, in general, this is not the case: Duplicator may have a winning strategy in an infinite Ehrenfeucht-Fraïssé game adequate for some modal language and the models need not be bisimilar [4].

Corollary 1 (decidability of topo-bisimulations). In the case of polygonal topological models over the real plane, the problem of identifying whether two models are topo-bisimilar or not is decidable.

4   The IRIS Prototype

The topo-distance is a building block of an image retrieval system, named IRIS Image RetrIeval based on Spatial relationships, coded in Java and enjoying a Swing interface (Figure 4). The actual similarity measure is built in IRIS to both index and retrieve images on the basis of:

1. the spatial intricacy of each region,
2. the binary spatial relationships between regions, and
3. the textual description accompanying the image.

Referring to Figure 3, one can get a glimpse of the conceptual organization of IRIS. A spatial model, as defined in Section 2, and a textual description (central portion of the figure) are associated with each image of the collection (on the left). Each topological model is represented by its topo-distance vector, as built by the algorithm in Section 3 and by a matrix of binary relationships holding between regions. Similarly, each textual description is indexed holding a representative textual vector of the text (right portion of the figure). In Figure 4, a screen-shot from IRIS after querying a database of about 50 images of men and cars is shown. On the top-right is the window for sketching queries. The top-center window serves to write textual queries and to attach information to the sketched regions. The bottom window shows the results of the query with the thumbnails of the retrieved images (left to right are the most similar). Finally, the window on the top-left controls the session.

   We remark again the importance of moving from games to a distance measure and of identifying the topo-vectors for actually being able to implement the spatial framework. In particular, in IRIS once an image is place in the database the topo-vector for its related topological model is computed, thus off-line, and it is the only data structure actually used in the retrieval process. The representation is quite compact both if compared with the topological model and with the image itself. In addition, the availability of topo-vectors as indexing structures enables us to use a number of information retrieval optimizations, [12]. In IRIS, the similarity consists of three components:

$$sim(I_q, I_j) = \frac{1}{k_n}(k_u^{\text{topo}} \cdot d_{\text{topo}}(I_q, I_j) + k_u^{\text{b}} \cdot d_{\text{b}}(I_q, I_j) + k_u^{\text{text}} \cdot d_{\text{text}}(I_q, I_j))$$

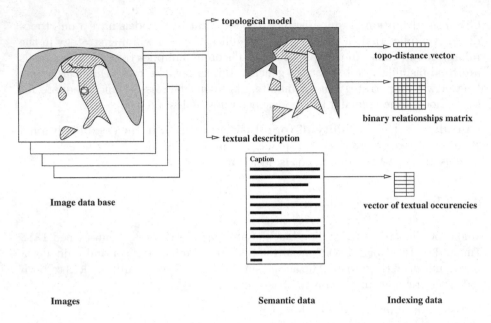

Fig. 3. The conceptual organization of IRIS together with the indexing data structures.

where I_q is the query image (equipped with its topological model and textual description), I_j is the j-th image in the visual database, k_u^{topo}, k_u^{b}, and k_u^{text} are user defined factors to specify the relative importance of topological intricacy, binary relationships and text in the querying process, k_n is a normalizing factor, $d_{\text{topo}}(I_q, I_j)$ is the topo-distance between I_q and I_j, $d_{\text{b}}(I_q, I_j)$ and $d_{\text{text}}(I_q, I_j)$ are the distances for the binary spatial relationships and for the textual descriptions, respectively.

5   Concluding Remarks

We have recalled a general mereotopological framework. We addressed issues of model equivalence and especially of model comparison, thus, looking at mereotopology from a new angle. Defining a distance that encodes the mereotopological difference between spatial models has important theoretical and application implications, in this paper we have focused on the latter. We have shown the actual decidability of the devised similarity measure for a practically interesting class of models.

Having implemented a system based on the above framework is also an important step in the presented research. Experimentation is under way, but some preliminary considerations are possible. We have noticed that the prototype is very sensible to the labeling of segmented areas of images, i.e., to the assignment

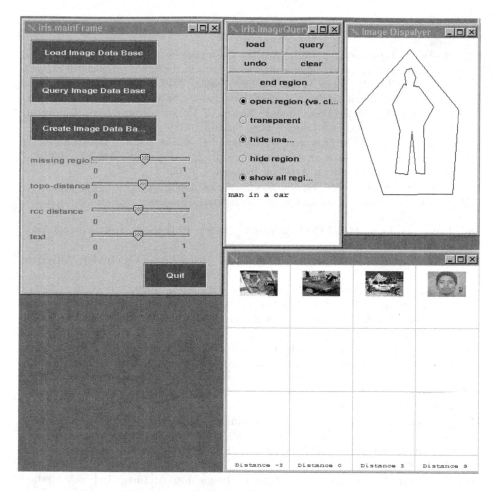

Fig. 4. The result of querying a database of men and cars.

of propositional letters to regions. We have also noticed that the mereotopological expressive power appears to enhance the quality of retrieval and indexing over pure textual searches, but the expressive power of $S4_u$ is still too limited. Notions of qualitative orientation, shape or geometry appear to be important, especially when the user expresses his desires in the form of an image query or of a sketch. The generality of the framework described in the paper allows for optimism about future developments.

Acknowledgments

The author is thankful to the anonymous referees for their helpful comments. This work was supported in part by CNR grant 203.7.27.

References

[1] M. Aiello. Topo-distance: Measuring the Difference between Spatial Patterns. In G. Brewka and L. Moniz Pereira, editors, *Logics in Artificial Intelligence (JELIA 2000)*, LNAI, 1919, pages 73–86. Springer Verlag, 2000.

[2] M. Aiello and J. van Benthem. Logical Patterns in Space. In D. Barker-Plummer, D. Beaver, J. van Benthem, and P. Scotto di Luzio, editors, *Logic Unleashed: Language, Diagrams and Computation*, Stanford, 2001. CSLI.

[3] N. Asher and L. Vieu. Toward a Geometry of Common Sense: a semantics and a complete axiomatization of mereotopology. In *IJCAI95*, pages 846–852. International Joint Conference on Artificial Itelligence, 1995.

[4] J. Barwise and L. Moss. *Vicious Circles*. CSLI, 1996.

[5] B. Bennett. Modal Logics for Qualitative Spatial Reasoning. *Bulletin of the IGPL*, 3:1 – 22, 1995.

[6] J. van Benthem. *Modal Correspondence Theory*. PhD thesis, University of Amsterdam, 1976.

[7] P. Blackburn, M. de Rijke, and Y. Venema. *Modal Logic*. Cambridge Univeristy Press, 2001.

[8] R. Casati and A. Varzi. *Parts and Places*. MIT Press, 1999.

[9] S.K. Chang and S.H. Liu. Picture indexing and abstraxtion techniques for pictorial databases. *IEEE Trans. on Pattern Analysis and Machine Intelligence*, 6(7):475–484, 1984.

[10] M. de Berg, M. van Kreveld, M. Overmars, and O. Schwarzkopf. *Computational Geometry: Algorithms and Applications*. Springer-Verlag, 2000. Second edition.

[11] A. Del Bimbo. *Visual Information Retrieval*. Morgan Kaufmann Publishers, 1999.

[12] W. Frakes and R. Baeza-Yates, editors. *Information Retrieval, Data Structures and Algorithms*. Prentice Hall, 1992.

[13] V. Goranko and S. Pasy. Using the universal modality: gains and questions. *Journal of Logic and Computation*, 2:5–30, 1992.

[14] D. Park. Concurrency and Automata on Infinite Sequences. In *Proceedings of the 5th GI Conference*, pages 167–183, Berlin, 1981. Springer Verlag.

[15] E. Petrakis, C. Faloutsos, and L. King-Ip. ImageMap: An Image Indexing Method Based on Spatial Similarity. *IEEE Transactions on Knowledge and Data Engineering*, 2001. To appear.

[16] I. Pratt and O. Lemon. Ontologies for Plane, Polygonal Mereotopology. *Notre Dame Journal of Formal Logic*, 38(2):225–245, 1997.

[17] D. Randell, Z. Cui, and A. G. Cohn. A Spatial Logic Based on Regions and Connection. In *Proc. of Int. Conf. on Principles of Knowledge Representation and Reasoning (KR'92)*, pages 165–176. San Mateo, 1992.

[18] S. Santini and J. Ramesh. Similarity measures. *IEEE Transactions on Pattern Analysis and Machine Intelligence*, 21(9):871–883, 1999.

[19] O. Stock, editor. *Spatial and Temporal Reasoning*. Kluwer Academic Publishers, 1997.

[20] H. Tagare, F. Vos, C. Jaffe, and J. Duncan. Arrangement: A spatial relation between part for evaluating similarity of tomographic section. *IEEE Transactions on Pattern Analysis and Machine Intelligence*, 17(9):880–893, 1995.

[21] A. Tarski. Der Aussagenkalkül und die Topologie. *Fund. Math.*, 31:103–134, 1938.

An Analysis of Backjumping and Trivial Truth in Quantified Boolean Formulas Satisfiability

Enrico Giunchiglia[1], Massimo Narizzano[1], and Armando Tacchella[2]

[1] DIST, Università di Genova, Viale Causa, 13 – 16145 Genova, Italy
[2] CS Dept., Rice University, 6100 Main St. MS 132, 77005-1892 Houston, Texas

Abstract. Trivial truth and backjumping are two optimization techniques that have been proposed for deciding quantified boolean formulas (QBFs) satisfiability. Both these techniques can greatly improve the overall performance of a QBF solver, but they are the expression of opposite philosophies. On one hand, trivial truth is a "look-ahead" policy: it is applied when descending the search tree to (try to) prune it. On the other hand, backjumping is a "look-back" policy: it is applied when backtracking to (try to) avoid useless explorations. Neither of these optimizations subsumes the other: it is easy to come up with examples in which trivial truth behaves much better than backjumping, and the other way around. In this paper we experimentally evaluate these two optimizations both on randomly generated and on real world test cases.

1 Introduction

Trivial truth [1, 2] and backjumping [3] are two optimization techniques that have been proposed for deciding quantified boolean formulas (QBFs) satisfiability. Both these techniques can greatly improve the overall performance of a QBF solver, but they are the expression of two opposite philosophies. On one hand, trivial truth is a "look-ahead" policy: it is applied when descending the search tree to (try to) prune it. On the other hand, backjumping is a "look-back" policy: it is applied when backtracking to (try to) avoid useless explorations. Neither of these two optimizations subsumes the other: it is easy to come up with examples in which trivial truth behaves much better than backjumping, and the other way around. In this paper we experimentally compare trivial truth and backjumping. The comparison is done using the QuBE system [4]. While trivial truth is implemented by various QBF solvers like EVALUATE [1] and QSOLVE [5], QuBE is –as far as we know– the only system with a backjumping optimization built in. The experimental analysis is performed on a combination of random kQBFs (see [2]), generated according to "model A" proposed by Gent and Walsh in [6], and on the real world instances proposed by Rintanen in [7]. The conclusions are that

- on random kQBFs, backjumping becomes more effective as the value of k increases, while trivial truth is more effective for specific values of k;
- on real world QBFs, trivial truth does not improve the performance, while backjumping enables QuBE to cope with some instances which could not be solved otherwise.

F. Esposito (Ed.): AI*IA 2001, LNAI 2175, pp. 111–122, 2001.
© Springer-Verlag Berlin Heidelberg 2001

All the aforementioned issues are the subject of the next three sections. In particular, Section 2 is devoted to the preliminaries, which include a formal presentation of QBFs; a presentation of QUBE decision algorithm(s), including a high-level description of backjumping and trivial truth; and a presentation of the testing methodology. Section 3 is devoted to the experimental evaluation of backjumping and trivial truth. In Section 4 we experiment with QUBE, QKN [8], EVALUATE [1], DECIDE [7], and QSOLVE [5] in order to assess the impact of QUBE's optimizations given the current state of the art in QBF solvers.

2 Preliminaries

Consider a set P of propositional letters. An *atom* is an element of P. A *literal* is an atom or the negation of an atom. For each literal l, (i) $\bar{l}$ is x if $l = \neg x$, and is $\neg x$ if $l = x$; (ii) $|l|$ is the atom occurring in l. A *clause* C is a p-ary $(p \geq 0)$ disjunction of literals such that no atom occurs twice in C. A *propositional formula* is an m-ary $(m \geq 0)$ conjunction of clauses. As customary, we represent a clause as a set of literals, and a propositional formula as a set of clauses.

A *QBF* is an expression of the form

$$Q_1 x_1 \ldots Q_n x_n \Phi, \qquad (n \geq 0) \tag{1}$$

where every Q_i $(1 \leq i \leq n)$ is a quantifier, either existential $\exists$ or universal $\forall$; $x_1, \ldots, x_n$ are pairwise distinct atoms in P; and Φ is a propositional formula in the atoms $x_1, \ldots, x_n$. $Q_1 x_1 \ldots Q_n x_n$ is the *prefix* and Φ is the (quantifier-free) *matrix* of (1).

Consider a QBF of the form (1). A literal l occurring in Φ is:

- *existential* if $\exists|l|$ belongs to the prefix of (1), and is *universal* otherwise.
- *unit* in (1) if l is existential, and, for some $k \geq 0$,
  - a clause $\{l, l_1, \ldots, l_k\}$ belongs to Φ, and
  - each expression $\forall|l_i|$ $(1 \leq i \leq k)$ is at the right of $\exists|l|$ in the prefix of (1).
- *monotone* if either l is existential, l occurs in Φ, and $\bar{l}$ does not occur in Φ; or l is universal, l does not occur in Φ, and $\bar{l}$ occurs in Φ.

A clause C is *contradictory* if no existential literal belongs to C. For example, the empty clause (i.e., the clause with no literals) is contradictory.

The semantics of a QBF φ can be defined recursively as follows. If φ contains a contradictory clause then φ is not satisfiable. If the matrix of φ is empty then φ is satisfiable. If φ is $\exists x \psi$ (resp. $\forall x \psi$), φ is satisfiable if and only if φ_x or (resp. and) $\varphi_{\neg x}$ are satisfiable. If $\varphi = Qx\psi$ is a QBF and l is a literal, φ_l is the QBF obtained from ψ by deleting the clauses in which l occurs, and removing $\bar{l}$ from the others. It is easy to see that if φ is a QBF without universal quantifiers, the problem of deciding φ satisfiability reduces to propositional satisfiability (SAT).

Notice that we allow only for propositional formulas in conjunctive normal form (CNF) as matrices of QBFs. Indeed, by applying standard CNF transformations (see, e.g., [9]) it is always possible to rewrite a QBF into an equisatisfiable one satisfying our restrictions.

```
 1  φ = ⟨the input QBF⟩;
 2  Stack= ⟨the empty stack⟩;

 3  function Simplify() {
 4    do {
 5      φ' = φ;
 6      if (⟨a contradictory clause is in φ⟩)
 7        return FALSE;
 8      if (⟨the matrix of φ is empty⟩)
 9        return TRUE;
10      if (⟨l is unit in φ⟩)
11        { |l|.mode = UNIT; Extend(l); }
12      if (⟨l is monotone in φ⟩)
13        { |l|.mode = PURE; Extend(l); }
14    } while (φ' != φ);
15    return UNDEF; }
```

```
16  function Backtrack(res) {
17    while (⟨Stack is not empty⟩) {
18      l = Retract();
19      if (((|l|.mode == L-SPLIT) &&
20          ((res == FALSE && |l|.type == ∃) ||
21           (res == TRUE && |l|.type == ∀)))
22        {|l|.mode = R-SPLIT; return l̄; }}
23    return NULL; }

24  function QubeSolver() {
25    do {
26      res = Simplify();
27      if (res == UNDEF) l = ChooseLiteral();
28      else  l = Backtrack(res);
29      if (l != NULL)  Extend(l);
30    } while (l != NULL);
31    return res; }
```

Fig. 1. The pseudo-code of QUBE.

2.1 QUBE

QUBE is implemented in C on top of SIM [10], an efficient library for propositional satisfiability developed by our group. A C-like high-level description of QUBE is shown in Figure 1. Inspection of QUBE's main routine (*QubeSolver* in Figure 1) reveals that the solver works in the usual way, trying to simplify φ as much as possible (line 26) before choosing how to branch on truth values (line 27), or backtracking to some previous choice point (line 28) whenever a contradictory clause or an empty formula is reached. Clearly, the order in which *ChooseLiteral* picks its choice depends on how literals are arranged in the prefix of φ. Outermost literals are selected first, unless they appear in a contiguous sequence of literals under the scope of the same kind of quantifier: in this case we are free to instantiate the literals in such a sequence with an arbitrary order. In Figure 1 we used the following conventions and notations:

- φ is a global variable initially set to the input QBF.
- *Stack* is a global variable storing the search stack, and is initially empty.
- ∃, ∀, FALSE, TRUE, UNDEF, NULL, UNIT, PURE, L-SPLIT, R-SPLIT are pairwise distinct constants.
- for each atom x in the input QBF, (*i*) $x.mode$ is a variable whose possible values are UNIT, PURE, L-SPLIT, R-SPLIT, and (*ii*) $x.type$ is ∃ if x is existential, and ∀ otherwise.

QUBE relies on a set of primitives on φ (and *Stack*) to solve the input QBF. The basic services have the purpose of assigning a truth value to a literal and of undoing such assignments. In particular:

- *Extend*(l) first pushes l and φ in the stack; then deletes the clauses of φ in which l occurs, and removes $\bar{l}$ from the others.

- *Retract*() pops the literal and the corresponding QBF that are on top of the stack: the literal is returned, while the QBF is assigned to φ.

Extend() and *Retract*() are thus the finest grained operations that can be performed on QUBE data structure. At a coarser level, QUBE relies on:

- *Simplify*() (detailed in Figure 1) simplifies φ till a contradictory clause is generated (line 6), or the matrix of φ is empty (line 8), or no simplification involving unit clauses and monotone literals is possible (lines 5, 14).
- *ChooseLiteral*() returns a literal l occurring in φ such that for each atom x occurring to the left of $|l|$ in the prefix of φ, x does not occur in φ, or x is existential iff l is existential. *ChooseLiteral*() also sets $|l|.mode$ to L-SPLIT.
- *Backtrack*(*res*) (detailed in Figure 1) pops all the literals and the corresponding QBFs (line 18) from the stack, till a literal l is reached such that $|l|.mode$ is L-SPLIT (line 19), and either (i) l is existential and *res* = FALSE (line 20); or (ii) l is universal and *res* = TRUE (line 21). If such a literal l exists, $|l|.mode$ is set to R-SPLIT, and $\bar{l}$ is returned (line 22). If no such literal exists, NULL is returned (line 23).

The trivial truth optimization is implemented in QUBE as follows. After the simplifications following the branch on an universal variable have been performed, QUBE checks whether the formula obtained from φ by deleting universal literals is satisfiable. If it is, then φ is satisfiable [2]. This optimization can produce dramatic speed-ups, particularly on randomly generated QBFs (see, e.g. [2]). Notice that ours is an optimized version of trivial truth as described in [2], where the check is performed at each branching node. In our version, such a check is not performed after branches on existential variables.

Backjumping comes into play when QUBE reaches a leaf node in the search tree, be it a contradictory clause or an empty formula. At this point, QUBE builds a reason for the current status, i.e., the set of literals directly causing it; then, while bactracking, QUBE refines such reason and tries to understand the branches that indirectly determined the satisfiability status in the leaf. In this way, QUBE can skip the other side of branches on existential literals which would lead again to a contradictory clause, and the other side of branches on universal literals that would lead again to an empty formula. Therefore, the procedure that we implemented in QUBE is a generalization of conflict-direct backjumping as it is usually implemented in SAT solvers. It turns out that, exactly as in SAT, backjumping has some overhead, but it can produce significant speed-ups [3].

Currently QUBE is distributed in two fashions: QUBE-BT, featuring standard chronological backtracking, and QUBE-BJ featuring non-chronological, conflict-directed backjumping. The choice between these two versions determines whether we are running the backjumping optimization or not. As for the trivial truth optimization, it is performed by default in both versions: we denote with "QUBE-BT -tt" and "QUBE-BJ -tt" the procedures corresponding, respectively, to QUBE-BT and QUBE-BJ with trivial truth turned off. QUBE's options other than backjumping and trivial truth are set according to their default values. As matter of fact, all the experiments have been run with the same version of *ChooseLiteral*, i.e., Böhm's heuristic [11] for SAT, modified as in [5] to consider existential literals only. Other configurations of QuBE, including those that we do not take into account here, are described in [4] to which we refer the reader for further details.

2.2 Testing Methodology

To experiment with various settings of QuBE and to compare it with other state-of-the-art solvers,[1] we have considered sets of random QBFs generated according to the "model A" as described in [6]. With this model, each QBF has the following 4 properties: (i) the prefix consists of k sequences, each sequence has n quantifiers, and each two quantifiers in a same sequence, are of the same type, (ii) the rightmost quantifier is $\exists$, (iii) the matrix consists of l clauses, (iv) each clause consists of h literals of which at least 2 are existential. In our experiments we fix $h = 5$ and we run the solvers with (some of) the settings $k = 2, 3, 4, 5$ and $n = 50, 100, 150$, in order to understand how the effectiveness of backjumping and trivial truth is related to a change of those parameters. The choice of $h = 5$ is motivated by the analysis presented in [6]: here the authors show that "model A" instances with $h = 5$ turn out to be challenging on average. On the other hand, smaller values of h are not quite as good: for instance, according to [6], in the case of $h = 3$ only a few samples turn out to be really difficult for the current state-of-the-art solvers.

For every problem, i.e., every specific value of k and n, the range of l is experimentally chosen to cover at least the 100%-satisfiable - 100% unsatisfiable transition. In order to meet this requirement and to compare performances among different settings, we fixed $1 \leq l/n \leq 20$ for all the problems. Given a point, i.e., a specific value of k and l/n, we generate 100 samples; for each sample and for all the solvers we measure the running time in CPU seconds. For QuBE, we also count the number of times that *ChooseLiteral* is called, i.e., the number of nodes in the search tree. Notice that when trivial truth is enabled, this includes the nodes explored by QuBE when running the "look-ahead" search. In order to save time, the execution of a solver on a sample is timed out after 1200s. Even more, for any point $k, l/n$, the execution of a solver is stopped after it exceeds the timeout on more than 50% of the samples, or:

- up to 6 were attempted so far and at least 5 timed out, or
- up to 10 were attempted so far and at least 8 of them timed out, or
- up to 20 were attempted so far and at least 13 of them timed out.

In the following, we say that a point cannot be solved whenever any of the above conditions is met. For each point we consider the Q-percentiles for $Q = 50, 60, 70, 80, 90,$ 100, the Q-percentile being the value such that $Q\%$ of the observations falls at or below it [12]. Our main statistical tool is the 50-percentile – best known as the *median* value – which we use as a resistant estimate for the average behaviour of the solvers on each point. The percentiles for $Q \geq 60$ serve the purpose of showing the behaviour on the hardest instances: in particular the 100-percentile corresponds to the worst case

[1] Experiments run on several identical Pentium III, 600MHz, 128MBRAM equipped with Linux Suse 6.x, kernel release 2.2.14. QuBE is compiled with GNU C release 2.95.2.

behaviour of the solvers on each point. When a point cannot be solved, the values of all the Q-percentiles default to 1200s.

Our experimental analysis includes the 38 problems contributed by Rintanen in [7].[2] The problems are translations from planning problems into the language of QBFs. They are interesting because:

- none of them can be solved by all the solvers at hand, and
- they share some "structure" with the original planning problem.

The second point is particularly relevant when comparing results on Rintanen's problems with results on "model A" instances. In SAT (see, e.g., [10]) it is often the case that the performance of some heuristics and optimizations is quite different when changing from randomly generated instances to real world ones. Therefore, although there is not yet any evidence in this direction for QBF, we included real world instances to get a wide-spectrum evaluation of QUBE and other state-of-the-art solvers.

3   Backjumping vs. Trivial Truth

We start the review of our experimental results with the comparison showed in Figure 2 among the four versions of QUBE giving all possible combinations of backjumping and trivial truth, including QUBE-BT -tt, i.e, QUBE's "vanilla" algorithm. The plots are arranged in two columns, running times are reported on the left and nodes are reported on the right; going from top to bottom, we show the results of problems $k = 2, 3, 4, 5$ with $n = 50$. In every plot, the x-axis is the range of l/n, and the y-axis is either the running time or the number of nodes, both in logarithmic scale. The percentage of satisfiable samples is represented by the dotted curve in the background. Notice that in the plots we omit the points which could not be solved.

By looking at the plots in Figure 2 and focusing on the running times for $k = 2$ (top-left), we immediately notice that trivial truth causes at least 3 orders of magnitude speed-up for the hardest formulas, i.e., those with $l/n = 4$. As a matter of fact, QUBE-BT median running time peaks at slightly less than 1s, while QUBE-BT -tt cannot solve more than 50% of the samples within the time limit. Still with $k = 2$, but looking at the number of nodes (Fig. 2 top-right), we see that the good performance of trivial truth is readily explained by a similar order-of-magnitude difference in the number of nodes: the difference is even more impressing if we consider that such number includes the nodes explored by trivial truth. On the other hand, backjumping does not seem to pay off: although the median number of nodes for QUBE-BJ (resp. QUBE-BJ -tt) is always less than or equal to the same statistic for QUBE-BT (resp. QUBE-BJ -tt), the difference is not enough to pay off the additional overhead. Indeed, it turns out that backjumping alone (QUBE-BT -tt) is not able to decrease the median running time of QUBE below the 1200s threshold for $l/n = 4$.

The situation is quite different for all values $k \geq 3$. Indeed, trivial truth has a much more limited impact, in particular for $k = 3$ (Fig. 2 second row) and $k = 5$ (Fig. 2 bottom row), while backjumping is delivering order-of-magnitude speed-ups on the same

---

[2] Available at www.informatik.uni-freiburg.de/~rintanen/qbf.html.

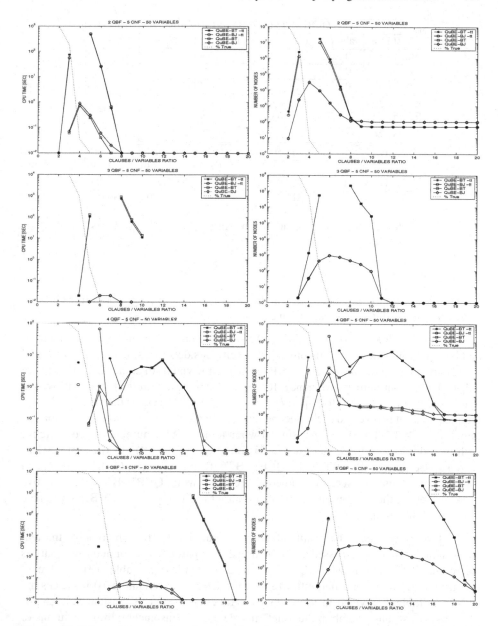

Fig. 2. QUBE median running time (left) and number of nodes (right) with $n = 50$, $k = 2, 3, 4, 5$.

settings. This is utterly evident by looking at the running times for $k = 5$ (Fig. 2 bottom-left), where QUBE-BJ and QUBE-BJ -tt curves both peak at less than 0.1s, while QUBE-BT and QUBE-BT -tt both peak – possibly well – above the timeout threshold.

Test File	Value	QuBE-BT -tt Time	QuBE-BJ -tt Time	QuBE-BT Time	QuBE-BJ Time
B..3ii.4.3	0	-	5.690	-	7.900
B..3ii.5.2	0	-	97.450	-	128.460
B..3iii.4	0	-	1.630	-	2.540
C..21v.22	1	140.630	163.950	-	-
C..22v.23	1	292.900	341.330	-	-
C..23v.24	1	605.050	701.300	-	-
T..6.1.iv.11	0	32.500	6.940	40.220	8.460
T..6.1.iv.12	1	14.610	1.830	19.330	2.330
T..7.1.iv.13	0	753.020	139.720	941.300	144.280
T..7.1.iv.14	1	311.830	28.910	416.700	36.090

Table 1. QUBE optimizations on (some) real world instances.

Again, it is a similarly large reduction in the search space size (Fig. 2 bottom-right) that determines the difference in performance.

The plots with $k = 4$ (Fig. 2 third row) are even more interesting, since trivial truth and backjumping show to be incomparable even considering a single setting of k and l/n. Neither backjumping alone (QUBE-BJ -tt) nor trivial truth alone (QUBE-BT) are able to achieve optimum performances for $k = 4$. Looking at running times (left) we see that in the first part of the plot, up to $l/n = 6$, QUBE-BT is faster than QUBE-BJ -tt, but the situation is reversed in the second half of the plot, with the two curves rejoicing only for $l/n \geq 17$. The situation is similar when looking at the number of nodes (right), with the additional remark that QUBE-BJ (resp. QUBE-BJ -tt) always explores less search space than QUBE-BT (resp. QUBE-BT -tt). Interestingly, QUBE-BT median running time does not exceed the timeout threshold, while QUBE-BJ -tt peaks above it; nevertheless, the two optimizations can interact positively, since QUBE-BJ is able to solve all the points.

In Table 1 we show the results obtained by running QUBE on some of the real world samples that we discussed in Subsection 2.2. In particular we omit those instances (there are 28 of them) in which QUBE is either able (11) or not able (17) to solve all the instances, no matter what optimizations are tried. The remaning 10 instances are shown in Table 1, divided in three classes: "blocks-world" ("B" instances), "chain" ("C" instances), and "bomb in the toilet" problems ("T" instances). In the columns of Table 1, besides the satisfiability status, we report for each version of QUBE the running time in seconds: instances exceeding the time limit are denoted with a dash. In the case of "B" instances, backjumping is the optimization of choice: QUBE-BJ -tt as well as QUBE-BJ are able to solve all the three instances, while QUBE-BT -tt and QUBE-BT are not. We also notice that trivial truth is causing a performance degradation in QUBE-BJ which turns out to be slower than QUBE-BJ -tt. With "C" instances, even QUBE's vanilla version is able to solve the corresponding QBFs, while backjumping does not seem to pay off. Noticeably, the versions featuring trivial truth are not able to solve the

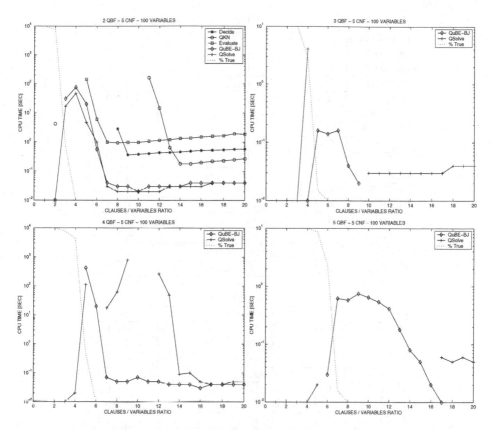

Fig. 3. QUBE and state-of-the-art solvers on $k = 2, 3, 4, 5$ and $n = 100$ problems.

instances within the time limit. With "T" instances, QUBE-BJ -tt is again the fastest on all the problems, thus confirming the effectiveness of backjumping.

4   QUBE and State-of-the-Art QBF Solvers

In Figure 3 we review the experiments comparing state-of-the-art solvers with QUBE. Going from left to right, top to bottom, we show the problems $k = 2, 3, 4, 5$ with $n = 100$. The plots are arranged in the same way as in Figure 2. We run QUBE-BJ and QSOLVE [5] with all the settings, while for $k = 2$ we also tested DECIDE [7], EVALUATE [1] and QKN [8]. Looking at Figure 3 (top left) we immediatly see that QUBE and QSOLVE perform roughly the same (with QSOLVE being slightly better than QUBE) and better than all the other solvers that we tested: EVALUATE, QKN and DECIDE all fail to solve the hardest points. Still in Figure 3, for $k \geq 3$ we further observe that QUBE is always faster than QSOLVE, sometimes by orders of magnitude. Since QSOLVE runs trivial truth (and trivial falsity), but no backjumping, we take this as further evidence on the effectiveness of backjumping for values of $k \geq 3$. In particular,

Test File	Value	QuBE-BJ -tt Time	QSolve Time	Evaluate Time	QKN Time	Decide Time
B..3i.4.4	0	-	-	-	-	0.11
B..3i.5.3	0	-	-	-	-	49.72
B..3i.5.4	1	-	-	-	-	7.53
B..3ii.4.3	0	5.690	-	-	-	0.07
B..3ii.5.2	0	97.450	-	-	-	0.41
B..3ii.5.3	1	-	-	-	-	1.80
B..3iii.4	0	1.630	-	-	-	0.02
B..3iii.5	1	-	-	-	-	0.56
B..4i.6.4	0	-	-	-	-	3.72
B..4ii.6.3	0	-	-	-	-	3.10
B..4ii.7.2	0	-	-	-	-	8.79
B..4iii.6	0	-	-	-	-	1.51
B..4iii.7	1	-	-	-	-	729.11
C..12v.13	1	0.220	6.45	-	-	0.07
C..13v.14	1	0.470	20.1	-	-	0.10
C..14v.15	1	0.970	63.47	-	-	0.12
C..15v.16	1	2.020	199.31	-	-	0.16
C..16v.17	1	4.200	624.97	-	-	0.19
C..17v.18	1	8.920	-	-	-	0.23
C..18v.19	1	18.480	-	-	-	0.28
C..19v.20	1	38.590	-	-	-	0.31
C..20v.21	1	85.400	-	-	-	0.36
C..21v.22	1	163.950	-	-	-	0.40
C..22v.23	1	341.330	-	-	-	0.48
C..23v.24	1	701.300	-	-	-	0.56
T..10.1.iv.20	1	-	-	-	-	6.30
T..16.1.iv.32	1	-	-	-	-	43.15
T..2.1.iv.3	0	0.000	0	-	0.147	0.01
T..2.1.iv.4	1	0.000	0	-	-	0.02
T..6.1.iv.11	0	6.940	11.81	-	-	36.17
T..6.1.iv.12	1	1.830	8.53	-	-	0.91
T..7.1.iv.13	0	139.720	426.93	-	-	428.20
T..7.1.iv.14	1	28.910	203.53	-	-	1.64

Table 2. QUBE and state-of-the-art solvers on (some) real world instances.

we remark the qualitative similarity between QSOLVE with $k = 4$ and $n = 100$ in Figure 3 and QUBE-BT with $k = 4$ and $n = 50$ in Figure 2, and the fact that all the considerations that we did on $n = 50$ seems to carry over to $n = 100$.

We conclude the comparison between QUBE and the other state-of-the-art solvers with the results presented in Table 2. In the Table, we report the running times of QUBE and other solvers on 33 out of 38 problems: the remaining instances could not be solved by any of the systems. As we can see from Table 2, the best solver overall turns out to be DECIDE with 33 problems solved and 42.28s average running time (on solved samples), followed by QUBE, with 18 problems solved and 73.21s, and QSOLVE with 11 problems solved and 149.29s. QKN and EVALUATE with, respectively, 1 and 0 problems solved, trail the list. In this regard, we point out that DECIDE features "inversion of quantifiers" and "sampling" mechanisms which are particularly effective on these benchmarks. Athough QUBE does not feature such mechanisms its performances are quite good on these tests: on "C" instances this is entirely due to its heuristics and efficient implementation, while backjumping turns out to be the crucial factor in the solution of "B" and "T" instances.

5 Conclusions

Summing up, the results of our experimental evaluation of backjumping and trivial truth, largely confirm that they are of incomparable strengths, but they both help in obtaining substantial speed-ups. In more details:

- on random kQBFs, backjumping is more effective with $k \geq 3$ and, in particular, with $k = 2i + 1$; trivial truth is very effective on $k = 2$ and less effective on $k \geq 3$. $k = 4$ is an example where, on the same setting of k and n, trivial truth and backjumping show a different behaviour, as well as the ability to interact positively. On this class of problems they can both be used to cope with instances that are hardly solved by using them separately;
- on real world QBFs, trivial truth does not improve the performances, while backjumping enables QUBE to solve some "blocks world" and "bomb in the toilet" instances which could not be solved otherwise.

Thanks to its optimizations, QUBE turns out to be very competitive with state-of-the-art solvers on "model A" instances for all values of k and n that we tried, but in particular for $k = 3, 4, 5$ and $n = 100$. In the case of real world samples, QUBE with backjumping comes second best after DECIDE which is indeed highly tuned to solve those problems.

Acknowledgments

We wish to thank Marco Cadoli, Rainer Feldmann, Theodor Lettman, Jussi Rintanen, Marco Schaerf, Stefan Schamberger, for providing us with their systems and helping us to figure them out during our experimental analisys.

The first two authors are supported by MURST and ASI. The last author is supported by NSF grants CCR-9700061 and CCR-9988322, BSF grant 9800096, and by a grant from the Intel Corporation.

References

[1] M. Cadoli, A. Giovanardi, and M. Schaerf. An algorithm to evaluate quantified boolean formulae. In *Proc. of AAAI*, 1998.

[2] M. Cadoli, M. Schaerf, A. Giovanardi, and M. Giovanardi. An Algorithm to Evaluate Quantified Boolean Formulae and its Experimental Evaluation. In *Highlights of Satisfiability Research in the Year 2000*. IOS Press, 2000.

[3] E. Giunchiglia, M. Narizzano, and A. Tacchella. Backjumping for Quantified Boolean Logic Satisfiability. In *Proc. of IJCAI*, 2001. To appear.

[4] E. Giunchiglia, M. Narizzano, and A. Tacchella. QuBE: a system for Deciding Quantified Boolean Formulas Satisfiability. In *Proc. of IJCAR*, 2001.

[5] R. Feldmann, B. Monien, and S. Schamberger. A Distributed Algorithm to Evaluate Quantified Boolean Formulae. In *Proc. of AAAI*, 2000.

[6] Ian Gent and Toby Walsh. Beyond NP: the QSAT phase transition. In *Proc. of AAAI*, pages 648–653, 1999.

[7] J. T. Rintanen. Improvements to the Evaluation of Quantified Boolean Formulae. In *Proc. of IJCAI*, pages 1192–1197, 1999.

[8] H. Kleine-Büning and M. Karpinski and A. Flögel. Resolution for quantified boolean formulas. *Information and Computation*, 117(1):12–18, 1995.

[9] D.A. Plaisted and S. Greenbaum. A Structure-preserving Clause Form Translation. *Journal of Symbolic Computation*, 2:293–304, 1986.

[10] E. Giunchiglia, M. Maratea, A. Tacchella, and D. Zambonin. Evaluating search heuristics and optimization techniques in propositional satisfiability. In *Proc. of IJCAR*, LNCS. Springer Verlag, 2001. To appear.

[11] M. Buro and H. Kleine-Büning. Report on a SAT competition. Technical Report 110, University of Paderborn, November 1992.

[12] D. S. Moore and G. P. McCabe. *Introduction to the Practice of Statistics*. W. H. Freeman and Co., 1993.

Abduction with Penalization
in Logic Programming

Nicola Leone[1], Simona Perri[1], and Francesco Scarcello[2]

[1] Department of Mathematics, University of Calabria
I-87030 Rende (CS), Italy
leone@unical.it, sperri@si.deis.unical.it
[2] D.E.I.S., University of Calabria
87030 Rende (CS), Italy
scarcello@deis.unical.it

Abstract. Abduction, first proposed in the setting of classical logics, has been studied with growing interest in the logic programming area during the last years.

In this paper we study *abduction with penalization* in logic programming. This form of abductive reasoning, which has not been previously analyzed in logic programming, turns out to represent several relevant problems, including optimization problems, very naturally. We define a formal model for abduction with penalization from logic programs, which extends the abductive framework proposed by Kakas and Mancarella. We show the high expressiveness of this formalism, by encoding a couple of relevant problems, including the well-know Traveling Salesman Problem from optimization theory, in this abductive framework. The resulting encodings are very simple and elegant. We analyze the complexity of the main decisional problems arising in this framework. An interesting result in this course is that "negation comes for free." Indeed, the addition of (even unstratified) negation does not cause any further increase to the complexity of the abductive reasoning tasks (which remains the same as for not-free programs).

1 Introduction

Abduction is an important kind of reasoning which has been first studied in depth by Peirce [19]. Given the observation of some facts, abduction aims at concluding the presence of other facts, from which, together with an underlying theory, the observed facts can be explained, i.e., deductively derived. Thus, roughly speaking, abduction amounts to an inverse of modus ponens.

For example, medical diagnosis is a typical abductive reasoning process: From the symptoms and the medical knowledge, a diagnosis about a possible disease is abduced. Notice that this form of reasoning is not sound (a diagnosis may turn out to be wrong), and that in general several abductive explanations (i.e., diagnoses) for observations may be possible.

During the last years, there has been increasing interest in abduction in different areas of computer science. It has been recognized that abduction is an

F. Esposito (Ed.): AI*IA 2001, LNAI 2175, pp. 123–134, 2001.

important principle of common-sense reasoning, and that abduction has fruitful applications in a number of areas such diverse as model-based diagnosis [20], speech recognition [12], maintenance of database views [15], and vision [3].

In the past, most research on abduction concerned abduction from classical logic theories. However, we argue that the use of logic programming to perform abductive reasoning can be more appropriate in several applicative domains.

For instance, consider the following scenario. Assume that it is Saturday and is known that Joe goes fishing on Saturdays if it's not raining. This may be represented by the following theory T:

$$go\_fishing \leftarrow is\_saturday \wedge \neg rains \; ; \quad is\_saturday \leftarrow$$

Now you observe that Joe is not out for fishing. Intuitively, from this observation we conclude that it rains (i.e, we abduce *rains*), for otherwise Joe would be out for fishing. Nevertheless, under classical inference, the fact *rains* is not an explanation of $\neg go\_fishing$, as $T \cup \{rains\} \not\models \neg go\_fishing$ (neither can one find any explanation). On the contrary, if we adopt the semantics of logic programming, then, according with the intuition, we obtain that *rains* is an explanation of $\neg go\_fishing$, as it is entailed by $T \cup \{rains\}$.

In the context of logic programming, abduction has been first proposed by Kakas and Mancarella [14] and, during the recent years, common interest in the subject has been growing rapidly [4,16,14,13,6,5,21], also for the observation that, compared to deduction, this kind of reasoning has some advantages for dealing with incomplete information [5,1].

In this paper we study *abduction with penalization* in logic programming. This form of abductive reasoning, well studied in the setting of classical logics [7], has not been previously analyzed in logic programming.

We define a formal model for abduction with penalization from logic programs, which extends the abductive framework proposed by Kakas and Mancarella [14]. Roughly, a penalty is assigned to each hypothesis. An abductive solution S is weighted by the sum of the penalties of the hypotheses in S.[1] Mimimum-weight solutions are preferred over the other solutions since they are considered more likely to occur.

We show that some relevant problems, including, e.g., the classical *Traveling Salesman Problem* from optimization theory, can be encoded very simply and elegantly by abduction with penalization; while they cannot be encoded at all in (function-free) logic programming even under the powerful stable model semantics.

We analyze the computational complexity of the main decisional problems arising in this framework. An interesting result in this course is that "negation comes for free." Indeed, the addition of (even unstratified) negation does not cause any further increase to the complexity of the abductive reasoning tasks (which remains the same as for not-free programs). Thus, abduction with penalization over general logic programs has precisely the same complexity as

---

[1] Actually, in this paper, we consider also forms of weighting functions more general than Sum.

abduction with penalization over definite Horn theories of classical logics. Consequently, the user can enjoy the knowledge representation power of nonmonotonic negation without paying any additional cost in terms of computational overhead.

2   Preliminaries on Logic Programming

2.1   Syntax

A *term* is either a constant or a variable[2]. An *atom* is $a(t_1, ..., t_n)$, where a is a *predicate* of arity n and $t_1, ..., t_n$ are terms. A *literal* is either a *positive literal* a or a *negative literal* $\neg A$, where a is an atom. Two literals are *complementary* if they are of the form p and $\neg p$, for some atom p. Given a literal L, $\neg.L$ denotes its complementary literal (the complement of an atom A is literal $\neg A$ and vice versa). Accordingly, given a set A of literals, $\neg.A$ denotes the set $\{\neg.L \mid L \in A\}$.

A *program clause* (or *rule*) r is

$$a \leftarrow b_1, \cdots, b_k, \neg b_{k+1}, \cdots, \neg b_m, \qquad n \geq 1, \; m \geq 0$$

where $a, b_1, \cdots, b_m$ are atoms. Atom a is the *head* of r, while the conjunction $b_1, ..., b_k, \neg b_{k+1}, ..., \neg b_m$ is the *body* of r.

A *(logic) program* is a finite set of rules. A $\neg$-free program is called *Horn program* or *positive program*. A term, an atom, a literal, a rule or program is *ground* if no variable appears in it. A ground program is also called a *propositional* program.

2.2   Stable Model Semantics

Let LP be a program. The *Herbrand Universe* U_{LP} of LP is the set of all constants appearing in LP. The *Herbrand Base* B_{LP} of LP is the set of all possible ground atoms constructible from the predicates appearing in the rules of LP and the constants occurring in U_{LP} (clearly, both U_{LP} and B_{LP} are finite). Given a rule r occurring in a program LP, a *ground instance* of r is a rule obtained from r by replacing every variable X in r by $\sigma(X)$, where σ is a mapping from the variables occurring in r to the constants in U_{LP}. We denote by $ground(LP)$ the (finite) set of all the ground instances of the rules occurring in LP. An *interpretation* for LP is a subset I of B_{LP} (i.e., it is a set of ground atoms). A positive literal a (resp. a negative literal $\neg a$) is true with respect to an interpretation I if $a \in I$ (resp. $a \notin I$); otherwise it is false. A ground rule r is *satisfied* (or *true*) w.r.t. I if its head is true w.r.t. I or its body is false w.r.t. I. A *model* for LP is an interpretation M for LP such that every rule $r \in ground(\mathcal{P})$ is true w.r.t. M.

Given a logic program LP and an interpretation I, the *Gelfond-Lifschitz transformation* of LP with respect to I is the logic program LP^I consisting of all rules $a \leftarrow b_1, ..., b_k$ such that   (1) $a \leftarrow b_1, ..., b_k, \neg b_{k+1}, ..., \neg b_m \in LP$ and   (2) $b_i \notin I$, for all $k < i \leq m$.

---

[2]   Note that function symbols are not considered in this paper.

Notice that $\neg$ does not occur in LP^I, i.e., it is a positive program. Each positive program LP has a least model (i.e., a model included in every model), denoted by $lm(LP)$.

An interpretation I is called a *stable model* of LP iff $I = lm(LP^I)$ [11]. The collection of all stable models of LP is denoted by $\mathrm{STM}(LP)$ (i.e., $\mathrm{STM}(LP) = \{I \mid I = lm(LP^I)\}$).

Example 1. Consider the following (ground) program LP:

$$a \leftarrow \neg b \quad b \leftarrow \neg a \quad c \leftarrow a \quad c \leftarrow b$$

The stable models of LP are $M_1 = \{a, c\}$ and $M_2 = \{b, c\}$. Indeed, by definition of Gelfond-Lifschitz transformation, $LP^{M_1} = \{\ a \leftarrow,\ c \leftarrow a,\ c \leftarrow b\ \}$ and $LP^{M_2} = \{\ b \leftarrow,\ c \leftarrow a,\ c \leftarrow b\ \}$; thus, it is immediately recognized that $lm(LP^{M_1}) = M_1$ and $lm(LP^{M_2}) = M_2$.

In general, a logic program may have more than one stable model or even no stable model at all. In the logic programming framework (under stable model semantics) there are two main notions of reasoning:

Brave reasoning (or *credulous reasoning*) infers that a literal Q is true in LP (denoted $LP \models^b Q$) iff Q is true with respect to M for some $M \in \mathrm{STM}(LP)$.

Cautious reasoning (or *skeptical reasoning*) infers that a literal Q is true in LP (denoted $LP \models^c Q$) iff Q is true with respect to M for all $M \in \mathrm{STM}(LP)$.

The inference relations $\models^b$ and $\models^c$ extend to sets of literals as usual.

Example 2. For the program LP of Example 1, a, b and c are brave inferences ($LP \models^b \{a, b, c\}$); the only cautious inference is c ($LP \models^c c$).

In this paper, we are mainly interested in brave reasoning, even if our definitions can be easily extended to cautious reasoning.

3   A Model of Abduction with Penalization

In this section, we describe our formal model for abduction with penalizations over logic programs.

Definition 1. A problem of abduction $\mathcal{P}$ consists of a triple $\langle H, LP, O \rangle$, where H is a finite set of ground atoms *(hypotheses)*, LP is a logic program, and O is a finite set of ground literals *(observations, or manifestations)*.

A set of hypotheses $S \subseteq H$ is an *admissible solution* (or *explanation*) to $\mathcal{P}$ if there exists a stable model M of $LP \cup S$ such that, $\forall o \in O$, o is true w.r.t. M (i.e., $LP \cup S \models^b O$).

The set of all admissible solutions to $\mathcal{P}$ is denoted by $Adm(\mathcal{P})$.   ∎

The following example shows a classical application of abduction for diagnosis purposes.

Example 3. (NETWORK DIAGNOSIS) Suppose that we are working on machine *a* (and we therefore know that machine *a* is online) of the computer network in Figure 1, but we observe machine *e* is not reachable from *a*, even if we are aware that *e* is online. We would like to know which machines are offline. This can be easily modeled in our abduction framework defining a problem of abduction $\langle H, LP, O\rangle$, where the set of hypotheses is $H =\{$*offline(a), offline(b), offline(c), offline(d), offline(e), offline(f)*$\}$, the set of observations is $O = \{\neg$ *offline(a)*, $\neg$ *offline(e)*, $\neg$ *reaches(a,e)*$\}$, and LP is the logic program

> *reaches(X, X)* $-node(X), \neg$ *offline(X).*
> *reaches(X, Z):* $-reaches(X, Y),$ *connected(Y, Z),* $\neg$ *offline(Z).*

Note that the admissible solutions for $\mathcal{P}$ corresponds to the network configurations that may explain the observations in O. In this example, $Adm(\mathcal{P})$ contains five solutions $S_1 = \{$*offline(f), offline(b)*$\}$, $S_2 = \{$*offline(f), offline(c), offline(d)*$\}$, $S_3 = \{$*offline(f), offline(b), offline(c)*$\}$, $S_4 = \{$*offline(f), offline(b), offline(d)*$\}$, $S_5 = \{$*offline(f), offline(b), offline(c), offline(d)*$\}$.

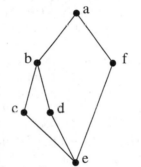

Fig. 1. Computer network

Note that Definition 1 concerns only the logical properties of the hypotheses, and it does not take into account any kind of minimality criterion. We next define the problem of abduction with penalizations, which allows us to make finer abductive reasonings, by expressing preferences on different sets of hypotheses and single out the most plausible abductive explainations.

Definition 2. A problem of abduction with penalization (*PAP*) $\mathcal{P}$ is a tuple $\langle H, LP, O, \gamma, cost\rangle$, where $\langle H, LP, O\rangle$, is a problem of abduction, γ is a function from H to the set of positive reals *(the penalty function)*, and $cost : 2^{R^+} \to R^+$ is a function computable in polynomial time. The set of admissible solutions for $\mathcal{P}$ is the same as the set of solutions of the embedded abduction problem $\langle H, LP, O\rangle$, i.e., we define $Adm(\mathcal{P}) = Adm(\langle H, LP, O\rangle)$.

For a set of atoms A, we denote by $\gamma(A)$ the set $\{\gamma(a) \mid a \in A\}$. Then, S is an *(optimal) solution* (or *explanation*) for $\mathcal{P}$ if (i) $S \in Adm(\mathcal{P})$ and (ii) $cost(\gamma(S)) \leq cost(\gamma(S'))$, for all $S' \in Adm(\mathcal{P})$.

The set of all (optimal) solutions for $\mathcal{P}$ is denoted by $Opt(\mathcal{P})$. ∎

To simplify the notation, we will write $cost_\gamma$ to denote the composition of the cost function $cost$ with the penalty function γ, i.e., for a set of hypotheses S, $cost_\gamma(S) = cost(\gamma(S))$.

Example 4. (MINIMUM-CARDINALITY CRITERION) Consider again the network and the problem of abduction $\langle H, LP, O \rangle$ in Example 3. From this problem, we define a problem of abduction with penalization $\mathcal{P} = \langle H, LP, O, \gamma, cost \rangle$, where the cost and the penalty functions are defined as follows. For each $S \subseteq H$, $cost_\gamma(S) = \sum_{x \in S} \gamma(x)$ and, for each $h \in H$, $\gamma(h) = 1$.

This way, we prefer the explanations with the minimum numbers of offline machines. Since $cost_\gamma(S_1) = 2$, $cost_\gamma(S_2) = cost_\gamma(S_3) = cost_\gamma(S_4) = 3$, $cost_\gamma(S_5) = 4$, it follows that S_1 is the unique optimal solution for $\mathcal{P}$.

Example 5. (PROBABILISTIC CRITERION) Minimizing the number of offline machines is not necessarily the best strategy. If the reliability of the machines is very different, one should take it into account. To this end, for each machine x in the network of Figure 1, the penalty function γ assigns the probability of x to be offline to the hypothesis $offline(x)$. Let these values be $\gamma(offline(a)) = \gamma(offline(e)) = 0.2$, $\gamma(offline(b)) = 0.64$, $\gamma(offline(f)) = 0.4$ and $\gamma(offline(c)) = \gamma(offline(d)) = 0.8$.

In this case, a good cost function should prefer solutions corresponding to the sets of machines that are most likely down simultaneously. We can reasonably assume these events to be independent each other. Thus, our cost function should prefer sets of machines such that the product of the probabilities (i.e., of the penalties) is the maximum. This is clearly equivalent to minimize the following cost function: $cost_\gamma(S) = 1 - \prod_{x \in S} \gamma(x)$, for any $S \subseteq H$. Thus, we have $cost_\gamma(S_1) = 0.74$, $cost_\gamma(S_2) = 0.74$, $cost_\gamma(S_3) = 0.80$, $cost_\gamma(S_4) = 0.80$, $cost_\gamma(S_5) = 0.84$. In this case, the optimal solutions for $\mathcal{P}$ are S_1 and S_2.

The following properties of a hypothesis in a *PAP* $\mathcal{P}$ are of natural interest with respect to computing abductive solutions.

Definition 3. Let $\mathcal{P} = \langle H, LP, O, \gamma, cost \rangle$ be a *PAP* and $h \in H$. Then, h is relevant for $\mathcal{P}$ iff $h \in S$ for some $S \in Opt(\mathcal{P})$, and h is necessary for $\mathcal{P}$ iff $h \in S$ for every $S \in Opt(\mathcal{P})$.

Example 6. In example 5, the only *necessary* hypothesis is *offline(f)*; while the *relevant* hypotheses are *offline(f)*, *offline(b)*, *offline(c)* and *offline(d)*.

The main decisional problems arising in the context of abduction with penalizations are the following. Given a *PAP* $\mathcal{P} = \langle H, LP, O, \gamma, cost \rangle$,

1. does there exist a solution for $\mathcal{P}$? (*Consistency*)
2. is a given set of hypotheses an optimal solution for $\mathcal{P}$? (*Optimality*)
3. is a given hypothesis $h \in H$ relevant for $\mathcal{P}$, i.e., does h contribute to some optimal solution of $\mathcal{P}$? (*Relevance*)

4. is a given hypothesis $h \in H$ necessary for $\mathcal{P}$, i.e., is h contained in all optimal solutions of $\mathcal{P}$? (*Necessity*)

The complexity of the consistency, optimality, relevance, and necessity problems is studied in Section 5.

4   An Example: The Traveling Salesman Problem

In [8], Eiter, Gottlob and Mannila show that Disjunctive Datalog (function-free logic programming with disjunction in the heads and negation in the bodies of the rules) is highly expressive, as it can express every problem in Σ_2^P (that is, recognizable in polynomial time by a non-deterministic Turing machine which uses an NP oracle). Moreover, the authors strenght the theoretical analysis of the expressiveness by proving that problems relevant in practice like, e.g., the *Traveling Salesman Problem (TSP)* and *Eigenvector*, can be programmed in Disjunctive Datalog, while they cannot be expressed by disjunction-free programs. Nevertheless, the logic programs implementing these problems in Disjunctive Datalog highlight, in our opinion, a weakness of the language for the representation of optimization problems. The programs are very complex and tricky, the language does not provide a clean and declarative way to implement these problems.[3]

We show below how the TSP problem can be encoded in our abductive framework. A comparison of our encoding against the encoding of this problem in (plain) disjunctive Datalog described in [8] clearly shows that abduction with penalizations provides a simpler, more compact, and more elegant encoding of TSP. Moreover, note that using this form of abduction even normal (disjunction-free) programs are sufficient for encoding such optimization problems.

Example 7. (TRAVELING SALESMAN BY ABDUCTION WITH PENALIZATIONS) It is well-known that finding an optimal solution to the Traveling Salesman Problem (TSP) is intractable. Recall that the problem is, given cities $c_1, \ldots, c_n$, find a round trip that visits all cities in sequence and has minimal traveling cost, i.e., a permutation τ of $1, \ldots, n$ such that

$$w(\tau) = \sum_{i=1}^{n-1} w(\tau(i), \tau(i+1)) + w(\tau(n), \tau(1))$$

is minimum, where $w(i, j)$ is the cost of traveling from c_i to c_j, given by an integer.

Computing an optimal tour is both NP-hard and co-NP-hard. In fact, in [17] it was shown that deciding whether the cost of an optimal tour is even is Δ_2^P-complete. Hence, this is not possible in or-free logic programming even if unstratified negation is allowed (unless PH collapses).

---

[3] We refer to standard Disjunctive Datalog here. As shown in [2], the addition of *weak constraints*, implemented in the DLV system [10], is another way to enhance Disjunctive Datalog to naturally express optimization problems.

Suppose that the cities are encoded by $1, \ldots, n$ and, for each pair of cities $1 \leq i, j \leq n$, The set of hypotheses is $H = \{C(i,j) \mid 1 \leq i, j \leq n\}$, where $C(i,j)$ encodes the fact that the salesman visits city j immediately after city i. The penalty function $\gamma(C(i,j)) = w(i,j)$ encodes the cost of traveling from j to i.

Let LP be the program consisting of the following rules:[4]

$$
\begin{aligned}
&(1) &City(i) &\leftarrow &1 \leq i \leq n \\
&(2) &Visited(I) &\leftarrow City(I), C(J,I), C(I,K) \\
&(3) &MissedCity &\leftarrow City(I), \neg Visited(I) \\
&(4) &BadTour &\leftarrow C(I,J), C(I,K), J \neq K \\
&(5) &BadTour &\leftarrow C(J,I), C(K,I), J \neq K
\end{aligned}
$$

Consider the *PAP* $\mathcal{P} = \langle H, \gamma, LP, O, cost \rangle$, where $O = \{\neg MissedCity, \neg Bad\text{-}Tour\}$, and the cost function is the sum, i.e., $cost_\gamma(S) = \sum_{h \in S} \gamma(h)$, for any set of hypotheses $S \subseteq H$.

It is easy to see that every optimal solution $S \in Opt(\mathcal{P})$ corresponds to an optimal tour and vice versa. Intuitively, the facts (1) of LP define the set of the cities to be visited. Rule (2) states that a city i has been visited if it has been both reached and left by the traveling salesman (i.e., there exist two cities j and k such that $C(j,i)$ and $C(i,k)$ are in the solution). Rule (3) says that there is a missed city if at least one of the cities has not been visited. Atom $BadTour$, defined by rules (4) and (5), is true if some city is in two or more connection endpoints or connection startpoints. The observations $\neg MissedCity, \neg BadTour$ enforce that the tour is complete (no city is missed) and it is legal (no city is visited twice).

Thus, admissible solutions in $Adm(\mathcal{P})$ correspond one-to-one to the admissible (legal and complete) tours. Since optimal solutions minimize the sum of the connection costs, abductive solutions in $Opt(\mathcal{P})$ correspond one-to-one to the optimal tours. $\square$

5   Computational Complexity

5.1   Preliminaries on Complexity Theory

For NP-completeness and complexity theory, cf. [18]. The classes Σ_k^P, Π_k^P and Δ_k^P of the Polynomial Hierarchy (PH) are defined as follows:

$$
\Delta_0^P = \Sigma_0^P = \Pi_0^P = \mathrm{P} \quad \text{and for all } k \geq 1,
$$
$$
\Delta_k^P = \mathrm{P}^{\Sigma_{k-1}^P}, \quad \Sigma_k^P = \mathrm{NP}^{\Sigma_{k-1}^P}, \quad \Pi_k^P = \mathrm{co}\text{-}\Sigma_k^P.
$$

In particular, $\mathrm{NP} = \Sigma_1^P$, co-$\mathrm{NP} = \Pi_1^P$, and $\Delta_2^P = \mathrm{P}^{\mathrm{NP}}$. Here P^C and NP^C denote the classes of problems that are solvable in polynomial time on a deterministic (resp. nondeterministic) Turing machine with an oracle for any problem π in the

---

[4] The symbol $\neq$ represents the inequality predicate, we consider inequality a built-in without loss of generality, as it can be easily simulated in our formalism.

class C. The oracle replies to a query in unit time, and thus, roughly speaking, models a call to a subroutine for π that is evaluated in unit time. If C has complete problems, then instances of any problem π' in C can be solved in polynomial time using an oracle for any C-complete problem π, by transforming them into instances of π; we refer to this by stating that an oracle for C is used. Notice that all classes C considered here have complete problems.

The classes Δ_k^P, $k \geq 2$, have been refined by the class $\Delta_k^P[O(\log n)]$, in which the number of calls to the oracle is in each computation bounded by $O(\log n)$, where n is the size of the input. Notice that for all $k \geq 1$,

$$\Sigma_k^P \subseteq \Delta_{k+1}^P[O(\log n)] \subset \Delta_{k+1}^P \subseteq \Sigma_{k+1}^P \subseteq \text{PSPACE};$$

each inclusion is widely conjectured to be strict.

Note that the computational complexity of abduction with penalization in the setting of classical logics has been carefully investigated in [7]. They have shown that, for general logic theories, the consistency problem is Σ_2^P-complete, and both the relevance and the necessity problems are Δ_3^P-complete. Moreover, they studied some restrictions in order to reduce the computational complexity of these tasks. In particular, they considered Horn theories. In this case, the consistency problem is NP-complete (and actually polynomial for definite Horn theories), while both the relevance and the necessity problems are Δ_2^P-complete.

The computational complexity of some abduction tasks from logic programs has been investigated in [9]. They determined the complexity of relevance and necessity problems considering subset-minimal and minimum-size explanations. However, they did not consider abduction with penalization, which is the subject of the present work.

5.2   Complexity Results

We study the computational complexity of the main decision problems arising in the framework of abduction with penalization from logic programs. Throughout this section, we consider propositional *PAP*, i.e., we assume that the logic program of the *PAP* is ground.

Theorem 1. (Consistency) *Deciding whether a PAP is consistent is* NP-*complete.*

Proof. (Sketch.) Let $\mathcal{P} = \langle H, LP, O, \gamma, cost \rangle$ be a *PAP*. Membership in NP can be proved by a simple guess-and-check algorithm. We can guess a set of hypotheses $S \subseteq H$ and a set of ground atoms M, and then check in polynomial time that (i) M is a stable model of $LP \cup S$, and (ii) O is true w.r.t. M. Hardness for NP can be proved by reducing the NP-hard problem of deciding if a logic program has a stable model to the consistency problem for a *PAP*.   ∎

Theorem 2. (Optimality) *Deciding whether a set of atoms S is an optimal solution for a PAP $\mathcal{P}$ is* co-NP-*complete. Hardness holds even if the logic program of $\mathcal{P}$ is positive.*

Proof. (Sketch.) Let $\mathcal{P} = \langle H, LP, O, \gamma, cost \rangle$ be a *PAP* and let S be a set of atoms. We can prove that S is not an optimal solution for $\mathcal{P}$ by guessing a set of atoms $S' \subseteq H$ and then checking in polynomial time that (i) either $cost(\gamma(S')) < cost(\gamma(S))$ and $S' \in Adm(\mathcal{P})$, or (i) $S \notin Adm(\mathcal{P})$. It follows that deciding whether S is optimal belongs to co-NP.

For the hardness part, recall the TSP encoding described in Example 7. This example shows how to construct, from an instance T of the traveling salesman problem, a *PAP* $\mathcal{P}(T) = \langle H, LP, O, \gamma, cost \rangle$ such that the solutions of T are in a one-to-one correspondence with the optimal solutions of $\mathcal{P}(T)$. Note that this construction is clearly feasible in polynomial time. Therefore, the co-NP-hard problem of deciding whether a tour for T is a solution for T (i.e., is a minimum-weighted tour) is (polynomial time) reducible to the problem of deciding whether a solution is optimal for a *PAP*. It follows that the optimality problem for a *PAP* is also co-NP-hard, and hence co-NP-complete.

Note that program LP of the *PAP* $\mathcal{P}(T)$ above is not positive. Consider the positive program LP' obtained from LP by deleting rule (3), and let $O' = \{\neg BadTour\} \cup \{ Visited(i) \mid 1 \leq i \leq n \}$ and $\mathcal{P}'(T) = \langle H, LP', O', \gamma, cost \rangle$. It is easy to verify that the solutions of T are in a one-to-one correspondence with the optimal solutions of $\mathcal{P}'(T)$, and hence hardness holds even if negation cannot occurs in the logic program of the *PAP*.   ∎

Given a *PAP* $\mathcal{P} = \langle H, LP, O, \gamma, cost \rangle$, let $max\_cost(\mathcal{P})$ denote the maximum value that the function $cost$ may return over all sets $H' \subseteq H$. In the following complexity results, we assume that $max\_cost(\mathcal{P})$ is polynomial-time computable from $\mathcal{P}$. Note that this is actually the case for all the considered examples, e.g., it is 1 for the network example. Moreover, it is always true if $cost$ is a monotonic function, i.e., if $X_1 \subseteq X_2$ entails $cost_\gamma(X_1) \leq cost_\gamma(X_2)$. Indeed, in this case, $max\_cost(\mathcal{P}) = cost_\gamma(H)$. For instance, the sum function, classically used as the cost function in the framework of abduction with penalties, is clearly monotonic.

Theorem 3. (Relevance) *Deciding whether an hypothesis h is relevant for a PAP $\mathcal{P}$ is Δ_2^P-complete. Hardness holds even if the logic program of $\mathcal{P}$ is positive.*

Proof. (Sketch.) We next show that relevance is in Δ_2^P. Let $\mathcal{P} = \langle H, LP, O, \gamma, cost \rangle$ be a *PAP* and let $h \in H$ be a hypothesis. We first compute the minimum value for the $cost$ function over the set of admissible solutions for $\mathcal{P}$. We proceed by binary search on $[0 \dots k]$, where $k = max\_cost(\mathcal{P})$. Roughly, we perform at most $\log k$ calls to an NP oracle telling whether there exists an admissible solution whose cost is less than a given number or not. Once we know the cost c of the optimal solutions, we make a further call to a NP oracle to determine whether there exixts an admissible solution containing h whose cost is c.[5]

Hardness can be derived from the Δ_2^P-hardness of relevance for abduction with penalties in the restricted case where the theory is Horn [7].   ∎

The complexity of the necessity problem can be proved in a very similar way.

---

[5] Note that the number of calls is polynomial in the input size, since $\log k$ is $O(|\mathcal{P}|)$ due to the succint representation of numbers encoding penalties.

Theorem 4. (Necessity) *Deciding whether an hypothesis $h \in H$ is necessary for a PAP $\mathcal{P}$ is Δ_2^P-complete. Hardness holds even if the logic program of $\mathcal{P}$ is positive.*

6   Conclusion

We have defined a formal model for abduction with penalization from logic programs. We have shown that the proposed formalism is highly expressive and it allows to encode relevant problems in an elegant and natural way. We have carefully analyzed the computational complexity of the main decisional problems arising in this framework. The complexity analysis shows some interesting properties of the formalism: (1) "negation comes for free," that is, the addition of (even unstratified) negation does not cause any further increase to the complexity of the abductive reasoning tasks (which is the same as for positive programs); (2) abduction with penalization over general logic programs has precisely the same complexity as abduction with penalization over definite Horn theories of classical logics. Consequently, the user can enjoy the knowledge representation power of nonmonotonic negation without paying any additional cost in terms of computational overhead. Moreover, the complexity analysis indicates that abduction with penalization has the same complexity as reasoning in (or-free) logic programming with weak constraints [2]. Future work indeed concerns the implementation of the proposed formalism on top of the DLV system [10] by exploiting weak constraints.

References

1. C. Baral and M. Gelfond. Logic Programming and Knowledge Representation *Journal of Logic Programming*, 1994.
2. F. Buccafurri, N. Leone, and P. Rullo. Enhancing Disjunctive Datalog by Constraints. *IEEE Transactions on Knowledge and Data Engineering*, 12(5):845–860, 2000.
3. E. Charniak and P. McDermott. *Introduction to Artificial Intelligence*. Addison Wesley, Menlo Park, Ca, 1985.
4. L. Console, D. Theseider Dupré, and P. Torasso. On the Relationship Between Abduction and Deduction. *Journal of Logic and Computation*, 1(5):661–690, 1991.
5. M. Denecker and D. De Schreye. Representing incomplete knowledge in abductive logic programming. In *Proc. of the International Symposium on Logic Programming*, pp. 147–163, 1993.
6. P. Dung. Negation as Hypotheses: An Abductive Foundation for Logic Programming. In *Proceedings ICLP-91*. MIT Press, 1991.
7. Eiter, T., Gottlob, G.. The Complexity of Logic-Based Abduction. *Journal of the ACM*, 42(1):3–42, 1995.
8. Eiter, T., Gottlob, G., and Mannila, H.. Disjunctive Datalog. *ACM Transactions on Database Systems*, 22(3):364–418, 1997.
9. Eiter, T., Gottlob, G., and Leone, N.. Abduction from Logic Programs: Semantics and Complexity. *Theoretical Computer Science*, 189(1-2): 129-177, 1997.

10. T. Eiter, W. Faber, N. Leone, and G. Pfeifer. Declarative Problem-Solving Using the DLV System. *Logic-Based Artificial Intelligence*. Kluwer Academic Publishers, 2000.

11. M. Gelfond and V. Lifschitz. The Stable Model Semantics for Logic Programming. In *Proc. Fifth Logic Programming Symposium*, pp. 1070–1080. MIT Press, 1988.

12. J. R. Hobbs and M. E. Stickel. Interpretation as Abduction. In *Proc. 26th Annual Meeting of the Assoc. for Computational Linguistics*, 1988.

13. A. Kakas and R. Kowalski and F. Toni. Abductive Logic Programming. *Journal of Logic and Computation*, 2(6):719–771, 1992.

14. A. Kakas and P. Mancarella. Generalized Stable Models: a Semantics for Abduction. In *Proc. of ECAI-90*, pp. 385–391, 1990.

15. A. Kakas and P. Mancarella. Database Updates Through Abduction. In *Proceedings VLDB-90*, pp. 650–661, 1990.

16. K. Konolige. Abduction versus closure in causal theories. *Artificial Intelligence*, 53:255–272, 1992.

17. Papadimitriou, C.. The Complexity of Unique Solutions. *Journal of the ACM* 31, 492–500, 1984.

18. C. H. Papadimitriou. *Computational Complexity*. Addison-Wesley, 1994.

19. C. S. Peirce. Abduction and induction. In J. Buchler, editor, *Philosophical Writings of Peirce*, chapter 11. Dover, New York, 1955.

20. D. Poole. Normality and Faults in Logic Based Diagnosis. In *Proceedings IJCAI-89*, pp. 1304–1310, 1989.

21. C. Sakama and K. Inoue. On the Equivalence between Disjunctive and Abductive Logic Programs. In *Proc. of ICLP-94*, pp. 88–100, 1994.

Causal Simulation and Diagnosis of Dynamic Systems

Andrea Panati[1] and Daniele Theseider Dupré[2]

[1] Dipartimento di Informatica
Università di Torino
Corso Svizzera 185, 10149 Torino, Italy
panati@di.unito.it
[2] Dipartimento di Scienze e Tecnologie Avanzate
Università del Piemonte Orientale
Corso Borsalino 54, 15100 Alessandria, Italy
dtd@mfn.unipmn.it

Abstract Previous work in model-based reasoning and in reasoning about action and change has shown that causal knowledge is essential to perform proper inferences about discrete changes in a system modeled by a set of logical or qualitative constraints.

In this work we show that causal information can also be conveniently used to greatly improve the efficiency of qualitative simulation, pruning spurious behaviors and guiding the computation of the "successor" relation, yet maintaining the ability to deal with ambiguous predictions. The advantages of the approach are demonstrated on test cases, including one from a real application, using a diagnostic engine based on a causal-directed constraint solver.

1 Introduction

A significant part of recent research in Model-Based Diagnosis focused on dynamic systems with automated control [9, 10, 11], since most of the technical systems that demand for some form of automated diagnosis share these properties.

In this paper we address the task of simulation and diagnosis of continuous dynamic systems modeled as a system of qualitative deviation equations [9].

In [11] we showed that the causal structure of the modeled system can be conveniently used to model discontinuous behavior as a consequence of an abrupt fault, and can lead to better fault identification for relevant classes of dynamic systems. This is related to the way causality is used in reasoning about action and change [5, 8, 14].

Here we show how the same causal structure of the model can be used to improve the efficiency of constraint-based reasoning, leading to a backtrack-free strategy which maintains the ability to deal with ambiguous predictions.

The paper is organized as follows. Section 2 introduces the relevant concepts of qualitative modeling. Section 3 discusses efficient reasoning strategies based

F. Esposito (Ed.): AI*IA 2001, LNAI 2175, pp. 135–146, 2001.

on the causal structure of the model. In section 4 we apply the methodology to
a real-world application, the Common Rail fuel injection system. In section 5 we
discuss related work.

2   Qualitative Deviations

Qualitative Reasoning (QR) about continuous systems requires abstracting the
domain of values for variables. Many systems described in the QR literature
are based on a set of 3 qualitative values $S = \{-, 0, +\}$, which correspond
to real number signs. Arithmetic operations, such as qualitative addition ($\oplus$),
subtraction ($\ominus$) and multiplication ($\otimes$), can be defined on this domain.

Applying model-based diagnosis to dynamic controlled systems is one of the
main focuses of research in the field. In [9] an approach based on qualitative
deviations has been introduced. A qualitative deviation of a variable x represents
whether the actual value of x is less than, greater than, or equal to a reference
value for x, which may be varying over time.

This form of qualitative modeling is suitable for dynamic systems in which
some variables are continuously varying (especially under electronic control) according to a number of inputs, therefore a predefined partition of the set of
possible real values into e.g. *normal*, *low* and *high* ranges cannot be given. A
main problem in applying this approach is however the choice of the reference
behavior. We regard the reference behavior as the evolution of the system when
all components are not faulty.

As discussed in [11], this choice has strong influences on fault detection.

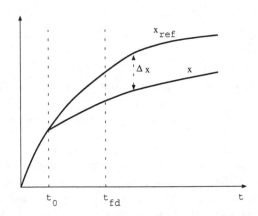

Fig. 1. The example observation; t_0 is the (unknown) time when the fault occurs,
t_{fd} is the time when it is detected.

In particular, a diagnostic problem arises when a deviation of an observable
variable is observed, i.e. the values of some of the variables in the qualitative

deviation model are known and at least one of them is a non-zero value of a deviation.

We assume here that such a *fault detection* is performed independently of the qualitative deviation modeling; e.g. it is performed using a (maybe approximate) quantitative model, or, as suggested in [13], it is provided by subjective observation of a human who detects that some variable is less than or greater than it should be. In figure 1 we show an example. Notice that the deviation cannot be detected immediately, and also the derivative of the variable has a negative deviation.

Qualitative deviation modeling is done as follows. The system is modeled in terms of differential equations that include appropriate *parameters* for components, whose values correspond to different (correct or faulty) *behavior modes* of the component. From these equations, corresponding equations on qualitative deviations are derived as follows:

1. for each variable x, its deviation $\Delta x(t)$ is defined as $\Delta x(t) = x(t) - x_{ref}(t)$, where $x_{ref}(t)$ is a reference behavior;
2. from any equation $A = B$, the deviation equation $\Delta A = \Delta B$ is derived;
3. the corresponding qualitative equation $[\Delta A] = [\Delta B]$ is derived; it equates the signs of the two deviations ($[.]$ is the sign operator). There are rules to transform an expression $[\Delta A]$ into an equivalent one where Δ and $[.]$ are only applied to variables.

As an example, the equation

$$dp/dt = c(f_{in} - f_{out} - f_{leak}) \tag{1}$$

models pressure change in a container, depending on inflow and outflow (plus possibly a leak flow). The corresponding qualitative deviation equation is:

$$\partial \Delta p \longleftarrow= \Delta f_{in} \ominus \Delta f_{out} \ominus \Delta f_{leak} \tag{2}$$

where $\partial \Delta p$ is the qualitative derivative of Δp, i.e. the sign of the derivative of Δp, which also corresponds to the qualitative deviation of the derivative of p. The reference value of f_{leak} is 0, so $\Delta f_{leak} = [f_{leak}]$. The container has 2 behavior modes: the "ok" mode which imposes $\Delta f_{leak} = 0$ (i.e., there is no leak flow), an the fault mode "leaking" which imposes $\Delta f_{leak} = +$.

Equation 2 is a compact representation of a number of situations. E.g. the fact that $\partial \Delta p = -$ may correspond to any of the following cases:

- the pressure should be increasing, and it is increasing less than it should be, or it is steady, or decreasing;
- the pressure should be steady, and it is decreasing;
- the pressure should be decreasing, and it is decreasing more.

In any case, given equation 2, if $\partial \Delta p = -$, then $\Delta f_{in} = -$ or $\Delta f_{out} = +$ or $\Delta f_{leak} = +$, i.e. there is less inflow than expected, or more outflow, or a leak.

3   Causal Reasoning

The basic relations of qualitative addition and subtraction ($\oplus$ and $\ominus$) are satisfied by 13 combinations of values, out of the 27 possible ones. In [3] it is shown that the hardest Constraint Satisfaction Problems (CSPs) are often those where constraints are satisfied by about 50% of the possible value assignments. Then we can expect that solving CSPs in the sign algebra would not be easy. Moreover, $\oplus$ and $\ominus$ are not functional relations, even though they are abstractions of functions; e.g. the sign of the addition of a positive and a negative number is not determined. This is well-known in qualitative reasoning, since the qualitative abstraction over real numbers introduces a loss of information.

In order to solve sign CSPs in an efficient way, we should exploit some structural property of the problem at hand. An approach to do this based on CSP heuristics, in particular a cycle cutset decomposition of the constraint graph, was presented in [12].

In this paper we present a different approach, based on causal information, which, as shown in [11], is also useful to achieve the proper reasoning results, in particular in characterizing the effects of abrupt faults (see also section 3.3).

3.1   Causal Semantics

A qualitative equation, e.g. $a = b \oplus c$, is a constraint, i.e. a non-directional relation among the variables, which can be used to make (perhaps ambiguous) inferences on any variable given the other two. However, we usually have a causal understanding of the behavior of a physical system. For instance, by adding causal semantics to the container pressure equation we write:

$$\partial \Delta p \longleftarrow = \Delta f_{in} \ominus \Delta f_{out} \ominus \Delta f_{leak} \tag{3}$$

where the arrow from the right hand side to the single variable on the left hand side means that the (deviation of the) pressure derivative $\partial \Delta p$ can change its value only if at least one of Δf_{in}, or Δf_{out} or Δf_{leak} changes, and a variable on the right hand side of the equation cannot change, at least as a direct result of this relation, if one of the other variables changes; it could change as an indirect result due to a feedback loop involving other equations.

This gives a stronger semantics to qualitative equations, restricting the set of solutions for each constraint, given the way the constraint was satisfied in the previous state [11].

For example, starting from a state in which all deviations are zero, if Δf_{in} becomes "$-$" for some reasons (e.g. a fault), then the causal semantics imposes that in the successor state $\partial \Delta p = -$ while the other variables do not change, i.e. $\Delta f_{out} = 0$ and $\Delta f_{leak} = 0$. Other possible combinations of values that would satisfy the equation given that $\Delta f_{in} = -$ (e.g. $\partial \Delta p = 0$, $\Delta f_{out} = -$, $\Delta f_{leak} = 0$) are filtered out by the causal constraint.

Notice that the constraint may still be used for inference in several directions, e.g. if from observation we infer $\partial \Delta p = -$, then from the equation we know it must have been caused by one of $\Delta f_{in} = -$ or $\Delta f_{out} = +$ or $\Delta f_{leak} = +$. But inferences from effects to causes should not be arbitrarily mixed with inferences from causes to effects.

In [11] we showed how causal information can be used to appropriately restrict the set of diagnoses. In this paper we show how the causal structure is also used to develop an efficient strategy for intra-state reasoning, i.e. a linear time algorithm for backtrack-free constraint propagation.

In the following we suppose that all Qualitative Deviations Differential Equations (QDDEs) are of the form $v \longleftarrow= expr$, where we intend that variable v causally depends on variables in the expression $expr$. Therefore such an equation can be seen as "defining" v [5]; all the variables influencing v should appear on the right hand side. Then no variable should appear on the left hand side of more than one equation. Each equation of this form is easily translated into a set of ternary constraints on variables.

A directed graph (the *causal graph*) is derived from the set of equations as follows: there is an edge from a to b if and only if a occurs on the right hand side of an equation where b is on the left hand side, i.e. a influences b. We impose that the causal graph does not contain cycles. In the terminology of control theory, this means there are no algebraic loops.

Several approaches [4, 6, 10] exist for introducing this causal information, which is essential to an adequate representation of the behavior of the system. Our causal graph is similar to temporal causal graphs in [10] except that temporal *integrating* edges are not made explicit, so that feedback loops do not appear (as loops) in the graph.

3.2   Using Causality to Improve Reasoning

The causal semantics for QDDEs allows us to develop efficient qualitative simulation algorithms, taking advantage of the following two facts:

- The causality added to each QDDE imposes a direction on the standard relation, which means it reduces the number of tuples that are consistent with the constraint, given valid tuples in the previous state.
- Moreover, the set of causal rules defines a partial order on the set of constraints, which can be used to efficiently solve the model using a backtrack-free constraint propagator.

Causal-Directed Constraint Propagation The causal information embedded in the model induces a partial "causal" order on the set of model variables, and also on the set of constraints. Here we show how to compute this order, and how it can be used to greatly improve constraint solving and reasoning.

Let C be the set of ternary constraints (with causal meaning) of the causal QDDE model. Let $c_i : x \longleftarrow= y \ OP \ z$ be the generic constraint, where OP denotes a qualitative operator. Assign a degree to each $c_i \in C$ as follows: $deg(c_i) = 1 + max(deg(c_j)), c_j \in C_i$, where C_i is the set of constraints in which

y or z appear on the left side. Then, sort constraints in C in "causal order", i.e. non-decreasing order of $deg(c_i)$; let C_{causal} be this sorted list of constraints.

The resulting order is a total order that refines the partial order of the causal graph. Leaves in this graph, i.e. variables that do not depend on any other variable, have a special role since once their values are set, values of all other variables can be computed; in some cases the result is ambiguous, but if x depends directly on y and z, and values for y and z are given, after the constraint relating x, y and z is processed, in case x cannot be assigned a single value, we know that its domain cannot be restricted any longer by processing equations where x occurs, because those are equations where x *influences* other variables, and is not influenced by them.

Leaves in the graph could be state variables, i.e. variables whose derivative occurs in the model, or parameters related to behavior modes of components.

If the system is in a given qualitative state (an assignment of values to qualitative variables — including derivatives and deviations occurring in the model), it moves to a different state when:

1. (*abrupt fault change*): a fault occurs, i.e. a parameter changes its qualitative value;
2. (*dynamics change*): a state variable changes according to its derivative.

In both cases these are the *primary* changes; more changes in the same state will occur as side effects and can be computed given the new values for leaves, according to the causal order. More than one successor state can be computed, because derivative constraints are not functional, and side effects may also be ambiguous.

Since constraints are evaluated according to the causal order, we can solve the model (i.e. find a consistent state or prove the inconsistency of the CSP) without backtracking, then in $O(|C_{causal}|)$ (linear time in the number of constraints, as well as the number of variables).

Causal Simulation Algorithm We first show how causal simulation is defined for a *dynamics change*.

Let S_i be the current qualitative state. Simulation should compute possible successor states of S_i. We will express the algorithm as a nondeterministic one; different choices will lead to different successor states. We will denote a successor state as S_{i+1}. Let V_D be the subset of variables for which a qualitative derivative is explicitly represented in the model. The CD relation (continuity and derivative constraints) shown in table 1, relates the values of (v, v') in state S_i with the value of v in S_{i+1}.

A successor state for a given qualitative state is computed as follows:

1. Consider all possible "primary changes" to state variables, i.e. possible values for v_{i+1} given (v_i, v_i') according to relation CD.
2. Generate all possible *partial* states resulting from such primary changes, i.e. all assignments to state variables where at least one variable changes with respect to the previous state. Select nondeterministically one partial state.

v_i	v_i'	v_{i+1}
-	-	-
-	0	-
-	+	-, 0
0	-	-
0	0	0
0	+	+
+	-	0, +
+	0	+
+	+	+

Table 1. The CD relation.

3. Create the causally ordered list C_{list} of constraints for which a right-hand side variable is a primary change in the partial successor state:

$$C_{list} = \{x \longleftarrow= y \ OP \ z \in C | (y \in V_D \land y_{i+1} \neq y_i) \lor (z \in V_D \land z_{i+1} \neq z_i)\}$$

4. While C_{list} is not empty do the following:
   - Extract the first constraint in C_{list}, let it be $c_i : x \longleftarrow= y \ OP \ z$.
   - If variables y or z have not yet been assigned a value, let $y_{i+1} = y_i$, $z_{i+1} = z_i$, i.e. retain the same values they have in the previous state S_i. This corresponds to assuming *no change for which there is no cause*.
   - Evaluate the constraint c_i to compute x given y and z; this is done efficiently since y and z are now necessarily already instantiated.
   - Use the derivative of x in state S_i (x_i', if available) to filter admissible values for x_{i+1} according to the CD constraints.
   - If the derivative of x is not explicitly modeled, then estimate its value using y' and z'. If y' (resp. z') is not explicitly modeled, then estimate its value using values for y_i and y_{i+1}, which are now necessarily known.

$$y_{i+1} > y_i \rightarrow y_i' = +$$
$$y_{i+1} < y_i \rightarrow y_i' = -$$
$$y_{i+1} = y_i = 0 \rightarrow y_i' = 0$$
$$y_{i+1} = y_i \neq 0 \rightarrow y_i' =?$$

In case the result allows to infer a value for x', use it to filter values for x_{i+1} as above.
   - If $x_{i+1} \neq x_i$ or $x_{i+1}' \neq 0$ then add to C_{list} constraints in which x appears in the right-hand side.
   - If more than one value is admissible for x_{i+1} then select non deterministically a single value.

We notice that the complexity of generating a single successor state is $O(|C|)$; no backtracking is required for constraint evaluation. In other words, each constraint is never evaluated again.

3.3   Diagnosis

Causal simulation is applied to diagnosis of dynamic systems as follows (see figure 2):

- The initial state S_0 is a state with no deviations, and consistent with the correct fault modes for all components.
- State S_1 is obtained from S_0 setting as primary changes the values for component mode parameters for a specific fault F_i, and computing side effects using the causal structure, but relaxing the CD continuity constraints (we intend that F_i occurs abruptly, then introducing a discontinuity).
- Subsequent states are computed using causal simulation as described in the previous section, searching a state matching observations OBS. If such a state is found, then fault F_i is a candidate diagnosis. The search space is pruned when a state with detectable deviations inconsistent with OBS is reached.

The approach is similar to [11], which also provides a formal definition of simulation based diagnosis under the assumptions specified above. However, in this paper we show how processing constraints in causal order can be used both to compute the immediate results of a fault and to compute changes due to system dynamics.

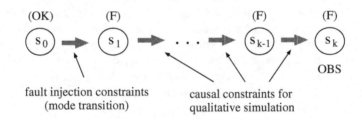

Fig. 2. Causal constraints for both fault injection and continuous change modeling.

When checking OBS consistency, we take into account the fact that S_i can be an "instantaneous" state, and in this case we do not require that it matches observations, because such state is not supposed to be detected by a real-world diagnostic system.

4   The Example System

In this section we present a fragment of a case study: a continuous dynamic controlled system studied within an automotive application project.

4.1   The Common Rail System

The Common Rail is a fuel injection system for diesel engines which is designed to control the injection pressure, as well as the injection amount and timing; this allows better engine performance and lower noise and emissions. To this end, pressurized fuel is stored in a container, the "Common Rail", where its pressure is controlled by an Electronic Control Unit (ECU) through a pressure regulator.

If the rail pressure, measured by the pressure sensor, deviates from the target value, the command to the pressure regulator is varied in order to reduce the difference between the measured pressure and the target value. For a more detailed description of the system, including possible recovery actions and diagnostic tests, refer to [1].

4.2   The Qualitative Deviations Causal Model

Qualitative deviations modeling has been chosen for this system especially because the fuel pressure in the rail is rapidly varying, according to the position of the accelerator pedal and a number of other inputs, therefore a *normal range* of values cannot be given.

A block diagram of the model used for our experiments is shown in figure 3. Variable names on the arcs correspond to pairs of interface variables of components, which are imposed to be equal by the connection. Observable variables are in italic.

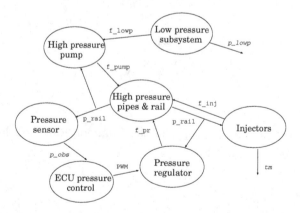

- f_{lowp}: flow from low pressure system;
- p_{lowp}: pressure in low pressure system;
- f_{pump}: outflow of high pressure pump;
- p_{rail}: pressure in the rail;
- p_{obs}: pressure sensor in the rail;

- pwm: command to pressure regulator;
- f_{pr}: flow through pressure regulator;
- f_{inj}: flow through the injectors;
- tm: torque measurement.

Fig. 3. Block diagram of the Common Rail and meaning of interface variables.

The qualitative deviations model for the general behavior of the example system is shown in table 2.

High pressure pump	$\Delta f_{pump} \longleftarrow = c_p \otimes \Delta f_{lowp} \oplus \Delta c_p \ominus \Delta p_{rail}$	(4)
High pressure pipes and rail	$\partial \Delta p_{rail} \longleftarrow = \Delta f_{pump} \ominus \Delta f_{pr} \ominus \Delta f_{inj} \ominus \Delta f_{leak}$	(5)
Pressure regulator	$\Delta f_{pr} \longleftarrow = open_{pr} \otimes \Delta p_{rail} \oplus \Delta open_{pr}$	(6)
	$\Delta open_{pr} \longleftarrow = c_{reg} \ominus \Delta pwm \otimes k_{reg}$	(7)
Pressure sensor	$\Delta p_{obs} \longleftarrow = \Delta k_s \oplus \Delta p_{rail} \oplus \Delta c_s$	(8)
Injectors	$\Delta f_{inj} \longleftarrow = i \otimes \Delta p_{rail} \oplus \Delta i \oplus \Delta f_{inj\_rec}$	(9)
Low pressure system	$\Delta f_{lowp} \longleftarrow = \Delta p_{lowp}$	(10)
Electronic Control Unit	$\partial \Delta pwm \longleftarrow = \ominus \Delta p_{obs}$	(11)

Table 2. Qualitative deviations model of the Common Rail

In addition to the model of general behavior, we considered 13 fault modes for the Common Rail components; all fault modes assing a non-zero deviation to some parameter (see [1] for more details).

Figure 4 contains the causal graph of the model augmented with temporal edges (shown as dotted edges).

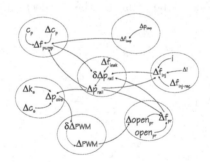

Fig. 4. Causal graph for the Common Rail model

4.3   Results

We compare the results of performing diagnosis with causal-based constraint propagation with respect to a standard constraint propagation algorithm, AC-3 in [7]. The overall reduction for checking consistency of the 13 considered fault modes fo all the 27 possible combinations of observations is from 28802 to 5669 states generated (i.e. more than 80% reduction of search when the causal approach is used, in the average), with an even better ratio for execution times. This last result is due to the gain in extending partial states to complete solutions without backtracking obtained through causal-directed constraint propagation, i.e. improved intra-state reasoning.

The models and algorithms described here have been implemented using C++. We developed a user-friendly diagnostic engine, including a graphical interface for interactive qualitative simulation. The user can control the search method (depth first or breadth first), and the interface highlights the causal chains of changes.

5   Discussion and Related Work

As mentioned before, the modeling approach is similar to temporal causal graphs in [10]. Algorithms in that approach are efficient because they do not reason on complete states of the system, but just on chaining deviations caused by each other within a single state or across states.

However, the approach in [10] does not deal with interaction of causes, which can give rise to ambiguous results: e.g. a cause for a deviating negatively and one for it deviating positively. For example, given an equation $a \leftarrow= b \oplus c$, corresponding to two positive edges $b \rightarrow a$ and $c \rightarrow a$ in the temporal causal graph, and given the observation $a = +$, the algorithm in [10] considers two immediate causes $b = +$ and $c = +$, implicitly assuming $c = 0$ in the former case and $b = 0$ in the latter. If the two backward chaining paths from b and c converge on a shared node, assumptions on b and c cannot be considered independently[1]. Similarly, if there are other observations which involve assumptions on b or c, such assumptions should be combined with those due to a.

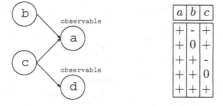

a	b	c
+	-	+
+	0	+
+	+	-
+	+	0
+	+	+

Table 3. Ambiguous prediction scenario and values for b and c given $a = +$.

In our case, the result $a = +$ can be due to 5 different cases for the combination of values of b and c, including ambiguous combinations (see table 3) all of which can be considered depending on other intra-state or inter-state constraints on b and c.

A component-based model decomposition approach for qualitative simulation, similar to our [12] cutset decomposition into subproblems, has been proposed in [2] to cope with complexity and scalability issues in QSIM-like systems.

---

[1] From personal communication with the authors of [10], these issues are being dealt with in latest versions of the algorithms.

6   Conclusions

We have shown how structuring the model can provide efficient ways of reasoning on physical systems; in particular, a causal structure allows reasoning efficiently on the dynamics of the system, yet maintaining the ability of dealing with interaction of causes and with the ambiguities associated with qualitative abstractions.

References

[1] F. Cascio, L. Console, M. Guagliumi, M. Osella, A. Panati, S. Sottano, and D. Theseider Dupré. Generating on-board diagnostics of dynamic automotive systems based on qualitative models. *AI Communications*, 12(1,2):33–43, June 1999. Special issue on Model-Based Reasoning.

[2] D. Clancy and B. Kuipers. Qualitative simulation as a temporally-extended constraint satisfaction problem. In *Proc. AAAI 98*, 1998.

[3] A. Davenport and E. Tsang. An empirical investigation into the exceptionally hard problems. *Proc. Workshop on Constraint-based Reasoning*, pages 46–53, 1995.

[4] Johan de Kleer and John Seely Brown. Qualitative physics based on confluences. *Artificial Intelligence*, 24:7–83, 1984. Also in *Readings in Knowledge Representation*, Brachman and Levesque, editors, Morgan Kaufmann, 1985, pages 88-126.

[5] M. Denecker, D. Theseider Dupré, and K. Van Belleghem. An inductive definition approach to ramifications. *Electronic Transactions on Artificial Intelligence*, 2(1-2), 1998.

[6] Yumi Iwasaki and Herbert A. Simon. Causality in device behavior. *Artificial Intelligence*, 29(1):3–32, 1986.

[7] V. Kumar. Algorithms for constraint satisfaction problems: A survey. *AI Magazine*, 13(1):32–44, 1992.

[8] Fangzhen Lin. Embracing causality in specifying the indirect effects of actions. In C.S. Mellish, editor, *Proceedings of the International Joint Conference on Artificial Intelligence*, pages 1985–1991, 1995.

[9] A. Malik and P. Struss. Diagnosis of dynamic systems does not necessarily require simulation. In *Proc. 7th Int. Workshop on Principles of Diagnosis*, 1996.

[10] P.J. Mosterman and G. Biswas. Diagnosis of continuous valued systems in transient operating regions. *IEEE Trans. on Systems, Man and Cybernetics*, 29(6):554–565, 1999.

[11] A. Panati and D. Theseider Dupré. State-based vs simulation-based diagnosis of dynamic systems. In *Proc. ECAI 2000*, 2000.

[12] Andrea Panati. Non binary CSPs and heuristics for modeling and diagnosing dynamic systems. In *Proc. 6th Congress of the Italian Association for Artificial Intelligence*, September 1999. Also in Lecture Notes in Artificial Intelligence 1792.

[13] P. Struss. Fundamentals of model-based diagnosis of dynamic systems. In *Proc. IJCAI 97*, pages 480–485, 1997.

[14] Michael Thielscher. Ramification and causality. *Artificial Intelligence*, 89(1-2):317–364, 1997.

Critical Parallelization of Local Search for MAX-SAT

Andrea Roli[1]* and Christian Blum[2]

[1] DEIS
Università degli Studi di Bologna
Viale Risorgimento, 2 – Bologna (Italia)
aroli@deis.unibo.it
[2] IRIDIA
Université Libre de Bruxelles
Av. Roosvelt, 50 – Bruxelles (Belgium)
cblum@ulb.ac.be

Abstract. In this work we investigate the effects of the parallelization of a local search algorithm for MAX-SAT. The variables of the problem are divided in subsets and local search is applied to each of them in parallel, supposing that variables belonging to other subsets remain unchanged. We show empirical evidence for the existence of a critical level of parallelism which leads to the best performance. This result allows to improve local search and adds new elements to the investigation of criticality and parallelism in combinatorial optimization problems.

1 Introduction

Combinatorial Optimization Problems constitute an important challenge for Artificial Intelligence and related fields. Even though the most difficult ones are NP-hard and they require exponential computational time in the worst case, the design of efficient and effective algorithms is a very active research field. Especially for very large instances, *complete* algorithms (i.e., they find the optimal solution in bounded time) may require too much computational time, and *incomplete (approximate)* algorithms are preferred. Those algorithms do not guarantee to find the optimal solution in bounded time, but they are generally efficient in finding suboptimal solutions.

Approximate algorithms often employ *Local Search* (LS) as a very powerful tool for solution quality and speed improvement. LS algorithms start with an initial solution and they try to improve it by local changes; those *moves* change a coded solution into a neighboring solution. For example, if a solution is coded as set of binary variables, a possible local move is changing the value of one variable. The drawback is that LS gets trapped in *local optima* which can be very poor with respect to *global optima*; therefore, LS requires a strategy which helps to

---

* Corresponding author. This work was partially developed during a visiting period at IRIDIA – Université Libre de Bruxelles.

F. Esposito (Ed.): AI*IA 2001, LNAI 2175, pp. 147–158, 2001.
© Springer-Verlag Berlin Heidelberg 2001

escape from poor local optima and guides the search toward good ones. General strategies for local search are extensively used in *metaheuristics*. Among these we mention Tabu Search [7], Simulated Annealing [12], Evolutionary Computation and Memetics Algorithms [2, 17], Ant Colony Optimization [5], Iterated Local Search [20] and Variable Neighborhood Search [8]. Surveys and current research results on metaheuristics can be found in [21, 3].

Beside general strategies, an effective yet simple way to improve LS is the *parallelization* of search, introduced and discussed in [13, 4, 11, 10]. The common idea among those approaches is to perform more than one local move in parallel[1]. This local search variant can be also embedded in metaheuristic algorithms.

In [11, 10] the set of binary variables of the problem is decomposed in subsets (called *patches*) and for each subset the value of a variable is changed if this improves the objective function restricted to that subset. A local move can be improving for a subset, but since relations among variables remain unchanged, it can be non-improving for other subsets. Nevertheless, it has been shown that when the system is not divided in patches, LS often leads to poor local optima; but as parallelism increases, LS is able to find better and better solutions, up to a point where the performance starts to decrease again. The conclusion is that there exists an optimum degree of parallelism, which allows to get the best average solution quality. In [13] the authors apply a LS move to each variable with probability p. This means that in each iteration pn moves are performed on average, where n is the number of variables. Hence, the parallelism of the algorithm is pn. They show that there is a critical value p_c such that the average solution value reached is the best for $p = p_c$.

The aim of the present work is to probe whether similar effects can be found also with other local search algorithms and in different kinds of problems. In this paper we investigate the effects of parallelizing a local search algorithm applied to MAX-SAT problems. MAX-SAT is an optimization version of the Satisfiability Problem [6] and it is defined by a set of clauses, which are disjunctions of literals (binary variables negated or not): the objective is to minimize the number of unsatisfied clauses (or, equivalently, maximize the number of satisfied clauses). We applied a parallel version of a local search procedure [19] to MAX-SAT and we discovered the existence of an optimal degree of parallelism which allows LS to reach the best performance. This result supports the general conjecture that the optimization of a system composed of conflicting elements can be improved by dividing the system into an optimal number of components and optimize each of them as if it was the whole system. Additionally, parallel local moves improve algorithm effectiveness, especially for large instances.

This paper is organized as follows: in Sect. 2 we introduce the basic concepts and principles of parallel local search, while in Sect. 3 we describe their application to MAX-SAT problems. In Sect. 4 we show experimental results, which are discussed in Sect. 5. Finally, in Sect. 6 we present conclusions and further work.

---

[1] Moves are performed *synchronously* and they can be implemented either in sequential or parallel algorithms.

2 Local Search and Parallelism

A Constraint Optimization Problem (COP) can be defined as follows:

- a set of variables $X = \{x_1, \ldots, x_n\}$;
- variable domains $D_1, \ldots, D_n$;
- constraints among variables;
- an *objective function* to be minimized $F : D_1 \times \ldots \times D_n \to \mathbb{R}^+$;

Local search (LS) algorithms require the definition of *states*, which are (feasible) configurations of variables and of a *neighborhood function*, which assigns to each state s a set of feasible states $\mathcal{N}(s)$. The simplest LS constructs a path in the state space by moving from a state s to another state in $\mathcal{N}(s)$. The transition from a state to the successor is the result of the application of a *move operator* M (implicitly defined by the neighborhood function) on s. The search stops either when it reaches a local optimum, or when the maximum number of iterations or non-improving moves has been reached.

In [13, 4, 10, 11] some studies on the parallelization of local search algorithms are described. In [13], the authors apply a parallel version of Simulated Annealing [12] to the optimization of NK-landscapes [9, 10]. Suppose to have a minimization problem on N boolean variables; the search space can be represented as an *energy landscape*: the goal is to find a minimum in this landscape. Every variable x_i is associated to an energy value e_i, which is a function of x_i and other K variables. The objective function of the system (total energy) is $E = \frac{1}{N} \sum_{i=1}^{N} e_i$. A move from state s_1 to state s_2 results in an energy difference $\Delta E = E(s_2) - E(s_1)$. The application of the move operator is, in this case, simply a *flip* of a variable (i.e., $x_i \leftarrow \sim x_i$). The basic algorithm behaves as follows: it randomly selects a variable and flips it; it accepts this move with probability 1 if $\Delta E \leq 0$ and with probability $\exp(-\Delta E/T)$ if $\Delta E > 0$. T is a *temperature* parameter, which controls the annealing schedule: the higher T, the higher the probability to choose a non-improving move. In the parallel version, every variable x_i ($i = 1, 2, \ldots, n$) has probability p of being selected, that is, at each iteration pn parallel variable flips are tested on average. Hence, the degree of parallelism of search is $\tau = pn$. The authors discover that there is a p_{opt} for which the algorithm finds the solution with the lowest E: higher or lower values of p on average produce higher total energy values.

Since the effect of a variable flip on the objective function value is evaluated as if it was the only one to change, parallel (i.e., simultaneous) flips introduce a kind of noise in the energy evaluation. As observed in [14], the introduction of noise increases the effectiveness of local search, since it helps to escape from local optima. It is worth to note that [14] shows that the quality of solutions found increases as noise increases, up to a critical value above which the performance decreases again. However, differences and similarities between parallel LS and LS with noise have still to be completely discovered and explained.

Analogous results are reached in [10, 11], where yet a different approach is chosen. The COP is, in this case, the optimization of a NK-landscape with variables arranged in a bidimensional lattice; every variable corresponds to a cell in the lattice and K indicates the number of neighboring cells linked to it. The lattice is divided in P nonoverlapping patches and a simple local search is applied in parallel to each patch. A variable is flipped if it decreases the energy of the patch to which it belongs. The authors find an optimal number of patches which allows the search to reach the lowest total energy value.

The underlying principle of the last approach is that, in order to optimize systems composed of conflicting elements, it is generally useful dividing the system in subsystems and optimize each of them independently. One of the effects of simultaneous changes is to help the search to avoid local optima, as they introduce a kind of *noise* due to the fact that each subset performs a local move supposing the other subsets do not change. Moreover, the authors claim that the optimal subdivision drives the system in a state such that subsystems coordinate themselves for a global optimization goal.

These works on parallelization of search propose very useful ideas for the improvement of local search for COPs and suggest new directions to understand local search behavior. In the following, we present an application of LS parallelization applied to MAX-SAT and we show empirical evidence for the existence of a critical level of parallelism.

We would like to stress that the algorithm of the above-cited and present works are implemented sequentially. With "parallel moves" we mean "synchronous moves". Anyhow, these results could benefit also implementations on parallel architectures.

3   Parallel Local Search for MAX-SAT

MAX-SAT is an optimization version of the Satisfiability Problem (SAT). SAT belongs to the class of NP-complete problems [6] and can be stated as follows: given a set of clauses, each of which is the logical disjunction of $k > 2$ *literals* (a literal is a variable negated or not), we ask whether an assignment to the variables exists that satisfies all the clauses. It is possible to define a representation of MAX-SAT according to the definition of COP given in Sect. 2:

- a set of binary variables $X = \{x_1, \ldots, x_n\}$;
- variable domains $D_1 = \ldots = D_n = \{0, 1\}$;
- no constraints among variables;
- an *objective function* to be minimized: $E =$ number of unsatisfied clauses;

In the literature, effective local search algorithms to solve MAX-SAT have been proposed [15, 1, 22]. In this paper we investigate the parallelization of a simple, yet effective, local search algorithm: MAX-GSAT. MAX-GSAT is a MAX-SAT version of GSAT, a well-known local search procedure for SAT [19]. The high-level description of MAX-GSAT is reported in Fig.1. MAX-GSAT works as follows: at each iteration, it flips the variable which decreases the number of unsatisfied clauses the most. It is not a pure hill climbing algorithm, as it accepts also moves which either produce the same objective function value or increase

procedure MAX-GSAT
Input: a set of clauses α, $MAXMOVES$
Output: a truth assignment of α
begin
    $T :=$ initial truth assignment;
    $MOVES := 0$; $besterror := Eval(\alpha, T)$; $bestsolution := T$;
    while $MOVES < MAXMOVES$ **do**
        if T satisfies α **then return** T;
        $p :=$ a propositional variable such that a change in its truth assignment
            gives the largest decrease in number of clauses of α
            that are not satisfied by T;
        $T := T$ with p reversed;
        $MOVES := MOVES + 1$;
        $error := Eval(\alpha, T)$;
        if $error < besterror$ **then**
        begin
            $MOVES := 0$; $bestsolution := T$; $besterror := error$;
        end
    end while
return $bestsolution$;
end

Fig. 1. High-level description of MAX-GSAT algorithm

it. The search stops when the maximum number of non-improving moves is reached (or a satisfying assignment is found, i.e., $E = 0$). In our implementation this number is equal to the number of variables.

Our parallelization of MAX-GSAT (thereafter referred to as MAX-PGSAT) is straightforward: variables are divided in τ subsets of equal cardinality and for each subset the variable which fulfills the GSAT criterion is flipped. This results in the application of τ simultaneous variable flips. It is important to stress that the evaluation of a variable flip is done as if all the other variables did not change. Relations between variables are still valid, as variable flips are evaluated by taking into account all the clauses a variable is in. The basic MAX-PGSAT algorithm is described in Fig.2.

The composition of subsets can be either decided before starting the algorithm and kept fixed, or it can be reconfigured at each iteration. In our experiments we adopted the second choice, to make results independent of a particularly (un)favourable subdivision of variables.

4   Experimental Results

In this section we describe the experimental analysis on the performance of MAX-PGSAT as a function of parallelism. We tested MAX-PGSAT on random generated unsatisfiable instances with three literals per clause (3-SAT), retrieved

procedure MAX-PGSAT
Input: a set of clauses α, τ, $MAXMOVES$
Output: a truth assignment of α
begin
    $T :=$ initial truth assignment;
    $MOVES := 0$; $besterror := Eval(\alpha, T)$; $bestsolution := T$;
    while $MOVES < MAXMOVES$ **do**
        if T satisfies α **then return** T;
        Divide the set of variables in τ subsets according to a chosen criterion;
        parfor each subset X_k of variables $(k = 1, 2, \ldots, \tau)$
            $p_k :=$ a propositional variable in X_k such that a change in its truth
                        assignment gives the largest decrease in the number of clauses
                        of α that are not satisfied by T;
        end parfor
        $T := T$ with $p_1, p_2, \ldots, p_\tau$ reversed;
        $MOVES := MOVES + 1$;
        $error := Eval(\alpha, T)$;
        if $error < besterror$ **then**
        begin
            $MOVES := 0$; $bestsolution := T$; $besterror := error$;
        end
    end while
return $bestsolution$;
end

Fig. 2. High-level description of MAX-PGSAT, the parallelized version of MAX-GSAT

from SATLIB[2]. We considered nine sets, from 50 to 250 variables and each set is composed of ten instances with a ratio between clauses (m) and variables (n) approximately equal to 4.3 (the *critical region* [16]). The number of subsets τ varies from 1 (only the best flip among all the variables is performed) to $n/2$; at the beginning of each iteration, a number of τ subsets is randomly generated[3].

The graph in Fig.3 reports the average error (number of unsatisfied clauses) as a function of τ for an instance with 100 variables and 430 clauses. This graph shows the typical behavior of the algorithm. Observe that the original algorithm ($\tau = 1$) reaches an average error of 4 and, as τ increases, the error decreases until a minimum at $\tau = \tau_{opt} = 6$; above that value the average error starts to increase.

For all sets of instances, a similar behavior has been noticed.

---

[2] http://www.intellektik.informatik.tu-darmstadt.de/SATLIB.
[3] All subsets have equal cardinality, except for one which contains $\tau + n \bmod \tau$ variables.

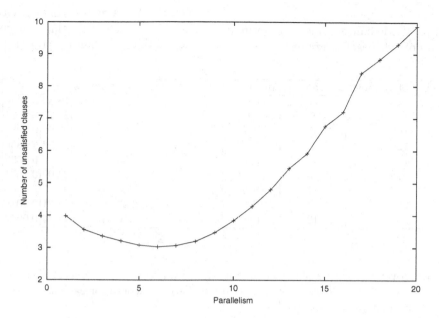

Fig. 3. Average error vs. τ. Instance with 100 variables and 430 clauses. Results are averaged over 10000 runs.

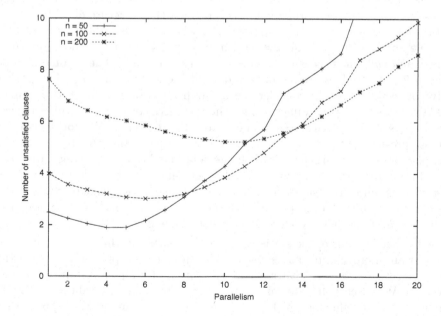

Fig. 4. Average error vs. τ. Instances with 50,100,200 variables and 218,430,860 clauses respectively. Results are averaged over 10000 runs.

Table 1. Median and mean of optimal values of τ for each set of instances.

number of variables	Median τ_{opt}	Mean τ_{opt}
50	4	4.18
75	6	5.9
100	6	6.3
125	7	7.5
150	8	9.4
175	10	10.33
200	11	10.7
225	12	12.36
250	12	12.6

Table 2. Average connectivity and its normalized value for typical 3-SAT random generated instances.

number of variables	q	$\bar{q}$
50	19.88	0.3976
75	21.76	0.2901
100	22.88	0.2288
125	23.33	0.1866
150	23.99	0.1599
175	24.00	0.1371
200	24.11	0.1206
225	24.21	0.1076
250	24.34	0.0973

Moreover, as can be observed in Fig.4, the higher the number of variables, the higher τ_{opt}. This result is summarized in Table 1, where for each set median and mean of τ_{opt} are reported[4].

We conjecture that the fact that τ_{opt} increases as n increases, while m/n remains constant, is due to the decrease of the average amount of *connections* between variables. We define *average connectivity q* as the average number of variables connected with any variable (two variables are connected if they are in a same clause). More formally, let us represent the structure of a MAX-SAT instance as an undirected graph $\mathcal{G} = (\mathcal{V}, \mathcal{A})$, where each $v \in \mathcal{V}$ corresponds to a variable and arc $(v_i, v_j) \in \mathcal{A}$ $(i \neq j)$ if and only if variables v_i and v_j are in a same clause. q is then the average number of arcs per node. The minimum value for q is 0 (all variables are disconnected) and the maximum is $n - 1$ (i.e., $\mathcal{G}$ is fully connected). We will consider the normalization of q, defined as $\bar{q} = q/n$. Table 2 shows the typical values of $\bar{q}$ for the instances considered in this analysis. Fig.5 shows the graphic combination of Table 1 and Table 2. We notice that the curve representing τ_{opt} vs. $\bar{q}$ is monotonically non increasing. As explanation of this phenomenon we argue that when the relations between variables are loose (i.e., $\bar{q}$ is low), a variable flip affects a relatively small number of other variables, thus the system can be subdivided into several nearly independent subsets. On the contrary, tight relations produce a large network of dependencies among the variables and thus they are more sensitive to single flips.

A further analysis of the statistics presented earlier in this section, allows to discover an interesting phenomenon. For example, the graph of Fig.6 shows the average error and the error variance as a function of τ for an instance with 100 variables. We observe that the minimum error is obtained for a value of τ slightly smaller than the value for which the variance has a minimum. We suppose that

---

[4] The average error has been evaluated over 100 runs and then median and mean of τ_{opt} over the 10 instances of each set have been considered.

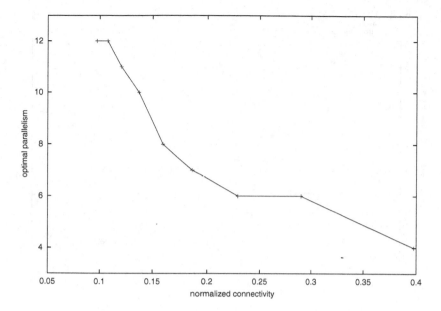

Fig. 5. Optimal parallelism τ_{opt} vs. normalized average connectivity $\bar{q}$.

near the critical value τ_{opt} the algorithm achieves the highest effectiveness and thus it converges toward a smaller region around the best value it can find.

5 Discussion

We think that an explanation for the existence of an optimum level of parallelism can be given in terms of optimal trade-off between *exploration* and *exploitation*, as explained in the following. Exploration is achieved by long jumps in the search space, thus high number of simultaneous flips. Exploitation is obtained by an intensified search in a promising region of the search space. This is achieved with very few parallel variable flips.

It is worth mentioning that analogous results have been discovered in the parallelization of GSAT applied to satisfiable instances of SAT [18]. In this case, τ_{opt} corresponds to the best overall performance, not only as number of solved instances, but also iterations and computational time.

Finally, some considerations about the computational time[5]. The algorithm presented has been implemented sequentially and the complexity introduced by the application of τ simultaneous flips is low. The evaluation of the effect of a flip in the objective function requires a constant computational time, thanks to

---

[5] The algorithm has been implemented in C, compiled with *gcc* (Linux) and ran on a Pentium II 400MHz with 512 MB of RAM and 512 KB of cache memory.

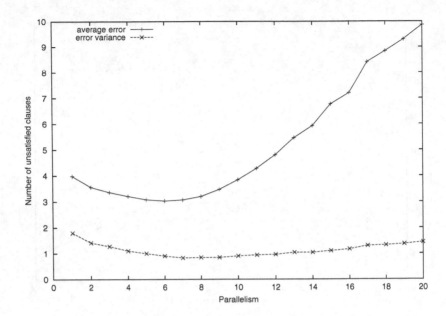

Fig. 6. Average error and variance vs. τ. Instance with 100 variables. Results are averaged over 10000 runs.

an efficient data structure implementation[6]. Thus, the evaluation phase for τ subsets is proportional to $\tau \cdot n/\tau = n$. However, additional computational time is required for updating data structures after τ flips; this time is proportional to τm, because for each variable flip the data structures of all the connected variables have to be updated. Anyway, on the average, this does not introduce a significant overhead; for example, for the largest instances (250 variables, 1065 clauses) the average time ranges from $70ms$ for $\tau = 1$ to $110ms$ for $\tau_{opt} = 12$.

6   Conclusion and Future Work

We have shown that implicit parallelization in local search applied to MAX-SAT leads to a better average performance of search. The parallelization is controlled by a parameter for which there exists a critical value which determines the optimal algorithm performance. These results are adding to previous ones on criticality and parallelism in combinatorial optimization problems, which show that parallelism, system connectivity and quality of solutions are strictly related. Further analyses are required to know whether the phase transition discovered in [13, 10, 11] is present also in the case of MAX-PGSAT on MAX-SAT instances.

---

[6] Data structures are similar to those used in the WalkSAT code retrieved from SATLIB.

We are currently extending the experiments to other MAX-SAT benchmark sets, including structured instances. Moreover, we are testing MAX-PGSAT on very large instances and results are very promising, especially if the parallel phase is subject to a *schedule*, whereby τ is progressively decreased. In this case, the balance between exploration and exploitation is varied during the search process. In a first phase, a high level of parallelism allows to reach a promising region of the search space faster. Then, a progressive decrease of parallelism leads the search to converge toward a good local optimum in that region.

Future work is focused on the study of problem parameters which are linked to the behavior of parallel local search and to the formal analysis of local search algorithms in the context of dynamic systems. In particular, the analysis of the properties of the graph defined by variables relations is very promising. Parameters and properties such like *average connectivity*, *diameter*, *stability* and *percolation flows* can be used to divide the system in clusters of correlated variables and thus find the optimal *ad hoc* subdivision. They also could be useful to extract information about the problem itself.

Acknowledgments

We would like to thank Michela Milano for her suggestions and useful discussions; we also thank Thomas Stützle for having provided part of the code. This work was partially supported by the "Metaheuristics Network", a Research Training Network funded by the Improving Human Potential programme of the CEC, grant HPRN-CT-1999-00106. Andrea Roli acknowledges support from the CEC through a "Marie Curie Training Site" (contract HPMT-CT-2000-00032) fellowship. The information provided is the sole responsibility of the authors and does not reflect the Community's opinion. The Community is not responsible for any use that might be made of data appearing in this publication.

References

[1] Roberto Battiti and Marco Protasi. Reactive Search, a history-base heuristic for MAX-SAT. *ACM Journal of Experimental Algorithmics*, 1997.

[2] Patrice Calegari, Giovanni Coray, Alain Hertz, Daniel Kobler, and Pierre Kuonen. A taxonomy of evolutionary algorithms in combinatorial optimization. *Journal of Heuristics*, 5:145–158, 1999.

[3] David Corne, Marco Dorigo, and Fred Glover, editors. *New Ideas in Optimization*. Advanced topics in computer science series. McGraw-Hill, 1999.

[4] Frank-Michael Dittes. Optimization on rugged landscapes: A new general purpose Monte Carlo approach. *Physical Review Letters*, 76(25):4651–4655, June 1996.

[5] Marco Dorigo and Gianni Di Caro. The Ant Colony Optimization meta-heuristic. In D. Corne, M. Dorigo, and F. Glover, editors, *New Ideas in Optimization*, pages 11–32. McGraw-Hill, 1999. Also available as Technical Report IRIDIA/99-1, Université Libre de Bruxelles, Belgium.

[6] Michael R. Garey and David S. Johnson. *Computers and intractability; a guide to the theory of NP-completeness*. W.H. Freeman, 1979.

[7] Fred Glover and Manuel Laguna. *Tabu Search*. Kluwer Academic Publichers, 1997.

[8] Pierre Hansen and Nenad Mladenovic. An introduction to Variable Neighborhood Search. In Stefan Voss, Silvano Martello, Ibrahim Osman, and Catherine Roucairol, editors, *Meta-heuristics: advances and trends in local search paradigms for optimization*, chapter 30, pages 433–458. Kluwer Academic Publishers, 1999.

[9] Stuart A. Kauffman. *The origins of order*. Oxford University Press, New York, 1993.

[10] Stuart A. Kauffman. *At home in the universe*. Oxford Press, 1995.

[11] Stuart A. Kauffman and William Macready. Technological evolution and adaptive organizations. *Complexity*, 26(2):26–43, March 1995.

[12] S. Kirkpartick, C. D. Gelatt, and M. P. Vecchi. Optimization by simulated annealing. *Science, 13 May 1983*, 220(4598):671–680, 1983.

[13] William G. Macready, Athanassios G. Siapas, and Stuart A. Kauffman. Criticality and parallelism in combinatorial optimization. *Science*, 271:56–59, January 1996.

[14] David McAllester, Bart Selman, and Henry Kautz. Evidence for invariants in local search. In *Proceedings of the 14th National Conference on Artificial Intelligence and 9th Innovative Applications of Artificial Intelligence Conference (AAAI-97/IAAI-97)*, pages 321–326, Menlo Park, July 27–31 1997. AAAI Press.

[15] Patrick Mills and Edward Tsang. Guided Local Search for solving SAT and weighted MAX-SAT Problems. In Ian Gent, Hans van Maaren, and Toby Walsh, editors, *SAT2000*, pages 89–106. IOS Press, 2000.

[16] David G. Mitchell, Bart Selman, and Hector J. Levesque. Hard and easy distributions of sat problems. In *Proceedings, Tenth National Conference on Artificial Intelligence*, pages 459–465. AAAI Press/MIT Press, July 1992.

[17] P. Moscato. Memetic algorithms: A short introduction. In F. Glover D. Corne and M. Dorigo, editors, *New Ideas in Optimization*. McGraw-Hill, 1999.

[18] Andrea Roli. Criticality and parallelism in GSAT. In Henry Kautz and Bart Selman, editors, *Electronic Notes in Discrete Mathematics*, volume 9. Elsevier Science Publishers, 2001.

[19] Bart Selman, Hector J. Levesque, and David G. Mitchell. A new method for solving hard satisfiability problems. In Paul Rosenbloom and Peter Szolovits, editors, *Proceedings of the Tenth National Conference on Artificial Intelligence*, pages 440–446, Menlo Park, California, 1992. American Association for Artificial Intelligence, AAAI Press.

[20] Thomas Stützle. *Local Search Algorithms for Combinatorial Problems - Analysis, Algorithms and New Applications*. DISKI - Dissertationen zur Künstliken Intelligenz. infix, 1999.

[21] Stefan Voss, Silvano Martello, Ibrahim H. Osman, and Catherine Roucairol, editors. *Meta-Heuristics - Advances and Trends in Local Search Paradigms for Optimization*. Kluwer Academic Publishers, 1999.

[22] Benjamin W. Wah and Yi Shang. Discrete Lagrangian-Based Search for Solving MAX-SAT Problems. In *Proc. 15th Int'l Joint Conf. on Artificial Intelligence, IJCAI*, pages 378–383, Aug. 1997.

Product Design as Product Revise: The Case of Chemical Compounds

Stefania Bandini and Sara Manzoni

Dipartimento di Informatica, Sistemistica e Comunicazione
Università di Milano–Bicocca
{bandini,manzoni}@disco.unimib.it

Abstract. This paper presents a model for chemical formulation called Abstract Compound Machine (ACM). The ACM permits to explicitly represent, compute and integrate (as adaptation module) in a Case–Based Reasoning architecture the knowledge about design of chemical compound. The specific application domain described here concerns the design of rubber compounds as product revise in tire industry.

1 Introduction

Product design is a process whose aim is the creation of a new product that has to meet a set of requirements and to offer some needed properties. In many cases, an existing and already developed product can be used as starting point, and, in order to fit new conditions, revised and modified into the new product.

The design of products for which *chemical formulation* is a central issue in the production process is a common problem for a wide range of industrial domains. It involves heterogeneous core competencies (e.g. chemistry, engineering) sharing final goals, although from very different perspectives. The competence involved is strongly based on past experiences and cases (successful and not), and on the ability to adapt previously adopted choices to new market scenarios.

Chemical formulation in industry is a particular problem solving activity for product design, and the knowledge involved has two main goals: to guarantee the reproducibility and the reuse of previously designed successful products (namely, *cases*), and to achieve innovation by the creation of new products, without altering the strong constraints imposed by the industrial production process, in other words, by *adaptation*.

Case–Based Reasoning (CBR) [1] approaches to the area of chemical formulation have yielded very promising results, and several formal and applicative proposals have been developed so far ([2,3,4,5,6]). The adaptation to new situations of solutions from previously solved cases is one of the basic tasks of the CBR approach to problem solving [7].

The main aim of this paper is to describe the implementation of a chemical formulation model for the innovative adaptation of previously developed products to new scenarios and/or constraints in the process of product design. A general model for chemical formulation has been developed by the creation

F. Esposito (Ed.): AI*IA 2001, LNAI 2175, pp. 159–164, 2001.

of a representation formalism called Abstract Compound Machine (ACM). The ACM permits to explicitly represent, compute and integrate in a CBR architecture the knowledge about the chemical formulation of a product. The specific domain that will be presented as an example of the implementation of the ACM model, used as adaptation module, concerns the innovative design of rubber compounds in tire industry. Rubber compounds belong to the class of the so–called *core products*, that is, those components or subassemblies that actually contribute to the value of end products [8]. Anyway, the generality of this abstract model makes it suitable also for other cases of chemical formulations, as long as the basic ingredients in the formulation can be expressed with discrete quantities.

2   Chemical Formulation for Product Revise

Chemical formulation is the design of a chemical compound. Basically, a chemical compound can be described by a "recipe", defining the quantities of some basic ingredients that have to be combined in order to achieve a required property, being "properties in action" the final performance of a compound. Thus, any change in the properties required from the compound implies that some modifications have to be made in its chemical formulation, that is, the corresponding recipe has to be revised. Therefore, the main purpose of product revise is to satisfy some new performance requirements for the product.

The Abstract Compound Machine (ACM) is a model created for the representation and the computation of the chemical formulation of a compound. In the ACM model, a *recipe* of n ingredients is a finite non ordered set $\{Q_1, ..., Q_n\}$, where each element Q_i represents the quantity of the i-th ingredient. A given ingredient belongs to one or more families of ingredients. Each family F_k is described by a set $\{A_1^k, ..., A_m^k\}$ of attributes. Each ingredient, that is each element i of a family F_k, is thus described by a value V_{ij}^k for each of its own attributes A_j^k. If an ingredient i does not belong to a family F_k, the corresponding values V_{ij}^k are undefined. For each attribute A_j^k a constant of tolerance T_j^k is defined. The latter is used in the comparison of two attribute values: two values $V_{i'j}^k$ and $V_{i''j}^k$ (respectively the j-th attribute values for ingredients i' and i'' belonging to family F_k) are considered different only if $|V_{i'j}^k - V_{i''j}^k|$ is greater than T_j^k. These constants are necessary, given the empirical nature of attribute values, and are also used to reduce the effect of possible errors introduced by empirical measurement processes (e.g. lab tests measurements). Starting from a recipe R, a *revised* recipe is a recipe R' where some quantities have been changed. Compound revision follows the application of four sets of rules:

1. *Description Rules*, describing a product already developed as a recipe according to the ACM model, that is, as a vector of quantities of ingredients.
2. *Performance–Properties Rules*, defining which changes are needed in the properties of the recipe, in order to obtain a change in performance.

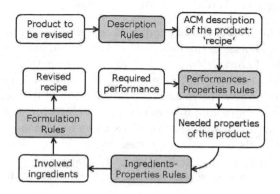

Fig. 1. Activation order for ACM rules

3. *Ingredients–Properties Rules,* defining which attributes of the ingredients of a recipe are involved in the modification of the properties of the recipe.
4. *Formulation Rules,* generating a revised recipe R' starting from R. Three types of formulation rules have been defined:
   (a) *Substitution,* replacing the quantity of an ingredient i with an equal quantity of another ingredient l of the same family F_k (chosen by the Ingredients–Properties Rules), in order to change the value of one or more attributes (V_{ij}^k):

$$if \ (Q_i \neq 0); \ (i \in F_k); \ (l \in F_k); (|V_{ij}^k - V_{lj}^k| > T_j^k) \ then$$

$$\{Q_1, \ldots, Q_{i-1}, Q_i, Q_{i+1}, \ldots, Q_l, \ldots, Q_n\} \rightarrow$$

$$\{Q_1, \ldots, Q_{i-1}, 0, Q_{i+1}, \ldots, Q_i + Q_l, \ldots, Q_n\}$$

   (b) *Increase in quantity,* adding to the quantity of an ingredient a given constant U_k, defined according to the family F_k of the ingredient:

$$if \ (i \in F_k) \ then$$

$$\{Q_1, \ldots, Q_i, \ldots, Q_n\} \rightarrow \{Q_1, \ldots, Q_i + U_k, \ldots, Q_n\}$$

   (c) *Reduction in quantity,* decreasing the quantity of an ingredient by a constant U_k, defined as in the previous point:

$$if \ (i \in F_k); \ (Q_i > U_k) \ then$$

$$\{Q_1, \ldots, Q_i, \ldots, Q_n\} \rightarrow \{Q_1, \ldots, Q_i - U_k, \ldots, Q_n\}$$

Compounds adaptation follows the application of the sets of ACM rules described above, according to the sequence shown in Fig. 1. Within each set, the choice of the rules determines how the recipe is revised in order to reach the desired performance.

3   The Design of Rubber Compounds

A rubber compound is a chemical compound whose main ingredients are artificial or natural elastomers. In tire industry, rubber compounds (in jargon *batch*) is a typical example of core product: it is a basic component of a tire (other components are structural elements) determining its final value and performance. Innovation in tire industry often concerns the revision of its core products. The revision of a rubber compound implies changes in its recipe, that is, a modification in the quantity or quality of some of its basic ingredients (e.g. elastomers, fillers, accelerants, oils, and others). Generally, batch revision aims to change some of its chemical–physical properties (e.g. hysteresis) in order to achieve some needed tire performance (e.g. thermal or mechanical stability).

3.1   Rubber Compounds for Motorsport Car Tires

The case of chemical compound formulation we studied, in collaboration with the Motorsports Department of Pirelli Tires, concerns tread batches for car racing. The competence involved in the design of tires for racing, owned by race engineers, tire designers and rubber compound designers, consists mainly of their experience in the field and their knowledge about a very complex decision making problem. Since they have to make a choice in each single race (where a specific product has been designed and developed ad hoc), their decisions are usually strongly related to performance (e.g. thermal and mechanical stability, resistance to wear) and results obtained in previous races on "similar" tracks (usually in previous championship seasons). The general problem solving mechanism used to solve a new problem is thus strongly based on reasoning about past cases. The use of *episodic knowledge* is one of the main characteristics determining the final choice of a rubber compound.

All the knowledge involved in this problem–solving process can be roughly divided into two main roles. The main aim of the first one is to capture the similarity between past cases and the current one, and to decide how to improve the solution adopted in the past; the second is concerned with the adaptation of a retrieved solution to the new situation according to the improvements required (i.e., the chemical formulation of the new rubber compound). Competencies very different in their nature are present in the two roles. For the first one, no model can be created (if we follow the example of car racing, it is impossible to create a formal model representing the knowledge of a race engineer: a classical CBR approach is the best one for capturing the episodic knowledge characterizing this problem). In the second, a creation of a formal model based on the chemical formulation knowledge owned by professional chemical competence is instead possible, while a pure CBR approach (where each recipe represened a different case [5]) would not be feasible.

3.2   Applying the CBR Approach

In order to support the competencies of the Motorsports Department of Pirelli Tires, a dedicated system (*P-Race*) has been developed (for more details see [6,9]).

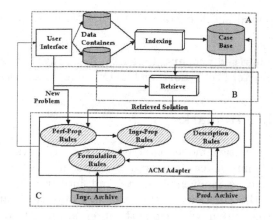

Fig. 2. The role of the ACM Adapter in the CBR–based approach

In particular, it supports the tread batch design activity involving race engineers and rubber compound designers. From the application of the CBR approach to the problem of the design of tread batch for car racing tires we have obtained:

1. A *Case Base*, where each case represents a set of domain data concerning a race or a trial. Each case contains descriptive information (date, time and location of a racing event) and a set of parameters used by the system to retrieve from the Case Base the most similar cases (the description of the parameters can be both quantitative and qualitative, that is, expressed by a fuzzy representation performed by an *Indexing Module* [10]). The solution for a case is the recipe of the tread batch used in that situation. Moreover, a set of attributes specify the performance obtained when the batch was applied.

2. A *Retrieval Module* designed to evaluate the similarity between the current case and the ones stored in the Case Base [10].

3. A *ACM Module*, that adapts retrieved solutions to the current problem. It activates the integration interface with the recipes archive in order to provide to the ACM module the decoded recipe expressed in terms of ingredient quantities (applying *Description Rules*). Moreover, it modifies the recipe of a rubber compound in order to obtain needed performance.

The main components of the P-Race system are outlined in Figure 2. The system execution starts with the representation of the current problem as a case to be solved (part A). The system examines the Case Base containing past cases and retrieves a list of similar cases (part B). The list of solutions proposed by the system could, at this point, include a feasible solution for the problem at hand that could be directly applied. Otherwise, adaptation process (part C) revises the proposed solution, applying ACM–like rules. For example, an Ingredients–Properties Rule encoding the relation between the hysteresis of the rubber compound and the Transition Glass of the polymer is expressed as follows:

if desired_property(high_increase_hysteresis)
then ingredient(polymer) and attribute(transition_glass)

4   Concluding Remarks

The chemical formulation model as adapter in a CBR system described here has been included into a real industrial application (P–Pace system [6]). The chemical formulation component has been put into use after an experimental campaign testing the reliability of the responses on past solutions. The future development of the system will include the integration of P–Race with software systems devoted to the acquisition and the description of track data with telemetric devices in order to support rallies. Moreover, the ACM model will be also employed in the design of rubber compounds for large–scale production of tires dedicated to trucks.

References

1. J. Kolodner, *Case–Based Reasoning*, Morgan Kaufmann Pu., San Mateo (CA), 1993.
2. M.L. Maher, M. Balachandran, D.M. Zhang, *Case–Based Reasoning in Design*, Laurence Erlbaum Ass. Pu., Hove, UK, 1985.
3. K. Börner, *CBR for Design*, in M. Lenz, B. Bartsch-Spörl, H. Burkhard, S. Wess (Eds.), Case–Based Reasoning Technology, Lecture Notes in Artificial Intelligence 1400, Springer, pp 201-233, 1998.
4. W. Cheetham, J. Graf, *Case–Based Reasoning in Color Matching*, in D.B. Leake, E. Plaza (Eds.), Case–Based Reasoning Research and Development, Proceedings of the 2nd International Conference on CBR, Springer-Verlag, Berlin, 1997.
5. S. Craw, N. Wiratunga, R. Rowe, *Case–Based Design for Tablet Formulation*, Proceedings of the 4th European Workshop on Case–Based Reasoning, Springer-Verlag, Berlin, pp 358-369, 1998.
6. S. Bandini, S. Manzoni, *A Support System Based on CBR for the Design of Rubber Compounds in Motor Racing*, LNCS/LNAI 1898, Springer Verlag, Berlin, 2000.
7. D. B. Leake, *Combining Rules and Cases to Learn Case Adaptation*, Proc. of the Seventeenth Annual Conference of the Cognitive Science Society, 1995.
8. Prahalad C. K. and Hamel, G., *The core competence of the corporation*, in R. L. Cross and S. B. Israelit (eds.) *Strategic Learning in a Knowledge Economy*, Butterworth Einemann, Boston, 2000.
9. S. Bandini, S. Manzoni, *CBR Adaptation for Chemical Formulation*, Proc. of the 4th ICCBR, Aha, D.W., Watson, I. & Yang, Q. (Eds.), *Case–Based Reasoning Research and Development*, Vancouver, LNCS/LNAI, Springer, 2001.
10. S. Bandini, S. Manzoni, *Application of Fuzzy Indexing and Retrieval in Case Based Reasoning for Design*, Proc. 16th ACM Symposium on Applied Computing (SAC 2001), Neuro–Fuzzy Applications Track, March 11-14, Las Vegas, USA, 2001.

Belief Revision and the Ramsey Test: A Solution

Laura Giordano[1], Valentina Gliozzi[2], and Nicola Olivetti[2]

[1] DISTA, Università del Piemonte Orientale "A. Avogadro"
Corso Borsalino 54 - 15100 Alessandria, Italy,
laura@mfn.unipmn.it
[2] Dipartimento di Informatica - Università di Torino
C.so Svizzera 185 - 10149 Torino, Italy,
{gliozzi, olivetti}@di.unito.it

Abstract. We offer a solution to the *triviality result* by Gärdenfors. His result claims that there are no non-trivial belief revision systems which satisfy the AGM postulates and are compatible with the Ramsey Test. We show that this result does no longer apply if we restrict some of the AGM postulates to deal only with the non-conditional part of epistemic states.

1 Introduction

In [1] Alchourrón, Gärdenfors and Makinson have proposed a set of rationality postulates, called AGM, that govern *belief revision*, a particular form of belief change. The process of revision modifies the original epistemic state by inserting a new piece of information represented by a formula. The new epistemic state resulting from revision has to be consistent if so is the incoming formula, and it has to differ as little as possible from the original epistemic state. The latter requirement is the so-called Minimal Change Principle.

More precisely, the AGM postulates characterize the revision of *belief sets*, i.e. deductively closed sets of *propositional* formulas: if K is a belief set, and A is a propositional formula, the belief revision operators characterized by AGM postulates return a new belief set $K * A$ in which A has been consistently added. The belief sets considered by the AGM postulates are therefore rather simple knowledge structures in which only factual knowledge of the world can be represented. On the contrary, all the knowledge, such as plausibility judgements, expectations, "revision strategies" that influence the result of a belief revision, are left outside the belief sets.

In [6] Gärdenfors has proposed to enrich the notion of belief set. To this purpose, he has proposed to extend the propositional language $\mathcal{L}$ with the conditional operator $>$, and to consider belief sets as deductively closed sets of formulas of $\mathcal{L}_>$ rather than of $\mathcal{L}$. These enriched belief sets contain therefore two kinds of formulas: propositional and conditional formulas. According to Gärdenfors, the meaning of conditional formulas can be expressed in terms of belief revision by means of the so-called Ramsey Test (RT). The Ramsey Test suggests an acceptability criterion for conditional formulas, which informally claims that the

F. Esposito (Ed.): AI*IA 2001, LNAI 2175, pp. 165–175, 2001.
© Springer-Verlag Berlin Heidelberg 2001

conditional sentence "if A, then B" is accepted in the belief set K if and only if B belongs to the revision of K by A. Ramsey Test has been expressed by Gärdenfors as follows:

(RT) $A > B \in K$ iff $B \in K * A$,

where $*$ represents a belief revision operator.

The importance of the Ramsey Test is twofold. By the Ramsey Test, conditionals and belief revision become two sides of the same coin. On the one hand, the Ramsey Test may provide a semantics of conditionals (i.e. conditional sentences) in terms of epistemic dynamics. This is actually the formalization, in the context of belief revision theory, of the seminal ideas by the philosopher F.P. Ramsey [16] about the meaning of conditional sentences.

On the other hand, the Ramsey Test postulates a correspondence between conditional formulas and belief revision which might be used to represent the "revision strategies" within the belief sets. By means of the Ramsey Test, one could define explicitly a revision operator by a set of conditional formulas. In this way, conditional formulas could provide a way of axiomatizing revision.

Unfortunately, the Ramsey Test is incompatible with the AGM postulates for belief revision, and in particular with the Minimal Change Principle. More precisely, the Ramsey Test entails the Monotonicity Principle according to which given two belief sets K and K', if $K \subseteq K'$, then $K*A \subseteq K'*A$. The Monotonicity Principle, combined with the rationality postulates for belief revision leads to a well known *triviality result* by Gärdenfors [6] according to which there are no significant belief revision systems compatible with the Ramsey Test.

Gärdenfors' negative result has stimulated a wide debate and literature aiming to reconcile the two sides of the coin: belief revision and conditional logic. The proposals can be divided in a few categories. Some authors maintain that the Ramsey Test links conditionals and *belief update*, which is another kind of belief change operation, different from belief revision. [10]. Other authors suggest to avoid the triviality result by considering a weaker version of the Ramsey Test [17,13]. Others, finally, propose to exclude conditional formulas from belief sets, ascribing them a different epistemic status [12].

In this paper we show that the correspondence postulated by the Ramsey Test can be safely assumed (avoiding the triviality result) if we weaken some of the revision postulates so that they only apply to the propositional (i.e.non-conditional) part of an epistemic state.

Moreover, our weakened reformulation of the AGM postulates has an intuitive support. Learning new information may change our expectations and plausibility judgements about the world. In short, even if consistent, new information may change our revision strategies. This means that we cannot assume the Minimal Change Principle on the revision strategies themselves. Since by the Ramsey Test the revision strategies are represented by conditional formulas, we cannot assume the Minimal Change Principle on conditional formulas.

The following examples show that even in the case of consistent revision conditional sentences might be naturally added or removed.

Example 1. A woman has been murdered last night. Mary and John, her neighbours, are the main suspects. To solve up his doubts about who is the murder, the detective decides to look for the gun, believing that if the gun is found in John's room, then John is the culprit, and if it is found in Mary's room, Mary is the culprit. His knowledge base can be formalized as follows:

$$K = (gun\_John > John), (gun\_Mary > Mary)$$

Suppose now that the gun is found in John's room, but with Mary's fingerprints. The detective would conclude that Mary is the culprit and therefore abandon his conditional belief $(gun\_John > John)$. This contrasts with the Minimal Change Principle (and more precisely with AGM postulate (K*4)), according to which the detective's knowledge base after learning the information $gun\_John \wedge fingerprint\_Mary$ has to differ as little as possible from his original knowledge base, and, in particular, it has to contain all the conditional sentences previously believed.

The next example comes from Darwiche and Pearl [2]

Example 2. The same murder than in example 1. The detective in charge of the inquiry believes that only one out of John and Mary is the culprit, and therefore that if Mary has killed, then John has not and, viceversa, if John has killed, then Mary has not. His knowledge can be represented as follows:

$$K = \{(Mary > \neg John), (John > \neg Mary)\}$$

Suppose that he learns that John has killed the woman. He would conclude that John, and not Mary, has killed. However, his new knowledge base cannot be represented by:

$$K * John = \{John, \neg Mary, (Mary > \neg John), (John > \neg Mary)\}$$

like the Minimal Change Principle would impose.

Indeed, suppose that later the detective discovers that also Mary is involved in the murder. Would he conclude that John is no longer involved? No, he would rather conclude that they both have participated in the murder. Therefore, the right representation of the detective's knowledge base after learning that John is the culprit is the following:

$$K * John = \{John, \neg Mary, (Mary > John \wedge Mary), (John > \neg Mary).\}$$

in which conditionals have changed, in spite of the fact that the revision has been done with a consistent information. This clearly violates the Minimal Change Principle, and more precisely AGM postulates (K*3) and (K*4).

The plan of the paper is the following. In section 2 we present our restricted formulation of AGM postulates; in section 3 we show that there is a non-trivial belief revision system satisfying our postulates and the Ramsey Test; in section 4 we consider some related works.

2   Belief Revision

Let the conditional language $\mathcal{L}_>$ be the extension of the propositional language $\mathcal{L}$ by the conditional operator $>$. Let S be a set of formulas of $\mathcal{L}_>$, we define $Cn_{PC}(S) = \{A \in \mathcal{L}_> \text{ s.t. } S \models_{PC} A\}$; the relation $S \models_{PC} A$ means that A is a propositional consequence of S, where conditional formulas are treated as atoms.

An *epistemic state* is any set of formulas of $\mathcal{L}_>$ which is deductively closed with respect to Cn_{PC}. A *belief set* is a deductively closed set of formulas of $\mathcal{L}$. We introduce a belief function $[\,]$ that associates to each epistemic state K its corresponding belief set $[K] = K \cap \mathcal{L}$. A revision operator $*$ is any function that takes an epistemic state and a formula in $\mathcal{L}$ as input, and gives an epistemic state as output. The *expansion* of an epistemic state K by a formula A is the set $K + A = Cn_{PC}(K \cup \{A\})$.

Definition 1. *A belief revision system is a triple $\langle \mathbf{K}, *, [\,] \rangle$, where $\mathbf{K}$ is a set of epistemic states closed under the revision operator $*$, and $[\,]$ is the belief function. The operator $*$ satisfies the following postulates:*

- $(B * 1)$ $K * A$ *is an epistemic state;*
- $(B * 2)$ $A \in K * A$;
- $(B * 3)$ $[K * A] \subseteq [K + A]$;
- $(B * 4)$ *if* $\neg A \notin [K]$, *then* $[K + A] \subseteq [K * A]$;
- $(B * 5)$ $K * A \vdash_{PC} \bot$ *only if* $\vdash_{PC} \neg A$;
- $(B * 6)$ *if* $A \equiv B$, *then* $K * A = K * B$;
- $(B * 7)$ $[K * (A \wedge B)] \subseteq [(K * A) + B]$;
- $(B * 8)$ *if* $\neg B \notin [K * A]$, *then* $[(K * A) + B] \subseteq [K * (A \wedge B)]$
- $(B * \top)$ *for any K consistent, $K * \top = K$.*

Postulates (B*1), (B*2), (B*5), (B*6) are AGM postulates (K*1), (K*2), (K*5), (K*6). Postulates (B*3), (B*4), (B*7), (B*8) are the restriction of AGM postulates (K*3), (K*4), (K*7), (K*8) to belief sets. Postulates (K*3),(K*4) represent the Minimal Change Principle. The restriction of (K*3), (K*4) means that the Minimal Change Principle is restricted to the non-conditional part of epistemic states. As we have argued in the introduction, the Minimal Change Principle cannot be assumed for conditional formulas. A similar remark applies to (K*7) and (K*8) that are a generalization of (K*3),(K*4)[1]. Postulate $(B * \top)$ expresses a rather unquestionable property of revision. It comes for free from the original AGM postulates (K*3),(K*4); we have introduced it as we can no longer derive it from our corresponding (B*3), (B*4).

The restriction we have put on AGM postulates have an impact on the closure properties of belief revision systems. AGM postulates entail that belief revision systems are closed with respect to expansion, i.e. if $\mathbf{K}$ is the set of all the epistemic states of a belief revision system, then for any epistemic state K, if $K \in \mathbf{K}$, then also $K + A \in \mathbf{K}$. This property follows immediately from $(K * 3), (K * 4)$

---

[1] Given $(B * \top)$, (K*3),(K*4) derive respectively from (K*7),(K*8) by taking $A = \top$.

together with the closure with respect to the revision operator. In contrast, this property cannot be derived from our modified postulates. In our setting, the closure with respect to revision does not imply the closure with respect to expansion. As we have argued in the introduction, the revision of an epistemic state with a formula A, even when A is consistent with the state, may affect the *conditional formulas* holding in that state in a way that is not reflected by the simple expansion operation.

As we will see in the next section, these restrictions are sufficient to avoid the *triviality result* by Gärdenfors.

3   Non-triviality

In this section, we show that there is a non-trivial belief revision system satisfying postulates $(B * 1) - (B * \top)$ and the Ramsey Test.

Definition 2. *A belief revision system* $\langle \mathbf{K}, *, [\,] \rangle$ *is non-trivial if there are three formulas A, B, C in $\mathcal{L}$, which are pairwise disjoint (i.e. such that $\vdash_{PC} \neg(A \land B)$, $\vdash_{PC} \neg(B \land C)$, $\vdash_{PC} \neg(A \land C)$), and an epistemic state $K \in \mathbf{K}$ such that $\neg A \notin K$, $\neg B \notin K$, and $\neg C \notin K$.*

To fit our result in its proper place, we recall Gärdenfors's triviality result.

Theorem 1 ([4], page 85). *There is no non-trivial belief revision system which satisfies AGM postulates (K*1)-(K*8) and (RT).*

Actually, Gärdenfors result is stronger, as he has shown that the AGM postulates (K*1),(K*2),(K*4), (K*5) alone, together with (RT) imply the triviality of the belief revision system. In contrast, we show that our reformulated postulates $(B * 1) - (B * \top)$ are compatible with the Ramsey Test, in the sense that they do not entail the triviality of the belief revision system.

We proceed as follows. We consider a Spohn system as defined in [19,2] and we show how to build a belief revision system satisfying postulates $(B * 1) - (B * \top)$ and (RT). Since we have proved in [9] that there is one non-trivial Spohn system, we will be able to conclude that there is one non-trivial belief revision system.

A Spohn system is a structure $\langle \mathbf{R}, *_s \rangle$, where

- $\mathbf{R} = \{k : W \to Ord\}$ is a set of functions from the set W of all classical interpretations to the set of ordinals. The elements k of $\mathbf{R}$ are called *rankings*, and the elements w of W are called *worlds*. It is assumed that for all rankings $k \in \mathbf{R}$, there is a world w such that $k(w) = 0$.
- $k(A) = \min\{k(w) : w \models A\}$.
- The operator $*_s$ of type: $\mathbf{R} \times \mathcal{L} \longrightarrow \mathbf{R}$ is defined as follows [2]:

$$k *_s A(w) = \begin{cases} k(w) - k(A) \text{ if } w \models A \\ k(w) + 1 \text{ otherwise} \end{cases}$$

---

[2] This is the simplified version of Spohn's function proposed in [2]

Given a Spohn system , let $Bel : \mathbf{R} \to P(\mathcal{L})$, be defined as follows

$$Bel(k) = \{A \in \mathcal{L} \mid \forall w \in W \ (k(w) = 0 \to w \models A)\}.$$

Starting from a Spohn system $\langle \mathbf{R}, *_s \rangle$, we can define a belief revision system like the one described in section 2, in which epistemic states are deductively closed sets of formulas in $\mathcal{L}_>$, and the revision operator satisfies postulates $(B *$ $1) - (B * \top)$ as follows.

Definition 3 (Construction).

- *Let $\mathcal{L}*_>$ be the subset of $\mathcal{L}_>$ defined as follows:*
  - *if $A \in \mathcal{L}$, then $A \in \mathcal{L}*_>$;*
  - *if $A \in \mathcal{L}$ and $B \in \mathcal{L}*_>$, then $A > B \in \mathcal{L}*_>$.*
- *First, we define the set $S(k)$ by stipulating:*
  - *let $A \in \mathcal{L}$. If $A \in Bel(k)$, then $A \in S(k)$;*
  - *let $A > B \in \mathcal{L}*_>$ If $B \in S(k *_s A)$, then $A > B \in S(k)$;*
  - *no other formula is in $S(k)$.*
- *Then, we let $K = Cn_{PC}(S(k))$ and*
  $$\mathbf{K} = \{K \mid K = Cn_{PC}(S(k)) \text{ and } k \in \mathbf{R}\}.$$
  We define an operator $*$ on $\mathbf{K}$ as follows
  $$K * A = Cn_{PC}(S(k *_s A))$$
  We finally consider the structure $\langle \mathbf{K}, *, [\ ]\rangle$.

We now show that, given any Spohn system $< \mathbf{R}, *_s >$ the corresponding structure built as indicated in the previous definition is a belief revision system. To this aim, we start noticing that the sets K of $\mathbf{K}$ are epistemic states, as they are closed with respect to Cn_{PC} by definition. Furthermore, we show that the revision operator satisfies postulates $(B * 1) - (B * \top)$. To this purpose, we need the two following lemmas.

Lemma 1. *Given $K \in \mathbf{K}$, with $K = Cn_{PC}(S(k))$, for $k \in \mathbf{R}$, we have that if $\perp \notin Bel(k)$ then $\perp \notin K$.*

Lemma 2. *. Let $K \in \mathbf{K}$, with $K = Cn_{PC}(S(k))$, where $k \in \mathbf{R}$. For any formula $A \in \mathcal{L}*_>$, $A \in K$ if and only if $A \in S(k)$.*

Proof. $\Leftarrow$ It holds by definition.
$\Rightarrow$ By definition, in $S(k)$ there are only formulas of $\mathcal{L}*_>$. If $A \in K$ then $S(k) \vdash_{PC} A$, thus there exist formulas $D_1, \ldots, D_n, E_1, \ldots, E_k \in S(k)$ such that $D_1, \ldots, D_n \in \mathcal{L}$, $E_1, \ldots, E_k \in \mathcal{L} *_> -\mathcal{L}$, and $D_1, \ldots, D_n, E_1, \ldots, E_k \vdash_{PC} A$.
We distinguish two cases: (i) if $A \in \mathcal{L}$, then $D_1, \ldots, D_n, E_1, \ldots, E_k \vdash_{PC} A$ iff $D_1, \ldots, D_n \vdash_{PC} A$, for $E_1, \ldots, E_k$ do not occur in $\{D_1, \ldots, D_n\}$, nor in A. Since $\{D_1, \ldots, D_n\} \subseteq S(k)$ iff $\{D_1, \ldots, D_n\} \subseteq Bel(k)$ and $Bel(k) = Cn_{PC}(Bel(k))$, we can conclude that $A \in Bel(k)$, and therefore $A \in S(k)$.
(ii) If $A \in \mathcal{L} *_> -\mathcal{L}$, then $D_1, \ldots, D_n, E_1, \ldots, E_k \vdash_{PC} A$ iff $A = E_i \in \{E_1, \ldots, E_k\}$, and therefore re $A \in S(k)$.

We now show that the revision operator $*$ defined above satisfies the revision postulates of section 2.

Theorem 1 *The structure defined in 3 is a belief revision system.*

Proof. In light of the previous lemmas and considerations, we have to show that the operator $*$ satisfies postulates $(B * 1) - (B * \top)$.

- **(B ∗ 1)** $K * A$ is an epistemic state.
  This follows from the definition of $K * A$.
- **(B ∗ 2)** if $A \in \mathcal{L}$, then $A \in K * A$.
  By the definition of Spohn operator, if $k *_s A(w) = 0$ then $w \models A$, since if $w \not\models A$, then it would be $k *_s A(w) = k(w) + 1 > 0$. By the definition of Bel, it follows that $A \in Bel(k *_s A)$ and, by the definition of $K * A$, we have that $A \in K * A$.
- **(B ∗ 3)** $[K * A] \subseteq [K + A]$.
  By definition of $*_s$, for any w such that $k(w) = 0$ and $w \models A$, $k *_s A(w) = 0$. Therefore, $\{w : k(w) = 0 \text{ and } w \models A\} \subseteq \{w : k *_s A(w) = 0\}$.
  By definition of Bel, it follows that $Bel(k *_s A) \subseteq Cn_{PC}(Bel(k) \cup \{A\})$.
  By lemma 2, we know that $[K * A] = \{B \in \mathcal{L} : B \in K * A\} = \{B \in \mathcal{L} : B \in S(k *_s A)\} = Bel(k *_s A)$.
  By the same reasoning, we also know that $[K] = Bel(k)$.
  Moreover, we can show that K, $[K + A] = [K] + A$. To see this, suppose the contrary holds. Then there would be a formula $B \in \mathcal{L}$ such that $B \in [K+A]$, but $B \notin [K] + A$. Therefore, there would be some formulas $E_1 \dots E_n \in \mathcal{L} *_, -\mathcal{L}$ such that $E_1 \dots E_n, A \vdash_{PC} B$. But since $B \in \mathcal{L}$, it would follow that $A \vdash_{PC} B$ and that therefore $B \in [K] + A = Bel(k) + A$. We can therefore conclude that $[K * A] \subseteq [K + A]$.
- **(B ∗ 4)** if $\neg A \notin [K]$, then $[K + A] \subseteq [K * A]$.
  If $\neg A \notin [K]$, then $\neg A \notin Bel(k)$. Therefore, there is a world w such that $k(w) = 0$ and $w \models A$. By definition of $k(A)$, this entails that $k(A) = 0$. From this fact and the definition of $*_s$, it follows that for any w, if $k *_s (w) = 0$ then $k(w) = 0$ and $w \models A$. We can conclude that $\{w : k *_s A(w) = 0\} \subseteq \{w : k(w) = 0 \text{ and } w \models A\}$. By definition of Bel, it follows that $Bel(k) + A \subseteq Bel(k *_s A)$.
  Moreover, by definition of S and by lemma 2, we know that $Bel(k *_s A) = [K * A]$, and $Bel(k) + A = [K] + A = [K + A]$. Thus, if $\neg A \notin [K]$ then $[K + A] \subseteq [K * A]$.
- **(B ∗ 5)** $K * A \vdash_{PC} \bot$ only if $\vdash_{PC} \neg A$.
  Since the set W of a Spohn system is the set of all classical interpretations, if $\not\vdash_{PC} \neg A$, then there exists $w : w \models A$. In particular, there exists w such that $w \models A$ and $k(w) = k(A)$. By definition of $*_s$, for any such w, $k *_s A(w) = k(w) - k(A) = 0$. It follows that there exists one w such that $k *_s A(w) = 0$. Therefore $Bel(k *_s A) \not\vdash \bot$. By the definition of $*_s$ and by lemma 1, we can conclude that $K * A \not\vdash_{PC} \bot$.
- **(B ∗ 6)** if $\vdash_{PC} A \leftrightarrow B$, then $K * A = K * B$.
  This follows directly by the fact that, by definition of $*_s$, we have that if $\vdash_{PC} A \leftrightarrow B$, then $k *_s A = k *_s B$.

- **(B ∗ 7)** $[K * (A \wedge B)] \subseteq [(K * A) + B]$.
  By definition of $k(A)$, we know that $k(A \wedge B) \geq k(A)$. By definition of $*_s$, it follows that for any w such that $w \models A \wedge B$, we have $k *_s (A \wedge B)(w) = k(w) - k(A \wedge B) \leq k(w) - k(A) = k *_s A(w)$. Therefore, for any w such that $w \models A \wedge B$, if $k *_s A(w) = 0$, then $k *_s (A \wedge B)(w) = 0$.
  Since $\{w : k *_s A(w) = 0 \text{ and } w \models B\} \subseteq \{w : w \models A \wedge B\}$, it follows that $\{w : k *_s A(w) = 0 \text{ and } w \models B\} \subseteq \{w : k *_s (A \wedge B)(w) = 0\}$. Therefore $Bel(k *_s (A \wedge B)) \subseteq Bel(k * A) + B$ and, by lemma 2, it follows that $[K * (A \wedge B)] \subseteq [K * A] + B = [(K * A) + B]$.

- **(B ∗ 8)** if $\neg B \notin [K * A]$, then $[(K * A) + B] \subseteq [K * (A \wedge B)]$.
  If $\neg B \notin [K * A]$, then $\neg B \notin Bel(k * A)$, and by definition of Bel $\{w : k *_s A(w) = 0\} \cap [[B]] \neq \emptyset$. Let $w \in \{w : k *_s A(w) = 0\} \cap [[B]]$. From the fact that $k *_s A(w) = 0$ we can easily obtain that, first, $w \models A$, and therefore $w \models A \wedge B$; second, that $k(w) = k(A)$. Furthermore, since by definition of $k(A \wedge B)$ and $k(A)$ we know that $k(A \wedge B) \geq k(A)$, we have that $k(A \wedge B) \geq k(w)$, but since $w \models (A \wedge B)$, we conclude that $k(A \wedge B) = k(w) = k(A)$. It follows that $\{w : k *_s (A \wedge B)(w) = 0\} \subseteq \{w : k *_s A(w) = 0\}$. Moreover, since $\{w : k *_s (A \wedge B)(w) = 0\} \subseteq [[B]]$, we obtain that $\{w : k *_s (A \wedge B)(w) = 0\} \subseteq \{w : k *_s A(w) = 0\} \cap [[B]]$. From this, we can conclude that $Bel(k *_s (A)) + B \subseteq Bel(k *_s (A \wedge B))$. By lemma 2, it follows that $[K * A] + B \subseteq [K * (A \wedge B)]$ and therefore that $[K * A + B] \subseteq [K * (A \wedge B)]$.

- **(B ∗ ⊤)** $K = K * \top$. For all k, $k * \top = k$, therefore $S(k) = S(k * \top)$ and $K = K * \top$.

We can now show that the belief revision system of definition 3 satisfies the Ramsey Test, as far as the formulas in $\mathcal{L}^*_>$ are concerned.

Theorem 2 *In the belief revision system of definition of 3, for all formulas $A > B \in \mathcal{L}*_>$, and for all $K \in \mathbf{K}$, we have that $A > B \in K$ iff $B \in K * A$.*

Proof. ⇒ If $A > B \in \mathcal{L}*_>$ and $A > B \in K = Cn_{PC}S(k)$, by lemma 2, $A > B \in S(k)$. Then, by definition of S, $B \in S(k *_s A)$ and, by definition of $K * A$, $B \in K * A$.
⇐ If $B \in K * A = Cn_{PC}(S(k *_s A))$ and $B \in \mathcal{L}*_>$, then by lemma 2, $B \in S(k *_s A)$. It follows, by the definition of $S(k)$, that $A > B \in S(k)$ and therefore $A > B \in K$.

We collect the previous results to show that there is one non-trivial belief revision system satisfying the Ramsey Test.

Theorem 3 *There is a non-trivial belief revision system.*

Proof. (Sketch) As shown in [9], there is a non-trivial Spohn system. We sketch the proof. Let us consider the language $\mathcal{L}'$ containing only the propositional variables p_1, p_2, p_3, p_4. Let $A = \neg p_2 \wedge \neg p_3 \wedge p_4; B = p_2 \wedge \neg p_3 \wedge \neg p_4; C = \neg p_2 \wedge p_3 \wedge \neg p_3$.
Clearly, $\vdash_{PC} \neg(A \wedge B), \vdash_{PC} \neg(B \wedge C)$ and $\vdash_{PC} \neg(A \wedge C)$.

Notice that the set W of all the classical interpretations of $\mathcal{L}'$ will be the set $\{w : w \in 2^{\{p_1,p_2,p_3,p_4\}}$. Consider now Spohn system S' that contains a ranking k' such that $k'(w) = 0$ iff $w \models p_1$.
Clearly, $Bel(k') = \{p_1\}$, and $\neg A \notin Bel(k')$, $\neg B \notin Bel(k')$, $\neg C \notin Bel(k')$. Therefore S' is non-trivial.

Consider now the belief revision system $\langle \mathbf{K}, *, [\ ] \rangle$ obtained from S' by the construction described in definition 3. By construction, there will be in $\mathbf{K}$ an epistemic state $K' = Cn_{PC}(S(k'))$. By the fact that $\neg A \notin Bel(k')$, $\neg B \notin Bel(k')$, $\neg C \notin Bel(k')$, by definition of $S(k')$, and by lemma 2, we can conclude that $\neg A \notin K'$, $\neg B \notin K'$, and $\neg C \notin K'$.

We have shown that there is a non-trivial belief revision system which satisfies the Ramsey Test. Therefore the triviality result does not apply to our belief revision systems. The conflict between the Minimal Change Principle and the Monotonicity Principle has been solved by giving up the first one as far as conditional formulas are concerned (while retaining it for non conditional formulas). As we have seen in section 2, this has been obtained by weakening some AGM postulates.

As a final remark, we have shown that there are non-trivial belief revision systems that satisfy the Ramsey Test with respect to formulas in $\mathcal{L}*_>$, i.e. formulas which do not have nested conditionals (on the left). Since we consider the revision operation as defined only for propositional formulas, a more general form of Ramsey Test involving arbitrary $\mathcal{L}_>$-formulas would have been meaningless. In [4] Gärdenfors does not consider this limitation, as he allows revision by conditional formulas as well. He shows that there is no non-trivial belief revision system which satisfies the Ramsey Test for arbitrary formulas of $\mathcal{L}_>$. However, the restriction on formulas of $\mathcal{L}*_>$ does not affect Gardenfors' argument, for the triviality proof works exactly the same even if RT is restricted to $\mathcal{L}*_>$ formulas.

4   Conclusions

In this paper we have shown how the triviality result by Gärdenfors can be avoided by restricting some of the revision postulates to propositional formulas. In the introduction we have argued that these restrictions have an intuitive support.

The triviality result by Gärdenfors has been widely investigated in the literature. A possible way out to the triviality result consists in considering a different notion of belief change, called "belief update"[11,10], which does not enforce the Minimal Change Principle (not even for propositional formulas). Grahne [10] has proposed a conditional logic which combines updates and counterfactuals and which does not entail triviality.

Recently Ryan and Schobbens [18] have established a link between updates and counterfactuals, by regarding them as existential and universal modalities. The Ramsey rule is an axiomatization of the inverse relationship between the two sets of modalities.

Makinson [14] has analyzed the triviality result in the case the inference operator is non-monotonic and he has proved that triviality still holds in this case.

Rott has suggested that triviality could perhaps be avoided by weakening the Ramsey rule which, in the formulation used by Gärdenfors in the proof of the triviality result, leads to the counterintuitive conclusion that if $A \in K$ and $B \in K$ then $A > B \in K$. However, Gärdenfors [5] has shown that this is not the case, as he has considered several ways of weakening the Ramsey rule that avoid the counterintuitive conclusion but still lead to triviality.

Lindström and Rabinowicz in [13] discuss some alternative solutions to Gärdenfors negative result such as questioning preservation, weakening the Ramsey rule, leaving the conditional formulas out of the belief sets, and making the evaluation of conditionals dependent on the epistemic state.

Levi [12] has proposed a way out to the triviality problem based on a strict separation between conditional and non-conditional beliefs. The triviality is avoided by assuming that conditional sentences cannot be members of belief sets, consequently the belief operator only applies to sets of propositional beliefs and therefore revision postulates are naturally restricted to propositional belief sets. In this respect our approach has some similiarity with Levi's one. As a difference, we only restrict *some* of the postulates and we allow the occurrence of conditionals in epistemic states, including iterated conditionals whose acceptance (whence meaning) is not defined in Levi's framework.

The last approach is close to the one proposed in [9] to define a conditional logic for revision, as well as to the one developed in [3], which defines a logical framework for modeling both revision and update. The fact that in both [9] and [3] triviality does not occur seems to be explainable by the fact that, besides leaving the conditional formulas out of the belief sets (so that postulates are only required to hold for propositional formulas), epistemic states are considered to be complete with respect to some conditional formulas and that, in essence, a stronger version of the Ramsey Test is adopted. In this paper we have shown that a solution to the Triviality Result can be found also in the case in which epistemic states are not assumed to be complete with respect to conditional formulas.

References

1. C.E. Alchourrón, P. Gärdenfors, D. Makinson, On the logic of theory change: partial meet contraction and revision functions, *Journal of Symbolic Logic*, 50:510–530, 1985.
2. A. Darwiche, J. Pearl, On the logic of iterated belief revision, *Artificial Intelligence* 89: 1-29, 1997.
3. N. Friedman, J.Y. Halpern, Conditional Logics of Belief Change, *in* Proceedings of the National Conference on Artificial Intelligence (AAAI 94):915-921, 1994.
4. P. Gärdenfors, Belief Revision and the Ramsey Test for Conditionals, *The Philosophical Review*, 1996.

5. P. Gärdenfors, Variations on the Ramsey Test: more Triviality Results, *Studia Logica* 46: 319-325, 1987.
6. P. Gärdenfors, Knowledge in flux: modeling the dynamics of epistemic states, MIT Press, Cambridge, Massachussets, 1988.
7. L. Giordano, V. Gliozzi, N. Olivetti, A Conditional Logic for Belief Revision, in Proc. JELIA'98, LNAI 1489, Springer, 294–308, 1998.
8. L. Giordano, V. Gliozzi, N. Olivetti, A Conditional Logic for Iterated Belief Revision, in ECAI2000, Proc. 14th European Conference on Artificial Intelligence, W. Horn (ed.), IOS Press, Berlin, 2000.
9. L. Giordano, V. Gliozzi, N. Olivetti, Conditional Logic and Iterated Belief Revision, *Studia Logica*, Special Issue on Belief Revision, 2001.
10. G. Grahne, Updates and Counterfactuals, *Journal of Logic and Computation*, Vol 8 No.1:87-117, 1998.
11. H. Katsuno, A.O. Mendelzon, On the Difference between Updating a Knowledge Base and Revising it, *in* Proceedings of the Second International Conference on Principles of Knowledge Representation and Reasoning, 1991
12. I. Levi, Iteration of Conditionals and the Ramsey Test, *Synthese*, 76: 49-81, 1988.
13. S. Lindström, W. Rabinowicz, The Ramsey Test revisited, *in* Crocco, Fariñas del Cerro, Herzig (eds.) Conditionals from Philosophy to Computer Science, Oxford University Press, 1995.
14. D. Makinson, The Gärdenfors impossibility theorem in non-monotonic contexts, *Studia Logica*, vol 46: 1-6, 1990.
15. W. Nejdl, M. Banagl, Asking About Possibilities- Revision and Update semantics for Subjunctive Queries, *in* Lakemayer, Nebel, Lecture Notes in Artificial Intelligence: 250-274, 1994.
16. F.P. Ramsey, *in* A. Mellor (editor), Philosophical Papers, Cambridge University Press, Cambridge, 1990.
17. H. Rott, Ifs, though and because, *Erkenntnis*, vol.25, pp.345-370.
18. M. D. Ryan and P.-Y. Schobbens. Counterfactuals and updates as inverse modalities. *Journal of Logic, Language and Information*, 6, pp. 123-146, 1997.
19. W. Spohn, Ordinal conditional functions: a dynamic theory of epistemic states, *in* W. L. Harper and B. Skyrms, (eds.), Causation in Decision, Belief Change and Statistics 2, 105-134, 1987.

Supporting Product Configuration in a Virtual Store

Diego Magro and Pietro Torasso

Dipartimento di Informatica, Università di Torino
Corso Svizzera 185; 10149 Torino; Italy
{magro, torasso}@di.unito.it

Abstract. In the present paper we shall analyse the main requirements and the general architecture of a system able to support a customer in configuring a complex product in a virtual store on the Web. Moreover, we shall present the conceptual language adopted for modelling the application domains and we shall sketch the main reasoning mechanisms involved in the interactive configuration process.

1 Introduction

Recent development in Web technologies has opened important opportunities for developing new interactive services. Among others, the possibility for a customer to access a wide variety of information about products or services has paved the way for systems which embed an intelligent component for supporting the customer in such activity. Both user-adaptive systems and recommender systems have been developed [9]. In most of these systems (included the work done at "Dipartimento di Informatica" in developing SeTA [2]) the attention is mainly devoted to the technique for acquiring (and learning) the user needs and in selecting the products (or services) which best match these needs. In most cases there is the implicit assumption that the product or the service cannot be modified to mach the user requirements (i.e. it is not configurable), and therefore the problem is to propose the user with the products that satisfy some of her/his needs or preferences.

Whilst this approach is adequate for some relevant domains, it is does not fully exploit the experience gained in the last two decades in developing knowledge-based systems in a variety of tasks (from diagnosis to planning, from design to configuration). In particular, in the last decade several innovative approaches to configuration have been investigated and efficient systems able to configure very complex technical systems have been developed (see [11] for a review). This experience is potentially quite useful for supplementing recommender systems with the ability of configuring a product by assembling it starting from a set of simpler devices and subcomponents. However, it is worth noting that several important differences exist between systems devoted to technical and physical configuration and tools for supporting configuration in the interactive environment of the Web. In particular, technical configuration can start just

F. Esposito (Ed.): AI*IA 2001, LNAI 2175, pp. 176–188, 2001.

when the specifications on the functions and the requirements of the complex system to build have been identified;

moreover, the result is often a physical configuration in terms of a detailed description of the connections between the different devices that compose the system. These assumptions do not always hold when we consider the role of a system able to support a customer in configuring a complex product in a virtual store on the Web.

In the present paper we analyse the main requirements of such a system and we describe the general architecture of a system we have developed. Such a system acts as an intelligent configurator agent in a Web accessible virtual store. In particular, we discuss the representation language adopted for modelling the domain entities and the constraints among them. Furthermore, the paper sketches the main reasoning mechanisms involved in the interactive configuration process. In the discussion section, we briefly comment on the similarities and differences between the proposed approach and the ones used in technical configuration. In the paper, we use the PC domain as a running example.

2 $\mathcal{FPC}$: A Conceptual Modelling Language

Basic Domain Concepts. An important distinction concerns the dichotomy between *atomic* and *complex* products. All products that are sold "as they are" (e.g. a CD writer or a keyboard) are considered as *atomic* (i.e. their internal structure, that can be quite complex, is of no interest for the task). A *complex product* can be viewed as a structured entity whose subparts can be complex products in their turn or atomic ones. Complex products are not directly available to a customer, but they can be built by assembling a set of atomic products. Thus a configuration process is responsible for specifying how the atomic products should be assembled in order to build an instance of a complex product satisfying a set of requirements. The configuration process has to take into account the *constraints* restricting the set of valid combinations of components and subcomponents. Let us consider for example the PC domain: a PC is a complex product made up of (among other components) a case, one or two disk drives and a motherboard. In the motherboard (a complex object) there can be a controller SCSI. However, if the main printed circuit board is of type SCSI no additional controller SCSI is needed, while such a controller is mandatory in a PC having a SCSI device (e.g. a SCSI CD writer) and whose main printed circuit board is of type EIDE. The representation formalism should have sufficient expressive power to capture these constraints. Since both atomic and complex products have *properties* and features characterizing them, the representation formalism has to provide the typical tools for structuring a domain: *taxonomic* relations and inheritance of properties. More important, the formalism has to model the *whole-part relation* between a complex product and each one of its components since this is a special kind of property that plays a central role in the considered task.

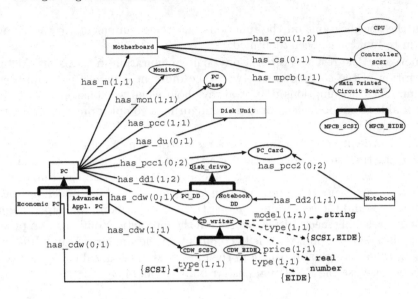

Fig. 1. A sample (portion of a) conceptual model

It is worth pointing out that the basic requirements and distinctions in the representation formalism are only those relevant to the particular task.

If, for example, the task were the technical configuration of the products, also the concepts of *physical connection* and *port* would be important and thus they should be modelled. Moreover, the granularity of the entities could vary from one task to another: the internal structure of some products that are considered *atomic* for this task (e.g. a monitor) would be important if the task were, for example, repair or manufacturing.

The Conceptual Language $\mathcal{FPC}$. $\mathcal{FPC}$ (Frames, Parts and Constraints), on the one hand, is a simple frame-based language able to represent the *classes* of products as well as the *taxonomic relations* among them. On the other hand, it offers the facility of building the *partonomies* that (recursively) express the *whole-part relations* between each complex product and any one of its components. Moreover, $\mathcal{FPC}$ allows one to represent the *constraints* among the components and the subcomponents of complex products.

Frames and Parts. Each *frame* represents a *class* of products (either *atomic* or *complex*) and it has a set of *member slots* associated to it. Each slot represents a *property* of the products belonging to the class and it can be of type either *partonomic* or (alternatively) *descriptive*. Any slot p of a class C is described via a value restriction (that can be another class or a set of values of a predefined kind) and a number restriction (i.e. an integer interval $[m,n]$ with $m \leq n$), as usual in the KL-ONE like representation formalisms. In the following, given a slot p of a class C, we indicate the value restiction of p (also called the *codomain* of the slot p) with $cod(C, \langle p \rangle)$, while $C_{min}(C, \langle p \rangle)$ and $C_{max}(C, \langle p \rangle)$ indicate, respectively, the lower bound m and the upper bound n of the number restriction.

Formally, a slot p with value restriction $cod(C, \langle p \rangle) = D$ and number restriction $[m,n]$ captures the fact that the property p for any product of type C is expressed by a (multi)set of values of type D whose cardinality belongs to the interval $[m,n]$.

Partonomic slots are used for capturing the *whole-part relation* between a complex object and a subcomponent. This relation corresponds to the *complex-component relation* described in [4] and it is asymmetric and transitive. Formally, any partonomic slot p of a class C is interpreted as a relation from C to $cod(C, \langle p \rangle) = D$ such that $(\forall c \in C)(C_{min}(C, \langle p \rangle) \leq |p(c)| \leq C_{max}(C, \langle p \rangle))$; the meaning is straightforward:

any complex product of type C has from a minimum of $C_{min}(C, \langle p \rangle)$ up to a maximum of $C_{max}(C, \langle p \rangle)$ subparts of type D via a whole-part relation named p. [1] Figure 1 contains a small (simplified) portion of a conceptual model relevant to the PC domain. Each rectangle represents a class of complex products and each oval represents a class of atomic products; any thin solid arrow corresponds to a partonomic slot whilst each thin dashed arrow corresponds to a descriptive slot. In the figure, it is stated that each PC contains exactly one motherboard, one or two disk drives, an optional CD writer and so on. A CD writer is described by its model (denoted by a string), its type (either SCSI or EIDE) its price (expressed as a real number), etc.

In order to simplify the notation adopted in the next sections we introduce the notion of *slot chain*: a slot chain $\gamma = \langle p_1, \ldots, p_n \rangle (n \geq 0)$, starting in a class C is interpreted as the relation composition $p_n \circ p_{n-1} \circ \ldots \circ p_1$. The empty slot chain $\langle \rangle$ is interpreted as the identity function. If p_n is a partonomic slot, the chain represents the subcomponents of a complex product $c \in C$ via the *whole-part relations* named $p_1, \ldots, p_n$. If p_n is a descriptive slot, this chain represents the values of the property p_n for the subcomponents of c via the *whole-part* relations $p_1, \ldots, p_{n-1}$. Given $\gamma = \langle p_1, \ldots, p_n \rangle$ starting in C ,let $cod(C, \langle p_1 \rangle) = D_1, \ldots, cod(D_{n-1}, \langle p_n \rangle) = D_n$. D_n is the *codomain* of the slot chain γ starting in C and it is indicated with $cod(C, \gamma)$ $(cod(C, \langle \rangle) = C)$. Similarly, a set of slot chains $R = \{\gamma_1, \ldots, \gamma_m\}(m \geq 1)$ (each one starting in C) is interpreted as the relation union $\bigcup_{i=1}^{m} \gamma_i$ (we have $cod(C, R) = \bigcup_{i=1}^{m} cod(C, \gamma_i)$). For example, the chain $\langle has\_m, has\_CPU \rangle$ starting in the class PC, in figure 1, represents the set of CPUs of a PC and $cod(PC, \langle has\_m, has\_CPU \rangle) = CPU$. The set of slot chains starting in PC $\{\langle has\_m, has\_CPU \rangle, \langle has\_m, has\_cs \rangle\}$ represents the set containing the CPU(s) and the controller SCSI (if any) of any PC. We have $cod(PC, \{\langle has\_m, has\_CPU \rangle, \langle has\_m, has\_cs \rangle\}) = CPU \cup Controller\_SCSI$.

In our formalism, the partonomy plays a major role in defining the inferential mechanisms (in particular configuration). However, also the taxonomy can be useful for modelling the domain. For this reason, we have adopted a simplified

---

[1] To be precise, we should always distinguish between a *frame*, which is a language element, and the *class* that it describes. However, in order to simplify the presentation, we use the words *frame* and *class* as synonyms. Analogously, we don't distinguish between a *slot* and the *property*, either descriptive or partonomic, that it represents (defined as a *mathematical relation*).

version of the taxonomic links present in the KL-One like languages, but we have maintained a strict notion of inheritance [1]. More specifically, the *taxonomy* has a root representing the class of all products, each class (but the root) has exactly one superclass and the direct subclasses of any class C always represent a partitioning of C. Each subclass can refine the description of its superclass by adding new slots (w.r.t. those inherited from its superclass) or by *restricting* the number restriction interval or the codomain of any inherited slot. In figure 1 the subclass links are represented by thick solid arrows. Following that conceptual model, a generic PC has an *optional* CD writer, but an Advanced Applications PC has *exactly one* CD writer (i.e. the number restriction interval of the slot *has_cdw* has been restricted) that must be of type CDW_SCSI (i.e. the codomain of the slot *has_cdw* has been restricted too). We note that if $\delta = \langle has\_cdw, type \rangle$, we have $cod(PC, \delta) = \{SCSI, EIDE\}$, $cod(Economic\_PC, \delta) = \{EIDE\}$ and $cod(Adv.\_Appl.\_PC, \delta) = \{SCSI\}$.

In any conceptual model, no cycle involving subclass links, partonomic links or both is allowed.

<u>Constraints</u>. A set (possibly empty) of *constraints* is associated to each class of complex objects. These constraints allow one to express those restrictions on the components and the subcomponents of the complex products that can't be expressed by using only the frame portion of $\mathcal{FPC}$, in particular the inter-slot constraints that cannot be modelled via the number restrictions or the value restrictions.

Each constraint cc associated to C is of the form $\alpha \Rightarrow \beta$, where α is a conjunction of predicates or the boolean constant *true* and β is a predicate or the boolean constant *false*. The meaning is that for every complex product $c \in C$, if c satisfies α then it must satisfy β. It should be clear that if $\alpha = true$, then, for each $c \in C$, β must always hold, while if $\beta = false$, then, for each $c \in C$, α can never hold. The constraint *true* $\Rightarrow$ *false* is forbidden.

Each subclass inherits all the constraints of its superclass, and it can introduce new constraints (w.r.t. those inherited).

In order to give an idea of the constraint language we first introduce some of the basic predicates that can occur in a constraint:

Let $R = \{\gamma_1, \ldots, \gamma_m\} (m \geq 1)$, where each $\gamma_i = \langle p_{i_1}, \ldots p_{i_n} \rangle (n \geq 1)$ is a slot chain starting in a class of C complex products. For any $c \in C$, $R(c)$ indicates the values of the relation R computed for c. The last slots of the chains occurring in R can either be all descriptive or all partonomic. In the former case, $R(c)$ can, in general, be a multiset of property values, while in the latter it represents a set of components.

1) $(R)(h;k)$. $c \in C$ satisfies the predicate *iff* $h \leq |R(c)| \leq k$, where h, k are non negative integers with $h \leq k$ and $R(c)$ is a set of components.

2) $(R)(inI)$. $I = I_1 \cup \ldots \cup I_s (s \geq 1)$ and each $I_j (j = 1, \ldots, s)$ is a class. $c \in C$ satisfies the predicate *iff* $R(c) \subseteq I$. $R(c)$ can be a set of components or a (multi)set of property values.

3) $(R)(inI(h; k))$. $I = I_1 \cup \ldots \cup I_s$ and each $I_j (j = 1, \ldots, s)$ is a class. $c \in C$ satisfies the predicate *iff* $h \le |R(c) \cap I| \le k$, where h, k are non negative integers with $h \le k$ and $R(c)$ is a set of components.

4) $(\Sigma(R))$ *RelOp* n. $c \in C$ satisfies the predicate *iff* $(\sum_{i \in R(c)} i)$ *RelOp* n, where n is a number, *RelOp* $\in \{=, <, >, \le, \ge\}$ and $R(c)$ is a (multi)set of numeric properties values.

These types of predicates are sufficient for building many constraints that capture typical restrictions and interdependencies in the PC domain. Some examples are listed below:

[co1]: *"In any Motherboard, if the main printed circuit board is of type SCSI, there mustn't be any additional controller SCSI"*:
$(\{\langle has\_mpcb\rangle\})(inMPCB\_SCSI) \Rightarrow (\{\langle has\_cs\rangle\})(0; 0)$ (associated to the Motherboard class)

[co2] *"In any PC, if there is a CD writer of type SCSI and the main printed circuit board is of type EIDE, then a controller SCSI is needed"*:
$(\{\langle has\_cdw\rangle\})(inCDW\_SCSI(1; 1)) \wedge (\{\langle has\_m, has\_mpcb\rangle\})(inMPCB\_EIDE) \Rightarrow (\{\langle has\_m, has\_cs\rangle\})(1; 1)$ (associated to the PC class)

[co3] *"The total price of all the atomic components of an economic PC must be less than 1000 EUROs"* (assuming that each class of atomic products has the slot *price*):
$true \Rightarrow$
$(\Sigma(\{\langle has\_m, has\_cpu, price\rangle, \langle has\_m, has\_cs, price\rangle,$
$\langle has\_m, has\_mpcb, price\rangle, \ldots \})) < 1000$ (associated to the Economic PC class)

[co4] *"Any PC for advanced applications must have two CPUs"*
$true \Rightarrow (\{\langle has\_m, has\_cpu\rangle\})(2; 2)$ (associated to the Advanced Appl. PC class).

3   System Functions and Problem Solving Capabilities

As stated in the introduction, the goal of the system is to support a customer in selecting the set of components that can be configured to form a complex product satisfying her/his needs. This goal can be achieved by combining reasoning mechanisms able to perform configuration with mechanisms for interacting with the customer. Figure 2 sketches the information and the control flows in the system. The system provides three main functions

(Hypothesize, Configure, Change/Expand configurations), each one exploiting suitable reasoning mechanisms (detailed below) and using the conceptual model of the domain represented in the $\mathcal{FPC}$ language. It is worth noting that the process is iterative since, at the end of each activity, the customer can revise her/his requirements (as depicted by the control arrows).

(1). The system interacts with the customer in order to get from her/him both the set $\mathcal{PRODS}$ of complex product types the customer is interested in and the set $\mathcal{CH}$ of atomic components that the customer wants to be included in the complex product. Since the system cannot assume that the customer is an expert of the domain and that she/he knows exactly from the real beginning what kind of product she/he needs, the interaction has the goal of eliciting

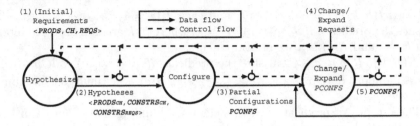

Fig. 2. System Overview

other kinds of information that can in some way restrict $\mathcal{PRODS}$. Thus, the system allows the customer to include into $\mathcal{PRODS}$ more than one kind of complex product (all those that the customer feels they might satisfy her/his needs). If the customer isn't able to indicate any set of complex product types, $\mathcal{PRODS}$ contains all those ones available in the store. Moreover, the system presents the customer with a (predefined) set of requirements about the most relevant features of the complex products, so that the customer can select the ones she/he is more interested in ($\mathcal{REQS}$).

(2). The task *hypothesize* exploits the set $\mathcal{CH}$ of atomic products chosen by the customer for performing a preliminary test of consistency with the set of complex products $\mathcal{PRODS}$ [2] indicated by the customer and for figuring which complex products mentioned in $\mathcal{PRODS}$ are suitable candidates for configuration. In particular, the set $\mathcal{PRODS}_{\mathcal{CH}}$ is inferred by means of the *Hypothesis Formulation* reasoning mechanism.

Hypothesis Formulation. This mechanism filters out those classes in $\mathcal{PRODS}$
whose instances *can't* have as (sub)parts all the atomic products of the kinds chosen by the customer. All the other classes of products are considered as *plausible hypotheses*.

This inference mechanism makes use of the following relation (recursively defined). Let C_1 and C_2 be two product classes of a conceptual model. A nonempty slot chain γ starting in C_1 is an *actual path* from C_1 to C_2 (written $C_1[\gamma] \rhd C_2$) *iff*:

– if $\gamma = \langle p_1 \rangle$ then $(\exists C_1', C_2')(leaf(C_1') \wedge leaf(C_2') \wedge C_1$ subsumes $C_1' \wedge$
C_2 subsumes $C_2' \wedge cod(C_1', \langle p_1 \rangle)$ subsumes $C_2' \wedge C_{max}(C_1', \langle p_1 \rangle) \neq 0)$;
– if $\gamma = \langle p_1, p_2 \ldots, p_n \rangle$ $(n \geq 2)$ then $(\exists D)(leaf(D) \wedge C_1[\langle p_1 \rangle] \rhd D \wedge D[\langle p_2, \ldots, p_n \rangle] \rhd$
$C_2)$.

We write $C_1 \rhd C_2$ to indicate that $(\exists \gamma)(C_1[\gamma] \rhd C_2)$. It is worth noting that this relation expresses the fact that $C_1 \rhd C_2$ iff, *by considering only the taxo-partonomic descriptions of the classes* (i.e. by ignoring the constraints associated to each class), it is possible to build a description of an instance of the class C_1 having as component an instance of the class C_2.

---

[2] Without loss of generality, we can assume that we have $leaf(C)$ for each $C \in PRODS$ (where $leaf(C)$ means that C is a leaf class in the taxonomy of products).

Let $\mathcal{CH} = \{ch_1, \ldots, ch_n\}$ $(n \geq 1)$ be a set of class of atomic products representing the kinds of atomic components chosen by the customer (we assume $leaf(ch)$ for each $ch \in \mathcal{CH}$).

The algorithm can be sketched (declaratively) as follows:

INPUT: the conceptual model CM, $\mathcal{PRODS}$, and $\mathcal{CH}$.

OUTPUT: $\mathcal{PRODS_{CH}}$.

$\mathcal{PRODS_{CH}} := \{C/C \in \mathcal{PRODS} \wedge (\forall ch \in \mathcal{CH})(C \triangleright ch)\}$;

return $\mathcal{PRODS_{CH}}$.

(It should be clear that if $\mathcal{CH} = \emptyset$, then $\mathcal{PRODS_{CH}} = \mathcal{PRODS}$).

Let's consider, for example, the case where $\mathcal{CH} = \{PC\_DD, PC\_Card\}$ and $\mathcal{PRODS} = \{Economic\_PC, Advanced\_Appl\_PC, Notebook\}$. In this case, *Hypothesis Formulation* infers that the only complex product types that can contain the choices expressed by $\mathcal{CH}$ are $Economic\_PC$ and $Advanced\_Appl\_PC$. Notebook is ruled out because of inconsistency between $\mathcal{CH}$ and the taxo-partonomic knowledge (see fig. 1). In fact, Notebook $\not\triangleright$ PC_DD and this means that the taxo-partonomic knowledge forbids any Notebook to have any PC_DD as a part.

It is worth noting that in this way a filtering in the products can be performed with a limited computational effort by taking into account only the taxo-partonomic portion of the domain knowledge. The full use of the constraints is left to the configuration step. Despite the use of the taxo-partonomic knowledge only, in some cases, it is possible to detect the inconsistency of $\mathcal{CH}$ without performing any configuration step.

For example, it is easy to verify that *Hypothesis Formulation* returns $\mathcal{PRODS_{CH}} = \emptyset$, if $\mathcal{CH} = \{PC\_Case, Notebook\_DD\}$ and $\mathcal{PRODS} = \{Economic\_PC, Advanced\_Appl\_PC, Notebook\}$.

If $\mathcal{PRODS_{CH}}$ is not empty (that is, the preliminary consistency check has been satisfied by at least one of the complex product types in $\mathcal{PRODS}$), all other pieces of information collected so far have to be translated into a uniform representation language. In particular, $\mathcal{CH}$ is translated into a set of constraints $\mathcal{CONSTRS_{CH}}$ (expressed in the constraint language described in paragraph 2) that capture the fact that each complex product C in $\mathcal{PRODS_{CH}}$ must contain (at least) all the atomic components that the customer has selected. The way in which this translation is performed is described in [5].

The translation of the set of general requirements $\mathcal{REQS}$ into the set of constraints $\mathcal{CONSTRS_{REQS}}$ is straightforward. In fact, a set of constraints (expressed in the constraint language described in paragraph 2) corresponds to each predefined requirement presented to the customer. These associations are part of the conceptual model and are used to substitute each requirement in $\mathcal{REQS}$ with the corresponding constraints.

(3). In the *configure task*, for each complex product type in $\mathcal{PRODS_{CH}}$, the system tries to build a complex product of that type satisfying the requirements and the choices of the customer. *configure* (described below) returns a set $\mathcal{PCONFS}$ of configurations. Note that $\mathcal{PCONFS} = \emptyset$ iff the requirements are inconsistent and no complex product satisfying them can be built. Actually, the configurations in $\mathcal{PCONFS}$ are *partial configurations*, in the sense that they contain only those components and subcomponents related in some way to the requirements and they can be considered as the proposals of the system to the customer. **(4), (5).** The customer can request to the system to change some partial con-

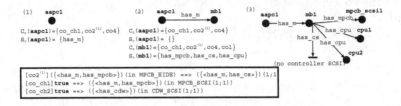

Fig. 3. Three snapshots of the configuration process

figurations in $\mathcal{PCONFS}$ or to expand them (returning the new set $\mathcal{PCONFS'}$ of partial configurations).

The iteration of these two steps can lead to a set of complete configurations. [3]

4   A Configuration Example

In the following, for each $C \in \mathcal{PRODS}_{CH}$, with $\mathcal{CONSTRS}_{CH}(C)$ (respectively, $\mathcal{CONSTRS}_{REQS}(C)$) we indicate the set of constraints in $\mathcal{CONSTRS}_{CH}$ (respectively, in $\mathcal{CONSTRS}_{REQS}$) relevant to the class of products C. Given the conceptual model CM, a class $C \in \mathcal{PRODS}_{CH}$ of complex products and the set of input constraints $\mathcal{CONSTRS}_I(C) = \mathcal{CONSTRS}_{CH}(C) \cup \mathcal{CONSTRS}_{REQS}(C)$, expressing the customer's requirements for the product of type C, the configuration mechanism produces (if possible) a (partial) instance $\mathcal{PCONF}$ of a complex product of type C, satisfying the input constraints. If no such (partial) instance can be produced, it means that the customer expressed an inconsistent (w.r.t. CM, assumed consistent) set of requirements for C.

Any instance of a complex product is represented as a tree. Each node represents a component (either atomic or complex) and each edge labelled p from a node $m1$ to a node $m2$ means that the component $m2$ is a part of $m1$ via the *whole-part relation* p (see [5]). The configuration activity is performed by means of a search process with a backtracking mechanism. The process starts with a configuration (tree) containing only the root (representing the target product) and it tries to expand it until all the considered constraints are satisfied. The configuration algorithm is described in [5] and in [6]; here we illustrate it by means of an example.

Let's consider the (portion of) conceptual model consisting of the taxopartonomy of figure 1 plus the constraints from $co1$ to $co4$ (that we suppose to be the only ones contained in the conceptual model) in section 2 and let's

---

[3] Due to space constraints, we can't describe how the configuration mechanism can be used in these two activities.

suppose that we want to configure an Advanced_Appl._PC (AAPC, in the follow-ing) containing a SCSI Main Printed Circuit Board and a SCSI CD Writer. For the sake of simplicity, we assume that $REQS = \emptyset$, thus $CONSTRS_{\mathcal{I}}(AAPC) = CONSTRS_{\mathcal{CH}}(AAPC) = \{co\_ch1, co\_ch2\}$ (see fig. 3). The process starts with the root of the configuration (tree) representing an instance $aapc1$ of an AAPC (fig. 3 (1)). The set $C_c(aapc1)$ of the current constraints for the (root) compo-nent (initially containing all the constraints that must be considered for that component) is computed. As expected, the input constraint co_ch1 belongs to that set, while co_ch2 doesn't. In fact, given the taxo-partonomy of fig. 1, we are sure that co_ch2 is always satisfied by any AAPC, thus this constraint can be ignored. Since the constraint $co4$ refers to the same subcomponent as co_ch1 (i.e. the motherboard), it must be considered too; for the same reason, the constraint $co2$ is taken into consideration, but in the form $co2^{(1)}$ obtained by eliminating the predicate $(\{\langle has\_cdw\rangle\})(inCDW\_SCSI(1;1))$ from its antecedent (in fact, this predicate is satisfied by any AAPC respecting the taxo-partonomic descrip-tion of the domain). Then, the set $S_c(aapc1)$ of the partonomic slots that have to be considered for that component is computed on the basis of $C_c(aapc1)$. The only slot of AAPC mentioned by the current constraints is has_m. In the snap-shot of fig. 3 (2) a motherboard $mb1$ has been introduced into the configuration and the current constraints and the current partonomic slots are computed for it. While expanding the $mb1$ component, the constraints co_ch1, $co2^{(1)}$ and $co4$ must be considered, since they mention some components of $mb1$ (by means of the slots has_mpcb, has_cs and has_cpu). Moreover, the constraint $co1$ has to be considered too, since it mentions the same components of $mb1$ as co_ch1 (via the has_mpcb slot) and as $co2^{(1)}$ (via the has_mpcb and has_cs slots). These con-straints entail the set $S_c(mb1)$ of slots (those of the Motherboard class mentioned in the constraints $C_c(mb1)$). The snapshot of fig. 3 (3) illustrates the produced partial configuration. It is easy to see that this partial configuration satisfies the following properties: **(a)** it contains only those components related to the input constraints. In fact, only those constraints related to the input one(s) are taken into consideration and any introduced component is relevant to some slot mentioned by the considered constraints; **(b)** it satisfies the input constraints: co_ch1 is satisfied, since a MPCB_SCSI appears in the configuration (as said, co_ch2 is satisfied by any AAPC); **(c)** it can be expanded in a complete configu-ration (still satisfying the input constraints), in fact: all the constraints related to the input ones were considered and are satisfied by the final configuration, thus, given the consistency of the conceptual model, the configuration can be completed in some way that it satisfies the taxo-partonomic description and all the other constraints.

Coming back to the example, we can suppose that the customer asks for the completion of the produced partial configuration (see the *change/expand* task in figure 2). If she/he doesn't put any additional requirement, such a complete con-figuration can be produced without revising any choice made during the compu-tation of the partial configuration. This means that the main problem of building an AAPC satisfying the constraints $CONSTRS_{\mathcal{I}}(AAPC) = \{co\_ch1, co\_ch2\}$

had been split into two independent subproblems: that of configuring the PC
motherboard in order to satisfy the input constraints and that of choosing the
other atomic components and (possibly) of configuring the (optional) Disk Unit.

The subdivision of the main problem into two independent subproblems is
still possible if the customer, during the *change/expand* task imposes a new set of
requirements not directly involving the partonomic slots occurring in the partial
configuration (e.g. if she/he puts a set of requirements on the Disk Unit complex
component). However, in this last case, if the new requirements are inconsistent
w.r.t. the conceptual model, no complete configuration can be produced.

The capability of producing such kinds of partial configurations (that in [6]
we called *laziness*) is important for the two following main reasons: firstly, the
configuration process can be expensive from the computational point of view;
if the customer needs only to check the consistency of her/his requirements it
would be an useless effort to consider those (sub)parts of the target product not
involved in the satisfaction of the requirements. Secondly, the system shouldn't
be too autonomous in configuring the product, since the customer should be
involved in this process (see the *change/expand* task).

5   Discussion

The paper describes some aspects of a system able to support a customer (possibly inexperienced) of a virtual store in configuring complex products. In particular, the system supports the customer in individuating the kind of product
that might satisfy her/his needs, in verifying the consistency of her/his requirements for the target product and in building a (possibly partial) configuration
for that product. To perform these tasks, the system uses two main problem
solving mechanisms: the *hypothesis formulation* and the *configuration* ones.

As concerns the configuration problem, many approaches that have been proposed in the last decade can be roughly classified into two different classes: the
logic-based and the *CSP-based* frameworks. Among those belonging to the first
category we find, for example, the formalization of the configuration process as
a problem of finding a stable model for a logical theory of *weight constraint
rules* representing the domain knowledge [12]; the *consistency-based* definition
of the configuration problem [3] and the *description logic-based* approach described in [7]. In the CSP-based approaches to configuration the components
and their properties are represented by means of variables. Since the number of
components that will appear in a configuration can't be known a priori, in [8] a
technique is presented to dynamically change the CSP problem by introducing
new variables. Another extension to CSP framework is proposed in [10] in order
to express also the *structure* (e.g. the partonomic knowledge) of a complex object.
[13] describes a way of capturing both the dynamic and the structural aspects
of the configuration problems in the classical CSP framework. While CSP-based
configurators had got significant results in terms of efficiency, they require that
the domain knowledge is translated in terms of variables and constraints. Since
any component has to be modelled by means of a number of variables the advan-

tages of object-centered representation can be lost. In interactive configuration, the need of maintaining a close relation between the view of the user in terms of components and subcomponents and the view of configurator has suggested a development of a hybrid approach where most of the knowledge is represented in terms of taxo-partonomy and the constraints are used only to capturing inter-dependencies among subcomponents. While the semantics of the $\mathcal{FPC}$ language is inspired to that of description logics, the reasoning mechanism benefit from some techniques derived from CSP. [6] describes the use of specific constraint propagation mechanisms in order to focus the search during the configuration process. Moreover, in that same paper, the way of subdividing the configuration problem into a set of independent subproblems and the mechanisms used to produce the above-mentioned *partial configurations* are also presented.

A prototype of the system whose core we have described here has been implemented in Java. Besides this core, it consists of a knowledge acquisition tool supporting the knowledge engineer in building the $\mathcal{FPC}$ conceptual model and of a tool to be used by the owner of the virtual store for the window-dressing and for the introduction of the atomic products models (i.e. of their most specific description) into the catalogue. The customer can access the store through a web browser and the dialogue with the system is handled by a set of Java Server Pages.

References

[1] R. J. Brachman and J. G. Schmolze. An overview of the kl-one knowledge representation system. *Cognitive Science*, (9):171–216, 1985.

[2] L. Ardissono et al. Agent technologies for the development of adaptive web stores. *LNAI*, 1991:197–216, 2000.

[3] G. Friedrich and M. Stumptner. Consistency-based configuration. In *AAAI-99, Workshop on Configuration*, 1999.

[4] P. Gerstl and S. Pribbenow. Midwinters, end games, and body parts: a classification of part-whole relations. *Int. J. Human-Computer Studies*, (43):865–889, 1995.

[5] D. Magro and P. Torasso. Description and configuration of complex technical products in a virtual store. In *Proc. of the Configuration Workshop held at the ECAI 2000*, pages 50–55, 2000.

[6] D. Magro and P. Torasso. Interactive configuration capability in a sale support system: Laziness and focusing mechanisms. In *Proc. of the Configuration Workshop held at the IJCAI-01 (to appear)*, 2001.

[7] D. L. McGuinness and J. R. Wright. An industrial-strength description logic-based configurator platform. *IEEE Intelligent Systems*, (July/August 1998):69–77, 1998.

[8] S. Mittal and B. Falkenhainer. Dynamic constraint satisfaction problems. In *Proc. of the Eigth National Conference on Artificial Intelligence*, pages 25–32, 1990.

[9] P. Resnick and H. Varian (Eds.). Recommender systems. *Comm. ACM*, 40(3):56–89, 1997.

[10] D. Sabin and E.C. Freuder. Configuration as composite constraint satisfaction. In *Proc. Artificial Intelligence and Manufacturing. Research Planning Workshop*, pages 153–161, 1996.

[11] D. Sabin and R. Weigel. Product configuration frameworks - a survey. *IEEE Intelligent Systems*, (July/August 1998):42–49, 1998.

[12] T. Soininen, I. Niemelä, J. Tiihonen, and R. Sulonen. Unified configuration knowledge representation using weight constraint rules. In *Proc. of the Configuration Workshop held at the ECAI 2000*, pages 79–84, 2000.

[13] M. Veron and M. Aldanondo. Yet another approach to ccsp for configuration problem. In *Proc. of the Configuration Workshop held at the ECAI 2000*, pages 59–62, 2000.

Characterising Concept's Properties in Ontologies

Valentina A.M. Tamma and Trevor J.M. Bench-Capon

Department of Computer Science, The University of Liverpool
Liverpool L69 7ZF, United Kingdom
{valli,tbc}@csc.liv.ac.uk

Abstract. This paper presents and motivates an extended ontology conceptual model which represents explicitly semantic information about concepts. This model results from explicitly representing information which precisely characterises the concept's properties and expected ambiguities, including which properties are prototypical of a concept and which are exceptional, the behaviour of properties over time and the degree of applicability of properties to subconcepts. This enriched conceptual model permits a precise characterisation of what is represented by class membership mechanisms and helps a knowledge engineer to determine, in a straightforward manner, the meta-properties holding for a concept. Moreover, this enriched semantics facilitates the development of reasoning mechanisms on the state of affairs that instantiate the ontologies. Such reasoning mechanisms can be used in order to solve ambiguities that can arise when ontologies are integrated and one needs to reason with the integrated knowledge.

1 Introduction

In the last decade ontologies have moved out of the research environment and have become widely used in many expert system applications not only to support the representation of knowledge but also complex inferences and retrieval. [McG00]. The extensive application of ontologies to broader areas has affected the notion of what ontologies are: they now range from light-weight ontologies, that is taxonomies of non-faceted concepts to more sophisticated ones where not only concepts but also their properties and relationships are represented.

More and more often ontologies are the efforts of many domain experts and are designed and maintained in distributed environments. For this reasons research efforts are now devoted to merging and integrating diverse ontologies [PGPM99]. Lastly, the growing use of ontologies in expert systems requires that ontologies provide a ground for the application of reasoning techniques that result in sophisticated inferences such as those used to check and maintain consistency in knowledge bases.

The interest in designing ontologies that can be easily integrated and provide a base for applying reasoning mechanisms has stressed the importance of suitable conceptual models for ontologies. Indeed, it has been made a point that the

F. Esposito (Ed.): AI*IA 2001, LNAI 2175, pp. 189–200, 2001.

sharing of ontologies depends heavily on a precise semantic representation of the concepts and their properties [FM99, McG00, TBC00].

This paper presents and motivates an extension to the classic conceptual model for ontologies, which describes entities in the domain by a set of concepts defined in terms of some exhibited properties or *attributes*, and the relationships connecting these concepts. The enriched ontology model presented in this paper proposes to encompass additional semantic information concerning the concept, which consists of a precise characterisation of the concept's properties and expected ambiguities, including which properties are prototypical of a concept and which are exceptional, the behaviour of the property over time and the degree of applicability of properties to subconcepts. This enriched conceptual model aims to provide enough semantic information to deal with problems of semantic inconsistency that arise when reasoning with integrated ontologies.

The paper is organised as follows: section 2 and subsections presents the motivations for adding semantics to the conceptual model, section 3 presents an OKBC-based [CFF+98] knowledge model instantiating the proposed conceptual model while section 4 discusses the model. An example of concept description using the proposed model is given in section 5 and finally section 6 draws conclusions.

2   Encompassing Semantics in the Conceptual Model

The motivation for enriching semantically the ontology conceptual model draws on three distinct arguments that are analysed in the reminder of this section.

2.1   Integrating Diverse Ontologies

The first argument concerns the integration of ontologies. Integrating ontologies involves identifying overlapping concepts and creating a new concept, usually by generalising the overlapping ones, that has all the properties of the originals and so can be easily mapped into each of them. Newly created concepts inherit properties, usually in the form of attributes, from each of the overlapping ones. One of the key points for integrating diverse ontologies is providing methodologies for building ontologies whose taxonomic structure is clean and untangled in order to facilitate the understanding, comparison and integration of concepts. Several efforts are focussing on providing engineering principles to build ontologies, for example [GP98, GP99]. Another approach [GW00] concentrates on providing means to perform an ontological analysis which gives prospects for better taxonomies. It is based on a rigorous analysis of the *ontological meta-properties* of taxonomic nodes, which are based on the philosophical notions of *unity, identity, rigidity* and *dependence* [GW00].

When the knowledge encompassed in ontologies built for different purposes needs to be integrated inconsistencies can become evident. Many types of ontological inconsistencies have been defined in the literature, for instance in [VJBCS98]

and the ontology environments currently available try to deal with this inconsistencies, such as SMART [FM99] and CHIMAERA [MFRW00]. Here we broadly
classify inconsistencies in ontologies into two types: structural and semantic. We
define structural inconsistencies as those that arise because of differences in the
structure of the concept definitions. Structural inconsistencies can be detected
and resolved automatically with limited intervention from the domain expert.
Semantic inconsistencies are caused by the knowledge content of diverse ontologies which differs both in semantics and in level of granularity of the representation. They require a deeper knowledge on the domain [MFRW00, TBC00].
Adding semantics to the concept descriptions can be beneficial in solving this
latter type of conflict, because a richer concept description provides more scope
to resolve possible inconsistencies.

2.2   Reasoning with Ontologies

The second argument to support the addition of semantics to ontology conceptual models turns on the need to reason with the knowledge expressed in the
ontologies. Indeed, when different ontologies are integrated, new concepts are created from the definitions of the existing ones. In such a case conflicts can arise
when conflicting information is inherited from two or more general concepts and
one tries to reason with these concepts. Inheriting conflicting properties in ontologies is not as problematic as inheriting conflicting rules in knowledge bases,
since an ontology is only *providing the means for describing explicitly the conceptualisation behind the knowledge represented in a knowledge base* [BLC96]. Thus,
in a concept's description conflicting properties can coexist. However, when one
needs to reason with the knowledge in the ontology, conflicting properties can
hinder the reasoning process. In this case extra semantic information on the
properties, such as the extent to which the property applies to the members of
the class, can be used to derive which property is more likely to apply to the
situation at hand.

2.3   Nature of Ontologies

The last argument is based on the nature of ontologies. An ontology *explicitly*
defines the type of concepts used to describe the abstract model of a phenomenon
and the constraints on their use [SBF98]. It is an *a priori* account of the objects
that are in a domain and the relationships modelling the structure of the world
seen from a particular perspective. In order to provide such an account one has
to understand the concepts that are in the domain, and this involves a number
of things. First it involves knowing what can sensibly be said of a thing falling
under a concept. This can be represented by describing concepts in terms of
their properties, and by giving a full characterisation of these properties. Thus,
when describing the concept *Bird* it is important to distinguish that some birds
fly and others do not.
It has been argued that such information is not, strictly *ontological* but it is more
of *epistemic* nature (Guarino, personal communication). From a philosophical

viewpoint an ontology is an *a priori* description of what constitues *necessary truth* in any possible world [Kri80]. Such a formal standing on ontologies permits to add a meta-level of description to ontologies and thus to reason about *meta-properties* [GW00]. We believe that in order to be able to share and reuse ontologies and to reason with the knowledge expressed in ontologies, the formal meta-level of the description should be complemented by a richer concept description, more oriented to the knowledge sharing task. If we consider the different ways in which the term *ontology* has been used in artificial intelligence, we obtain a spectrum where formal ontologies are at one end, while something close to knowledge bases are at the other end of the spectrum. Our view on ontology is somewhere in the middle: ontologies should provide enough information to enable knowledge engineers to have a full understanding of a concept *as it is in the actual world*, but should also enable knowledge engineers to perform a formal ontological analysis. For this reason, we believe in ontologies that provide an a priori account of necessary truth on all the possible worlds but also some information on the *actual world and all the worlds accessible from it*.

A full understanding of a concept involves more than this, however: it is important to recognise which properties are *prototypical* [Ros75] for the class membership and, more importantly, which are the permitted exceptions. There are, however differences in how confident we can be that an arbitrary member of a class conforms to the prototype: it is a very rare mammal that lays eggs, whereas many types of well known birds do not fly. Understanding a concept also involves understanding how and which properties change over time. This dynamic behaviour also forms part of the domain conceptualisation and can help to identify the *meta-properties* holding for the concept.

3   A Knowledge Model Representing the Enriched Conceptual Model

In this section we illustrate a frame-based model which results by representing the elements of the conceptual model in terms of the frame paradigm. We have chosen to extend a frame-based, OKBC-like [CFF+98] knowledge model, since the frame-based paradigm applied to ontologies is thought of being easy to use because closer to the human way of conceptualise, and providing a rich expressive power (a discussion on frame-based languages for ontologies can be found in [LM01]).

In this model properties are characterised with respect to their behaviour in the concept description. The knowledge model is based on *classes*, *slots*, and *facets*. *Classes* correspond to concepts and are collections of objects sharing the same properties, hierarchically organised into a multiple inheritance hierarchy, linked by *IS-A* links. Classes are described in terms of *slots*, or attributes, that can either be sets or single values. A slot is described by a name, a domain, a value type and by a set of additional constraints, here called *facets*. Facets can contain the documentation for a slot, constrain the value type or the cardinality of a slot, and provide further information concerning the slot and the way in which the slot is to be inherited by the subclasses. The set of facets provided by OKBC has been extended in order to encompass descriptions of the attribute and its behaviour in the concept description and changes over time. The facets we use are listed below, where we distinguish *epistemic nature* facets from *ontological nature* ones, and are discussed in the next section:

- **Defining Values**: It associates a value $v \in$ **Domain** with an attribute in order to represent a property. However, when the concept that is defined is very high in the hierarchy (so high that any conclusion as to the attribute's value is not possible), then it is more likely to associate with the slot **Defining Values** either the whole domain (when no decision at all can be made on the attribute's value) or a subset of the domain (when a concept is defined by means of inheritance from a parent, thus the concept inherits the slot's filler from its parent but specialises it by identifying a subset of the domain characterising the parent concept), that is **Defining Values** = Domain or **Defining Values** = Subdomain $\subset$ Domain. For example, when describing a generic concept such as *Person* in terms of the attribute *Age*, we can associate with this slot the **Defining Values**=[0, 120], expressing the fact that a person's age can range between 0 and 120. In such a case [0, 120] coincides with **Domain**. The concept is too generic in order to associate a single value with the slot *Age*. If, then, we define the concept *Teenager* as subconcept of *Person*, this inherits from *Person* the slot *Age*, but the child concept is qualified by associating with this slot the **Defining Values**=[11, 18] which is a subset of [0, 120]. This is an ontological facet;
- **Value descriptor**: The possible filler for this facet are *Prototypical, Inherited, Distinguishing, Value*. An attribute's value is a *Prototypical* one if the value is true for any prototypical instance of the concept, but exceptions are permitted with a degree of credibility expressed by the facet **Modality**. An attribute's value can be *Inherited* from some super concept or it can be a *Distinguishing* value, that is a value that differentiates among siblings. If this facet is set to *Value* this means that the value is neither prototypical, nor inherited or distinguishing. Note that inherited and distinguishing values are incompatible in the same concept description, that is a value is either inherited or distinguishing, but cannot be both. On the other hand a value can be prototypical and inherited. Distinguishing values become inherited for subclasses of the class. This is an ontological facet;
- **Exceptions**: It can be either a single value or a subset of the domain. It indicates those values that are permitted in the concept description because they are in the domain, but deemed exceptional from a common sense viewpoint. The exceptional values are not only those which differ from the prototypical ones but also any value which is possible but highly unlikely. This property is epistemic;
- **Modality**: An integer describing the degree of confidence of the fact that the attribute takes the value specified in the facet **Value**. It describe the class membership condition. The possible values are 1: *All*, 2: *Almost all*, 3: *Most*, 4: *Possible*, 5: *A Few*, 6: *Almost none*, 7: *None*. The value *None* associated

with this facet tantamounts to negation. For example, in the description of the concept *Bird* the slot *Ability to Fly* takes value Yes with *Ranking* 3, since not all birds fly. This facet is epistemic;

- **Change frequency**: Its possible values are: *Regular, Once only, Volatile, Never*. This facet describes how often an attribute's value changes. If the information is set equal to *Regular* it means that the change process is continuous, for instance the age of a person can be modelled as changing regularly. If the facet is set equal to *Once only* it means that only one change over time is possible, while if the facet is set equal to *Never* it indicates that the value is set only once and then it cannot change again, for example a person's date of birth once set cannot change again, and finally *Volatile* means that the change process is discrete and can be repeated, that is the attribute's value can change more than once, for example people can change job more than once. This property is epistemic;
- **Event**: Describes conditions under which the value changes. It is the set $\{((E_j, S_j, V_j), R_j)|j = 1, \cdots, m\}$ where E_j is an event, S_j is the state of the pair attribute-value associated with a property, V_j defines the event validity and R_j denotes whether the change is reversible or not. This facet is epistemic. The semantics of this facet is explained in the section below.

4   Relating the Extended Knowledge Model to the Motivations

The knowledge model presented in the previous section permits the characterisation of concepts by providing means to understand and detect also the *meta properties* holding for a concept. By adopting the proposed conceptual model knowledge engineers are assisted in performing the ontological analysis which is usually demanding to perform, and they are forced make ontological commitments explicit. Indeed, real situations are information-rich complete events whose context is so rich that, as it has been argued by Searle [Sea83], it can never be fully specified. Many assumptions about meaning and context are usually made when dealing with real situations [Ros99]. These assumptions are rarely formalised when real situations are represented in natural language but they have to be formalised in an ontology since they are part ontological commitments that have to be made explicit. Enriching the semantics of the attribute descriptions with things such as the behaviour of attributes over time or how properties are shared by the subclasses makes some of the more important assumptions explicit. The enriched semantics is essential to solve the inconsistencies that arise either while integrating diverse ontologies or while reasoning with the integrated knowledge. By adding information on the attributes we are able to better measure the similarity between concepts, to disambiguate between concepts that *seem* similar while they are not, and we have means to infer which property is likely to hold for a concept that inherits inconsistent properties. The remainder of this section describes the additional facets and relates them to the discussion in section 2.

4.1   Behaviour over Time

In the knowledge model the facets *Change frequency* and *Event* describe the behaviour of properties over time, which models the changes in properties that are permitted in the concept's description without changing the essence of the concept. Describing the behaviour over time involves also distinguishing properties whose change is *reversible* from those whose change is *irreversible*.

Property changes over time are caused either by the natural passing of time or are triggered by specific event occurrences. We need, therefore, to use a suitable temporal framework that permits us to reason with time and events. The model chosen to accommodate the representation of the changes is the *Event Calculus* [KS86]. Event calculus deals with local event and time periods and provides the ability to reason about change in properties caused by a specific event and also the ability to reason with incomplete information.

We can distinguish *continuous* versus *discrete properties*. *Continuous properties* are those changing regularly over time, such as the age of a person, while *discrete properties* are those characterised by an event which causes the property to change. If the value associated with change frequency is *Regular* then the property is continuous, if it is *Volatile* the property is discrete and if it is *Once only* then the property is considered discrete and the triggering event is set equal to *time-point=T*.

Since most of the forms of reasoning for continuous properties require discrete approximations, we transform any regular occurrence of time in form of an event, by representing the event triggering the change in property as the passing of time from the instant t to the instant t'. Each change of property is represented by a set of quadruples $\{((E_j, S_j, V_j), R_j)|j = 1, \cdots, m\}$ where E_j is an event, S_j is the state of the pair attribute-value associated with a property, V_j defines the event validity while R_j indicates whether the change in properties triggered by the event E_j is reversible or not. The model used to accommodate this representation of the changes adds reversibility to *Event Calculus*, where each triple (E_j, S_j, V_j) is interpreted either as *the concept is in the state S_j before the event E_j happens* or *the concept is in the state S_j after the event E_j happens* depending on the value associated with V_j. The interpretation is obtained from the semantics of the event calculus, where the former expression is represented as $Hold(before(E_j, S_j))$ while the latter as $Hold(after(E_j, S_j))$.

Events in this representation are always *point events*, and we consider *durational events* (events which have a duration) as being a collection of *point events* in which the state of the pair attribute-value as determined by the value of V_j, holds as long as the event lasts. The duration is determined by the definition of an *event* in *Event Calculus*, where for each event is given an initial and a final time point. We realise that this representation oversimplify the dynamic of process changes and we aim to investigate a more sophisticated change representation as future work.

The idea of modelling the permitted changes for a property is strictly related to the philosophical notion of *identity*. In particular, the knowledge model addresses the problem of modelling identity when time is involved, namely *identity through change*, which is based on the common sense notion that an individual may remain the same while showing different properties at different times [GW00]. The knowledge model we propose explicitly distinguishes the properties that can change from those which cannot, and describes the changes in properties that an individual can be subjected to, while still being recognised as an instance of a certain concept.

The notion of changes through time is also important to establish whether a property is *rigid*. A *rigid property* is defined in [GCG94] as: *"a property that is essential to* all *its instances, i.e.* $\forall x \phi(x) \rightarrow \Box \phi(x)"$. The interpretation that is usually given to *rigidity* is that if x is an instance of a concept C than x has to be an instance of C in every possible world. Time is only one of these systems of possible worlds, however characterising a property as rigid even if only with respect to time gives a better angle on the *necessary* and *sufficient* conditions for the class membership.

4.2 Modality

The term modality is used to express the way in which a statement is true or false, which is related to establish whether a statement constitute a *necessary truth* and to distinguish necessity from possibility [Kri80]. The term can be extended to qualitatively measure the way in which a statement is true by trying to estimate the number of possible world in which such a truth holds. This is the view we take in this paper, by denoting the degree of confidence that we can associate with finding a certain world with the facet *Modality*. This notion is quite similar to the one of *Ranking* as defined by Goldszdmidt and Pearl [GP96]: *Each world is ranked by a non-negative integer representing the degree of surprise associated with finding such a world* .

Here we use the term modality to denote the degree of surprise in finding a world where the property P holding for a concept C does not hold for one of its subconcepts C'. The additional semantics encompassed in this facet is important to reason with statements that have different degrees of truth. Indeed there is a difference in asserting facts such as "Mammals give birth to live young" and "Bird fly". The ability to distinguish facts whose truth holds with different degrees of strength is important in order to find which facts are true in every possible world and therefore constitute *necessary truth*. The concept of necessary truth brings us back to the discussion about *rigidity*, in fact it can be assumed that the value associated with the *Modality* facet together with the temporal information on the changes permitted for the property lead us to determine whether the property described by the slot is a rigid one. Good candidate to be rigid properties are those whose *Modality* facet is equal to *All* and that cannot change in time, that is whose *Change frequency* facet is set to *Never*.

The ability to evaluate the degree of confidence in a property describing a concept is also related to the problem of reasoning with ontologies obtained by integration. In such a case, as mentioned in Section 2.2 inconsistencies can arise if a concepts inherits conflicting properties. In order to be able to reason with these conflicts some assumptions have to be made, concerning on how likely it is that a certain property holds; the facet *Modality* models this information by modelling a qualitative evaluation of how subclasses inherit the property. This estimate represents the common sense knowledge expressed by linguistic quantifiers such as *All, Almost all, Few, etc.*.

In case of conflicts the property's degree of truth can be used to rank the possible alternatives following an approach similar to the non-monotonic reasoning one developed by [GP96]: in case of more conflicting properties holding for a concept description, properties might be ordered according to the degree of truth, that is a property holding for all the subclasses is considered to have a higher rank than one holding for few of the concept subclasses.

4.3   Prototypes and Exceptions

In order to get a full understanding of a concept it is not sufficient to list the set of properties generally recognised as describing a typical instance of the concept but we need to consider the expected exceptions. Here we denote by *prototype* those values that are prototypical for the concept that is being defined; in this way, we partially take the cognitive view of prototypes and graded structures, which is also reflected by the information modelled in the facet *Modality*. In this view all cognitive categories show gradients of membership which describe how well a particular subclass fits people's idea or image of the category to which the subclass belong [Ros75]. Prototypes are the subconcepts which best represent a category, while exceptions are those which are considered exceptional although still belong to the category. In other words all the sufficient conditions for class membership hold for prototypes. For example, let us consider the biological category *mammal*: a *monotreme* (a mammal who does not give birth to live young) is an example of an exception with respect to this attribute. Prototypes depend on the context; there is no universal prototype but there are several prototypes depending on the context, therefore a prototype for the category *mammal* could be *cat* if the context taken is that of *animals that can play the role of pets* but it is *lion* if the assumed context is *animals that can play the role of circus animals*. In the model presented above we explicitly describe the context in natural language in the *Documentation* facet, however, the context can be also described by the roles that the concept which is being described is able to play.

Ontologies typically presuppose context and this feature is a major source of difficulty when merging them.

For the purpose of building ontologies, distinguishing the prototypical properties from those describing exceptions increases the expressive power of the description. Such distinctions do not aim at establishing default values but rather to guarantee the ability to reason with incomplete or conflicting concept descriptions.

The ability to distinguish between prototypes and exceptions helps to determine which properties are necessary and sufficient conditions for concept membership. In fact a property which is prototypical and that is also inherited by all the subconcepts (that is it has the facet *Modality* set to *All*) becomes a natural candidate for a necessary condition. Prototypes, therefore, describe the subconcepts that best fit the cognitive category represented by the concept *in the specific context given by the ontology*. On the other hand, by describing which properties are exceptional, we provide a better description of the class membership criteria in that it permits to determine what are the properties that, although rarely hold for that concept, are still possible properties describing the cognitive category. Here, the term *exceptional* is used to indicate something that differs from what is normally thought to be a feature of the cognitive category and not only what differs from the prototype.

Also the information on prototype and exceptions can prove useful in dealing with inconsistencies arising from ontology integration. When no specific information is made available on a concept and it inherits conflicting properties, then we can assume that the prototypical properties hold for it.

5   A Modelling Example

We now provide an example to illustrate how the previously described knowledge model can be used for modelling a concept in the ontology. The example is taken from the medical domain and we have chosen to model the concept of *blood pressure*. Blood pressure is represented here as an ordered pair (s, d) where s is the value of the *systolic pressure* while d is the value of the *diastolic pressure*. In modelling the concept of blood pressure we take into account that both the systolic and diastolic pressure can range between a minimum and a maximum value but that some values are more likely to be registered than others. Within the likely values we then distinguish the *prototypical* values, which are those registered for a healthy individual whose age is over 18, and the *exceptional* ones, which are those registered for people with pathologies such as hypertension or hypotension. The prototypical values are those considered normal, but they can change and we describe also the permitted changes and what events can trigger such changes. Prototypical pressure values usually change with age, but they can be altered depending on some specific events such as shock and haemorrhage (causing hypotension) or thrombosis and embolism (causing hypertension). Also conditions such as pregnancy can alter the normal readings.

Classes are denoted by the label **c**, slots by the label **s** and facets by the label **f**. Irreversible changes are denoted by I while reversible property changes are denoted by R.

c: Circulatory system;
  s: Blood pressure
    f: Domain: [(0,0)-(300,200)];
    f: Defining verb Values : [(90,60)-(130,85)];
    f: Value descriptor: prototypical;
    f: Exceptions: [(0,0)-(89,59)] ∪ [(131,86)-(300,200)];
    f: Modality: 3;
    f: Change frequency: Volatile;
    f: Event: (Age=60,[(0,0)-(89,59)] ∪ [(131,86)-(300,200)],after, I);

f: Event: (haemorrhage,[(0,0)-(89,59)],after, R);
f: Event: (shock,[(0,0)-(89,59)],after, R);
f: Event: (thrombosis,[(131,86)-(300,200)],after,R);
f: Event: (embolism,[(131,86)-(300,200)],after,R);
f: Event: (pregnancy,[(0,0)-(89,59)] ∪ [(131,86)-(300,200)],after,R);

6   Conclusions

This paper has presented an extended conceptual model for ontologies that encompasses additional semantic information aiming to characterise the behaviour of properties in the concept description. We have motivated this enriched conceptual model by discussing the problems that require additional semantics in order to be solved.

The novelty of this extended conceptual model is that it explicitly represents the behaviour of attributes over time by describing the permitted changes in a property that are permitted for members of the concept. It also explicitly represents the class membership mechanism by associating with each slot a qualitative quantifier representing how properties are inherited by subconcepts. Finally, the model does not only describe the prototypical properties holding for a concept but also the exceptional ones.

We have also related the extended knowledge model to the formal ontological analysis by Guarino and Welty [GW00], which is usually difficult to perform and we believe our model can help knowledge engineers to determine the meta-properties holding for the concept by forcing them to make the ontological commitments explicit.

A possible drawback of this approach is the high number of facets that need to filled when building ontology. We realise that this can make building an ontology from scratch even more time consuming but we believe that the outcomes in terms of better understanding of the concept and the role it plays in a context together with the guidance in determining the meta-properties at least balances the increased complexity of the task.

References

[BLC96]   A. Bernaras, I. Laresgoiti, and J. Corera. Building and reusing ontologies for electrical network applications. In *Proceedings of the 12th European Conference on Artificial Intelligence (ECAI)*, pages 298–302, 1996.

[CFF+98]   V.K. Chaudhri, A. Farquhar, R. Fikes, P.D. Karp, and J.P. Rice. OKBC: A programmatic foundation for knowledge base interoperability. In *Proceedings of the Fifteenth American Conference on Artificial Intelligence (AAAI-98)*, pages 600–607, Madison, Wisconsin, 1998. AAAI Press/The MIT Press.

[FM99]   N. Fridman Noy and M.A. Musen. SMART: Automated support for ontology merging and alignment. In *Proceedings of the 12th Workshop on Knowledge Acquisition, Modeling and Management (KAW)*, Banff, Canada, 1999.

[GCG94]   N. Guarino, M. Carrara, and P. Giaretta. An ontology of meta-level-categories. In *Principles of Knowledge representation and reasoning: Proceedings of the fourth international conference (KR94)*. Morgan Kaufmann, 1994.

[GP96]   M. Goldszmidt and J. Pearl. Qualitative probabilistic for default reasoning, belief revision, and causal modelling. *Artificial Intelligence*, 84(1-2):57–112, 1996.

[GP98]   A. Gómez-Pérez. Knowledge sharing and reuse. In J. Liebowitz, editor, *The Handbook of Applied Expert Systems*. CRC Pres LLC, 1998.

[GP99]   A. Gómez-Pérez. Ontological engineering: A state of the art. *Expert Update*, 2(3):33–43, Autumn 1999.

[GW00]   N. Guarino and C. Welty. A formal ontology of properties. In R. Dieng, editor, *Proceedings of the 12th EKAW Conference*, volume LNAI 1937. Springer Verlag, 2000.

[Kri80]   S.A. Kripke. *Naming and necessity*. Harvard University Press, 1980.

[KS86]   R. Kowalski and M. Sergot. A logic-based calculus of events. *New Generation Computing*, 4:67–95, 1986.

[LM01]   O. Lassila and D. McGuinness. *The Role of Frame-Based Representation on the Semantic Web*, volume Vol. 6(2001), number not yet determined of *Linkping Electronic Articles in Computer and Information Science. ISSN 1401-9841*. 2001.

[McG00]   D.L. McGuinness. Conceptual modelling for distributed ontology environments. In *Proceedings of the Eighth International Conference on Conceptual Structures Logical, Linguistic, and Computational Issues (ICCS 2000)*, 2000.

[MFRW00]   D.L. McGuinness, R.E. Fikes, J. Rice, and S. Wilder. An environment for merging and testing large ontologies. In *Proceedings of KR-2000. Principles of Knowledge Representation and Reasoning*. Morgan-Kaufman, 2000.

[PGPM99]   H.S. Pinto, A. Gómez-Pérez, and J.P. Martins. Some issues on ontology integration. In V.R. Benjamins, editor, *Proceedings of the IJCAI'99 Workshop on Ontology and Problem-Solving Methods: Lesson learned and Future Trends*, volume 18, pages 7.1–7.11, Amsterdam, 1999. CEUR Publications.

[Ros75]   E.H. Rosch. Cognitive representations of semantic categories. *Journal of Experimental Psychology: General*, 104:192–233, 1975.

[Ros99]   E.H. Rosch. Reclaiming concepts. *Journal of Consciousness Studies*, 6(11-12):61–77, 1999.

[SBF98]   R. Studer, V.R. Benjamins, and D. Fensel. Knowledge engineering, principles and methods. *Data and Knowledge Engineering*, 25(1-2):161–197, 1998.

[Sea83]   J.R. Searle. *Intentionality*. Cambridge University Press, Cambridge, 1983.

[TBC00]   V.A.M. Tamma and T.J.M Bench-Capon. Supporting inheritance mechanisms in ontology representation. In R. Dieng, editor, *Proceedings of the 12th EKAW Conference*, volume LNAI 1937, pages 140–155. Springer Verlag, 2000.

[VJBCS98]   P.R.S. Visser, D.M. Jones, T.J.M. Bench-Capon, and M.J.R. Shave. Assessing heterogeneity by classifying ontology mismatches. In N. Guarino, editor, *Formal Ontology in Information Systems. Proceedings FOIS'98, Trento, Italy*, pages 148–182. IOS Press, 1998.

Reasoning about Dynamic Scenes Using Autonomous Agents

Paolo Remagnino, Graeme A. Jones, and Ndedi Monekosso

Digital Imaging Research Centre,
School of Computing and Information Systems,
Kingston University, United Kingdom
{p.remagnino,g.jones,n.monekosso}@king.ac.uk
http://www.king.ac.uk/dirc

Abstract. The scene interpretation system proposed below integrates computer vision and artificial intelligence techniques to combine the information generated by multiple cameras on typical secure sites. A multi-agent architecture is proposed as the backbone of the system within which the agents control the different components of the system and incrementally build a model of the scene by merging the information gathered over time and between cameras. The choice of a distributed artificial intelligence architecture is justified by the need for scalable designs capable of co-operating to infer an optimal interpretation of the scene. Decentralizing intelligence means creating more robust and reliable sources of interpretation, but also allows easy maintenance and updating of the system. The scene model is learned using Hidden Markov models which capture the range of possible scene behaviours. The employment of such probabilistic interpretation techniques is justified by the very nature of surveillance data, which is typically incomplete, uncertain and asynchronous.

1 Introduction

Understanding the evolution of a dynamic scene entails the interpretation of events occurring in the overlapping fields of view of a set of cameras monitoring the environment [11, 9]. For instance, a security guard is interested in identifying potential crime incidents such as people breaking into secure areas, tampering with parked vehicles or violent and destructive behaviour in public spaces. Shopping mall operators are interested in determining customer flow to specific shops and through shopping aisles. Such examples need the ability to detect of relevant events and tracking of moving objects, and the behavioural analysis of these objects and their interactions over time. The scene interpretation problem - characterized by the existence of multiple sensors and cameras scattered across a potentially large geographic area - is ideally implemented as a distributed system [9, 4]. The sensors, which perceive the environment, can be of different type (*e.g.* motion detectors and cameras) each generating asynchronous and highly redundant data streams. Events occurring in the field of view of these sensors can be defined as stochastic processes that may or may be not independent.

The agent paradigm makes use of latest object-oriented technology. Designing a system using the object-oriented methodology means describing the system in terms

F. Esposito (Ed.): AI*IA 2001, LNAI 2175, pp. 201–211, 2001.

of objects representing the basic elements that constitute the problem in hand. Agent programming extends the passive character of these objects to create agent objects, or simply agents - self-contained software modules capable of independent reasoning and self-adaptation to an evolving external world. Despite the often-heated nature of the debate over the definition of agents, there are some well-defined common characteristics. Agents must be autonomous and capable exchanging knowledge about the environment. An agent must be able to adapt its plans to both internal changes (*e.g.* faults) and external changes, by modifying its own model of the perceived world, and adapt its own goals.

Computer vision has always required intelligent software to extract information and encode it in the simplest form. Scene understanding entails the extraction of semantic information about the viewed scene. The process of bridging the gap between data and information has always created a chasm between low level image analysis and high level interpretation. Agent orientation lends itself very well to the interpretation of a scene based on computer vision. The work of Buxton [4] is a good example of an event-based detection system for surveillance situations using Bayesian networks as a simple yet effective classification technique. Intille [13] used a more orthodox agent-based system to classify American football actions again using Bayesian networks to identify the events. Remagnino [11] used Bayesian networks to model behaviours and interactions between objects in a typical car park scenario. Rosario [12] have modeled interactions using coupled hidden Markov models which assume that interaction behaviours are well represented by interwoven stochastic processes.

2   Overview of Agent Architecture

The physical installation is designed around a secured environment monitored by a number of cameras with overlapping views. A number of PCs distributed around the site are expected to process the incoming video. Each camera is managed by a camera agent responsible for detecting and tracking all moving objects traversing the camera's view volume. For each new event (initiated by a scene object entering a camera's view volume), an object agent is instantiated with the responsibility of providing a continuously updated description of the temporal event. All cameras are calibrated to a common ground plane coordinate system to enable information to be integrated across multiple cameras. For each temporal event, the camera agent computes the 3D trajectory of the object and extracts the set of subimages containing the event in each frame. These data are continuously streamed to the appropriate object agent and used to update a classification of the event object itself - *e.g.* vehicle person - and a semantic commentary on the object behaviour. Since an event may be detected in more than one field of view, multiple object agents may be instantiated for a single event. Consequently object agents must also collaborate to identify these multiple instantiations. Any pair of object agents that detect such equivalence merge to create a single object agent inheriting data channels from multiple camera agents. Object agents are terminated once tracking information from attached camera agent(s) has been terminated.

2.1 Camera Agent

Digital cameras are set to challenge the dominance of analogue technology as reducing costs increase access and even small companies wanting forensic quality imagery to monitor limited areas are willing to invest money to install sets of digital sensors. Cameras will soon have on-board hardware able to host software to process and analyse video footage in real-time. Currently a camera agent is hosted on a PC using the camera as a resource. As intelligent cameras become computationally more powerful, the centre of gravity of a camera agent will migrate towards the camera. In addition to instantiation of object agent processes and the reliable transport of trajectory and pixel information to these objects, to track events reliably, each camera agent must also enjoy sufficient algorithmic intelligence to perform the following tasks.

The camera agent is charged with the detection and tracking of all moving objects within the field of view. In brief the tracker works as follows. First the pixels in each new frame are classified as moving or not-moving by comparison with a temporally updated mean and variance frame. Regions within the resultant event map are extracted and used to validate current events. Regions which cannot be accounted for by current events are used to hypothesise a new event using an expected appearance model [2, 7]. Event hypotheses which are continuously validated for a preset number of frames are promoted by instantiating a new object agent. While introducing a latency in the generation of scene knowledge, such a threshold is necessary to avoid the costly overhead of creating new object agent threads/processes for false alarm events.

2.2 Object Agent

Once instantiated, the object agent is obliged to pursue the goal of classifying the event with which it is associated and classifying it's behaviour from a limited number of domain-specific activities. This knowledge is derived from the trajectory and pixel information provided by the camera agents(s). A trajectory estimator is employed to integrate the stream of 3D ground plane observations - possibly supplied by more than one camera agent - to generate smoothed position and velocity estimates of object. In addition, the projected 3D width and height of an object can be temporally tracked by combining the region dimensions extracted from the event map with the position of an object on the ground plane. Classification and behavioral analysis is performed by the following intelligent algorithms:

Object Classification People and vehicles enjoy distinct 3D velocity and 3D projected width characteristics. Figure 1 illustrates the class conditional probability distributions of vehicle and people in this classification space. Since to some extent these distributions are overlapping, it is necessary to integrate velocity and width observations over the history of a tracked object to avoid false classification. This can be illustrated by overlaying the trajectories in classification space of a typical person and vehicle event. A simple maximum a posteriori decision rule is employed to update the probability of classification given each new observation $a_t = (v_t, w_t)$ of the velocity v_t and width to height ratio w_t.

$$\omega = \arg\max_{\omega \in \Omega} P(\omega | a_t, \ldots, a_1) \tag{1}$$

where Ω is the set of possible event classifications $\{person, \; vehicle\}$. Assuming each observation $\mathbf{a}_t$ is independent of previous observations, the *a posteriori* probability $P(\omega|\mathbf{a}_t, \dots, \mathbf{a}_1)$ may be expressed temporally as

$$P(\omega|\mathbf{a}_t, \dots, \mathbf{a}_1) \approx p(\mathbf{a}_t|\omega)P(\omega|\mathbf{a}_{t-1}, \dots, \mathbf{a}_1) \qquad (2)$$

$$P(\omega|\mathbf{a}_1 \approx p(\mathbf{a}_1|\omega)P(\omega) \qquad (3)$$

where the class conditional probabilities $p(\mathbf{a}|person)$ and $p(\mathbf{a}|vehicle)$, and the prior probabilities $P(person)$ and $P(vehicle)$ are derived from training data such as that shown in figure 1.

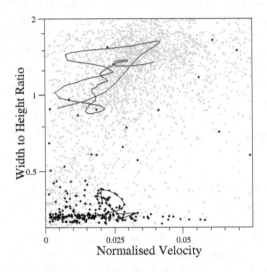

Fig. 1. Recovering class conditional and prior probabilities: a estimates for the *Vehicle* and *Person* class are shown as point clouds. Vehicles tend to enjoy larger width to height ratios and velocities. Velocity estimates are normalised by image row position to account for the near linear relationship between visual velocity and distance to object.

2.3   Behavioural Classification

Object agents are also responsible for identifying the behaviour of the event with which it is associated. The approach adopted here is to employ the trajectory information of an object to identify the likely behaviour of the event for an application specific domain such as car entering, person leaving car, car parking, etc. The hidden Markov model (HMM) methodology [6] is used to construct stochastic models of behaviour during a training phase. At run-time, a newly created object agent uploads the relevant models (*i.e.* some models are more probable at different time of the day) and repeatedly computes the likelihood of each model given the current trajectory. Such an approach not only provides a complement event classification technique but, crucially, identifies the event behaviour.

3   Scene Modelling Using HMMs

In the proposed framework object agents continuously co-operate to provide an optimal interpretation of the scene. The scene model is learned using hidden Markov models (HMMs). Models are learned for different categories of objects in a training phase, however such models are automatically updated by the observations of new tracked events. All tracked events contribute to the overall interpretation of the analysed scene, updating the most probable activity model.

The underlying idea of building a scene model has a number of advantages. First and foremost the incremental construction of the scene model from raw data. Such bottom-up interpretation can then be used to guide object classification. Learned models can be used to determine what object type originated the event, by calculating the likelihood of each model conditioned to the current set of observations. More importantly, the use of a scene model allows the agent to predict all feasible object future trajectories, sort them by likelihood and, potentially, feed back useful information to the tracking process.

In addition to maintaining an estimate of its trajectory, each object agent attempts to interpret the activity of its event from a number of predefined activities that have been identified for the particular problem context. The proposed approach makes use of the Markov learning technique. A pre-classified training set of tracks for people and vehicles is acquired from which Markov models of the required activities occurring in the analysed environment are built. At run-time, each event agent loads a copy of the scene model (all built HMMs). For each set of observations, corresponding to the object tracks, the corresponding event agent calculates the likelihood of all the available models (and hence activity) to identify the most likely activity of the object, and its class.

3.1   Markov Models for Scene Understanding

The Markov model is an ideal probabilistic technique for learning and matching activity patterns. Each Markov model is a stochastic state automaton in which each state is associated with both a prior probability of a process starting in that state, and a set of transition probabilities describing the likelihood of a process moving into a new state. In a previous implementation of our work [10], these states mapped directly onto manually identified regions of interest in the scene by an operator in an offline procedure from a series of semantic labels *e.g.* parking areas, vehicle entrance, exit, pedestrian path, etc. This process of manual pre-selection is not ideal, as the resultant regions may not necessarily model the probability density of activity accurately. Consequently, the current implementation generates the states automatically by employing the expectation-maximisation (EM) algorithm [1] to cluster the activity landscape. The EM algorithm fits a number of Gaussian probability distributions (the clusters) to the set of object positions derived from the set of event trajectories in the training set.

Each type of activity for people or vehicle events may be characterised by a family of trajectories moving on the ground plane and, hence, can be represented in a hidden Markov model as a set of states and associated prior and transitional probabilities. During the training phase, the dynamics of objects moving in the scene are used to train each hidden Markov model by computing the prior probability π_i for each state S_i (representing the probability that a particular region *state* is the starting point for a trajectory), the transitional probabilities a_{ij} between two states S_i and S_j (capturing the probability that an object moves from one state to another given all possible transitions from that region), and finally the probability distribution function $b_j(\mathbf{o})$ of an observation vector $\mathbf{o}$ for a state S_j *i.e.* the conditional probability of a particular position $\mathbf{o}$ given the state S_j.

In the current implementation the hidden Markov models are built in two stages. First, for each type of event *e.g.* pedestrian or vehicle, the set of states are extracted from the appropriate training set by locating clusters of observations using an efficient implementation of the EM algorithm [3]. Second, trajectories from the training set are used to compute the HMM probabilities. Priors are readily learnt by counting the frequency of starting in a particular state. Similarly transitional probabilities are learnt by counting the number of times a transition between states (including within a state) occurs normalised by all occurring transitions. The formulae used to build the HMM's are normalised to cater for the common problem of probability values rapidly converging to zero.

3.2   Behavioural Classification

Once the hidden Markov models have been learned they can be used to describe the dynamic evolution of the scene. Model selection can be performed by finding the model λ which yields the highest *a posterior* likelihood $P(\lambda|\mathbf{O})$ given the sequence of N observations $\mathbf{O} = (\mathbf{o}_1, \ldots, \mathbf{o}_N)$ associated with each new trajectory. Reproducing the work of Rabiner [6], this probability can be calculated by introducing the random variable $\mathbf{q}$, a possible sequence of states followed by the trajectory $\mathbf{O}$, and summing over all possible state sequences as follows

$$P(\mathbf{O}|\lambda) = \sum_{\forall \mathbf{q}} [P(\mathbf{O}|\mathbf{q}, \lambda)P(\mathbf{q}|\lambda)] \tag{4}$$

which can be re-written as

$$P(\mathbf{O}|\lambda) = \sum_{\forall q_1, \ldots, q_T} \pi_{q_1} b_{q_1}(\mathbf{o}_1) a_{q_1 q_2} \cdots a_{q_{T-1} q_T} b_{q_T}(\mathbf{o}_T) \tag{5}$$

see [6] for further details. At each moment in time, each object agent calculates the likelihood of a model given the current set of observed features about the object. The model λ which yields the highest a posterior probability is the one currently providing the most likely interpretation of object activity *i.e.*

$$\lambda' = \arg \max_{q_1, \ldots, q_T} P(\mathbf{O}|\lambda) \tag{6}$$

The most likely model is calculated using the classical *forward iterative procedure* provided by the HMM framework [6]. The procedure makes use of intermediate *forward* variables $\alpha_t(S_i), \forall i$ defined as the likelihood that a set of observations finishing in state S_i are described by the model λ. The procedure makes use of induction and is repeated until the termination stage in which the a posterior probability of a model λ is computed by summing over all final values of the α variable

$$P(\lambda|\mathbf{O}) \approx P(\mathbf{O}|\lambda)P(\lambda) \tag{7}$$

$$P(\mathbf{O}|\lambda) = \sum_{\forall i} \alpha_t(S_i) \tag{8}$$

where $P(\lambda)$ is the a priori probability of the model λ. However, rather than using $P(\lambda)$, the more accurate classification probability $P(\omega|\mathbf{a}_t, \ldots, \mathbf{a}_1)$ (derived in equation 3 of section 2.2 enables the classification procedure to directly influence the selection of the appropriate behavioural model as follows

$$P(\lambda|\mathbf{O}) \approx P(\mathbf{O}|\lambda)p(\lambda|\omega)P(\omega|\mathbf{a}_t, \ldots, \mathbf{a}_1) \tag{9}$$

where $p(\lambda|\omega)$ is the conditional probability of a particular behaviour given a classification ω of the event.

4   Results

Some preliminary behaviour classification results are presented. Trajectories for two behaviours - vehicle entering and person entering - were extracted by hand from over five hours of video data and used to construct HMM models. Three different sets of models were constructed using the EM algorithm for 5, 10 and 20 Gaussians to assess the performance for increasing complex models. Superimposed on a frame from the video sequence, the resultant states are shown as projected ellipses in figures 2 to 5. Figures 2, 3 and 4 present the results for the person model for 20, 10 and 5 Gaussians. A similar figure 5 presents the states for the vehicle model with 10 Gaussians. Note that the footfalls for the person behaviour model have correctly been identified on the pavement on the left despite the occlusion problems created by the wall.

A typical state transition matrix is presented pictorally in Figure 6. It should be noted that, particularly for the person entering model, the object tends to spends more time within a state than moving to a new state.

Behavioural Classification To illustrate the effectiveness of the classification process, the models were tested against a vehicle and person set of test trajectories for each of the three sets of models - 5, 10 and 20 Gaussians. Performance may be assessed for each of the three cases by producing a scatter matrix detailing the percentage of behaviours correctly and incorrectly explained by the behavioural models. These matrices are presented in Table 1 left, Table 1 right and Table 2 left for the 20, 10 and 5 Gaussian cases respectively. These tables illustrate that as the number of Gaussians used to model the activity on the ground increases, the classification accuracy rises. For the 5-state model,

Fig. 2. Person Model (20 Gaussians)   **Fig. 3.** Person Model (10 Gaussians)

Fig. 4. Person Model (5 Gaussians)   **Fig. 5.** Vehicle Model (10 Gaussians)

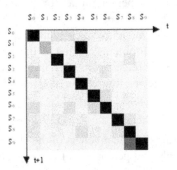

Fig. 6. Example state transition matrix for person model using 10 Gaussians (or states). Probabilities are mapped onto greyscales such that black represents a probability of unity while white represents zero.

Scatter Matrix	Vehicle Model	Person Model	Scatter Matrix	Vehicle Model	Person Model
Vehicle Data	77%	23%	Vehicle Data	63%	37%
Person Data	27%	73%	Person Data	28%	72%

Table 1. *Left :* Classification Results for 20 Gaussians, *Right :* Results for 10 Gaussians

Scatter Matrix	Vehicle Model	Person Model	Scatter Matrix	Vehicle Model	Person Model
Vehicle Data	52%	48%	Vehicle Data	93%	7%
Person Data	39%	61%	Person Data	9%	91%

Table 2. *Left :* Classification Results for 5 Gaussians, *Right :* Combined Classification Results ·

the EM algorithm has poorly modelled the activity within the scene resulting in the essentially random classification of vehicle data.

Classification accuracy can be significantly improved by firstly increasing the number of states. Greater separation is achieved by including greater numbers of states. However, such gains are likely to reduce as the number increases beyond 20 states. Indeed there is an increasing likelihood of over-training in which the HMM no longer generalizes but rather begins to model the specific training set. A second improvement can be achieved by adopting the a posteriori probability expression in equation 9 which integrates the object classification evidence. Since we have only one activity per object type, this rule may be written as

$$P(\lambda|\mathbf{O}) \approx P(\mathbf{O}|\lambda)P(\omega|\mathbf{a}_t, \ldots, \mathbf{a}_1) \tag{10}$$

Using this rule with the 20 Gaussian HMM generates the following scatter matrix which represents a significant improvement in classification accuracy.

5 Discussion

The paper has presented the design criteria and methodology for a system dedicated to the interpretation of a dynamic scene. Artificial Intelligence techniques have been proposed to handle the distributed nature of the application and the uncertain nature of the acquisition process. Modular software has been suggested as the most suitable solution to the fusion of asynchronous information and the incremental creation of an event model able to capture scene dynamics and allow the classification of typical scene events. Distributed systems are more reliable, easier to update and maintain. The distributed nature of the monitoring system, based on cameras scattered across large areas lends itself very well as an Artificial Intelligence system. Intelligence can be distributed across the monitoring system towards the cameras and sensors, to identify objects and track only those deemed of some interest. Intelligence can also be distributed towards processing units closer to the sensors to analyse locally the information gathered by the cameras, and broadcast only that part of some interest to the user. As it stands the presented methodology is still at the beginning. Its design is ready, but a full implementation is still needed to test all its characteristics and limitations. The authors think that in the near future the following will represent the major challenges

- Use of more cluttered scenes, including near field video footage
- The design and implementation of techniques to handle interaction between more events
- The use of mobile cameras and adaptation of scene model
- A study on the degradation of the system in cases of internal and external faults

Although the design of intelligent monitoring techniques seems to be one the current major trends in Computer Vision, it is the belief of the authors that this paper presents a novel methodology which encompasses the latest AI techniques and the latest trends in distributed systems. It is the belief of the authors that the methodology can be employed to implement a truly modular, fault tolerant and scalable architecture for scene interpretation.

6   Answering the Reviewers' Comments

The reviewers request a better justification of the use of agency for the autonomous reasoning of a complex scene, the details of the agent communication language (ACL) and information about the platform used.

First of all let us repeat that the system is in an early development stage, this paper presents more concrete and advanced ideas and a more robust system prototype than what was presented at the previous AI*IA conference.

Agent-oriented technology superseeds the object-oriented paradigm: it comes with active ways to deal with the situation in hands, it is augmented with intelligent functionality (reasoning/planning), it allows superior communication between agents (shared reasoning) and at the same time inherits all the standard object-oriented features, including modularity and encapsulation.

The authors have already proposed a three-tiered design of the agent [5]. This includes three interacting modules controlling the inter-agent communication (shared reasoning), the automatic tuning of algorithms (adaptation to environment) and the choice between algorithms (planning/reasoning). Each independent tier is modular and in theory could be logically promoted to agent status, being autonomous. Object-orientation does not provide sufficient flexibility and interactivity to be used as a development paradigm. Agent-orientation, on the other hand, meets the design and implementation requirements: each agent is endowed with planning and reasoning capability.

At present reasoning is merely implemented at the geometric level, in terms of a combination of visual evidence over time. The current design can be easily extended to combine evidence from multiple sensors. The process of combining evidence and disambiguating hypotheses takes us to the second query of the reviewers, the communication language. A document is curently in preparation which describes a communication language based on Bayesian formalism to serve the co-operation of agents in solving visual tasks. Computer vision research mainly concerns the understanding of complex scenes, including object recognition and dynamics analysis. There has been a wide interest in the community in combining logic and probabilistic formalisms [8] to create a stronger language to describe objects and events relating them. The authors are still studying the strength of the standard Bayesian formalism to combine and propagate evidence, and disambiguate over interpretations of complex events. The communication layer of the agent design is therefore still limited, but capable of great improvements. The synergy of a multitude of agents is simplified as the evidence can be dealt with probabily calculus, maintaining a plausible and consistent set of hypotheses about the scene dynamics.

The platform used at present comprises high specification personal computers running the WindowsNT operating system. The system prototype was implemented in C++. The vision modules run real-time, tracking moving objects at frame-rate (25 fps), while, at present, the reasoning module is implemented in C++ and runs off line.

References

[1] A.Dempster, M.Laird, and D.Rubin. Maximum likelihood from incomplete data via the em algorithm. *J.R.Stat. Soc., B*, 39:1–38, 1977.

[2] A. Bakowski and G.A. Jones. Video surveillance tracking using colour adjacency graphs. In *IEE Conference on Image Processing and its Applications*, pages 794–798, 1999.

[3] V. Cadez, S. Gaffney, and P. Smyth. A general probabilistic framework for clustering individuals and objects. In *Proceedings of the ACM KDD*, 2000.

[4] H.Buxton and S. Gong. Visual surveillance in a dynamic and uncertain world. *Artificial Intelligence*, 78:431–459, 1995.

[5] L.Marchesotti, P.Remagnino, and G.A.Jones. Evaluating centralised and distributed multi-agent architectures for visual surveillance. In *Proceedings of European Signal Processing Conference*, 2000.

[6] L.Rabiner and B-H. Juang. *Fundamentals of Speech Recognition*. Prentice-Hall, 1993.

[7] J. Orwell, P. Remagnino, and G.A. Jones. From connected components to object sequences. In *First IEEE International Workshop on Performance Evaluation of Tracking and Surveillance*, pages 72–79, 2000.

[8] H. Pasula and S. Russell. Approximate inference for first-order probabilistic languages. In *Proceedings of the International Joint Conference of Artificial Intelligence*, 2001.

[9] P.Remagnino. Situated and ubiquitous behaviours: Layers of abstract for scene understanding. In *Proceedings of Artificial Intelligence and Soft Computing (IASTED)*, pages 234–240, 2000.

[10] P.Remagnino, J.Orwell, D.Greenhill, G.A.Jones, and L.Marchesotti. An agent society for scene interpretation. In G.Foresti, P.Mahonen, and C.S. Regazzoni, editors, *Multimedia Video-based Surveillance Systems, Requirements, Issues and Solutions*, pages 108–117. Kluwer, 2000.

[11] P.Remagnino, T.Tan, and K.Baker. Agent orientated annotation in model based visual surveillance. In *Proceedings of IEEE International Conference on Computer Vision*, pages 857–862, 1998.

[12] B. Rosario, N. Oliver, and A. Pentland. A synthetic agent system for bayesian modeling of human interactions. In *Proceedings of Conference on Autonomous Agents*, pages 342–343, 1999.

[13] S.S.Intille and A.F.Bobick. A framework for recognizing multi-agent action from visual evidence. In *Proceedings of the Sixteenth National Conference on Artificial Intelligence*, pages 518–525, 1999.

Tuning the Collaboration Level with Autonomous Agents: A Principled Theory

Rino Falcone[1], Cristiano Castelfranchi[2]

[1]IP-CNR, ROMA - Italy
falcone@ip.rm.cnr.it
[2]University of Siena - Italy
castel@ip.rm.cnr.it

Abstract. In this paper, we address the problem of adjustable autonomy: this is the real general problem with and among autonomous agents. We discuss how modifying the assigned/received delegation entails a proper enlargement or restriction of autonomy (and at which level); and we show how the theory of autonomy adjustment is strictly related to the theory of levels and kinds of delegation and help. We show how adjustability of delegation and autonomy is actually 'bilateral', since not only the delegator can adjust the delegee's autonomy, but also the delegee can have (cooperative) reasons and the ability to change the received delegation and modify its own autonomy in it. Adjustment is also 'bidirectional' (from more autonomy to less autonomy, or vice versa), and multi-dimensional. Finally we analyze the reasons for modifying the assigned autonomy.

1 Introduction: Agents' Autonomy

In this paper we are going to analyze the complex scenario in which a cognitive agent has the necessity to decide if and how to delegate/adopt a task to/from another agent in a given context. How much autonomy is necessary for a given task.

Autonomy [Castelfranchi, 2000] is very useful in collaboration (why having an intelligent collaborator without exploiting its intelligence?) and even necessary in several cases (situatedness, different competencies, local information and reactivity, decentralization, etc.), but it is also risky because of misunderstandings, disagreements and conflicts, mistakes, private utility, etc.. A very good solution to this conflict is maintaining a high degree of interactivity *during* the collaboration, by providing *both* the man/delegator/client and the machine/delegee/contractor the possibility of having initiative in interaction and help (*mixed initiative* [Ferguson&Allen, 1998; Hearst, 1999]) and of *adjusting* [Hexmoor, 2000] the kind/level of delegation and help, and the degree of autonomy run time. We will analyze a specific view of autonomy strictly based on the notions of delegation and adoption [Castelfranchi&Falcone, 1998].

Software and autonomous agents will not be useful only for relieving human agents from boring and repetitive tasks; they will be mainly useful for situations where delegation and autonomy are necessary (*'strong dependence'*) because the delegator will not have the local, decentralised and updated knowledge, or the expertise, or the just-in-time reactivity, or some physical skill that requires some local control-loop.

F. Esposito (Ed.): AI*IA 2001, LNAI 2175, pp. 212-224, 2001.

Thus autonomy and initiative are not simply optional features for *agents*, they are necessary requirements, and obligatory directions of study. However, *control cannot be completely lost and delegation cannot be complete*, not only for reasons of confidence and trust, but for reasons of distribution of goals, of knowledge, of competence, and for an effective collaboration. In this sense the possibility to control and adjust the autonomy of the agents is becoming a growing and interesting research field [Martin&Barber, 1996; Hexmoor, 2000]. Our claim is that *in studying how to adjust the level of autonomy and how to arrive to a dynamic level of control, it is necessary an explicit theory of delegation (and trust), which specifies different dimensions and levels of delegation, and relates the latter to the notion and the levels of autonomy.*

This will provide a principled base for modelling adjustment and its dimensions, not simply an empirical base. In several cases of collaboration among agents an *open delegation* is required, that is the delegation «to bring it about that ...». The agent is supposed to use its knowledge, its intelligence, its ability, and to exert some degree of discretion.

Moreover, since the knowledge of the client concerning the domain and its helping agents is limited (possibly both incomplete and incorrect), some *delegated task* (the requested or the elicited behaviour) might be not so useful for the client itself while perhaps the contractor is able to provide greater help with its own knowledge and ability, going beyond the *literally* delegated task. We will call *extension of help* or *critical help* this kind of help.

However, possible conflicts arise between a client and its contractor; conflicts which are either due to the intelligence and the initiative of the contractor or to an inappropriate delegation by the client. We do not consider here the contractor's *selfish reasons* for modifying delegation.

We have designed a complex model of the relationships among trust, control and autonomy: where autonomy is based on trust and the dynamic evolution of trust is strictly linked with control and with the possibilities of the delegation (autonomy) adjustments.

For the purpose of this paper we use a practical and not very general notion of autonomy. In particular, we refer to the *social* autonomy in a *collaborative* relationship among agents. We distinguish between:

- a *meta-level autonomy* that denotes how much the agent is able and in condition of negotiating about the delegation or of changing it (to this regard, a slave, for example, is not autonomous: he cannot negotiate or refuse);

- a *realization autonomy*, that means that the agent has more or less discretion in finding a solution to an assigned problem, or a plan for an assigned goal.

Both are forms of goal-autonomy, the former at the higher level, the latter at the sub-goals (instrumental) level. We consider part of the same notion the fact that the lower is the client's control (monitoring or intervention) on the execution, the more autonomous is the contractor.

In section 2 we present our delegation/adoption theory and the various dimensions of delegation and help, in particular the interaction and specification dimensions. This (quite long) analysis is very relevant because it introduces a very large and multidimensional spectrum of the possibilities for allocating tasks and for helping another agent to achieve its own goals; it is also shown how these possibilities are, in fact, characterized by the mental components of the agents involved in the interaction. In section 3, we analyze how both delegator and delegee can adjust the previous delegation/adoption action. We see what adjustments are possible and which of them are really interesting. We also analyze the channels and the ways of interaction. In section 4, the relationships between autonomy and delegation are shown. Finally, in section 5, we consider classes of reasons and principles on which adjustments are based.

2 Delegation/Adoption Theory

Let $Act=\{\alpha_1, .., \alpha_n\}$ be a set of *actions*, and $Agt=\{Ag_1, .., Ag_m\}$ a set of *agents*. The *general plan library* is $\Pi = \Pi^a \cup \Pi^d$, where Π^a is the abstraction hierarchy rule set and Π^d is the decomposition hierarchy rule set. An action $\alpha'\in Act$ is called *elementary action* in Π if there is no a rule r in Π such that α' is the left part of r. We will call *BAct* (*Basic Actions*) the set of elementary actions in Π and *CAct* (*Complex Actions*) the remaining actions in *Act*

Given α_1, α_2 and Π^d, we introduce the *Dom-c(α_1 α_2)* operator to say that α_1 *dominates* α_2 (or α_2 *is dominated by* α_1) in Π^d: *Dom-c(α_1 α_2)* = *True* if there is a set of rules $(r_1, .., r_m)$ in Π^d, such that: $(\alpha_1 = Lr_1)\wedge(\alpha_2\in Rr_m)\wedge(Lr_i\in Rr_{i-1})$, where: Lr_j and Rr_j are, respectively, the left part and the right part of the rule r_j and $2\leq i\leq m$ (in the same way it is possible to define the *Dom-a(α_1 α_2)* operator considering the abstraction hierarchy rule set Π^a). We call R the operator that, when applied to an action α, returns the set of the *results* produced by α.

The *notion of delegation* is already explicitly present in the domain of MAS, of collaboration [Haddady, 1996], and team-work.

Informally, *in delegation (reliance) an agent Ag_1 needs or likes an action of another agent Ag_2 and includes it in its own plan. In other words, Ag_1 is trying to achieve some of its goals through Ag_2's actions; thus Ag_1 is relying upon and has the goal that Ag_2 performs a given action. Ag_1* is constructing a MA plan and Ag_2 has a "part" in this plan: Ag_2's task (either a state-goal or an action-goal). On the other hand: *in adoption (help) an agent Ag_2 acquires and has a goal as (long as) it is the goal of another agent Ag_1, that is, Ag_2 usually has the goal of performing an action since this action is included in the plan of Ag_1.* So, also in this case Ag_2 plays a part in Ag_1's plan (sometimes Ag_1 has no plan at all but just a need, or a goal) since Ag_2 is doing something for Ag_1.

We assume that *to delegate an action necessarily implies delegating some result of that action* (i.e. expecting some results from Ag_2's action and relaying on it for obtaining those results). Conversely, *to delegate a goal state always implies the delegation of at least one action (possibly unknown to Ag_1) that produces such a goal state as result* (even when Ag_1 asks Ag_2 to solve a problem, to bring it about that g, without knowing or specifying the action, Ag_1 necessarily presupposes that Ag_2 should and will do some action and relies on this).

Thus, we consider the action/goal pair $\tau=(\alpha,g)$ as the real object of delegation, and we will call it 'task'. Then by means of τ, we will refer to the action (α), to its resulting world state (g), or to both.

We introduce an operator of delegation with three parameters:

$Delegates(Ag_1 \; Ag_2 \; \tau)$, where Ag_1, Ag_2 are agents and $\tau=(\alpha,g)$ is the task. This means that Ag_1 delegates the task τ to Ag_2. In analogy with delegation we introduce the corresponding operator for adoption: $Adopts(Ag_2 \; Ag_1 \; \tau)$. This means that Ag_2 adopts the task τ for Ag_1: helps Ag_1 by caring about τ.

We consider three main dimensions of delegation/adoption: interaction-based types of delegation/ adoption; specification-based types of delegation/ adoption, and control-based types of delegation/ adoption. Let us analyze these cases more in detail.

2.1 Interaction-Based Types of Delegation

We have three general cases: *weak*, *mild* and *strong delegation*. They represent different degrees of strength of the established delegation. More precisely, we call *weak delegation* the delegation simply based on exploitation for the achievement of the task. In it there is no agreement, no request or even (intended) influence: Ag_1 is just exploiting in its plan a fully autonomous action of Ag_2. We call *mild delegation* that based on induction. In it there is no agreement, no request, but Ag_1 is itself eliciting, and inducing in Ag_2 the desired behaviour in order to exploit it. We call *strict delegation*, that based on explicit agreement, i.e. on the achievement by Ag_1 of the task through an agreement with Ag_2.

More precisely, we introduce the *W-Delegates* operator for representing *weak delegation*. So the expression $W\text{-}Delegates(Ag_1 \; Ag_2 \; \tau)$ represents the following *necessary* mental ingredients:

---

a) The achievement of τ (the execution of α and its result g) is a *goal* of Ag_1

b) Ag_1 believes that there exists another agent Ag_2 that has the *power of* achieving τ.

c) Ag_1 believes that Ag_2 will achieve τ in time and by itself (without any Ag_1's intervention).

c-bis) Ag_1 believes that Ag_2 *intends* (in the case that Ag_2 is a cognitive agent) to achieve τ in time and by itself, and that will do this in time and without any Ag_1's intervention.

d) Ag_1 *prefers* to achieve τ through Ag_2

e) The achievement of τ through Ag_2 is the choice (goal) of Ag_1

f) Ag_1 has the goal (*relativized* to (e)) of not achieving τ by itself.

We consider (a, b, c, and d) what the agent Ag_1 views as a "*Potential for relying on*" the agent Ag_2, its *trust* in Ag_2; and (e and f) what Ag_1 views as the "*Decision to rely*" *on*" Ag_2. We consider "Potential for relying on" and "Decision to rely on" as two constructs temporally and logically related to each other.

We introduce the *M-Delegates* operator for representing *mild delegation*. *M-Delegates$(Ag_1 Ag_2 \tau)$* represents the following necessary mental ingredients:

---

a') The achievement of τ is a *goal* of Ag_1

b') Ag_1 believes that there exists another agent Ag_2 that has the *power of* achieving τ.

c') Ag_1 does not believe that Ag_2 will achieve τ by itself (without any Ag_1's intervention).

d') Ag_1 believes that if Ag_1 realizes an action α' then as a consequence it will be more probable that Ag_2 intends τ. Where Ag_2 does not adopt the Ag_1's goal that Ag_2 intends τ.

e') Ag_1 *prefers* to achieve τ through Ag_2.

f') Ag_1 intends to do α' relativized to (d').

g') The achievement of τ through Ag_2 is the goal of Ag_1.

h') Ag_1 has the goal (*relativized* to (g')) of not achieving τ by itself.

We consider (a', b', c', d' and e') what the agent Ag_1 views as a "*Potential for relying on*" the agent Ag_2; and (f, g' and h') what Ag_1 views as the "*Decision to rely on*" Ag_2

With respect to weak and mild delegation it is interesting to analyze the possibilities of the Ag_2's mind. We should distinguish between two main cases: Ag_2 knows *(W)or(M)-Delegates$(Ag_1 Ag_2 \tau)$* and Ag_2 does not know *(W)or(M)-Delegates$(Ag_1 Ag_2 \tau)$*. In other words, a delegation is possible even if the delegee knows it.

We introduce the *S-Delegates* operator for representing *strong delegation*. So the expression *S-Delegates$(Ag_1 Ag_2 \tau)$* represents the following *necessary* mental ingredients:

---

a") The achievement of τ is a *goal* of Ag_1

b") Ag_1 believes that there exists another agent Ag_2 that has the *power of* achieving τ.

c") Ag_1 does not believe that Ag_2 will achieve τ by itself (without any Ag_1's intervention).

d") Ag_1 believes that if Ag_1 realizes an action α' there will be this result: Ag_2 will intend τ as the consequence of the fact that Ag_2 adopts the Ag_1's goal that Ag_2 would intend τ (in other words, Ag_2 will be socially committed [Jennings, 1993] with Ag_1).

e") Ag_1 *prefers* to achieve τ through Ag_2.

f") Ag_1 intends to do α' relativized to (d").

g") The achievement of τ through Ag_2 is the goal of Ag_1.

h") Ag_1 has the goal (*relativized* to (g')) of not achieving τ by itself.

We consider (a", b", c", d" and e") what the agent Ag_1 views as a "*Potential for relying on*" the agent Ag_2; and (f', g" and h") what Ag_1 views as the "*Decision to rely on*" Ag_2.

Also in adoption, as for delegation, we must identify the mental states of the interacting agents, the actions that follow and their results in the world and in the cognitive state of the agents. On the basis of the kind of interaction between the adopting agent and the adopted one, it is possible to define various types of adoption.

Let us call *weak adoption* the adoption just based on spontaneous initiative, on the intended interference of Ag_2 that permits (contributes to) the achievement by Ag_1 of the task.

W-Adopts($Ag_1 Ag_2 \tau$) represents the following *necessary* mental ingredients:

---

a''') Ag_2 believes that the achievement of τ is a *goal* of Ag_1.

b''') Ag_2 believes that Ag_2 has the *power of* achieving τ.

c''') Ag_2 *intends* to achieve τ for Ag_1 (i.e., Ag_2 has the goal to achieve τ relativized to the previous beliefs (*a'''* and *b'''*)).

In analogy with the weak delegation we consider (*a'''* and *b'''*) what the agent Ag_2 views as a "*Potential for weak adoption*" of the agent Ag_1; and (*c'''*) what Ag_2 views as the "*Choice of weak adopting*" Ag_1. There is no agreement, no information or even influence: Ag_2 unilaterally and spontaneously has the goal of performing a given action because this action is either contained in Ag_1's plan or is (according to Ag_2) an interest of Ag_1. Notice that this kind of help may be even ignored by Ag_1. In other words, Ag_2 can adopt some of Ag_1's goals independently of Ag_1's delegation, request or conscious need.

We will call *strong adoption* the adoption based on explicit agreement about the achievement by Ag_2 of the task delegated/requested by Ag_1. It is based on Ag_2's adopting Ag_1's task in response to Ag_1's request/order or Ag_2's offer and Ag_1's acceptance. The expression *S-Adopts($Ag_1 Ag_2 \tau$)* represents the following *necessary* mental ingredients:

---

a'''') Ag_2 believes that the achievement of τ is a *goal* of Ag_1.

b'''') Ag_2 believes that Ag_2 has the *power of* achieving τ.

d'''') Ag_2 believes that Ag_1's goal is "Ag_2 would intend τ"

c'''') Ag_2 *intends* to achieve τ for Ag_1 (i.e., Ag_2 has the goal to achieve τ relativized to the previous beliefs (*a''''*, *b''''*, *d''''*)).

We consider (*a''''*, *b''''* and *d''''*) what Ag_2 sees as a "*Potential for strong adoption*" of the agent Ag_1; and (*c''''*) what Ag_2 sees as the "*Choice of strong adopting*" Ag_1.

Strong delegation is implied and implies *strong adoption*.

2.2 Specification-Based Types of Delegation

The object of delegation (τ) can be minimally specified (*open delegation*), completely specified (*close delegation*) or specified at any intermediate level. Let us consider two cases:

i) *Pure Executive (Close) Delegation:* when the client (or the contractor) believes it is delegating (adopting) a completely specified task; what Ag_1 expects from Ag_2 is just the execution of a sequence of elementary actions (or what Ag_2 believes Ag_1 delegated to it is simply the execution of a sequence of elementary actions).

ii) *Open Delegation:* when the client (contractor) believes it is delegating (adopting) a non completely specified task: either Ag_1 (Ag_2) is delegating (adopting) an abstract action, or it is delegating (adopting) just a result (state of the world). Ag_2 can realize the delegated (adopted) task by exerting its autonomy. We can have several possible level of openness of the delegated (adopted) task.

2.3 Control-Based Types of Delegation

The various possibilities to control the delegated task. We can say that control is a (meta) action:

a) aimed at ascertaining whether another action has been successfully executed or if a given state of the world has been realized or maintained (*feedback*, checking);

b) aimed at dealing with the possible deviations and unforeseen events in order to positively cope with them (*intervention*).

3 The Adjustment of Delegation/Adoption

In section 5 we will analyze the general reasons for delegation/adoption adjustment; let us here consider part of the taxonomy of the adjustments, their nature and their importance.

We do not consider in this paper the delegation/adoption adjustments with respect to the interaction dimention. We are just going to analyze the adjustments with respect to the specification dimension.

3.1 Delegee's Adjustments

Suppose that *Delegates(Ag_1 Ag_2 τ)* and the task (τ) is included in a more general Ag_1's plan aimed at achieving goal g' through a complex action α'. Moreover, *Dom-c(α' α)*, $\tau=(\alpha,g)$, and $\tau'=(\alpha',g')$. We have three main delegee's adjustments (that could be also crossed):

A. *Reduction of Help* (the delegee provides less help on τ than delegated)
if *Adopts(Ag_2 Ag_1 τ_1) AND Dom-c(α α_1)*
with $\tau_1=(\alpha_1,g_1)$, the delegee reduces the task to a subpart of the requested task.

B. *Extension of Help* (the delegee provides more help on τ than delegated)
if *Adopts(Ag_2 Ag_1 τ_1) AND Dom-c(α_1 α) AND (Dom-c(α' α_1) OR ($\alpha'\equiv\alpha_1$)*

with $\tau_1=(\alpha_1,g_1)$; the delegee goes beyond what has been delegated by the client without changing the delegator's plan. In fact, the delegee chooses a task that satisfies a higher level task (within the general delegator's intended plan) compared with the delegated task.

C. *Critical Help (the delegee provides a qualitatively different action/help than what delegated)*

Let us mention only the simplest case: *Simple Critical help*

if *Adopts(Ag_2 Ag_1 τ_x) AND g$\in$R(α_x)*

with $\tau_x=(\alpha_x,g)$; the delegee achieves the goal(s) of the delegated plan/action, but it changes that plan/action.

3.2 Delegator's Adjustments

Suppose that *Delegates(Ag_1 Ag_2 τ)*, and that Ag_1 itself intends to change (to adjust) that delegation. Suppose also that Ag_1 is achieving goal g' through plan τ', with *Dom-c(α' α)*. We can have five main delegator's adjustments:

A. Reduction of Delegation (with respect to the previous delegated plan)

if *Delegates(Ag_1 Ag_2 τ_1) AND Dom-c(α α_1)*

with $\tau_1=(\alpha_1,g_1)$, the delegator adjusts the original delegation, by reducing the task that the contractor must realize (the client reduces the task to a subpart of the previous task requested).

B. *Extension of Delegation (with respect to the previous delegated plan)*

if *Delegates(Ag_1 Ag_2 τ_1) AND Dom-c(α_1 α) AND (Dom-c(α' α_1) OR $\alpha'\equiv\alpha_1$)*

with $\tau_1=(\alpha_1,g_1)$, the delegator adjusts its delegation in such a way that its new request goes beyond what has been previously delegated without changing the previous plan.

C. *Modification of Delegation*

In analogy with the delegee's adjustments, it consists of four subcases (modification of the previous delegated task just changing the previous goal, modification of the previous delegated task considering a super-goal and changing the plan to obtain that goal, modification of the previous delegated task considering a sub-goal and changing the plan to obtain that goal, modification of the previous delegated task changing both the plan and the goal). In this paper, for reasons of brevity, we do not analyze them.

D. *Openness of Delegation*

if *Delegates(Ag_1 Ag_2 τ_x) AND Dom-a(α_x α)*

in words, the delegator adjusts its own delegation so that the new delegated plan is more abstract.

E. *Closening of Delegation*

if *Delegates(Ag_1 Ag_2 τ_x) AND Dom-a(α α_x)*

in words, the delegator adjusts its own delegation so that the new delegated plan is more specified.

For adjusting delegation and help are necessary channels and protocols - on the user/client's side- for monitoring (reporting, observing, inspecting), and for intervention (instructions, guidance, helps, repair, brake); and -on the delegee's side- some room for discretion and practical innovation; for both channels and protocols for communication and re-negotiation during the role-playing and the task execution.

4 The Adjustment of Delegation/Adoption

As we said, not always a delegation adjustment produces a change in the delegee's autonomy (by limiting, restricting or vice versa enlarging, expanding it). The main causes of Autonomy Adjustment are the following ones:
- there is a change of the Ag_2's entitlement at the meta-level (Ag_2 can refuse, negotiate, change the delegation); or it is not entitled but in fact takes such an initiative (*meta-autonomy adjustment*);
- the new task is more or less *open* than the former (*realization-autonomy adjustment*);
- there is more or less control on Ag_2 (*control-dependent autonomy adjustment*);
- there is a change in delegation strength (*interaction-dependent autonomy adjustment*).
Each of these autonomy adjustments are both *bilateral* (realized by either the client or the contractor) and *bidirectional* (either augmenting or reducing the autonomy itself).
In general we can say that:
- *When there is a delegee's adjustment there is always a change of its meta-autonomy* (the delegee decides with its initiative to change the client's delegation); while not always there is a change in its realization autonomy. For example, in the *reduction of help,* realization autonomy remains the same because the delegee realizes just a part of the delegated task (but this part was also included in the previously delegated task). In other words, the delegee does not have more autonomy in how to realize τ. Conversely in the *extension of help*, there are two possibilities: i) the delegee has more realization autonomy when the adopted plan includes some (not delegated) part which is non completely specified (thus the delegee has more discretion in its realization); ii) the delegee has the same realization autonomy if the adopted plan does not need more discretion than the delegated one. Finally, in the *critical help*, there is always more realization autonomy given the possibility to choose new actions.
- *When there is a client's adjustment the delegee's meta-autonomy never changes* (in fact, the client itself takes the initiative of modifying the delegation). As for the delegee's realization autonomy we can say that: in the case of *reduction of delegation*, Ag_2's autonomy of execution (if its discretionary power is reduced with the new delegation) is reduced or it remains unchanged (suppose that the old task was completely specified in all details). In the case of *extension of delegation*, either the autonomy of realization increases (if the new task presupposes some action -not included in the old one- with a certain degree of openness) or it remains unchanged (if this new task was completely specified in all details). In the case of *critical delegation*, the autonomy of realization of the delegee increases or not depending on whether respectively the new actions are more or less open than the old ones. In the case of *openness of delegation*, the autonomy of realization of the delegee always increases (openness is in fact a factor that increases the discretion of the delegee). Vice versa, in the case of *closing of delegation*, the delegee's autonomy of realization is always reduced.
Another very interesting dimension of autonomy adjustment -which we do not consider here- is that linked to the strength of delegation.

4.1 Adjusting Autonomy by Modifying Control

As we said a very important *dimension* of autonomy is related to the control activity of the adopted/delegated task. Given that control is composed by feedback plus intervention, adjusting it means to adjust (at least one of) its components. Let us consider some relevant aspects.

Adjusting the Frequency of Feeback
The *frequency of the feedback on the task* could be:
- *purely temporal* (when the monitoring or the reporting is independent of the structure of the activities in the task, they only depend on a temporal choice);
- *linked with the working phases* (when the activities of the task are divided in phases and the monitoring or the reporting is connected with them).
Client and contractor could adjust the frequency of their feedback activity in three main ways:
- by *changing the temporal intervals* fixed at the beginning of the task delegation/adoption (when the monitoring/reporting was purely temporal);
- by *changing the task phases* in which the monitoring/reporting is realized with respect to those fixed at the beginning of the task delegation (when monitoring/reporting was linked with the working phases);
- by *moving from* the purely temporal monitoring/reporting to the working phases monitoring/reporting (or vice versa).

Adjusting the Frequency and Kind of Intervention
As explained above, the intervention is strictly connected with the presence of the monitoring/reporting on the task, even if, in principle, both the intervention and the monitoring/reporting could be independently realized. In addition, also the frequencies of intervention and of monitoring/reporting are correlated. More precisely, the frequency of intervention could be: 1) *never*; 2) *just sometimes* (phase or time, a special case of this is at the end of the task); 3) *at any phase or at any time (depending of the necessity)*.
The adjustment of the frequency of intervention by the client is an important case of adjustment of contractor's autonomy. Suppose that at the beginning there is an agreement about the fact that *never* is the established frequency of intervention, and suppose that the client intervenes one or more times during the contractor's task realization: the contractor's autonomy has been reduced. In general, a contractor is more autonomous if the frequency of client's intervention is low.
So the adjustments by the client in this direction (low frequency of interventions) produce an increase of contractor's autonomy.

5 Principles and Reasons for Autonomy Adjustment

We will examine in this section the general basic reasons (criteria) for adjusting (restricting or expanding) the delegee's autonomy by both the user/client, and the delegee.

5.1 Why the Client Should Reduce the Delegee's Autonomy

In this preliminary identification of reasons for autonomy adjustment we prefer a more qualitative and simplified view, not necessarily related with a probabilistic framework. Of course, to be more precise, one should specify that what changes are the subjective probabilities assigned to those events (beliefs). For example, at the moment of delegation Ag_1 has believed that the probability of mistakes by Ag_2 was p (and this expectation was compatible with the decision of delegating with a given degree of autonomy), while now Ag_1 realizes that this probability is higher than expected.

Let us simplify the issue in the following schema:

WHEN (classes of reasons):
- Ag_1 believes that Ag_2 is not doing (in time) what Ag_1 has delegated to it; and/or
- Ag_1 believes that Ag_2 is working badly and makes mistakes (because of lack of competence of knowledge, of control, etc.); and/or
- Ag_1 believes that there are unforeseen events, external dangers and obstacles that perhaps Ag_2 is not able to deal with; and/or
- Ag_1 believes that Ag_2 is going beyond its role or task, and Ag_1 is not happy about this (because of lack of trust or of conflict of power)
THEN (reduction of autonomy)
Ag_1 will reconsider his/her/its delegation to Ag_2, and Ag_2's level of autonomy in order to reduce it by either specifying the plan (task) or by introducing additional control, or constraining the interaction (strong delegation), etc..

5.2 Why the Client Should Expand the Delegee's Autonomy

WHEN (classes of reasons):
- Ag_1 believes that Ag_2 is doing or can do better than previously expected (predicted); and/or
- Ag_1 believes that the external conditions are better than expected; and/or
- Ag_1 believes that Ag_2 is working badly and makes mistakes (because of lack of possible flexibility, or because too much control, etc.) and/or
- Ag_1 believes that Ag_2 can do more than previously assigned, or can find its own situated way of solving the problem
THEN (expansion of autonomy)
Ag_1 will reconsider his/her/its delegation to Ag_2, and Ag_2's level of autonomy in order to expand it by either letting the plan (task) less specified or reducing control or doing weaker the interaction, etc..

5.3 Why Limiting Its Own Autonomy

Let us now consider some (collaborative) reasons of adjustment on the delegated agent's side.

WHEN (classes of reasons):
- Ag_2 arrives to believe that it is not able to do all the task (level of self-confidence); and/or
- Ag_2 arrives to believe that there are unforeseen events, external dangers and obstacles that it is not able to deal with
THEN (reduction of autonomy)
Ag_2 will reconsider the received delegation (for example providing sub-help and doing less than delegated) and its level of autonomy in order to reduce it by either asking for the specification of the plan (task) or for the introduction of additional control (example: "give me instructions, orders; monitor, help, or substitute me").

5.4 Why Expanding Its Own Autonomy

WHEN (classes of reasons):
- Ag_2 arrives to believe that it is able or in condition for doing more or providing a significantly better solution for the delegated goal (within the Ag_1 plan, or relatively also to other Ag_1's desires and interests), and
- Ag_2 is rather sure about this (both about Ag_1's plan and needs; the optimality of the new solution; and its own capability), and
- it is not forbidden or is (explicitly or implicitly) permitted by Ag_1 that Ag_2 takes such a collaborative initiative, and/or
- Ag_2 believes that Ag_1 will accept and enjoy its initiative (because convenience largely exceeds surprise or distress)
THEN (expansion of autonomy)
Ag_2 will reconsider the received delegation and level of autonomy in order to go beyond those limits by directly providing for example over-help or critical -help (doing more and better).

(When the 2nd, 3rd and 4th of the above conditions are not realized, Ag_2 could take the initiative of communicating for offering the new solution or in asking for the permission, and in fact for re-negotiating the delegation).

6 Conclusions

Our rationale was as follows: i) autonomy is very useful in collaboration (why having an intelligent collaborator without exploiting its intelligence?) and even necessary in several cases (situatedness, different competencies, local information and reactivity, decentralization, etc.); ii) but it is also risky -because of misunderstandings, disagreements and conflicts, mistakes, private utility, etc.; iii) a very good solution to this conflict is maintaining a high degree of interactivity *during* the collaboration, by providing *both* the man/delegator/client and the machine/delegee/contractor the possibility of having initiative in interaction and help (*mixed initiative*) and of *adjusting* the kind/level of delegation and help, and the degree of autonomy run time.

Our claim is that in order to adjust autonomy one should in fact adjust the delegation/help relationship. Moreover, adjustment is *bi-directional* (one can expand or reduce the delegee's autonomy) and is *bilateral*. This means that also the delegee, the machine (the 'agent') can change or try to change its level of autonomy by modifying the received delegation or the previous level/kind of help. This is an additional and important aspect of its autonomy.

We have discussed: different types and levels of delegation and help, and their relationships; different kinds of transitions among delegation and adoption levels (adjustments); different reasons for adjusting a previous kind of delegation or help and level of autonomy; and how also control represents a crucial dimension.

In our view, to neglect or reduce the mental characterization of delegation (allocation of tasks) and adoption (to help another agent to achieve its own goals) means, on the one hand, loose a set of possible interesting kinds and levels of reliance and help, and, on the other hand, do not completely satisfy the needs and the nature of human interaction that is strongly based on these categories of cooperation.

7 References

[Castelfranchi, 2000] Castelfranchi C., (2000) Founding Agent's Autonomy on Dependence Theory, in Proceedings of ECAI'00,. Berlin, August 2000.

[Castelfranchi&Falcone, 1998] Castelfranchi, C., Falcone, R. (1998), Towards a Theory of Delegation for Agent-based Systems, *Robotics and Autonomous Systems*, Special issue on Multi-Agent Rationality, Elsevier Editor. Vol. 24, pp. 141-157.

[Ferguson&Allen, 1998] Ferguson, G., Allen J., (1998) TRIPS: An Integrated Intelligent Problem-Solving Assistant, Proc. National Conference AI (AAAI-98), AAAI Press, Menlo Park, Calif.

[Haddadi, 1996] A. Haddadi, Communication and Cooperation in Agent Systems (the Springer Press, 1996).

[Hearst, 1999] Hearst M. (editor), Mixed-initiative interaction - Trends & Controversies, IEEE Intelligent Systems, September/October 1999.

[Hexmoor, 2000] Hexmoor H. (editor), Special Issue on Autonomy Control Software, Journal of Experimental & Theoretical Artificial Intelligence, Vol.12 N°2, April-June 2000.

[Jennings, 1996] Jennings N.R. 1993. Commitments and conventions: The foundation of coordination in multi-agent systems. *The Knowledge Engineering Review*, 3, 223-50.

[Martin&Barber, 1996] Martin C. E., Barber K. S., (1996), Multiple, Simultaneous Autonomy Levels for Agent-based Systems, in Proc. Fourth International Conference on Control, Automation, Robotics, and Vision, Westing Stamford, Singapore, pp.1318-1322.

The Definition of Legal Relations in a BDI Multiagent Framework

Guido Boella, Leonardo Lesmo

Dipartimento di Informatica and Centro di Scienza Cognitiva
Università di Torino - Cso Svizzera 185 - Torino ITALY
guido@di.unito.it

Lyda Favali

Dipartimento di Scienze Giuridiche
Università di Torino - V. S.Ottavio 54 - Torino ITALY
lyfavali@tin.it

Abstract. This paper aims at linking the AI notion of multi agent system with the notion of LEGAL RELATION [Allen & Saxon 95]. The paper is based on the idea that legal rules concern actions to accomplish or to exclude and states to achieve or to avoid or actions for changing existing legal relations. The body of the rule establishes who and under which conditions must respect the obligation. The notion of 'obligation' has been defined elsewhere [Boella & Lesmo 01] and will be reviewed here. In this paper it is used as an ontological basis to define the LEGAL RELATIONS appearing in the A-Hohfeld language, and the concepts of 'bearer of the obligation' (who undergoes the rule) and of 'normative agent' (who watches on the rule) are connected to an ontology of legal entities.

Introduction

In recent years, there have been two parallel lines of research in AI and law. Intelligent agents have been one of the mainstreams in AI. Legal Relations have been shown to be one of the main tools to rationalize legal reasoning. This paper aims at building a bridge between the two fields.

Multiagent systems are based on a similarity to human behavior. So it is not strange that agent theories have evolved to model not only software agents, but also their human counterpart. This is useful from a twofold perspective: human agents (i.e. the users of computer systems) must interact with software tools, so it is important that such tools have understandable (on their side) models of their human users, in order to devise the ways to serve them better; second, if software agents are modelled in a way similar to human users, the users can have a better understanding of their behavior and find them more friendly and usable.

On the legal side, it has been claimed that many legal terms, as 'right' are often used in an approximate way so that as early as at the beginning of this century, it has been tried to determine a set of basic legal terms able to define in an unambiguous way legal rules. This early attempt has evolved in a more precise formalization, i.e. the A-Hohfeld language [Allen & Saxon 95]. This language was born as a semi-formal definition of the basic LEGAL RELATIONS, and developed into a complex system

F. Esposito (Ed.): AI*IA 2001, LNAI 2175, pp. 225-236, 2001.

of EXTENDED LEGAL RELATIONS, claimed to cover all concepts useful for describing legal rules [Allen & Saxon 98, 99].

But legal rules aim at constraining the behavior of the individual subject to them, in order to make it compatible with a desired social harmony. So, there is an apparent relationship between the legal system and multi agent systems. It seems reasonable to try and connect the two points of view: formal models of behavior, and formal models of constraints on behavior.

Most works in the field of AI and law have focused on the representational issues of legal rules (see [Tiscornia & Turchi 97]) or on the problem of the possible combinations of normative positions [Sergot 98]. On the contrary, in the MAS community, more and more attention is being devoted to the problem of generating norm abiding behavior and of modeling the decision process of agents under obligations ([Dignum 96], [Castelfranchi 98] [Sartor 01]).

In the past years, we have developed a model of agents, able to account for some complex phenomena concerning human behavior in dialogue [Ardissono et al. 00], and for the basic principles of rational behavior in the interaction with other agents [Boella 00]. More recently, we have shown that this model is able to cope with obligations [Boella & Lesmo 01].

In this paper, we want to draw a connection between these two fields by introducing our treatment of norms and obligations in the definition of the Legal Relations of the A-Hohfeld language [Allen & Saxon 95]. The main contribution of this attempt is to make explicit the *operational* component underlying legal reasoning, which is left implicit in many works, starting from [Allen & Saxon 95]. A new link is established between a rule expressed in terms of Legal Relations, and the required behavior of the individuals mentioned in the rule. On this basis, it is possible to define rules which are applicable both to human and to software agents, and to introduce new formal ways to reason about the applicability of rules.

The paper is organized as follows: the next section introduces the basic concepts of the underlying model of agents; the third section gives a short introduction to A-Hohfeld; the fourth section presents a formal definition of obligations; the last section shows how LEGAL RELATIONS can be specified in terms of actions and obligations; finally, the Conclusions close the paper.

Agents, Actions, and Obligations

Although the theory of BDI (Belief-Desires-Intentions) agents need not be examined in depth in the present context, there are some aspects which are relevant. Perhaps, the most important are that agents have goals and are capable to act in order to achieve these goals. An aspect that is usually disregarded is where these goals come from. It is usually assumed that an agent has personal desires that concur in forming his goals; moreover, the social desire to maintain good relations with other agents (i.e. social goals), or the necessity to coordinate cooperation (goal adoption [Castelfranchi 98]) can lead to the formation of goals. But there is at least another source of goals which should be considered: it consists in *obligations*.

In previous papers, we outlined a theory of norms and a reasoning framework for taking deliberations dealing with obligations, which is inspired by the work of

[Goffman 70] in the sociological field. According to Goffman, a norm is a kind of guide to action which is supported by social sanctions. Moreover, he defines as *sanction* a reaction of others to the behavior of an individual or a group, a reaction aiming at enforcing the respect of a given norm. Hence, from the point of view of sociology, norms come always together with sanctions; since sanctions are actions, they presuppose, in turn, someone to perform them. As noted in [Tiscornia & Turchi 97]: "in general, every prescription requires a sanction. [...] prescriptions are autonomous norms, while sanctions exist in as far as there is also a prescription to which they refer" (p.65)[1]. So, there is a strict dependence between sanctions and norms, at least in most cases[2].

We founded our theory of *obligations* on the following assumptions:

1. There exists a *Bearer* who must fulfill the prescription(s) carried by the obligation.
2. The prescription is represented as an *Action to be done,* an *Action not to be done,* a *State to achieve,* or a *State to avoid.*
3. There exists a *Sanction,* which can be applied in case the prescription is not fulfilled. In principle, the sanction is an action which affects the bearer in a negative way.
4. There exists a *Normative Agent* who acts in case the obligation is not fulfilled and possibly her action results in the application of the sanction to the Bearer.

We have shown that such a formalization of obligations can be embedded in a MAS which is based on the notion of *goal adoption, anticipatory coordination* [Castelfranchi 98] and *decision theoretic planning* as the one presented in [Boella 00].

As stated above, the agent's goals do not depend only on his own objectives but he also has to take into account other agents' goals, such as those involved in obligations. But the decision about which goal to pursue cannot be made only on the basis of the effects of the plan for achieving the different goals. In a multiagent setting, the agent's choices directly affect the behavior of other agents. As [Goffman 70] notices in his discussion on *strategic interaction,* when an agent considers which course of action to follow, before he takes a decision, he will depict in his mind the consequences of his action for the other involved agents, their likely reaction, and the influence of this reaction on his own welfare. He will adapt his actions to the other agents' reaction before it can even happen.

If we want to cope with this kind of reasoning we need both a criterion for comparing actions and some form of *anticipatory coordination* to predict the reactions of the other agents involved in the interaction. To meet the first requirement, we adopted *decision theory* so that we can characterize the preferences of an agent by means of a *utility function.* On the other hand, anticipatory coordination means that the state that results from the execution of an action (or, in general, a plan) cannot be used to evaluate the utility of the action. Rather, each outcome of the agent's action

---

[1] Similar comments in the economical field are made in [Axelrod 86].

[2] Of course, there are exceptions; for instance, the so called 'blank norms' or 'natural obligations' lack an explicit sanction component. Moreover, sanctions are not the only motivation for fulfilling a norm, as we show in [Boella & Lesmo 01]. For instance, an agent can get a direct advantage from the fulfillment of the norm, as a personal satisfaction in complying with social rules.

must be first updated with the effects of the (predicted) reaction of the other agent. The other agent must be (recursively) modeled as a BDI agent, with his own beliefs, goals and preferences.

This is particularly relevant in the case of obligations. In this case, the 'other agents' can be reduced to the Normative Agent, so that, in choosing what to do, the Bearer of the obligation must try to foresee whether the Normative Agent will sanction him in case he does not fulfill the obligation which the Normative Agent must enforce.

It may well happen that the choice falls on a plan which does not fulfill the obligation, in case all plans that fulfill it lead to a very negative state for the agent. More interestingly, the Bearer could also devise plans to mislead (or corrupt) the Normative Agent, so that the Sanction is not applied even if the obligation has not been fulfilled. We have also argued that this modelling of dishonest agents (even if morally questionable) could be essential in order to let Normative Agents recognize dishonest behaviors.

As a consequence, norms need not be represented by another primitive propositional attitude with a distinct ontological status, but as a combination of beliefs and goals of the agent subject to the norm and of the agent who has to enforce the respect of the norm: in particular, the goal of avoiding sanctions, the goal of not violating the norm and the belief that there is another agent who has the goal of sanctioning violations.

The technical tools we adopted to implement the model is decision theoretic planning (i.e., non classical planning based on decision theory and/or game theory, see [Haddawy & Hanks 98]). It is useful to remember that decision and game theoretic planning have an important role in modelling multi agent situations, as, for example, [Boutilier 99] and [Gmytrasiewicz & Durfee 00] have recently argued.

Legal Relations

It is not possible to describe here in any detail the organization of the A-Hohfeld language. However, we need to introduce the basic principles.

The language is organized around eight Basic Legal Relations: Duty , Right, Privilege, No Right, Power, Inability, Liability, Immunity. The goal of the language is to overcome a problem associated with these relations, i.e. the difficulty of providing for them a clear definition. So, A-Hohfeld is a semi-formal language enabling one to express such definitions (an example is reported below in the subsection on *Directed Obligations*).

A second, more recent goal of the inventors of A-Hohfeld is to provide the language with the ability to express, by means of the Legal Relations all Legal Concepts. This has been achieved by the definition of Enriched Legal Relations, which, via the introduction of some quantifiers ranging on the involved agents and of some negations (which may be present or absent), brought the total number of Legal Relations up to about 1600.

It is clear that the goal of the present paper cannot be to redefine A-Hohfeld, or to introduce a different language. On the contrary, the goal is to look for the underlying ontology of the LEGAL RELATIONS, and the proposal is to adopt, as the basic ontological concept, the concept of *obligation*. In other words, this paper aims at showing that all the LEGAL RELATIONS can be defined operationally on the basis of a formal of definition of obligations, as the one we introduced for modelling agent behavior; so, artificial agents can be said to have DUTIES, RIGHTS, etc., and rational motivations for reasoning about them, as human agents do.

A Formal Definition of Obligations

In the definition of obligation, we assumed that it consists in a situation where an agent N (the *Normative Agent*) has a goal G that another (or more than one) agent B (the *Bearer*) satisfy a goal G', and who, in every case the agent B acts without adopting the goal G', has to decide whether to perform an action Act which (negatively) affects some aspect of the world which (presumably) interests B. Both agents know these facts.

Differently from what appears at first sight, this definition covers not only "institutional" cases, but also other situations like obligations in dialog (see [Boella et al. 99] and [Ardissono et al. 00]) which share the characteristic that new goals are acquired as a consequence of social inputs.

Formally, we define an agent C as a 6-tuple {IB, G, f, L, KP, P}, where:

- *IB* are the agent beliefs (including the beliefs about the possible *normative agents*);
- *G* is the set of private goals of *C*;
- f is the utility function of *C* (a function from states to real numbers); it is used to evaluate the outcomes of *C*'s actions. f applies to states expressed as sets of attributes. We restrict it to functions expressed as the weighed sum of unary functions, each of which takes as argument the value of one of the attributes describing the current status of the world; each unary function expresses the desirability degree of the values of an attribute;
- *L* is a set of tuples representing the obligations known by *C* of which he is the *bearer*;
- *KP* is the set of plan recipes which *C* knows (see, for example, [Carberry 90]);
- P is a (probabilistic) planner which, given a set containing goals and states, produces the plans that may possibly be executed by an agent (the agent's *candidate plans*) in any situation.

In the *L* component of an agent, an obligation Ω is represented as a 5-tuple {*B, N, O, CO, R*} where:

1. *B* is the *bearer* of the obligation (actually the description of the class of individuals to which the obligation applies; i.e. it is the *type* of the potential bearers)
2. *N* is the *normative agent* (actually the type of the authorized normative agents)

3. *O* is the *content* of the obligation, i.e., the state or action goal which *N* wants to be adopted by *B*,
4. *CO* is the *condition* of the obligation, i.e., the set of predicates specifying in which states the obligation must be fulfilled,
5. *R* is an action (the *sanction*) which *N* will presumably bring about in case he detects a violation of the obligation.

The content of the obligation Ω, i.e. *O*, is not necessarily a state (e.g., ``the tank must be full"), but it can be also an action where B is the agent (e.g., ``the agent should send the credit card number") or not (e.g., ``The parent of the agent must submit his personal certificate"). But it can also be the prescription of not executing an action (``you should not send huge files by mails") or, almost equivalently, the prescription not to achieve a state (``the tank must not be empty") or to maintain it true as in the current situation (``the door must remain closed").

Of course, the sanction is executed only in case the normative agent believes that there is a violation: in order to establish whether a violation occurred the normative agent has to perform a monitoring action. For this reason, in our model, the sanction *R* is represented by a plan to be executed by the normative agent that consists of a monitoring action followed by the very action of affecting the world in a way that is (negatively) relevant for the bearer agent.

Directed Obligations

One of the features which are present in the Language of LEGAL RELATIONS (LLR) is the concept of *directed obligation* (an in-depth analysis of this concept appears in [Herrestad & Krogh 95]). The idea is that most LR are directed to a counterparty. This is not prescribed by the definition of obligation presented above. Obviously, it is possible to extend the definition of obligation by introducing a third privileged individual (beyond the bearer and the normative agent), who plays the role of the beneficiary of the obligation. However, a closer inspection of the role of Normative Agent suggests another solution.

The *Normative Agent* was introduced to model the institutional figure who has the task to check that a particular set of obligations is respected (e.g., policemen)[3]. However, it seems that this same role, complemented with the notion of utility we introduced above, can play the role of the counterparty. In fact, there is the possibility that two conditions hold (in the definition of the obligation):

1. The Normative Agent is *positively affected* by the *content O* of the obligation (i.e., he occurs among the Action Participants of *O* and the execution/achievement of *O* provides him with an increase of utility).
2. The sanction consists in opening a legal procedure against the bearer (e.g. a complaint).

---

[3] Actually, there exists another important institutional figure, the *Sovereign*, who created the obligation. Since the model presented in this paper is mainly intended as a model of action under the constraints of obligations, the Sovereign and the Defender Agents have been merged in a single *Normative Agent*. See, however, the comments on the POWER relation and the Conclusions.

In case these conditions hold, we say that the normative agent plays the role of *counterparty* of the bearer of the obligation, and we call the obligations such that these conditions hold *Directed Obligations*.

We claim that the concept of utility and the action-based formalization give substance to the notion of *benefit* (note that these two notions are already present in our framework for independent reasons): "when expressing such a preference, the legal authority regards A to be a *benefit* for j (and j be the *beneficiary* of A)" [Herrestad & Krogh, p.212] (in the quotation, A corresponds to our O, and j to our Normative Agent). Of course, the evaluation of the utility is not carried out by A, but by the legal authority (the Sovereign), who created the rule.

The conditions listed above mirror rather closely a clause in the definition of RIGHT given in [Allen & Saxon 95, p.223]. But what is more important, [Allen & Saxon 95] directly relates deontic notions with the behavior of the normative agent and, in turn, of the legal system:

"Person-p1 has a Right that Person-p2 do s" means [...] "IT IS OBLIGATORY THAT s be done for Person-p1 by Person-p2" *which, in turn, means operationally* [...]
IF   A. IT IS NOT SO THAT Person-p2 does s for Person-p1
THEN B. Person-p2 has violated her DUTY to Person-p1, AND
       C. IF   Person-p1 seeks remedy in the legal system by Litigating
           THEN the legal system will provide a remedy to
           Person-p1 with respect to Person-p2

This is reported as an *operational* definition of RIGHT, *in terms of how the legal system will treat the matter*. Since our perspective is operational, in the sense that we model the behavior of agents, it is not strange that there is a strict correspondence. In fact, our sanctioning of the failure to respect an obligation produces the same effect in two steps: first, the counterparty sanctions the bearer by *seeking remedy in the legal system*; then, the legal system will have the duty (expressed as a general obligation to sanction who does not fulfill an obligation) to *provide remedy*. Note that, in general, the sanction is not 'obligatory', unless explicitly stated, so that no counterparty has the obligation to seek remedy. When the bearer of the obligation has to decide whether to comply with the obligation he has to simulate the decision process of the counterparty and see if he will choose to seek remedy (i.e., if he will become aware of a violation, if he knows how to seek remedy, if he can seek remedy, and if it is useful for him to do so). Note that the normative agent, either with the role of counterparty or not, is not necessarily the *sovereign* agent who created the norm (but see Footnote 3).

Finally, in case there is a counterparty, the act of seeking remedy is not an exercise of POWER (see the definition in the next Section), since no new obligation of the legal system is created, but just one of the conditions of application of an existing obligation of the legal system (to provide remedy) is made true. In this case, the Bearer will have to (recursively) simulate not only the reasoning of the Normative agent but also how the legal system will decide to fulfill his obligation to provide remedy to the violation (see [Boella & Lesmo 01] for a discussion on multiple levels of recursive modelling).

In other situations, where the normative agent watches over the norm on the behalf of some institution (e.g., a policeman), the sanction can be an exercise of POWER (e.g., creating the duty to pay a fine) or even some form of punishment affecting the utility of the bearer of the norm.

Obligations and Legal Relations

Given the definition of obligation described in the previous section, it is now possible to provide a definition of the LEGAL RELATIONS. We will show the definition of some of the 8 basic Relations. This should not be seen as a principled choice, but it depends on space constraints. The dual versions can easily be produced.

The relation which is closer to the definition of obligation is DUTY:

Agent D has the **DUTY** to P iff
1. There exists an obligation Ω, such that
    - The Bearer B_Ω of Ω is of type T_{B_Ω}
    - The applicability condition of Ω is CO_Ω
    - The content of Ω, O_Ω is equal to P
2. D is of type T_{B_Ω}
3. The condition CO_Ω holds in the current situation

Clauses 2 and 3 are remarkable, since they impose some conditions on the definition of DUTY. Clause 2 simply transfers to duties the requirement we set forth for obligations that they are defined for specific subclasses of individuals. Clause 3 specifies that any duty is subject to certain conditions. This is partially in contrast with the separation maintained in A-Hohfeld between basic and CONDITIONAL LEGAL RELATIONS. We believe that in most cases DUTIES (as any other LEGAL RELATION) is conditioned to a particular state of affair; clearly, in some special cases, the condition can simply coincide with the truth value "True" (i.e. it always holds), but we claim that these are just exceptions to the more common cases. Notice that it is not specified if CO_Ω must be true at the outset or it can become true after some particular action or event. In case there is an event that makes true a condition previously false, then the DUTY comes about for the agent: operationally, this means that from that moment the Bearer must adopt the goal specified by Ω and decide to pursue it under the light of the anticipation of a possible sanction. Finally, we must observe that there is a universal quantification implicit in the *iff* operator "For each D and P, then ...", and that the agent variable D can occur in CO_Ω.

Agent A has the **RIGHT** to P towards agent D iff
1. There exists an obligation Ω, such that
    - The Bearer B_Ω of Ω is of type T_{B_Ω}
    - The Normative Agent N_Ω of Ω is of type T_{N_Ω}
    - The applicability condition of Ω is CO_Ω
    - The content of Ω, O_Ω is equal to P
2. D is of type T_{B_Ω}

3. The condition CO_Ω holds

4. N_Ω has the role of Counterparty (i.e. it is positively affected by P and may apply the sanction – seeking remedy against B_Ω)

5. A is of type T_{N_Ω}

This is "directed" RIGHT, as the presence of Counterparty (defined above) in clause 4 shows. It can be observed that the condition CO_Ω, being any general proposition concerning the situation at hand, could require that N_Ω be in a given relation R with the bearer of the obligation B_Ω; in this case, the RIGHT applies just in case A is in relation R with D.

Agent D has the **PRIVILEGE** to P iff

1. There exists no obligation O, such that
   - The Bearer B_Ω of Ω is of type T_{B_Ω}
   - The applicability condition of Ω is CO_Ω
   - The contents of Ω, O_Ω is equal to $\neg P$

2. Or, if such an obligation exists, either

3. D is not of type T_{B_Ω}, or

4. The condition CO_Ω does not hold in the current situation

In other words, D has the PRIVILEGE to P if there is no obligation that prevents P, or if such an obligation exists, it does not apply to D, or it does not apply in the current situation. It can be observed that there is a difference between the explicit statement of a privilege and the realization that a given action (P) is not explicitly forbidden. In our view, this is an important matter, which concerns consistency in law. As stated above, we assume that our proposal is in line with the basic assumptions of Hohfeldian Legal Relations[4]. So, we do not argue against the opportunity to include in the language relations as PRIVILEGE. In fact, it seems clear that checking that there are no duties that forbid a given action is a difficult task; so it is not unreasonable that the legislator carries out this check just once, and then states explicitly the existence of the privilege. The next time a case must be examined, the full check of existing duties can be bypassed, and the privilege can be applied. However, it seems also clear that stating a PRIVILEGE of D to P, while the current set of rules also state that, in the same situation, D has the DUTY to $\neg P$ is an inconsistency that should be avoided. Finally, notice that this is a liberal view of law: you can do everything which is not explicitly forbidden. In principle, it is possible to revert to a restrictive view: privileges are defined as basic, and duties as derivative. In this case, you obtain something as: you cannot do anything, unless you are explicitly allowed to[5].

---

[4] It must be observed that some scholars have challenged the view of Allen and Saxon, claiming that *Privilege* is not the absence of obligations, but the fact that no obligation affecting the privilege can be created ("there should not exists any obligation such that …").

[5] Actually, what should be done is to substitute the basic concept of obligation with the inverse concept of permission (actions that one can do without sanctions). Then, privileges are defined in terms of permissions and duties in terms of absence of permissions. But the underlying idea is the same.

In order to define the next LEGAL RELATION, POWER, we need to introduce a particular subset of actions. This does not affect the underlying ontologic assumptions, but it simply enables us to introduce the recursion required by POWER[6]: An Obligation-Affecting-Action related to the LEGAL RELATION P is an action such that, among its effects there is:
1. either a modification of the current set of obligations that produces P,
2. or the modification of the set of Obligation-Affecting-Actions   such that this modification produces P.

So in the first case, it is possible to introduce a new obligation (thus creating, for instance, a new DUTY); in the second case, it is possible to introduce an action whose agent creates an obligation (creating the POWER to create a DUTY), or an action whose agent can introduce an action for creating an obligation (two-level application of POWER, in LR terms), etc.

Agent D has the **POWER** to bring about that P iff
1. There exists an obligation-affecting-action R related to P, such that
    - The Agent X_R of R is of type T_R
    - The applicability condition of R is CO_R
2. D is of type T_R
3. CO_R holds in the current situation

It can be observed that this definition is rather simple, with respect to the complexity of the concept of POWER. A first reason is that it is not necessary to introduce the notion of *authority*, since the fact that the action exists (with the specified consequences) is sufficient: the ontology of actions is such that the presence of an action says by itself that (under the defined conditions) the action will produce the specified effects; it is just the type of effects which keeps apart the exercise of POWER from any other action.

A second reason for the simplicity of the definition is that the definition of Obligation-Affecting-Actions has far-reaching implications. First of all, it is not explicitly required that P does not hold before D exploits its power, neither it is stated that after D executes R, D looses his power. This is not needed, since the definition involves a *modification* in the set of existing obligations. If, for instance, the effect of R is to introduce a new obligation, it is clear that the execution of R by D has no effect if such obligation is already enforced, so that the definition does not apply (no modification to the set of existing obligation is produced), and D does not have any POWER about P. Analogously, after D has exercised his POWER, P will be present among the existing obligations, so that any subsequent execution of R by D will have no effect (D has lost his POWER). Second, it does not seem that we need to keep apart various kinds of POWER (power of creating duties, power of creating privileges, power of creating power, etc.). In fact, these differences depend on the kind of modifications to the set of obligations or actions. In case a new obligation is added, then it usually produces new duties for some agents (the agents of the required type, and when the condition of application holds). In case an existing obligation is cancelled, then new privileges may be created (all the privileges concerning actions that were previously forbidden by the cancelled obligation). In case the condition of

---

[6] Intuitively, POWER is the right to create some new obligations.

application or the type of the bearer is modified, we can have that, with a single application of POWER, both some duties (for some agents) and some privileges (for other agents) are created. For instance, if there is an obligation such that all young people under 16 cannot enter a disco after midnight, and this obligation is changed into the obligation that no young people under 15 can enter a disco after eleven, we obtain that the DUTY is created for young under 15 not to enter a disco between eleven p.m. and midnight and that the PRIVILEGE is created for young between 15 and 16 to enter discos after midnight.

Finally, the recursive character of POWER is mirrored in the use of the recursive obligation-affecting-action within the definition of POWER.

As [Jones & Sergot 96] discuss, the notion of power must be kept separate from those of *permission* and *practical possibility*. In our model, the first notion is clearly distinct from POWER, since one can have a POWER while having the DUTY not to exercise it: if, instead, he does so, the violation of the DUTY may lead the normative agent to sanction him according to the specification of the related obligation. On the other hand, the *practical possibility* depends on the truth of the applicability conditions of the obligation-affecting-action involved in the POWER.

Conclusions

In this paper, we have shown that a theoretical framework based on actions and agents can provide a useful basis for expressing the meaning of the LEGAL RELATIONS appearing in the A-HOHFELD language. We claim that this enterprise is useful for connecting the AI concept of agent-based system, and the legal concepts of rule and obligation.

One of the main points that must be investigated concern the source of obligations. According to the A-Hohfeld definition of LEGAL RELATIONS, the set of obligations can be modified by means of the exercise of POWER. However, because of the recursive character of POWER, it is clear that a given POWER is assigned to a particular type of individuals by means of another application (at a higher level) of POWER. The top-level organization of POWER is the subject to studies of social and political character; currently, the POWER of introducing new obligation in a society of artificial agents is reserved to the human who implemented the system; the formalization in terms of obligations can be a tool for enforcing a social organization on a society of autonomous computer agents, who can create by themselves their own duties and privileges.

Acknowledgements

This work has been partially supported by Italian CNR project "Conoscenza, intenzioni e comunicazione".

References

[Allen & Saxon 95] L.E.Allen, C.S.Saxon: "Better Language, Better Thought, Better Communication: The A-HOHFELD Language for Legal Analysis". *Proc. 5th Int. Conf. on AI and Law*, College Park, Md., 219-228 (1995)

[Allen & Saxon 98] L.E.Allen, C.S.Saxon: "The Legal Argument Game of LEGAL RELATIONS". *E Law –Murdoch Univ. Electronic J. Of Law, 5, n.3* (1998).

[Allen & Saxon 99] L.E.Allen, C.S.Saxon: "Application of Enriched Deontic LEGAL RELATIONS: Federal Rules of Civil Procedure Rule 7(a), Pleadings". *Proc. 7th Int. Conf. on AI and Law*, Oslo, 80-89 (1999)

[Ardissono et al. 00] L.Ardissono, G.Boella, L.Lesmo: "Plan Based Agent Architecture for Interpreting Natural Language Dialogue", *Int. J. Of Human-Computer Studies 52*, (2000)

[Axelrod 86] R.Axelrod: "An Evolutionary Approach to Norms", *American Political Science Review 80, 4, 1095-1111 (1986)*.

[Boella 00] G.Boella: *Cooperation among Economically Rational Agents*. PhD thesis. Univ. of Torino (2000)

[Boella et al. 99] G.Boella, R.Damiano, L.Lesmo, L.Ardissono: "Conversational Cooperation: the Leading Role of Intentions". *Proc. Amstelogue'99 Workshop*, Amsterdam (1999)

[Boella & Lesmo 01] G. Boella, L. Lesmo: "Deliberate Normative Agents", in R. Conte and C. Dellarocas: *Social Order in multi-agent systems*, Kluwer (to appear)

[Boutilier 99] C.Boutilier: "Multiagent Systems: Challenges and Opportunities for Decision-Theoretic Planning". *AI magazine 20*, 35-43 (1999)

[Carberry 90] S.Carberry: *Plan Recognition in Natural Language*. MIT Press (1990).

[Castelfranchi 98] C.Castelfranchi: "Modeling social action for {AI} agents". *Artificial Intelligence 103*, 157-182 (1998).

[Cohen & Levesque 90] P.R.Cohen, H.J.Levesque: "Intention is Choice with Commitment". *Artificial Intelligence 42*, 213-261 (1990)

[Conte & Castelfranchi 95] R.Conte, C.Castelfranchi: *Cognitive and Social Action*. UCL Press (1995)

[Dignum 96] F.Dignum: "Autonomous agents and social norms". *Proc. of ICMAS'96 Workshop on Norms, Obligations and Conventions* (1996)

[Gmytrasiewicz & Durfee 00] P.J.Gmytrasiewicz, E.H.Durfee: "Rational Coordination in Multi-Agent Environments". *Autonomous Agents and Multi-Agent Systems 3*, 319-350 (2000)

[Goffman 70] E. Goffman, *Strategic Interaction*, Basic Blackwell, Oxford (1970)

[Haddawy & Hanks 98] P.Haddawy, S.Hanks: "Utility models for goal-directed, decision-theoretic planners". *Computational Intelligence 14*, 392-429 (1998)

[Herrestad & Krogh 95] H.Herrestad, C.Krogh: "Obligations Directed from Bearers to Counterparties". *Proc. 5th Int. Conf. on AI and Law*, College Park, Md., 210-218 (1995)

[Jennings 00] N.R.Jennings: "On Agent-Based Software Engineering". *Artificial Intelligence 117*, 277-296 (2000)

[Jennings et al. 98] N.R.Jennings, K.Sycara, M. Wooldridge: "A Roadmap of Agent Research and Development", *Autonomous Agents and Multi-Agent Systems 1*, 275-306 (1998).

[Jones & Sergot 96] A.Jones, M.J.Sergot: "A Formal Characterisation of Institutionalised Power". *Journal of IGPL* 4(3), 429-455 (1996)

[Sartor 01] G.Sartor: "Why Agents Comply with Norms, and why they Should", in R. Conte and C. Dellarocas: *Social Order in multi-agent systems*, Kluwer (to appear)

[Sergot 98] M.J. Sergot, Normative positions. In P.McNamara, H.Prakken (eds): *Norms, Logics and Information Systems*. IOS Press (1998)

[Tiscornia & Turchi 97] D.Tiscornia, F.Turchi: "Formalization of Legislative Documents Based on a Functional Model". *Proc. 6th Int. Conf. on AI and Law*, Melbourne, 63-71 (1997)

Reasoning about Actions
in a Multiagent Domain

Laura Giordano[1], Alberto Martelli[2], and Camilla Schwind[3]

[1] DISTA, Università del Piemonte Orientale "A. Avogadro"
laura@mfn.unipmn.it
[2] Dipartimento di Informatica - Università di Torino
mrt@di.unito.it
[3] Faculté des Sciences de Luminy, LIM-CNRS
schwind@lim.univ-mrs.fr

Abstract. In this paper we present a theory for reasoning about actions which is based on the Product Version of Dynamic Linear Time Temporal Logic (denoted $DLTL^{\otimes}$) and allows to describe the behaviour of a network of sequential agents which coordinate their activities by performing common actions together. $DLTL^{\otimes}$ extends LTL, the propositional linear time temporal logic, by strengthening the until operator by indexing it with the regular programs of dynamic logic. Moreover, it allows the formulas of the logic to be decorated with the names of sequential agents, taken from a finite set.
The action theory we propose is an extension of the theory presented in [8], which is based on the logic DLTL, and allows reasoning with incomplete initial states and dealing with postdiction, ramifications as well as with nondeterministic actions. Here we extend this theory to cope with multiple agents synchronizing on common actions.

1 Introduction

An approach to reasoning about actions that recently gained renewed attention is the one based on the use of dynamic logic and of temporal logic. The suitability of modal logic for reasoning about actions has been pointed out by several authors in the last years [3,7]. On the one hand, Dynamic Logic [11] adopts essentially the same ontology as McCarthy's situation calculus, by taking the state of the world as primary, and encoding actions as transformations on states: actions can be represented in a natural way by modalities, and states as sequences of modalities. On the other hand, the adoption of a temporal logic for action theories allows general goals, like achievement and maintenance goals to be specified through temporal modalities.

The need of temporally extended goals has been motivated by Bacchus and Kabanza [1] and by Kabanza et al. [14], who proposed an approach to planning based on a linear time temporal logic. The formalization of properties of planning domains as temporal formulas in CTL has also been proposed in [10], where the idea of planning as model checking in a temporal logic has been explored. Other

F. Esposito (Ed.): AI*IA 2001, LNAI 2175, pp. 237–248, 2001.

authors have made use of the μ-calculus for reasoning about actions [21,4,5]. The μ-calculus allows complex goals to be formalized in a planning context, including achievement and maintenance goals [21].

In [8] the modal action theory developed in [7] has been enhanced by moving to the setting of temporal logics. More precisely, an action theory has been proposed based on the linear time temporal logic, DLTL (Dynamic Linear Time Temporal Logic [13]), which is, essentially, a dynamic logic equipped with a linear time semantics. It provides a simple way of constraining the (possibly infinite) evolutions of the system by making use of regular programs. The temporal projection problem and the planning problem can be modelled as satisfiability problems in DLTL.

In this paper we want to further exploit the expressiveness of temporal logic to extend our action theory for modelling a collection of interacting agents. To this purpose, we will make use of the Product Version of DLTL ($DLTL^{\otimes}$) to reason about a fixed number of finite state sequential agents, that coordinate their activities by performing their actions together. In [12] $DLTL^{\otimes}$ has been shown to be expressively equivalent to the regular product languages and to admit an exponential time decision procedure. In particular, the satisfiability and model checking problems for $DLTL^{\otimes}$ can be solved by product Büchi automata. A nice property of $DLTL^{\otimes}$ is that every formula of $DLTL^{\otimes}$ is trace consistent, so that properties defined by $DLTL^{\otimes}$ formulas can be verified efficiently by making use of partial order based reduction techniques.

$DLTL^{\otimes}$ does not allow to describe global properties of a system of agents, since the truth of a formula is evaluated at a local state (that is, a state local to an agent) and the temporal modalities define causal relationships among local states. However, it allows the specification of the dynamic of the system to be given through the separate specification of the different agents in the domain description.

Our action theory allows reasoning with incomplete initial states, and dealing with postdiction, ramifications and nondeterministic actions, which are captured by possibly alternative extensions (temporal models). Moreover, it provides a formalization of complex actions through the regular programs of dynamic logic and, in particular, it allows modelling the behaviour of different agents, which interact by executing common actions.

2   The Logic

We first shortly recall the definition of the logic $DLTL$ and, then, the definition of its product version.

2.1 $DLTL$

In this section we shortly define the syntax and semantics of DLTL as introduced in [13]. In such a linear time temporal logic the next state modality is indexed by actions. Moreover, (and this is the extension to LTL) the until operator is indexed by programs in Propositional Dynamic Logic (PDL) [11].

Let Σ be a finite non-empty alphabet. The members of Σ are actions. Let Σ^* and Σ^ω be the set of finite and infinite words on Σ, where $\omega = \{0, 1, 2, \ldots\}$. Let $\Sigma^\infty = \Sigma^* \cup \Sigma^\omega$. We denote by σ, σ' the words over Σ^ω and by τ, τ' the words over Σ^*. Moreover, we denote by $\leq$ the usual prefix ordering over Σ^* and, for $u \in \Sigma^\infty$, we denote by $prf(u)$ the set of finite prefixes of u.

We define the set of programs (regular expressions) $Prg(\Sigma)$ generated by Σ as follows:

$$Prg(\Sigma) ::= a \mid \pi_1 + \pi_2 \mid \pi_1; \pi_2 \mid \pi^*$$

where $a \in \Sigma$ and π_1, π_2, π range over $Prg(\Sigma)$. A set of finite words is associated with each program by the mapping $[[]] : Prg(\Sigma) \to 2^{\Sigma^*}$, which is defined in the standard way, as follows:

- $[[a]] = \{a\}$;
- $[[\pi_1 + \pi_2]] = [[\pi_1]] \cup [[\pi_2]]$;
- $[[\pi_1; \pi_2]] = \{\tau_1 \tau_2 \mid \tau_1 \in [[\pi_1]] \text{ and } \tau_2 \in [[\pi_2]]\}$;
- $[[\pi^*]] = \bigcup [[\pi^i]]$, where
  - $[[\pi^0]] = \{\varepsilon\}$
  - $[[\pi^{i+1}]] = \{\tau_1 \tau_2 \mid \tau_1 \in [[\pi]] \text{ and } \tau_2 \in [[\pi^i]]\}$, for every $i \in \omega$.

Let $\mathcal{P} = \{p_1, p_2, \ldots\}$ be a countable set of atomic propositions. The set of formulas of $\mathrm{DLTL}(\Sigma)$ si defined as follows:

$$\mathrm{DLTL}(\Sigma) ::= p \mid \neg \alpha \mid \alpha \vee \beta \mid \alpha \mathcal{U}^\pi \beta$$

where $p \in \mathcal{P}$ and α, β range over $\mathrm{DLTL}(\Sigma)$.

A model of $\mathrm{DLTL}(\Sigma)$ is a pair $M = (\sigma, V)$ where $\sigma \in \Sigma^\omega$ and $V : prf(\sigma) \to 2^\mathcal{P}$ is a valuation function. Given a model $M = (\sigma, V)$, a finite word $\tau \in prf(\sigma)$ and a formula α, the satisfiability of a formula α at τ in M, written $M, \tau \models \alpha$, is defined as follows:

- $M, \tau \models p$ iff $p \in V(\tau)$;
- $M, \tau \models \neg \alpha$ iff $M, \tau \not\models \alpha$;
- $M, \tau \models \alpha \vee \beta$ iff $M, \tau \models \alpha$ or $M, \tau \models \beta$;
- $M, \tau \models \alpha \mathcal{U}^\pi \beta$ iff there exists $\tau' \in [[\pi]]$ such that $\tau\tau' \in prf(\sigma)$ and $M, \tau\tau' \models \beta$. Moreover, for every τ'' such that $\varepsilon \leq \tau'' < \tau'^1$, $M, \tau\tau'' \models \alpha$.

A formula α is satisfiable iff there is a model $M = (\sigma, V)$ and a finite word $\tau \in prf(\sigma)$ such that $M, \tau \models \alpha$.

The formula $\alpha \mathcal{U}^\pi \beta$ is true at τ if "α until β" is true on a finite stretch of behaviour which is in the linear time behaviour of the program π.

The derived modalities $\langle \pi \rangle$ and $[\pi]$ can be defined as follows: $\langle \pi \rangle \alpha \equiv \top \mathcal{U}^\pi \alpha$ and $[\pi] \alpha \equiv \neg \langle \pi \rangle \neg \alpha$. It is easy to see that $M, \tau \models \langle \pi \rangle \alpha$ iff there exists $\tau' \in [[\pi]]$

---

[1] We define $\tau \leq \tau'$ iff $\exists \tau''$ such that $\tau\tau'' = \tau'$. Moreover, $\tau < \tau'$ iff $\tau \leq \tau'$ and $\tau \neq \tau'$.

such that $\tau\tau' \in prf(\sigma)$ and $M, \tau\tau' \models \alpha$. Also, $M, \tau \models [\pi]\alpha$ iff for all $\tau' \in [[\pi]]$ such that $\tau\tau' \in prf(\sigma)$ it holds that $M, \tau\tau' \models \alpha$.

Furthermore, if we let $\Sigma = \{a_1, \ldots, a_n\}$, the $\mathcal{U}$, O (next), $\Diamond$ and $\Box$ of LTL can be defined as follows: $O\alpha \equiv \bigvee_{a \in \Sigma}\langle a \rangle \alpha$, $\alpha\mathcal{U}\beta \equiv \alpha\mathcal{U}^{\Sigma^*}\beta$, $\Diamond\alpha \equiv \top\mathcal{U}\alpha$, $\Box \equiv \neg\Diamond\neg\alpha$, where, in $\mathcal{U}^{\Sigma^*}$, Σ is taken to be a shorthand for the program $a_1 + \ldots + a_n$. Hence both LTL(Σ) and PDL are fragments of DLTL(Σ). As shown in [13], DLTL(Σ) is strictly more expressive than LTL(Σ).

2.2   A Product Version of *DLTL*

We shortly recall the definition of $DLTL^\otimes$ from [12]. Let $Loc = \{1, \ldots, K\}$ be a set of locations, the names of the agents synchronizing on common actions. A *distributed alphabet* $\tilde{\Sigma} = \{\Sigma_i\}_{i=1}^K$ is a family of (possibly non-disjoint) alphabets, with each Σ_i a non-empty, finite set of actions (Σ_i is the set of actions which require the participation of agent i). Let $\Sigma = \bigcup_{i=1}^K \Sigma_i$. For $\sigma \in \Sigma^\infty$, we denote by $\sigma \uparrow i$ the projection of σ down to Σ_i. Moreover, we define $Loc(a) = \{i \mid a \in \Sigma_i\}$, the set of agents which participate in each occurrence of action a.

Atomic propositions are introduced in a local fashion, by introducing a non-empty set of atomic propositions $\mathcal{P}$. For each proposition $p \in \mathcal{P}$ and agent $i \in Loc$, p_i represents the "local" view of the proposition p at i, and is evaluated in the local state of agent i.

Let us define the set of formulas of $DLTL^\otimes(\tilde{\Sigma})$ and their locations:

- $\top$ is a formula and $loc(\top)=\emptyset$;
- if $p \in P$ and $i \in Loc$, p_i is a formula and $loc(p_i) = \{i\}$;
- if α and β are formulas, then $\neg\alpha$ and $\alpha \vee \beta$ are formulas and $loc(\neg\alpha) = loc(\alpha)$ and $loc(\alpha \vee \beta) = loc(\alpha) \cup loc(\beta)$;
- if α and β are formulas and $loc(\alpha), loc(\beta) \subseteq \{i\}$ and $\pi \in Prg(\Sigma_i)$, then $\alpha\mathcal{U}_i^\pi\beta$ is a formula and $loc(\alpha\mathcal{U}_i^\pi\beta) = \{i\}$.

Notice that no nesting of modalities $\mathcal{U}_i$ and $\mathcal{U}_j$ (for $i \neq j$) is allowed, and the formulas in $DLTL^\otimes(\tilde{\Sigma})$ are boolean combinations of formulas from the set $\bigcup_i DLTL_i^\otimes(\tilde{\Sigma})$, where

$$DLTL_i^\otimes(\tilde{\Sigma}) = \{\alpha \mid \alpha \in DLTL^\otimes(\tilde{\Sigma}) \text{ and } loc(\alpha) \subseteq \{i\}\}.$$

A model of $DLTL^\otimes(\tilde{\Sigma})$ is a pair $M = (\sigma, V)$, Where $\sigma \in \Sigma^\infty$ and $V = \{V_i\}_{i=1}^K$ is a family of functions V_i, where $V_i : prf(\sigma \uparrow i) \to 2^\mathcal{P}$ is the valuation function for agent i.

The satisfiability of formulas in a model is defined as above, except that propositions are evaluated locally. In particular, for all $\tau \in prf(\sigma)$:

- $M, \tau \models p_i$ iff $p \in V_i(\tau \uparrow i)$;
- $M, \tau \models \alpha\mathcal{U}_i^\pi\beta$ iff there exists a τ' such that $\tau' \uparrow i \in [[\pi]]$, $\tau\tau' \in prf(\sigma)$ and $M, \tau\tau' \models \beta$. Moreover, for all τ'' such that $\varepsilon \leq \tau'' < \tau'$, $M, \tau\tau'' \models \alpha$.

Satisfiability in $DLTL^\otimes$ is defined as above. In [12] $DLTL^\otimes$ has been shown to be expressively equivalent to the regular product languages and to admit an exponential time decision procedure.

3   Action Theories

In this section we extend to a multiagent setting the action theory developed in [8]. In the following the behaviour of the global system will emerge as the product of the behaviours of the single agents which interact by synchronizing on common actions. The behaviour of each agent i is specified by a domain description D_i, which describes the atomic actions the agent may perform by means of a set of action laws, causal rules, precondition laws and a set of general constraints. Such constraints also provide a description of the complex behaviour of the agent, given by means of regular programs of dynamic logic. The agents interact by performing common actions together, where each agent participating in the action execution has its own local description of the action determining the action effects on its local state.

In our action theories we call *fluent names* the atomic propositions in $\mathcal{P}$ indexed by an agent name i. Namely, for each $p \in P$ and $i \in Loc$, p_i is a fluent name local to i. A *fluent literal* l is a fluent name f or its negation $\neg f$. Given a fluent literal l, such that $l = f$ or $l = \neg f$, we define $|l| = f$. We will denote by Lit_i the set of all fluent literals local to i.

A *(distributed) domain description* D is a family of domain descriptions D_i, one for each agent i. A *domain description D_i for agent i* is defined as a tuple $(\Pi_i, Frame_i, \mathcal{C}_i)$, where Π_i is a set of *action laws* and *causal laws*; $\mathcal{C}_i$ is a set of *constraints*; $Frame_i$ provides a classification of fluents as frame fluents and nonframe fluents as we will define below.

Action laws in Π_i have the form: $\Box_i(\alpha \rightarrow [a]_i\beta)$, with $a \in \Sigma_i$ and $\alpha, \beta \in DLTL_i^{\otimes}$, meaning that executing action a in a local i state where precondition α holds causes the effect β to hold.

Causal laws in Π_i have the form: $\Box_i(\bigwedge_{a\in\Sigma}([a]_i\alpha \rightarrow [a]_i\beta))$, with $a \in \Sigma_i$ and $\alpha, \beta \in DLTL_i^{\otimes}$, meaning that, for all actions a, if α holds (in the local i state) after the execution of a, then β also holds after its execution. Such laws are intended to expresses "causal" dependencies among fluents (see [18,17,22,7]), and, intuitively, their directionality makes them similar to inference rules: if we are able to derive α then we can conclude β.

Constraints in $\mathcal{C}_i$ are arbitrary formulas of $DLTL^{\otimes}$. Constraints not only put conditions on the value of fluents at the different states, but they also determine which are the possible behaviours of the agent in a state. We do not put any restrictions on the kind of constraints that we allow in $\mathcal{C}_i$, which include both safety and liveness constraints. Let us only mention some constraints that are usually discussed in reasoning about actions literature. *Domain constraints* of the form **always** α, as introduced in [15], which enforce the condition α to hold on all possible states, are safety constraints which can be formalized by the formula $\Box_i\alpha$. *Precondition laws*, which put conditions on the executability of actions in a state, can be formalized, in a linear time temporal logic, by formulas of the form $\Box_i(\alpha \rightarrow [a]_i\bot)$, meaning that action a cannot be executed in all reachable states in which α holds[2]. *Observations* about the value of fluents in different states can be formalized as state constraints of the form $[a_1; \ldots; a_j]_i \alpha$, meaning that $\alpha \in DLTL^{\otimes}$ holds in the state obtained after executing the action sequence $a_1, \ldots, a_j$ (and, in particular, in the initial state when the action sequence is empty).

Constraints in $\mathcal{C}_i$ can be used to describe the sequences of actions which are possible for the agent. For instance, the liveness constraint $\langle \pi \rangle_i \top$ constrains all the executions of agent i in the system to start with a finite sequence of actions which is a possible behaviour of the program π.

We assume that for each causal law $\Box_i(\bigwedge_{a \in \Sigma}([a]_i \alpha \rightarrow [a]_i \beta))$ in Π, there is a corresponding constraint formula $\alpha \rightarrow \beta$ in the set $\mathcal{C}_i$, which assures that also in the initial state if α holds, β holds too.

$Frame_i$ is a set of pairs (p_i, a), where p_i is a fluent for agent i, and $a \in \Sigma_i$ is an action to which agent i participates. $(p_i, a) \in Frame_i$ means that, for agent i, p_i is a frame fluent for action a, that is, p_i is a fluent to which persistency applies when action a is executed. Those fluents which are not frame with respect to a do not persist and may change value in a nondeterministic way, when executing a. Note that it may occur that $(p_i, a) \in Frame_i$ while $(p_j, a) \notin Frame_j$ for $i \neq j$.

As $DLTL^{\otimes}$ does not include test actions, we introduce them in the language as atomic actions in the same way as done in [8]. Test actions allow the choice among different behaviours to be controlled. To allow agent i to test the value of a proposition ϕ in its local state, we introduce the modality $[\phi?]_i$ (regarded as an atomic action in Σ_i), ruled by the following laws:

$$\Box_i(\neg \phi \rightarrow [\phi?]_i \bot)$$
$$\Box_i(< \phi? >_i \top \rightarrow (L \leftrightarrow [\phi?]_i L)), \text{ for all fluent literals } L \in Lit_i.$$

The first law is a precondition law, saying that action $\phi?$ is only executable in a state in which ϕ holds. The second law describes the effects of the action on the state: the execution of the action $\phi?$ leaves the state unchanged[3]. In the following we will assume that, for all test actions occurring in the examples, the corresponding action laws are implicitly added (as constraints) to the domain description.

We remark that the global state of the system can be regarded as a set of local states, one for each agent i. The action laws and causal rules in D_i describe how the local i state changes when an action $a \in \Sigma_i$ is executed. An action a which is common to agents i and j is executed synchronously by the two agents, which update their local states separately, according to their action specification given in D_i and D_j. Moreover, the behaviour of each agent i, a subsequence σ_i of the system behaviour σ, must satisfy the constraints in $\mathcal{C}_i$. In particular, the action must be executable for both the agents i and j.

---

[2] In a branching time logic, precondition laws are usually formalized by laws of the form $\Box_i (\alpha \rightarrow \langle a \rangle_i \top)$. However, this formalization is not well suited for a linear time logic, in which only a single action can be executed at each state.

[3] Note that, as a difference with PDL, the execution of test actions causes the state to change, though the value of propositions in the state is kept unaltered.

Though action laws and causal laws can themselves be regarded as special kinds of constraints, we have distinguished them from all other constraints as they are given a special treatment when dealing with the frame problem. As in [8], to deal with the frame problem we make use of a completion construction which, given a domain description, introduces frame axioms for all the frame fluents in the style of the successor state axioms introduced by Reiter [20] in the context of the situation calculus. The completion construction is applied only to the action laws and causal laws and not to the constraints. In fact, we assume that frame fluents only change values according to the immediate and indirect effects of actions described by the action laws and causal laws. For lack of space we refer to [8] for the details on the completion construction. We just mention that, in this multiagent setting, the action laws and causal rules in the Π_i's have to be considered separately for each i, by introducing different frame axioms for the different agents. Given a domain description D, we call $Comp(D)$ be the set of formulas including all frame axioms as well as the constraints C_i for all agents i. The extensions of the domain description D are defined as the models of $Comp(D)$.

The temporal projection problem and the planning problem can be modelled as satisfiability problems in $DLTL^\otimes$, as it has been done in [8] in the single agent context. In particular, the *planning problem* "is there a sequence of actions leading to a state where a given formula α_i holds for agent i ?" can be solved by checking if the query $\Diamond_i \alpha_i$ has a solution in D, that is, if there is a model $M = (\sigma, V)$ satisfying the query and the completion of the domain description $Comp(D)$. The plan which makes α_i true can be extracted from the model M[4]. It is a "concurrent plan" and it contains the actions which have to be performed by the different agents to reach the goal. Some of the actions are common to different agents and must be executed by the different agents together. Other actions are local to a single agent. Though the plan which is extracted from a model is a linear plan, it represents a class of equivalent plans which can be obtained by permutations of adjacent independent actions (where two actions a and b are independent when there is no agent participating in both of them, i.e. $Loc(a) \cap Loc(b) = \emptyset$)[5]. Thus a linear plan can be regarded as a plan in which the actions of the different agents are partially ordered.

Example 1. Let us first consider an example of two robots which must move a set of blocks from a room to another using a table [2]. The robots can put individually the blocks on the table, but they must lift and move the table simultaneously, otherwise the blocks will fall off.

---

[4] In general, one may want to find a plan in which the different agents achieve different goals. Hence, the query to be satisfied may have the form $\Diamond_i \alpha_i \wedge \ldots \wedge \Diamond_K \alpha_K$, where α_i is the goal of agent i.

[5] In [12] it has been shown that the behaviours described by the temporal logic $DLTL^\otimes$ (i.e. regular product languages) lie within the domain of regular Mazurkiewics trace languages. Thus $DLTL^\otimes$ provides a flexible and powerful means for specifying trace consistent properties of distributed programs, which can be verified efficiently by making use of partial order based reduction techniques.

Each robot has a private state consisting of a set of fluents, which specify what the robot knows about the world. In a simplified formulation we assume that there are only two blocks $Block_1$ and $Block_2$, and each robot knows the position of one of them, besides knowing its own position and that of the table. In the following, p, q, r will range in the set $\{Room_1, Room_2\}$, while b will range in the set $\{Block_1, Block_2\}$.

The set of fluents of the i-th robot is[6]: $P_i = \{at_i(Block_i, p), at_i(Robot_i, p), at_i(Table, p), table\_up_i, on\_table_i(Block_i)\}$ for all values of p. Each one of the two robots has the following alphabet of actions: $\Sigma_i = \{put\_on\_table_i(Block_i), lift\_table, move\_table(p)\}$, for all p and $i = 1, 2$, where $put\_on\_table_i(Block_i)$, the action of putting block $Block_i$ on the table, is private of each robot, whereas the two other actions of lifting the table and moving it to a position p are shared by them and must be executed simultaneously.

We introduce the following precondition and action laws (for all p, q, r, b):

$\Box_i((at_i(Table, p) \wedge at_i(Robot_i, q) \wedge at_i(b, r)) \vee on\_table_i(b)) \rightarrow$
$[put\_on\_table_i(b)]_i \bot)$ with $p \neq q$ or $p \neq r$.
$\Box_i([put\_on\_table_i(b)]_i on\_table_i(b))$
$\Box_i((at_i(Table, p) \wedge at_i(Robot_i, q)) \rightarrow [lift\_table]_i \bot)$ with $p \neq q$.
$\Box_i([lift\_table]_i table\_up_i)$
$\Box_i((at_i(Table, p) \vee \neg table\_up_i) \rightarrow [move\_table(p)]_i \bot$
$\Box_i([move\_table(r)]_i at_i(Table, r))$

As we have pointed out before, precondition laws specify when actions *cannot* be executed. Note that when executing a shared action each robot will update its state separately according to its action law. Furthermore we need some constraints. For all possible values of x and for $p \neq q$, $\Box_i(\neg(at_i(x, p) \wedge at_i(x, q))$ Finally, the fact that a box on the table moves with it can be described by the causal law: $\Box_i([a]_i at_i(Table, p) \wedge on\_table_i(b)) \rightarrow [a]_i at_i(b, p))$, for each action $a \in \Sigma_i$.

We assume that all fluents are frame fluents. Let us now add formulas describing the initial state of $Robot_1$ and $Robot_2$:

$at_1(Robot_1, Room_1) \wedge at_1(Block_1, Room_1) \wedge at_1(Table, Room_1) \wedge \neg table\_up_1 \wedge$
$\neg on\_table_1(Block_1)$
$at_2(Robot_2, Room_1) \wedge at_2(Block_2, Room_1) \wedge at_2(Table, Room_1) \wedge \neg table\_up_2 \wedge$
$\neg on\_table_2(Block_2)$

Assume now that we want the robots to move both boxes to the other room. This can be expressed as a satisfiability problem: Given the query:

$$\Diamond_1 at_1(Block_1, Room_2) \wedge \Diamond_2 at_2(Block_2, Room_2)$$

find a model (of the domain description $Comp(D)$) satisfying it. For instance the model beginning with

$put\_on\_table_1(Block_1), put\_on\_table_2(Block_2), lift\_table, move\_table(Room_2)$

---

[6] Identifiers beginning with a capital letter denote constants.

is a possible solution. From this solution we can extract the two plans for the two robots, by projecting the solution on the two alphabets. Note that, as we have pointed out before, the relative order among private actions of different agents (as, for instance, $put\_on\_table_1(Block_1)$ and $put\_on\_table_2(Block_2)$), is not important so that they can also be executed in a different order and the above plan can be regarded as only specifying a partial ordering of actions.

In this example each robot can only reason about the effects of its own actions and cannot know what the other robot is doing. In a more realistic setting the actions of the robots might interfere and thus a robot should be able to acquire knowledge about the effects of the actions of other robots. This can be modeled by introducing an environment which keeps track of the changes caused by all robots, and by providing the robots with *sensing* actions allowing the value of a fluent to be asked to the environment. In the next example, reasoning about actions allows properties of a system of agents to be verified.

Example 2. Two robots have to lift a table [6] and their actions must be synchronized so that the table does not tip so much that objects on it fall off. Differently from the previous example there are no shared actions between the two robots, and they can lift the table separately.

We model the two robots, $robot_1$ and $robot_2$ and their interaction with the environment E. Here we have three locations $\{1, 2, E\}$ and a distributed alphabet $\tilde{E} = \{\Sigma_1, \Sigma_2, \Sigma_E\}$ where $\Sigma_1 = \{$ $grab\_left, vmove\_left, sense\_vpos\_right\}$ contains the actions which $robot_1$ executes to lift the left part of the table; Σ_2 $= \{grab\_right, vmove\_right, sense\_vpos\_left\}$ contains the actions which $robot_2$ executes to lift the right part of the table; $\Sigma_E = \{vmove\_right, vmove\_left, sense\_vpos\_right, sense\_vpos\_left\}$ contains the actions which the environment executes, to record the modifications produced by the robot actions. The two actions $sense\_vpos\_right$ and $sense\_vpos\_left$ are informative actions (usually called "sensing actions") which allow the robots to acquire up to date knowledge about the part of the environment which is not under their control. For instance, we can expect that $robot_1$ has to do a sensing action to know the vertical position of the right end of the table which is under the control of $robot_2$.

The set of atomic propositions $\mathcal{P}$ is the following $\{holding\_right, holding\_left, vpos\_right(d), vpos\_right(d), up\_right, up\_left\}$, for all the possible (finite and discrete) values d of the vertical position. In the following we will assume that there are 10 different vertical positions possible for the right end of the table $vpos\_right(1), \ldots, vpos\_right(10)$, and the same for the left one.

The set Π contains the following action laws for $robot_1$ (for all $d \in \{1 \ldots 10\}$ and d' successors of d):

$\Box_1([grab\_left]_1 holding\_left_1)$
$\Box_1(vpos\_left(d)_1 \rightarrow [vmove\_left]_1 vpos\_left(d')_1)$
$\Box_1([sense\_vpos\_right(d)]_1 vpos\_right(d)_1).$

The $grab\_left$ action has the effect of $robot_1$ holding the left end of the table. The $vmove\_left$ action increases the vertical position of the left end. The $sense\_vpos\_right(d)$ action provides the position d of the right end.

The set $\mathcal{C}$ contains the following precondition laws and constraints:

$\Box_1(holding\_left_1 \rightarrow [grab\_left]_1\bot)$

$\Box_1(\neg holding\_left_1 \rightarrow [vmove\_left]_1\bot)$

$\Box_1(\neg[sense\_vpos\_right(d)]_1\bot)$

$\Box_1(up\_left_1 \leftrightarrow vpos\_left(10)_1)$

$\Box_1(safetolift_1 \leftrightarrow vpos\_left(d)_1 \wedge vpos\_right(f)_1 \wedge d \leq f + Tot)$

The $grab\_left$ action is possible only if $robot_1$ is not holding the left end of the table. The $vmove\_left$ action is possible only if $robot_1$ is holding the left end of the table. As far as $robot_1$ is concerned the $sense\_vpos\_right(d)$ action is always executable. The left end of the table is up if its vertical position is 10. It is safe for $robot_1$ to lift the table if the difference between the vertical positions of the left and the right ends of the table is less then a certain value.

The following program π_1 describes the possible behaviours of $robot_1$:

$$\pi_1 = grab\_left; (\neg up\_left_1?; (sense\_vpos\_right(1) + \ldots + sense\_vpos\_right(10)); $$
$$((safetolift?; vmove\_left) + \neg safetolift?))^*; up\_left_1?$$

Analogous action laws and constraints are provided for the robot 2 (just exchange left and right and replace 1 with 2). Concerning the environment, we have the following actions laws Π (for all $d \in \{1 \ldots 10\}$ and d' successors of d):

$\Box_E(vpos\_right(d)_E \rightarrow [vmove\_right]_E vpos\_right(d')_E)$

$\Box_E(vpos\_left(d)_E \rightarrow [vmove\_left]_E vpos\_left(d')_E)$

and constraints $\mathcal{C}$:

$\Box_E(\neg[vmove\_right]_E\bot)$

$\Box_E(\neg[vmove\_left]_E\bot)$

$\Box_E(\neg vpos\_right(d)_E \rightarrow [sense\_vpos\_right(d)]_E\bot)$

$\Box_E(\neg vpos\_left(d)_E \rightarrow [sense\_vpos\_left(d)]_E\bot)$

$\Box_E(up\_right_E \leftrightarrow vpos\_right(10)_E)$

$\Box_E(up\_left_E \leftrightarrow vpos\_left(10)_E)$

The $sense\_vpos\_right(d)$ action is executable if d is the vertical position of the right end of the table. It has no effect on the environment, but it is how the environment provides information to $robot_1$ about the value of $vpos\_right$. The $vmove\_right$ action is always executable by the environment. When it is executed by $robot_2$, it has the effect of changing the value of $vpos\_right$ in the environment.

By adding the constraints $< \pi_1 >_1 \top$ and $< \pi_2 >_2 \top$ we specify that we will accept only sequences of actions where the programs of both robots terminate.

Assuming that in the initial state both ends of the table are down, we can formalize the fact that in any execution of the system the ends of the table are always at the same height to within a threshold Tot until both ends are up, by the following formula: $Level\ \mathcal{U}_E(up\_left_E \wedge up\_right_E)$, where $Level \equiv_{def} vpos\_right(d)_E \wedge vpos\_left(f)_E \wedge | d - f | \leq Tot$. The formula has to be true in all models of $Comp(D)$. While in the previous example we wanted to find a plan and the problem was formalized as a satisfiability problem, here we want to verify some property α of the system of agents, which can be formalized as the problem of verifying the validity of a formula (namely, $Comp(D) \rightarrow \alpha$).

4   Conclusions

In this paper we have proposed a temporal logic approach for reasoning about actions and change in a multiagent context. Our action theory extends the one presented in [8], which is based on Dynamic Linear Time Temporal Logic (DLTL), by moving to the Product Version of DLTL: the behaviours of the system are generated by a network of sequential agents that coordinate their activities by performing common actions together. In our action theory the frame and the ramification problem are both addressed by lifting to the multiagent case the solution developed in [8]. More precisely, (modal) successor state axioms are introduced which are obtained by a completion construction and which are similar to those introduced by Sheila McIlraith in [19] for dealing with ramifications in the situation calculus. A similar kind of transformation has also been used by Enrico Giunchiglia in [9] to translate action theories to first order logic theory to model planning as satisfiability in first order logic. As a difference with these proposals, our action theory deals with the multiagent case and it allows constraints (which are arbitrary temporal formulas) and queries to include program expressions. Under this respect, the language is related to the language ConGolog [6], an extended version of the language Golog [16] that incorporates a rich account of concurrency, in which complex actions (plans) can be formalized as Algol-like programs in the situation calculus. A substantial difference with ConGolog, apart from the different logical foundation, is that here we model agents with their own local states, while in Congolog the agents share a common global environment and all the properties are referred to a global state.

In [2] Boutilier and Brafman address the problem of planning with concurrent interacting actions. They show that, the STRIPS action representation can be augmented to handle concurrent interacting actions and they develop an extension of the UCPOP algorithm to solve a multiagent planning problem. Also in this case, differently from our approach, all action affect the same global state. Though the presence of a global environment is very natural in a robotic context (and, in fact, in our second example we had to explicitly introduce a model of the environment), this is not always the case. For instance, when modelling the interaction between software agents, it is reasonable to assume that each of them has its own local state on which actions have effect.

References

1. F. Bacchus and F. Kabanza. Planning for temporally extended goals. in *Annals of Mathematics and AI*, 22:5–27, 1998.
2. C. Boutilier and R.I. Brafman. Planning with Concurrent Interacting Actions. in *AAAI-97*, Providence, August 1997.

3. G. De Giacomo, M. Lenzerini. PDL-based framework for reasoning about actions. In *LNAI 992*, pages 103–114, 1995.

4. G. De Giacomo and X.J.Chen. Reasoning about nondeterministic and concurrent actions: A process algebra approach. In Artificial Intelligence, 107:63-98,1999.

5. G. De Giacomo and R. Rosati. Minimal knowledge approach to reasoning about actions and sensing. In *Proc. of the 3rd Workshop on Nonmonotonic Reasoning, Action, and Change (NRAC'99)*, Stockholm, Sweden, August 1999.

6. G. De Giacomo, Y. Lespérance, H. J. Levesque. ConGolog, a concurrent programming language based on the situation calculus. *Artificial Intelligence* 121(2000), pp.109-169.

7. L. Giordano, A. Martelli, and C. Schwind. Ramification and causality in a modal action logic. In *Journal of Logic and Computation*, 10(5):625-662, 2000.

8. L. Giordano, A. Martelli, and C. Schwind. Reasoning About Actions in Dynamic Linear Time Temporal Logic. *Proceedings FAPR'2000, Int. Conf. on Pure and Applied Practical Reasoning*, London, September 2000. To appear on the Logic Journal of the IGPL.

9. E. Giunchiglia. Planning as satisfiability with expressive action languages: Concurrency, Constraints and Nondeterminism. In Seventh International Conference on Principles of Knowledge Representation and Reasoning (KR'00). Breckenridge, Colorado, USA 12-15 April 2000.

10. F. Giunchiglia and P. Traverso. Planning as Model Checking. In Proc. The 5th European Conf. on Planning (ECP'99), pp.1–20, Durham (UK), 1999.

11. D. Harel. First order dynamic logic in *Extensions of Classical Logic, Handbook of Philosophical Logic II*, pp. 497–604, 1984.

12. J.G. Henriksen and P.S. Thiagarajan A product Version of Dynamic Linear Time Temporal Logic. in *CONCUR'97*, 1997.

13. J.G. Henriksen and P.S. Thiagarajan Dynamic Linear Time Temporal Logic. in *Annals of Pure and Applied logic*, vol.96, n.1-3, pp.187–207, 1999

14. F. Kabanza, M. Barbeau and R.St-Denis Planning control rules for reactive agents. In *Artificial Intelligence*, 95(1997) 67-113.

15. G.N. Kartha and V. Lifschitz. Actions with Indirect Effects (Preliminary Report). In *Proc. KR'94* , pages 341–350, 1994.

16. H. J. Levesque, R. Reiter, Y. Lespérance, F. Lin, and R. B. Scherl. GOLOG: A Logic Programming Language for Dynamic Domains. *J. of Logic Prog.*, 31, 1997.

17. F. Lin. Embracing Causality in Specifying the Indirect Effects of Actions. In *Proc. IJCAI'95*, pages 1985–1991, 1995.

18. N. McCain and H. Turner. A Causal Theory of Ramifications and Qualifications. In *Proc. IJCAI'95*, pages 1978–1984, 1995.

19. S. Mc Ilraith Representing Actions and State Constraints in Model-Based Diagnosis. AAAI'97, pp. 43–49, 1997.

20. R. Reiter. The frame problem in the situation calculus: a simple solution (sometimes) and a completeness result for goal regression. In *Artificial Intelligence and Mathematical Theory of Computation: Papers in Honor of John McCarthy*, V. Lifschitz, ed.,pages 359–380, Academic Press, 1991.

21. Munindar P. Singh. Applying the Mu-Calculus in Planning and Reasoning about Actions. In *Journal of Logic and Computation*, 1998.

22. M. Thielscher. Ramification and Causality. Artificial Intelligence Journal, vol. 89, No. 1-2, pp. 317-364, 1997.

L*MASS
A Language for Situated Multi-agent Systems

Stefania Bandini[1], Sara Manzoni[1], Giulio Pavesi[1], and Carla Simone[2]

[1] Dipartimento di Informatica, Sistemistica e Comunicazione
Università di Milano–Bicocca
{bandini,manzoni,pavesi}@disco.unimib.it
[2] Dipartimento di Informatica
Università di Torino
simone@di.unito.it

Abstract. The main aim of this paper is to present a language for the description of systems of reactive agents situated in an environment. This language for Multi–Agent Situated Systems (MASS) has been inspired by a previously introduced Reaction–Diffusion Machine (RDM). It will be shown that it can describe heterogeneous systems of reactive agents, that is agents with different capabilities through an action model based on reaction–diffusion metaphor. Moreover we show how the model has been applied to the location of suitable sites for extra–urban shopping centres.

1 Introduction

The main aim of this paper is to introduce the *L*MASS* language, developed for the description of systems of reactive agents situated in an environment. The formal semantic of L*MASS can be found in [1] and a preliminary implementation in [2]. This kind of Multi–Agent System (MAS) is based on a action–deliberation–reaction mechanism, that allows to describe agents characterized by a set of possible actions and a mechanism for the selection of the action to be undertaken based on the internal state of the agents themselves. Agents described with L*MASS are *situated*, that is, their actions are strongly influenced by their position in the environment. The position in the space defines the situation in which the agents are acting, where "situation" refers to a potentially complex combination of internal and external events and states [3]. Reactive situated agents are very sensitive to the spatial relationships that determine constraints and capacities for actions as well as privileged cooperation relationships. The space where agents are situated can reproduce a physical space, but it is nevertheless possible to define a "virtual space" that agents can roam and where they interact. Interactions take place when two or more agents are brought into a dynamic relationship through a set of reciprocal actions and have an influence on the future behaviour of the agents [4].

The application of the language will be shown in the domain of the Multi–Agent Based Simulation (MABS). MABS is based on the idea that it is possible

F. Esposito (Ed.): AI*IA 2001, LNAI 2175, pp. 249–254, 2001.

to represent a phenomenon as the result of the interactions of an assembly of simple and autonomous agents with their own operational autonomy. MAS can be used to simulate many types of artificial worlds as well as natural phenomena [4]. In particular, their application to the problem of the localization process for shopping centres will be shown. Finding a "good" location for a shopping centre, that is, close enough to widely populated areas and roads, and far away from other centres, is a problem that has been widely studied by urbanists and economists, and many different approaches have been proposed [5]. In particular, the idea we implemented with agents is based on the gravitational model, where shopping centres are seen as masses that emit gravitational fields that attract consumers and repel other installations. This kind of model has been previously implemented with Cellular Automata [6,7], but in the most significant examples the strict CA uniformity requirements of CA formalism have been removed. In this paper it will be shown how the MAS approach fits more naturally to this problem and domain.

2 L*MASS

In this section each component of L*MASS, a modeling language for systems of situated agents will be briefly and informally described. L*MASS describes a *Space* as a connected undirected graph representing an adjacency relation among its nodes. Each node constitutes a *site*, and can contain at most one agent.

L*MASS defines the set of *Fields* acting in the space as the means by which agents asynchronously communicate. Fields are generated by agents active in the space, or have a source outside the space, in the latter case representing the interaction between agents and the environment. A field is characterized by a *distribution function* and by a *signature* allowing to compose and compare its values. Fields propagate along the edges of the graph and leave on sites information about their passage.

The space of L*MASS is populated by a set of individuals called *agents*. Each agent is defined by a *type* τ, describing the set X_τ of *states* the agent can assume, and a list θ_τ of *thresholds* to express its current sensitivity to fields. Moreover, the type specifies the set A_τ of *actions* it can perform. Actions define whether and how the agent changes its state and/or its position, how it interacts with other agents, and how neighboring agents can influence it. An agent a is characterized by a triple $\langle \tau, p_a, x_a \rangle$ where p_a is the site of the space where the agent is located and $x_a \in X_\tau$ is its current state.

L*MASS defines the actions agents can perform according to five basic *primitives* whose parameters specify how the involved agent(s) or field values are modified.

– **Reaction** A reaction primitive takes the following format:

$$\mathbf{reaction}((p_1, \tau_1, x_1), \ldots, (p_k, \tau_k, x_k); (p_1, \tau_1, \bar{x}_1), \ldots, (p_k, \tau_k, \bar{x}_k))$$

where the set of sites $p_1 \ldots p_k$ forms a clique in the space graph. *Reaction* defines a *synchronous interaction* among a set of agents pair-wise situated on adjacent sites, if their type and state match the first argument. The second argument specifies how the involved agents change their states.

- **Emit** An emit primitive takes the following format:

$$\mathbf{emit}(\langle \tau, p, x \rangle; F_i)$$

Emission defines the one side of an *asynchronous interaction* among agents: that is, the sending of broadcast messages by the agent specified by the first parameter, if its current state is such to make it a source of field F_i. The values of the latter propagate in the sites of the space according to the distribution function associated with it.

- **Perceive** A perceive primitive takes the following format:

$$\mathbf{perceive}(\langle \tau, p, x \rangle; F_i)$$

Perception defines the second side of an *asynchronous interaction* among agents: that is, the possible reception of broadcast messages conveyed through F_i, by the agent specified in the first argument, according to its type and state. This means that a message can be neglected if its value is below the sensitivity level of the agent receiving it, that is expressed by the threshold associated with its type. Otherwise, the message is ininfluencial since it cannot be perceived: the function returns the undefined value denoted by $\perp$. This is the very essence of the broadcast interaction pattern, in which messages are not addressed to specific receivers but potentially to all agents populating the space.

- **Trigger** A trigger primitive takes the following format:

$$\mathbf{trigger}(\langle \tau, p, x \rangle; F_i, \langle \tau, p, \bar{x} \rangle)$$

Trigger defines how the reception of a field causes a change of state in the receiving agent espressed by the first argument. This means that if perceive$(F_i) \neq \perp$ then the agent becomes $a = \langle \tau, p, \bar{x} \rangle$.

- **Transport** A transport primitive takes the following format:

$$\mathbf{transport}(\langle \tau, p, x \rangle; F_i, \langle \tau, \bar{p}, x \rangle)$$

Transport defines how the reception of a field causes a change of position in the receiving agent espressed by the first argument. This means that if perceive$(F_i) \neq \perp$ and $\bar{p}$ is empty then the agent becomes $a = \langle \tau, \bar{p}, x \rangle$, that is moves to site $\bar{p}$.

There are some additional linguistic features allowing to specify the environment of an agent system. The first one concerns the possibility to construct a constellation of such systems and the second one the possibility of let them interact. The resulting agent system is thus multi–layered (MMASS) but not hierarchical. Let $MASS_i$, for i belonging to $\{1...n\}$, denote a Multi–Agent Situated System. Hence, the primitive

$$\mathbf{Compose}(MASS_1, ..., MASS_n)$$

allows the construction of the resulting MMASS.

In order to allow the interaction across the constituent MASS's, L*MASS uses the notion of *interface*. The interface specifies which external fields are imported or exported from each MASS and takes the following format:

$$\textbf{Interface}(\textbf{export} : E_1, ..., E_k; \textbf{import} : I_1, ..., I_h)$$

with the obvious meaning. Imported fields are used in the previously mentioned primitives as internal fields do. Hence, they can be mentioned in them and used in agent type definition. By definition, the value of an external field in any site of a local space is the value at its source. Moreover, the receiving MASS has to define if and how this value has to be internally propagated by means of local fields defined for this purpose. In fact, their distribution function is highly dependent on the structure of the local space which is completely hidden to the external MASS's.

3   Application

L*MASS language has been applied in the domain of Multi–Agent Based Simulation to the problem of the location of suitable sites for extra–urban shopping centres [8]. Simulations can be useful when suitable space is available and a good location for a new shopping centre has to be chosen, or when the possibility of success in locating a new shopping centre in an area already served by other retailers has to be evaluated. Geographical factors, such as the proximity of other centres and residential areas, are essential for the choice of a suitable location for a shopping centre. Moreover, once some centres have settled in a given area, other factors like competition should be taken into account. For example, one centre could start low price special sales in order to attract consumers, or invest heavily on advertisement. We now show how the design of a MMASS composed by two MASS's allows the simulation of the two aspects involved in this problem. Two MASS's have been defined: the territorial MASS and the strategic MASS. In the former, the formation or the disappearance of a shopping centre is modeled by considering only geographical factors. In the latter, already existing centres compete with one another trying to attract consumers. Each shopping centre is represented in both the territorial and the strategic MASS. Interaction between the two MASS's is performed through field emission by agents belonging to a MASS and their perception as external fields by agents of the other MASS.

3.1   The Territorial MASS

The territorial MASS represents the territory where the simulation is performed. It is defined as a regular grid, that is, the territory is divided into square blocks, each one populated by an agent. The different agent types reproduce the different types of area that can be found in an urban environment, that is: *ResidentialArea*, *IndustrialArea*, *NotBuildableArea* (e.g. mountains or rivers or parks), *Road* and *SuitableArea*. The first four types have only one possible state, which does not change during simulations. On the contrary, agents of type *SuitableArea* model the formation (or the disappearance) of shopping centres by changing their state that can assume one of three possible values: *Empty, SmallCentre* and *Large-Centre*.

Agents of each type emit two different fields, namely F_0 and F_1, according to their type and state. Field F_0 models the attractive or repulsive effect that the presence of an agent of a given type has on small shopping centre, while F_1 is used in an analogous way for large centres. The values of the fields, and their distribution function, change according to the type of the emitting agent. Positive values favor the formation of a shopping centre, while negative values have a negative influence. For instance, the presence of a large shopping centre has a negative impact on the location of other centres in its surroundings, while highly populated areas strongly encourage the formation of shopping centres with positive field values. For both fields, the field composition function is the sum of the different field values.

Fields F_0 and F_1 are perceived only by agents of type *SuitableArea* that, as a consequence, change their state. For instance if an agent representing an empty area perceives a value of F_0 higher than a given threshold, it changes its state and becomes a small shopping centre. In the same way, if the value of F_1 is higher than a corresponding threshold, the agent becomes a large shopping centre. That is:

$$when\ \mathbf{perceive}(\langle SuitableArea, p, Empty \rangle; F_0) \neq \perp$$

$$\mathbf{trigger}(\langle SuitableArea, p, Empty \rangle; F_0; \langle SuitableArea, p, SmallCentre \rangle)$$

Conversely, if a small shopping centre agent perceives a negative value of the field F_0, it could become an empty space, and in the same way a large shopping centre perceiving a field F_1, could change its state to *SmallCentre*.

Moreover *SuitableArea* agents representing small or large shopping centres emit an additional field (F_2) when some changes in their state happens. This field cannot be perceived by the agents of the territorial MASS but, as will be better described in next subsection, is exported to the *Strategic MASS*. In analogous way field F_3 is imported into the territorial MASS from the strategic MASS. Agents belonging to the strategic MASS emit F_3 whenever their power in the competition among shopping centres has decreased or increased. The consequence of the perception of F_3 by a *SuitableArea* agent is a change of its state according to field value and agent state. For instance, if the field value is lower than the corresponding threshold the state changes from *SmallCentre* to *Empty*, while it changes to *LargeCentre* when the field value is greater than another threshold.

3.2   The Strategic MASS

The number of nodes of the space of the strategic MASS is equal to the number of *SuitableArea* agents of the territorial MASS. The graph is complete, that is, each pair of nodes is connected by an edge. An agent of type *Strategic* inhabits each node of the space. Agent states are denoted by the couple $(x, f(x))$ where x is an integer value expressing the power of the agent and $f(x)$ is a function of the agent power and can assume one of the three values *Inactive, Defensive,* and *Aggressive.* Each strategic agent corresponding to an empty area on the territorial MASS has power zero and is in the inactive state.

Competition among shopping centres is modelled as a reaction between agents characterized by defensive or aggressive state located on adjacent sites. The consequence of a reaction is a change in the states of involved agents. The rule we adopted is simple: the most powerful wins, and increases its power by a given value set by the user, while the loser has its power decreased by the same value. Since all pairs of nodes on the strategic level are neighbouring, this rule is applied in a non–deterministic way, that is, random pairs execute the reaction primitive.

Field F_3 is emitted by strategic agents in state defensive or aggressive and is exported to the territorial MASS in order to signal to *SuitableArea* agents about changes in their state. The intensity of field F_3 corresponds to the power value of the agent and it is perceived by its counterpart on the territorial MASS. Strategic agents in *Inactive* state are sensitive to field F_2 imported from the territorial MASS, and as a consequence of its perception, they can be activated and change their state; if the perceived value is greater than the given threshold, the agent power changes proportionally to the intensity of the field perceived, and as a consequence it changes either to aggressive or defensive.

References

1. Bandini, S. and Simone, C. *Integrating Forms of Interaction in a Distributed Coordination Model* Foundamentae Informaticae in press.
2. Bandini, S., De Paoli F., Manzoni, S. and Simone, C. *OO Reactive Agents for RDM–Based Simulations* Proceedings of the Workshop "Dagli oggetti agli agenti: tendenze evolutive dei sistemi software" Parma, 29-30 maggio 2000.
3. Connah, D. *The Design of Interacting Agents for Use in Interfaces* Brouwer–Janse, D. & Harringdon, T. L. (eds.), Human–Machine Communication for Educational Systems Design, Computer and Systems Sciences, 129, Heidelberg: Springer Verlag, 1994.
4. Ferber, J. *Multi–Agents Systems: An Introduction to Distributed Artificial Intelligence* Addison–Wesley, Harlow (UK), 1999.
5. Gentili, G. Principi di concezione e progettazione dei centri commerciali I Centri Commerciali al Dettaglio, 1981.
6. Engelen, G., White, R., Uljii, I. and Drazan., P. *Using cellular automata for integrated modelling of socio–environmental systems* Environmental Monitoring and Assessment, 34:203–214, 1995.
7. Couclelis, H. *From Cellular Automata to Urban Models, New Principles for Model Development and Implementation,* in Batty, M., Couclelis, H. and M. Eichen *Urban systems as Cellular Automata,* Special issue of Environment and Planning: Planning and Design, vol. 24 n. 2, Pion, London, 1997.
8. Bandini, S., Manzoni, S., Pavesi, G. and Simone, C. Location of Extra–Urban Shopping Centres: A Multi–Agent based Approach Proceedings of INPUT 2001: Informatica e pianificazione urbana e territoriale Isole Tremiti, June, 2001.

An Interactive System for Generating Arguments in Deceptive Communication

Valeria Carofiglio[1], Cristiano Castelfranchi[2], Fiorella de Rosis[1], and
Roberto Grassano[1]

[1] Department of Informatics, University of Bari
Bari, Italy
{carofiglio, derosis, grassano }@di.uniba.it
http://aos2.uniba.it:8080/IntInt.html
[2] Department of Communication Sciences, University of Siena
Siena, Italy
castel@www.ip.rm.cnr.it

Abstract. We describe an interactive system that enables constructing
and evaluating arguments when communication is not necessarily sincere.
The system considers the possible differences between its own beliefs and
the beliefs it ascribes to the interlocutor, to exploit them at its advantage; this can be done by representing uncertainty in the mental state
of the interlocutor and in the reasoning process. In order to select the
argument(s) that best achieve the deception goal, a list of 'candidates to
deception' is selected according to a few defined strategies and various
'weights' are attached to each of them. We describe how the prototype
enables verifying the appropriateness of the methods employed in simulating various forms of deceptive argumentation.

keywords: belief ascription, belief networks, dialog simulation, deception.

1   What Is a 'Deceptive' Communication?

Let us start from the following, basic question: "What is it that makes 'deceptive'
the communication of a Speaker S to a Addressee A?". Contrary to a common
view, it is not necessarily a contradiction between what S believes and what
he says: he might very well deceive A while saying the truth or without saying
anything; deception is a more general category of lie, that is of 'saying the
false'. The difference between a 'sincere' and a 'deceptive' act is in the difference
between the Speakers' belief about the communicated fact and the goal he aims
at achieving, with this communication, in the mind of the Addressee. Again, this
difference does not necessarily require 'inverting the truth value of A's belief':
S might very well desire to leave A in (or induce her into) ignorance about a
fact, or to just influence her a bit, either positively or negatively. Obviously, if
communication directly concerns the fact that is the 'deception object', S will
be led to lie, in order to deceive A. But, if S applies 'indirect' forms of deception

F. Esposito (Ed.): AI*IA 2001, LNAI 2175, pp. 255–266, 2001.

by talking about facts (that we will call 'deception media') that are related to the deception object, then his choice of what to say will be larger and he will not necessarily lie. The first case corresponds to answering to precise questions, of the type *'Is that true?'*; the second one may be encountered in other situations, such as responding to *'Why?'* or *'Tell me something about that problem'* question types.

In this second category of cases, S will have the opportunity of selecting his answer among various alternatives. In previous papers, we examined the deception forms that were applied in some 'natural' dialogs in the medical domain [4] and considered, in particular, deception in responding to *'Why?'* questions [6]. In this paper, we wish to examine which models of the Addressee the Speaker needs to build, when planning indirectly deceptive communicative acts to respond to *'Tell me something about that problem'* questions: we will show, in particular, the advantages of choosing belief networks to represent mental models of the two participants to the information exchange.

2   The Art of Deception

Humans apply a large variety of deception forms, in their communicative acts, and they are not necessarily 'uncooperative' in doing that, as they may even deceive 'for the benefit of their interlocutors' [2,3]. Deception may be *active* or *passive*, according to whether something is done, by S, to achieve his goal or not. It may be applied *directly* to the deception object or *indirectly* to it, through some deception medium; in this second case, it may be applied to causes or to effects of the deception object or may be aimed at diverting the interlocutor's attention towards a fictitious cause or effect: for a more detailed analysis of this large range of deception forms, see [7]. Beyond intentionally insincere assertions, there is always some interest of the Speaker, the need to achieve some goal about the domain-state. S selects the communication that best achieves this goal based on a joint evaluation of the following aspects:

- *efficacy* of the deception object in achieving the domain goal and *impact* of the deception medium on the deception object. The combination of the two measures formalises the fact that not all moves or strategies, not all proposed evidences or beliefs produce the same effects on the Addressee's mental state;
- *plausibility* of the communicative act to A: this relates to the likelihood that A will get convinced about the fact after S's communication, that she will come to believe it;
- *safety* of the communicative act : this is linked to the risk, to S, of being discovered, by A, in a deception attempt. This feature combines two risks: the risk of not being believed and the risk of being blamed. The risk of being suspected in an attempt to deceive depends, in its turn, on various factors, the most important of which are the following: (i) how plausible might be, to A, that S believes in what he says and (ii) whether A may come to understand

that her believing in that fact is in S's interest and advantage. In addition, even if A suspects S of a deception attempt, she might not necessarily blame him for this, for instance because she hasn't got enough evidence;
- *reliability* of the mentioned information source: in communicating the fact, S may mention an *information source* to support his statement; in doing so, S will consider the reliability of this source, again according to A.

3   A Deception Simulator: Mouth of Truth

Mouth of Truth is a system that enables simulating the way that a potentially deceptive communicative act may be planned. The System plays the role of the Speaker (the potential 'deceiver') and the User the role of the Addressee. The problem considered may be stated as follows. Given:

- a domain;
- a mental state of S, as a set of beliefs about the domain that we represent with a bayesian network OWN-S;
- a set T of domain facts that the Addressee declares to know;
- a domain fact p that is taken as the 'deception object';

plan a communicative act that responds to a given goal (for S) about the Addressee's belief in p: $(G_S B_A p)$ or $(G_S \neg BW_A p)$. The System interacts with the User through a web interface which enables her to select a domain and to declare what she knows about it. S builds a image of the mental state of A $(IM-S-A)$, consistently with his own mental state (OWN-S); this image differs from OWN-S in the number of nodes and, consequently, of arcs connecting them. The two models are built so as to be probabilistically compatible: this means that the prior probabilities associated with the nodes they share are the same. Once IM-S-A has been built, the truth values of the facts in T are propagated in it, and the System looks at the probability that A assigns to p, in her present state of knowledge. The candidates to communication are selected, by S, by considering the factors we mentioned in Section 2: efficacy, impact, plausibility and safety of the candidate; the system justifies its choice in terms of the deception strategy that would bring to select every candidate in the list. We now examine in more detail some of the steps that the system follows in its reasoning.

4   Which Beliefs to Ascribe to A

"An obvious way to ascribe beliefs to other agents is by using their utterances (and actions) as a basis.... One method is to have stereotypical models,... A second method is to take the system's beliefs as a basis, and perturb them in some fashion to generate the beliefs of other agents" [1]. If the second approach is adopted and both models are represented as belief networks, the following alternatives in the relationship between OWN-S and IM-S-A may be identified:

– an *identical model*, in which the structure of the two models is the same;
– an *overlay model*, in which IM-S-A is a sub-network of OWN-S;
– a *shift model*, in which IM-S-A is partially overlapped to OWN-S.

The two models may be either 'probabilistically compatible' or may differ in their parameters, and therefore in the prior probabilities of the nodes they share.

What is there of particular, then, when a potentially deceiving act is planned? How should IM-S-A be built in this case? The assumption we make is that, if S wants to leave unvaried the Addressee's belief about the deception object, he will be particularly prudent in evoking facts that are not 'in focus' and will behave so as to avoid to saw doubts in the Addressee's mind. Therefore, his communicative acts will try to keep 'as close as possible' to the beliefs that he may consider as 'active', in the given phase of interaction, in A's mind[1]. This strategy is convenient also when S's goal is to change A's belief about p: in fact, by avoiding to talk about facts that are not 'active' in that phase, S reduces the risk of deceiving unnecessarily, by not mentioning facts to which A was not thinking at the moment and whose truth value might become evident in a future phase of interaction. Obviously, the set of active beliefs is inherently dynamic: some of them may become 'inactive' after some time, other may activate as far as the dialog goes on. When deception may occur, S will tend to keep a memory of all facts that have been active 'not too much long ago', in order to insure the safety of his communicative acts. Let us see how the belief ascription module is implemented, in Mouth Of Truth.

4.1   Creating a Structure for IM-S-A

Given a belief network D, we call:

– $N_D = \{n_1, ..., n_m\}$ the set of nodes in D and p_i an assignment of value to the multivalued variable associated with n_i; the deception object corresponds, in particular, to an assignment of value to the node n_d ;
– $C_D = \{(n_i, n_j) \mid i, j = 1, ..., m; i \neq j\}$ the set of the arcs belonging to D.

The process of building IM-S-A includes two steps: *"Creating IM-S-A's structure"* and *"Assigning parameters to IM-S-A"*.

As we said, in S's image of A's mental state, only the active beliefs of her mind are represented: this set includes the nodes that A declared to know and the node n_d. As, in the present prototype, IM-S-A is built as an 'overlay model' of OWN-S, by taking the assumption of 'commonality' [1], nodes in T are linked to n_d in the same way as they are in OWN-S. IM-S-A is then built by applying to OWN-S a 'pruning' algorithm that saves the nodes in T and the node n_d. Given OWN-S and $M = T \cup \{n_d\}$ the algorithm explores all the edges of OWN-S to check if a path between each pair of nodes in M exists. The algorithm

---

[1] We call active beliefs the subset of the agent's beliefs that, in a given context or situation, the agent is considering, using or evaluating, for a given decision or a given problem-solving.

is a generalization of the breath-first algorithm extended to $|M|$ (cardinality of M) nodes, and it insures that the output is Minimal Tree (MT) in OWN-S connecting every element of T to n_d.

4.2   Assigning Parameters to IM-S-A

Two models are probabilistically compatible if the prior probabilities associated with the nodes they share are identical. Application of the Bayes theorem allows to insure compatibility between OWN-S and IM-S-A: the procedure outlined in figure 1 considers the case of a node having two parent nodes, one of which is deleted; it may be easily extended to the case in which more than one parent node is deleted.

```
Let BN be a Belief Network such that:
   N_BN = {n_i,n_h,n_k} is the set of nodes of BN;
   C_BN ={{( n_i,n_k),(n_h,n_k)}is the set of arcs of BN;
   {P_BN(n_k|n_i,n_h),P_BN(n_k|¬n_i,n_h),P_BN(n_k|n_i,¬n_h),P_BN(n_k|¬n_i,¬n_h)}
are the conditional probabilities associated with the node n_k;
   {P_BN(n_i),P_BN(n_h)} are the prior probabilities associated with    the nodes n_i,n_h.
Let BN-r be the probabilistically compatible (with BN) belief network that is obtained
from BN by deleting the node n_h and the arc (n_h,n_k).BN-r is defined by associating, with
the arc (n_i,n_k) and the node n_i, the following parameters:

P_BN-r(n_i)= P_BN(n_i),
P_BN-r(n_k| n_i)=P_BN(n_k| n_i, n_h)*P_BN(n_h)+P_BN(n_k| n_i,¬ n_h)*P_BN(¬n_h),
and alike for P_BN-r(n_k|¬ n_i).
```

Fig. 1. The algorithm to assign parameters to IM-S-A.

5   How to Select a Communicative Act

Once IM-S-A has been built, S propagates in this network the evidences in T that A declared to know and looks at the probability that A assigns to n_d, in her present state of knowledge. A list L of 'candidates to communication' is then built and the measures mentioned in Section 2 are computed for every node in L.

5.1   Listing Candidates

In choosing candidates to communication, S considers only the facts that are unknown to A, in his view. He exploits the Addressee's ability to reason from causes to effects and vice-versa. So, candidates to communication are all the nodes that are either included in IM-S-A, with uniform probability distribution over their states, or are 'parents', 'children' or 'brothers' of the nodes of IM-S-A not included in this model. Figure 2 outlines the algorithm for producing the list of candidates.

```
current_node ← first_node(T);
while current_node ≠ NULL
      parents← get_parents(current_node);
      current_parent← first_node(parents);
      while current_parent ≠ NULL
            if Unknown(current_parent)
                  push current_parent in L;
            brothers← get_childrens(current_parent);
            current_brother← first_node(brothers);
            while current_ brother ≠ NULL
                  if Unknown(current_brother)
                        push current_brother in L
                  current_brother ←next_node(current_brother);
            current_parent← next_node(current_parent);
      children← get_children(current_node);
      current_children← first_node(children);
      while current_children ≠ NULL
            if Unknown(current_children)
                  push current_children in L;
            current_children←next_node(current_children);
current_node ←next_node(current_node);
```

Fig. 2. The algorithm to select candidates to deception.

5.2   Analysing the Impact of Candidates on the Deception Object

From the list L of candidates to communication, S extracts a sub-list of the 'optimal ones'. To this purpose, for each candidate node p_j, S builds a 'temporary' new IM-S-A, by adding the node (with its links, if necessary) to the original IM-S-A. It then evaluates the impact of the candidate p_j on the deception object p_i by propagating, in the temporary IM-S-A, the evidence corresponding to every state of p_j and by observing the posterior probability of the p_j. We implemented two different notions of impact:

– in the first one, the impact corresponds to *the degree of achievement of S's goal about A's belief in p_i* and is a function of the difference between the probability of the deception object that S would like to achieve in A's mind and the posterior probability of the this node after coming to believe in p_j:

$$Imp^1(p_j \hookleftarrow p_i) = 1 - \mid G_S B_A P(p_i) - B_S B_A P(p_i \mid p_j) \mid$$

– in the second one, the impact corresponds to *the degree of change in the belief of A about p_i* that is induced by believing in the current candidate node p_j: it is therefore measured as a function of the difference between the prior and posterior probability of A's belief in pi:

$$Imp^2(p_j \hookleftarrow p_i) = (B_S B_A P(p_i \mid p_j) - B_S B_A P(p_i))$$

5.3   Analysing the Plausibility of Candidates

We implement two different notions of plausibility:

– the *local plausibility* is a function of the difference between what S presumes to be the Addressee's belief about the candidate p_j and the communication he/she receives from S:

$$Plau^1_{S,A}(p_j) = 1 - \mid B_S B_A P(p_j) - B_S P(p_j) \mid$$

– the *global plausibility* is a function of the same difference, extended to all facts p_l that are 'connected to p_j', in the context of 'active beliefs':

$$Plau_{S,A}^2(p_j) = 1 - 1/w(\Sigma_{l=1,...w} \mid B_S B_A P(p_l) - B_S P(p_l) \mid),$$
$$\text{with } p_l \in \{\text{active beliefs}\}.$$

In this case, the idea is to see the plausibility of a fact as the overall compatibility of new knowledge induced by p_j with the previous one, in the mentioned context.

5.4 Supporting the Communication with a 'Reliable' Information Source

The credibility of a fact p referred by an information source IS may be defined, probabilistically, as: $Cred(p, IS) = P(p \mid Say(IS, p))$ (and alike for $\neg p$). It may be measured as a function of the reliability of the source ($Rel(IS, p) = P(Say(IS, p) \mid p)$) and of the prior probability of p. S may combine information sources in various ways to support his communication: he may cite 'reliable' (to A) sources or may combine reliable with unreliable ones, to try to confound her ideas.

6 An Example: The Tale of "Scratchy and Itchy"

Although, as we said, Mouth of Truth is a domain-independent tool, in this paper we will consider, as an example, the fictitious murder scenario that is described in [9].

"*Scratchy, a notorious spy from Vulcan, was found murdered in his bedroom, which is in the second floor of his house. Indentations were found on the ground right outside Scratchy's window, and they were observed to be circular. In addition, one set of footprints was found outside Scratchy's window, but the bushes were undisturbed. Itchy and Scratchy were long term enemies, and Itchy's fingerprints were found on the murder weapon (a gun discovered at the scene and registered to Itchy). Itchy, who is the head of the INS, has a ladder with oblong supports, which he was planning to use to paint his house. Poochie, the town's major, has a cylindrically-supported ladder which is available to him*".

Let us now suppose that S knows that Itchy (I) is innocent but that, for some reason, he doesn't want the truth to come out: the deception object is therefore the node 'I-murdered' ('*Itchy murdered Scratchy*') and S's goal is that A ignores its truth value. Let us now suppose that A declares to know that '*One single person was out of Scratchy's windows*' (node 'single-per'), that "*Itchy used his own gun*" (node 'I-used-his') and that "*Itchy and Scratchy have been seen to fight, some days before*" (node 'I-Sc-seen'). S builds a image of the mental state of A, by starting from these facts (the list T) and from the node 'I-murder'. Figure 3 displays the result of this step and shows that, in S's view, A tends to believe that Itachy is guilty ($P(I\_murdered) \approx 0.7$); to achieve its goal, S will then try to find arguments in favour of Itchy's innocence.

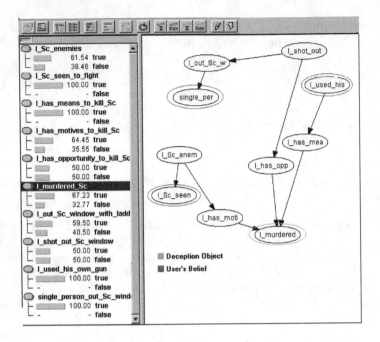

Fig. 3. IM-S-A

As S presumes that the node *"Itchy and Scratchy simulated a conflict"* ('I-SC-sim') is not 'active', he does not insert this node in IM-S-A and updates the probability table associated with its child-node 'I-Sc-see'.

To *increase the doubt*, in A's mind, about I being guilty, S needs to decrease P(I-murdered) from .7 towards .5. Let us assume that he decides to argue by exploiting A's ability of "reasoning from causes to effects": he will apply a strategy of 'deception on a cause of the Interlocutor's belief' or of 'diversion from the real cause to other causes that might be convenient to achieve the deception goal'. He will then put, in the list of candidates, the parents of the facts (in T) that A already knows. Let 'single-per' be the first element of this list; its parents, in OWN-S, are 'I-out-Sc-w' (Itachy was out of the Scratchy's windows with his ladder) and 'S-out-Sc-' (Someone else was out of the Scratchy's windows with Itachy's ladder): only the first of them is included in IM-S-A, with an equidistribution of its values; both parent-nodes of 'single-per' are therefore candidates to deception. S tries to understand which will be the impact, on the deception object, of each of the values the two variables may assume. He adds to IM-S-A the node 'S-out-Sc-'. Setting this variable as 'true' equates, for S, to saying: *"As you know, there was a single person out of Scratchy's windows that night; however, this doesn't mean that that person was Itchy: someone else could have been there, instead"*. If, on the contrary, S takes, as candidate, 'I-out-Sc=false' ('Itchy was not out of Scratchy's window'), this equates to saying: *"As you know, there was a single person out of Scratchy's windows that night: well, this person was not Itchy".*

Other deception strategies may take, as candidates, the 'children' of nodes in T or their brothers. The choice of 'children' may correspond to a strategy of 'deception on a consequence' of the Interlocutor's belief or of 'diversion from the real consequences towards other consequences that might be convenient to achieve the deception goal'. The choice of 'brothers' corresponds to a strategy of 'indirect deception on a cause' of the Interlocutor's belief': 'indirect' because it is applied to the consequences of this cause rather than directly on the cause itself."

Figure 4 shows the results of examining the mentioned deception strategies. As far as 'deception on the causes' is concerned, it shows that "Someone else was out of Scratchy windows" is, in fact, the most convenient choice, as far as the combination of impact (.97) and plausibility (.79) are concerned; this statement is not very riskful, to S, as it does not require him to lie.
Other candidates in the Table are less convenient: for instance, saying that 'Itchy was not out the Scratchy's windows' would imply, for S, lying, at the risk of being discovered. The Table shows, as well, that selecting the best combination of impact and plausibility is not always easy. To increase this value, S might evoke some supporting information source; he might say, for instance: *"Everybody knows, in this village, that Itchy's ladder may be used by anyone who needs it!".*

The system justifies its choice of the candidates by generating a natural language message that relates each of them to the specific 'deception strategy' which brough to select it. The following is an example of such an explanation text:

'The following candidates have been selected because you said that the Interlocutor believes that 'A single person was out of Scratchy's window':

— *Itchy was out of Scratchy's window with a ladder' and 'Someone else was out of Scratchy's window with a ladder'. These nodes are possible causes of the interlocutor's belief; the choice of one of them may correspond to a strategy of 'deception on a cause of the Interlocutor's belief' or of 'diversion from the real cause to other causes that might be convenient to achieve the deception goal'.*
— *'Oblung indentations were found out of Scratchy's window' and 'Only one set of footprints was found out of Scratchy's window'. These nodes are consequences of the Interlocutor's belief. The choice of one of them may correspond to strategy of 'deception on a consequence' of the Interlocutor's belief or of 'diversion from the real consequences towards other consequences that might be convenient to achieve the deception goal'.*

"The following candidates have been selected, in addition, because you said that the Interlocutor believes that 'Itchy and Scratchy have been seen to fight':

Deception media		Deception object		Impact		Plausibility		Safety
		prior belief	post belief	goal achievement	belief change	local plausibility	global plausibility	
I_out_Sc_window_with_ladder	true	0.672258	0.769847	0.730153	0.0975882	0.595	0.884018	0.595
	false	0.672258	0.528888	0.971112	-0.14337	0.405	0.829607	0.405
S_out_Sc_window_with_ladder	true	0.672258	0.528888	0.971112	-0.14337	0.405	0.791007	0.5
	false	0.672258	0.769846	0.730154	0.0975882	0.595	0.857744	0.5
oblung_indentations_out_Sc_win	true	0.672258	0.672258	0.827742	0	0.7	0.972727	0.47525
	false	0.672258	0.672258	0.827742	0	0.3	0.936364	0.52475
bush_undisturbed	true	0.672258	0.672258	0.827742	0	0.6	0.963636	0.5
	false	0.672258	0.672258	0.827742	0	0.4	0.945455	0.5
one_set_of_footsprints_out_window	true	0.672258	0.672258	0.827742	0	0.999	0.999909	0.5
	false	0.672258	0.672258	0.827742	0	**0.001**	0.909182	0.5
I_Sc_enemies	true	0.672258	0.845	0.655	0.172742	**0.615385**	**0.909716**	**0.5**
	false	0.672258	0.395872	0.895872	-0.276387	0.384615	0.855545	0.5
I_Sc_simulate_a_conflict	true	0.672258	0.645387	0.854613	-0.026871	0.692308	0.959261	0.5
	false	0.672258	0.732718	0.767282	0.0604596	0.307692	0.908336	0.5
I_has_motives_to_kill_Sc	true	0.672258	0.85	0.65	0.177742	0.644517	0.913691	0.540872
	false	0.672258	0.35	0.85	-0.322258	0.355483	0.843515	0.459128
I_Sc_holydays_together	true	0.672258	0.397304	0.897304	-0.274954	0.192923	0.795988	0.2505
	false	0.672258	0.737983	0.762017	0.0657248	0.807077	0.951233	0.7495
I_gun_used_kill_Sc	true	0.672258	0.672258	0.827742	0	0.75	0.977273	0.625
	false	0.672258	0.672258	0.827742	0	0.25	0.931818	0.375
I_fingerprints_on_gun	true	0.672258	0.672258	0.827742	0	0.9225	0.992955	0.71
	false	0.672258	0.672258	0.827742	0	0.0775	0.916136	0.29
I_has_means_to_kill_Sc	true	0.672258	0.672258	0.827742	0	1	1	0.5
	false	0.672258	0.672258	0.827742	0	0	1	0.5

Fig. 4. Impact, Plausibility and Safety measures on candidates to deception

- 'Itchy and Scratchy were enemies' and 'Itchy and Scratchy simulated a conflict'. These nodes are possible causes of the interlocutor's belief (see previous comment).
- 'Itchy has motives to kill Scratchy' and 'Itchy and Scratchy frequently spend their holydays together'. The choice of these nodes corresponds to a strategy of 'indirect deception on a cause' of the Interlocutor's belief ('Itchy and Scratchy were enemies'): 'indirect because it is applied to the consequences of this cause rather than directly on the cause itself."

7   Concluding Remarks

Although modeling of deception is a necessary step in building a 'natural' dialog system, we are not surprised that this problem received so little attention so far: after some years of study, we feel we are only at the beginning of our way to the solution. Tackling this problem from the point of view of bayesian networks seems to us a very promising approach, though. If examined from a purely logical viewpoint, the problem involves a high-complexity reasoning: in mentioning dialog models that they label as not 'cooperative'[2], Taylor and colleagues [8] claim that modeling these dialogs would require reasoning at 'deeply-nested belief levels' level (higher that the third one). They also claim that deeply-nested beliefs are 'awkward and contrary to intuitions in human-human dialogs', and support their statement with the results of psychological research. The approach we describe in this paper enables avoiding deeply-nested belief reasoning by starting from the following basic assumptions: (i) beyond intentionally insincere assertions, there is always some interest of the Speaker, the need to achieve some domain-goal; (ii) deception results from a conflict (between S and A) about this goal and finally (as a consequence of the two previous hypotheses (iii) S is interested to do his best to hide his deception attempts. The consequence of these assumptions is, first of all, that deceiving does not coincide with lying, and therefore discovering contradictions in the interlocutor enlights only a subset of the large variety of deception attempts: this entails the need of tackling the problem from an 'uncertain belief' viewpoint and to attach, to beliefs, a system of weights that formalize the aspect we mentioned in Section 3. In Mouth of Truth, given a candidate p to communication, the efficacy is a measure of the effect produced by p on the System's goal; the impact enables measuring the convenience of indirect deception, the plausibility enables forecasting the short-term success of the deception attempt and the safety its long-term success; the first three measures require second-level nesting of beliefs, the third one third-level nesting. Finally, the introduction of a reliable information source enables reinforcing the deception attempt when this risks to be unsuccessful. Belief networks seemed to us, once again, a powerful method to model the interlocutor in dialogs: besides representing the inherently uncertain process of 'arousal of suspicion', the possibility they offer to apply various forms of reasoning (from causes to effects and vice-versa) enables simulating the deception forms we mentioned in Section 2. The assumption of 'probabilistic compatibility' between the two models (of S and of A) reduces the range of deceptions we may simulate, at present: in Mouth of Truth, S cannot exploit, in his deceptive attempts, the different strength that, in his view, A applies to some relation among beliefs. This is one of the (very many) aspects that we plan to investigate in the near future. The works with which our research has more relations are Demolombe's research on trust in information sources [5] and Zukerman's NAG Project, with its subsequent extensions [9,10]: there are similarities between our algorithms and some modules of this system, such as its "Attentional Mechanism" and its "Analyser". However, deception is an exception to 'plain' dialogs that are usually considered in HCI: we therefore owe ideas, as well, to those who worked on politeness, bluff and other unusual aspects of dialog modeling. Rather than evaluating our Simulator, we wish to use this tool to assess whether the theory

---

[2] To these authors, 'cooperative dialogues' are "defined by their lack of any commitment, on the part of any participants, to any form of deception, malicious or otherwise".

about deception planning we apply is effective in enabling the generation of the most common deception forms: for this reason, we designed this tool so as to be domain-independent, and plan to apply it to a variety of domains.

References

1. Ballim, A., Wilks, Y.: Beliefs, stereotypes ad dynamic agent modeling. User Modeling and User-Adapted Interaction, 1, 1, 1991.
2. Castelfranchi, C., Poggi, I.: Lying as pretending to give information. Pretending to Communicate. H. Parret (Ed), Springer Verlag, 1993.
3. Castelfranchi, C., Poggi, I.: Bugie, finzioni e sotterfugi. Carocci Publ Co, 1998.
4. Castelfranchi, C., de Rosis, F., Grasso, F.: Deception and suspicion in medical interactions; towards the simulation of believable dialogues. Machine Conversations, Y Wilks (Ed), Kluwer Series in Engineering and Computer Science, **511**, 1999.
5. Demolombe, R.: Can computers deliberately deceive? To trust information sources; a proposal for a modal logic framework. In Proceedings of the Workshop on Deception, Fraud and Trust in Multiagent Systems. Autonomous Agents, 1998.
6. de Rosis, F., Castelfranchi, C. Which User Model do we need to relax the hypothesis of 'sincere assertions' in HCI?. UM99, Workshop on 'Attitudes, personality and emotions in User-Adapted Interaction', Banff, 1999.
7. de Rosis, F., Castelfranchi, C., Carofiglio, V.: Can computers deliberately deceive? A simulation attempt of Turing's Imitation Game. Sumbitted for publication.
8. Taylor, J.A., Carletta, J., Mellish, C.: Requirements for belief models in Cooperative dialogue. User Modeling and User-Adapted Interaction, 6, 1, 1996.
9. Zukerman, I., McConachy, R., Korb, K., Pickett, D.: Exploratory interaction with a bayesian argumentation system. Proceedings of IJCAI 1999.
10. Zukerman, I., Jinath, N., McConachy, R., George, S.: Recognising intentions from rejoinders in a bayesian interactive argumentation system. In PRICAI 2000 Proceedings, Melbourne. 8.

An Agent Based Approach to Virtual Market Place Simulation

Filippo Neri

Marie Curie Fellow at Unilever Research Port Sunlight, UK
University of Piemonte Orientale, Italy
Address: Unilever Research Port Sunlight
Quarry Road East Bebington Wirral CH633JW UK
Filippo.Neri@unilever.com, filipponeri@yahoo.com

Abstract. A virtual market place for the qualitative simulation of how product awareness spreads among consumers is described. Potentially this methodology could allow the investigation of hypothetical economic mechanisms underlying tradeoff among product advertisement effort, consumers' memory span and duration, and passing word among friends in determining a product market share. Preliminary experiments showing the potentialities of this approach are reported.

Keywords: Models of rationality for economic models, virtual agent-based institutions of e-commerce, dynamics of info-economies.

1 Introduction

The diffusion of an Internet based economy, that includes even the less valuable transactions, is day by day more evident. The existing information infrastructure has allowed the exploitation of new methods to contract the purchases of goods and services, the most notable of which is probably the agent mediated electronic commerce [Kephart et al., 1998, Maes, 1994]. In this economy, autonomous agents become the building block for developing electronic market places or for comparing offers across several seller's websites (shopbots) [Maes, 1994, Rodriguez-Aguilar et al., 1998]. Our aim is to use an agent-based market place to qualitatively simulate the diffusion of products' awareness across the Internet and its impact on customer choices. As many commercial scenarios could be selected, we chose to investigate a simple commercial interaction. Different groups of consumers have to choose one product between a set of perfect substitutes that differ in price, advertised lifestyle associated with the product and the advertising effort to initially penetrate the market. Our objective is the to understand how a sequence of repeated purchases is affected by the trade off among the previous variables, the consumers' desires and limits, and the diffusion of the awareness about the existing products. The ultimate goal would be to capture the common experience of choosing, for instance, among alternative

F. Esposito (Ed.): AI*IA 2001, LNAI 2175, pp. 267–272, 2001.

brands of Italian Pasta packages displayed in the webpage or on the physical shelf of our grocery store.

Some researchers take a very long term view about the ecommerce phenomena envisioning economies of shopbots [Kephart et al., 1998, Maes, 1994, Rodriguez-Aguilar et al., 1998]. For instance, Kephart et al. [Kephart et al., 1998] try to model large open economies of shopbots by analysing the an economy based on information filtering and diffusion towards targeted shopbots (customers). Quite differently, we try to capture the commercial phenomena in more near future where customers are human beings with their intrinsic limit in information processing, having the need to trust the bought product and to feel supported, and reassured about their purchasing choice as their best possible choice. We share, however, with Kephart et al. the desire to analyse and understand how the information flow can affect such economy. Academics in business schools already report preliminary studies of these situations. For instance, Lynch and Ariely [Jr. and Ariely, 2000] try to understand the factors behind purchases made in a real world experiment of wine selling across different retailers' websites and Brynjolfsson et al. [Smith et al., 2001] discuss which factors seems to be more likely to impact the consumer choices in the electronic market place. However, we are not currently aware of other agent based modelling approaches dealing with these issues. To further extend our work, a more sophisticated approach to modelling the electronic market place may have to be selected in order to take into account negotiation protocols or virtual organisation formation as, for instance, described in [Rocha and Oliveira, 1999] or to account for additional brokering agents as described in [Viamonte and Ramos, 1999]. In the near future, we would like to investigate the emergence of information diffusion strategies by using a distributed genetic algorithm [Neri and Saitta, 1996].

The paper is organised has follow: in section 2 a description of the market place is reported, in section 3 the performed experiments are commented and, finally, some conclusions are drawn.

2   The Virtual Market Place

The architecture of our virtual market place is straightforward: round after round, groups of consumers, modelled as software agents, select which product to buy according to an internal status that takes into account the consumers' preferences for a product and their awareness about the product's benefits and image. This sketchy description of the buying experience should match what most people experience when selecting among wholemeal bread choices or plain milk chocolate bars made by different companies at the local grocery store. The description of how products and consumers are represented follows. A product is view as a collection of an identifier, a price, an effort to describe its features/benefits on the package, an effort to bound the product to the image of a lifestyle (brand) and an initial advertisement effort to penetrate the market. It is important to note that the scope of this work is to consider products that are substitute one for the others but differ in price or other characteristics. A consumer is a (software) agent operating on the market and she is driven in her purchase by a target price, a need for understanding the product benefits, the lifestyle conveyed by the product brand, and the initial marketing effort put into placing the product in the market. The consumer can remember only a constant number of products (memory limit) for a constant number of rounds (memory duration), and she may share with her friends her opinion about the known products. During this interaction, she may review her opinions about the products by updating her set of known products. It is worthwhile to note that the memory span limits the consumer awareness of the available products. For instance, if a consumer had a memory limit of 3, she would be aware of 3 products at most and she would make her purchasing choice only among those three products. The memory span also influences the exchange of information during the after shopping chat. In our series of experiments, all the products prices and characteristics are a priori fixed in order to cover a range of significant offers. The list of the available products follows:

Product(Id, Price, Description, Image, InitialAdvertisement): Product(0, LowValue, LowValue, LowValue, LowValue), ..., Product(15, HighValue, HighValue, HighValue, HighValue)

Each product is defined by an identifier (Id), a selling price (Price), an effort in describing its benefits on its package, an effort to convey a lifestyle (image), and an effort to initially penetrate the market. The constants 'LowValue' and 'HighValue' correspond to the values 0.2 and 0.8. The Price, Description and Image parameters are used to evaluate a customer's preference for the product, whereas the InitialAdvertisement parameter defines the initial awareness of the product among the customers. So, for instance, a product defined as Product(x, LowValue, LowValue, LowValue, LowValue) is especially targeted toward price sensitive consumers that do not care about knowing much on the product. And with an initial penetration rate of 0.2, on average, 20% of the consumers are aware of its availability at the beginning of the first buying round. It is worthwhile to note that, in the above list, 16 products are listed but, actually, odd and even products differs only because of a different initial advertising effort. Our model does not currently consider advertising effort during the lifetime of the product after the market penetration one. A similar choice has been made to represent the customers. The four groups of consumers considered are:

Customer(Price, Description, Image), Customer(LowValue, LowValue, LowValue) (bargain hunters), Customer(LowValue, LowValue, HighValue) (image sensitive), Customer(LowValue, HighValue, LowValue) (description sensitive), Customer(LowValue, HighValue, HighValue) (image and description sensitive)

For the scope of this paper, we concentrate on customers whose target product has a low price but differs in the other features. Through our selection of target values, we tried to capture the following categories of customers: the bargain hunters, the brand sensitive ones, the package sensitive ones (i.e. are interested in its nutrition values, its composition, its ecological impact, etc.), and those that are both brand and package sensitive. As the customer chooses to buy that product that most closely match her target preferences, we defined the following distance measure:

$Preference(product) = (max(product.Price, target.Price) - target.Price)^2 +$
$(min(product.Description, target.Description) - target.Description)^2 +$
$(min(product.Image, target.Image) - target.Image)^2$

The selected product is then the one with the lowest value, according to the above expression, among the ones known by the customer. Alternative expressions for the preference measure are under study.

3   Experimental Results

Goal of the experimentation is to demonstrate that our tool can capture some of the inherent complexity behind the determination of the product market shares by considering a variety of factors that impact on this economic phenomena. These factors include the customers' expectations for a product, the limited memory span and duration that consumers reserve to remember available products, and the diffusion of the product awareness among consumers by initial advertisement and further passing by word. All the reported experiments are based on the following basic settings. During each round, 400 consumers (one hundred for each of the four consumer types) select which of the 16 products to buy. Only products that the consumer remembers (i.e. appearing in its memory list) compete for being purchased. The economic process is repeated for 100 rounds. For each experiment, the reported figures are averaged over 3 runs. As a baseline for evaluating the economic process, we consider the situation where each consumer is fully aware of all the available products since the first round. As all the consumers are oriented towards products with low price but with different characteristics, it is straightforward to calculate that the product market shares stay constant over the 400 rounds and correspond to the values reported in Fig. 1a. In the picture, the product identifiers appear on the x axis, and the market shares on the y axis. Thus for instance, Product 6 will achieve a 9.3% market share. It is worthwhile to note that the product from 9 to 16 have a 0% market share because, in the range from 1 to 8, there exists a product with identical features but with lower price. If we were in this ideal situation, every consumer would be able to make the best pick among the available products. Unfortunately, in the real world, full knowledge about the available choices is not common and product awareness is the result of a variety of factors including advertisement, passing by word among friends and memory capacity. The impact of these factors on the product market shares is taken into account in the following experiments. Let us consider the case where consumers do not have any friends or do not talk about products to friends (average number of friends or avgf =0), they can remember only 2 products at the time (memory limit or ml=2), and they remember each product for 20 rounds unless either they keep buying it or they are told about by their friends. The initial (end of round 1) and final market shares (end of round 100) appear in Fig. 1b. It appears that the initial and final market shares are very alike and that the higher the effort

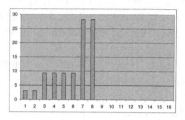
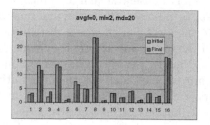

Fig. 1. (a) Ideal market shares in presence of a perfect product awareness. (b) Product market shares when consumers not talk to their friends about their shopping (avgf=0), remembering at most 2 products (ml=2) and with memory duration of 20.

in penetrating the market the better the market share (compare odd and even numbered products). The market share distribution is biased toward low priced product, this is to be expected given the customers' preferences. But, still, some high price products achieve a significant portion of market because of the limited memory span of the consumers that would prevent them to compare and choose among more alternatives. If we alter the previous scenario just by increasing the number of friends to 20, we obtain quite a different distribution of market shares, Fig. 2a. The pattern of the initial market shares is similar to that of the previous

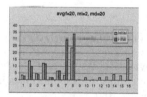
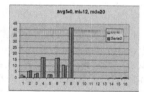
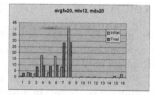

Fig. 2. (a) Product market shares (Pms) in the case of consumers talking to about 20 friends about their shopping (avgf=20), remembering at most 2 products (ml=2) and with memory duration of 20. (b) Pms in the case of consumers not talking to their friends about their shopping (avgf=0), remembering at most 12 product (ml=12) and with memory duration of 20. (c) Pms in the case of consumers talking to about 20 friends about their shopping (avgf=20), remembering at most 12 products (ml=12) and with memory duration of 20.

scenario but the final shares tend to converge towards the ideal ones. This can be interpreted that having many friends does actually empower the customer in making the best selection. It is interesting to note that the only initial advertisement cannot compensate for the further product comparisons communicated among the consumers. However, the initial product advertising effort results in the consumers remembering and, then, choosing the more advertised products among the low priced ones. An alternative scenario would be to keep an average number of friends equal to 0, but increase the consumer memory limit to 12, Fig. 2b. In this case, the initial and final distribution look alike and tend to converge to the ideal market shares distribution but a bias toward the products investing in the initial advertising is evident.

Finally, if both the average number of friends (avgf=20) and the memory limit (ml=12) increase, then the initial and final distribution differ, the final one most closely matching the ideal ones, Fig. 2c. Comparing the initial and final distributions of market shares it appears that exchanging information about products with friends and remembering a number of them is the key to make a successful choice in this scenario.

4   Conclusion

A virtual market place to qualitatively observe a set of factors influencing product market shares has been described. The main experimental finding is that enhancing information diffusion, in the hypothesized market place, results in the consumers being able to make the "wisest choice" among the available offers. This means that they are able to select the most suitable product at the lowest price. The reported experimentation shows the potentialities of the simulator in visualizing complex interactions such those behind economic processes. We are currently working toward understanding to what extent this approach could be used to model a real world situation.

References

[Jr. and Ariely, 2000] Jr., J. G. L. and Ariely, D. (2000). Wine online: search costs and competiotion on price, quality and distribution. *Marketing Science*, pages 1–39.

[Kephart et al., 1998] Kephart, J. O., Hanson, J. E., Levine, D. W., Grosof, B. N., Sairamesh, J., Segal, R., and White, S. R. (1998). Dynamics of an information-filtering economy. In *Cooperative Information Agents*, pages 160–171.

[Maes, 1994] Maes, P. (1994). Agents that reduce work and information overload. *Communications of the ACM*, pages 31–40.

[Neri and Saitta, 1996] Neri, F. and Saitta, L. (1996). Exploring the power of genetic search in learning symbolic classifiers. *IEEE Trans. on Pattern Analysis and Machine Intelligence*, PAMI-18:1135–1142.

[Rocha and Oliveira, 1999] Rocha, A. P. and Oliveira, E. (1999). Agents advanced features for negotiation in electronic commerce and virtual organisations formation process. *Agent Mediated Electronic Commerce - An European Perspective*.

[Rodriguez-Aguilar et al., 1998] Rodriguez-Aguilar, J. A., Martin, F. J., Noriega, P., Garcia, P., and Sierra, C. (1998). Towards a test-bed for trading agents in electronic auction markets. *AI Communications*, 11(1):5–19.

[Smith et al., 2001] Smith, M. D., Bailey, J., and Brynjolfsson, E. (2001). Understanding digital markets: review and assessment. *Draft available at http://ecommerce.mit.edu/papers/ude*, pages 1–34.

[Viamonte and Ramos, 1999] Viamonte, M. J. and Ramos, C. (1999). A model for an electronic market place. *Agent Mediated Electronic Commerce - An European Perspective*.

Open Domain Question/Answering on the Web

Bernardo Magnini, Matteo Negri and Roberto Prevete

ITC-irst, Istituto per la Ricerca Scientifica e Tecnologica
Via Sommarive, 38050 Povo (TN), Italy
{magnini|negri|prevete}@irst.itc.it

Abstract. This paper presents a question/answering system for searching the web. The system accepts natural language questions in Italian and returns as answer a ranked list of document passages together with the URL of the whole document. Three crucial aspects related to the web scenario have been investigated: the linguistic expansion of the query, the optimization of the search boolean expression, the evaluation of the results.

1   Introduction

Textual Question Answering (QA) aims at identifying the answer of a question in large collections of documents. QA systems are presented with natural language questions and the expected output is either the actual answer identified in a text or small text fragments containing the answer.

In the last years, under the promotion of the TREC-8 [20] and TREC-9 [21] competitions, there has been a large interest in developing QA systems. A common architecture includes three basic components: a *question processing* component, generally based on some kind of linguistic analysis; a *search component*, based on information retrieval techniques; an *answer processing* component, which exploits the similarity between the question and the documents to identify the correct answer. A variety of approaches have been implemented to support the linguistic analysis needed for question processing. Among the others, LASSO [16] makes use of a taxonomy of question types with the aim of identifying both the question type and answer type. The QALC system [6] developed at LIMSI emphases the term extraction capabilities based on the use of FASTR [11]. The approach presented in [9] and [10] demonstrates that the use of linguistic knowledge, particularly for question processing, significantly improves the system performance. The approach developed at the University of Sheffield [17] makes use of a revisited version of LaSIE, an information extraction system. Finally, it has been demonstrated [18] that the ability of performing anaphora resolution on the retrieved documents brings important information in the answer identification process.

Despite of the large use of linguistic technologies made by the above mentioned systems, it seems that some issues, crucial for the web scenario, have not been addressed. In this paper we want to investigate specific topics deriving by the application of QA techniques in the web scenario. Our contribution involves three major areas:

F. Esposito (Ed.): AI*IA 2001, LNAI 2175, pp. 273-284, 2001.
© Springer-Verlag Berlin Heidelberg 2001

☐ *Linguistic expansion of the query.* A significant difference in web based QA is that there is no guarantee that either the answer is actually present in at least one document or that there is some linguistic implication between the answer and the question, as it is assumed in the TREC initiative, where questions are manually derived from the text collection. As a consequence some form of enrichment of the query is necessary to improve the retrieval of relevant documents. In particular we emphasize the role of word sense disambiguation, as a necessary step toward query expansion.

☐ *Search modalities.* Searching the web forces to interface the QA system with existing search engines. It becomes important taking advantage in the best way of the "advance search" capabilities available, such as boolean expressions. Moreover, as for the output of the search, many linguistically based techniques are not suitable to be used in analyzing documents retrieved from the web in real time.

☐ *Evaluation.* The implication of an answer with respect to its question for a web user is generally weaker than for controlled text collections, where human judges apply rigid tests. A reason for this is that the relevance of a web document relies on several factors. For instance, a retrieved document could not include the answer in itself, but could nevertheless provide links to other documents useful to find the answer. Elements that provide implicit knowledge are the document structure, hypertextual links, multimedia co-reference, and generally, a strong use of contextual information. We propose a metric that takes into account the context the document is able to provide.

The paper is structured as follows. Section 2 introduces the global architecture of the system. Section 3 addresses the linguistic analysis of the question, including word sense disambiguation, answer type identification, and query expansion. Section 4 illustrates the proposed solution for the composition of a boolean expression for the search engine.

2   Architecture

The system has three main components, illustrated in Figure 1.

The *question processing* component is in charge of the linguistic analysis of the Italian input question, which is performed sequentially by the following modules.

☐ *Tokenization and pos tagging.* First the question is tokenized and words are disambiguated with their lexical category by means of a statistical part of speech tagger developed at Irst.

☐ *Multiwords recognition.* About five thousand multiwords (i.e. collocations, compounds and complex terms) have been extracted from a monolingual Italian dictionary [4] and are recognized by pattern matching rules.

☐ *Word sense disambiguation.* This module disambiguates words in the query with respect to their senses. This module, described in Section 3.1, is crucial for providing reasonable keyword expansions and, eventually, English translations.

☐ *Answer type identification.* The answer type for a question represents the entity to be searched as answer. The module is based on a answer type classification and on a rule system, both described in Section 3.2.

☐ *Keywords expansion.* Two kind of expansions, described in Section 3.3, are carried out: word synonyms and morphological derivations.

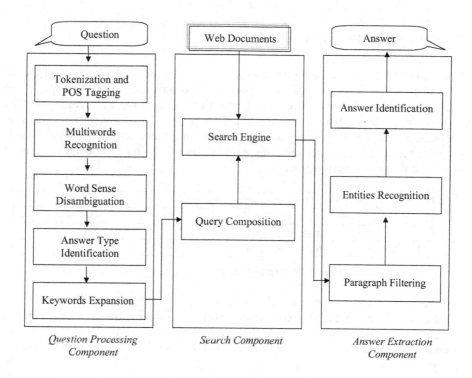

Fig. 1. System Architecture.

The *search component* first composes a boolean expression from the question keywords, then performs the document retrieval on the web. We are currently using Inktomi[1], with a direct and efficient access. The output is a ranked list of documents.

The *answer extraction* component implements a paragraph filtering module that extracts text paragraphs from the top scored retrieved documents. This is done maximizing the number of keywords and expansions, produced in the question processing phase, within a window of a fixed length of words. The output are the text paragraphs that should contain the answer to the question. The *named entities recognition* module identifies the entities in the text paragraphs corresponding to the answer type category. We are using an adaptation of Learning Pinocchio [3], which makes use of learning algorithms to recognize named entities, such as persons, organizations, locations, measures and dates. Finally, the *answer identification*

---

[1] The work reported in this paper has been partially supported by Kataweb, an Italian web portal. We thank both Kataweb and Inktomi Corporation for kindly having placed the search engine for the experiments at our disposal.

module highlights the portion of text containing the answer to the question, which will be presented to the user.

3   Linguistic Expansions

In the last TREC-9 set up *reformulation questions* were included which asked for the same answer (i.e. the same string in a particular document of the collection). As an example, questions in table 1 are all reformulations. QA on the web presupposes the opposite situation, in that for a certain question we may have several *reformulation answers*, in different documents, and all of them appropriate for the question. In this scenario the ability to make linguistic expansions on the query becomes a crucial aspect for the system performance.

Q-711: What tourist attractions are there in Reims?
Q-712: What do most tourists visit in Reims?
Q-713: What attracts tourists in Reims?
Q-714: What are tourist attractions in Reims?

Table 1. Reformulation questions (from [10]).

For the experiments reported in this paper we have translated into Italian the 200 questions used in the TREC-8 competition (for the complete list and for a detailed description of the acquisition procedure see [20]. The set includes typical wh-questions whose answer is supposed to be a certain fact described in a small portion of text.

3.1   Semantic Disambiguation

Identifying the correct sense of a word in a question is necessary if we want to add either synonyms or translations for that word without the risk of introducing disturbing elements in the search query. There are two crucial questions to address: first, a repository of word senses has to be identified; second, it is important to develop a disambiguation technique able to cope with the specificity of questions, particularly with the availability of a limited context (i.e. few words).

As for sense repository we have adopted MultiWordNet [1], a multilingual lexical database including information about English and Italian words. MultiWordNet is an extension of the English WordNet [5], a semantic network of English words grouped into synonym sets called synsets. Two kinds of relations are provided: semantic relations (i.e. among synsets), and lexical relations (i.e. among words). The main lexical relations represented in WordNet are synonymy and antonymy, while hyponymy, hypernymy, meronymy, entailment and conceptual opposition are the main semantic relations among synsets. MultiWordNet has been developed keeping as much as possible of the semantic relations available in the English WordNet: Italian synsets have been created in correspondence with English synsets, importing the semantic relations from the corresponding English synsets. The Italian part of MultiWordNet currently covers about 40,000 lemmas, completely aligned with the English WordNet 1.6 (i.e. with correspondences to English senses).

As far as word disambiguation is concerned we have applied Word Domain Disambiguation (WDD), a technique already experimented for the disambiguation of short news [14], and further extended by adding domain frequency information. Word Domain Disambiguation is a variant of WSD where for each word in a text a *domain* label, (among those allowed by the word) has to be chosen instead of a *sense* label. Domain labels, such as MEDICINE and ARCHITECTURE, provide a natural way to establish semantic relations among word senses, grouping them into homogeneous clusters. In MultiWordNet the synsets have been annotated with one or more domain labels selected from a set of about two hundred labels hierarchically organized (see [12] for the annotation methodology and for the evaluation of the resource).

The WDD algorithm works in two steps. First, for each content word in the query and for each sense of the word, the correspondent domain labels in MultiWordNet are collected with a score determined by the frequency of the label among the senses of the word. Let us consider as example an ambiguos query from the TREC corpus. In "Quale è la stella più luminosa visibile dalla Terra?" (*"What is the brightest star visible from Earth?"*): the situation after the first step of the WDD algorithm is represented in Figure 2.

stella	stella#1: celestial body	ASTRONOMY
	stella#2: an actor who play	ART
luminoso	luminoso#1: bright brilliant shining	PHYSICS
	luminoso#2: popular glorious	FACTOTUM
	luminoso#3: promising auspicious	FACTOTUM
visibile	visibile#1: conspicuous obvious	PHYSICS
	visibile#2: visible seeable	ASTRONOMY
terra	terra#1: Earth world globe	ASTRONOMY
	terra#2: estate land landed_estate acres	ECONOMY
	terra#3: clay	GEOLOGY
	terra#4: soil dirt	GEOLOGY
	terra#5: ground_earth	ELECTRICITY
	terra#6: dry_land earth solid_ground	GEOGRAPHY
	terra#7: land ground soil	GEOGRAPHY
	terra#8: earth ground	GEOLOGY

Fig. 2. Word Domain Disambiguation.

At the second step, all the possible tuples of domain labels for each word are scored by means of a similarity function, and the best tuple is selected. The similarity between two domains is computed according to the probability of the two domains to co-occur within a text. This information has been computed over several balanced corpora, both for English (i.e. the Brown corpus, the LOB corpus and the Reuters news corpus) and for Italian (i.e. the Elsnet corpus and a large collection of newspaper news). In our example, the algorithm selects ASTRONOMY for "stella", PHYSICS for "luminoso", ASTRONOMY for "visibile" and ASTRONOMY for "terra", which correspond to our intuition about the involved word senses.

Results obtained over the 200 Italian questions, previously manually annotated with the correct domain label for each keyword, are very encouraging, showing a limited lost in accuracy with respect to WDD over longer texts, where larger pieces of context are available for disambiguation.

3.2   Answer Type Identification

The answer type for a question represents the entity to be searched as answer. To extract this information, a taxonomy of *answer types* was manually defined starting from the 200 TREC-8 questions. The taxonomy includes categories such as "LOCATION", "PERSON", "TIME-PERIOD", "MEASURE" and "GENERIC". Then, each category is associated to a set of rules that check different features of the question; in particular a rule may detect the presence of a particular word occurrence, of words of a given part of speech, and of words belonging to a given semantic category. For instance, the rule described in (1) matches any question starting with "quale" ("*what*"), whose first noun, if any, is a person.

(1)   RULENAME: QUALE-CHI
        TEST: ["quale" [¬NOUN]* [NOUN:person-p]ⱼ +]
        OUTPUT: ["PERSON" J]

The rule matches questions like "Quale famoso leader comunista è morto a Città del Messico?" (*"What famous communist leader died in Mexico City?"*), because the first noun encountered after "quale" (i.e. "leader") satisfies the person-p constraint. The same rule does not match the question "Quale grande città americana ha avuto il più alto tasso di omicidi nel 1988?" (*"What large U.S. city had the highest murder rate for 1988?"*), because "città" does not satisfy the person-p predicate. Semantic predicates (e.g. location-p, person-p, time-p, etc.) are defined on the MultiWordNet taxonomy, already described in Section 3.1. Each predicate checks if the sense of a word referred in a rule is subsumed by at least one high level synset manually defined for that predicate. As an example, for person-p, we identified synsets like person#1 ("human being") and group#1 ("any number of entities considered as a unit"). Then the predicate is satisfied if leader#1 is subsumed by at least one of these synsets.

While rules are mostly language dependent, semantic predicates defined on the MultiWordNet conceptual hierarchy are reusable for different languages. For instance, rule (2) is the English realization of rule (1) for Italian:

(2)   RULENAME: WHICH-WHO
        TEST: ["which" [¬NOUN]* [NOUN:person-p]ⱼ +]
        OUTPUT: ["PERSON" J]

The output of a rule gives two pieces of information: the category of the answer type and the focus of the question [16], i.e. the word that expresses the answer type in the question. In the examples above, the answer type is the category PERSON, while the focus is the word "leader". This information will be used to retrieve the correct answer to the question in the documents retrieved by the search engine. In particular, the category of the entity we are looking for (e.g. a PERSON) is used as input to the named entity recognition system, which individuate a set of candidate answers (i.e. person names). Then the focus information (e.g. "leader") allows to restrict the candidate set to those person names that are placed close to the focus or to a synonym of it in MultiWordnet.

Currently we use about 90 answer type rules for Italian and 70 for English. They have been checked on the TREC corpus resulting respectively in a 93% and 91% accuracy. Failures are mainly due to pos-tagging and disambiguation errors.

3.3   Keywords Expansion

At this step of the linguistic processing of the question, a stop words filter is applied that cuts off both non content words and non relevant content words. The remaining words (we call them "basic keywords") are then passed to an expansion phase, which considers both morphological derivations and synonyms, as they can potentially improve the system recall, i.e. the answer to the question might contain either variations or synonyms of the basic keyword of the question.

Morphological derivation. The approach adopted is answer oriented, in that it considers the expansions with the higher probability to appear in the answer. For instance, given the question "Chi ha inventato la luce elettrica?" ("*Who invented the electric light?*"), five expansions are automatically generated for the basic keyword "inventare": the past participle masculine "inventato", because this is the actual form of the lemma; the past participle female "inventata", because the direct object of the verb is female; the past indicative "inventò", because in Italian it can substitute the past participle; the noun "inventore", because it is the nominalization of the subject of the verb; finally, the noun "invenzione", because it is the nominalization of the object of the verb. Derivations have been automatically extracted from an Italian monolingual dictionary [4].

Synonyms. The use of query expansions for text retrieval is a debated topic. Flank [7] shows that wordnet expansions from a semantically hand tagged corpus improve search precision of 10% with respect to expansions computed without any disambiguation. Moldovan [15] reports a number of experiments where WordNet is successfully used to build similarity lists that expand the query, increasing the number of the retrieved documents. Voorhees [19] argues that WordNet derived query expansions are effective for very short queries, but that they do not bring any improvements for long queries. In [8] are pointed out some more weaknesses of WordNet for Information Retrieval purposes, in particular the lack of domain information and the fact that sense distinctions are excessively fine-grained for the task.

The approach adopted for disambiguation, i.e. word domain disambiguation, is in line with these suggestions: domains allow the clustering of related wordnet senses. Once a domain label for a word is selected by the disambiguation algorithm, synonyms are collected from all the MultiWordNet synsets for that word belonging to the selected domain. For instance, given the morphological expansions described above for the verb "inventare", a number of synonyms extracted from MultiWordNet are added, including "scoprire" ("*discover*") and "scopritore" ("*discoverer*").

4   Search Component

Once the basic keywords and their correspondent expansions have been identified, they are composed in a boolean expression, which is then passed to the web search engine. We considered a baseline and two alternative composition strategies:

☐ **Keyword "and" composition search (KAS)**. The baseline corresponds to the default method that most search engines implement. Given a list of basic keywords, no expansion is performed and keywords are composed in an AND clause.

NL-QUESTION: Chi è stato l'inventore della luce elettrica?
BASIC-KEYWORDS: inventore luce_elettrica
EXPANSIONS:
inventore

   $\xrightarrow{\text{synonyms}}$ scopritore, ideatore

   $\xrightarrow{\text{derivation}}$ invenzione

      $\xrightarrow{\text{synonyms}}$ scoperta

   $\xrightarrow{\text{derivation}}$ inventare

      $\xrightarrow{\text{synonyms}}$ scoprire

luce_elettrica

  $\xrightarrow{\text{synonyms}}$ lampada_a_incandescenza

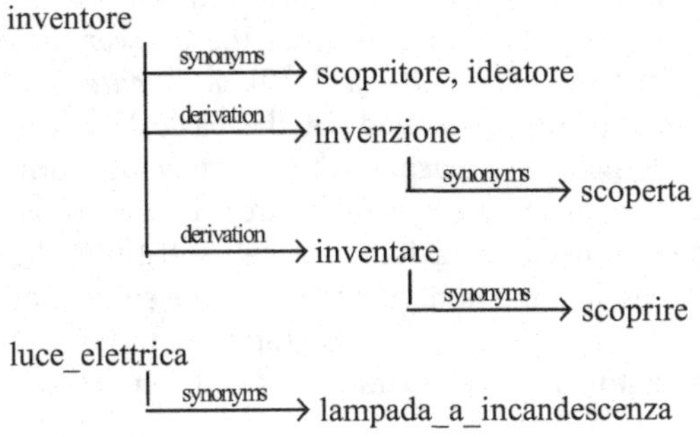

COMPOSITION:
(OR (inventore AND luce_elettrica) OR (inventore AND lampada_a_incandescenza)
OR (scopritore AND luce_elettrica) OR (scopritore AND lampada_a_incandescenza)
OR (ideatore AND luce_elettrica) OR (ideatore AND lampada_a_incandescenza)
OR (invenzione AND luce_elettrica) OR (invenzione AND lampada_a_incandescenza)
OR (scoperta AND luce_elettrica) OR (scoperta AND lampada_a_incandescenza)
OR (inventare AND luce_elettrica) OR (inventare AND lampada_a_incandescenza)
OR (scoprire AND luce_elettrica) OR (scoprire AND lampada_a_incandescenza)
OR inventore OR luce_elettrica))

Fig. 3. Example of Cartesian composition search.

- **Keyword expansion insertion search (KIS)**. In this composition modality a disjunctive expression is constructed where each disjoint element is an AND clause formed by the base keywords plus the insertion of a single expansion. In addition, to guarantee that at least the same documents of the KAS modality are retrieved, both an AND clause with the basic keywords and all the single basic keywords are added as disjoint elements.
- **Keyword Cartesian composition search (KCS)**. In this composition modality a disjunctive expression is constructed where each disjoint element is an AND clause formed by one of the possible tuple derived by the expansion set of each base keyword. In addition, to guarantee that at least the same documents of the KAS modality are retrieved, the single basic keywords are added as disjoint elements. Figure 3 reports an example.

An experiment has been carried out to see which composition modality performs better. We worked with twenty questions, with different number of expansions. Documents were retrieved by the search engine for each question and for each of the three composition modalities. Then a set of 15 human judges was asked to rank the first 10 documents retrieved along the following five value scale:

1. *answer_in_context*: The answer corresponding to the question is recovered and the document context is appropriate. For example, if the question is «Who is the inventor of the electric light?» then «Edison» is reported in the document, in some way, as the inventor of the electric light and the whole document deals with inventions and/or Edison's life.
2. *answer_no_context*: The answer to the question is recovered but the document context is not appropriate. (e.g. the document does not deal neither with inventors nor with Edison's life).
3. *no_answer_in_context*: The answer corresponding to the question is not recovered but the document context is appropriate.
4. *no_answer_no_context*: The answer corresponding to the question is not recovered and the document context is not appropriate.
5. *no_document*: The requested document is not retrieved.

For each question k we obtained three sets $V_{KAS,k}$, $V_{KIS,k}$ and $V_{KCS,k}$ of (*pos, assessment*) pairs corresponding to the three search methods, where *pos* is the position of the document in the ordered list returned by the search method, and *assessment* is the assessment of one participant. We eliminated all the (*pos, assessment*) pairs whose *assessment* was equal to *no_document*.
Said *i* a (*pos, assessment*) pair belonging to $V_{KAS, k}$, $V_{KIS, k}$ or $V_{KCS, k}$ we define the function $r: N \rightarrow \{0,1,2,3\}$ so that $r(i)=0$ if *assessment* is *no_answer_no_context*, $r(i)=1$ if *assessment* is *no_answer_in_context*, $r(i)=2$ if *assessment* is *answer_no_context*, $r(i)=3$ if *assessment* is *answer_in_context*.
Given a question *k* and a set V_k of (*pos, assessment*) pairs corresponding to an ordered list L_k of documents, the evaluation of the relevance of L_k with respect to *k* has been defined by means of the following two relevance functions: f_+ that considers the document position and f that does not.

$$f-(k) = \frac{\sum_{i \in V_k} v(i)}{m} \qquad f+(k) = \frac{\sum_{i \in V_k} v(i) / p(i}{\sum_{j=1}^{m} 1 / j}$$

Where:
- $p(i)$ is the position of the web document in the ordered list.
- $v(i) = \alpha(r(i)) \cdot r(i) + \beta(r(i))$
  $\alpha(x), \beta(x) : \{0,1,2,3\} \rightarrow (0,1)$ are *tuning functions* that allow to weight the assessments.
- m is the maximum length of an ordered list of web documents.

Starting from the relevance functions, f_+ and f_- we compared the three search methods KAS, KIS and KCS.

The experiment results (see Table 2) were that the KCS method performed better than the baseline (relevance of documents increased by 33% without considering the position of the document and 22% considering it) and also better than the KIS method.

We also measured the degree of contextual information provided by the document with respect to the question, because context increases the probability that other relevant documents can be found following hypertextual links, possibly with the correct answer to the question. Results obtained with KIS and KCS confirmed that they provide a significant increase of context retrieval score with respect to the baseline (37% and 41% respectively). Details of the experiment are provided in [13].

	KAS		KIS		KCS	
Total URLs	146		200		200	
Total retrieved	137		191		188	
% retrieved	94%		95%		94%	
			% KAS		% KAS	
	f_- (- pos.)	f_+ (+ pos.)	f_- (- pos.)	f_+ (+ pos.)	f_- (- pos.)	f_+ (+ pos.)
Relevance	0.21	0.23	+19 %	+13 %	+33 %	+22 %

Table 2. Composition modalities compared

At this point the boolean expression is submitted to the web search engine. Several parameters can usually be set; among them, the maximum number of documents returned, the search domain and information concerning the presentation of the search results. The order of the document presentation reflects the number of AND clauses that have been satisfied in the search.

5   Conclusion and Future Work

A question/answering system for searching the web has been presented. The system accepts natural language questions in Italian and returns as an answer a ranked list of document passages together with the URL of the whole document. Some crucial aspects related to the web scenario have been investigated: the linguistic processing of the question, where we make use of MultiWordNet both for disambiguation and for the answer type identification; the optimization of the search boolean expression, which is given in input to an existing search engine on the web.

One crucial issue for the future is the automatic evaluation of a QA system, i.e. without having humans judging thousands of answers. Although there is some recent work in this direction [2], the approach we are testing considers the web as the main information source to evaluate the relevance of an answer. The basic idea is the following: if an certain answer is relevant with respect to given question, then there should be many documents containing keywords extracted both from the question and from the answer. Moreover these documents should be semantically similar documents, i.e. they should maximise the overlapping of semantic features, such as the set of domains labels (see Section 3.2) extracted from each text.

References

1. Artale, A., Magnini, B., Strapparava, C.: WordNet for Italian and Its Use for Lexical Discrimination. In Lenzerini, M. (Ed.) AI*IA 97: Advances in Artificial Intelligence, Proceeedings of the 5th Congress of the Italian Association for Artificial Intelligence, Rome, Italy, Springer Verlag (1997).
2. Breck, E.J., Burger, J.D., Ferro, L., Hirschman, L., House, D., Light, M., Mani, I.: How to Evaluate Your Question Answering System Every Day ...and Still Get Real Work Done. Proceedings of LREC-2000, Second International Conference on Language Resources and Evaluation (2000) 1495-1500.
3. Ciravegna, F.: Learning Pinocchio: User Manual. Technical Report, IRST, Trento (2000).
4. Disc. Dizionario Italiano Sabatini Coletti. Giunti, Firenze (1997).
5. Fellbaum, C.: WordNet, An Electronic Lexical Database. The MIT Press (1998).
6. Ferret, O., Grau, B., Hurault-Plantet, M., Illouz, G., Jacquemin, C., Masson, N., Lecuyer, P.: QALC – The Question Answering System of LIMSI-CNR. Proceedings of the Ninth Text Retrieval Conference (TREC-9), Gaithersburg, MD. (2000).
7. Flank, S.: A Layered Approach to NLP-Based Information Retrieval. Proceedings of COLING-ACL'98, Université de Montréal, Canada (1998) 397-403.
8. Gonzalo, J., Verdejo, F., Peters, C., Calzolari, N.: Applying EuroWordnet to Cross-Language Text Retrieval. Computers and the Humanities, 32, 2-3 (1998) 185-207
9. Harabagiu, S., Pasca, M., Maiorano, S.: Experiments with Open-Domain Textual Question Answering. Proceedings of Coling-2000 (2000a).
10. Harabagiu, S., Moldovan, D., Pasca, M., Mihalcea, R., Surdeanu, M., Bunescu, R., Girju, R., Rus, V., Morarescu, P.: Falcon: Boosting Knowledge for Answer Engines. Proceedings of the Ninth Text Retrieval Conference (TREC-9), Gaithersburg, MD. (2000b).
11. Jacquemin, C.: Syntagmatic and Paradigmatic Representations of Term Variation. Proceedings of ACL-99, University of Maryland (1999) 341-348.

12.Magnini, B., Cavaglià, G.: Integrating Subject Field Codes into Wordnet. Proceedings of LREC-2000, Second International Conference on Language Resources and Evaluation (2000) 1413-1418.
13.Magnini, B., Prevete, R.: Exploiting Lexical Expansions and Boolean Compositions for Web Querying (2000).
14.Magnini, B., Strapparava, C.: Experiments in Word Domain Disambiguation for Parallel Texts. Proceedings of the ACL workshop on Word Senses and Multilinguality, Hong Kong (2000) 27-33.
15.Moldovan, D., Mihalcea, R.: A WordNet-Based Interface to Internet Search Engines. Proceedings of FLAIRS-98, Sanibel Island, FL (1998).
16.Moldovan, D., Harabagiu, S., Pasca, M., Mihalcea, R., Goodrum, R., Girju, R., Rus, V.: Lasso: A Tool for Surfing Answer Net. Proceedings of the Eight Text Retrieval Conference (TREC-8) (1999) 65-74.
17.Scott, S., Gaizauskas, R.: University of Sheffield TREC-9 Q&A System. Proceedings of the Ninth Text Retrieval Conference (TREC-9), Gaithersburg, MD. (2000).
18.Vicedo, J.L., Ferrández, A.: Applying Anaphora Resolution to Question Answering and Information Retrieval Systems. Proceedings of WAIM-2000, First International Conference On Web-Age Information Management, Shanghai, China (2000) 344-355.
19.Voorhees, E.M.: Using WordNet for Text Retrieval, in Fellbaum C. (ed): WordNet, an Electronic Lexical Database. MIT Press (1998).
20.Voorhees, E.M., Tice, D.M.: The TREC-8 Question Answering Track Evaluation. Proceedings of the Eight Text Retrieval Conference (TREC-8) (1999).
21.Voorhees, E.M., Tice, D.M.: The Ninth Text REtrieval Conference (TREC 9) http://trec.nist.gov/pubs/trec9/t9_proceedings.html (2001).

User-Adapted Image Descriptions from Annotated Knowledge Sources

Maria Teresa Cassotta[1], Berardina De Carolis[1] and Fiorella de Rosis[1]

Chiara Andreoli[2] and M. Luisa De Cicco[2]

[1]Intelligent Interfaces, Department of Computer Science, University of Bari,
70126 Bari, Italy
{cassotta, decarolis, derosis}@di.uniba.it
[2] Department of Experimental Medicine and Pathology, University "La Sapienza" of Rome,
Italy

Abstract. We present the first results of a research aimed at generating user-adapted image descriptions from annotated knowledge sources. This system employs a User Model and several knowledge sources to select the image attributes to include in the description and the level of detail. Both 'individual' and 'comparative-descriptions' may be generated, by taking an appropriate 'reference' image according to the context and to an ontology of concepts in the domain to which the image refers; the comparison strategy is suited to the User background and to the interaction history. All data employed in the generation of these descriptions (the image, the discourse) are annotated by a XML-like language. Results obtained in the description of radiological images are presented, and the advantage of annotating knowledge sources are discussed.

1 Introduction

The amount of heterogeneous information available on the Web is growing exponentially; this growth makes increasingly difficult to find, access, present and maintain information. From research about how to make these tasks easier, methods for making machine understandable multimedia web resources have emerged: these methods require associating semantics to information, through the use of metadata. The description of such metadata is typically based on a domain conceptualization and a definition of a domain-specific annotation language.

An annotation can be loosely defined as "any object that is associated with another object by some relationship" (from the W3C Annotation Working Group). In particular, XML is a standard, proposed by the W3C, to create mark-up languages for a wide variety of application domains; developing such languages favours universal storage and interchange formats, re-use and share of resources for web distributed knowledge representation and programming [11]. Metadata annotation of web resources is essential for applying AI techniques for *searching* and *extracting* relevant information (by improving a semantic contextualized search), for *maintaining* web resources (by keeping them consistent, correct and up-to-date). More recently, there is

F. Esposito (Ed.): AI*IA 2001, LNAI 2175, pp. 285-296, 2001.

a tend to employ it, as well, for *automatic document generation* especially when user-adaptation has to be considered (a machine accessible representation of the semantics of these information sources is useful for generating web sites which enable their dynamic reconfiguration according to user profiles and other relevant aspects [12]). This paper investigates on this last aspect: how annotations could be used in web-based NLG systems and, in particular, in generating user-adapted explanations from annotated concept ontologies.

Introducing annotations in a NLG systems requires two main steps: 1) *defining annotations for knowledge sources* in the application domain and for the intermediate results of the generation process; whenever possible, already existing and shared annotation languages should be employed (especially as far as application domain data are concerned); 2) *revising the NLG algorithms* so as to enable every generation module to read annotated data and to produce annotated results.

As far as user adaptation is concerned, annotating resources increases the possibility of finding information of interest to a particular user and to denote which particular piece of information is relevant for a particular interaction context. Annotating the steps of the generation process (for instance, the discourse plan) enforces a distributed vision of the process and enables rendering the final output as a function of the device through which the User interacts.

This vision become particularly attractive when the resource to be described and explained to the user is an image. There are millions of images on the web that could be accessed for different uses and purposes, understanding their semantics would give the possibility of using them in several ways: for instance, for searching an image, for extracting useful information related to it, for creating image ontologies, for describing them verbally or textually, and so on.

In this paper, we will focus on this last aspect and in particular on the generation of user-adapted image descriptions related to concept explanations in a web-based consultation systems. For this purpose, we need: i) to "understand" images, ii) to organize them into appropriate ontologies, iii) to define a user modelling component that formalizes the user features that are relevant for adapting the description, iv) to relate the image description attributes to user features and iv) to generate the description more appropriate to the user and to the interaction context. This adaptation process may be seen as follows: given a metadata describing the image through a set of attributes, a user model containing information about the user level of knowledge in the application domain, a list of already seen images during the interaction and the interaction context:

- select the attributes to include in the description and the level of detail of their description;
- select the appropriate description strategy (an image can be described individually or by comparison with an image in the ontology that is known to the User);
- define the appropriate way to present the relevant information according to the context (i.e. web vs. wap);

To test our approach, we choose the medical domain in which image-based examples are very common to describes normal anatomical sites as well as particular pathologies. In particular, in order to show example of how it works in real domain application, we choose the context of web-based consultation medical guidelines

(ARIANNA, for more details see [3]) whose potential users may be classified as i) *students*, who may learn diagnostic and therapeutic procedures to follow in specific situations; ii) *doctors* with several degrees of competence, who may apply correct diagnostic and therapeutic procedures; iii) *patients*, who may get information about the scope and the efficacy of the health treatment they have to undergo. In this context we used an image annotation tool to generate an XML structure correspondent to the metadata associated to it. For this purpose, we defined a XML-based mark-up language for radiological images and we developed an algorithm for interpreting its semantics. Then, starting from a set of annotated images, the information contained in the user model and a given communicative goal that formalises the user request of seeing an image example, a discourse plan is produced. This plan is built by taking into account the User's information needs and her background knowledge, and specifies the information content and the structure of the description text [3,10]: it is written also as an XML-structure, according to a mark-up language that we defined for this purpose. The annotated plan is the input of the surface generator that, according to the interaction context and to the user characteristics, decides how to render it.

The paper is structured as follows. Section 2 presents our strategy for annotating images and in particular radiological ones. Section 3 is devoted to the description of the description generation process. Section 4 presents the User Modeling component, Section 5 describes, in particular, the planning approach and Section 6 the surface generation component. Comparison strategies are illustrated in Section 7 and, finally, conclusions and future work are drawn in Section 8.

2 Understanding the Image

Understanding an image means extracting the features that characterize the information needed for its description: typically, these features are regions with their shape, texture, edges and so on. Since we do not use automatic image recognition techniques to extract these features, we use content-descriptive metadata to define the image components, their attributes and the relationships among them. To build these metadata, we use an annotation tool (Inote [8]) in Java that is available on line and provides a way of annotating images with a XML-based mark-up language. Inote allows the User to attach textual annotations to an image and to store them in a text file as XML data, through a XML structure that organizes them appropriately. With this tool, expert radiologists can mark-up a digital radiological image by directly "writing on it" and without altering it; once a image has been loaded, the borders of one or more regions in the image may be outlined interactively, and a number of attributes may be associated with each of them. Regions are called "details" and attributes "annotations", and may be given a name; a text may be associated with every annotation of every detail, by filling a text field. The details may be organized into as many "overlays" as needed. Inote's mark-up language is very general, and may be applied to every kind of image. To tailor it to radiological images, we defined an ad hoc markup language that allows us to identify overlays and details in our images, with their attributes, in a unique and unambiguously interpretable way. For instance, a radiological image has some "General Properties" that identify it: the technique with which the image was produced, the body region on which the exam was performed and the diagnosis (diagnostic remarks). Its main information content then consists in a list of details that correspond to the regions of interest (anatomic structures); a set of morphological characteristics (morphology, density, shape, etc.) is associated with each of them.

```
<overlay>
    <title>parenchymal organs</title>
    <detail >
        <title>liver</title>
        <annotation>
            <title>position</title>
            <text>left</text>
        </annotation>
        <annotation>
            <title>morphology</title>
            <text>ellipsoidal</text>
        </annotation>
        <annotation>
            <title>volume</title>
            <text>normal</text>
        </annotation>
        <annotation>
            <title>margins</title>
            <text>regular</text>
        </annotation>
    </detail>
</overlay>
```

Fig. 1. An example of XML structure produced by Inote.

Then, the first overlay in the Inote file then defines the "General Properties"; it is followed by other overlays, representing groups of visible details.

For instance, in the CT of abdominal organs, the following overlays may be defined:

- parenchymal organs
- hollow organs
- vascular structures
- muscular structures
- skeletal structures

The overlay named 'parenchymal organs' includes, as details, the organs in the image that belong to this category: the liver, the spleen and the lung parenchyma.

For each organ or detail, the following attributes may be specified: position in the image, relation with other parts, morphology, volume, density and margins. Each of them corresponds to an annotation. The example in Fig. 1 is a portion of the XML structure produced by Inote for a CT-scan (Computerised Tomography) of the abdomen. The XML structure produced by Inote represents the knowledge base for our description generator. Before generating texts, our XML-application has to interpret the Inote tags and the detail and the overlay to which every annotation belongs, so that sentences describing the image can be built correctly.

3 Generation of Image Descriptions

Two main strategies are used to generate an image description: an "individual" and a "comparative" description strategy. In the first case, the generated text provides a complete user-adapted description of the image itself, in which overlays, details and attributes of the image are provided according to the user features.

In the second case, a comparison strategy is used to describe the image by analogy or by difference with a reference image that is already known by the user. As a default, the non-pathological case is used in order to provide a comparative description of pathological ones, according to teaching approach used in radiology when they explain case-based reasoning to students. The comparison of two images includes in the description the 'commonalities' and the 'alignable' and 'non alignable' differences

[9] between the two metadata. Only properties appropriate to the user level of knowledge are mentioned in the text and they are grouped in commonalities, alignable and non-alignable differences. All or some of these group of properties and attributes are presented in description according to the strategy that is more suited to the context. This approach will be explained in more details later on in the paper and corresponds to what we consider a systematic description of concepts, which is typical of learning tasks, as opposed to information-seeking ones [7].

4   User Modeling

The decision of what to model and how to model it is driven by the decision of *what to adapt* and *how to adapt it*. As concern the *what to adapt* issue, in the context explained in the Introduction, we decide to include the following system features:

- the system *goal* (decision-support vs training): in the first case, users are provided with a textual description relative to the image that the user asked for, while   in the second case, users receive a very concise description of the image and then they can explore it interactively by asking questions about a particular detail or area of the image;
- the *image description mode*: an image may be explained either individually or by comparison or contrast with other known images;
- the *individual image description*: this may include a selected subset of the image attributes, as well as the way in which each attribute is described.
- the *final rendering of the description*: an image description can be verbal, textual, multimodal according to some context features.

The system goal, as well as the image description, are adapted to the user level of education and experience in the domain: the 'training mode' is reserved to students, the 'decision-support' mode to doctors; attributes introduced in the descriptions addressed to different users are different; the image description mode is adapted to knowledge of other images in the ontology and the way in which the description is rendered at the surface level is adapted to the interaction context (i.e. device).

In order to adapt these system features, we need to model the following user and context characteristics: i) the user *level of experience* in the application domain and the *level of education*: these are important in order to decide the granularity of the description (in terms of level of details provided) and to achieve a satisfying level of comprehension of the description (in terms of strategy to be followed and terms to be employed); ii) the *interaction history*: it is used to have an idea of what the user has seen and then presumably knows during the interaction in order to use this knowledge for generating more relevant description in which comparison techniques can be used to explain an image content by analogy or difference to already known ones that are related to the one being currently described; iii) the *context*: in our case it is mainly the device through which the user interacts with the system, but it could include more modeling of more complex features;

The user modeling component uses a technique based initially on the activation of a *stereotype,* that is triggered from answers to 'educational level', 'years of experience' and 'type of specialisation' questions. The stereotype's body includes a list of default properties of the type: *KnowAbout (U I-k)* , where I-k is an image in one of the ontologies in the application domain KB of the system. The sterotypical knowledge is set up according to what we did in ARIANNA for providing user-adapted explanation about concepts mentioned during a clinical guideline consultation: stereotypes are such that: (i) undergraduate students are presumed to ignore all images, (ii) graduating students are presumed to know only the images at the highest level, in the ontologies that correspond to their specialisation; (iii) general practitioners know highest level images in all taxonomies, (iv) specialist doctors are presumed to know all images, in the taxonomy that corresponds to their specialisation and, finally, (v) radiologists are presumed to know all images. Immediately after activation, the stereotype is copied into a *User Profile* which is updated dynamically during interaction, by revising the list of *KnowAbout* properties and the interaction history, for the guideline the user is examining. Updating of the user knowledge is based, in particular, on the rule: *Describe (S U I-k)* $\Rightarrow$ *KnowAbout (U I-k)*. We know that this question has long been debated in the hypermedia generation environment, where it is claimed that no certainty exists that a user really reads the displayed information and really learns it: to repair to such a wrong default assumption, we insert an anchor to description of attributes (or images) the user is presumed to know, so as to give her the possibility to access this information.

5 Planning the Image Description

Given a communicative goal corresponding to the user request for an image description ("Explain (System User I)" where I denotes a specific image in the domain KB), the planner selects according to this goal and to the user characteristics, a presentation plan from a library of non-instantiated plans that are represented as XML structures too; the generic plan is, then, instantiated by filling the slots of its steps with available data in XML-domain-files corresponding to image metadata. The library of plans has been built by abstraction from a corpora of written image explanation provided by expert radiologists addressed to the user categories described in Section 4. The DTD definition of our Discourse Plan Markup Language is shown in Fig.2. In this specification, a discourse plan is a tree identified by its name; its main components are the nodes, identified by a name, containing mandatory attributes describing the communicative goal and the rhetorical elements (role in the RR of its father and rhetorical relation) attached to it. Then the 'info' element, that is not mandatory, describes additional information, related to a node, concerning the focus of the discourse and the complexity of the sub-tree departing from it. These optional information elements are not used in this particular application, but they are necessary in other NLG systems developed by our research group [4, 5]. The XML-based annotation of the discourse plan is driven by two reasons, the first is that in this way it is possible to build a library of standard explanation plan that can be instantiated when needed and used by several applications working in several contexts; the second one is that XML is used as a standard interface between all the modules constituting our generators, favouring in this way the distribution of resources and computation.

```
DPML 1.0 – Discourse Plan Markup Language
<!DOCTYPE d-plan[
<!ELEMENT tree (node+) <!ATTLIST tree name CDATA #REQUIRED>
<!ELEMENT node (node*, info*)>
  <!ATTLIST node name CDATA #REQUIRED goal  CDATA #REQUIRED
              role (root|nucleus|sat) #REQUIRED RR CDATA #IMPLIED>
<!ELEMENT info EMPTY)>
<!ATTLIST info focus  CDATA #REQUIRED compl (H|M|L) #REQUIRED >
  ]>
```

Fig.2. Discourse Plan Markup Language DTD.

The selected plan structure will correspond either to an individual description plan or to a comparison plan. A small portion of the XML-Instantiated-Plan describing the individual description of a C.T. scan of the abdomen is shown in Fig. 3. In this case, the XML-annotated plan has been instantiated according to the information relative to 'img1.xml' (as it is possible to notice from the goal of the tree root 'Explain(image, img1.xml)').

```
<d-plan name="CT-abdomen.xml">
  <node name="n1" goal="Explain(Image, img1.xml)" role="root" RR="Sequence">
    <node name="n2" goal="Describe(General Features, image)" role="nucleus" RR="ElabGenSpec">
      <node name="n4" goal="Inform(diagnosis,normal liver)" role="nucleus" RR="null"/>
      <node name="n5" goal=" Describe(Exam, C.T.)" role="sat" RR="Joint">
        <node name="n6" goal="Inform(name, C.T. Abdomen)" role="nucleus" RR="null"/>
        <node name="n8" goal="Inform(level, spleen)" role="nucleus" RR="null"/>
      </node>
    </node>
    <node name="n3" goal="Describe(Specific Features, image)" role="nucleus" RR="OrdinalSequence">
      <node        name="n9"goal="Describe(ComplexStructure-1,        parenchymal_organ)"        role="nucleus"
      RR="OrdinalSequence">
        <node name="n10" goal="Describe(detail,liver)" role="nucleus" RR="ElabGenSpec">
          <node name="n12" goal="Describe(attribute,liver)" role="sat" RR="Joint">
            <node name="n13" goal="Inform(position,left)" role="nucleus" RR="null"/>
            <node name="n16" goal="Inform(rel_position,medialpart_abdomen)" role="nucleus" RR="null"/>
            <node name="n17"goal="Inform(morphology,ellipsoidal)"role="nucleus" RR="null"/>
            <node name="n18" goal="Inform(volume,normal)" role="nucleus" RR="null"/>
            <node name="n19" goal="Inform(margins,regular)" role="nucleus" RR="null"/>
          </node>
          <node name="n11" goal="Inform(name,liver)" role="nucleus" RR="null"/>
      </node>
          ...
</d-plan>
```

Fig. 3. An example of XML-Instantiated-Plan.

5.1.   Comparing Images

Let's now see how we generate the description of a image by comparing it with a selected reference image. The general strategy we apply is the following: for every detail in a overlay, we mention first commonalities, second alignable differences and finally non-alignable differences. In the case of image descriptions, we distinguish, at the moment, three types of comparisons, that depend on what the User already knows and on the images she has already seen. Then, given a Image I to be described to a User U and a Reference-Image RI, three different comparison plans may be activated:

Comparison 1.   KnowAbout(U, RI) AND Remember(U, RI) ⇒ Exec(S, cplan_1);

If the user, according to its background knowledge, profession and level of expertise or according to what she has already seen, knows RI and is presumed to remember its description, the first comparison plan (cplan_1) is applied. This plan corresponds to the following strategy: for each overlay and for each detail, only the attribute values of I that are different from the ones in RI are mentioned (alignable differences). After them, the values of the attributes that are not present in RI are presented (non-alignable differences). This plan is applied, for instance, to describe pathological cases to radiologists.

Comparison 2.   KnowAbout(U,RI) AND ¬Remember(U,RI) ⇒ Exec(S, cplan_2);

If the user knows RI but does not remember it in all its details, the second comparison plan (cplan_2) is applied. This plan corresponds to the following strategy: for each overlay and for each detail, the attributes of I that take different values from those of RI are mentioned, by describing both values (for I and for RI). After them, also in this case, non-alignable differences are presented. This plan is applied, for instance, to general practitioners.

Comparison 3.   ¬KnowAbout(U,RI) ⇒ Exec(S, cplan_3);

If the user does not know RI, the third comparison plan (cplan_3) is applied. This plan corresponds to the following strategy: for each overlay and for each detail, all attributes in the two images are described, by emphasizing commonalities, alignable and not-alignable differences. This plan is applied, for instance, to students.

6   Rendering the Image Description

This functionality of our Image Describer is very simple; the XML-Instantiated-Plan is the input of a Surface Realisator that, using flexible templates, produces the image explanation as an HTML file. This process is mainly driven by the Rhetorical Relations (RR) between portions of the plan. The plan is explored in a depth-first way; for each node, a linguistic marker is placed between the text spans that derive from its children, according to the RR that links them. For instance, the following sentence:

> *"Inside the parenchyma, tubular shaped, hyperdense and white images are visible (the superhepatic veins)"*

is obtained from a template for the *ElabGenSpec* RR. In this template, the satellite is obtained through the application of the *Joint* template to the attributes <position>, <shape>, <density> and <colour>; this satellite is followed by the nucleus, which specifies the name of the object in focus, between brackets ("the superhepatic veins", in the example).   The decision of rendering this template in this way is driven by common patterns we extracted from a corpus of explanations written by expert radiologists; from the same corpus, we extracted also the generation rules for the templates corresponding to other RRs. At present, we generate the text in HTML; however, our approach is general enough to produce descriptions in different formats and, therefore, for different interaction contexts. It is also domain independent, since it is only driven by the Rhetorical structure of the discourse plan. We choosed to develop our surface generator instead of using existing standard techniques (such as XSLT stylesheet templates) because these approaches would not allow us to produce the complex textual descriptions matching the style of the corpus we analysed. This limit it is also underlined by Cawsey and colleagues [1,2], who used XML coupled with XSLT stylesheets for generating user tailored tabular presentations of online resources from selected metadata. In addition, in this system, as we will seen later on, we generate also description by comparison with other images, and this requires a more complex reasoning that is difficult to reduce to XSLT application to an XML file. Fig. 4 shows an example of the description that was generated from the discourse plan in Fig. 3.

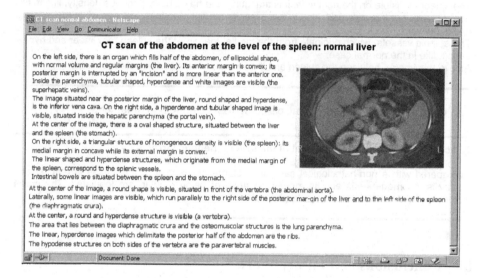

Fig 4. An example of individual image description.

7   Comparing Images

Let us see some examples of comparisons that were generated with our system: in all these examples, the reference image is a CT scan of the abdomen for a 'non-pathological' case, while the image to be described is a case of hepatic cirrhosis, obtained with the same technique. The first text is generated by cplan_3: alignable differences are emphasized in italics, while, in this example, there are no 'non alignable differences' between the two images; only the first part of the text is shown, for space reasons.

CT scan of the abdomen at the level of the spleen: hepatic cirrhosis.

As in the non-pathological case, the liver is the organ situated on the left side of the image, which fills half of the abdomen, of ellipsoidal shape. *In this case, however, its volume is reduced, its density is inhomogeneous and its margins, instead of being regular, are lobulated.* Like in the normal case, the anterior margin is convex while the posterior one is more linear and is interrupted by an incision. Superhepatic veins are visible inside the parenchyma; they are tubular shaped, hyperdense and white, like in the normal case.
As in the normal vein, the inferior vena cava is situated near the posterior margin of the liver, round shaped and hyperdense. The portal vein lies inside the hepatic parenchyma: it is hyperdense and tubular shaped like in the normal case, *but is enlarged.*
As in the normal case, the stomach is visible at the center of the image, between the–liver and the spleen, and is oval-shaped.
The spleen is visible on the right side; it is triangular and has a homogeneous density, like in the normal case, *but it is enlarged.* Also in this case, its medial margin is concave while the external one is convex.
The splenic vessels, which originate from the medial margin of the spleen, are linear and hyperdense, like in the normal case.
Also in this image, between the spleen and the stomach, intestinal bowels are visible.
....

If c_plan2 is applied to the same case, the following text is obtained:

CT scan of the abdomen at the level of the spleen: hepatic cirrhosis.

If compared with a non-pathological case, the volume of the liver in this image is reduced, its density is inhomogeneous and its margins, instead of being regular, are lobulated. The portal vein is enlarged and the spleen is enlarged too.
....

8   Conclusions and Future Work

In this paper, we presented the first prototype of Image Descriptor, a software to generate image descriptions from annotated knowledge sources: this prototype was built in Java using the IBM-XML4J parser and will be integrated in a system (ARIANNA) that dynamically generates hypermedia presentations of clinical guidelines; ARIANNA is already in use and an experimental evaluation study has been performed, to check how physicians react to it. The methods and the techniques we employed for generating image descriptions aim at favouring sharing and re-use of information. In particular, annotating images has several advantages: first of all, it enables retrieving images from Web databases according to ad hoc criteria; in addition, once a image has been retrieved, it may be described in a natural language text whose content, structure, and style may be adapted to the context in which retrieval was made.

The annotation of linguistic resources favours, in general, their re-use and distribution: their semantics can be interpreted and rendered in different ways according to the interaction context; for instance, plain text, HTML or WML. Our research efforts go in this direction: we plan to introduce, in ARIANNA, a Conversational Agent with the role of an "Explainer" that supports the User at different levels; we already developed a similar Agent in another context, the generation of 'Animated User Manuals' for software applications [4]. In passing from hypertexts to Animated Agents, most of the techniques described in this paper will not change: for instance, the DTD for representing discourse plans is the same, and therefore also the planning component remains invaried; we only add a 'Sentence Planner' that revises the XML-plan files and substitute the surface text generator with a module that generates what we call the "Agent's behaviours".

We claim that, to enable sharing of resources and methods among various research centers and to produce outputs in context and application-dependent forms, establishing standards in the NLG field is a promising approach. This may foster reuse of methods in different applications and settings: let's think about new UMTS phones or wearable computers, whose particular graphical interface will require revising the generation methods that many of us developed so far. The work described in this paper is a step in this direction.

Acknowledgments

This work was founded by the CNR grant 21.15.01 on the topic: "Digital Processing of Radiological Images" and by the NationalCo-founded Project on "Intelligent Agents: Knowledge Acquisition and Interaction".

References

1. Cawsey, A. Presenting tailoed resource descriptions: Will XSLT do the job? In Proceedings of the 9th International WWW Conference, 2000.
2. Cawsey A., Bental D., Bruce E. and McAndrew, P.: Generating resource descriptions from metadata to support relevance assessments in retrieval. Proceedings of RIAO 2000.
3. De Carolis, B., de Rosis, F., Andreoli, C., Cavallo, V. and De Cicco, M.L.: The dynamic Generation of Hypertext Presentations of Medical Guidelines. The New Review of Hypermedia and Multimedia, 67-88 (1998).
4. De Carolis, B., de Rosis, F., Pizzutilo, S.: Generating User-Adapted Hypermedia from Discourse Plans. Fifth Congress of the Italian Association of Artificial Intelligence (AI*IA 97), Roma , (1997).
5. B. De Carolis, C. Pelachaud, I. Poggi, Verbal and non verbal discourse planning. Workshop on Achieving Human-like Behaviors. Autonomous Agents 2000. ACM Press.
6. de Rosis, F., De Carolis, B., Pizzutilo, S.: Automated Generation of Agent's Behavior from Formal Models of Interaction. To appear in proceedings of AVI 2000, Palermo, Italy (2000).
7. Hammond, N. and Allinson, L.: Extending Hypertext for Learning: an Investigation of Access and Guidance Tools. People and Computers V, HCI 89, Cambridge University Press (1989).
8. Inote: Image Annotation Tool. http://jefferson.village.edu/iath/inote.html.
9. Markman., A.B. and Gentner., D.: Commmonalities and Differences in Similarity Comparisons. Memory and Cognition, 24, 2 (1996).

10. Moore, J., D. Participating in Explanatory Dialogues. Interpreting and Responding to Question in Context. ACL-MIT Press series in NLP, (1995).W3C: eXtensible Markup Language (XML). http://www.w3.org/xml/
11. Marcu, D.: Extending a Formal and Computational Model of Rhetorical Structure Theory with Intentional Structures à la Grosz and Sidner. The 18th International Conference on Computational Linguistics COLING'2000, Luxembourg, July 31-August 4, 2000.
12. M. Perkowitz, and O. Etzioni. Towards Adaptive Web Sites: Conceptual Framework and Case Study. Artificial Intelligence, 118(1-2), 2000.

Wide Coverage Incremental Parsing by Learning Attachment Preferences

Fabrizio Costa[1], Vincenzo Lombardo[2], Paolo Frasconi[1], and Giovanni Soda[1]

[1] DSI, Università di Firenze, ITALY
{costa, paolo, giovanni}@dsi.unifi.it
[2] DiSTA, Università del Piemonte Orientale, ITALY
vincenzo@di.unito.it

Abstract. This paper presents a novel method for wide coverage parsing using an incremental strategy, which is psycholinguistically motivated. A recursive neural network is trained on treebank data to learn first pass attachments, and is employed as a heuristic for guiding parsing decision. The parser is lexically blind and uses beam search to explore the space of plausible partial parses and returns the full analysis having highest probability. Results are based on preliminary tests on the WSJ section of the Penn treebank and suggest that our incremental strategy is a computationally viable approach to parsing.

1 Introduction

The most successful approaches to wide coverage parsing are the history-based algorithms, where the parse tree is viewed as a sequence of decisions (a derivation), and the probability of the tree is calculated by combining single decision probabilities. The resolution of structural ambiguity in probabilistic terms relies on a learning process over large text corpora annotated with syntactic structures (treebanks). History-based parsers are generally modeled upon probabilistic context-free grammars, and produce more accurate results if they learn about bilexical dependencies between head words of constituents [2, 3]. Though in general these approaches use specialized machine learning techniques, general learning frameworks are also applicable (ID3 algorithm [7], maximum entropy model [14]). The most common control structure is the chart-based (or dynamic programming) technique.

This paper explores the possibility that a psycholinguistically motivated parser can also perform well on freely occurring text. Our reference theories in the psycholinguistic literature are those theories that rely on learning parse decisions from the past experience (e.g., [13]). Specifically, we have developed an incremental history-based parsing model that relies on a dynamic grammar, and solves attachment ambiguities by using a general machine learning technique (recursive neural networks).

The incrementality hypothesis assumes that humans process language from left to right, and proceed by chunking partial parses that span the initial fragment of the sentence (we can call these partial parses *incremental trees*). Wide

F. Esposito (Ed.): AI*IA 2001, LNAI 2175, pp. 297–307, 2001.
© Springer-Verlag Berlin Heidelberg 2001

coverage parsing models are rarely based on the incrementality hypothesis. An exception to this claim is the work of [15], who have implemented a predictive parser, which selects the parses to expand with a probabilistic best-first method and a beam search algorithm. An alternative connectionist approach to the incremental parsing problem is given by [9], where a Simple Synchrony Network is used to generate rather than process the syntactic tree.

With the incremental strategy, the probabilistic model follows the chain of rule predictions that allow the linking of the next input word. A natural way to encode such linguistic knowledge is the dynamic grammar approach. A dynamic grammar characterizes the syntactic knowledge in terms of states, and transitions between states [12], thus forming a framework where competence and performance can be easily put in relation (derivation steps and parsing actions coincide). In our approach, the states of the dynamic grammar are the incremental trees, and the transitions between states are the attachment operations of partial structures that extend an incremental tree to include the next input word.

The probabilistic model that informs the parsing decisions relies on a learning technique that involves a neural network model, called *recursive neural network* [5]. Recursive neural networks can adaptively process labeled graphs, and exploit the supervised learning paradigm on structured data. The incremental trees are the instances in the learning domain, and the prediction task consists in estimating the probability that a given incremental tree is the correct one.

The paper is organized as follows: Section 2 introduces the basic notions of incremental processing, and illustrates the parsing strategy. In section 3 we formulate the learning task, and specialize the basic network architecture to solve the learning problem considered here. In section 4 we describe the experimental setup, and discuss the results.

2   Incremental Parsing with Connection Paths

Incremental processing of natural language (incrementality for short) is a widely held hypothesis upon the parsing actions of the human language processor. According to incrementality, the semantic interpretation of some fragment of the sentence occurs as the scan of the input material proceeds from left to right. This incrementality hypothesis has received a large experimental support in the psycholinguistic community over the years: from the shadowing experiments [11], to the data about head-final language processing [1, 6, 8], to the eye-movement studies of visual object recognition [4]. In this section, we provide an operational definition of incrementality, which forms the core of the parsing process.

The operational account of the incrementality hypothesis we are going to pursue here is called *strong incrementality*, and is a parsimonious version of incrementality (see [16]). This proposal shares some commonalities with a number of psycholinguistic models [17, 18] and the broad coverage predictive parser described in [15]. Parsing proceeds from left to right through a sequence of incremental trees, each spanning one more word to the right. No input is stored in a disconnected state.

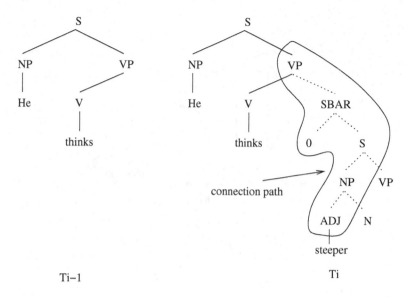

Fig. 1. The connection path for "steeper" in "He thinks steeper prices are to come."

The connection of the next input word to the existing structure (what is called the *left context*) requires the construction of a substructure called the *connection path* (see Figure 1). In parsing naturally occurring text, this results in a high number of candidate connection paths, which yields a hard search problem.

Before describing the parsing algorithm, we provide some basic definitions. Given a sentence $s = w_0 w_1 \cdots w_i \cdots w_{|s|-1}$ and a tree T for it, we define recursively the *incremental trees* $T_i (i = 0, 1, ..., |s| - 1)$ spanning $w_0 \cdots w_i$ as follows:

- T_0 consists of the node w_0;
- T_i consists of all the nodes and edges in T_{i-1} and the chain of nodes and edges from w_i to N, where N is
  - either a node of T_{i-1},
  - or the lowest node of T dominating both the root of T_{i-1} and w_i (in this case T_i also includes the edge from N to the root of T_{i-1}).

Given two incremental trees T_1 and T_2, we define the *difference* between T_1 and T_2 as the tree formed by all the edges which are in T_1 and not in T_2, and all the nodes touched by such edges. Now, given a sentence $s = w_0 w_1 \cdots w_{|s|-1}$ and a tree T for it, the *connection path* for w_i is the difference between the incremental trees T_i and T_{i-1}. Moreover,

- A node both in T_i and in T_{i-1}, and touched by an edge only in T_i, is called an *anchor* (that is, a node where the connection path anchors to T_{i-1}).
- The node labeled by the POS tag of w_i is called a *foot*.

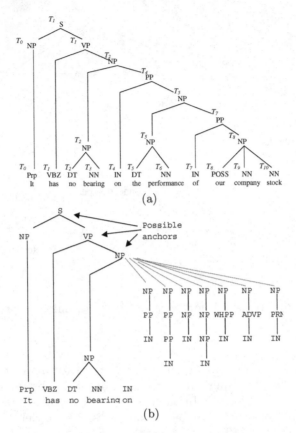

(a)

(b)

Fig. 2. (a) The incremental trees of the sentence "It has no bearing on the performance of our company stock." Nodes are labeled with the incremental tree that includes them for the first time. (b): Local ambiguity in incremental processing of the same sentence. The figure shows the incremental tree T_3, with its potential anchors and the connection paths compatible with one of the anchors (NP).

In Figure 2a, we show the sequence of incremental trees for a sentence of the corpus. The notions introduced so far underlie a parsing schema that operates incrementally with a grammar composed of connection paths. The grammar of connection paths is a sort of *dynamic grammar* [12], that is a grammar that defines the linguistic knowledge in the form of possible transitions between parsing states.

In order to implement a wide coverage parser, we have collected a large basic grammar of connection paths. We have run a simulation algorithm on sections 2-21 of the Penn treebank (about 40,000 sentences). The simulation algorithm collects all the incremental trees associated with the trees in the sample, by simulating the building of the syntactic structure as it would be built by a perfectly informed incremental parser (a similar approach has been described in [10]). The data base (or universe) of connection paths extracted from the dataset counts 5.348. The connection paths as defined here do not include any information beyond the structural commitments which are necessary to incorporate the new word in input (see Figures 1 and 2a). Linguistically informed connection paths would include further nodes required by constraints posed by the individual words. For example, in Figure 1 the node SBAR would be predicted by the subcategorization frame of the word "thinks", and so it would not be part of the connection path for linking "steeper".

2.1   Parsing Strategy

Let us consider the parsing search space $\mathcal{S}(s)$ associated with a given sentence $s = w_1, \ldots, w_n$. States in this space consist of incremental trees, and state transitions (search operators) correspond to legal attachments of connection paths to incremental trees. The initial state is the empty tree. Goals are all the states whose associated parse trees span the whole sentence under consideration. Clearly, the generic *parse* tree at depth i of the *search* tree spans $w_1, \ldots, w_i$. The search space $\mathcal{S}(s)$ is a tree for every sentence s, and any incremental tree for $w_1, \ldots, w_i$ can be identified by the unique sequence of connection path attachments $j_1, j_2, \ldots, j_i$ in its derivation. We denote by $T_{j_1,\ldots,j_i}$ the resulting incremental tree. Note that only one derivation $j_1^*, \ldots, j_n^*$ leads to the correct tree for $w_1, \ldots, w_n$. Our method consists of defining a probability distribution over the space of possible derivations and then seeking the most likely derivation. The probability distribution over derivation is factorized using the psycholinguistic notion of preference in the first pass attachment, modeled as the conditional probability

$$P(T_{j_1,\ldots,j_i}|T_{j_1,\ldots,j_{i-1}}) \tag{1}$$

Given an incremental tree spanning $w_1, \ldots, w_{i-1}$, several candidate incremental trees can be built to accommodate the next word w_i. We denote by $F_{j_1,\ldots,j_{i-1}}$ the forest of candidate parse trees obtained by linking w_i to $T_{j_1,\ldots,j_{i-1}}$. We assume this set of candidates is exhaustive and contains the correct incremental tree for $w_1, \ldots w_i$. Hence:

$$\sum_{T_{j_1,\ldots,j_i} \in F_{j_1,\ldots,j_{i-1}}} P(T_{j_1,\ldots,j_i}|T_{j_1,\ldots,j_{i-1}}) = 1 \tag{2}$$

Since derivations are unambiguous, we can recursively apply equation 1, obtaining

$$P(T_{j_1,\ldots,j_i}) = P(T_{j_1,\ldots,j_i}|T_{j_1,\ldots,j_{i-1}})P(T_{j_1,\ldots,j_{i-1}}). \tag{3}$$

where in the base step we assign probability one to the empty tree spanning the empty sentence. As a result, the probability of a full parse $T_{j_1,\ldots,j_n}$ is

$$P(T_{j_1,\ldots,j_n}) = \prod_{i=1}^{n} P(T_{j_1,\ldots,j_i}|T_{j_1,\ldots,j_{i-1}}). \tag{4}$$

Conditional probabilities in Eq. 1 are empirically estimated from a treebank and modeled by a recursive neural network, a machine learning architecture that can solve the supervised learning problem when instances are represented by labeled acyclic graphs [5]. The algorithm for learning first pass attachments is outlined in the next section.

Finding the most likely analysis in this framework is computationally expensive due to the large size of the state space. We found that the average branching factor (corresponding to the number of first pass attachment alternatives) is about 132 in the set of 40k sentences mentioned above. Since exhaustive search is computationally unfeasible, a beam search algorithm is employed for selecting a pool of candidate analyses receiving high probability according to the above model. The outer loop of the algorithm sweeps the sentence word by word, from left to right. At each stage i, we create a beam of B_i best candidates by expanding and scoring each candidate selected in the previous stage. Branches of search space with low probability incremental trees are thus pruned, based on the rationale that they are unlikely to appear as the left fragment of the most likely full analysis.

3   Formulating Parse Decisions with a Neural Network

Ambiguity comes in two forms: the number of possible anchors on the right edge of T_{i-1}, and the number of different paths that can link w_i with T_{i-1} from some anchor (see Figure 2b). A selection procedure chooses the best connection path and anchor for continuation, and instantiates it to generate the new incremental tree T_i. Now we first formulate the learning task, and then we illustrate the network architecture.

3.1   The Learning Task

The instances of the learning domain are the incremental trees. We start from a core corpus of parsed sentences, which is denoted as $\boldsymbol{B} = \{(s^{(p)}, T(s^{(p)})), p = 1, \cdots, P\}$ where $s^{(p)}$ is a generic sentence and $T(s^{(p)})$ its parse tree. The *universe of connection paths* $U(\boldsymbol{B})$ is the set of all connection paths that can be extracted from $T(s^{(p)}), p = 1, \cdots, P$ by running the simulation algorithm described above. The universe $U(\boldsymbol{B})$ effectively plays the role of a dynamic grammar for the sentences in $\boldsymbol{B}$.

Given a sentence $s = w_0, \ldots, w_{|s|-1}$ (not in the corpus $\boldsymbol{B}$), at stage i of parsing we know the correct incremental tree $T_{i-1}(s)$ spanning $w_0, \ldots, w_{i-1}$. The goal of an incremental parser is then to compute the next tree $T_i(s)$ in order to accommodate the next word w_i. $T_i(s)$ can be obtained by joining $T_{i-1}(s)$ to one of the connection paths in $U(\boldsymbol{B})$. However, other trees spanning $w_1, \cdots, w_i$ can be generated by legally attaching other connection paths. The set of trees obtained by legally attaching $T_{i-1}(s)$ to any path in $U(\boldsymbol{B})$ is called the *forest of candidates* for word w_i within sentence s, denoted $\boldsymbol{F}_i(s) = \{T_{i,1}(s), \ldots, T_{i,m_i}(s)\}$. Of course, only one of the trees in $\boldsymbol{F}_i(s)$, $T_{i,j^*}(s)$, is the correct one (and maybe none, in case of incompleteness of the grammar).

The learning algorithm relies on a statistical model that assigns probabilities of correctness to each candidate tree. Parameters of the model are estimated from examples. Then the model can be effectively employed to rank alternative trees, sorting them by increasing probability of correctness.

The learning task is formulated as follows: Each instance is the whole forest of candidate trees $\boldsymbol{F}_i(s)$. The task consists of learning the correct member of the forest, which can be identified by a multinomial variable with realizations in $\{1, \ldots, m_i(s)\}$. Training examples are pairs $(\boldsymbol{F}_i(s), j_i^\star(s))$, where the input portion is the candidate forest and the output portion (supervision) is the integer $j_i^\star(s) \in [1, m_i(s)]$ identifying the correct tree.

One learning instance is a "bag" of objects (trees), which contains exactly one positive instance, and such instance can be always identified in the training set. In a probabilistic setting this means that the learner should make decisions about *multinomial* output variables $O_i(s)$ whose realizations are integers in $[1, \cdots, m_i(s)]$ identifying the correct tree in the bag associated with word w_i in sentence s. In particular, for each position i within s and for each alternative j, the learner should predict the quantity

$$y_{i,j}(s) = P(O_i(s) = j | \boldsymbol{F}_i(s)) \tag{5}$$

where $O_i(s) = j$ means that $T_{i,j}(s)$ is the correct tree. Predictions are conditional to the whole set of candidates thus introducing competition among trees in the forest. In the following subsection we shall explain how this learning task can be solved using a connectionist approach. To simplify notation, reference to the particular sentence s will be omitted in the following discussion.

3.2   Neural Network Architecture

We use an architecture, called *recursive* neural network, which is suitable for dealing with labeled directed acyclic graphs [5]. The input I in the present case is a labeled ordered forest of m-ary trees, where labeled means that each vertex has a label from a finite alphabet $\mathcal{I} = I_1, \ldots, I_N$ (namely, the current set of non-terminal symbols in the universe of connection paths), and ordered means that for each vertex v, a total order is defined on the m children of v ($ch[v]$ denotes the ordered m-tuple of vertices that are v's children; $I(v)$ denotes the label attached to vertex v). The basic network computation is based on the following recursive state space representation:

$$\begin{aligned} \boldsymbol{x}(v) &= f(\boldsymbol{x}(ch[v]), I(v)) \\ a &= g(\boldsymbol{x}(r)). \end{aligned} \tag{6}$$

$\boldsymbol{x}(v) \in \mathbb{R}^n$ denotes the state vector associated with node v; $\boldsymbol{x}(ch[v]) \in \mathbb{R}^{m \cdot n}$ is a vector obtained by concatenating the components of the state vectors contained in v's children; $f : \mathcal{I} \times \mathbb{R}^{m \cdot n} \to \mathbb{R}^n$ is the state transition function that maps states at v's children and the label at v into the state vector at v;

$g : I\!R^n \rightarrow I\!R$ is the output function, that maps the state $x(r)$ (at the root r of the input tree) into a real number a. States in Eq. (6) are updated bottom-up, traversing the tree in post-order. If a child is missing, the corresponding entries in $x(\text{ch}[v])$ are filled with the *frontier* state $\bar{x}$, which is associated with the base step of recursion. Functions f and g are implemented by two multilayered perceptrons. After all $m_i(s)$ trees in the forest $F_i(s)$ have been processed by the same network, we obtain a vector of $m_i(s)$ real outputs $a_{i,j}(s)$. These real numbers are eventually passed through the softmax function (normalized exponentials) to obtain the probabilities that will be used to rank trees in the forest.

Supervised learning is based on the maximum likelihood principle as in many other neural network models. The cost function has the form of a cross-entropy (negative log-likelihood according to the multinomial model) and is written as follows:

$$J(\mathcal{D}) = -\sum_{p=1}^{P} \sum_{i=0}^{|s^{(p)}|-1} \log y_{i,j*} \tag{7}$$

where $\mathcal{D}$ denotes the training set, the first sum ranges over sentences in the training set, the second sum ranges over words within each sentence, and j^* is the index of the correct incremental tree in the candidate list (which is known in the training set). Optimization is solved by gradient descent. In this case, gradients are computed by a special form of backpropagation on the feedforward network obtained by unrolling the state transition network according to the topology of the input graph I [5].

4   Implementation and Results

In this section, we illustrate the experiments we carried out to demonstrate the viability of the method. We have carried on two experiments to evaluate two different subcomponents of our systems. The first experiment has been the verification that the network can generalize appropriately over incremental trees in order to predict the correct connection path for the expansion. In the second experiment we have combined neural network predictions with the simple search strategy described above.

4.1   Dataset

The reference grammar is the data base of 5,348 connection paths extracted from the sections 2-21 of the WSJ Collection of the Penn II Treebank (39,831 sentences, about 1 million words). For the training set section 2-21 was used (about 40,000 sentences), for the validation set section 24 (about 3,500 sentences), and for the test set section 23 (about 2,500 sentences). Each sentence of the three sets was processed in the following manner. For each word w_i, we have examined a forest of candidate incremental trees F_i, formed by identifying the possible anchor nodes on the right frontier of T_{i-1} and the foot category of w_i, and composing T_{i-1} with all the connection paths in the universe $U(\boldsymbol{B})$ that are compatible with the anchor category and the foot category (see Figure 2b) [1]. we do not consider individual words and semantic affixes of non-terminal labels. For example, both NP-PRD and NP-MNR have been collapsed to NP. The total number of non-terminal symbols is 72.

In our runs, the average cardinality of a candidate set $\boldsymbol{F}_i$ is 133, and the maximum cardinality is 2542. This gives a precise idea of the amount of ambiguity that occurs for the connection of each word. In the training set (40k sentences), the total number of words is about 1 million and the total number of candidates is 126 millions. In the test set (2416 sentences), the total number of words is 51,433 and the total number of candidates is 7 millions.

The recursive network used for the experiments implements the model described in Section 3.2, and has the following specifications: $m = 15$ (maximum outdegree), $N = 72$ labels (one-hot encoded), and $n = 20$ state components, yielding a total of 7,440 adjustable parameters. Each tree in the forest is processed separately by a recursive network with one linear output unit. The resulting numbers are then normalized with the softmax function. All the trees (both the correct and the incorrect ones) are grouped into 1 million forests and are employed to train the network in each epoch.

In all the experiments, we estimated generalization (the average position R of the correct candidate) by running the partially trained networks in recall mode on the 3,676 validation sentences. Gradient descent was stopped when the performance on the validation set was maximum. This early stopping is expected to be useful in order to prevent overfitting. Due to the redundancy in our large training set, 4 epochs were sufficient.

4.2   Results on Learning First Pass Attachments

The output of the trained network is employed to rank candidate trees by increasing probability of correctness. Hence, the performance measure of our approach to parse decisions is based on the rank position assigned to the correct tree in each forest $\boldsymbol{F}_i$.

A synthesis of results on the 2,416 test sentences is reported in Table 1. Each time the parser tries to attach a word, it must select a connection path (actually an incremental tree) out of a certain number that can range from 1 (unique selection) to 2542. In order to rate the performance of the network in selection, we have gathered the possible cases in bins: so, the first row includes the cases which require the selection of one connection path out of two, three, four and up to seven, respectively; the second row includes the cases which require the selection of one connection path out of eight to fourteen, respectively; etc. The actual bins originate from the effort of balancing their cardinality (around 3000, see the last column). R is the average position of the correct incremental tree, after having sorted candidates according to network predictions. $R = 1$ would

---

[1]   Notice that the model does not make use of lexical and semantic information, which are considered very relevant in wide coverage parsing.

Table 1. Performance of the network in positioning the correct incremental tree.

Bin	R	1 pos %	Num	Bin	R	1 pos %	Num
2 – 7	1.18	88%	2727	90 – 103	1.56	84%	2885
8 – 14	1.22	90%	2738	104 – 123	1.69	83%	2974
15 – 20	1.27	88%	2734	124 – 145	1.61	83%	2909
21 – 29	1.27	88%	2913	146 – 176	1.68	82%	2995
30 – 39	1.57	84%	2895	177 – 207	1.93	79%	2984
40 – 49	1.43	84%	2974	208 – 255	1.82	81%	2969
50 – 61	1.51	85%	2845	256 – 330	1.86	82%	2998
62 – 75	1.70	79%	2790	331 – 476	2.26	77%	2989
76 – 89	1.64	82%	2810	477 – 2542	3.74	67%	2304

yield a perfect predictor that always ranks the correct tree in first position. The third column reports the percentage of times that the correct incremental tree was in the first position. The fourth column reports the cardinality of the bin. Globally, 82.67% of the trees are correctly assigned in first position and the global average position is 1.70.

4.3   Preliminary Results on Incremental Parsing

We have run the parser on the 2,416 test sentences with a beam of 100. We are perfectly aware that this number is very low compared with the base beam factor (10,000) used by Roark and Johnson. 97% of the sentences were parsed (that is, reached the end)[2]. The performance of the parser on the 2,416 test sentences was 64.89% labeled precision and 57.84% labeled recall with an average crossing of 2.76 (that becomes precision/recall 70.27/62.62 if we consider only sentences shorter than 30 words). Of course these preliminary results still do not compete against the level of performance of many current history-based parsing systems (precision/recall 76%/76% and average crossing of 2.26 for parsers that operate only with POS tags, without lexical information). However, we believe that the results are encouraging, and we are currently investigating how to incorporate lexical dependency information and grammatical transformations.

5   Conclusions

The paper has presented a novel methodology for parsing unrestricted text based upon the incrementality hypothesis. The results are quite preliminary. The method currently takes into account only the syntactic structure labeled with non terminal categories. The insertion of a number of linguistic heuristics should improve the performances presented here.

---

[2] The fact that 3% were not parsed is to be accounted to the incapability of the recursive neural network to process trees containing nodes with outdegree greater than the maximum specified (in our case 15).

References

[1] M. Bader and I. Lasser. German verb-final clauses and sentence processing. In C. Clifton, L. Frazier, and K. Reyner, editors, *Perspectives on Sentence Processing*, pages –. Lawrence Erlbaum Associates, 1994.

[2] E. Charniak. Statistical parsing with a context-free grammar and word statistics. In *Proc. of AAAI97*, 1997.

[3] M. Collins. A new statistical parser based on bigram lexical dependencies. In *Proc. of 34th ACL*, pages 184–191, 1996.

[4] K. M. Eberhard, M. J. Spivey-Knowlton, J.C. Sedivy, and M. K. Tanenhaus. Eye movements as a window into real-time spoken language comprehension in natural contexts. *Journal of Psycholinguistic Research*, 24:409–436, 1995.

[5] P. Frasconi, M. Gori, and A. Sperduti. A general framework for adaptive processing of data structures. *IEEE Trans. on Neural Networks*, 9(5):768–786, 1998.

[6] L. Frazier. Syntactic processing: Evidence from dutch. *Natural Language and Linguistic Theory*, 5:519–559, 1987.

[7] U. Hermjakob and R. J. Mooney. Learning parse and translation decisions from examples with rich context. In *Proceedings of ACL97*, pages 482–489, 1997.

[8] Y. Kamide and D. C. Mitchell. Incremental pre-head attachment in japanese parsing. *Language and Cognitive Processes*, 14(5–6):631–662, 1999.

[9] P.C.R. Lane and J.B. Henderson. Incremental syntactic parsing of natural language corpora with simple synchrony networks. *IEEE Transactions on Knowledge and Data Engineering*, 13(2):219–231, 2001.

[10] V. Lombardo and P. Sturt. Incrementality and lexicalism: A treebank study. In S. Stevenson and P. Merlo, editors, *Lexical Representations in Sentence Processing*. John Benjamins, 1999.

[11] W. Marslen-Wilson. Linguistic structure and speech shadowing at very short latencies. *Nature*, 244:522–533, 1973.

[12] D. Milward. Dynamic dependency grammar. *Linguistics and Philosophy*, 17(6), 1994.

[13] D.C. Mitchell, F. Cuetos, M.M.B. Corley, and M. Brysbaert. Exposure-based models of human parsing: evidence for the use of coarse-grained (nonlexical) statistical records. *Journal of Psycholinguistics Research*, 24, 1995.

[14] A. Ratnaparkhi. A linear observed time statistical parser based on maximum entropy models. In *Proceedings of EMNLP97*, 1997.

[15] B. Roark and M. Johnson. Efficient probabilistic top-down and left-corner parsing. In *Proc. of ACL99*, 1999.

[16] E. P. Stabler. The finite connectivity of linguistic structure. In C. Clifton, L. Frazier, and K. Reyner, editors, *Perspectives on Sentence Processing*, pages 303–336. Lawrence Erlbaum Associates, 1994.

[17] M. J. Steedman. Grammar, interpretation and processing from the lexicon. In W. M. Marslen-Wilson, editor, *Lexical Representation and Process*, pages 463–504. MIT Press, 1989.

[18] P. Sturt and M. Crocker. Monotonic syntactic processing: a cross-linguistic study of attachment and reanalysis. *Language and Cognitive Processes*, 11(5):449–494, 1996.

Flexible Parsing Architectures for NLP Applications

Roberto Basili, Maria Teresa Pazienza, and Fabio Massimo Zanzotto

Dipartimento di Informatica, Sistemi e Produzione,
Universita' di Roma Tor Vergata (ITALY)
{basili,pazienza,zanzotto}@info.uniroma2.it

Abstract. The requirements of different NLP applications have strong implications on the design and implementation of the related syntactic recognisers. In this paper, a fine-grained modular parser design framework is presented. Our aim is to reduce the design of a parsing processors to the composition of a pool of basic modules. Results over sample parsers and criteria for optimising coverage and accuracy are discussed.

1   Introduction

NLP applications (as Information Extraction, Text Classification, Document Indexing, etc.) employ grammatical analysers in activities ranging from the recognition of simple structures (Proper Nouns, noun phrases, etc.) to the detection of more complex phenomena (events). This heavily required flexibility has deep implications on the design and implementation of the target recognisers: different applications often have very different focus and performance needs.

The performance of the overall parsing process is a trade-off between linguistic quality of the produced material, on the one side, and the computational complexity, on the other. *Lexicalisation* of the grammatical rules and the *decomposition* of the parsing process are widely used approaches to control the quality of the results. However, sublanguage effects affecting subcategorisation lexicons have to be considered to make lexicalisation an effective means for controlling the performances. On the other hand, the *decomposition* of the parsing process (as often proposed in literature [1]) has suitable effects on the control of the overall parsing complexity, beeing too *a clear and reliable principle for the engineering of NLP applications*.

The design of a parsing processor can benefit from a fine-grained modular understanding of the syntactic recognition that models the overall (monolithic) process as a composition of dedicated components (e.g. POS tagging, noun phrase extraction, PP-attachment resolution). The design may simply proceed through elicitation of some of the available parsing components if they do not add value to the overall process in term of performance gain or recognition of interesting phenomena. Furthermore, in a modular framework, benchmarking of the different processors can be undertaken independently, and specific measures for the different potential architectures are enabled. Independent measurements

F. Esposito (Ed.): AI*IA 2001, LNAI 2175, pp. 308–313, 2001.

can thus justify the selection of an optimal architecture among a pool of potential configurations. Performance evaluation as well as optimisation can enter the design process since its earlier stages, as traditionally suggested in software engineering practice.

2   A Flexible Framework for Parser Design

A design model that supports a fine-grained modular parser development requires clear indications on the representation scheme of syntactic information exchanged between the modules and on a the compositions of the parser modules. Furthermore, a criterion inspiring the decomposition of the monolithic parsing process is desirable. As a consequence of this criterion, a pool of processors can be developed as the basic modules supporting for the composition of different parser instances.

2.1   Extended Dependency Graph

The uniform formalism should be able to represent partial analysis and show to the modules only the relevant information. The constituency-based approach has a limitation: the notion of *continuous* constituent. For instance, a pp-attachment resolution module should be free to draw the conclusion that a PP-kernel is attached to the VP-kernel without postulating the structure of the rests of NPs/PPs between the two. A dependency-based annotation scheme is more indicated to cope with this kind of problems, but it is not conceived for the information hiding: the nodes of the graph are always words, no encapsulation of the information is foreseen.

The formalism we have defined is a mixture inheriting the positive aspects of the two (apparently diverging) approaches: the *data encapsulation* and the *partial analysis storage attitude*. The proposed annotation scheme is an extended dependency graph (XDG): a graph whose nodes C are *constituents* and whose edges D are the *grammatical relations* among the constituents, i.e. $\mathcal{XDG} = (C, D)$. The $\mathcal{XDG}$ set is completely defined when the node tags, Γ, and the edge tags, Δ, are fully specified, i.e. it will be denoted by $\mathcal{XDG}_{\Gamma\Delta}$. The Γ and Δ tag sets depend upon the level of the syntactic analysis (and the underlying grammatical theory). The formalism efficiently models the syntactic ambiguity. In general, alternative interpretations for dependencies are represented by alternative $d \in D$. However, *planarity* [6] can be used to select unambiguous sentence (eventually partial) interpretations.

2.2   Composition of Parsing Modules

A generic syntactic processor MP is a *linguistic processing module* that (may) exploit syntactic knowledge stored in (possibly lexicalised) rule set R. MP processes a sentence S in order to augment it with syntactic information producing a richer representation S'. The same applies to the parsing sub-processors P_i, i.e.

$$P : R \times \mathcal{XDG}_{\Gamma\Delta} \rightarrow \mathcal{XDG}_{\Gamma'\Delta'} \tag{1}$$

so that $P(r, xdg) = xdg'$, where xdg and xdg' are the input and the enhanced graph, respectively. The first argument of a function P_i can be omitted for sake of synthesis (since it is defined for a given parser instance). The equation 1 will be written $P_i(xdg) = P(xdg; r_i) = xdg'$. The overall modular parser MP is a cascade of processing modules $(P_1, ..., P_n)$ obtained via composition operator

$$MP(xdg) = P_n \circ P_{n-1} \circ \ldots \circ P_2 \circ P_1(xdg)$$

Parsing sub-processors can be classified according to their attitude to pre-serve pre-existent choices (*monotonicity*), the actions performed on the graph (*constituent gathering*, for processors grouping set of words into larger con-stituents, and *dependency gathering*, where nodes are left untouched and only dependencies are added), and, finally, with respect the knowledge R_i used (*lex-icalised* or *grammar-driven*). This classification gives indications both on the development and tuning costs and on the possible use in the chain of each single module.

2.3   Lexicalised Syntactic Processors

The decomposition adopted is inspired by the principle that subcategorisation lexicons are valuable resources for controlling the performances. Furthermore, the possibility of reducing the costs for building lexicons via automatic acqui-sition [4] makes *lexicalised* modules more attractive. In this framework, two lexicalised modules are adopted: a verb argument matcher and a adjective mod-ifier matcher. These require a module, *the chunker* P_1 [1], for producing an intermediate sentence representation able to hide unrelevant ambiguities. The intermediate representation is $\mathcal{XDG}_{\Gamma\Delta}$ whose nodes are chunks (Γ and Δ are Γ={VPK, NPK, PPK, ...} and Δ={SUBJ, DIROBJ, PPMOD, }). More for-mally, $P_1 : \mathcal{XDG}_{\Gamma'\Delta'} \rightarrow \mathcal{XDG}_{\Gamma\Delta}$ where Γ'={Noun, Prep, Verb, ...} and $\Delta' = \emptyset$.

The specific processor for matching verb argument structures, P_2, is a *de-pendency lexicalised* processor able to work at different levels of lexicalisation. It processes $\mathcal{XDG}_{\Gamma\Delta}$, i.e. $P_2 : \mathcal{XDG}_{\Gamma\Delta} \rightarrow \mathcal{XDG}_{\Gamma\Delta}$. Successful matches add to the target xdg dependency edges also called *icds*, i.e. *inter-chunk dependencies*. An original feature is the specific combination of the argument matching with the clause recognition [3]. The role of lexical information is not only to fill slots in va-lency lexical entries, but also to control, via planarity constraints, the matching for other verbs.

The second dependency-gathering lexicalised processor, P_3, has been de-signed to deal with adjectival subcategorisation. The recognition of dependencies whose heads are adjectives may well employ adjective subcategorisation frames. Let us take, as an example, an excerpt of the sentence # 0439(63) of the Penn Tree bank:

An increasing number of references by the Soviet press to opposition groups now active in the U.S.S.R., particularly the Democratic Union, allege that ...

The processor will augment the grammatical information detected in the sentence by adding the dependency between *active* and *in the U.S.S.R.* according to the subcategorisation frame *[active [PP [P in] [NP _]]* .

3 Evaluating Alternative Parsing Architectures

The flexible architecture gives the possibility to investigate different parsing processors. In order to understand the value of the lexical information, the following configurations have been analysed:

- a base (non lexicalized) processor, i.e. $P_1 \circ P_4$, hereafter called *BASE*
- a strictly lexicalized processor, made of the composition of the chunker P_1 with P_2 and P_3 components referred to as *LEXICAL*
- a processor integrating lexicalized and shallow parsing, i.e. $P_1 \circ P_2 \circ P_3 \circ P_4$, hereafter called *COMBINED*

where P_4 ($P_4 : \mathcal{XDG}_{\Gamma\Delta} \rightarrow \mathcal{XDG}_{\Gamma\Delta}$) is a non-lexicalized *shallow analyzer* [2], mainly used for lexical acquisition from corpora. Thus, it follows a $recall - first$ policy and retains ambiguous dependencies. Conflicting syntactic readings are preserved in the output graph. This affects the precision of the *BASE* and *COMBINED* configuration. As our goal is also to study precision, a PP-disambiguation module P_5 ($P_5 : \mathcal{XDG}_{\Gamma\Delta} \rightarrow \mathcal{XDG}_{\Gamma\Delta}$) has been also integrated in the parsing chains. P_5 implements a simple disambiguation strategy, i.e. the minimal attachment choice. P_5 is thus a non monotonic dependency-gatherer as it removes some of the previously assigned links in the input *xdg*. We have tested also two augmented configurations MA^- ($P_1 \circ P_4 \circ P_5$) and MA^+ ($P_1 \circ P_2 \circ P_3 \circ P_4 \circ P_5$) obtained by integrating the disambiguation processor.

For the performance evaluation in terms of quality of derived linguistic information, a metrics oriented to an *annotated-corpus* has been adopted. In particular the used formalism is *Parseval*-like where the *Parseval scheme* [5] has been adapted to the particular annotation paradigm. The comparison between the *oracle* information, i.e. the treebank-information, and the parser syntactic material is carried on a dependency-annotation base. The annotated corpus is the *Penn Treebank* [8], and the metrics adopted are then *Recall*, *Precision* and *F*-measure. Constituency-based annotated information of the oracle has been translated in a dependency formalism. Translation algorithms have been settled in other works [7, 4]. In the present work the adopted translation algorithm left not translated about 10% of the *oracle trees*(i.e. reference corpus trees).

Metrics are settled on this representation and they are targeted over given grammatical relation τ (e.g. *NP_PP*), as follows:

$$R^\tau(S) = \frac{card((A_o^\tau(S) \cap A_s^\tau(S)))}{card(A_o^\tau(S))} \qquad P^\tau(S) = \frac{card((A_o^\tau(S) \cap A_s^\tau(S)))}{card(A_s^\tau(S))} \qquad (2)$$

where $A_o^\tau(S)$ are the correct syntactic relations of type τ for the sentence S, and $A_s^\tau(S)$ are the syntactic relations of type τ extracted by the system. In particular, given the set of test sentences Ω, global values for recall and precision are derived as follows:

$$R^\tau(\Omega) = \frac{1}{\sum_{s\in\Omega}\gamma_s}\sum_{s\in\Omega}\gamma_s R^\tau(s) \qquad P^\tau(\Omega) = \frac{1}{\sum_{s\in\Omega}\omega_s}\sum_{s\in\Omega}\omega_s P^\tau(s) \qquad (3)$$

where γ_s and ω_s are weighting factors associated depending on the characteristics of sentences. Notice that another global definition, *cumulative recall* and *precision* respectively, is possible where cumulative phenomena are taken into account:

$$R^\tau(\Omega) = \frac{card(\bigcup_{S\in\Omega}(A_o^\tau(S)\cap A_s^\tau(S)))}{card(\bigcup_{S\in\Omega}A_o^\tau(S))} \qquad P^\tau(\Omega) = \frac{card(\bigcup_{S\in\Omega}(A_o^\tau(S)\cap A_s^\tau(S)))}{card(\bigcup_{S\in\Omega}A_s^\tau(S))}$$

$$(4)$$

The F-measure synthetic metric is defined for the whole corpus Ω as follows:

$$F_\alpha^\tau(\Omega) = \frac{1}{(\alpha\frac{1}{P^\tau(\Omega)} + (1-\alpha)\frac{1}{R^\tau(\Omega)})} \qquad (5)$$

The target test bed Ω is a subset of 500 sentences out from the 40,000 translated interpretations. It has been set up in order to selectively measure the effects of the lexicalized processors in the parsing chains.

Our evaluation goal here is to compare the accuracy of different configurations. By using equation 3, we averaged precision and recall (i.e. γ_S and ω_S are set to 1, $\forall S$), and we measured the F-measure of the different architectures. Values of 72.23% and 78.19% characterizes the $BASE$ and $COMBINED$ configuration respectively. If disambiguation is adopted (i.e. in MA^+), the result is $F_{0.5}(\Omega) = 81.48\%$. It is clear here that combination of lexicalized processors, plus a simple disambiguation strategy, outperforms in general the $BASE$ parser.

In order to selectively analyse syntactic dependencies (τ) several runs have been carried out. The measures of R_τ and P_τ, as in equations 4, are reported in Table 1.

The $BASE$ processor is the less precise, as it preserves all the potential attachments. Its recall represents an upper-bound for the other processors. Notice that the $LEXICAL$ configuration has an high precision (on specific phenomena, V_PP and Adj_PP) but its recall suggests that it is insufficient to fully "cover" the wide phenomena related to prepositional dependencies.

The best performing architecture is the $COMBINED$ cascade, where lexical knowledge is firstly employed and it constraints the scope of the shallow analyzer. This is true not only on prepositional modifiers but also on the attachment of direct object ($\tau = V\_NP$).

Several relevant consequences can be drawn. First, different types of phenomena with respect to the contributions of lexicalized processors can now be selectively studied. Secondly, optimal configuration for specific phenomena can be outlined, even in the design phase, and this supports and eases the systematic configuration of novel parsing architectures within new application scenarios. Finally, factorising lexical processes has proofed beneficial in the overall parsing process. This allows to (1) estimate the role of some lexicalised components and, if strictly required by the new application, (2) assess them via specific customisation actions during porting. The results suggest that modular parsing is viable

Table 1. Evaluation: Parsing configuration vs. different syntactic phenomena

	ADJ_PP		NP_PP		V_NP		V_PP	
	R	P	R	P	R	P	R	P
BASE	11,63%	100,00%	87,23%	26,81%	91,07%	44,94%	70,39%	37,50%
LEXICAL	25,58%	100,00%	-	-	86,51%	80,06%	38,55%	76,38%
COMBINED	27,91%	100,00%	80,84%	37,38%	87,74%	73,25%	68,16%	44,15%

within the defined framework and that even shallow approaches (widely employed within robust parsing systems) improve significantly their performances: they help to increase coverage, even when poor lexical knowledge is available.

References

[1] Steven Abney. Part-of-speech tagging and partial parsing. In G.Bloothooft K.Church, S.Young, editor, *Corpus-based methods in language and speech*. Kluwer academic publishers, Dordrecht, 1996.

[2] Roberto Basili, Maria Teresa Pazienza, and Paola Velardi. A shallow syntactic analyser to extract word association from corpora. *Literary and linguistic computing*, 7(2):114–124, 1992.

[3] Roberto Basili, Maria Teresa Pazienza, and Fabio Massimo Zanzotto. Efficient parsing for information extraction. In *Proc. of the ECAI98*, Brighton, UK, 1998.

[4] Roberto Basili, Maria Teresa Pazienza, and Fabio Massimo Zanzotto. Evaluating a robust parser for italian language. In *Proc. of the Workshop on Evaluation of Parsing Systems, held jointly with 1st LREC*, Granada, Spain, 1998.

[5] E. Black, S. Abney, D. Flickenger, C. Gdaniec, R. Grishman, P. Harrison, D. Hindle, R. Ingria, F. Jelinek, J. Klavans, M. Liberman, M. Marcus, S. Roukos, B. Santorini, and T. Strzalkowski. A procedure for quantitatively comparing the syntactic coverage of english grammars. In *Proc. of the Speech and Natural Language Workshop*, pages 306–311, Pacific Grove, CA, 1991.

[6] D. Grinberg, J. Lafferty, and D. Sleator. A robust parsing algorithm for link grammar. In *4th International workshop on parsing tecnologies*, Prague, 1996.

[7] D. Lin. A dependency-based method for evaluating broad-coverage parsers. In *Proc. of the 14th IJCAI*, pages 1420–1425, Montreal, Canada, 1995.

[8] M. P. Marcus, B. Santorini, and M. A. Marcinkiewicz. Building a large annotated corpus of english: The penn treebank. *Computational Linguistics*, 19:313–330, 1993.

Information Presentation Adapted to the "User in Context"

Berardina De Carolis, Pietro Di Maggio, and Sebastiano Pizzutilo

Intelligent Interfaces, Department of Computer Science, University of Bari
Via Orabona 4, 70126 Bari, Italy
{decarolis, derosis, pizzutilo}@di.uniba.it

Abstract. In the optics in which the computer disappears and provides its services to users through portable and wearable devices, access to these services will depend on the situation in which the interaction takes place. Therefore, the adaptation to the context as well as to the user is increasing of importance in achieving an effective communication of information and provision of services. To this aim, besides users' experience (character, interests,...) other features have to be considered in the adaptation process: their location, activity, emotional state and the device they are using. This paper presents methods and techniques at the basis on a *Personal Presentation Agent,* whose task is the selection and presentation of relevant information adapted to the "User in Context".

1   Introduction

User-tailored information communication was the goal of research on adaptive systems in the last ten years. Features such as the user interests, background knowledge and preferences were considered to settle, at the same time, the information to be included in the message and its 'surface' realisation [2,4].

With the evolution of devices for interacting with information services (mobile phones, wearable computers, "augmented everyday objects"), the access to these services will depend on the situation in which they and their users are. Context-awareness is, then, increasing of importance in achieving an effective communication of information and provision of services [1]. This means that adapting information presentation to user's features is not enough: the user location, her/his current activity, emotional state and the characteristics of the used device are important parameters for establishing how the information has to be accessed and presented.

This paper presents a *Personal Presentation Agent,* whose task is to select the information that is appropriate to the "user in context" and present it in a clear, coherent and complete way. To this aim, information included in the various sources needs to be understandable by a software agent and this requires defining and using 'annotation languages' that allow to interpret appropriately the semantics of data. Our Presentation Agent combines a standard annotation of domain knowledge based on XML with two context-sensitive modules: a Presentation Planner, that establishes the information to present and its structure and a Surface Generator that sets up the output layout. The result is the personalization of the communication at both the content and the layout levels according to the user characteristics and to context features.

F. Esposito (Ed.): AI*IA 2001, LNAI 2175, pp. 314-319, 2001.

2   'User in Context' Models

Let us consider, as an example, the case of an information server about *medical first-aid*. It may be accessed through two different devices (PC and mobile phone) and protocols (HTTP and WAP). In the first case, one may assume that web-based first-aid information is presented in the form of an *instruction manual*, eventually adapted to the user knowledge and level of experience, with links to detailed first-aid procedures through figures, videos and so on. The same information, if accessed from a mobile phone, might be provided by assuming an *emergency* situation; this requires a layout adaptation due to the device and a quick access to the most essential data (for instance: the address of the nearest first-aid service or the most urgent action to make). This example allows distinguishing between *two families of factors that influence adaptivity* of the presentation:

- *factors that persists during time or evolve slowly*: these long-term factors are related to the user's background knowledge, cognitive capacity, experience, personality, job, sex, age, interests about topic families and so on. This type of knowledge may be acquired through standard stereotype-triggering methods [18]; starting from the activated stereotype, an individual User Model can be built and updated dynamically along the interaction sessions;
- *factors related to a particular interaction session or situation*: these short-term factors depend on the context in which the user is and moves [14]. Context-awareness regards three main points: the environment, the activity and the device employed [1]: a) the *environment* in which the application operates is identified by the physical and social surroundings of the user, her emotional state, the location, the activities going on in the environment and other external properties; b) the *activity* describes the task the user is performing or, more generally, her behavior and habits; c)the *device* can be a PC, a PDA, a mobile phone, a TV, a watch, and so on.

3   Presentation Aspects to Be Varied

The aspects of the information presentation may be varied according to the context. Adaptation may generally be introduced in the following phases of the generation process: *a.) when planning the presentation content*, that is when deciding "what to say" to the user, at which level of detail and by using which media; *b.) when rendering the presentation at the surface level*, that is when deciding "how to display information" to the user, by selecting an appropriate presentation structure and layout. Considering context in addition to the user characteristics requires adding to the usual adaptation criteria other issues; for instance: 1) *activity*; the task the user is performing influences the type of information, the way information is accessed, and so on. Providing a search or a browsing access modality or pushing relevant information for emergency are examples of adaptation to activity; 2) *emotional state*; factors concerning the emotional state influence the way in which the emotion is displayed. This does not mean that the expression relies on an embodiment of the software agent. Affective expression can be conveyed through speech or text style, figures, colours etc. For instance: if a user accesses to information in conditions of emergency, the Presentation Agent will have to avoid engendering panic, by using "ensuring" expressions or voice timbre. 3) *device*; display capacity affects how the information is selected, structured and rendered; for instance, natural language texts may be more or less verbose, complex figures may be avoided or replaced by ad hoc parts or written/spoken comments; 4) *environment*; texts, images and other multimedia may be selected according to the environment. For instance: a contextualization of the NLG step allows to generate sentences of the type "The first-aid service closest to you is in the "St. John Hospital", at about 1 km north".

4   Our Presentation Agent

The architecture of our presentation agent is inspired to classical NLG systems [10]. It provides a *Presentation Planner*, which is responsible of deciding *what to present* to the user and according to *which* discourse *structure* and a *Surface Generator*, which is responsible for rendering appropriately the discourse plan at the surface level. Input of the Presentation Agent are the **communicative goal**, which represents the user request, the **context features** and a set of **knowledge sources** representing the *application domain, linguistic resources* and *context models*. The domain knowledge and linguistic resources (plans in particular) are formalized using XML-based annotation languages. To reduce the complexity of this phase, we abstract a library of standard plans from a corpus of 'natural' presentations in the application domain. This library will represent the discourse structure achieving a given communicative goal (i.e. describe an object, explain an action, and so on). In this way, a discourse plan can be selected, dynamically pruned, hierarchically composed and instantiated, by filling the variable slots with domain data [5]. XML representation of plans has been made according to a Document Type Definition (DTD) defined for this purpose. This approach derives from the operationalization of Mann and Thompson's "Rhetorical Structure Theory" (RST) and from classical definitions of discourse plan [10,15,16].

The strategies for producing the information layout from the discourse plan are based on the basic idea that information is presented to the user in the form of information units, which are aggregations of information tokens (written or spoken sentences, multimedia displays etc). Therefore, the Surface Generator decides:
1) **how to *aggregate*** D-Plan nodes into information units; 2) **how to *display*** an information unit, according to the device. For instance: a web page includes a title, a body and a footer as typical tokens while, in a WAP page, the title appears only at the beginning of the navigation session, the body tends to be composed of homogenous information items – links only, textual information only, images only, etc - and the footer depends on the programmability of the softkeys, that is related to the telephone type; 3) **which *media to select*** for conveying every information token: some media are preferable to convey particular information tokens, according to the user characteristics and to the device employed. For instance: text is preferred over images on small devices. To this aim, textual descriptions may be generated from the metadata associated with the image. 4) **which *type of navigation*** through the hypermedia (free/guided), structure (linear, hierarchical or circular) and level of orientation support to provide.   These features may be adapted to the user experience

(guided-mode with strong orientation for non-expert users, free-mode for expert users; strong orientation support for instructional purposes, less orientation for information [6,7]). The device influences, as well, this choice. In a WAP based application, the poor usability of the device (small display, limited bandwidth, small memory capacity) suggests structuring menus so as to propose a guided navigation structure with step-by-step interaction, feedback provided only in negative cases, appropriate use of softkeys [3,11,13,20]. The surface generation algorithm uses information in the discourse plan (RR, goals, complexity, focus) to produce a presentation that is appropriate to the situation. If the context requires a very short message, we extract from Dplan a tree representing the 'essence' of the overall discourse. The 'most nuclear part of the discourse' may be obtained by exploring Dplan in a top-down way and by recursive pruning all the RR's satellites [8]. If the whole Dplan has to be transformed into a network of information units, the tree is examined in a top-down way and nodes are aggregated recursively into information units. When the user does not follow the suggested navigation path, follow-up guidelines are generated, again, from the items associated with Dplan nodes.

5   An Example

As far as the device is concerned, we will take two cases that may be considered as representatives of the 'tabs' and 'pads' envisaged by Weiser [21]: a PC and a WAP-phone. The Fig.1 shows a portion of the XML Dplan for first-aid procedure. The main goal (n1) is to explain to the user how to deal with emergencies in patients with a head injury; the RR associated with this node is a 'Motivation' whose 'nucleus' (n2) describes the procedure to apply in this situation, while its 'satellite' describes why the suggested procedure should be applied.

```
<d-plan>
<tree name="del-with-emergency">
<node name="n1" goal="Explain(S.U. Deal-emergency(head-injury)) RR="Motivation" role=root>
<info focus="head-injury" compl=M/>
    <node name="n2" goal="Describe(SU Emergency-treatment(head-injury)) RR="Joint" role=N>
    <info focus="head-injury" compl=L/>
        <node name="n3"goal="Reccomend(SU Avoid(panic))" RR="null" role=N/>
        info focus="panic" compl=L/>
        <node name="n4"goal="Reccomend(SU Avoid-remove(casuality))"RR="Joint" role=N>
        info focus="casuality" compl=L/>
.........
```

Fig 1: A part of the discourse plan describing how to deal with emergencies

5.1.   Procedural Information Presentation

Case 1: a User browses with a PC in the 'first-aid' information system
In this case, two hypermedia, with a different structure and navigation style, may be generated, according to the user experience. A hierarchical-circular structure, accessible through structured menus, is more appropriate to expert users, who may

navigate in a free way within the hypermedia, by looking for the particular items they want to know. Alternatively, an overall index that points to all information units may be created as the home page. If, instead, the user is a novice, a guided navigation mode is preferable: the intentional structure of Dplan is mirrored in a hierarchy of 'structure' pages (Fig. 2). In the guided mode, the user is guided to examine the process in detail step by step through the buttons in the Footer, until reaching a unit that fully describes a particular step. Buttons in the footer indicate the alternative units to visit and may be labelled according to the goal of the next unit or to the RR between the origin and the destination unit, to reduce the risk of cognitive disorientation of the user.

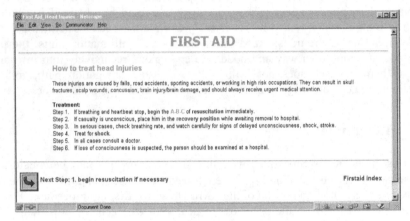

Fig. 2: a 'structure' page in the 'guided' mode.

Case 2: a novice User requests assistance from a mobile device, in an emergency situation:

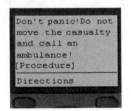

As mentioned previously, in this case, the 'most nuclear part of the discourse' is extracted from Dplan (Fig.3). The 'Procedure' link gives information about the first aid treatment of the head injury, while the 'Direction' softkey inform about the closest hospital. If the user requests additional information, the system guides her in a sequential exploration of the subtasks of the procedure using softkeys.

Fig. 3: Essential emergency information

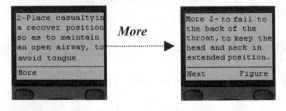

Softkeys labels emphasise the fact that the display concerns the same topic (More), a subsequent step (Next) or a image about the same topic. Two cards are generated from the subtree linked by the "More" softkey.

Fig. 4: Some more detail about how to deal with emergency.

6   Conclusions

This work is our first step towards adapting the presentation of information to the 'user in context'. Even if the shown example is still displayed on a PC and on a WAP-phone, we claim that the approach adopted is general enough to be device independent by providing the right amount of contextualized information in an appropriate presentation form. This is a first prototype and obviously a lot of work has to be done to test the efficacy of the algorithms developed and to validate the assumptions we made.

References

1. Abowd G.D., Dey A. K., Orr R. J., and Brotherton J. Context-awareness in Wearable and Ubiquitous Computing Virtual Reality, Vol. 3 (1998), pp. 200-211.
2. Brusilovsky P. (1996). Methods and Techniques of Adaptive Hypermedia. *UMUAI*, 6: 87-129.
3. Buyukkokten O., Molina H.G, Paepcke A., Winograd T. Power Browser: Efficient Web Browsing for PDAs. The 9th International WWW Conference (WWW9)., 1999.
4. Dale R Oberlander J. Milosavljevic M. and Knott A. Integrating Natural Language Generation and Hypertext to Produce Dynamic Documents Interacting with Computers, 10, 1998.
5. De Carolis B., de Rosis F., Berry D C and Michas I. Evaluating plan-based hypermedia generation. *7th European Workshop on Natural Language Generation.* Toulouse, 1999,
6. De Carolis B., de Rosis F, Pizzutilo S. Generating user-adapted hypermedia from discourse plans. *AI*IA 97: Advances in Artificial Intelligence*, LNAI Maurizio Lenzerini (eds), Springer, 334-345, 1997.
7. De Rosis F, Grasso F and Berry D. Refining instructional text generation after evaluation. *Artificial Intelligence in Medicine.* 17, 1999.
8. Hovy E. H. Automated Discourse Generation using Discourse Structure Relations. Artificial Intelligence, 63, (1993), 341-385.
9. http://www.Phone.com . Application Style guide for gsm 900-1800.
10. Jones M, Marsden G, Mohd-Nasir N, Boone K, Buchanan G.. Improving Web Interaction on Small Displays. http://www.handheld.mdx.ac.uk/www8/www8.pdf.
11. Jörding, T. Temporary User Modeling for Adaptive Product Presentation on the Web. Proceedings of UM99, Banff, Canada, pp. 333-334.
12. Mann W.C., Matthiessen C.M.I.M., Thompson S. (1989). Rhetorical Structure Theory and Text Analysis.*ISI Research Report- 89- 242.*
13. Moore J.D. and Paris C. (1993). Planning Text for Advisory Dialogues: Capturing Intentional and Rhetorical Information. *Computational Linguistics*, 19(4): 651-694.
14. Rich, E.: User Modeling via Stereotypes, Cognitive Science, 3, pp. 329-354, 1979.
15. Schmidt A., Schröder H and Frick O. WAP - Designing for Small User Interfaces. ACM CHI 2000 Extented Abstracts, Conference on Human Factors in Computing Systems. April 2000. pp 187-8. ISBN 1-58113-216-6.
16. Weiser M. The Computer for the 21st Century. *Scientific American*, september 1991.

A Hybrid Approach to Optimize Feature Selection Process in Text Classification

Roberto Basili, Alessandro Moschitti, and Maria Teresa Pazienza

University of Rome Tor Vergata
Department of Computer Science, Systems and Production
00133 Roma (Italy)
{basili,moschitti,pazienza}@info.uniroma2.it

Abstract. Feature selection and weighting are the primary activity of every learning algorithm for text classification. Traditionally these tasks are carried out individually in two distinct phases: the first is the global feature selection during a corpus pre-processing and the second is the application of the feature weighting model. This means that two (or several) different techniques are used to optimize the performances even if a single algorithm may have more chances to operate the right choices. When the complete feature set is available, the classifier learning algorithm can better relate to the suitable representation level the different complex features like linguistic ones (e.g. syntactic categories associated to words in the training material or terminological expressions). In [3] it has been suggested that classifiers based on generalized Rocchio formula can be used to weight features in category profiles in order to exploit the selectivity of linguistic information techniques in text classification. In this paper, a systematic study aimed to understand the role of Rocchio formula in selection and weighting of linguistic features will be described.

1 Natural Language Processing and Text Classification

Linguistic content in Text Classification (TC) aims to define specific and selective *features* with respect to training and test documents. Previous works on NLP-driven text classification (e.g. [1]) suggest that word information (e.g. morphology and syntactic role) improve performances. In particular, lemmatization and POS tagging provide a linguistically principled way to compress the features set (usually obtained by traditional crude methods like stop lists or statistical thresholds, e.g. χ^2). Statistical unsupervised terminological extraction has been also applied to TC training [2]. It allows to detect more complex and relevant features, i.e. complex nominal groups typical of the different target classes. The results are improved TC performances, although the contribution given by such modules has not yet been accurately measured. When more complex features (e.g. words and their POS tag or terminological units) are captured it is more difficult to select the relevant ones among the set of all features. Data sparseness effects (e.g. the lower frequency of n-grams wrt simple words) interact with wrong recognitions (e.g. errors in POS assignment) and the overall information

F. Esposito (Ed.): AI*IA 2001, LNAI 2175, pp. 320–326, 2001.

may not be enough effective. The traditional solution is the *feature selection*, discussed for example in [7]. By applying statistical methods, (information gain, χ^2, mutual information ...), non relevant features are removed. The Major drawback is that features irrelevant for a class can be removed even if they are important for another one. The crucial issue here is how to give the right weight to a given feature in different classes. This is even more important when NLP (and, mainly, terminology recognition) is applied: some technical terms can be perfectly valid features for a class and, at the same time, totally irrelevant or misleading for others.

In this paper a systematic study aimed to understand the role of Rocchio formula in the selection and weighting applied to standard and linguistic features (e.g. terminological expressions), will be described.

2   A Hybrid Feature Selection Model

2.1   The Problem of Feature Selection

Automatic feature selection methods foresee the removal of noninformative terms according to corpus statistics (e.g. *information gain, mutual information* and χ^2), and the construction of new (i.e. reduced or re-mapped) feature space. A distinctive characteristic is the selection of features based on their relevance in the whole corpus instead of in a single category. Moreover, in [6], feature selection appears as a distinct phase in building text classifier. In order to account for differences in the distribution of relevance throughout classes, we should depart from the idea of a unique ranking of all corpus features. Features should be selected with respect to a single category. This can lead to retain features only when they are truly informative for some classes. In next section an extension of the Rocchio formula aiming to obtain feature weights that are also, at the same time, optimal selectors for a given class is presented.

2.2   Generalizing Rocchio Formula for Selecting Features

The Rocchio's formula has been successfully used for building profile of text classifier as follows. Given the set of training documents R_i classified under the topics C_i, the set $\bar{R}_i$ of the documents not belonging to C_i, and given a document h and a feature f, the weight Ω_f^h of f in the profile of C_i is:

$$\Omega_f^i = \max\left\{0, \frac{\beta}{|R_i|}\sum_{h \in R_i} \omega_f^h - \frac{\gamma}{|\bar{R}_i|}\sum_{h \in \bar{R}_i} \omega_f^h\right\} \tag{1}$$

where ω_f^h represent the weights of features in documents[1]. In Eq. 1 the parameters β and γ control the relative impact of positive and negative examples and determine the weight of f in the i-th profile. In [4], Equation 1 has been firstly

---

[1] Several methods are used to assign weights of a feature, as widely discussed in [5]

used with values $\beta = 16$ and $\gamma = 4$: the task was categorization of low quality images. In the next section a procedures for selecting an optimal γ, keeping fixed β to 1 value, will be presented.

Selecting Features via Rocchio's Formula Parameters The relevance of a feature deeply depends on the corpus characteristic and, in particular, on the differences among the training material for the different classes, i.e. size, the structure of topics, the style of documents, ... This varies very much across text collections and across the different classes within the same collection. Notice that, in Equation 1, features with negative difference between positive and negative relevance are set to 0. This implies a discontinuous behavior of the Ω_f^i values around the 0. This aspect is crucial since the 0-valued features are irrelevant in the similarity estimation (i.e. they give a null contribution to the scalar product). This form of selection is rather smooth and allows to retain features that are selective only for some of the target classes. As a result, features are optimally used as they influence the similarity estimation for all and only the classes for which they are selective.

As feature weights relies on the γ and β setting, fitting them with respect to the classification performance has two main objectives:

- First, noise is drastically reduced without direct feature selection (i.e. without removing any feature).
- Second, the obtained ranking provides scores that can be directly used as weights in the associated feature space.

Notice that each category has its own set of relevant and irrelevant features and Eq. 1 depends for each class i on γ and β. Now we assume the optimal values of these two parameters can be obtained by estimating their impact on the classification performance, independently for each class i. This will result in a vector of (γ_i, β_i) couples each one optimizing the performance of the classifier over the i-th class. Hereafter we will refer to this model as the $Rocchio_{\gamma_i}$ classifier. Finally, it has to be noticed that combined estimation of the two parameters is not required. For each class, we fixed one parameter (β_i indeed) and let γ_i vary until the optimal performance is reached. The weighting, ranking and selection scheme used for $Rocchio_{\gamma_i}$ classifier is thus the following:

$$\Omega_f^i = \max\left\{0, \frac{1}{|R_i|} \sum_{h \in R_i} \omega_f^h - \frac{\gamma_i}{|\bar{R}_i|} \sum_{h \in \bar{R}_i} \omega_f^h\right\} \tag{2}$$

In our experiments, β has been set to 1, Equation 2 has been applied given the parameters γ_i that for each class C_i lead to the maximum breakeven point[2] over a test set. By using this formula, when γ_i is increased only features very representative for the target class i assume a relevant weights. Alternatively features

---

[2] It is the threshold values for which precision and recall coincide (see [6] for more details).

that are moderately informative for a category i but that are at same time poor relevant for all other categories may be heavily weighted. In this perspective γ_i parameter acts as a domain concept selector. In next sections the above characteristic of γ_i is verified over (possibly complex) features extracted by Natural Language Processing techniques. As such features are more representative than simple words the effectiveness of $Rocchio_{\gamma_i}$ selection can be emphasized and measured.

2.3   The Role of NLP in Feature Extraction

Main objective of this section is to describe the role of linguistic information in the representation of different classes in a TC task. We underline that these latter are often characterized by sets of *typical* concepts usually expressed by multi-words expressions, i.e. linguistic structures synthesizing widely accepted definitions (e.g. *"bond issues"* in topics like *"Finance* or *Stock Exchange"*). These sets provide useful information to capture semantic aspects of a *topics*. The multi-word expressions are at least in two general classes useful for TC: Proper Nouns (PN) (e.g. like locations, persons or artifacts) and Terminological expressions, which are more relevant triggers than PN for the classification decisions. Their detection results in a more precise set of features to be included in the target vector space. The identification of linguistically motivated terminological structures usually requires external resources (thesaura or glossaries): as extensive repositories are costly to be developed and simply missing in most domains, an enumerative approach cannot be fully applied. Automatic methods for the derivation of terminological information from texts can thus play a key role in content sensitive text classification.

Previous works in the NLP research area suggest that the semantic classes related to terms depend strongly on the underlying domain. As terms embody domain specific knowledge we expect that their derivation from a specialized corpus can support the matching of features useful for text classification. Once terms specific to a given topics C_i are available (and they can be estimated from the training material for C_i), their matching in future texts d should strongly suggest classification of d in C_i. In this work, the terminology extractor described in [2] has been adopted in the training phase. Each class (considered as a separate corpus) gives rise to a set of terms, T_i. When available, elements in T_i can be matched in future test documents. They are thus included in the final set of features of the target classifier. Other features provided by linguistic processing capabilities are lemmas and their associated POS information able to capture word syntactic roles (e.g. *adjective, verb, noun*). Those irrelevant features, that are not necessarily produced via complex linguistic processing (e.g. single words), are correctly smoothed by Eq. 2 and this also helps in a more precise weight of the NLP contribution. This results in a hybrid feature selection model where grammatical and statistical information are nicely investigated.

3   Experimenting Hybrid Feature Selection in Text Classification

In these experiments the Equation 2 is applied to several sets of linguistically derived features. Reuters, version 3, corpus prepared by Apté [6] has been used as reference corpus. It includes 11,099 documents for 93 classes, with a fixed splitting between test (TS) and learning data (3,309 vs. 7,789). The linguistic features described in Section 2.3 have been added to the standard set. They consist of:

- Proper Nouns: +PN indicates that the recognized proper nouns are used as features for the classifiers; -PN is used instead to indicate that proper nouns recognized in texts are removed from the set of valid features during training
- Terminological Expressions (+TE)
- Lemmas (-POS) and Lemmas augmented with their POS tags (+POS)

In Table 1 is reported the BEP of the three feature sets: the comparison is against the baseline, i.e. the best non linguistic result. Note that for each feature set, indicated in the table, re-estimation of the γ_i parameters has been carried out. The above table shows the overall positive impact (by microaveraging the

Table 1. Breakeven points of $Rocchio_{\gamma_i}$ on three feature set provides with NLP applied to Reuters version 3.

Base-Line	+POS-PN	+PN+TE	+PN+TE+POS
83.82%	83.86%	84.48%	85.13%

BEP of all 93 categories) of using diverse NLP capabilities. However, individual analysis for each category is required for a better understanding of the selectivity of γ_i. Figure 1 shows the performance (BEP) of some classes wrt the adopted γ for profile learning. Results show that $Rocchio_{\gamma_i}$ weighting scheme proposes as a robust filtering technique for sparse data in the training corpus. It is to be noticed that the behavior of the γ_i parameters is tightly related to the categories (i.e. to the training material available for them). Different categories show quite different values of γ_i able to optimize performances. This seems related to the inner conceptual nature of the categories themselves. A suitable setting represents thus a promising model to select relevant features, that well reflect the semantic role of each of them. For this reason, we applied the best obtained settings to weight linguistic features in profiles and carried on a contrastive analysis against the baseline figures derived by only using standard features.

A second major outcome, is that the comparative evaluation of simpler against linguistically motivated feature sets confirm the superiority of the latter. The $Rocchio_{\gamma_i}$ applied to linguistic material supports thus a computationally efficient classification. This is mainly due to the adoption of the optimal selection and weighting method proposed in Equation 2, which optimizes features

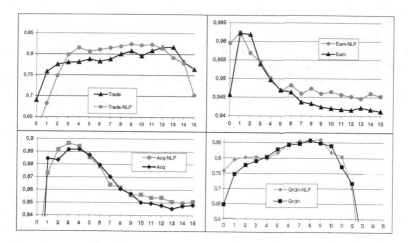

Fig. 1. Break-even point performances of the Rocchio classifier according to different γ values for some classes of Reuters 3 Corpus

vs. performances (see Figure 1). It seems that a suitable parameter setting for the γ_i provides a systematic way to filter (and emphasize) the source linguistic information. It has to be noticed that in the experiments we obtained a source set of 9,650 features for the Reuters 3 *acq* category. After γ_{acq} setting, only 4,957 features are assigned with a weight greater than 0.

Figure 1 also shows that the NLP plots (for the selected classes i) have values systematically higher than plots of tests over standard features. This is true for each γ_i value. Notice that if a non optimal γ is chosen for a given class, it is possible that classifiers trained with standard feature outperform those trained with NLP, as evidently data sparseness in linguistic data creates dangerous noise. This is the mainly reason for previous failures in the adoption of Rocchio weighting. The results show how setting of suitable γ_i values are critical for the optimal use of linguistic information. The suggested model (Eq. 2) thus represents an efficient approach to hybrid feature selection in operational (large scale) TC systems.

References

[1] R. Basili, A. Moschitti, and M.T. Pazienza. Language sensitive text classification. In *Proceeding of 6th RIAO Conference, Collège de France, Paris, France*, 2000.

[2] R. Basili, A. Moschitti, and M.T. Pazienza. Modeling terminological information in text classification. In *Proceeding of 7th TALN Conference*, 2000.

[3] R. Basili, A. Moschitti, and M.T. Pazienza. NLP-driven IR: Evaluating performances over text classification task. In *Proceeding of the 10th IJCAI Conference, Seattle, Washington, USA*, 2001.

[4] David J. Ittner, David D. Lewis, and David D. Ahn. Text categorization of low quality images. In *Proceedings of SDAIR-95*, pages 301–315, Las Vegas, US, 1995.

[5] G: Salton and C. Buckley. Term-weighting approaches in automatic text retrieval. *Information Processing and Management*, 24(5):513–523, 1988.

[6] Y. Yang. An evaluation of statistical approaches to text categorization. *Information Retrieval Journal*, May, 1999.

[7] Y. Yang and Jan O. Pedersen. A comparative study on feature selection in text categorization. In *Proceedings of ICML-97*, pages 412–420, Nashville, US, 1997.

Concepts for Anchoring in Robotics

Andrea Bonarini, Matteo Matteucci, and Marcello Restelli

Politecnico di Milano Artificial Intelligence and Robotics Project
Department of Electronics and Information
Politecnico di Milano, Milan, Italy
{bonarini,matteucc,restelli}@elet.polimi.it

Abstract. Anchoring is the activity an agent does to classify the objects
it perceives and to track them. With the increasing abilities of mobile
robots, anchoring is becoming a major research issue to make robots
perform their task in unstructured and partially unknown environments.
We propose a model to represent knowledge in an agent, possibly participating to a multi–agent system, showing that the anchoring problem can
be successfully faced by well known AI techniques. We discuss how this
model can reliably support the instantiation of concepts by aggregating
percepts affected by uncertainty, sensed by several sensors, and obtained
from different agents.

1   Introduction

Robotic agents operate in an environment containing other *physical objects*.
These are perceived by *smart sensors* that translate some physical features acquired by a *physical sensor*, into information (*features*) represented by an internal
formalism which can be understood by the other modules participating to the
action selection for the agent. When this information is used to maintain a model
of the environment, it is important that features referring to a physical object be
collected in an internal representation of the same object, referred to as *perceptual image*. It is relevant to relate the perceptual image with a *concept* present in
the agent knowledge, since this makes it possible to reason about the perceived
object with categories describing the corresponding concept. An embodied agent
anchors a physical object when it can instantiate a concept compatible with the
perceived features, and maintains the relationship between such an instance and
the physical object it refers to, during its activities.

Recently, the *anchoring problem* has been introduced [2][3] as a research topic
relevant to implement autonomous embodied agents able to perform their tasks
in unstructured environments, possibly interacting with other robots, smart sensors, and people. For non-trivial tasks, reactive behaviors (relying on signals from
sensors) have to be complemented by behaviors relying on reasoning that can
only be done on grounded symbols. The use of a symbolic model enables data
fusion among different sensors and agents operating in related environments.
Symbolic interpretations can be successfully shared, and make it possible to integrate in compact models distributed information. The anchoring problem still

F. Esposito (Ed.): AI*IA 2001, LNAI 2175, pp. 327–332, 2001.

needs a formal definition. In the next section, we introduce a general model to represent concepts and instances, and a procedure to relate them to the corresponding physical objects through the respective perceptual image. In the third section, we discuss how our model applies to multi-agent systems, by focusing on sharing knowledge.

2   Knowledge Representation and Anchoring

Among the properties that can be obtained by basing anchoring on a knowledge model we mention here: *noise filtering, sensorial coherence, virtual sensing, consistency in time,* and *abstraction*.

The knowledge representation model we propose for anchoring is based on the notion of *concept* and its *properties*. A property is a tuple

$$p \triangleq\ < label, \mathbb{D}, \rho >, \tag{1}$$

where *label* denotes the property, $\mathbb{D}$ is the set of all the possible values for that property given a specific representation code (e.g., for the colors we can use the set $\{red, green, blue, \ldots\}$ or the RGB space $\mathbb{N}^3_{[0,255]}$) and ρ represents a restriction of the domain $\mathbb{D}$ for that property in the specific concept.

Two properties p_1 and p_2 are *compatible*, $p_1 \sim p_2$, if they have the same label and domain or a mapping between the respective domains exists. A property p_1 includes p_2 if they are compatible and the restriction of domain $\rho_1(\mathbb{D})$ is included in the restriction of domain $\rho_2(\mathbb{D})$:

$$p_1 \subseteq p_2 \Leftrightarrow (p_1 \sim p_2) \wedge (\rho_1(\mathbb{D}) \subseteq \rho_2(\mathbb{D})) \tag{2}$$

A set of properties describes a *concept C*, which is used in our model to represent the knowledge about perceptual images of physical objects. Depending on the concept and on the specific domain a property can be classified as *substantial* or *accidental* (respectively S and A in equation 3).

$$C \triangleq \{< p, \mathtt{x} >\} : \ \mathtt{x} \in \{\mathtt{S}, \mathtt{A}\}. \tag{3}$$

Substantial properties characterize the immutable part of a concept; for a given object, their values do not change over time, and they can be used for object recognition since they explain the essence of the object they represent. Accidental properties are those properties that do not characterize a concept; their values for the specific instance can vary over time, they cannot be used for object recognition, but they are the basis of instance formation, tracking, and model validation.

We call the set of properties for a concept i as P_i, and the partial function defining the type of property ϕ:

$$\phi : \bigcup_i (C_i \times P_i) \rightarrow \{\mathtt{A}, \mathtt{S}\}. \tag{4}$$

The *extension* $\epsilon(C)$ of the concept C is the set of all its possible instances. The *intension* $\iota(C)$ of the concept C is the set of all its substantial properties.

The fundamental structural relationships between concepts are *specialization* and *generalization*. We say that a concept C_2 specializes a concept C_1 (we denote that with $C_2 = \sigma(C_1)$) when it is defined by a superset of the C_1 properties and compatible properties are included, i.e., when:

$$(\iota(C_2) \supseteq \iota(C_1)) \wedge (\epsilon(C_2) \subseteq \epsilon(C_1)),\tag{5}$$

Concepts C_2 and C_3 that specialize C_1 do that in a *partial* way or a *total* way; we have a total specialization iff

$$\epsilon(C_2) \cup \epsilon(C_3) = \epsilon(C_1),\tag{6}$$

otherwise we have a partial specialization. Concepts C_2 and C_3 that specialize C_1 do that in an *overlapping* way or an *exclusive* way; we have an exclusive specialization iff

$$\epsilon(C_2) \cap \epsilon(C_3) = \emptyset,\tag{7}$$

otherwise we have a overlapping specialization.

Using concepts it is possible to describe the knowledge used by the agent during the anchoring process. We introduce the notion of *model*: given the set of the known domains $\mathcal{D}$, a model $\mathcal{M}_d$ is the set of all the concepts known by the agent referring to the specific domain $d \in \mathcal{D}$, linked by (structural and domain specific) relationships. A relationship between concepts may represent:

1. a *constraint* that must be satisfied by concept instances in order to belong to the model
2. a *function* that generates property values for a concept from property values of another (inference function)
3. a *structural constraint* to be used when reasoning about classification and uncertainty

2.1   The Anchoring Process

Sensors produce a description of perceptual images in terms of set of features. Each feature f is represented as a pair

$$f \triangleq < label, value >,\tag{8}$$

where *label* is the symbolic name of the property the feature refers to, and *value* is the value of the feature belonging to an appropriate set of possible values $\mathbb{D}$. This activity can be considered as the *symbol grounding* phase in the anchoring process: percepts are interpreted as symbolic features to be classified as concept instances and maintained in time.

When enough information (i.e., features) is collected for an object in the environment, it is possible to detect, by a *classification* process γ, a concept matching the perceived object and to generate an instance of it, with the related degree of reliability:

$$\gamma : \wp(\{f\}) \rightarrow \{\overline{C}\} \times \Re_{[0,1]}, \tag{9}$$

where $\wp(\{f\})$ is the power set of all the features. In doing this, we use as classification criteria the *degree of matching* of the features perceived by sensors about the object and the substantial properties of the concepts. After classification, all the substantial and accidental properties associated to the concept can be used to reason about the concept instance.

In this phase we notice how *sensor fusion*– the aggregation of features from different sensors referring to the same object in the environment – can be easily implemented using *clustering* techniques considering the distance between the features values, common subsets of features, or domain specific knowledge represented by relationships among concepts.

The matching degree among concepts and features describing an object in the environment can be computed by any *pattern matching* algorithm that takes into account that: only partial descriptions of perceptual images may be available, only substantial properties are relevant, and not all properties have the same expressive power in describing a concept. Pattern matching for a concept C is done on the intension $\iota(C)$ of the concepts, but only instances belonging to the extension $\epsilon(C)$ of the concepts can be accepted.

Pattern matching, as symbol grounding, has to deal with uncertainty, since the classification process can be affected by noisy features, partial descriptions of objects, and partial contradictions among concept properties or in relationships among instances. We call θ the function that associates a concept instance to its reliability value. Concept instances related to more intensive concepts are in general less reliable, since they require matching more features and matching problems are common in real world applications:

$$\iota(C_1) \subseteq \iota(C_2) \Rightarrow \theta(\overline{C_1}) \geq \theta(\overline{C_2}) \tag{10}$$

From the instances of concepts $\overline{C}_i$ and the model $\mathcal{M}_E$ it is possible to infer new concept instances using relationships between concepts representing specific knowledge for the application domain. We define as instance of the environment model $\overline{\mathcal{M}}_E$ the set of all concept instances either derived from the classification process or from inference on concept instances that are compatible with the relationships contained in the model itself:

$$\overline{\mathcal{M}}_E \equiv \{\overline{C} : C \in \mathcal{M}_E\}. \tag{11}$$

The *state* of the system represented by the model instance $\overline{\mathcal{M}}_E$ is the set of all values of accidental properties – time variant and not – of concept instances belonging to the model itself. The *tracking* phase of anchoring consists of maintaining in time a coherent state of $\overline{\mathcal{M}}_E$ and a correct classification of instances. In doing this, accidental properties have to be monitored during time, using state prediction techniques such as linear regression or Kalman filtering.

3   Extension to Multi-agent Systems

So far, we have dealt with world modelling processes in a single–agent architecture. It is expected that in a multi–agent context each agent could take advantage of data perceived by its teammates. Having the opportunity to combine different local representations, it is possible to build a shared viewpoint of the common environment, that we call *global representation*. In doing this we suppose that each agent shares the same ontology containing *global concepts (GC)*.

The global representation builder receives as input the instances of models produced by the local processes. Each model instance contains a set of instances of concepts (e.g., wall, robot, person, etc.). The agent having those instances in its $\overline{\mathcal{M}_E}$ is the *owner* and specifies a reliability value associated to the anchoring process, considering reliability of sensors in the operating conditions, pattern matching, and so on.

The global representation building process achieves fusion of concept instances through a clustering process. We define *cluster* a set of concept instances related to concepts whose extensions have a non-null intersection and "similar" values for the accidental properties. The meaning of "similar" is given by the following partial function δ, defined only for compatible properties:

$$\delta : \rho_{p_1}(\mathbb{D}) \times \rho_{p_2}(\mathbb{D}) \mapsto \{\text{true}, \text{false}\}. \tag{12}$$

This function, given two values of compatible properties p_1 and p_2, returns true if the related concept instances can coexist in the same cluster, false otherwise.

Two concept instances $\overline{C}_1$ and $\overline{C}_2$ can belong to the same cluster if:

1. their accidental properties are similar:

$$\forall p_i \in P_1, \forall p_j \in P_2 :$$
$$(p_i \sim p_j) \wedge (\phi(C_1, p_i) = \mathsf{A}) \wedge (\phi(C_2, p_j) = \mathsf{A}) \Rightarrow \delta(\overline{p_i}, \overline{p_j}) = \text{true}$$

2. they have a different owner
3. the respective concepts are not mutually exclusive, i.e.,

$$\epsilon(C_1) \cap \epsilon(C_2) \neq \emptyset.$$

For instance, *person* and *man* are two compatible concepts, while *man* and *woman* cannot belong to the same cluster, since no man is a woman, but men are persons; moreover instances of concepts like *woman* and *soldier* can belong to the same cluster since some women are soldiers.

A new global concept instance $(\overline{GC})$ is extracted for each cluster, and its accidental properties are deduced from the accidental properties of the cluster elements by a fusion process that takes into consideration also their reliability values. A $\overline{GC}$ can be an instance of any concept among those relative to the concept instances belonging to the cluster and its reliability is evaluated by combining their reliability values; clusters having more elements and less intensive concepts produce more reliable $\overline{GC}$s.

A global representation gives to the MAS some interesting qualities (that justify the flourishing of several recent works about this topic [4][5]): *robustness*, *extensive sensing, fault tolerance*, and *cooperation*

4   Conclusions

In this paper we have presented the anchoring problem and a model to face it. Although a model for anchoring has been already proposed with some applications [3][2], we propose an alternative approach to establish a general framework for anchoring, suitable for sensor fusion and multi–agent communication, too. The main advantages and novelties introduced by the proposed solution to the anchoring problem are:

- *general unifying model*: our approach puts in evidence the relationships between anchoring and classical AI notions such as symbol grounding, pattern recognition, state estimation, and clustering
- *separation of concerns*: we propose a framework for automatic instantiaton of a symbolic model of the environment from sensorial percepts given a sound knowledge formalization, thus separating the design of the sensorial apparatus from control architecture
- *integrability of domain knowledge*: the use of classic knowledge representation languages allows to consider domain knowledge deriving also from designers

We consider our model as a possible general formalization of the anchoring problem. It is also suitable for triggering special, active sensing behaviors, working as active anchoring processes [6]. We have also discussed how it can be easily applied to multi–agent systems increasing robustness, reliability, and fault tolerance. More details are given in [1].

References

[1] A. Bonarini, M. Matteucci, and M. Restelli. Anchoring: do we need new solutions to an old problem or do we have old solutions for a new problem? In *Proc. of the AAAI Fall Symposium on Anchoring Symbols to Sensor Data in Single and Multiple Robot Systems*, page In press, Menlo Park, CA, 2001. AAAI Press.

[2] S. Coradeschi and A. Saffiotti. Anchoring symbols to vision data by fuzzy logic. In *Lecture Notes in Computer Science*, volume 1638, pages 104–112. Springer-Verlag, Berlin, D, 1999.

[3] S. Coradeschi and A. Saffiotti. Anchoring symbols to sensor data: Preliminary report. In *Proc. of AAAI*, pages 129–135, Cambridge, MA, 2000. MIT Press.

[4] L. Hugues. Grounded representations for a robots team. In *Proc. of the 2000 IEEE/RSJ Int. Conf. on Intelligent Robots and Systems*, pages 2248–2253, 2000.

[5] D. Jung and A. Zelinsky. Grounded symbolic communication between heterogeneous cooperating robots. *Autonomous Robots*, 8(3):269–292, 2000.

[6] A. Saffiotti and K. LeBlanc. Active perceptual anchoring of robot behavior in a dynamic environment. In *Proc. of the IEEE Int. Conf. on Robotics and Automation (ICRA)*, pages 3796–3802, San Francisco, CA, 2000.

Symbolic and Conceptual Representation of Dynamic Scenes: Interpreting Situation Calculus on Conceptual Spaces

Antonio Chella[1], Marcello Frixione[2], and Salvatore Gaglio[1]

[1] Dip. di Ingegneria Automatica e Informatica, Univ. of Palermo, Italy
and CERE-CNR, Palermo, Italy
{chella,gaglio}@unipa.it
[2] Dip. di Scienze della Comunicazione, Univ. of Salerno, Italy
frix@dist.unige.it

Abstract. In (Chella et al. [1,2]) we proposed a framework for the representation of visual knowledge, with particular attention to the analysis and the representation of scenes with moving objects and people. One of our aims is a principled integration of the models developed within the artificial vision community with the propositional knowledge representation systems developed within symbolic AI. In the present note we show how the approach we adopted fits well with the representational choices underlying one of the most popular symbolic formalisms used in cognitive robotics, namely the *situation calculus*.

1 Our Model of Visual Perception: An Overall View

In (Chella et al. [1,2]) we proposed a theoretical framework for the representation of knowledge extracted from visual data. One of our aims is a principled integration of the approaches developed within the artificial vision community, and the propositional systems developed within symbolic knowledge representation in AI. It is our assumption that such an integration requires the introduction of a *conceptual level* of representation that is in some way intermediate between the processing of visual data and declarative, propositional representations. In this note we argue that the conceptual representation we adopted for representing motion is compatible with one of the most influential symbolic formalisms used in cognitive robotics, namely the *situation calculus* (Reiter [10]). In the rest of this section we summarize the main assumptions underlying our proposal. Section 2 is devoted to a synthetic description of our conceptual level representation of motion. Section 3 shows how situation calculus can be mapped on the conceptual representation we adopted. A short conclusion follows.

On the one hand, the computer vision community approached the problem of the representation of dynamic scenes mainly in terms of the construction of 3D models, and of the recovery of suitable motion parameters, possibly in the presence of noise and occlusions. On the other hand, the KR community developed rich and expressive systems for representation of time, of actions and, in general, of dynamic situations.

F. Esposito (Ed.): AI*IA 2001, LNAI 2175, pp. 333–343, 2001.

Nevertheless, these two traditions evolved separately and concentrated on different kinds of problems. The computer vision researchers implicitly assumed that the problem of visual representation ends with the 3D reconstruction of moving scenes. The KR tradition in classical, symbolic AI usually underestimated the problem of grounding symbolic representations in the data coming from sensors.

It is our opinion that this state of affairs constitutes a strong limitation for the development of artificial autonomous systems (typically, robotic systems). It is certainly true that several aspects of the interaction between perception and behaviour in artificial agents can be faced in a rather reactive fashion, with perception more or less directly coupled to action, without the mediation of complex internal representations. However, we maintain that this is not sufficient to model all the relevant types of behaviour. For many kinds of complex tasks, a more flexible mediation between perception and action is required. In such cases the coupling between perception and action is likely to be "knowledge driven", and the role of explicit forms of representation is crucial. Our model can be intended as a suggestion to provide artificial agents with the latter of the above-mentioned functionalities.

We assume that a principled integration of the approaches of artificial vision and of symbolic KR requires the introduction of a missing link between these two kinds of representation. In our approach, the role of such a link is played by the notion of *conceptual space* (Gärdenfors [3]). A conceptual space (CS) is a representation where information is characterized in terms of a metric space defined by a number of *cognitive* dimensions. These dimensions are independent from any specific language of representation. According to Gärdenfors, a CS acts as an intermediate representation between subconceptual knowledge (i.e., knowledge that is not yet conceptually categorized), and symbolically organized knowledge.

According to this view, our architecture is organised in three *computational areas*. Figure 1 schematically shows the relations among them. The *subconceptual* area is concerned with the low level processing of perceptual data coming from the sensors. The term subconceptual suggests that here information is not yet organised in terms of conceptual structures and categories. In this perspective, our subconceptual area includes a 3D model of the perceived scenes. Indeed, even if such a kind of representation cannot be considered "low level" from the point of view of artificial vision, in our perspective it still remains below the level of conceptual categorisation.

In the *linguistic* area, representation and processing are based on a propositional KR formalism (a logic-oriented representation language). In the *conceptual* area, the data coming from the subconceptual area are organised in conceptual categories, which are still independent from any linguistic characterisation. The symbols in the linguistic area are grounded on sensory data by mapping them on the representations in the conceptual area.

In a nutshell, the performances of our model can be summarised as follows: it takes in input a set of images corresponding to subsequent phases of the

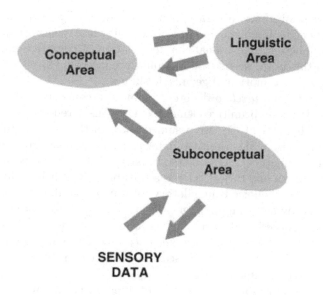

Fig. 1. The three areas of representation, and the relations among them.

evolution of a certain dynamic scene, and it produces in output a declarative description of the scene, formulated as a set of assertions written in a symbolic representation language. The generation of such a description is driven both by the "a priori", symbolic knowledge initially stored within the linguistic area, and by the information learned by a neural network component.

The purpose of this note is to show that the conceptual representation we adopted for dynamic scenes (and that is described in details in Chella et al. [2]) is homogeneous with the representational choices underlying one of the most popular symbolic formalisms used in cognitive robotics, namely the *situation calculus* (Reiter [10]). In this way, our dynamic conceptual spaces could offer a conceptual interpretation for situation calculus, which could help in anchoring propositional representations to the perceptual activities of a robotic system.

2   Conceptual Spaces for Representing Motion

Representations in the conceptual area are couched in terms of *conceptual spaces* (Gärdenfors [3]). Conceptual spaces provide a principled way for relating high level, linguistic formalisms on the one hand, with low level, unstructured representation of data on the other. A conceptual space CS is a metric space whose dimensions are in some way related to the quantities processed in the subconceptual area. Different cognitive tasks may presuppose different conceptual spaces, and different conceptual spaces can be characterised by different dimensions. Examples of dimensions of a CS could be colour, pitch, mass, spatial co-ordinates, and so on. In some cases dimensions are strictly related to sensory data; in other cases they are more abstract in nature. Anyway, dimensions do not depend on any specific linguistic description. In this sense, conceptual spaces come before any symbolic-propositional characterisation of cognitive phenomena. In particular, in this note, we take into account a conceptual space devoted to the representation of the motion of geometric shapes.

We use the term *knoxel* to denote a point in a conceptual space. A knoxel is an epistemologically primitive element at the considered level of analysis. For example, in (Chella et al. [1]) we assumed that, in the case of static scenes, a knoxel coincides with a 3D primitive shape, characterised according to some constructive solid geometry (CSG) schema. In particular, we adopted superquadrics (Pentland [7], Solina and Bajcsy [11]) as a suitable CSG schema. However, we do not assume that this choice is mandatory for our proposal. Our approach could be reformulated by adopting different models of 3D representation.

The entities represented in the linguistic area usually do not correspond to single knoxels. We assume that *complex entities* correspond to sets of knoxels. For example, in the case of a static scene, a complex shape corresponds to the set of knoxels of its simple constituents.

In order to account for the perception of dynamic scenes, we choose to adopt an intrinsically *dynamic conceptual space*. It has been hypothesised that simple motions are categorised in their wholeness, and not as sequences of static frames. According to this hypothesis, we define a dynamic conceptual space in such a way that every knoxel corresponds to a simple motion of a 3D primitive. In other words, we assume that simple motions of geometrically primitive shapes are our perceptual primitives for motion perception. As we choose superquadrics as geometric primitives, a knoxel in our dynamic conceptual space correspond to a simple motion of a superquadric.

Of course, the decision of which kind of motion can be considered "simple" is not straightforward, and is strictly related to the problem of motion segmentation. Marr and Vaina [4] adopted the term *motion segment* to indicate such simple movements. According to their SMS (State-Motion-State) schema, a simple motion is individuated by the interval between two subsequent overall rest states.

Such rest states may be instantaneous. Consider a person moving an arm up and down. According to Marr and Vaina's proposal, the upward trajectory of the forearm can be considered a simple motion, that is represented in CS by a single knoxel, say $\mathbf{k_a}$. When the arm reaches its vertical position, an instantaneous rest state occurs. The second part of the trajectory of the forearm is another simple motion that corresponds to a second knoxel, say $\mathbf{k_a'}$. The same holds for the upper arm: the first part of its trajectory corresponds to a certain knoxel $\mathbf{k_b}$; the second part (after the rest state) corresponds to a further knoxel $\mathbf{k_b'}$.

In intrinsically dynamic conceptual spaces, a knoxel $\mathbf{k}$ corresponds to a *generalised* simple motion of a 3D primitive shape. By *generalised* we mean that the motion can be decomposed in a set of components x_i, each of them associated with a degree of freedom of the moving primitive shape. In other words, we have:

$$\mathbf{k} = [x_1, x_2, \ldots, x_n]$$

where n is the number of degrees of freedom of the moving superquadric. In this way, changes in shape and size are also taken into account.

In turn, each motion x_i corresponding to the i-th degree of freedom can be viewed as the result of the superimposition of a set of elementary motions f_j^i:

$$x_i = \sum_j X_j^i f_j^i$$

In this way, it is possible to individuate a set of basis functions f_j^i, in terms of which any simple motion can be expressed. Such functions can be associated to the axes of the dynamic conceptual space as its dimensions. In this way, the dynamic CS results in a functional space. The theory of function approximation offers different possibilities for the choice of basic motions: trigonometric functions, polynomial functions, wavelets, and so on.

For our purposes, we are not interested in the representation of any possible motion, but only in a compact description of perceptually relevant kinds of motion. In the domain we are facing here, the motions corresponding to each degree of freedom of a superquadric can be viewed as the result of the superimposition of the first low frequency harmonics, according to the well-known Discrete Fourier Transform (DFT) (Oppenheim and Shafer [6], see also Chella et al. [2] for the details).

Figure 2 is an evocative representation of a dynamic conceptual space. In the figure, each group of axes f^i corresponds to the i-th degree of freedom of a simple shape; each axis f_j^i in a group f^i corresponds to the j-th component pertaining to the i-th degree of freedom.

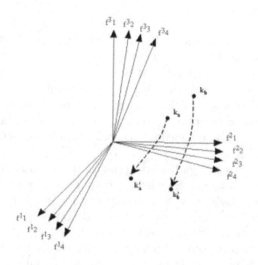

Fig. 2. A dynamic conceptual space.

In this way, each knoxel in a dynamic conceptual space represents a *simple motion*, i.e. the motion of a simple shape occurring within the interval between two subsequent rest states. We call *composite simple motion* a motion of a composite object (i.e. an object approximated by more than one superquadric). A composite simple motion is represented in the CS by the set of knoxels corresponding to the motions of its components. For example, the first part of the trajectory of the whole arm shown in figure 2 is represented as a composite motion made up by the knoxels k_a (the motion of the forearm) and k_b (the motion of the upper arm). Note that in composite simple motions the (simple) motions of their components occur simultaneously. That is to say, a composite simple motion corresponds to a single configuration of knoxels in the conceptual space.

In order to consider the composition of several (simple or composite) motions arranged according to some temporal relation (e.g., a sequence), we introduce the notion of *structured process*. A structured process corresponds to a series of different configurations of knoxels in the conceptual space. We assume that the configurations of knoxels within a single structured process are separated by instantaneous changes. In the transition between two subsequent configurations, the "scattering" of at least one knoxel occurs. This corresponds to a discontinuity in time, and is associated with an instantaneous event.

In the example of the moving arm, a scattering occurs when the arm has reached its vertical position, and begins to move downwards. In a CS representation this amount to say that knoxel k_a (i.e., the upward motion of the forearm) is replaced by knoxel k'_a, and knoxel k_b is replaced by k'_b. In fig. 2 such scattering is graphically suggested by the dotted arrows connecting respectively k_a to k'_a, and k_b to k'_b.

3   Mapping Symbolic Representations on Conceptual Spaces

In (Chella et al. [2]) the formalism adopted for the linguistic area was a KL-ONE like semantic net, equivalent to a subset of the first order predicate language. In this note we propose the adoption of the *situation calculus* as the formalism for the linguistic area. Indeed, the kind of representation it presupposes is in many respects homogeneous to the conceptual representation described in the previous section. In this section we suggest how a representation in terms of situation calculus could be mapped on the conceptual representation presented above.

Situation calculus is a logic based approach to knowledge representation, developed in order to express knowledge about actions and change using the language of predicate logic. It was primarily developed by John McCarthy [5]; for an up to date and exhaustive overview see (Reiter [10]).

The basic idea behind situation calculus is that the evolution of a state of affairs can be modelled in terms of a sequence of situations. The world changes when some *action* is performed. So, given a certain situation s_1, performing a certain action a will result in a new situation s_2. Actions are the sole sources of change of the word: if the situation of the word changes from, say, s_i to s_j, then some action has been performed.

Situation calculus is formalised using the language of predicate logic. Situations and actions are denoted by first order terms. The two place function *do* takes as its arguments an action and a situation: $do(a, s)$ denotes the new situation obtained by performing the action a in the situation s.

Classes of actions can be represented as functions. For example, the one argument function symbol *pick_up*(x) could be assumed to denote the class of the actions consisting in picking up an object x. Given a first order term o denoting a specific object, the term *pick_up*(o) denotes the specific action consisting in picking up o.

As a state of affairs evolves, it can happen that properties and relations change their values. In situation calculus, properties and relations that can change their truth value from one situation to another are called (relational) *fluents*. An example of fluent could be the property of being red: it can happen that it is true that a certain object is red in a certain situation, and it becomes false in another. Fluents are denoted by predicate symbols that take a situation as their last argument. For example, the fluent corresponding to the property of being red can be represented as a two place relation $red(x, s)$, where $red(o, s1)$ is true if the object o is red in the situation s_1.

Different sequences of actions lead to different situations. In other words, it can never be the case that performing some action starting form different situations can result in the same situation. If two situations derive from different situations, they are in their turn different, in spite of their similarity. In order to account for the fact that two different situations can be indistinguishable from the point of view of the properties that hold in them, the notion of *state* is introduced. Consider two situations s_1 and s_2; if they satisfy the same fluents, then we say that s_1 and s_2 correspond to the same state. That is to say, the state of a situation is the set of the fluents that are true in it.

In the ordinary discourse, there are lot of actions that have a temporal duration. For example, the action of walking from certain point in space to another takes some time. In the situation calculus all actions in the strict sense are assumed to be instantaneous. Actions that have a duration are represented as processes, that are initiated and are terminated by instantaneous actions (see Pinto [8], Reiter [10] chapter 7). Suppose that we want to represent the action of moving an object x from point y to point z. We have to assume that moving x from y to z is a process, that is initiated by an instantaneous action, say *start_move*(x, y, z), and is terminated by another instantaneous action, say *end_move*(x, y, z). In the formalism of situation calculus, processes correspond to relational fluents. For example, the process of moving x from y to z corresponds to a fluent, say *moving*(x, y, z, s). A formula like *moving*$(o, p1, p2, s1)$ means that in situation s_1 the object o is moving from position p_1 to position p_2.

This approach is analogous to the representation of actions adopted in the dynamic conceptual spaces described in the preceding section. In a nutshell, a scattering in the conceptual space CS corresponds to an (instantaneous) *action*. A knoxel corresponds to a particular *process*. A configuration of knoxels in CS corresponds to a *state*. Note that a configuration of knoxels does not correspond to a situation, because, at least in principle, the same configuration of knoxels could be reached starting from different configurations.

Consider for example a scenario in which a certain object o moves from position $p1p_1$ to position p_2, and then rests in p_2. When the motion of o from p_1 towards p_2 starts, a scattering occurs in the conceptual space CS, and a certain knoxel, say k_1, becomes active in it. Such a scattering corresponds to an (instantaneous) action that could be represented by a term like $start\_move(o, p1, p2)$. The knoxel k_1 corresponds in CS to the process consisting in the motion of the object o. During all the time in which o remains in such a motion state, the CS remains unchanged (provided that nothing else is happening in the considered scenario), and k_1 continue to be active in it. In the meanwhile, the fluent $moving(o, p1, p2, s)$ persists to be true. When o's motion ends, a further scattering occurs, k_1 disappears, and a new knoxel k_2 becomes active. This second scattering corresponds to an instantaneous action $end\_moving(o, p1, p2)$. The knoxel k_2 corresponds to o's rest. During the time in which k_2 is active in CS, the fluent $staying(o, p2, s1)$ is true.

In its traditional version, situation calculus does not allow to account for concurrency. Actions are assumed to occur sequentially, and it is not possible to represent several instantaneous actions occurring at the same time instant. For our purposes, this limitations is too severe. When a scattering occurs in a CS it may happen that more knoxels are affected. This is tantamount to say that several instantaneous actions occur concurrently. For example, according to our terminology (as it has been established in the preceding section), a composite simple motion is a motion of a composite object (i.e. an object approximated by more than one superquadric). A composite simple motion is represented in the CS by the set of knoxels corresponding to the motions of its components. For example, the trajectory of a whole arm moving upward (cfr. the example in the previous section) is represented as a composite motion made up by the knoxels $\mathbf{k_a}$ (the upward motion of the forearm) and $\mathbf{k_b}$ (the upward motion of the upper arm).

Suppose that we want to represent such a motion within the situation calculus. According to what stated before, moving an arm is represented as a process, that is started by a certain action, say $start\_move\_arm$, and that is terminated by another action, say end_move_arm. (For sake of simplicity, no arguments of such actions - e.g. the agent, the starting position, the final position - are taken into account here). The process of moving the arm is represented as a fluent $moving\_arm(s)$, that is true if in situation s the arm is moving. The scattering in CS corresponding to both $start\_move\_arm$ and end_move_arm involves two knoxels, namely $\mathbf{k_a}$ and $\mathbf{k_b}$, that correspond respectively to the motion of the forearm and to the motion of the upper arm. Consider for example $start\_move\_arm$. It is composed by two concurrent actions that could be named *start_move_forearm* and *start_move_upper_arm*, both corresponding to the scattering of one knoxel in CS (resp. $\mathbf{k_a}$ and $\mathbf{k_b}$).

Extensions of situation calculus that allows for a treatment of concurrency have been proposed in the literature (Reiter [9,10]; Pinto [8]). Pinto [8] adds to the language of the situation calculus a two argument function +, that, given two actions as its arguments, produces an action as its result. In particular, if a_1 and a_2 are two actions, $a_1 + a_2$ denotes the action of performing a_1 and a_2 concurrently. According to this approach, an action is *primitive* if it is not the result of other actions performed concurrently. In our approach, the scattering of a single knoxel in CS correspond to a primitive action; several knoxels scattering at the same time correspond to a complex action resulting from concurrently performing different primitive actions.

Therefore, according to Pinto's notation, the representation of the arm motion example in the formalism of the (concurrent) situation calculus involves four primitive actions:

$$start\_move\_forearm$$
$$start\_move\_upper\_arm$$
$$end\_move\_forearm$$
$$end\_move\_upper\_arm$$

and two non primitive actions:

$$start\_move\_arm = start\_move\_forearm + start\_move\_upper\_arm$$
$$end\_move\_arm = end\_move\_forearm + end\_move\_upper\_arm$$

In addition, the three following fluents are needed:

moving_arm (a formula like *moving_arm(s)* is true if in the CS configuration corresponding to the situation s both ka and kb are present);

moving_forearm (a formula like *moving_forearm(s)* is true if in the CS configuration corresponding to the situation s ka is present);

moving_upper_arm (a formula like *moving_upper_arm(s)* is true if in the CS configuration corresponding to the situation s kb is present).

4   Some Conclusions

In the above section we suggested a possible interpretation of the language of situation calculus in terms of conceptual spaces. In this way situation calculus could be chosen as the linguistic area formalism for our model, with the advantage of adopting a powerful, well understood and widespread formal tool. Besides this, we maintain that a conceptual interpretation of situation calculus would be interesting in itself. Indeed, it could be considered complementary with respect to traditional, model theoretic interpretations for logic oriented representation languages.

Model theoretic semantics (in its different versions: purely Tarskian for extensional languages, possible worlds semantics for modal logic, preferential semantics for non monotonic formalisms, and so on) has been developed with the aim of accounting for certain metatheoretical properties of logical formalisms (such as logical consequence, validity, correctness, completeness, and son on). However, it is of no help in establishing how symbolic representations are anchored to their referents.

In addition, the model theoretic approach to semantics is "ontologically uniform", in the sense that it hides the ontological differences between entities denoted by expressions belonging to the same syntactic type. For example, all the individual terms of a logical language are mapped onto elements of the domain, no matter of the deep ontological variety that may exist between the objects that constitute their intended interpretation. Consider the situation calculus. According to its usual syntax, situations, actions and objects are all represented as first order individual terms; therefore, they are all mapped on elements of the domain. This does not constitute a problem given the above mentioned purposes of model theoretic semantics. However, it becomes a serious drawback if the aim is that of anchoring symbols to their referents through the sensory activities of an agent.

In this perspective, it is our opinion that an interpretation of symbols in terms of conceptual spaces of the form sketched in the above pages could offer:

- a kind of interpretation that does not constitute only a metatheoretic device allowing to single out certain properties of the symbolic formalism; rather, it is assumed to offer a further level of representation that is, in some sense, closer to the data coming from sensors, and that, for this reason, can help in anchoring the symbols to the external world.
- A kind of interpretation that accounts for the ontological differences between the entities denoted by symbols belonging to the same syntactic category. This would result in a richer and finer grained model, that stores information that is not explicitly represented at the symbolic level, and that therefore can offer a further source of "analogic" inferences, offering at the same time a link between deliberative inferential processes, and forms of inference that are closer to the lower levels of the cognitive architecture (reactive behaviours, and so on).

Acknowledgements

This work has been partially supported by MURST "Progetto Cofinanziato CERTAMEN".

References

1. Chella, A., Frixione, M. and Gaglio, S.: A cognitive architecture for artificial vision, *Artificial Intelligence*, **89**, pp. 73-111, 1997.
2. Chella, A. Frixione, M. and Gaglio, S.: Undertsanding dynamic scenes, *Artificial Intelligence*, **123**, pp. 89-132, 2000.
3. Gärdenfors, P.: *Conceptual Spaces*, Cambridge, MA, MIT Press, 2000.
4. Marr, D. and Vaina, L.: Representation and recognition of the movements of shapes, *Proc. R. Soc. Lond. B*, **214**, pp. 501-524, 1982.
5. McCarty, J.: Situations, actions and causal laws. Technical Report, Stanford University, 1963. Reprinted in M. Minsky (ed.): *Semantic Information Processing*, MIT Press, Cambridge, Mass., pp. 410-417, 1968.
6. Oppenheim, A.V. and Shafer, R.W.: *Discrete-Time Signal Processing*, Englewood Cliffs, NJ, Prentice Hall, 1989.
7. Pentland, A.P.: Perceptual organization and the representation of natural forms, *Artificial Intelligence*, **28**, pp. 293-331, 1986.
8. Pinto, J.: Temporal Reasoning in the Situation Calculus. Ph.D. Thesis, Dept. of Computer Science, Univ. of Toronto, Jan. 1994.
9. Reiter, R.: Natural actions, concurrency and continuous time in the situation calculus. In: *Principles of Knowledge Representation and Reasoning: Proceedings of the Fifth International Conference (KR'96)*, Cambridge, Massachusetts, U.S.A. November 5-8, 1996.
10. Reiter, R.: *Knowledge in Action: Logical Foundations for Describing and Implementing Dynamical Systems*. MIT Press, Cambridge, Mass., 2001.
11. Solina, F. and Bajcsy, R.: Recovery of parametric models from range images: The case for superquadrics with global deformations, *IEEE Trans. Patt. Anal. Mach. Intell.*, **12**(2), pp. 131-146, 1990.

A Non-traditional Omnidirectional Vision System with Stereo Capabilities for Autonomous Robots

Giovanni Adorni, Luca Bolognini, Stefano Cagnoni, and Monica Mordonini

Department of Communications, Computers and System Science, University of Genoa
Department of Computer Engineering, University of Parma

Abstract. In this paper we describe a vision system based on the use of both an omnidirectional vision sensor and a standard CCD camera. This hybrid system is aimed at compensating for drawbacks of both sensors and at offering new opportunities deriving by their joint use. It can be used in several tasks, such as implementation of peripheral/foveal vision strategies, stereo vision, etc. The paper describes the device on which the vision system is based and its use as a stereo system for obstacle detection in a semi-structured environment, based on a perspective removal algorithm.

1 Introduction

The ever-growing computer performances, along with the ever-decreasing cost of video equipment allows nowadays for the development of robots that rely mostly, or even exclusively, on vision for real-time navigation and operation. In many cases, autonomous robot perception is based on the fusion of data coming from different sensory sources. However, such sensory systems require that navigation algorithms harmonize data of very different nature [1]. In fact, the use of vision as the only sensory input makes artificial perception closer to human perception with respect to the case in which other kinds of sensors, such as laser scanners or infra-red beams, are used. Therefore, vision-based navigation allows for more natural or even biologically-based approaches [2].

As robot navigation is moving to less and less structured environments, the need for sensory systems that provide a global, even if sometimes rough, description of the surrounding environment is increasing. This has stimulated growing interest in omnidirectional vision systems. In indoor semi-structured environments, cheap and fast self-localization strategies can be based on that kind of sensors. In [3], a 360° low-resolution image acquired through a very simple omnidirectional sensor is used in an approach based on a neuro-fuzzy control strategy.

Omnidirectional vision systems are usually based on a catadioptric sensor, consisting of an upwards-oriented camera that acquires the image reflected on a convex mirror hanging above it. Anyway, a number of such sensors are available and, consequently, a large number of approaches to omnidirectional vision are described in literature [4, 5].

Besides providing the widest possible field of view, omnidirectional vision systems can obviate the need for active cameras, that require complex control strategies. However, they suffer from two main limitations. The most relevant one is that the near field, which is the least distorted part of the image, is partially obstructed by the reflection

F. Esposito (Ed.): AI*IA 2001, LNAI 2175, pp. 344–355, 2001.

of the camera on the mirror. A further limitation is that the accumulation of the camera and system distortions makes it quite difficult either to find the resulting distortion law and to compensate it, or to design a mirror profile that can achieve a good trade-off between width of the field of view, image resolution and distortion. To reduce this effect, mirrors that produce a non-distorted image of a reference plane have been recently described [6, 7, 8].

Omnidirectional systems are therefore very efficient as concerns detection speed of the target position, but critical from the point of view of the accuracy with which the target is detected. For these reasons, in several cases, the omnidirectional vision sensor has been integrated with a different kind of sensor, to make object detection and robot self-localization more precise and robust (see, for example [9, 10, 11, 12]).

In this paper we present a vision system prototype (called HOPS, Hybrid Omni-directional/ Pin-hole Sensor), that consists of an omnidirectional sensor coupled with a standard CCD camera. HOPS was designed with the main intent of providing autonomous robots with the most useful features of both omnidirectional and traditional vision systems, to perform navigation tasks. The paper describes HOPS and an obstacle detection method that was implemented for use with the hybrid sensor.

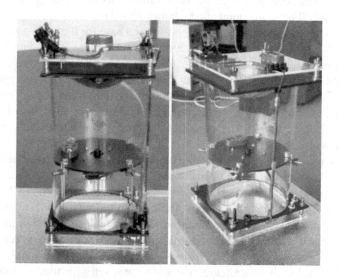

Fig. 1. Two views of the HOPS prototype.

2   HOPS: A Hybrid Omnidirectional/Pin-Hole Sensor

HOPS (shown in figure 1) is a hybrid vision sensor prototype that integrates omnidirectional vision with traditional pin-hole vision, to overcome the limitations of the two approaches. It can be best described as a color CCD camera mounted on top of an omnidirectional catadioptric sensor. Its lower part consists of an omnidirectional sensor

Fig. 2. Example of images that can be acquired through the omnidirectional sensor (left) and the top CCD camera (right).

that relies on a color CCD camera pointing upwards at a convex mirror, whose profile is given by the intersection between a cone and a sphere (see [13] for details). This mirror shape permits to image objects that are closer to the sensor with respect to classical off-the-shelf conical mirrors that are usually adopted for omnidirectional vision. This kind of design has been suggested by the requirements of RoboCup, in which robots need to see the ball up to the point at which they touch it.

The top of the omnidirectional sensor provides a base for the more traditional CCD-camera based sensor that leans on it. The traditional camera is fixed and looks down with a tilt angle of 60° with respect to the ground plane and has a field of view of about 80°. To allow for a higher stereo disparity between the two images it is positioned off the center of the device, as discussed in section 3.1. The "blind sector" caused by the upper camera cable on the lower sensor is placed at an angle of 180°, in order to relegate it to the "back" of the device. An example of the images that can be obtained by the two sensors is provided in fig. 2.

The aims with which HOPS was designed are accuracy, efficiency and versatility. The joint use of a standard CCD camera and of an omni-directional sensor provides HOPS with all their different and complementary features: while the CCD camera can be used to acquire detailed information about a limited region of interest, the omni-directional sensor provides wide-range, but less detailed, information about the sur-roundings of the system. HOPS, therefore, suits several kinds of applications as, for example, self-localization or obstacle detection, and makes it possible to implement pe-ripheral/foveal active vision strategies: the wide-range sensor is used to acquire a rough representation of a large area around the system and to localize the objects or areas of interest, while the traditional camera is used to enhance the resolution with which these areas are then analyses. The different features of the two sensors of HOPS are very use-ful for a stand-alone use (as we just described) as well as for a combined exploitation in which information gathered from both sensors is fused. In particular, HOPS can be used as a binocular sensor to extract three-dimensional information about the observed scene. This flexibility and versatility permits to use HOPS in several applications. As a first "building block" for a full HOPS-based robot navigation system, an obstacle detection method was implemented and is described in the following.

3 Obstacle Detection with a Hybrid Vision System

The idea of using inverse perspective for obstacle detection was first introduced in [14]. If one applies the inverse perspective transform (IPT) with respect to the same plane to a pair of stereo images, everything that lies on that plane looks the same in both views, while everything that does not is distorted differently, depending on the geometry of the two cameras through which the stereo pair is acquired. This property is particularly useful for tasks in which a relevant reference plane can be easily found. This is the case for navigation, either for vehicles traveling on roads (see, for example, [15, 16] and [17] for a review on the subject) or for indoor-operating autonomous robots [18, 19]. Three steps are usually required to detect obstacles based on stereo vision:

- Application of the inverse perspective transform to each of the two images;
- Subtraction of one image from the other one to compute differences;
- Remapping of the regions where obstacle candidates can be found on at least one of the acquired images, to label pixels either as obstacle or free space.

Stereo vision is usually obtained by two cameras slightly displaced from each other or through the acquisition of two images from a single sensor that can move to simulate the availability of two cameras displaced as above. The sensors can be traditional cameras or even omnidirectional sensors [18].

3.1 Computing Stereo Disparity

Information about the presence of obstacles in the observed scene can be derived from the stereo disparity between the two rectified images. Therefore it is necessary to set the geometry of the two sensors such that enough disparity is obtained, avoiding if possible the presence of any zero-disparity point. As shown below, it should be noticed that, in the case of HOPS, the disparity is not constant and depends on the position of the objects in the scene.

Figure 3 shows a general case study for stereo systems: the same point-obstacle P is observed from two points of view $O1$ and $O2$. The stereo disparity D can be defined as the distance between the two projections of the obstacle cast from $O1$ and $O2$ on the ground plane (the $z = 0$ plane), that is the two points of coordinates $(x_{p1}, y_{p1}, 0)$ and $(x_{p2}, y_{p2}, 0)$. Moreover, it is interesting to represent the disparity D as composed by the two components D_x and D_y since, to process the image for obstacle detection, the best situation is when D_y equals zero. In that case the disparity matching problem becomes one-dimensional. For a binocular sensor with two traditional CCD cameras, $O1$ and $O2$ are represented by the optical centers of the cameras and the stereo disparity is independent of the orientation of the cameras. Fixing the position of the two cameras, it is possible to compute D_x and D_y as functions of the coordinates of P:

$$D_x = h \, \frac{|z_1 - z_2|}{|z_1 z_2|} |X - X_0| = h \, K \, |X - X_0|$$
$$D_y = h \, \frac{|z_1 - z_2|}{|z_1 z_2|} |Y - Y_0| = h \, K \, |Y - Y_0|$$

where (x_1, y_1, z_1) and (x_2, y_2, z_2) represent the coordinates of $O1$ and $O2$, respectively, (X, Y, h) the coordinates of P and $X_0 = \frac{(x_2 z_1 - x_1 z_2)}{(z_1 - z_2)}$. This result shows that there is a

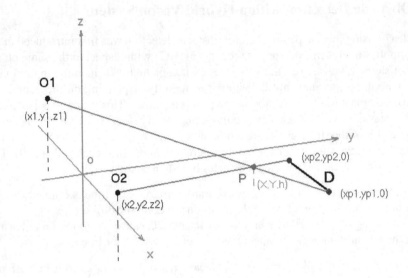

Fig. 3. Schematic representation of the stereo disparity D obtained by looking at the point-obstacle P from the two points of view $O1$ and $O2$. The $x - y$ axis plane is the ground reference plane.

straight line (of equation $X = X_0$) along which any obstacle produces a null disparity independently of its height. In the case of HOPS, $O1$ is the optical center of the upper CCD camera, while $O2$ is the point on the mirror surface that reflects the image of the point-obstacle P onto the second camera. This means that it is possible to reason as in the case of two traditional cameras, with the only difference that now the position of one of the two optic centers depends on the coordinates of the observed obstacle P. In this case we obtain that:

$$D_x = h \, \frac{|z_1 - f(X,Y,h)|}{|z_1 f(X,Y,h)|} |X - X_0(X,Y,h)|$$
$$D_y = h \, \frac{|z_1 - f(X,Y,h)|}{|z_1 f(X,Y,h)|} |Y - Y_0(X,Y,h)|$$

where $f(X,Y,h)$ is the z coordinate of $O2$, function of the position of the obstacle P. The only difference with the result reported above is that there exists a different straight line of null disparity for every possible position of the obstacle. As just shown above, the position of this line depends only on the coordinates of $O1$ and $O2$. If the CCD camera had been placed on the plane $(x = c)$ passing through the symmetry axis of the omni-directional sensor and parallel to the plane $x = 0$, X_0 would equal c where X equals c, so that all the central part of the visible area would have null or very low stereo disparity. That is the reason why the CCD camera was placed as left of this plane as possible.

3.2 Removing Perspective with HOPS

The problem dealt with by the inverse perspective transform consists of computing a correspondence function $P_{x,y} = \mathcal{C}(I_{i,j})$ that maps the pixels (with coordinates (i,j)) belonging to image I onto points of a new image P (with coordinates x, y) that shows a bird's view of a reference plane. From the view obtained by applying $\mathcal{C}(I)$ information about the relative positions of objects (e.g., distances between objects) that lie on the plane can be trivially extracted.

If all parameters related to the geometry of the acquisition systems and to the distortions introduced by the camera were known, the derivation of $\mathcal{C}$ could be straightforward [14, 16, 17, 20]. However, this is not always the case, most often because of the lack of a model of the camera distortion. In most cases, assuming an ellipsoidal model for the camera lens allows for an easy empirical derivation of the related parameters.

On one side, the computation of $\mathcal{C}_o$, the IPT for the catadioptric omnidirectional sensor, is complicated by the non-planar profile of the mirror, while on the other side it is simplified by the symmetry of the device geometry: it is enough to compute the restriction of $\mathcal{C}_o$ along a radius of the mirror projection on the image plane to compute the whole function. However, the mirror used in the HOPS prototype is characterized by a few slight manufacturing flaws that produce significant local distortions in the reflected image. This irregularities require that the IPT be derived empirically, or at least that the ideal model be corrected in the flawed points. Therefore, $\mathcal{C}_o$ was derived both from the ideal profile model and from empirical corrections to such a model.

After applying the IPT to both images acquired by HOPS, two "bird's view" images are obtained based on whose difference obstacle detection can be performed, as described in more details in [21].

3.3 Obstacle Detection with HOPS

The white regions that can be observed in the difference image (figure 4, bottom) obtained from an IPT stereo pair, derive from two kinds of discrepancies that can be found in stereo image pairs. If they derive from a lateral displacement of the two cameras, they are located to the left and/or right of obstacle projections in the IPT transformed images. When a vertical displacement of the two cameras occur instead, such regions are located above and/or below the obstacle projections. For HOPS applications the reference plane is the ground plane on which a robot that mounts the sensor is moving, and obstacles that are to be detected are supposed to be lying on it.

Therefore, using HOPS, typically: i) lateral differences are almost symmetrical and not particularly large; ii) no differences can be detected at the base of the obstacles, as obstacle bases lie on the reference plane; iii) vertical differences are particularly relevant corresponding to the top of obstacles, and directly proportional to the height of the obstacles.

Figure 2 shows an example in which the obstacles are a RoboCup ball and two trash bins. Such a scene will be used as a case study in describing the method.

The difference image D shown in figure 4 is the main input of the obstacle-detection method, even if color information contained in the input images is also used. The method is basically a segmentation method aimed at detecting image regions that have

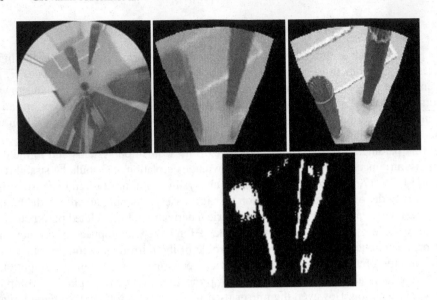

Fig. 4. IPT images obtained from the omnidirectional sensor (above, left) and the standard CCD camera (above, right). The region of the IPT omnidirectional image corresponding to the field of view of the standard camera (above, middle) and the resulting thresholded difference image (below) are also shown.

the obstacle features listed above. The analysis of image D is essentially a bottom-up approach in which fragmented segments of regions of interest are merged and matched together into larger regions, each of which eventually corresponds to an obstacle.

Therefore, after detecting connected regions in D and labelling them using a blob-coloring technique, a set of geometrical features is computed, that allows regions to be classified into one of four possible classes of interest, namely:

1. long vertically-elongated thick regions with two apices in their lower part, that directly identify an obstacle;
2. long vertically-elongated thin regions with a single lower apex, that may represent one of the two lateral difference segments of the typical obstacle "footprint" in D and that usually need to be matched with some other regions to identify an obstacle;
3. short vertically-elongated regions, that may be considered a sub-class of class 2, but to which a lower significance will be attributed in the matching phase;
4. small roundish regions that may represent small obstacles (typically having non-flat surfaces) or parts of them, which typically do not need any matching phase to identify the whole obstacle.

Once regions on the difference image have been classified, the next step is to try and match them (apart from the ones that belong to class 1 and 4, that directly identify obstacles) to detect "obstacle regions". This process is divided in two phases. The first attempts to merge two regions in the difference image and is based on the orientation and color of the neighboring background pixels in the IPT images. Two regions are merged if their orientation differ by less than 0.2 rad and have regions of the same color as neighbors. An example is shown in Figure 5, where the two regions highlighted with a square are merged. The second step is the main matching phase, in which two or more regions in the difference image are matched into an "obstacle region" on the basis of a heuristics that reasons upon orientation and color patterns in the neighboring background. The evaluation of color similarity is made according to a set of fuzzy rules that provide values ranging between 0 (total dissimilarity) to 1 (perfect equality).

 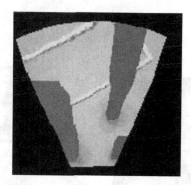

Fig. 5. Left: the results of the blob-coloring algorithm. The two regions highlighted with a square belong to class 3. The two elongated ones belong to class 2; all other regions belong to class 4. Right: the obstacle regions detected by "closing" the regions surrounded by, or corresponding to, the obstacle segments detected in the previous steps.

The final step in the obstacle-detection method can be divided in two phases. In the first one a preliminary rough "closure" of the obstacle regions is made. In the second phase, the region segmentation is refined, based on the assumption that obstacles have uniform color or, more generally, uniform pictorial features in the input images. In the case under consideration, taking color information into account was enough to perform this phase. If the maximum gradient falls below a preset threshold in one of the two IPT images the line is discarded: that is why the large round region on the left (the top of the trash can on the left in the IPT image of the upper camera) has almost completely disappeared in figure 5 (right), where the result of this last phase is shown.

4   Real-World Experiments

To test system performance in obstacle detection several experiments have been performed in indoor environments, like a RoboCup field, corridors and laboratories. In the tests HOPS was mounted on a mobile robot that was required to reach a goal avoiding obstacles, using a planning module that relies on information provided by HOPS as input. Several kinds of obstacles were scattered in the environment. As significant examples, we report the result of two such tests. The first one took place in a corridor (see figure 6). Several still obstacles (like a basket, a chair, a person) and false obstacles

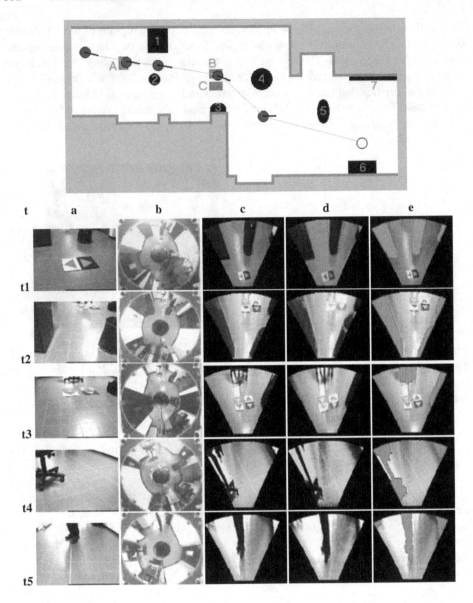

Fig. 6. Example of free space computation along a corridor (shown on top): a) frames acquired by the pin-hole vision sensor; b) frames acquired by the omnidirectional vision sensor; c), d) the inverse perspective transform of a) and b) with respect to the floor plane; in e) the detected obstacles are highlighted.

(flat patterns with high contrast lying on the floor) were present in the environment. The second experiment took place in a laboratory (see figure 7. In this case also mobile obstacles (i.e., a walking man) were present.

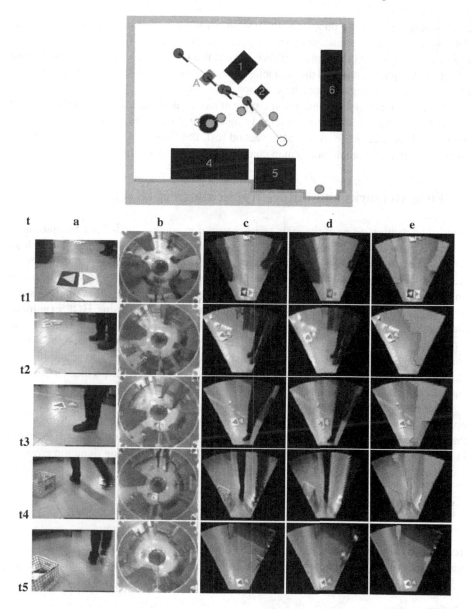

Fig. 7. Example of free space computation in a laboratory (shown on top): a) frames acquired by the pin-hole vision sensor; b) frames acquired by the omnidirectional vision sensor; c), d) the inverse perspective transform of a) and b) with respect to the floor plane; in e) the detected obstacles are highlighted.

The images shown in Figures 6 and 7 are taken in the most critical positions along the trajectory: the robot motion is clearly correlated to the result of the search for obstacles performed based on the HOPS system. In the figures one can see the maps of the test environment, the acquired images coming from the pin-hole vision system, the images coming from the omnidirectional sensor, the two images where the perspective effect has been removed, and the obstacles detected at each time t_i superimposed to the original image coming from pin-hole sensor.

As can be observed in Figure 6, the presence of real obstacles is correctly detected by the HOPS system, while the patterns lying on the floor plane disappear in the computation of the free space. Also in the second test, the false obstacles are not detected, while the detected volume of the man changes with his movements.

5   Final Remarks and Future Applications of HOPS

Obstacle detection is one of the main tasks required in autonomous-robot navigation. In the application described in the paper, HOPS has been used as a stereo sensor. Such an application was certainly not among the primary ones for which HOPS was designed. Actually, omnidirectional vision is a complicating factor for inverse-perspective based obstacle detection. However, we have focused on such a task to show that, besides more immediately perceivable advantages that can derive from using HOPS (namely, the joint availability of omnidirectional vision and high-resolution information about a region of interest), HOPS provides also the capabilities of a stereo system by which basic navigation sub-tasks can be accomplished in real-time: our prototype application can process about 3 frames/s on a 350 MHz K6 processor, which means that 10 frames/s can be easily achieved on more recent PCs.

Therefore, obstacle detection is one of the required "building blocks" we are developing in our way to designing, implementing and testing a full robot navigation system that relies on HOPS. Future work will be oriented towards integration of such a system in an autonomous robot architecture, to be used in rapidly changing dynamic environments as, for example, RoboCup competitions.

Acknowledgements

This work has been partially supported by CNR under the ART, Azzurra Robot Team (http://robocup.ce.unipr.it) grant, ASI under the "Hybrid Vision System for Long Range Rovering" grant, and by ENEA under the "Intelligent Sensors" grant.

References

[1] I. Bloch. Information combination operators for data fusion: a comparative review with classification. In *Proc. of the SPIE*, volume 2315, pages 148–159, 1994.

[2] O. Trullier, S. I. Wiener, A. Berthoz, and J. A. Meyer. Biologically based artificial navigation systems: review and prospects. *Progress in Neurobiology*, 51(5):483–544, 1997.

[3] J. Zhang, A. Knoll, and V. Schwert. Situated neuro-fuzzy control for vision-based robot localisation. *Robotics and Autonomous Systems*, 28:71–82, 1999.

[4] S. K. Nayar. Omnidirectional vision. In *Robotics Research. 8th International Symposium*, pages 195–202, 1998.

[5] T. Svoboda and T. Pajdla. Panoramic cameras for 3D computation. In *Proc. Czech Pattern Recognition Workshop*, pages 63–70, 2000.

[6] R. A. Hicks and R. Bajcsy. Reflective surfaces as computational sensors. In *Proc. 2nd Workshop on Perception for Mobile Agents*, pages 82–86, 1999.

[7] F. Marchese and D. Sorrenti. Omni-directional vision with a multi-part mirror. In *4th Int. Workshop on RoboCup*, pages 289–298, 2000.

[8] C. Marques and P. Lima. A localization method for a soccer robot using a vision-based omni-directional sensor. In *Proc. of EuroRoboCup Workshop*, Amsterdam, The Netherlands, June 2000. available in electronic form only.

[9] L. Delahoche, B. Maric, C. Pégard, and P. Vasseur. A navigation system based on an omnidirectional sensor. In *Proc. IEEE/RSJ Int. Conf. on Intelligent Robots and Systems*, pages 718–724, 1997.

[10] J. S. Gutmann, T. Weigel, and B. Nebel. Fast, accurate, and robust selflocalization in polygonal environments. In *Proc. 1999 IEEE/RSJ Int. Conf. on Intelligent Robots and Systems*, pages 1412–1419, 1999.

[11] M. Plagge, R. Günther, J. Ihlenburg, D. Jung, and A. Zell. The Attempto RoboCup robot team: Team-Tuebingen. In *RoboCup-99 Team Descriptions*, pages 200–209, 1999. available electronically at http://www.ep.liu.se/ea/cis/1999/006/cover.html.

[12] A. Clérentin, L. Delahoche, C. Pégard, and E. Brassart-Gracsy. A localization method based on two omnidirectional perception systems cooperation. In *Proc. 2000 ICRA. Millennium Conference*, volume 2, pages 1219–1224, 2000.

[13] A. Bonarini, P. Aliverti, and M. Lucioni. An omnidirectional vision sensor for fast tracking for mobile robots. *IEEE Trans. on Instrumentation and Measurement*, 49(3):509–512, 2000.

[14] H. A. Mallot, H. H. Bülthoff, J. J. Little, and S. Bohrer. Inverse perspective mapping simplifies optical flow computation and obstacle detection. *Biological Cybernetics*, 64:177–185, 1991.

[15] S. Bohrer, T. Zielke, and V. Freiburg. An integrated obstacle detection framework for intelligent cruise control. In *Proc. Intelligent Vehicles '95 Symp.*, pages 276–281, 1995.

[16] K. Onoguchi, N. Takeda, and M. Watanabe. Planar projection stereopsis method for road extraction. *IEICE Trans. Inf. & Syst.*, E81-D(9):1006–1018, 1998.

[17] M. Bertozzi, A. Broggi, and A. Fascioli. Stereo inverse perspective mapping: Theory and applications. *Image and Vision Computing Journal*, 16(8):585–590, 1998.

[18] C. Drocourt, L. Delahoche, C. Pégard, and C. Cauchois. Localization method based on omnidirectional stereoscopic vision and dead-reckoning. In *Proc. IEEE/RSJ Int. Conf. on Intelligent Robots and Systems*, pages 960–965, 1999.

[19] G. Adorni, S. Cagnoni, and M. Mordonini. Cellular automata based inverse perspective transform as a tool for indoor robot navigation. In E. Lamma and P. Mello, editors, *AI*IA99:Advances in Artificial Intelligence*, number 1792 in LNCS, pages 345–355. Springer, 2000.

[20] G. Adorni, S. Cagnoni, and M. Mordonini. An efficient perspective effect removal technique for scene interpretation. In *Proc. Asian Conf. on Computer Vision*, pages 601–605, 2000.

[21] G. Adorni, L. Bolognini, S. Cagnoni, and M. Mordonini. Stereo obstacle detection method for a hybrid omni-directional/pin-hole vision system. In *Robocup Symposium 2001*, 2001. In press.

Architectural Scenes Reconstruction from Uncalibrated Photos and Map Based Model Knowledge

Ignazio Infantino and Antonio Chella

Dipartimento di Ingegneria Automatica ed Informatica, Universitá di Palermo,
Viale delle Scienze, 90128, Palermo (PA), Italy
{infantino, chella}@csai.unipa.it
http://www.csai.unipa.it

Abstract. In this paper we consider the problem of reconstructing architectural scenes from multiple photographs taken from arbitrarily viewpoints. The original contribution of this work is the use of a map as a source of a priori knowledge and geometric constraints in order to obtain in a fast and simple way a detailed model of a scene. We suppose images are uncalibrated and have at least one planar structure as a façade for exploiting the planar homography induced between world plane and image to calculate a first estimation of the projection matrix. Estimations are improved by using correspondences between images and map. We show how these simple constraints can be used to calibrate the cameras, to recover the projection matrices for each viewpoint, and to obtain 3D models by using triangulation.

1 Introduction

The aim of the work in this paper is to be able to reconstruct architectural sites from uncalibrated images and using information from the facades and maps of buildings. Many approaches exist to attempt to recover 3D models from calibrated stereo images [14] or uncalibrated extended image sequences [1,15] by triangulation and exploiting epipolar [13] and trilinear constraints [9]. Other approaches consists of visualisation from image-based representations of a 3D scene [6,16,18]. Constructions of 3D model from a collection of panoramic image mosaics and geometrical constraints have also presented [10,17]. In this paper we adopt simple approach to construct a 3D model by exploiting strong constraints present in the scenes to be modelled.[3,4,12]. The constraints which can be used are parallelism and orthogonality, leading to simple and geometrically intuitive methods to calibrate the intrinsic and extrinsic parameter of the cameras and to recover Euclidean models of the scene from only two images from arbitrary positions. We propose an extension to [3] dealing with the problem of recovering 3D models from uncalibrated images of architectural scenes viewing façades by exploiting the planar homography induced between world and image and using a simple map.

F. Esposito (Ed.): AI*IA 2001, LNAI 2175, pp. 356–361, 2001.

2   Map-Based Model Knowledge

Map based model knowledge is required in order to reduce ambiguities which occur during the reconstruction process. It must comprise the scene and is therefore complex, and additionally difficult to acquire. A small set of descriptive features is added to the classic CAD representation of the map by the use of background knowledge. We have defined a simple language EDL (Environment Description Language) in order to have powerful representation of the scene viewed. The features are grouped in three main extensible classes:

1. ground-level objects (streets, lawns, footpath, etc.);
2. architectural objects (facades, roofs, windows, walls, gates, doors, etc.);
3. other objects (people, vehicles, trees, road signs, etc.).

For instance, a building is represented by a sub-set of architectural objects and their metric value. When the user indicates a map-image correspondence, the classification of the object drives the reconstruction process adding constraints related to geometric properties of it.

3   Modelling System

Our modelling system uses one or more pairs of images of a façade. For each pair, the user indicates line, point or plane correspondences between images and the map. The modelling system attempts to use all possible constraints in a consistent and coherent way. The goal is reached by decomposing the process into several linear steps. For a single view we perform:

1. Recovering the camera intrinsic parameters and rotation $\mathbf{R}$ from two vanishing points;
2. Recovering camera translation $\mathbf{t}$ from two known points on the map;
3. Rectification of the image based on the homography induced in the image of the planar structure.

In this way we have a first approximation of the projection matrix and the texture maps of planar structures [11]. These can be directly placed in a 3D model by the map correspondences. In order to have a better estimation of the projection matrix we use two strategies. The first one exploits two images viewing the same planar structure [18] and it deals with new homography estimation by automatically finding corner correspondences. Decomposition of inter-frame homography matrix gives the new estimation of the projection matrices of two views. The second one involves a global refinement using all possible map constraints. It allows reconstruction of points out of the planes used for calibration and rectification. The final steps are:

1. Global optimisation using map constraints (bundle adjustment);
2. Triangulation and raw 3D model;
3. Texture mapping and VRML model;

Fig. 1. Four of ten input images of an architectural scene and an example of line to line map constraint.

3.1   Calibration and Estimation of the Projection Matrix

For a pin-hole camera, perspective projection from Euclidean 3D space to an image can be represented in homogeneous coordinates by a 3 x 4 camera projection matrix $\mathbf{P}$ [5]:

$$\lambda_{\mathbf{i}} [u_i\ v_i\ 1]^T = \mathbf{P} [X_i\ Y_i\ Z_i\ 1]^T \qquad (1)$$

The projection matrix has 11 degrees of freedom and can be decomposed into a 3 x 3 orientation matrix $\mathbf{R}$ and a 3 x 1 translation vector $\mathbf{t}$ and a 3 x 3 camera calibration matrix, $\mathbf{K}$: $\mathbf{P} = \mathbf{K} [\ \mathbf{R}\ |\ \mathbf{t}\ ]$. From line correspondences given by the user, we can calculate vanishing points [3]. In the worst case we only have information about two perpendicular directions, but it is enough to estimate the scale factor α of the image plane if we suppose that the principal point coordinates are equal to image centre. Then we can calculate the camera calibration matrix $\mathbf{K}$ and the rotation matrix $\mathbf{R}$ for each image [2]. Moreover if we use two point correspondences between the map and the image (or a known length of a line on image) we also have the translation vector $\mathbf{t}$. From a common planar structure in the pair of images it is possible to automatically improve the estimated matrices above by exploiting the homography[5]. If we suppose points are on plane Z=0, we can write:

$$\begin{aligned} \lambda_1\ \mathbf{w}_1 &= \mathbf{K}_1\ [\mathbf{r}_1^1 | \mathbf{r}_1^2 | \mathbf{t}_1]\ \mathbf{X}^{\mathbf{P}} \\ \lambda_2\ \mathbf{w}_2 &= \mathbf{K}_2\ [\mathbf{r}_2^1 | \mathbf{r}_2^2 | \mathbf{t}_2]\ \mathbf{X}^{\mathbf{P}} \end{aligned} \qquad (2)$$

where r_1^1, r_1^2 are the two first columns of $\mathbf{R_1}, r_2^1, r_2^2$ are columns of $\mathbf{R_2}$, and $\mathbf{X^P}$ is a 3 x 1 vector which denote point is on plane $\Pi(Z = 0)$ in homogeneus coordinates. Let be

$$\mathbf{H_1} = \mathbf{K_1} \; [r_1^1 | r_1^2 | t_1]$$
$$\mathbf{H_2} = \mathbf{K_2} \; [r_2^1 | r_2^2 | t_2] \tag{3}$$

if $\mathbf{H_{21}} = \mathbf{H_2} \; \mathbf{H_1^{-1}}$ then

$$\lambda_2 \; \mathbf{w_2} = \lambda_1 \; \mathbf{H_{21}} \; \mathbf{w_1} \tag{4}$$

from which we can obtain $\mathbf{w_2} = [u_2 \; v_2]^T$:

$$u_2 = (\mathbf{h_1} \; \mathbf{w_1})/(\mathbf{h_3} \; \mathbf{w_1})$$
$$v_2 = (\mathbf{h_2} \; \mathbf{w_1})/(\mathbf{h_3} \; \mathbf{w_1}) \tag{5}$$

where $\mathbf{h_1}, \mathbf{h_2}, \mathbf{h_3}$ are rows of $\mathbf{H_{21}}$. Fixing for instance a façade, and using a Harris corners detector [7] we can find some correspondences between the two images. For each detected feature found in the first image we calculate where it is in second image by the homography. Only the stronger matches are selected and we suppose them belonging to viewed plane. In this way we have new estimates of correspondences on second image and we can improve estimate of homography. The decomposition of the homography matrix gives a new estimation of the inter-frame projection matrix.

3.2   Using Map Constraints

The map gives us important constraints to improve the estimation of the 3D model. We use the following constraints between geometric entities of image and map [18]:

1. point to point correspondences
2. point to line correspondences
3. line to line correspondences

For each image the user give some correspondences to a map and the system tries to improve the projection matrix estimation. Point to point correspondences are strong constraints because are directly related to the projection matrix:

$$\lambda_k \mathbf{w_k} = \mathbf{P} \mathbf{X_k} \tag{6}$$

Point to line correspondence is expressed by equation:

$$\mathbf{L} \mathbf{P_{4x4}^{-1}} [\lambda \mathbf{w} \; 1]^T = \mathbf{0_{3x1}} \tag{7}$$

where $\mathbf{L}$ is a 3x4 matrix of coefficients of 3 dimensional line equations and $\mathbf{P_{4x4}^{-1}}$ is inverse matrix of projection matrix $\mathbf{P}$ with adding the last row $[0\;0\;0\;1]$. 3d line trough points $\mathbf{X_2}$ and $\mathbf{X_1}$ can be expressed by:

$$(\mathbf{X_2} - \mathbf{X_1}) \wedge \mathbf{X} + (\mathbf{X_2} \wedge \mathbf{X_1}) = 0 \tag{8}$$

If we denote with $a = x_2 - x_1$, $b = z_2 - z_1$, $c = y_2 - y_1$, $d_1 = z_1 y_2 - y_1 z_2$, $d_2 = -z_1 x_2 + x_1 z_2$, $d_3 = y_1 x_2 - x_1 y_2$, line is described by a pair of equations from

$$\begin{aligned} by - cz + d_1 &= 0 \\ az - bx + d_2 &= 0 \\ cx - ay + d_3 &= 0 \end{aligned} \tag{9}$$

From equations system (7) we can eliminate λ and use 2 constraints.
Line to line correspondences are expressed as:

$$[a\ b\ c]^T = \mathbf{w_1} \wedge \mathbf{w_2} = (\mathbf{PX_3}) \wedge (\mathbf{PX_4}) \tag{10}$$

where a, b, c are coefficients of line equation $au + bv + c = 0$ on image passing trough generic points $\mathbf{w_1}$ and $\mathbf{w_2}$, and $\mathbf{X_{3i}}, \mathbf{X_{4i}}$ are two generic points of line map.

All constraints given by the user are used to define a minimisation problem in order to obtain new estimates of the projection matrices. Decomposing new matrices by QR decomposition we have also new estimates of camera calibration matrix $\mathbf{K}$, rotation matrix $\mathbf{R}$, translation vector $\mathbf{t}$ and camera position $\mathbf{X_c}$ of each image. In the process used to estimate better projection matrices we introduce also point to point correspondences which arise from the vanishing points calculated. The obtained 3D structure is rendered afterwards using a texture mapping procedure and the final model is stored in standard VRML 1.0 format.

Fig. 2. A panoranic view of the final VRML model reconstruction

4   Conclusion

The techniques presented have been successfully used to interactively build models of architectural scenes from pairs of uncalibrated photographs. Using only information from planar structure such as façades and a simple map, we can recover precise projection matrices with only a few point correspondences.

References

1. Beardsley, P., Torr, P., Zisserman, A.: 3D model acquisition from extended image sequences. ECCV 95, Cambridge, LNCS 1065, (2):683–695, Springer-Verlag, 1996.
2. Caprile, B., Torre, V.: Using vanishing points for camera calibration. IJCV, 127–140, 1990.
3. Cipolla, R., Drummond, T., Robertson, D.: Camera calibration from vanishing points in images of architectural scenes. In Proc. British Machine Vision Conference, Nottingham, vol. 2, 382–391, 1999.
4. Debevec, P. E., Taylor, C. J., Malik, J.: Modelling and rendering architecture from photographs: A Hybrid Geometry and Image-Based Approach. In ACM Computer Graphics (proc. SIGGRAPH), pp. 11-20, 1996.
5. Faugeras, O., Lustman, F.: Motion and structure from motion in a piecewise planar environment. Int. Journal of Pattern Recognition and Art. Int., 2(3):485–508, 1988.
6. Faugeras, O., Laveau, S., Robert, L., Csurka, G., Zeller, C.: 3-D reconstruction of urban scenes from sequences of images. Computer Vision and Image Understanding, n.69, vol.3,292–309,1998.
7. Harris, C., Stephens, M.: A combined corner detector and edge detector. Fourth Alvey Vision Conference, 147–151, 1988.
8. Hartley, R. I.: Estimation of relative camera positions for uncalibrated cameras. European Conf. on Computer Vision, pp. 579–587, S. M. Ligure, Italy, May 1992.
9. Hartley, R. I.: Lines and points in three views and the trifocal tensor. International Journal of Computer Vision, 22(2):125-140, 1996.
10. Kang, S. B.,Szeliski, R.: 3-D scene data recovery using omni-directional multibaseline stereo. In CVPR'96, 364–370, June 1997.
11. Liebowitz, D., Zisserman, A.: Metric Rectification for Perspective Images of Planes. In Proc. IEEE Conf. on Computer Vision and Pattern Recognition, 482–488, 1998.
12. Liebowitz, D., Criminisi, A., Zisserman, A.: Creating architectural models from images. Eurographics'99, vol.18, n.3, 1999.
13. Luong, Q. T., Viéville, T.: Canonical Representations for the Geometries of Multiple Projective Views. Computer Vision and Image Underst., 64(2):193–229, 1996.
14. Narayanan, P. J., Rander, P. W., and Kanade, T.: Constructing virtual worlds using dense stereo. In Proc. of Sixth IEEE Intl. Conf. on Computer Vision, Bombay (India), 3–10, January 1998.
15. Pollefeyes, M., Koch, R., Van Gool, L.: Self calibration and metric reconstruction inspite of varying an unknown internal camera parameters. In Proc. of Sixth IEEE Intl. Conf. on Computer Vision, Bombay (India), 90–95, January 1998.
16. Seitz, S. M., Dyer, C. R.: Toward image-based scene representation using view morphing. In Proc. of Intl. Conf. IEEE Conf. on Patt. Rec., Vienna (Austria), January 1996.
17. Shum, H. Y., Han, M., Szeliski, R.: Interactive construction of 3-D models from panoramic mosaics. In Proc IEEE Conf. On Computer Vision and Pattern Recognition, 427–433, Santa Barbara (USA), June 1998.
18. Szeliski, R., Torr, P.: Geometrically constrained structure from motion: Points on planes. In European Workshop on 3D Structure from Multiple Images of Large-Scale Environments (SMILE), 171–186, June 1998.

A SOM/ARSOM Hierarchy for the Description of Dynamic Scenes

Antonio Chella[1,2], Maria Donatella Guarino[2], and Roberto Pirrone[1,2]

[1] DIAI, University of Palermo, Viale delle Scienze,
I-90128 Palermo, Italy
{chella, pirrone}@unipa.it
[2] CERE-CNR, National Research Council,
Viale delle Scienze,
I-90128 Palermo, Italy
guarino@cere.pa.cnr.it

Abstract. A neural architecture is presented, aimed to describe the dynamic evolution of complex structures inside a video sequence. The proposed system is arranged as a tree of self-organizing maps. Leaf nodes are implemented by ARSOM networks as a way to code dynamic inputs, while classical SOM's are used to implement the upper levels of the hierarchy. Depending on the application domain, inputs are made by suitable low level features extracted frame by frame of the sequence. Theoretical foundations of the architecture are reported along with a detailed outline of its structure, and encouraging experimental results.

1 Introduction

Symbolic description of the objects inside a scene, and of their dynamic behavior is a crucial task in whatever vision system. Such a goal can be accomplished, in general, only using some a priori knowledge about the scene context along with various assumptions on the object models, and on their geometrical or physical constraints. We present a novel multi-layer neural architecture for dynamic scenes description where structural relations between the various elements are coded into the network topology. The proposed system has been developed as a part of the architecture prototype for the control of the ASI SPIDER robotic arm that will operate on the International Space Station [11]. The network is arranged to provide a symbolic description of the robot motion from a live video sequence taken by a fixed camera looking at the robot workspace. This description is in form of short assertions regarding the motion direction of the whole arm and of its components. Phrases are obtained after a labelling step performed over the units of the trained network. Inside the general framework of the robotic control architecture developed by some of the authors [1] the proposed system can be regarded as a way to implement the conceptual level: our architecture allows us to fill the gap between low level perceptual data, and their symbolic representation. This in turn can be useful to enrich the knowledge base defined for the application domain, and to guide planning activity and new sensing actions.

F. Esposito (Ed.): AI*IA 2001, LNAI 2175, pp. 362–368, 2001.

The architecture consists in a tree of self-organizing maps in order to encode the arm topology. Leaf nodes provide a description of the motion for single joints. This layer is made by ARSOM networks [8] to process dynamic image features extracted from the video input to describe joints motion. At the intermediate level, and at the topmost level some SOM networks are used to provide motion description for different groups of joints belonging to the shoulder, the elbow, the wrist/hand components, and the whole arm respectively. Several SOM-based multi-layer networks have been developed by various researchers, but our model is the only one dealing with dynamic inputs, and using a feed-forward scheme to propagate information along the maps hierarchy. In our model a vector representation of the internal state of each map is computed at each training step and is propagated from the child maps to the parent one, starting from the leaves of the tree structure. The most known multi-layer SOM-like networks are the WEBSOM, the PicSOM, and the TS-SOM models [5], [7], [6]. In all these models the lower layers maps can be regarded as a multi-resolution representation of the clusters that are present in the top most maps. Many other architectures have been developed that use multi-layer SOM [12], [10], [3], but all of them are very similar to the TS-SOM approach. In the HOSOM network [14] successive layers are dynamically grown starting from overlapping neighbourhoods of the root map, encoding data with some redundancy and increasing classification performance. In the HSOM network [9] the index value of the best match unit of the lower level map is propagated in a feed-forward scheme to the upper level one, thus allowing to obtain arbitrary cluster shapes. The rest of the paper is arranged as follows. In section 2 theoretical motivations for the choice of the architecture topology are explained. Section 3 is devoted to the detailed system description. In section 4 experimental results are reported, while in section 5 conclusions are drawn.

2   Theoretical Remarks

The main goal of the proposed system is to provide a symbolic interpretation for the dynamic evolution of a pattern of image features, making use of the a priori knowledge about the structure underlying the features themselves in the application domain. Due to the nature of the problem a hybrid architecture has been selected where the subsymbolic part provides a suitable coding for the input data, while the symbolic one is merely a labelling performed on the network activations pattern accordingly to our knowledge about the specific domain. The particular choice of the network topology is mainly inspired to the work that Gori and his associates [2][13] proposed as a general framework to build adaptive models for the symbolic processing of data structures. In this works, the authors focus their attention on a particular type of structure namely the directed ordered acyclic graph (DOAG). A DOAG D is a directed acyclic graph where a total order relation is defined on the edges. Structured information can be regarded as a labelled DOAG. We'll call $\mathbf{Y}_v$ the label attached to a vertex v. We'll denote with $\mathcal{Y}^{\#}$ the general space of the labels. A structural transduction

$\tau(\cdot)$ is a relation that is defined on two structured spaces $\mathcal{U}^{\#} \times \mathcal{Y}^{\#}$. A transduction admits a recursive state representation if there exist a structured space $\mathbf{X} \in \mathcal{X}^{\#}$ with $\mathrm{skel}(\mathbf{X}) = \mathrm{skel}(\mathbf{U}) = \mathrm{skel}(\mathbf{Y})$ and two functions defined as follows for each $v \in \mathrm{skel}(\mathbf{U})$ (here the notation $\mathrm{ch}[v]$ refers to the set of the children of vertex v).

$$\mathbf{X}_v = f(\mathbf{X}_{\mathrm{ch}[v]}, \mathbf{U}_v, v) \tag{1}$$
$$\mathbf{Y}_v = g(\mathbf{X}_v, \mathbf{U}_v, v) \tag{2}$$

3 Description of the System

The previous considerations about processing of structured data led us to develop our architecture as a tree of SOM/ARSOM networks. The tree structure fits to the topological structure of the robotic arm. In figure 1 is depicted a simple scheme of the architecture. The main difference with the approach proposed in [2] is the use of an unsupervised learning scheme to perform motion classification. On the other hand, complex and more descriptive labels are generated from primitive ones in correspondence of all the non-winner units. At the first level, the system processes the sequences obtained computing, for each frame, 2D projections of the arm joints onto the image plane $\mathbf{q}_i(t) = [x_i(t), y_i(t)]^T$ with $i = 0, \ldots, 4$. We consider only the last five joints even if the robot arm has 6 d.o.f. because the first one is projected always in a fixed position. The leaf networks provide a direct classification of the 2D motion. The error distribution over the units is propagated between the layers. In what follows, we'll proof that is possible to determine a structural transduction with a recursive state representation between the input feature space and the space of the symbolic output labels, and that the error distribution over the units can be regarded as the internal state of the system. Labels for input leaf nodes are given by

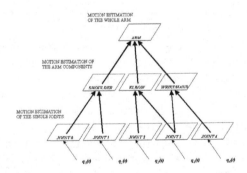

Fig. 1. An outline of the proposed system.

$\mathbf{U}_i = \{\mathbf{q}_i(t), \mathbf{q}_i(t-1), \ldots, \mathbf{q}_i(t-M)\}$ at the generic time instant t, while the generic SOM node label $\mathbf{U}_s$ consists in the name of the corresponding robotic arm component. Labels are mapped directly onto the output space, so we don't consider any extern input to the intermediate levels apart from the connections transmitting the state: this is equivalent to set $\mathbf{U}_s = \mathbf{0} \; \forall s$. We'll show that the transduction admits a recursive state representation. If we consider a generic ARSOM node, from [8] we can write the approximation error $\mathbf{e}_i^{(k)}$:

$$\mathbf{e}_i^{(k)} = \mathbf{q}_i(t) - \mathbf{Q}_i^T \tilde{\mathbf{w}}_i^{(k)}$$

where $\tilde{\mathbf{w}}_i^{(k)}$ is the weights vector, while $\mathbf{Q}_i$ represents the matrix whose rows are the $\mathbf{q}_i(\tau), \tau = t - 1, \ldots, t - M$. We can rewrite the label attached to the node $\mathbf{U}_i$, adding $\mathbf{q}_i(t)$ as the first row of the matrix, then it's possible to express the error as:

$$\mathbf{e}_i^{(k)} = \mathbf{U}_i^T \mathbf{w}_i^{(k)}$$

where $\mathbf{w}_i^{(k)} = [1| - \tilde{\mathbf{w}}_i^{(k)}]^T$. So the expression of the overall error can be written like in (1):

$$\mathbf{E}_i = f(\mathbf{0}, \mathbf{U}_i, \mathbf{W}_i) \tag{3}$$

In the previous equation $\mathbf{E}_i = [\mathbf{e}_i^{(k)}]_{k=1}^L$ is the overall error, while $\mathbf{W}_i = [\mathbf{w}_i^{(k)}]_{k=1}^L$ is the weight matrix, and is the node parametric representation as stated in [2]. For the generic SOM node s, we can write from [4] for each unit k at the training step n:

$$\mathbf{w}_s^{(k)}(n) = \mathbf{w}_s^{(k)}(n-1) + \gamma h_{bk}(\mathbf{e}_{ch[s]} - \mathbf{w}_s^{(k)}(n-1)) \tag{4}$$

here γ is the gain factor, h_{bk} is the neighbourhood coefficient, while b is the best matching unit index, and $\mathbf{e}_{ch[s]}$ is the input vector that correspond to error computed for all the children of node s. The matching error for the unit k can be written, according to (4):

$$\mathbf{e}_s^{(k)} = \mathbf{e}_{ch[s]} - \mathbf{w}_s^{(k)}(n-1) = \mathbf{e}_{ch[s]} + \frac{1 - \gamma h_{bk}}{\gamma h_{bk}} \mathbf{w}_s^{(k)}(n-1) \tag{5}$$

Then we can write the expression of the overall error in the same way of (1):

$$\mathbf{E}_s = f(\mathbf{e}_{ch[s]}, \mathbf{U}_s, \mathbf{W}_s) \tag{6}$$

In (6) $\mathbf{E}_s$ and $\mathbf{W}_s$ have the same meaning of the corresponding quantities in (3), while $\mathbf{U}_s$ has been set to the null vector. The output function g defined in (2) is implemented by means of the labelling process. Using the training episodes, labels are attached to the winner units at each layer of the network. Each label corresponds to the arm component motion description for the particular training episode. Complex labels, obtained as composition of the primitive ones in a neighbourhood, are attached to unlabelled units during the test. It can be noted that labelling depends from the units activation that, in turn, is related to the state as in (2).

4 Experimental Results

The proposed architecture has been developed as a monitoring system for the operations of the ASI SPIDER robotic arm. In our lab we couldn't acquire video sequences of the true arm because of its dimensions, so we have set up our experiments using a model of the real arm made with the ROBIX system (see figure 2). In the general case, a binary image is obtained subtracting the fixed background image and applying a threshold. The resulting blob is regularized with a morphological sequence of opening and closure operations. Then the skeleton is determined, and the approximating straight segments are extracted using the Hough transform. In figure 2 the various preprocessing steps are depicted.

Fig. 2. The ROBIX arm, and the feature points extraction process.

Starting from the lines intersections a simple decision scheme is implemented to determine the joints projections that makes use of our assumptions about the arm kinematics, and the projection geometry. The training episodes have been set up from 30 frames sequences regarding some basic movements of the robot arm: turning left, turning right, turn left or right and tilt toward the observer, go down to the left or right with all the arm extended. All the inverse movements have been also used in the training phase. All maps are 6×6 units wide, and use a learning rate of 0.1 for the ARSOM's and 0.6 for the SOM's. The neighbourhood initial size was 6 units for all the networks. We performed training in 600 epochs, and tested the system with 10 episodes obtained by partial composition of the training movements. In figure 3 some samples from a test episode are depicted together with the textual output of the system.

5   Conclusions

A novel hybrid approach for the symbolic description of dynamic structured scenes have been presented that can be used in several application domains where some a priori knowledge has been provided about the structure and the relations between the parts of the scene itself. Knowledge about the domain is used to guide the process of building the system structure. We stated that the proposed architecture is able to learn in an unsupervised way complex mappings between structured data spaces. We motivated our theoretical choices and, in particular, it has been proved that the feed-forward propagation scheme of the error pattern can be regarded as way to represent the internal state of the system so it's able to learn structural transductions. The proposed system has to be studied more in detail, and an extensive experimental phase is needed to fully evaluate its performance. In particular, we want to investigate the case of complex transductions between generic DOAG structures, and to experiment the system domains with a large amount of low level data like content based video indexing for multimedia databases.

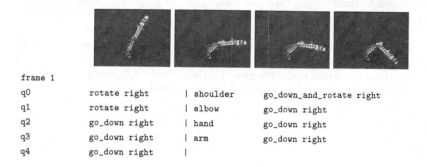

```
frame 1
q0        rotate right     | shoulder   go_down_and_rotate right
q1        rotate right     | elbow      go_down right
q2        go_down right    | hand       go_down right
q3        go_down right    | arm        go_down right
q4        go_down right    |
```

Fig. 3. A few samples from a test episode along with the textual output of the system.

References

[1] A. Chella, M. Frixione, and S. Gaglio. A Cognitive Architecture for Artificial Vision. *Artificial Intelligence*, 89:73–111, 1997.

[2] P. Frasconi, M. Gori, and A. Sperduti. A General Framework for Adaptive Processing of Data Structures. *IEEE Trans. on Neural Networks*, 9(5):768–786, September 1998.

[3] M. Hermann, R. Der, and G. Balzuweit. Hierarchical Feature Maps and Nonlinear Component Analysis. In *Proc. of ICNN'96*, volume 2, pages 1390–1394, Texas, 1996.

[4] T. Kohonen. The Self–Organizing Map. *Proceedings of the IEEE*, 78(9):1464–1480, September 1990.

[5] T. Kohonen, S. Kaski, K. Lagus, and T. Honkela. Very Large Two-Level SOM for the Browsing of Newsgroups. In *Proc. of International Conference on Artificial Neural Networks*, pages 269–274, Bochum, Germany, 1996.

[6] P. Koikkalainen and E. Oja. Self–Organizing Hierarchical Feature Maps. In *Proc. of International Joint Conference on Neural Networks*, pages 279–284, San Diego, CA, 1990.

[7] J. Laaksonen, M. Koskela, and E. Oja. PicSOM: Self–Organizing Maps for Content–Based Image Retrieval. In *Proc. of International Joint Conference on Neural Networks*, Washington D.C., USA, July 1999.

[8] J. Lampinen and E. Oja. Self–Organizing Maps for Spatial and Temporal AR Models. In *Proc. of the sixth SCIA Scandinavian Conference on Image Analysis*, pages 120–127, Helsinky, Finland, 1990.

[9] J. Lampinen and E. Oja. Clustering Properties of Hierarchical Self–Organizing Maps. *J. Math. Imaging Vision*, 2(3):261–271, 1992.

[10] T.C. Lee and M. Peterson. Adaptive Vector Quantization Using a Self–Development Neural Network. *IEEE J. Select Areas Commun.*, 8:1458–1471, 1990.

[11] R. Mugnuolo, P. Magnani, E. Re, and S. Di Pippo. The SPIDER Manipulation System (SMS). The Italian Approach to Space Automation. *Robotics and Autonomous Systems*, 23(1–2), 1998.

[12] G. Ongun and U. Halici. Fingerprint Classification through Self–Organizing Feature Map Modified to Treat Uncertainty. *Proceedings of the IEEE*, 84(10):1497–1512, October 1996.

[13] A. Sperduti and A. Starita. Supervised Neural networks for the Classification of Structures. *IEEE Trans. on Neural Networks*, 8(3):714–735, May 1997.

[14] P. N. Suganthan. Hierarchical Overlapped SOM's for Pattern Classification. *IEEE Trans. on Neural Networks*, 10(1):193–196, January 1999.

A Constraint-Based Architecture for Flexible Support to Activity Scheduling

Amedeo Cesta[1], Gabriella Cortellessa[1], Angelo Oddi[1], Nicola Policella[1], and Angelo Susi[1,2]

[1] IP-CNR, National Research Council of Italy, Viale Marx 15, I-00137 Rome, Italy
{cesta,corte,oddi,policella}@ip.rm.cnr.it
[2] Automated Reasoning Systems (SRA), ITC-IRST, Via Sommarive 18 - Loc. Pantè,
I-38050 Povo, Trento, Italy
susi@irst.itc.it

Abstract. The O-OSCAR software architecture is a problem solving environment for complex scheduling problem that is based on a constraint-based representation. On top of this core representation a problem solver module and a schedule execution system guarantee a complete support to address a scheduling problem. Furthermore, a rather sophisticated interaction module allows users to maintain control on different phases of schedule management.

1 Introduction

In several real application domains it is important that planning architectures support the user in all the phases a plan may go through, e.g., planning problem definition, solution synthesis, and execution monitoring. This kind of support is increasingly useful when the applications become critical, like for example in space missions support systems. We refer to all the phases of a plan with the term *"plan life-cycle"*. This paper is aimed at describing how artificial intelligence techniques for planning and scheduling can be integrated in a software architecture for offering services to users during plan life-cycle. We will show features of the software architecture O-OSCAR (for Object-Oriented SCheduling ARchitecture) and will underscore several of its recent developments aimed at creating a more complete supporting environment.

A key aspect in O-OSCAR design is the constraint-based reference model that we have intensively used to shape all the services it is able to offer. We have targeted a class of scheduling problems that involve quite complex time and resource constraints and applications domain related to automated management of space missions. Time constraints may model set-up times for instruments, target visibility windows, transmission times (e.g., to represent memory dump), deadline constraints, etc. Resource constraints can represent capacity of on board memory (e.g., tape recorder or solid state recorder), transmission channel capacity, and energy bounds (e.g., limitation on the number of active instruments in a space probe). From the scheduling literature point of view target problems have

F. Esposito (Ed.): AI*IA 2001, LNAI 2175, pp. 369–381, 2001.

been the so-called Resource Constrained Project Scheduling Problem (RCPSP) [2] and its variants with Generalized Precedence Relations (RCPSP/max) [7, 4] and with Inventory Constraints [9]. Such problems contain sophisticated constraints like maximum temporal separation between activities, and a variety of resource constraints for activities. In addition, specific attention has been deserved to the interaction of users with the scheduling systems. We have studied what kind of interaction services may contribute to enhance acceptance of the whole approach in real contexts.

This paper is organized as follows: Section 2 introduces the O-OSCAR architecture while the following sections describe specific aspects of the main software components: the constraint data base (Section 3), the problem solver (Section 4), the execution monitor (Section 5), and the user-interaction module (Section 6).

2   A CSP-based Software Architecture

In developing a complete solution to a planning/scheduling problem several basic aspects need to be integrated. They are sketched in Figure 1 that shows the different modules of O-OSCAR.

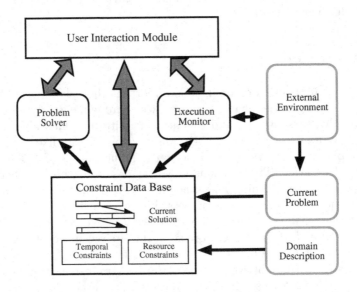

Fig. 1. A high level description of the O-OSCAR architecture

First of all we see (as typical in any computerized task) a box representing the "external environment" that is the part of the real world that is relevant for the problem the software architecture is aimed at supporting. Such an environment is modeled in the architecture according to two distinct aspects:

Domain Representation. The relevant features of the world (the domain) and the rules that regulate its dynamic evolution should be described in a symbolic language. This is the basic knowledge that allows the system to offer services.

Problem Representation. A description of the goals of a current problem is given to specify states of the real world that are "desired" and to be achieved starting from the current world state.

The core component of an architecture that uses a CSP (constraint-based problem solving) approach is the:

Constraint Data Base (CDB). This module offers an active service that automatically takes care of checking/maintaining the satisfaction of the set of constraints representing the domain and the problem. It is in charge of two strictly interconnected aspects:

Domain and Problem Representation. The Domain Representation Language allows the representation of classes of problems and the peculiar domain constraints in the class. At present O-OSCAR is able to solve the class of scheduling problems RCPSP and its variants mentioned before. The Problem Representation Language consists of a set of constraints specifying the activities and their constraints requirements specified in a RCPSP.

Solution Representation and Management. The CSP approach to problem solving is centered on the representation, modification and maintenance of a solution. Such solution in O-OSCAR consists of a representation designed on top of specialized constraint reasoners. The constraint model represents particular aspects of the domain (e.g., temporal features, resource availability) and is called into play when changes are performed by a problem solver, the execution monitor, or a user. The solution manager is usually endowed with a set of primitives for communicate changes and formulate queries.

The CDB is the key part of the approach and should be designed taking efficiency into account. Special functionalities built on it allow to obtain a complete support to plan life-cycle. Three modules contribute to complete the scenario and are in charge of the following tasks:

Automated Problem Solving. This module guides the search for a solution. It is endowed with two main features: (a) an open framework to perform the search for a solution; (b) heuristic knowledge (it is able to identify and represent heuristics to guide search and avoid computational burden).

Execution Monitoring. Once a solution to a given problem is obtained, this module closes the loop with the real world. It is responsible for dispatching the plan activities for execution and sensing the outcome of this execution and of the relevant aspect of the world. Sensed information (e.g., successful or delayed execution of activities, machine safe or fault status) is used to update the CBD and maintain a representation synchronized with the evolution of the real world.

User-System Interaction. This module allows the interaction of the user with
the CDB and the two previously described services. The interaction functionalities may vary from more or less sophisticated visualization services,
to a set of complex manipulation functionalities on the solution allowed to
the user.

The advantage of using CSP as the basic representation mechanism is that additional services can be added relying on the same representation. Furthermore,
the same basic service can be incrementally updated inserting more sophisticated
functionalities (for example a portfolio of solution algorithms relying on different
search strategies). In this way we have been able to incrementally evolve from an
architecture for solving only disjunctive scheduling problems [5], to the current
tool that solves more sophisticated problems.

3   The Constraint Data-Base

In developing the CDB for resource constrained scheduling problems two domain features need support: (a) quantitative temporal constraints where both
minimum and maximum separation constraints can be specified and (b) multi-
capacity resources (e.g., capacity greater than one). As shown in Figure 1 the
CDB contains two specialized constraint reasoners, the first for temporal constraint management (with an expressivity correspondent to the Simple Temporal
Problem [8]), the second for representing resource constraints and their status
of satisfaction. In particular data structures called *resource profiles* are dynamically maintained that represent the current resource consumption. This lower
layer is hidden to the external user by a more external layer that essentially
represent the features of the Domain Description Language. For the current
purposes the interface language at the higher level identifies the typical aspects
involved in a schedule, namely activities, resources, constraints and decisions.
Choosing a general representation allows us to interface our work not only with
constraint-based algorithms but also with typical abstractions from Operations
Research (the representation features are similar to those defined in [12] even if
with somehow different semantics).

3.1   Multi-capacity Resources

A peculiar feature of O-OSCAR is the type of resources and the corresponding
constraints that is possible to represent. We can represent both disjunctive and
cumulative resources and among the latter we can model both reusable and consumable resources.

Reusable Resources. Reusable resources can serve multiple requests at the
same time but have a maximum level of resource requirement (the capacity
level) that cannot be violated. Examples are very common in manufacturing,
and supply chain management but also when describing human resources. Typical behavior of reusable resources is that the resource requirement of an activity

happens during activity execution but when the activity ends the resource level is re-established at the previous level and it can be "reused".

Consumable resources. Resources are consumable when an activity can permanently destroy or produce a quantity of it. The fuel level in a car tank or the amount of money in a bank safe are examples of this kind of resources. The resource constraint to represent in such a case is that the level of resource cannot exceed a maximum value or assume values below a minimum level. The complexity introduced by this kind of resources is quite high although they are very common in nature and few works have explicitly dealt with them (exception being the work on inventory constraints [9, 1]).

It is worth specifying that the resource bounds are constant values in these problems and that a resource consumption is associated with activity start times, and a resource production with activity end times. We have studied the synthesis of specific resource constraint propagation rules to prune the search space of inconsistent solutions. Following an approach introduced in [6] and extending it, propagation rules are obtained computing upper and lower bounds for the resource consumption and reasoning about these bounds in any time-point in which a change in the resource level happens. Given t one of these time points, the activities can be subdivided in three sets: the set of activities that for sure precedes t, the set that follows, and the set that currently overlaps with t. Reasoning on the content of this last set allows to synthesize propagation rules that add new necessary temporal constraints to the problem description.

> **Example:** Given a single resource and three activities: a_1 that consumes 2 units of resource; a_2 that produces 1 unit; a_3 that produces 2 units. The resource is consumable with bounds $[0, 5]$. Let us suppose that according to current temporal constraints the possible start-time of activities may be in the following intervals:
> - a_1 $[0, 2]$
> - a_2 $[2, 8]$
> - a_3 $[1, 10]$
>
> If we consider the time instant $t = 2$, the activity a_1 precedes or coincides with t, while the other two activities are not ordered with respect to t. If we assume that a_3 happens after t the resource constraints are violated so we can detect the implicit constraints that the upper bound of a_3 $ub_3 \leq 2$. Imposing explicitly this constraint we prune the search space of useless potential assignments.

This is just an example of the propagation rules that are fully described in [11].

4 Constraint-Guided Problem Solving

The generic problem solving algorithm that is used within O-OSCAR follows the *profile-based schema* introduced in [3] and shown in Figure 2. It is a basic greedy algorithm that works on a temporally consistent solution, computes the resource violations (the conflicts) using the information on the resource profiles, and then tries to build a solution that is "resource consistent" by imposing some additional ordering constraints between activities to level the resource contention peaks. This is iterated until either a resource consistent solution is obtained or a dead-end encountered. The greedy algorithm can be inserted in an optimization schema for obtaining multiple, increasingly better, solutions. A technique we have used in various domains integrates the greedy search in a random sampling loop. The technique, introduced in [10], allows to escape local minima, taking advantage of the random restart biased by the heuristic estimation.

CreateSchedule(Problem)
1.   CDB ← BuildCspRepresentation(Problem)
2.   **loop**
3.   Conflicts ← ComputeConflicts(CDB)
4.   **if** (Conflicts = ∅)
5.   **then return**(CDB)
6.   **else**
7.   **if** ExistUnsolvableConflict(Conflicts)
8.   **then return**(Failure)
9.   **else**
10.   Conflict ← SelectConflict(Conflicts)
11.   Precedence ← SelectPrecedence(Conflict)
12.   Post&Update(Precedence,CDB)
13.   **end-loop**
14.   **end**

Fig. 2. A Basic One-Pass Profile-Based Algorithm

Relevant to study are not only the techniques for computing conflicts (function `ComputeConflicts` in Figure 2) but also the heuristic estimators for the choice points represented by `SelectConflict` and `SelectPrecedence`. In O-OSCAR, specific knowledge has been inserted from our own work fully described in [4]. It is worth noting that different search spaces are designed according to the kind of resources needed to represent a domain. Different heuristics are shown to be effective in capturing the structure of the search space of different problems like for examples problems with maximum separations and reusable resources (see [4]) and problems with consumable resources (see [11]).

5   The Plan Execution Monitor

When a schedule has to be executed in a real working environment, differences are possible between the modeled approximate reality used to produce the schedule and the real world. This can arrive to cause, in extreme cases, the impossibility to use the computed plan. To minimize the risk, two possible kinds of strategies are applicable: one predictive and another reactive. Predictive strategies act during problem solving and are based on the computation of schedules that are robust with respect to a specified set of unexpected events. Reactive strategies are based on methods that, during the execution phase, dynamically adjust the current schedule according to the evolution of its execution in the real environment. In O-OSCAR we have currently followed a reactive approach based on schedule repair. We have implemented an execution control module that continuously updates the constraint data-base representing the current status of the schedule to describe its variations at execution time. The execution module contains a basic portfolio of repair strategies that specifies the reaction methods to undesired events.

The Execution Algorithm. Figure 3 gives a very high level description of the regular activities of the execution monitor. Its input parameters represent the main communication channels that are open when it is working, namely the constraint data base (CDB) that contains the current solution to a problem, the external world (extEnvironment), and a new knowledge source, called RepairStrategies, that is internal to the execution monitor but can be object of specific interaction with the user.

ExecuteSchedule(CDB,extEnvironment,repairStrategies)
1. $t \leftarrow 0$;
2.   currentSchedule $\leftarrow$ EstractSolution(CDB)
3.   **loop**
4.   **if**(ExecutionFinished(currentSchedule)) **then Return**(TerminationSuccess)
5.   **else**
6.   SensingReport $\leftarrow$ SenseEnv(extEnvironment)
7.   ConflictSet $\leftarrow$ ConflictCheck(SensingReport, currentSchedule)
8.   **if** (ConflictSet $\neq \emptyset$) **then**
9.   CDB $\leftarrow$ Repair(CDB, ConflictSet, RepairStrategies)
10.   **if** (Inconsistent(CDB)) **then Return**(TerminationFailure)
11.   currentSchedule $\leftarrow$ ExtractSolution(CDB)
12.   DispatchSet $\leftarrow$ ComputeExecutableActions(currentSchedule)
13.   Dispatch(DispatchSet, extEnvironment)
14. $t \leftarrow t + 1$;
15.   **end-loop**.

Fig. 3. A Sketchy View of the Execution Algorithm

The executor, according to increasing time stamps, performs a basic cycle that consists of: (a) sensing the environment (Step 6); (b) computing conflicts with respect to the current represented scenario (Step 7); (c) in case of conflicts, updating the CDB and attempting at repairing the current schedule (steps 8-11); (d) in case of successful repair, continuing execution by dispatching actions in the external environment (steps 12-13).

The quite general abstraction of this presentation hides most of the work realized for constructing an executor for O-OSCAR. For the sake of space we add only few words aimed at clarifying the use of the CDB and the current repairing actions. After sensing the environment the executor generates a conflict report that is used to update the constraint data base. Information in the execution report is used to synchronize the representation in the CDB and the real word. At present the update information is purely temporal. It represents either delays in the start time of activities (additional separation constraint with respect to the beginning of the time-line) or delays in the termination of an activity (change of duration constraints). When the CDB contains the new propagated situation, if this is inconsistent an unrecoverable failure is declared, otherwise an updated schedule status is used by the monitor to continue execution. The interaction module updates the information visualization highlighting the differences with respect to nominal schedule (see next section for visualization features). In case the update of the schedule ends up in a consistent scenario the execution of the updated schedule continues. If the resulting schedule contains some conflicts (shifting activities may cause new contention peaks in the solution) the solution needs to be fixed before continuing execution. The user can influence the monitor fixing a particular repair strategy or leave complete initiative to the monitor to choose the repair policy. The current solution in this concern is rather simple but it can be seen as an enabling infrastructure to realize further features. On one hand we have to experiment different protocols for exchange of initiative between the user and the execution monitor to choose repairing actions, on another we need further investigation to understand better how to make the user more comfortable in doing direct modifications on the current schedule according to a problematic evolution of the execution process.

6   An Interaction Module for Continuous Support

As we said before, we aim at *putting the user in the loop* by creating supporting tools that allow the user to maintain control on the evolving situation represented in the CDB. Our aim is to study the possibility offered by the mixed environment in which human being and automated systems contribute to solving/managing complex problems (an area also referred to as *mixed-initiative problem solving*). In this view a scheduling architecture should be endowed with a specific module that takes care of the continuous communication between users and system. Goal of this module is to favor collaboration and to allow a synergetic interaction between the intuitions and specific knowledge of human beings from one hand and the computational power of the automated system from another.

Figure 4 gives an high level view of the kind of functionalities the interaction module is supposed to have. The idea is that users are supported in the whole plan life-cycle, having specialized support for Domain and Problem Definition, Problem Solving and Execution Monitoring.

The current status of the Interaction Module of O-OSCAR offers a first suit of functionalities for interacting with the different aspects of the systems. During each phase a set of specific supporting tools helps the user to perform basic tasks. We are evolving from an interaction module aiming at showing smart problem solving features [5], toward a tool in which the Interaction Module is a first citizen in the architecture adding value to the system as a whole.

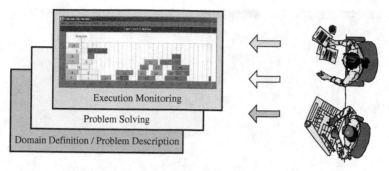

Fig. 4. Supporting Plan Life-Cycle

The most important goals of such a module are: (a) to give support to the scheduling problem definition; (b) to create a first set of features for mixed-initiative problem solving; (c) to take advantage of the flexibility of the CSP representation for offering services to the user for incremental and continuous intervention on the constraints represented in the CDB also during the execution phase, reacting to changes in the scheduling domain. (d) to offer basic inspection mechanisms to allow the user to monitor the plan execution phase.

A feature of the O-OSCAR interaction module is the ability to hide the system complexity to the user maintaining for him a level of intervention on the system. This is because it represents the constraint based schedule representation maintained in the system in a way understandable for the user.

The interaction module has also an object oriented design, is entirely written in Java and interacts with the C++ implementation of the rest of the architecture through a client-server protocol.

In the next subsection we describe how the big picture of Figure 4 is currently implemented in O-OSCAR and describe for each phase in the plan life-cycle which are the implemented services.

6.1   Current Visual Tools

The O-OSCAR Interaction Module made possible for the user to directly manipulate the graphical objects that represent the entities of the scheduling problem during the three phases described before. As said, the user can have distinct graphical environments for every phase but may also maintain a parallel view of the entire scheduling process. The interactive approach based on graphical object gives the system a level of "usability". The coordinated vision of all the available resources, in relation with all the three interaction phases, gives the user a "feeling of maintained control" on the system favoring the intermixing/shift of initiative.

Domain and Problem Definition. This graphical environment allows the user to manage the first part of the scheduling process. According with the CSP approach, used in the O-OSCAR system, a problem is represented as a graph of

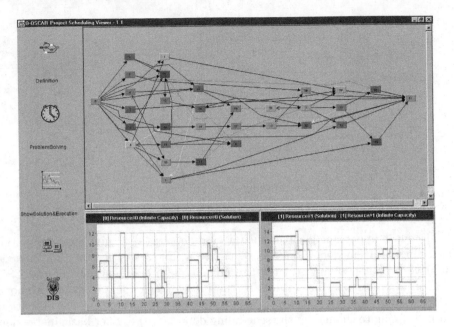

Fig. 5. Interaction for Problem Definition and Resolution

temporal constraints between activities. The system offers a graph manipulation window that allows the user to load and save the problem, add and remove activities, constraints and resources, modify the characteristics of every scheduling entity directly manipulating the graphical representation. In this way the user can manage dynamical situation, quite frequent in real contexts, in which either new activities arrive on-line and their accommodation in the existing schedule should be taken care of or resources breakdown and the schedule should be fixed in order to minimize total disruption.

Figure 5 shows the current interface for Problem Definition phase intermixed with features of the Problem Solving phase. In the upper part of the figure the graphical representation for a 30 activities scheduling problem. The problem graph is made of active graphical objects, and allow the user to change the problem interactively, for example adding new activities, modifying the temporal constraints network, etc.

Problem Solving. The Interface allows the user to ask for the solution of the represented problem. It is possible to select one solution strategy in a portfolio of specified strategies. Once a solution has been retrieved the system allows the user to choose between a certain number of possible Gantt diagrams, resource allocation diagrams or resource profile diagrams. The possibility of observing the solution from different perspectives, increase the user knowledge and stimulate in different ways his perception with respect to the problem at hand. In this way the user may have support for inserting his own intuition and experience in taking part in the decisional problem.

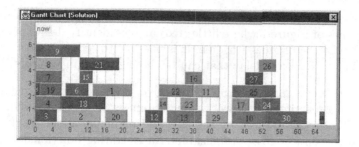

Fig. 6. Gantt Chart of a solved RCPSP problem

In addition the user can manually modify the solution while the system incrementally update the internal representation, automatically verifying its consistency.
Figure 6 shows one of the Gantt diagrams available for the problem specified
before. Additional information disaggregated in single resources is given in the
lower part of Figure 5 (the two small windows showing resource profiles) and
complete the picture of the current solution status.

Execution Control. Plan execution is dealt with as a separate working environment and represents the final step in the schedule life-cycle. The Interaction
Module allows to analyze the execution process in every instant until all operation are executed. In particular the Gantt window is used as the main source of
information (see also the upper part of the pictures in Figure 7. The user has as a
basic information the current time (a bar with label "time now" in the Figures 6
and 7. The bar evolve dynamically with time on the Gantt and activities change
colors according to their status of executed (grey) under execution (yellow) and
to be executed (original color). Figure 7 shows the execution status in different
time instant on the same problem.

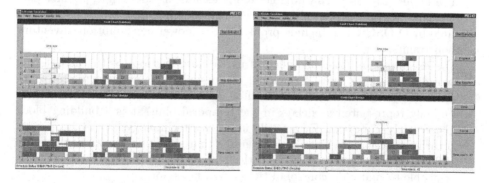

Fig. 7. Visual Inspection of the Execution

During the execution it is possible for the user to verify the differences between
the schedule computed during the solution phase and the real operation sequence

that is possible to execute in a given instant. This is shown in the lower windows in the pictures of Figure 7 where little (red) arrows identify delays of an activity with respect to the original schedule. It is possible to select the visualization of the operations execution delay that can be distinguished in two sets:

1. automatic delay, produced by the reactive strategies of the execution algorithm as a reaction to the working environment unexpected events;
2. manual delay, introduced by the user and manually added to the schedule representation using the graphical interfaces editing functionalities.

Further work is underway to endow the Execution Inspection interface with further views on the current problem. A further feature consists of the possibility of re-running off-line the execution of a schedule. In this way we create a sort of "simulation environment" in which the user can learn off-line the effects of certain choices he has made on-line on previous problems. These functionalities are very useful in a real dynamical working environment where decisions have to be taken very quickly and is very important that users has to be rapidly informed about the execution status and failures.

7   Concluding Remarks

In this paper we have reported a set of functionalities we have inserted in the O-OSCAR architecture. With respect to the initial work on O-OSCAR (see [5] for an overview) in our more recent work we have maintained the basic idea in this research project that is choosing constraints as the basic representation vehicle for problem solving, but have deeply scaled up in the kind of functionalities we are able to offer. In particular the main improvements we have described in this paper are:

- the representation of consumable resources adds a modeling capability particularly relevant. In fact it enlarges the class of scheduling problems addressable by O-OSCAR to include problems with power consumption, inventory constraints, etc.
- the execution monitor has allowed us to close the loop with the external world. This opens quite an amount of possibility for addressing real problems. Although at present the executor deals with a limited set of situations (mainly represented as delays in the temporal plan) it is a building block particularly important for actually using this technology.
- a rather sophisticated interaction module that allow the user to perceive the differences among three phases of the plan life-cycle, having different tools available to maintain control of the system behavior.

A lot of possibilities are opened by the current status of O-OSCAR, but a single feature is worth mentioning before closing the paper: the flexibility in manipulation the basic constraint representation with all the module that use the CDB. The fact that the constraint manager offers fully dynamic services has been a constant focus in our research work and is now somehow emphasized in O-OSCAR where they take the shape of additional service to the users grounded on the constraint representation.

Acknowledgments. This research has been supported by ASI (Italian Space Agency) as part of a joint effort among Dipartimento di Informatica e Sistemistica dell'Universita' di Roma "La Sapienza", Dipartimento di Informatica e Automazione della Terza Universita' di Roma, and IP-CNR [PST], Consiglio Nazionale delle Ricerche, Roma. O-OSCAR developments are currently partially supported by European Space Agency (ESA-ESOC) under contract No.14709/00/D/IM.

References

[1] J.C. Beck. Heuristics for Constraint-Directed Scheduling with Inventory. In *Proceedings of the Fifth Int. Conf. on Artificial Intelligence Planning and Scheduling (AIPS-00)*, 2000.

[2] P. Brucker, A. Drexl, R. Mohring, K. Neumann, and E. Pesch. Resource-Constrained Project Scheduling: Notation, Classification, Models, and Methods. *European Journal of Operations Research*, 1998.

[3] A. Cesta, A. Oddi, and S.F. Smith. Profile Based Algorithms to Solve Multiple Capacitated Metric Scheduling Problems. In *Proceedings of the Fourth Int. Conf. on Artificial Intelligence Planning Systems (AIPS-98)*, 1998.

[4] A. Cesta, A. Oddi, and S.F. Smith. A Constrained-Based Method for Project Scheduling with Time Windows. *Journal of Heuristics*, 2002.

[5] A. Cesta, A. Oddi, and A. Susi. O-OSCAR: A Flexible Object-Oriented Architecture for Schedule Management in Space Applications. In *Proceedings of the Fifth Int. Symp. on Artificial Intelligence, Robotics and Automation in Space (i-SAIRAS-99)*, 1999.

[6] A. Cesta and C. Stella. A Time and Resource Problem for Planning Architectures. In *Proceedings of the Fourth European Conference on Planning (ECP 97)*, 1997.

[7] B. De Reyck and W. Herroelen. A Branch-and-Bound Procedure for the Resource-Constrained Project Scheduling Problem with Generalized Precedence Relations. *European Journal of Operations Research*, 111(1):152–174, 1998.

[8] R. Dechter, I. Meiri, and J. Pearl. Temporal constraint networks. *Artificial Intelligence*, 49:61–95, 1991.

[9] K. Neumann and C. Schwindt. Project Scheduling with Inventory Constraints. Technical Report WIOR-572, Universität Karlsruhe, 1999.

[10] A. Oddi and S.F. Smith. Stochastic Procedures for Generating Feasible Schedules. In *Proceedings 14th National Conference on AI (AAAI-97)*, 1997.

[11] N. Policella. Problemi di scheduling con risorse consumabili, risoluzione con approccio a vincoli in una architettura software orientata agli oggetti. Master's thesis, Università di Roma "La Sapienza", March 2001. In Italian.

[12] G. Wolf. Schedule Management: An Object-Oriented Approach. *Decision Support Systems*, 11:373–388, 1994.

Planning and Execution in Dynamic Environments

Rosy Barruffi and Michela Milano

D.E.I.S., Università di Bologna - Italy
{rbarruffi, mmilano}@deis.unibo.it

Abstract. In this paper, we present an architecture for planning and executing in complex and dynamic environments. Such application domains are characterized by large amount of data, too wide and dynamic to be completely stored and maintained up-to-date. Planning and execution activities should deal with unpredictable action effects, unknown knowledge and dynamic information. We propose to use a planner and an executor based on the Interactive Constraint Satisfaction framework combining both search efficiency and data acquisition ability. Both planning and execution can be seen as search processes where constraint propagation, data acquisition and search are interleaved.

1 Introduction

Planning and executing in dynamic environments is a complex task. Plan construction should rely on high problem solving capabilities for searching the best solution in large search spaces. Also, domain information can change, action performed on the system could have non deterministic effects, not all data can be available at the beginning of the computation, since they can be computed or refined during the plan synthesis. Therefore, the execution of plans should be monitored and eventually refined/recomputed in case the system state is different from those expected.

Thus, the requirements of a planning architecture working in complex and dynamic environments are the following:

- efficiency in exploring large search spaces;
- reliability in producing correct solutions;
- ability to deal with incomplete knowledge;
- ability to interact with the environment to acquire unknown information;
- ability to deal with dynamic knowledge;
- ability to monitor the plan execution and react to domain changes.

We have developed an original planning architecture that fulfils these requirements by embedding two main components: a generative planner with problem solving and knowledge acquisition capabilities, and an executor that interleaves reactive planning and execution.

F. Esposito (Ed.): AI*IA 2001, LNAI 2175, pp. 382–387, 2001.
© Springer-Verlag Berlin Heidelberg 2001

The architecture is based on an extension of the Constraint Satisfaction framework [3], called *Interactive* Constraint Satisfaction framework [4]. On one hand, this extension maintains the advantages of Constraint Satisfaction techniques like their ability of pruning the search space thus increasing efficiency. On the other hand, it is able to work with partial and changing knowledge. The idea is to use variables defined on a partially known domain containing already known values and a variable representing further possible consistent values. When, either during plan computation or during plan execution, the available information is not enough or no longer consistent, acquisition of new values is performed. Acquisition can be guided by constraints the variables are subject to (i.e., *Interactive Constraints*) (ICs). ICs embed a filtering algorithm, as traditional constraints, and rely on sensors to retrieve constrained data when needed. Thus, two additional components should be added to the architecture: an acquisition component containing *sensors* to the environment and a constraint solver suitably extended to cope with partially know variable domains.

The architecture has been designed and developed within a project involving the University of Bologna and Hewlett Packard (HP Labs, Bristol). The aim of the project is to use Artificial Intelligence Planning techniques for solving distributed computer networks management tasks. For this reason, our architecture is called *PlanNet* (*Plan*ning for the *Net*work). However, the architecture is general purpose and can be applied to different application domains.

2 Design of a Planning Architecture

Four main components are considered to describe *PlanNet* architecture (see figure 1): the Generative Planner, the Reactive Executor, the Constraint Solver and the Information Gathering Module.

Given a desired final state (goal), the Generative Planner chains actions needed to achieve the goal (plan). Once a plan schema is built, the Executor is in charge of refining such plan schema, execute actions and check whether the effects are those expected. Both components are based on Interactive Constraint Satisfaction techniques requiring two additional architectural modules: a Constraint Solver and an Information Gathering Module to acquire information on the current domain state.

2.1 The Constraint Solver

The Constraint Solver (module **3** in figure 1) used in the architecture is based on an extension of traditional Constraint Satisfaction framework [3], called Interactive Constraint Satisfaction Problems (ICSP) [4], able to deal with both constrained data acquisition and propagation.

Intuitively, ICSPs allow to define constrained variables on partially or completely unknown domains. Constraints stated on those variables are called *Interactive Constraints* (ICs). When variables are defined on a completely known domain, ICs behaves as traditional constraint by pruning inconsistent values;

instead, if a variable domain is unknown, (only) consistent data is retrieved by querying the system. Thus, the Constraint Solver is responsible to check the consistency of such ICs and eventually require an interaction with the system when not enough data are available in variable domains. In this way, we can also deal with changing knowledge. If we leave the domain *open* (with a variable representing future acquisition), we can take into account cases where all consistent information at planning time is no longer consistent at execution time and new data can be available. For more details on the operational behaviour of ICs see [1].

2.2   The Information Gathering Module

As already mentioned, the IC propagation activity results in a traditional constraint propagation or information retrieval activity according to the available variable domain knowledge.

When domain values are not enough for standard propagation, the constraint solver queries an acquisition module (module **4** in figure 1) which is responsible of providing the needed information either by inferring it from a knowledge base, called Initial State (IS), or by retrieving it directly from the real world. The acquisition gathering component offers to the constraint solver an interface to the real world and performs additional pre and post processing of original data retrieved by sensors.

We can think of the constraint solver as a *client* invoking sensor acquisition indirectly by simply accessing the information gathering component. The information gathering activity is transparent to the constraint solver that does not have to change its constraints syntax to query the system nor to worry about when there is need for a remote access and when the desired information has been already stored in a knowledge base. IS represents a cache more than a proper knowledge base since it contains only information needed to build the plan. IS contains atomic formulas representing symbolic information translated from sensors to the external environment.

2.3   The Generative Planner

The generative planner (module **1** in figure 1) is in charge of building the plan needed to reach a given state (the goal) starting from the current state of the domain. It receives two inputs: (i) the goal to achieve, and (ii) the domain of actions that can be performed on the system (called *domain theory*)[6]. Both goal and actions are described in a formal language. The goal is a set of predicates representing properties that must be true at the end of the plan execution. The actions are represented in terms of pre and post-conditions containing variables. Thus, they represent action schema which can be specialized to obtain action instances.

While traditional planners require a completely known and static initial state, our planner dynamically acquires knowledge from the real system by exploiting

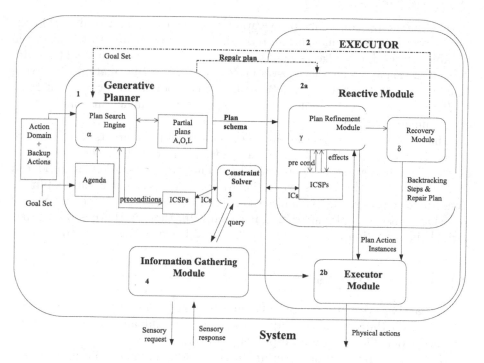

Fig. 1. Architecture

the ICSP framework. Thus, the planner relies on the Constraint Solver and Information Gathering Module described above.

The plan search engine (α) is a regressive non-linear planner performing least commitment planning [6]. It is sound and complete for its action representation, i.e., the planner is always able to return a correct plan if such a plan exists. This is true given a static initial state.

At each step of the planning process, the planner selects an open condition Q from the *Agenda* of open condition, checks if it is already satisfied in the initial state and, if not, tries to satisfy it by searching for an action whose post-conditions contain an effect unifying with Q. This action can be either an action already in the plan, or a new one. In this second case, a new set of pre-conditions are added to *Agenda*. In order to check if Q is satisfied in the initial state the planner interacts with the Constraint Solver (module **3** in figure 1) which is responsible for reporting to α about the state of the Interactive Constraint associated to Q.

We have mapped the planning problem in an Interactive CSP. Variables are those appearing in action pre-conditions and represent resources. Domains contain available resources on which the action can be performed. ICs are associated with action pre-conditions that should be true in order to execute the action. An IC fails if the corresponding relation is not true in the initial state. Otherwise, it returns a set of domain values that possibly satisfy the constraints.

The interactive constraint propagation activity results in a traditional constraint propagation or information retrieval activity according to the available variable domain knowledge as described in 2.1. Thus, in turn, it might require the interaction between the constraint solver and the Information Gathering module (module 4 in figure 1) for an acquisition of (potentially) consistent data.

If the constraint solver fails, the planner searches for an action containing an effect unifiable with Q.

The planner ends when the *Agenda* is empty and all threats (see [6]) have been solved and sends the plan schema to the executor in charge of refining and execute it. Note that, at this point, we are still not guaranteed that the produced plan is consistent. In fact, some variables still range on a domain containing some values representing available resource. Since these knowledge can change and since constraint propagation is not complete, there is the possibility that variable instantiation (called labelling) fails and backtracking is forced.

2.4   Reactive Executor

The **Reactive Module** (module **2a** in figure 1) is devoted to verify, before execution, whether action preconditions are still true and, after action execution, whether action effects have been properly executed.

A run-time precondition verification mechanism (module γ in figure 1) has been implemented by exploiting again IC propagation. Before action execution, variable domains contain a set of resources which were consistent and available during plan construction. IC propagation removes those values that are no longer consistent at execution time. After IC propagation, a still available resource is chosen and the action is performed on it.

The ICSP framework can also cope with non monotonic changes of variable domains. The idea is to leave domains *open* even after acquisition. If at execution time the entire set of known values (those acquired during plan construction) is deleted because of precondition verification, a new acquisition can start aimed at retrieving new consistent values. If no values are available, backtracking is performed in order to explore the execution of other branches in the search space of partial plans. If the overall process fails (and only in this case), a re-planning is performed.

Thus the plan execution process results in a search process in order to find the totally instantiated actions before performing them on the real world. Note that, while during the generative process the interactive constraints rely on the cache IS, in this phase they only interact with the real system since the information collected in IS is assumed to be out of date.

The second feature of the executor is an effect verification mechanism checks if the corresponding action has been properly executed. For this purpose, again, the plan refinement module (γ) calls the constraint solver. Each action effect is associated to an IC so as to query the underlying system and check whether the action has achieved the desired effect. If the verification succeeds, the execution of the plan goes on by selecting the next action. Otherwise, the executor (**2b**) fails and a backtracking mechanism is performed by the recovery module δ in order to select an alternative plan action instance.

Thus, the planner has to support repair activity also for dealing with irreversible action execution[1]. The problems of reactive planners [2] are mostly related with backtracking of irreversible actions. We are currently studying how to provide the action domain with *Backup* actions to add to the plan during the first phase of the planning process each time an irreversible action is instantiated.

Finally an **Executor** (module **2b** in figure 1) is represented by a module able to interact with the low level system in order to execute the ground actions.

3   Conclusion

In this paper, we have proposed an original, general purpose architecture for planning and executing in dynamic environments. The architecture relies on a planner producing plan schema and a reactive executor refining and executing it. Both components are based on interactive constraint satisfaction techniques, implemented by a constraint solver and a data acquisition component. The architecture has been successfully applied to system management tasks: it has been integrated in troubleshooting and intrusion detection systems [5]. Future works are aimed at providing a robust recovery mechanism based on backup actions that should be chained when a given plan fails. An interesting extension we are currently studying concerns the possibility of implementing the architecture on a multi-agent platform, by distributing planning, execution and data acquisition.

4   Acknowledgment

This project is partially supported by Hewlett Packard Laboratories of Bristol-UK (Internet Business Management Department).

References

[1] R. Barruffi, E.Lamma, P.Mello, and M. Milano. Least commitment on variable binding in presence of incomplete knowledge. In *Proceedings of the European Conference on Planning (ECP99)*, 1999.

[2] K. Golden. *Planning and Knowledge Representation for Softbots*. PhD thesis, University of Washington, 1997.

[3] P. Van Hentenryck. *Constraint Satisfaction in Logic Programming*. MIT Press, 1989.

[4] E. Lamma, M. Milano, P. Mello, R. Cucchiara, M. Gavanelli, and M. Piccardi. Constraint propagation and value acquisition: why we should do it interactively. *Proceedings of the IJCAI*, 1999.

[5] R. Montanari R. Barruffi, M. Milano. Planning in security management. *IEEE Intelligent Systems*, 16, 2001.

[6] D.S. Weld. An introduction to least commitment planning. *AI Magazine*, 15:27–61, 1994.

---

[1] An *irreversible* action is an action whose effects are not backtrackable after execution

An Agent Architecture for Planning in a Dynamic Environment

Giuliano Armano[1], Giancarlo Cherchi[1], and Eloisa Vargiu[2]

[1] DIEE, Dipartimento di Ingegneria Elettrica ed Elettronica, Università di Cagliari, Piazza d'Armi, I-09123, Cagliari, Italy
{armano, cherchi}@diee.unica.it
[2] CRS4, Centro di Ricerca, Sviluppo e Studi Superiori in Sardegna, VI Strada OVEST, Z.I. Macchiareddu I-09010 Uta (CA), Italy
eloisa@crs4.it

Abstract. This paper briefly describes a scalable architecture for implementing autonomous agents that act in a virtual world created for a computer game and must interact with it by suitably planning and executing actions in a dynamic and not-completely accessible environment. In particular, we are experimenting a two-pass vertically layered architecture that allows supporting an agent behavior through a clean hierarchical organization.

1 Introduction

In the last few years, AI researchers have concentrated their efforts in the field of intelligent autonomous agents, i.e., on systems capable of autonomous sensing, reasoning and acting in a complex environment. Suitable architectures have been devised to overcome the complexity problems that arise while trying to give agents a flexible behavior. Let us briefly recall that an agent architecture is essentially a map of the internals of an agent, i.e., its data structures, the operations that may be performed on them, and the corresponding control flows [9]. Among different kinds of architectures (see, for example: [1], [6], [5], [3]), we are particularly concerned with layered ones. In horizontally layered architectures each software layer is directly connected to the sensory inputs and action outputs. A great advantage of horizontally layered architectures (e.g., TOURINGMACHINES [4]) is their conceptual simplicity. However, as the layers are competing with one-another, there is the possibility that the overall behavior of the agent will become incoherent. In order to ensure consistency, such kind of architectures typically includes a mediator function, devoted to select the layer to be activated. In vertically layered architectures decision making is realized by means of several software layers, each of them being devoted to deal with the environment at different levels of abstraction. In particular, in two-pass vertically layered architectures, information flows up until a layer able to deal with the received stimulus is reached, and then the control flows back to the actuators (e.g., INTERRAP [7]).

In this paper, we briefly illustrate a two-pass vertically layered architecture that allows agents, designed for being used in a computer game, to exhibit planning capabilities in an environment whose complexity is comparable to the one that characterizes a real world domain.

F. Esposito (Ed.): AI*IA 2001, LNAI 2175, pp. 388–394, 2001.

2   A Layered Architecture for a Computer Game

The proposed architecture has been devised for a project aimed at developing a computer game. In particular, the game lets the users play within a virtual world populated by two different kinds of entities, i.e., "physical" and "network" entities. The former ones represent inhabitants of the virtual world (e.g., avatars), whereas the latter ones (e.g., computer viruses) live within a virtual, Internet-like, computer network. An agent can interact with the underlying environment, the player, and other agents. The environment in which the agents live is dynamic, not-completely observable, and must satisfy additional quasi real-time constraints. A prototype of the system has already been implemented and thoroughly tested. The current release is mainly aimed at experimenting how agents' planning capabilities cope with the complex environment that characterizes the game. Although most of the application code has been developed in C++, CLOS (Common Lisp Object System) has been adopted as the target language for implementing the agent-based prototype. In particular, the run-time support for agents is currently (and temporarily) embedded into the game in form of a DLL.

Defining or adopting a suitable architecture that allows agents to satisfy the constraints imposed by a dynamic environment has introduced several problems. To overcome them, we adopted an approach based on abstraction, which allows agents to exhibit their reactive, deliberative, and proactive behavior at different levels of granularity. To suitably support this conceptual mechanism, we devised a two-pass vertically layered architecture that can be equipped with an arbitrary number of layers (say N), depending on the domain characteristics and on the task complexity. In this way, any given abstraction can be naturally hosted by a proper layer of the architecture. Each layer exploits a local knowledge base (KB), and is numbered according to its level of abstraction (from 0=ground to N-1=most abstract). It is worth noting that, whereas in classical architectures any given layer usually exhibits different behaviors, in the proposed architecture all layers are –at least conceptually– identical, each of them embodying reactive, deliberative and proactive subsystems. Only the responsibilities of a layer change, depending on the level of abstraction being considered. According to the basic features that characterize a two-pass vertically layered architecture, the information flows from level 0 up to level N-1, whereas the control flows from level N-1 down to level 0.

2.1   Planning and Abstraction Hierarchies

Let us now focus our attention on the behavior of the hierarchical planner, as planning plays a central role in the overall agent behavior. As expected, plan generation is performed at different layers, each layer being equipped with a local planner, which is allowed to use its own operators only. The ground-level layer deals with atomic operations, whereas any other layer deals with abstract operations. For each layer, action schemata are suitably represented according to the PDDL syntax, and the behavior of each local planner follows an UCPOP-like strategy. As a default mechanism, each local planner is being activated on any goal imposed by its overlying planner (if any). Thus, a goal to be attained at level K>0 enforces other goals on the underlying K-1 level. That is why, an abstract operator that holds on a given level may actually be refined with a complex plan. In other words, the post-conditions of an abstract operator of level K>0 are considered as a goal by the planner located at level K-1.

Bearing in mind that agents must implement a proactive functionality in a dynamic environment, we can state that the whole architecture has been designed to make efficient and flexible this goal-oriented behavior. To be able to deal with the time constraints imposed by the environment, a hierarchical interleaved planning and execution (HIPE) approach has been devised and adopted. In other words, an agent repeatedly (and concurrently) performs planning, executes actions, and monitors any change occurred in the underlying environment, at different levels of granularity. After that an overall plan at the most abstract layer has been found, its first operator is refined at the underlying layer and so on, ending up with a corresponding plan that enforces a depth-first policy. In particular, execution starts as soon as the ground-level planner yields a local plan. Thus, a plan does not need to be complete before starting its execution, as operators refinement can be deferred until actually needed.

Note that the above strategy is feasible only under the assumption that the near-DRP [8] holds, i.e., that the ratio between "false" and "true" solutions at the most abstract level is reasonably low; if not, the agent would typically start activities actually not useful to reach the given goal. Whereas we assumed that the resulting abstraction mapping is "quasi-sound" (in the sense specified above), no assumption at all is made on its completeness. Of course, the absence of the latter property implies that not all ground solutions can be found starting from a search performed at a level K>0. Therefore –when a failure occurs at a the most abstract level– an attempt must be performed at the underlying level and so on, until a solution is found or the ground-level search ended with failure. Note also that, if a plan at a given layer fails due to environmental changes, local re-planning is attempted. If no solution is found, the failure is notified to the upper layer (if any), where local re-planning is attempted at a higher level of abstraction, and so on. The adopted approach exploits the architecture by moving any event that cannot be handled by the current layer up to the next (more abstract) one. In this way, local re-planning can be used as a general mechanism to deal with unexpected events, without being always compelled to start a global re-planning activity. It is also worth pointing out that, to be effective, the proposed HIPE approach requires an adaptive mechanism aimed at enlarging the space of solvable problems at abstract levels (i.e., at increasing their "degree of completeness"). This problem is addressed in a separate work (described in [2]), where new abstract operators, to be used in any subsequent planning activity, are discovered starting from already solved problems.

Each layer being equipped with a deliberative, a proactive, and a reactive module, both vertical and horizontal interactions (i.e., inter- and intra-layers, respectively) may occur while trying to reach a given objective. Figure 1 and 2 give a schematic description of the vertical and horizontal interactions that occur among these subsystems.

2.2   Vertical Interactions

Reactive Behavior. Any incoming event flows up from the ground-level to the most abstract layer, through the reactive modules. From an information-oriented perspective, the role played by a reactive module is to adapt any incoming event with the kind of information contained in the knowledge base of the corresponding layer. In particular, an incoming event usually needs to be suitably encoded at any level K>0, as the information dealt with by these levels is more abstract that the one coming from the underlying environment.

Proactive Behavior. As already pointed out, the proactive behavior is supported by a hierarchical planner distributed on N layers, each one devoted to cope with a different level of granularity. A bi-directional communication occurs among local planners. A planner at level K>0 can order its inferior to refine an abstract operator by passing it a triple *<pre,oper,post>* consisting of pre-conditions, operator, and post-conditions, respectively. Actually, only post-conditions (suitably translated to fit the syntax and semantics of the layer where the planner has been invoked) are exploited to set up a new (local) goal. On the other hand, to perform actions on the underlying environment, the ground-level planner uses the information carried out by the operator itself. A planner at level K<N-1 can inform its superior either that a plan has been successfully completed and executed or that a failure has occurred. At present, no information about the causes of the failure is supplied, but a more informative behavior –able to put into evidence why a plan has failed– is currently under study.

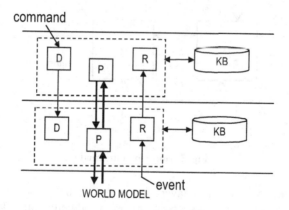

Fig. 1. Vertical interactions

Deliberative Behavior. Any incoming command, if accepted by the agent, flows towards the ground level, through the deliberative modules. This basically allows a user to send commands to an agent through a privileged input channel. From a control-oriented perspective, the role played by each deliberative module is to let an external command propagate down to a layer able to understand it. Another important feature embedded in the control chain that links deliberative modules is the capability of inhibiting any inferior, thus preventing it to undertake any decision. Note that the inhibition is automatically propagated from top to bottom (e.g., the deliberative module located at level N-1 is able to inhibit all inferior layers by issuing a single *inhibit* command). The inhibition capability is exploited by a deliberative module (of level K>0) when an external command or a reactive break request has been accepted.

In both cases any underlying activity must be stopped to let a new goal be served, and the usual way to do it is by issuing an *inhibit* command.

2.3   Horizontal Interactions

Reactive Behavior. Given a layer, its reactive module contains a partially-ordered set of rules, each rule having the general form *<pre,post,priority>*. Thus, a rule has an associated priority (range 1-10), and can be fired when its preconditions (*pre*) are verified. The main task of a reactive module is to check whether or not some rules exist that could be fired, according to the environmental changes caused by incoming events.[1] If at least one rule can be fired, the reactive module sends a *break* command to the planner and informs the deliberative module that a decision has to be undertaken (passing it the whole "firing-set"). If the deliberative module accepts the break request, the post-conditions of the selected rule become a new goal for the local planner, which tries to achieve it after stacking the current plan (to be typically restored on reactive behavior completion).

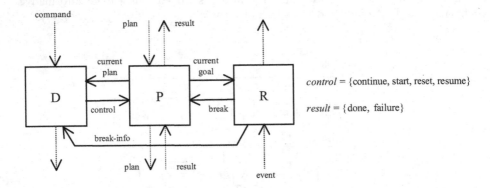

Fig. 2. Horizontal interactions.

Proactive Behavior. Given a layer, its proactive behavior may undergo heavy interactions with both the corresponding reactive and deliberative modules. In fact, it may receive a *break* command from the reactive module, resulting in the current activity being stopped while waiting for a command coming from the deliberative module. After receiving a *break* command, the local planner sends information about the current plan to the deliberative module, to help it deciding the policy to be undertaken. Depending on the command sent back by the deliberative module, the planner could alternatively *continue* its activity, *start* a new plan, become idle (*reset*) or *resume* the lastly-saved plan. It is worth pointing out that, due to the vertical interactions among local planners, the current (local) planning activity can also be restarted after receiving a failure notification by the inferior planner (or by a sensory

---

[1] Reactive rules are also designed to trigger any event that could make useless or impossible the current plan-and-execute activity.

input, at the ground-level layer). Furthermore, the planner can become idle after completing the current activity.

Deliberative Behavior. The current release of the deliberative module does not perform any complex reasoning activity, and interacts with the planner by sending a command in the set {*continue, start, reset, resume*}, as described above. In particular, when a new plan has to be activated, the deliberative module acts according to the following policy: after receiving a firing-set from the reactive module, the rule with the highest priority is selected (when several rules have the same high priority, a random choice is performed). Afterwards, a command for starting a new plan (after stacking the current one) is sent to the planner, provided that its priority is higher than the one associated with the current plan (the priority associated with a "non-reactive" plan being 0).

3 Conclusions and Future Work

In this paper, a two-pass vertically layered architecture for implementing autonomous agents within a computer game has been briefly outlined. Due to the constraints imposed by the underlying environment, a layered architecture –able to efficiently implement a hierarchical interleaved planning and execution strategy– appears to be a suitable solution for being able to cope with the complex virtual world that hosts agents. A simple architecture equipped with two layers has been implemented, thus allowing agents that populate the computer game to perform their tasks within the time slot imposed by the environment (i.e., possibly less than one second). As far as future work is concerned, we are currently investigating the problem of giving agents an adaptive behavior. In particular, the capability of learning abstract operators in order to better adapt themselves to the characteristics of the underlying dynamic environment is currently being addressed.

Acknowledgments

This work has been carried out under the joint project "Side-EffectZ", which involves CRS4[2] and Mediola.[3] We wish to thank M. Agelli (CRS4) and G. Dettori (Mediola) for their useful suggestions and valuable help.

References

1. Agre, P.E., Rosenchein, S.J. (eds.): Computational Theories of Interaction and Agency. The MIT Press (1996)

---

[2] Centro Ricerche Sviluppo e Studi Superiori in Sardegna.

[3] Mediola is a company that works on multimedia, games, and Internet-based applications.

2. Armano, G., Vargiu, E.: An Adaptive Approach for Planning in Dynamic Environments. In: 2001 International Conference on Artificial Intelligence, IC-AI 2001, Special Session on Learning and Adapting in AI Planning. Las Vegas, Nevada, June 25-28 (2001)

3. Brooks, R.A.: A robust layered control system for a mobile robot. In: IEEE Journal of Robotics and Automation, Vol. 2(1). (1986) 14-23

4. Ferguson, I. A., TouringMachines: An Architecture for Dynamic, Rational, Mobile Agents. PhD thesis. Clare Hall, University of Cambridge, UK (1992)

5. Georgeff, M.P., Lansky, A.L.: Reactive reasoning and planning. In: Proceedings of the Sixth National on Artificial Intelligence (AAAI-87). Seattle, WA (1987) 677-682

6. Lésperance, Y., Levesquue, H.J., Lin, F, Marcu, D., Reiter, R., and Scherl, R.B.: Foundations of a logical approach to agent programming. In: M. Wooldridge, J.P. Müller, and M. Tambe, editors, Intelligent Agents II, LNAI, Vol. 1037. Springer-Verlag (1996) 331-346

7. Müller, J.: A cooperation model for autonomous agents. In: J.P Müller, M. Wooldridge and N.R. Jennings (eds) Intelligent Agents III, LNAI, Vol. 1193. Springer-Verlag, Berlin Heidelberg New York (1997) 245-260

8. Tenenberg, J.D.: Abstraction in Planning. Ph.D. thesis, Computer Science Department, University of Rochester (1988)

9. Wooldridge, M.: Intelligent Agents. In: G. Weiss (ed) Multiagent Systems, MIT Press, Berlin Heidelberg New York (1999)

Author Index

Lecture Notes in Artificial Intelligence (LNAI)

Lecture Notes in Computer Science